Small Business Profiles

Small

Business

Profiles

A GUIDE TO TODAY'S
TOP OPPORTUNITIES
FOR ENTREPRENEURS

V o l u m e *1*

**Andrew Carnegie Library
Livingstone College
701 W. Monroe St.
Salisbury, NC 28144**

Suzanne M. Bourgoin,

Editor

Gale Research Inc. • *DETROIT* • *WASHINGTON, D.C.* • *LONDON*

127456

STAFF

Suzanne M. Bourgoin, *Editor*

David Collins, Nicolet V. Elert, L. Mpho Mabunda, Mary K. Ruby, *Associate Editors*

Marilyn Allen, *Editorial Associate*

Audra Avizienis, Virginia Barnstorff, Karen Bellenir, Barbara Carlisle Bigelow, Dean Boyer, Kerstan Cohen, Jeffrey L. Covell, Kristine Dailey, Thomas Derdak, Evelyn S. Dorman, Sina Dubovoj, Arthur Durivage, Tina Grant, Edna M. Hedblad, Marinell James, Janice Jorgensen, Paula Kepos, Michael L. LaBlanc, Mary McNulty, Dave Mote, Roger W. Roland, Julia M. Rubiner, Susan Salter, Francine Shonfeld Sherman, Roberta H. Winston, *Contributing Editors*

Peter M. Gareffa, *Senior Editor*

Mary Beth Trimper, *Production Director*
Mary Kelley, *Production Associate*
Cynthia Baldwin, *Art Director*
Mark C. Howell, *Graphic Designer*

While every effort has been made to ensure the reliability of the information presented in this publication, Gale Research Inc. does not guarantee the accuracy of the data contained herein. Gale accepts no payment for listing; and inclusion in the publication of any organization, agency, institution, publication, service, or individual does not imply endorsement of the editors or publisher. Errors brought to the attention of the publisher and verified to the satisfaction of the publisher will be corrected in future editions.

♾™ This book is printed on acid-free paper that meets the minimum requirements of American National Standard for Information Sciences— Permanence Paper for Printed Library Materials, ANSI Z39.48-1984.

This publication is a creative work fully protected by all applicable copyright laws, as well as by mis-appropriation, trade secret, unfair competition, and other applicable laws. The authors and editors of this work have added value to the underlying factual material herein through one or more of the following: unique and original selection, coordination, expression, arrangement, and classification of the information.

All rights to this publication will be vigorously defended.

Copyright © 1994 by Gale Research Inc.
835 Penobscot Bldg.
Detroit, MI 48226-4094

All rights reserved including the right of reproduction in whole or in part in any form.

Printed in the United States of America
Published simultaneously in the United Kingdom by Gale Research
International Limited (An affiliated company of Gale Research Inc.)

No part of this book may be reproduced in any form without permission in writing from the publisher, except by a reviewer who wishes to quote brief passages or entries in connection with a review written for inclusion in a magazine or newspaper.

ISBN 0-8103-9178-3

10 9 8 7 6 5 4 3 2 1

I(T)P™

The trademark ITP is used under license.

Small Business Profiles
Advisory Board

Irwin Friedman
Chairman Emeritus
Network of Small Businesses, Lyndhurst, Ohio

John Paul Galles
Executive Vice-President
National Small Business United, Washington, DC

Mark Leggett
Manager of Business, Science, and Technology Division
Indianapolis-Marion County Public Library, Indiana

Susan Neuman
Librarian
University of Pittsburgh Graduate School of Business Library, Pennsylvania

Dr. Norm Schlafmann
Director of Federal Relations
Office of the President, Wayne State University, Detroit, Michigan

Contents

Introduction

Small Business Profiles provides the aspiring entrepreneur with a unique source of concise, useful information for starting a small business. Rather than just offering general advice, *Small Business Profiles* presents detailed start-up instructions, including timely and accurate cost and profit figures, for a wide assortment of business opportunities. Each annually published volume fills the entrepreneur's need to secure the knowledge and skills necessary for achieving success in the world of small business.

Whether looking to capitalize on currently "hot" ventures or to reap profits from the perennial money-makers, the potential business owner will find *Small Business Profiles* an indispensable source. The types of businesses included in the series run the gamut from recycling consultant/broker and herb farm to car wash and dry cleaning service.

Small Business Profiles entries cover crucial aspects of business start-up, such as costs and expected profits; financing; marketing and advertising; obtaining licenses; deciding on insurance needs; and much more. *Small Business Profiles* also suggests numerous possibilities for obtaining more information and needed resources.

Some of *Small Business Profiles'* Many Valuable Features:

Small Business Profiles entries were designed with a user-friendly format to make learning about business start-up simple and interesting.

- **Attractive page design** incorporates textual subheads, making it easy to find specific information.

- **Instructive essays** present the user with clear and logical step-by-step guidelines for embarking on a particular business venture.

- **Easy-to-locate data sections** provide quick access to key information and cover such topics as Industry Statistics, Franchises Opportunities, and Trade Associations.

- **Sources for additional information** direct the user to selected books, magazines, and newspapers, where further reading on business start-up can be found.

Helpful Indexes

Small Business Profiles includes a Master Index, with cross-references that make it easy to locate entries, and a Franchise Index providing page references for additional information on franchises, including addresses and phone and fax numbers.

We Welcome Your Suggestions

Comments and suggestions for enhancing and improving *Small Business Profiles* can be mailed to:

The Editor
Small Business Profiles
Gale Research Inc.
835 Penobscot Bldg.
Detroit, MI 48226-4094
Phone: (800) 347-4253
Fax: (313) 961-6599

Accounting and Tax Preparation Service

Many people have heard the cliché "Nothing is guaranteed in this life except for death and taxes." Few, however, decide to exercise their entrepreneurial skills and exploit it. Considering that taxes are "guaranteed," can you imagine then how many millions of Americans each year must fill out tax forms? Preparing tax returns, as well as providing accounting services to individuals and small businesses, can be a very lucrative part- or full-time business.

The number of small businesses involved in tax preparation and basic accounting services has continued to grow over the years, due in large part to ever-changing tax laws and increasing time demands, which preclude millions of Americans from filing their own tax returns. The Internal Revenue Service (IRS) estimates that in a single year, between 45 and 60 million Americans pay for professional tax return preparation.

As a potential owner of a tax preparation business, it is important to remember that you will need to undergo special training and keep abreast of specific changes to the tax laws from year to year. Although you may wish to begin this business venture on a part-time basis, with the proper mix of financing, customer service, knowledge of the relevant laws, and a high quality level of work, there is enough money to be made in the business of tax preparation and accounting services for it to become a full-time profession.

COSTS AND PROFITS

Start-up costs for a tax preparation and accounting service business are minimal, ranging from $1,000 to $6,000 depending on the individual business owner's equipment needs. Fees range from a minimum of $75 for a simple state and federal tax return to approximately $300 for a more complex return involving limited partnerships, rental income, self-employment income, and various other "forms." As the industry is one focused on tax season—from late January through April 15 of each year—the earnings one can expect to realize from this business are indeed seasonal, and in fact may more appropriately be defined as part-time earnings. Tax preparation and accounting service businesses report earnings as little as $1,000 and up to as much as $50,000 per year.

Liabilities for a tax preparation business are small in comparison to many other businesses; however, they do include any monthly expenses, such as payroll and rent, as well as outstanding monthly obligations on any loans that you may have obtained to help you get started. Since many business owners consider an accounting service a part-time occupation, they may have the luxury of working out of their own home, thereby significantly decreasing the required operating expenses. Basic supplies for a tax preparation and accounting service are a computer, computer software, a few classes on tax preparation and basic accounting skills, and access to a photocopier—either at the local printing shop or one that you have leased or purchased on your own.

FINANCING

The attraction of starting a tax preparation and accounting service business is that it will not require significant, up-front start-up costs. There are several ways in which you can obtain financing, some of which are more obvious than others. Free advice is always the best place to start when looking for answers to your financing questions. It may be a family member, a former business or academic associate, or even professional associations and trade publications that you turn to for advice. Whatever the case, be certain to explore all of your financing options; you may be pleasantly surprised as to the available sources of financing for your business. Needing such a modest investment ($1,000 to $6,000 on average), you may find that a friend or family member will loan you the money.

It is important to have outlined a knowledgeable business plan prior to approaching anyone for financing. In the plan, you need to address the basics of how you are going to start and operate your business, from promotion and marketing strategy to location of business and pricing structure. A business plan will establish credibility for yourself and your business venture and illustrate why loaning you money would be a worthwhile investment for the financing source.

One place to begin is a publication of the **Small Business Administration (SBA)** called *Business Plan for Small Service Firms*. This is available from your nearest SBA or SCORE (Service Corps of Retired Executives) office. SCORE is an affiliate of the SBA, with offices throughout

FRANCHISE OPPORTUNITIES

Jackson Hewitt Tax Service: P.O. Box 65085, Virginia Beach, VA 23464-0995; phone: (800) 234-1040; founded, 1960; began franchising, 1985; 226 outlets; franchise fees start at $9,500. Franchisor provides computerized preparation and checking of income tax returns, bookkeeping, and financial operations. Jackson Hewitt retains arrangements with major retailers for seasonal franchise units to operate in stores and also offers complete package of services and systems of operation, including software, accounting methods, merchandising, advertising, sales, and promotional techniques; 7-day mandatory training program is provided.

Other Franchisors: H&R Block, Inc.: 4410 Main St., Kansas City, MO 64111; phone: (816) 753-6900. **Padgett Business Services U.S.A., Inc.:** 160 Hawthorne Park, Athens, GA 30606; phone: (404) 548-1040. **Peyron Associates, Inc.:** P.O. Box 175, Sellersburg, IN 47172; phone: (502) 637-7483. **Triple Check Income Tax Service:** 727 S. Main St., Burbank, CA 91506; phone: (213) 849-2273.

the country, that provides free consulting services, as well as moderately priced small business workshops. The SBA has a toll-free phone number, **1-800-U ASK SBA,** that is available to assist with your many questions, and can also be contacted by writing: **Small Business Directory, P.O. Box 1000, Ft. Worth, TX 76119.**

The SBA does have a "small loan" guarantee for loans of the $50,000 and under variety, which are made in cooperation with banks throughout the United States. Consult the SBA for a list of participating local banks in your area. An additional publication to turn to for financing help is the *SBA Hotline Answer Book,* a recommended reference guide for anyone who wishes to use the services of the SBA.

LAYOUT AND DESIGN

Layout and design are more critical to a store owner or franchisee than the business owner who operates out of his or her home. Regarding the franchisee, the layout and design of your store can make a very powerful statement to prospective clients. An office that is careful to pay attention to details, from the comfortable waiting space in the front of the store to the colorful yet modest artwork on the wall, will reflect the taste, personality, and most importantly, the level of seriousness of the business owner. Because tax preparation and accounting services are considered confidential, personal matters to your clients, make certain that your office is designed to allow for privacy during a one-on-one consultation with a customer. It would be very uncomfortable for those customers who may be in your waiting area to overhear the discussion that you may be having with another of your customers. The key issue of layout is to keep your store professional yet pleasant. A trip to the tax preparer can be very traumatic and downright confusing for many cus-

tomers, and the more at ease you can make clients feel, the more profitable it will be for your business.

For those who intend to operate out of their homes, many of these same principles of office layout and design apply. Your home office must place a heavy emphasis on organization, as this will make a lasting impression on your customers. Make sure you keep file folders in an easy-to-access position to allow for quick reference during a customer consultation. Also, provide comfortable chairs that allow for a more relaxed client and maintain a working desk free of clutter that contains only relevant reference manuals, a computer, a lamp, a calculator, a few pens and pencils, and a phone.

It is important to keep your home office isolated from the rest of the household so as to avoid any unnecessary interruptions and distractions from other family members. In general, the layout and design for any home business should display a "common sense" theme. Just as when you have visitors to your home and want the place to look neat, you should also attend to the tidiness of your home office, as potential business and profit can be made or destroyed depending on the condition of your office. Make the trip to your office as enjoyable an experience as possible for your customer. If a customer simply wants to pick up his or her completed statements or returns, have them ready ahead of time and easily accessed by your client.

Whether you have a store or a home office, it would be prudent to have extra tax forms, publications, and other items of interest available for your clients' reading pleasure and informational needs. Be careful not to encourage your customers to remain present in your office for a long period, though, as your time is precious and their charges could be increased.

STAFFING

How you staff your tax preparation and accounting service business will depend entirely on you and your ability to manage your clients' workload. The most important time of the year to have access to sufficient staffing is tax season. In the beginning you may wish to keep expenses down and operate alone; with the aid of a computer and a letter-quality, high-speed printer, you can eliminate the need for a typist and handle the production of various documents on your own. As your business expands, however, the need for typing help will increase, as you will find yourself spending more time researching tax laws, so as to apply them in the most advantageous way for your customers.

It is important to offer convenient business hours to your customers. Paying attention to the busy season, perhaps your home office hours will include evenings and weekends to accommodate your working clientele. Office hours for a franchise or store may also include evenings and weekends, but may open later in the morning during the week so as to avoid an excessive burden on the business owner, who is usually the primary laborer.

Regardless of your office hours, you must plan and staff accordingly. If you have a spouse or roommate, perhaps s/he could greet customers as they come to your home office. In a store, you may hire a part-time receptionist or assistant. Whatever the case, the message is to plan according to your customers needs. Whether your staff consists of 40 people or only one, the basic principles of customer service, which include a warm greeting and professional delivery, still apply and should be adhered to without hesitation.

MARKETING

You may ask the question, ''What does marketing have to do with my tax preparation and accounting service business?'' It has a great deal to do with your potential success and is as important to your overall business plan and strategy as licensing and financing. Marketing may take on many forms and extends itself to most areas of your business. As a business owner in a competitive field, you must develop a marketing strategy that will set your business apart from the competition.

Direct mail can be an effective marketing tool and should include any special services that make your business unique, such as personal pick-up and delivery. Something as simple as the voice mail greeting on your telephone answer-

ing service can be exploited to further market your services. A pleasant, professional greeting emphasizing the unique qualities your business offers can leave a very favorable impression on present and future customers.

Additional marketing opportunities may exist in the form of tie-in promotions. Your local credit union, for example, may allow you to hold a free seminar for members or may provide a small space in their member newsletter for you to offer free or discounted consultations to members only. Anything to isolate your business from the competition (in a positive manner) should be explored, and the power of successful marketing can make this happen.

ADVERTISING

In a service-oriented business such as accounting and tax preparation, word-of-mouth advertising will more than likely serve as the most effective method to promote your business. The power of word-of-mouth advertising should never be underestimated. *Dollars on Your Doorstep* magazine provided the example of a business owner who starts out with ten new clients. It was determined that each satisfied customer will likely tell two people about the business, and each one of them tell two others. Using simple math, ten customers becomes 20 new prospects, which in turn becomes 40 new prospects, then 80 until the ten original customers ultimately become 150 potential clients.

You may wish to contact the local churches in your area and ask them about advertising in their weekly church bulletin. Many customers feel strongly about supporting the businesses that advertise in their respective church bulletins. It is possible that such an advertisement will carry a hidden message for the customer that your business is a moral and ethical one, and should the customer decide to use your service, she or he will be treated fairly and with respect.

Still another source of advertising is the local ''hometown'' newspaper; it is generally less expensive than the major daily papers yet still reaches a large audience. This form of promotion can be effective as local papers tend to showcase more specialty services and trades, and obviously your business fits into this category nicely. Lastly, the Yellow Pages is yet another advertising vehicle for your business. When you consider the number of households in your area that have the Yellow Pages at their disposal, the retention rate of your advertisement is potentially enormous.

LICENSES AND INSURANCE

Before commencing operations of a tax preparation and accounting service, you will need to check with the local chamber of commerce and city zoning office about appropriate licensing required to operate your business, whether it be home-based or a public store. As a store owner, you will need to obtain a business license as well as relevant sales tax permits if applicable. In addition, insurance is extremely important, not only for the protection of yourself and your business, but also for your customers. Look into liability

---

PRIMARY ASSOCIATIONS AND SELECTED TRADE PUBLICATIONS

Associations:

National Association of Tax Consultants (NATC): 454 N. 13th St., San Jose, CA 95112; phone: (408) 298-1458.

National Society of Public Accountants (NSPA): 1010 N. Fairfax St., Alexandria, VA 22314; phone: (703) 549-6400.

America Taxation Association (ATA): c/o American Accounting Association (AAA), 5717 Bessie Dr., Sarasota, FL 34223-2399; phone: (813) 921-7747.

Periodicals:

Accounting News: Warren, Gorham and Lamont, Inc., 1 Penn Plaza, 40th Floor, New York, NY 10119; phone: (212) 971-5000.
CPA Client Bulletin: American Institute of Certified Public Accountants (AICPA), 1211 Avenue of the Americas, New York, NY 10036; phone: (212) 575-6200.
The CPA Journal: New York State Society of CPAs, 200 Park Avenue, 10th Floor, New York, NY 10166-0010; phone: (212) 973-8300.
Journal of Corporate Taxation: Warren, Gorham and Lamont, Inc., 1 Penn Plaza, 40th Floor, New York, NY 10119; phone: (212) 971-5000.
Taxes—The Tax Magazine: Commerce Clearing House, Inc., 2700 Lake Cook Rd., Riverwoods, IL 60015; phone: (708) 583-8500.

TRADE SHOWS AND CONVENTIONS

Accounting Management Computer Exposition:
Flagg Management, Inc., 369 Lexington Ave., New York,
NY 10017; phone: (212) 286-0333.

**American Institute of Certified Public Account-
ants Microcomputer Conference and Exhibition:**
American Institute of Certified Public Accountants, 1211
Avenue of the Americas, New York, NY 10036;
phone:(212) 575-6200.

American Taxation Association Convention:
American Taxation Association (ATA), 5717 Bessie Dr.,
Sarasota, FL 34233; phone: (813) 921-7747.

**Florida Association of Independent Account-
ants Convention:** P.O. Box 13089, Tallahassee, FL
32317; phone: (904) 878-3134.

**Midwest Accounting and Business Manage-
ment Show:** Illinois Certified Public Accounting Society
(ICPAS), 222 S. Riverside Plaza, 16th Floor, Chicago, IL
60606; phone: (312) 933-0393.

insurance for your property; if the insurance is for a home-based business, make sure it is adequate to guard against a client injuring herself or himself on your property. You may also wish to inquire about disability insurance and health insurance as the size of your business dictates.

A tax preparation and accounting service business, although competitive in its very nature and dominated in many areas by major franchises, can prove to be a profitable part-time or full-time small business venture. If you decide to become a franchise owner, make certain that you choose the franchise that represents the most profit potential combined with the best reputation and highest level of integrity. Whether you decide to be a franchisee or to go it alone, pay careful attention to creative means of marketing, advertising, and most importantly, personalized customer service. With the proper mix of these elements, you can expect to see your small business grow.

SOURCES:

Berle, Gustav, *SBA Hotline Answer Book,* Wiley Press, 1992.
Fox, Jack, *Starting and Building Your Own Accounting
   Business,* second edition, John Wiley & Sons, 1991.
Goodrich, Donna C., *How to Set Up and Run a Tax
   Preparation Service,* Wiley Press, 1985.
Harbert, Lee, ''Start a Tax Preparation Service,'' *Income
   Opportunities,* April 1990.
Miller, Robert E., Jr., *How to Compete Successfully in a Public
   Accounting Practice,* Prentice Hall, 1987.
''Mobile Bookkeeping,'' *Entrepreneur Magazine's 168 More
   Businesses Anyone Can Start and Make a Lot of Money,*
   second edition, Bantam, 1991.
Rausch, Edward N., *Financial Management for Small
   Businesses,* Amacom, 1988.
Schwartz, Carol A., editor, *Small Business Sourcebook,* sixth
   edition, Gale, 1993.
''Tax Preparation Service,'' *Entrepreneur Magazine's 111
   Businesses You Can Start for Under $10,000,* Bantam,
   1991.

—ARTHUR DURIVAGE

Animal Breeding Business

If you love animals and are willing to learn a lot about breeding and raising a certain species, there may be a business opportunity awaiting you. After all, what could be more rewarding than getting out of bed every morning knowing that you will spend your day working with and caring for your favorite pets or farm animals?

But, be aware of the risks involved in starting an animal breeding business; 80 percent of all commercial pet breeding operations are run by inexperienced people. As a result, millions of dogs and cats, for example, are destroyed every year because breeders are unable to find them a home. Numerous federal and local agencies have fashioned strict regulations and fines to discourage misguided breeders, and an increasing number of communities are simply outlawing pet breeding businesses. Nevertheless, several business opportunities exist for breeders of high-quality domestic animals and unique farm and commercial stock.

COSTS AND PROFITS

Most breeders of purebred pets make little or no money breeding dogs, cats, birds, and fish. They often view it as a hobby—an extension of their interest in a particular species or breed of animal. For example, one show dog enthusiast who owns a relatively large breeding operation started the sideline business after she became president of a midsized corporation. She employs a staff and supervises the business on evenings and weekends.

Pet breeding, though, can be lucrative. High quality puppies with good bloodlines typically sell for $500 to $1,500, depending on their breed. Championship adult dogs that have been professionally trained can bring between $1,000 and $10,000. Show cats typically sell for slightly less, depending on the breed.

To begin breeding valuable dogs and cats, you should be prepared to invest over $1,000 in a registered animal that can produce a good litter. In addition, veterinary expenses, professional obedience training, grooming, and supplies can push the minimum initial investment into the $2,000 range. It is not uncommon for breeders to cross the country to find the perfect mate for their animal. To impregnate your animal, you may spend anywhere from $1,000 to $3,000 on travel expenses and stud or insemination fees.

You will probably have a greater chance of profiting from the breeding of specialty farm and commercial animals. Show horses, for example, typically sell for about $5,000 as colts, and a top-notch adult can bring more than $100,000. Chinchilla breeders usually sell their animals for $150 to $350 apiece, though award-winning chinchillas can net over $1,000.

FINANCING

Bankers will generally be wary about loaning money for a start-up animal breeding operation, particularly if you don't have much breeding experience. Disease, infertility, and birthing problems are just a few of the factors that make breeding a risky business. But the biggest advantage of many breeding ventures is that you can get started on a low budget and let nature help you expand.

Government-backed loans may be available for some types of breeding operations. To find out if government funding exists for the breeding business you are considering, contact the major industry associations. The **Small Business Administration (SBA)** can help you research breeding businesses, and may even be able to help you write a business plan and secure a loan. Contact the SBA at **1-800-U ASK SBA,** or write: **SBA, P.O. Box 1000, Ft. Worth, TX 76119.** Check the Yellow Pages under ''U.S. Government'' to see if you have a local SBA office.

START-UP IDEAS

In contrast to the highly competitive pet breeding business, a plethora of unique and lucrative farm and commercial breeding enterprises offer excellent profit potential. One of the fastest-growing ventures in the mid-1990s was buffalo breeding. Although your first pair of animals will cost approximately $1 per pound, or a total of about $5,000, one buffalo hide alone can fetch over $3,000. Likewise, buffalo meat, which is lean and low in cholesterol, sells for over $5 per pound when it is ground and $13 per pound as steaks. You can even sell the teeth and hooves.

If your backyard is too small for a herd of buffalo, consider breeding chinchillas. There are only about 1,000 chinchilla ranchers in the United States, and you can buy a pair of these one-pound, 12-inch rodents for $300 to $700.

MAJOR ASSOCIATIONS AND TRADE GROUPS

Pet Breeding:

American Kennel Club: 51 Madison Avenue, New York, NY 10010; phone: (212) 696-8200.

National Congress of Animal Trainers and Breeders: Route 1, Box 32H, Oglebay Road, Grayslake, IL 60030.

United Kennel Club: 100 East Kilgore Road, Kalamazoo, MI 49001-5598; phone: (616) 343-9020.

Commercial and Farm Animal Breeding:

American Ostrich Association: 3840 Hulen St., Fort Worth, TX 76107; phone: (817) 731-8597.

American Buffalo Registry: 116 Executive Park, Louisville, KY 40207; phone: (502) 897-1650.

American Donkey and Mule Society: P.O. Box 865, Spindale, NC 28160; phone: (817) 382-6845.

Empress Chinchilla Breeders Cooperative: P.O. Box 402, Morrison, CO 80465; phone: (303) 697-4421.

Miniature Donkey Registry of the Unites States: 2901 N. Elm St., Denton, TX 76201; phone: (817) 382-6845.

National Pygmy Goat Association: 10000 Greenacres Dr., Bakersfield, CA 93312; phone: (805) 589-8081.

National Board of Farm Fur Organizations: 405 Sibley St., Ste. 120, St. Paul, MN 55101; phone: (612) 292-9629.

National Pedigree Livestock Council: 1 Holstein Place, Brattleboro, VT 05320-0808; phone: (802) 254-4551.

Their fur, which is more valuable than mink, sells for $55 to $75 pcr pclt and is uscd to makc fur coats that cost as much as $30,000. One of the largest U.S. chinchilla ranchers grosses between $200,000 and $400,000 annually and was able to trade 100 of his furry creatures for a Mercedes.

Butterfly breeding poses another unusual opportunity. One Pennsylvania butterfly farmer, Rick Mikula, started a breeding operation on a shoestring budget in his basement and was soon deluged with customers. He sells many of his insects to start-up butterfly breeders for six cents apiece. Butterfly releases at weddings are another profit center. Mikula also sells hundreds of butterflies weekly to zoos, aviaries, and flower gardens. Because the creatures live only two weeks, he enjoys steady demand. "I seem to be putting in 20 hour days," Mikula noted in the October 19, 1993 issue of *Northeast Pennsylvania Business Journal*.

If buffalos and butterflies aren't your style, maybe you will want to try giant, flightless birds. Indeed, many entrepreneurs were getting rich in the 1990s breeding emus and ostriches; the industry trade journal *Ratite Marketplace* boasted over 12,000 subscribers in 1994. A pair of adult breeding ostriches costs $45,000 to $60,000, and emus run approximately 20 percent less. But one pair of birds will produce about 40 chicks each year. As a result, raising these birds can be much more profitable than cattle ranching. At least one breeder had 1993 sales of more than $1 million.

Another unique business opportunity for animal lovers is breeding miniature and novelty livestock that are sold as pets and show animals. A lucrative market exists for miniature donkeys, horses, and cows that are less than three feet tall. Fainting goats—which stiffen and pass out for less than one minute when they are startled—are also big sellers. Although you will likely pay more for a good breeding animal, miniature horses typically sell for $1,000 to $2,500 and fainting goats go for about $1,000.

Worm ranching was one of the fastest-growing segments of the breeding business in the mid-1990s. This can be a great part-time home venture. Start-up costs are very low, and full-grown worms can be sold for fishing bait or as breeding specimens for about $2 per dozen. Most importantly, worm castings, or excrement, are a valuable soil additive used by greenhouses and to make potting mixes. Retail prices for castings are slightly less than $1 per pound, and bulk wholesale rates are about $250 per cubic yard. A 400-square-foot farm with 750,000 worms will require you to work about 20 hours per week, and will net between $10,000 and $15,000 annually.

SETTING UP YOUR BUSINESS

You can set up a simple dog breeding area in your home for one or two dogs. Several dogs will require a separate confinement area with access to dry, weatherproof housing and an area with a natural surface. A separate run for each dog of at least 100 square feet is ideal. Make sure that your dogs always have clean water available in dishes that won't tip or slosh. Feed your dogs at least once each day, and clean food bowls twice per week. A multi-dog confinement area will require individual feeding times to ensure that each dog is properly nourished.

A female dog will reach its whelping (birthing) date about two months after mating—watch for restlessness, swelling teats, and refusal to eat. The separated whelping area should have a warm bed protected from drafts and an infrared lamp in case extra warmth is needed. Buy a whelping box, or cover soft blankets with clean rags that can be changed and cleaned. Introduce the dog to the whelping area two weeks before the anticipated birth date. Each whelping area should be segregated.

Speak with your vet or read one of many books to learn how to help your dog if she has trouble during birth—she may fail to bite off the umbilical cord and clean the new pups, for example. You should also extensively research the care and training of puppies before they are born. Contact the **United Kennel Club (UKC)** about establishing proper records for your purebreds. Write: **UKC, 100 East Kilgore Road, Kalamazoo, MI 49001-5598; or call (616) 343-9020.**

If your interests are more in making money than in having a hobby, breeding chinchillas is a better bet than dog or cat breeding for a business that you can start at home. Chinchillas can be domesticated, and you can raise them in a cage much as you would a weasel or guinea pig. If your business grows, you can construct outdoor chinchilla houses. One chinchilla breeder keeps 3,500 animals on a five-acre spread. For more information about breeding and selling these squirrel-like creatures, contact the national Empress Chinchilla Breeders Cooperative.

About all you need to start your worm breeding business are worms and a few buckets. You can purchase African night crawler worms from a fellow breeder. Put the worms in a bucket and feed them a strict diet of peat, de-inked newspapers, and composted grains. The worms convert the food into castings, and you separate the worms and the castings using a special machine. The worms grow best at a temperature of 65 to 75 degrees Fahrenheit. As your worms multiply, you can sell them or expand your farm. The best way to learn about worm breeding is visit a worm farm. Ask a local bait shop for the name of the largest breeder in your area.

If you are thinking about starting or expanding a farm

SELECTED PUBLICATIONS AND PERIODICALS

Dog Breeding Publications:

American Kennel Club: American Kennel Club, 51 Madison Ave., New York, NY 10010; phone: (212) 696-8200. Covers dog care and training.

U.K.C. Kennel Requirements for Breeders of United Kennel Club Registered Dogs: United Kennel Club (UKC), 100 East Kilgore Road, Kalamazoo, MI 49001-5598; phone: (616) 343-9020.

Breeding Periodicals:

American Ostrich Association Newsletter: 3840 Hulen St., Fort Worth, TX 76107; phone: (817) 731-8597.

American Fur: National Board of Fur Farm Organizations, 405 Sibley St., Ste. 120, St. Paul, MN 55101; phone: (612) 292-9629.

Animals: 350 S. Huntington Ave., Boston, MA 02130; phone: (617) 522-7400.

Bison World: American Bison Association, P.O. Box 16660, Stockyard Station, Denver, CO 80216; phone: (303) 292-2833.

Bloodlines: UKC (see address above). Breeding information for dogs.

Cat World International: P.O. Box 35635, Phoenix, AZ 85069.

Dog World International: 300 W. Adams St., Chicago, IL 60606; phone: (312) 726-2802.

animal breeding business, there are several factors you will want to consider. Of course you will need a large area—perhaps even several thousand acres if you plan to graze animals. One elk breeder, for example, grazes about 330 animals on 5,000 acres, and finds elk three times cheaper to feed and graze than cattle. He sells some meat, but makes most of his money selling trophy hunting trips. The North American Elk Breeders Association can help you get started.

While buffalo don't necessarily require more room than cattle, each animal consumes about $1,000 worth of feed each year. In addition, a pair of buffalo will yield only one calf each year, so it might take a long time to build a profitable business. Ask the American Buffalo World Registry or the American Bison Association for more information.

If you have no experience breeding grazing animals and you have limited space, ostriches and emus may be the best way to break into the large animal breeding business. They are relatively easy to raise and a breeding pair requires only about three-quarters of an acre. Although they fare best in the U.S. Southwest, ostriches and emus are surprisingly adaptable and can do well in most climates if they have adequate shelter. But ostriches can grow ten feet tall and weigh more than 400 pounds. They can also break your ribs and kick down chain-link fences. The American Ostrich Association can supply you with advice on breeding the animals.

In contrast to ostriches, miniature and novelty farm animals are typically docile breeds; many were originally bred as pets for the children of royalty. They also require less space and food than normal stock, and are relatively easy to breed. For breeders with a little bit of livestock know-how, miniature breeds are an easy way to branch out into new markets.

MANAGEMENT ISSUES

The pet breeding business is crowded with both hobbyists and "puppy mills," which makes it difficult for start-up breeding businesses to turn a profit—even for breeders of race and hunting dogs. As evidence of this excess supply are millions of homeless animals that are destroyed each year, many of which are purebred (25 percent by one estimate). The problem is so bad that in 1993 the Humane Society of the United States proposed a two-year ban on all breeding of cats and dogs. In addition, many communities have started funding their animal shelters with heavy taxes on local breeders.

At the top end of the pet breeding spectrum are high-tech breeders that often use embryo-transfer and artificial insemination techniques to produce genetically superior show animals. Many of those breeders have been investing and working for years to perfect their animals and establish a reputation. They typically view their profession as a mix of art and science. For example, breeders will wait two years before breeding some types of dogs so that the Orthopedic

Foundation for Animals can certify an animal's ''hip soundness.''

If you think you may have what it takes to compete in the lucrative show dog breeding arena, contact the UKC, the largest dog registry in the world. The UKC can give you information on breeds, registration services, and breeders in your area and help you track down a high-quality stud that will complement your dog's physical characteristics and personality. Like most industry associations, the UKC discourages breeding pets for sale to retail shops, so don't expect help for a standard puppy-breeding business.

LICENSES AND REGISTRATION

Purebred dogs can be registered under a variety of programs that vary according to breed and bloodlines. Different registrations are available with the UKC, for example, for dogs with 14, 126, or 254 recorded ancestors, going back seven generations. Similar cat registration programs exist. The UKC and the American Kennel Club are the two largest purebred registries in the United States. In addition, most dog and cat breeds have a separate association that can help you register animals.

Dog, cat, bird, chinchilla, and other pet breeding businesses will need standard local and state business licenses. In addition, many communities require breeders to obtain special licenses and pay breeding fees. One community charges $70 per breeding animal annually, plus $25 for a license. Another city charges a flat fee of only $25. Some cities outlaw pet breeding entirely.

If you are going to breed commercial and farm animals, a variety of different licenses and laws will govern your business. Animals that are considered livestock, for example, are often subject to required testing for such diseases as tuberculosis. If you are going to graze your animals, you will need to obtain permission from local governing bodies. For enterprises such as elk hunting farms, your proposal may be subjected to a pubic hearing. Contact the associations that apply to your breeding operation for information on applicable state and federal laws. The business licensing department at your city hall can fill you in on local requirements.

Animal breeding can be a great way to make money and break the shackles of the nine-to-five routine. It offers a fulfilling hobby for enthusiasts and even affords nice profits for a select group of skilled breeders. But many animal lovers that try to make pet breeding a business become disillusioned. Specialty commercial and farm animals, on the other hand, offer an excellent opportunity to start a business on a small budget. With thorough research, a good business plan, and a little help from mother nature, you can reap big profits breeding the right animals.

SOURCES:

American Kennel Club: Dog Care and Training, MacMillan Publishing Company, 1991.

''Breeding,'' *Animals,* May/June 1993, p. 12.

Brekke, Ken, ''From Hobby to Champion Horses: Their 'Babies' Can Command Six Figures,'' *La Cross Tribune,* May 17, 1993.

Creedy, Steve, ''Worms Turning a Profit: Washington Farmers Tout Ecological Benefits,'' *Pittsburgh Post-Gazette,* March 21, 1993, p. C1.

Hoffman, Mark, ''Hazleton Man Has Winged Business Idea,'' *Northeast Pennsylvania Business Journal,* sec. 1, p. 18.

Lakes, Greg, ''Game Farm's Fair Game in West's Wild Debate,'' *Missoulian,* January 9, 1994, p. A1.

Lane, Bob, ''Sims Again Seeks Leash on Animal Breeding— Aim Is to Lower Number of Cats, Dogs Destroyed,'' *Seattle Times,* September 26, 1991, p. C1.

Loretz, John, ''A Question of Breeding,'' *Animals,* March/April 1993, p. 8.

Madden, Michael, editor, *Small Business Start-Up Index,* issue 1, Gale, 1991.

Neill, Michael, and Bill Shaw, ''A Life That No Dog Deserves,'' *People,* February 10, 1992, p. 67.

O'Boyle, Maureen, ''These Ranchers Ride on Chinchilla's Appeal,'' *Business First-Columbus,* January 31, 1994, p. 14.

Owen, Jack, ''This Bird's No Turkey: They're Mean, They're Lean, and They Could Just Make You Rich,'' *Miami Daily Business Review,* September 24, 1993, p. B1.

Segal, Troy ''It Takes a Special Breed to Play the Dog Game,'' *Business Week,* November 19, 1990, p. 176.

Smith, Rosalind, ''Breeders Hope Odd Animals Will Be a Cash Cow,'' *Press Enterprise,* December 26, 1994.

Stodder, Gayle Sato, ''Ostrich Ranching,'' *Entrepreneur,* May 1993, p. 186.

Sundby, Jill, ''Miniature Animals Give Big Rewards,'' *Billings Gazette,* April 4, 1993, p. D1.

U.K.C. Kennel Requirements For Breeders of UKC Registered Dogs, United Kennel Club, April 1993.

Ullman, Hans-Jochen, *The New Dog Handbook,* Baron's Educational Series, Inc., 1985.

Woy, Patricia A., *Small Businesses That Grow and Grow and Grow,* second edition, Betterway Publications, 1989.

—*DAVE MOTE*

Automobile Detailing Service

Automobile detailing has been called glorified car washing, but good detailing is really much more. Detailing attends to the specific maintenance needs of the high-tech materials used in modern automobiles. It does more than simply maintain a showroom shine; detailing helps preserve a car's value.

Changes within the automotive industry during the early 1990s resulted in a boom for auto detailers. As vehicle prices rose, owners kept their cars longer and became more interested in extending the value of their original investments. In addition, the development of innovative space-age materials created a demand for care beyond the scope of typical do-it-yourself, in-the-driveway car washes. Auto detailers reaped the rewards.

COSTS AND PROFITS

Auto detailing shops vary from small one-person operations working out of mobile units to large multi-bay centers servicing hundreds of cars annually. As a result, the costs of opening an auto detailing company depend on the type of shop envisioned. On the low end, detailers can set up a business for under $10,000, while on the high end, costs sometimes exceed $100,000. Average start-up costs are approximately $30,000.

According to Entrepreneur Group's *25 Hot Businesses for the Nineties,* in 1992 prices for the basic major equipment and initial supplies were between $5,000 and $17,000. Necessary auto detailing equipment includes rotary and orbital buffers, a wet/dry vacuum, a pressure cleaner, signs, a cash box or register, a security system, and office equipment. You will also need such supplies as cleaning solvents and soaps, polishes, waxes, buckets, rags, cotton swabs, toothbrushes, rubber gloves, aprons, and breathing filters. In addition, detailers require a place to work and space for customer parking.

Some companies eliminate the space requirements by operating mobile units. One source for mobile equipment is **National Detail Advanced Reconditioning Specialists, 801 Mitchell Road, Unit 108, Thousand Oaks, CA 91320; phone: (800) 356-9485.** The company offers two different self-contained systems, both assembled in trailers and designed to be pulled by a car or truck. The systems contain everything you need to enter the mobile auto detailing business. The smaller system, priced at $7,995, includes a 50-gallon water tank, a pressure washer, a steam cleaner, and canopies. The larger system comes with two 65-gallon water tanks, higher pressure capabilities, and extra items such as a carpet extractor and a hose reel. In addition to providing equipment, the company offers training, technical advice, and marketing assistance.

Because National Detail Advanced Reconditioning Specialists is not a franchise, system purchasers are under no obligation to pay licensing fees or royalties or to buy specified quantities of additional supplies and equipment. The company does, however, offer discounted products to people who have purchased its trailer systems.

On the other end of the auto detailing spectrum, business owners investing in a freestanding, full-service detailing center can expect start-up costs to run $100,000 and higher, depending on their location and other options. For example, in 1993 Ziebart TidyCar start-up costs were estimated to range between $99,000 and $161,000. Expenses include items such as the franchise license fee, equipment, site improvements, lease deposit, a computer system, grand opening advertising expenses, miscellaneous costs, and working capital as well as opening inventory and supplies, the first month's rent, and the first quarter's insurance premium.

Profit potential for automobile detailing shops depends on the type of establishment and its volume. For the industry as a whole, Entrepreneur Group reported that pretax profits in 1992 tended to range between 37 and 41 percent of sales, and the editors of *Entrepreneur* magazine estimated that during the early 1990s industrywide average net profit before taxes came to about $100,000, with high-end potential around $175,000.

In 1992 the average price for a thorough interior and exterior detailing job ran about $150 per vehicle, although some deluxe jobs fetched up to $550. As prices increase, however, the number of potential customers decreases. To help boost volume, some detailers offer a low-end product, such as washing by hand. The proper blend of services can help maximize profits.

from franchise to franchise, so make sure to get precise information from the companies you consider.

FRANCHISE OPPORTUNITIES

Endrust Auto Appearance & Detailing Centers:
1725 Washington Road, Suite 205, Pittsburgh, PA 15241; phone: (412) 831-1255. Founded, 1969; began franchising, 1975; reported 20 outlets in 1991; services include detailing, sound deadening, and car alarm installation. Franchisor provides on-site training program, advertising materials, and continuous releases of industry information. No franchise fee; initial investment estimated at $30,000; additional $20,000 required for working capital.

Geo Systems: 621 Lakeview Road, Suite C, Clearwater, FL 34616; phone: (813) 531-5400. Services include exterior Teflon protective coatings, detailing, glass tinting, power washing, interior steam cleaning, fabric protection, windshield repair, custom paint touch-ups, and security system installation. Complete mobile dealerships start at $1,995; financing available.

Shine Factory Systems, Inc.: 116 Monument Pl. SE, Calgary, Alberta, Canada T2A 1X3; phone: (403) 273-3525. Founded, 1979; began franchising, 1979; reported 26 Canadian outlets in 1991 and planned to expand in the U.S.; services include protective automotive paint finishes and detailing; franchisor provides hands-on two-week training program. Franchise fees start at $20,000 (Canadian).

Ziebart TidyCar: 1290 E. Maple Rd., Troy, MI 48007; phone: (810) 588-4100 or (800) 877-1312. Founded, 1963; more than 700 locations in 45 countries; offers full service auto improvement business featuring detailing and accessorizing for fleet and individual automobile owners; mobile service unit also available. Franchisor provides required 6-week training program and ongoing support. Franchise fee: $24,000.

FINANCING

If you are planning to open an independent shop, be sure to prepare thoroughly before approaching a lending institution for financing. You will need to make an assessment of your assets and be ready to disclose how much of a cash investment you can make. You will also be required to detail your projected expenses and justify income estimates. A solid business plan can encourage potential lenders to favorably evaluate your credit worthiness.

The **Small Business Administration (SBA),** which can be reached by calling **1-800-U ASK SBA,** and local community development authorities are other sources for funding. If you qualify for minority status, check with federal, state, and local government agencies for special lending programs. These sources, however, tend to require more paperwork than traditional lenders, and the approval process sometimes takes much longer.

In addition, several franchises offer financing to approved franchisees. You will, though, be expected to provide a percentage of the total start-up expenses from your own resources. The amount of your investment will vary

LOCATION AND SETUP

Store location will play a major role in your start-up costs. Premium locations demand premium prices. If you plan to focus your efforts on capturing a segment of the retail market, a location with a lot of traffic, good visibility, and easy access will be to your advantage. On the other hand, if most of your work will be done on a wholesale basis for car dealers or fleets, you may find a cheaper location off the beaten path more suitable.

When deciding on a location, analyze a region's car registrations. Although detailing customers can own any type of car, your best customers will probably be the owners of high value vehicles; look for places where these owners congregate. For example, if you locate your business in the garage area of an urban office complex, your customers can enjoy the convenience of having their cars serviced while they are at work. Proximity to a country club can also be a benefit, especially if you provide transportation.

Although you may choose to establish a freestanding facility for your business, you may find other options more beneficial and less expensive. One alternative is to rent space from a company whose products or services compliment your own. For example, high-traffic automatic car washes that do not already offer detailing may be glad to provide you with the space you need. Other possibilities include car dealerships, auto service centers, oil change or quick lube shops, repair shops, and body shops. Any place people leave cars for servicing or parking is potentially a good location.

Once you select your location you will probably need to modify the site to fit your needs. Although you will use most of the area for work space, you will also require a customer service area and an office for keeping your files and computer. Your customer area will include a cash register and counter space. If some of your customers will be waiting for their vehicles, provide a seating area and access to rest rooms. If you offer add-on products, a display area below or behind the counter can help bolster sales.

Make sure your store location is kept neat and shiny; your customers will get their first impression of your work from how you keep your shop. They will notice your attention to detail or lack of it. They will also make note of the service they receive. If you treat your customers poorly, they will get a negative impression about the type of care you will give their vehicles. Conversely, if you treat your customers well, they will develop confidence in the quality of your service.

If you decide to operate a mobile unit, instead of providing an environment where customers feel comfortable, you will be more concerned with route development and setting up a supply center. Check with your local zoning authority to determine whether or not you can use your home as a base for your business. Regulations may prohibit you from doing so, but you can usually rent warehouse space at prices far below the cost of premium locations. Developing routes and service schedules will enable you to use your time efficiently.

STAFFING

Mobile auto detailing can be done by a single person, but opening a store location will necessitate hiring employees. Even if you plan to do most of the work yourself, you will need extra help to answer the telephone or greet customers during busy seasons as well as to oversee the operation in your absence. If your strengths are in the administrative end of the business, your staffing requirements will focus on obtaining the right people to work on your customers' vehicles.

One of the most important people in your business will be the person who answers your telephone. Many of your customers will get their first impression of your company based on how they are treated when they call. Questions regarding your services and prices must be handled diplomatically because some potential customers may get "sticker shock" if you simply quote the price of your premium package. Kevin Rourke, owner of The Car Salon, Inc. in Atlanta, Georgia, suggested in *Professional Carwashing & Detailing,* "Ask each customer to describe their needs so you can recommend the best service."

INDUSTRY STATISTICS

- The International Carwash Association recommends detailing twice a year (source: *Business First of Buffalo,* July 22, 1991).
- There were an estimated 10,000 to 12,000 detailing shops operating in the U.S. during 1991; 90 percent were affiliated with a car wash (source: *Business First of Buffalo,* July 22, 1991).
- In 1971 the average age of cars on U.S. roads was 5.75 years; in 1992 the average age of cars on U.S. roads was 7.5 years (source: *Auto Detailing the Professional Way,* Chilton Book Co., 1992).
- New vehicle prices rose approximately 23 percent between 1986 and 1991 (source: Ziebart TidyCar, 1993).
- In 1992, the average full-service conveyor car-wash location received 11 percent of its revenue from an on-site detail shop; the average exterior-only conveyor location received 14 percent of its revenue from an on-site detail shop (source: *Professional Carwashing & Detailing* 1993 Automatic Carwash Survey).
- *Professional Carwashing & Detailing* reported a 3.6 percent increase in traffic at automatic carwashes between 1991 and 1992; gross revenues per car increased 1.4 percent for full-service facilities, but exterior-only tunnel washes experienced no growth; average extra service revenues were up 9 to 11 percent.

TRAINING EMPLOYEES

The employees you hire to work on your customers' vehicles require careful training. Improperly handled high-power buffers can cause serious damage to paint finishes. Different types of buffers present varying degrees of handling difficulty. In general, the higher the speed, the more skill required for safe operation. Orbital buffers are less powerful than rotary buffers and are less likely to damage a car's finish, but also lack the power needed to remove paint defects and oxidation. One type of buffer, a random orbital buffer, simulates the motion of hand polishing. Although hand buffing takes considerably longer than mechanical buffing, some detail shops specialize in hand operations that bring premium prices.

Your employees must also be knowledgeable about the chemical compatibility of various cleaning products. In addition, the chemicals selected must be compatible with various car finishes. For example, Nissan's Infiniti uses a high-tech clear coat finish made from a fluorine-based product. As a result, it requires the use of special fluorine compatible detailing products.

When you hire people, look for individuals who are conscientious, meticulous, precise, thorough, and even fussy. Auto detailing is called "detailing" because it deals with the intricacies of car maintenance. The success of an auto detailing shop is often found in its attention to small, often-overlooked things—the cleanliness of a wheel well or the repairing of a tiny scratch on a radio dial. The process of doing a good job requires hands-on and on-the-knees work.

To provide consistent services, you will want to establish long-term relationships with your employees. The car wash industry as a whole typically experiences high turnover. *Professional Carwashing & Detailing* reported in its 1993 Automatic Carwash Survey that average employee tenure for full-service conveyor car wash employees was only ten months. When you negotiate wage and benefit packages, keep in mind that the long-term benefits of developing a loyal, experienced staff may outweigh the short-term financial benefits of paying low wages.

MANAGEMENT ISSUES

One of the first decisions you will need to make when you decide to open an auto detailing establishment is whether to do business as an independent shop or as a franchise. The largest detailing franchise in North America in the early 1990s was Ziebart TidyCar, which offers a wide range of service packages from basic detailing to complete reconditioning. Ziebart TidyCar franchises also perform accessory installation of such items as sunroofs, security systems, and trailer hitches.

Another decision you will need to make is whether to provide your services to the wholesale market, retail market, or a blend of the two. Traditional wholesale customers include new- and used-car dealers. Detailers prep new cars

PRIMARY ASSOCIATIONS, TRADE PUBLICATIONS, AND CONVENTIONS

Associations:

International Carwash Association: 1 Imperial Place Building, 1 E. 22nd Street, Suite 400, Lombard, IL 60148-4915; phone: (708) 495-0100.

Professional Detailing Association: 4800 SW West Hills Drive, Topeka, KA; phone: (913) 273-5456. Publishes monthly technical bulletin and periodic newsletters.

Publications:

American Clean Car Magazine: 500 N. Dearborn, Suite 1100, Chicago, IL 60610; phone: (312) 337-7700. $33.00/year (six issues); free to qualifying industry participants.
ICA Letter: International Car Wash Association, 1 Imperial Place Building, 1 E. 22nd Street, Suite 400, Lombard, IL 60148-4915; phone: (708) 495-0100.
Professional Carwashing & Detailing: National Trade Publications, Inc., 13 Century Hill Drive, Latham, NY 12110-2197; phone: (518) 783-1281. Also publishes industry surveys.

Conventions:

International Carwash Association Convention and Exposition: International Carwash Association (ICA), 1 Imperial Place Building, 1 E. 22nd Street, Suite 400, Lombard, IL 60148; phone: (708) 495-0100.

prior to sale and recondition used cars. The work is often done on a contractual basis with provisions for adjustments based on a vehicle's condition. In addition to dealerships, wholesale customers include government agencies, highway patrols, ambulance services, daily car rental companies, school districts, funeral homes, and other fleet owners. Although wholesale customers generally pay a discounted rate, ranging from 20 to 40 percent less than retail, they supply a steady source of income. This can be of special significance if you are located in an area subject to climatic changes and seasons of inclement weather.

The bulk of your retail customers will be individual auto owners. Other potential clients include owners of recreational vehicles, boats, and airplanes. Traditionally, retail customers bring higher per car profits but less steady revenue. To maximize profits, many auto detailers market their services to a variety of customers. You will have to study the market in your area to determine the appropriate blend of wholesale and retail traffic through your shop. According to one estimate, the median annual volume for a detailing shop in 1992 was 300 cars wholesale and 400 cars retail.

To increase sales potential you may decide to offer add-on services such as installing cellular phones, audio equipment, vehicle alarms, auxiliary lighting, and sunroofs. As you evaluate the market demand for these kinds of services,

remember to consider your ability to perform them or calculate the costs associated with hiring an installer. In the event that you do hire an installer, make sure the quality meets your standards.

MARKETING

When your detailing shop first opens, you may find it beneficial to work primarily with car dealers even if you plan to eventually focus on the retail sector. This will help to establish your business name and reputation in the community. It will also provide you with a source of revenue while you build up a regular clientele.

New car dealerships are also an excellent source of leads for potential customers. You can have a brochure printed and arrange for local dealerships to distribute them to new car buyers. Some dealers will merely make your brochures available to new car buyers; others may actually sell detailing packages for you. In the latter case, make sure you price your services to include any sales commissions you will pay to the dealer.

Some detailers have found that the most effective brochures focus on how to protect the investment made in a new car. Literature describing detailing services educates new car buyers on the benefits of removing oxidation and filling in scratches to maintain the mirror-like shine of a showroom finish. Oxidation, a chemical reaction between a car's paint pigments and chemical agents in the atmosphere, creates a dull cover that is not removed by traditional washing and waxing. Tiny scratches caused by friction with particles in the air interfere with the ability to reflect light and, over time, dull even a clean car's finish.

Your literature can help potential customers understand that regular detailing pays off in real dollars. First, people tend to keep clean cars longer and thereby save on financing costs. Second, regularly detailed cars tend to fetch higher prices when they are traded in. Detailing can also pay off in reduced expenses for mechanical maintenance. On a well detailed car, maintenance problems such as leaks, worn belts, and hoses, are more easily noticed before they become major problems. As a result, a detailed car may last longer.

One way to help increase your business is to give away a complete detailing job. You can offer a standard or deluxe package as a prize in a benefit fund-raiser, or you can sponsor your own contest. People like to talk about their cars, and once you have demonstrated what you can do, word of mouth will help spread the news. One thing to remember, however, is that the tendency people have to talk about their cars can work against you if someone has a bad experience. Make certain all your employees maintain the standards you set.

Another marketing tool some detailers have used to increase sales volume is separating interior and exterior services. This practice enables them to offer detailing packages with lower prices than those necessary for complete jobs. Lower prices help overcome price resistance.

If you are operating a mobile detailing service, you will want to highlight convenience. When potential customers lack the time to visit a detailing shop, your ability to come to them will give you an advantage over your competition. If you are operating from a stationary shop, consider providing transportation for customers who must drop off their vehicles.

ADVERTISING

Advertising methods frequently used by auto detailers include direct mail, coupons, specials—such as discounts for senior citizens—and promotions with new-car dealers. One of the best sources for a direct mail advertising list is your existing customer base. Until you develop a list of regular customers, you can buy mailing lists. A sales representative from a mailing list company can help you determine what criteria will provide the best list for your needs. You may want to identify customers in a specific income bracket or target owners of certain types of automobiles.

In some franchises, you can join in national advertising campaigns. Depending on your specific franchise agreement, this participation may be optional or mandatory. When your involvement is voluntary, you will want to weigh its benefits against its costs. In urban areas with many advertising outlets, the cost of covering them can be very expensive, and you thus may gain from the franchise name recognition. In rural areas, it may be less expensive to handle all of your advertising yourself.

LICENSES AND INSURANCE

No matter where you locate your business, be sure to check with your local governing body to make sure you comply with all licensing and zoning rules. Some jurisdictions will also require you to carry specified amounts of liability insurance. One franchise estimated that quarterly insurance premiums ranged between $1,000 and $2,000 for its franchisees. Also, make sure you comply with all environmental regulations, especially those governing water discharge. It may be necessary for you to separate oil-contaminated water or water containing certain solvents for special handling. The costs of compliance can run into thousands of dollars, and fines for noncompliance can be hefty.

COMPUTER SYSTEM AND PROGRAMS

To help you run your auto detailing operation efficiently, some franchisors provide customized computer software. Independent shops can also benefit from computer technology by purchasing systems capable of maintaining customer records, performing bookkeeping tasks, keeping track of inventory, and generating invoices. Look for programs that will help you keep customer lists up to date so you can mail reminders when cars are due for service. In addition, Entrepreneur Group publishes a software package, *Auto Detailing,* designed specifically to help operate an auto detailing shop.

Many auto detailing shops are run by specialists in the craft, not business experts. In order to establish your business, you need to take a craftsperson's pride in the work you do, but you can outshine your competition by also becoming a savvy business owner. If you hone your entrepreneurial skills and build a reputation for quality, you can establish a successful auto detailing operation.

SOURCES:

"Auto Detailing: Cash in on a Showroom Shine," *25 Hot Businesses for the Nineties,* Entrepreneur Group, 1992, pp. 5-10.

Entrepreneur Magazine's 111 Businesses You Can Start for Under $10,000, Bantam Books, 1991, pp. 225-27.

Fink, James, "Car Owners Find Detail Shops Are Cut from a Different Cloth," *Business First of Buffalo,* July 22, 1991.

Horton, Cleveland, "Detailers Master Fine Points," *Advertising Age,* February 23, 1987.

Joseph, James, *Auto Detailing: The Professional Way,* Chilton Book Co., 1992.

Madden, Michael, editor, *Small Business Start-Up Index,* issue 2, Gale, 1991.

Martin, Susan Boyles, editor, *Worldwide Franchise Directory,* Gale, 1991.

"1993 Automatic Carwash Survey," *Professional Carwashing & Detailing,* 1993.

Reisert, Skip, "Selling Add-Ons Can Increase Sales," *Professional Carwashing & Detailing,* November 1993.

Rourke, Kevin, "Smart Detail Shop Marketing," *Professional Carwashing & Detailing,* November 1993.

Schwartz, Carol A., editor, *Small Business Sourcebook,* sixth edition, Gale, 1993.

Small Business Opportunities, November 1993.

Additional information for this profile was provided by Ziebart TidyCar, 1290 East Maple Road, Troy, MI 48007.

—KAREN BELLENIR

Automobile Oil Changing

Service

The decline of full-service gasoline stations in the early 1970s gave rise to an automobile maintenance and repair industry that specialized in many of the services that were once provided by neighborhood gas stations. Entrants into the market included tire dealers, transmission-repair businesses, and brake, muffler, and tune-up shops. A very lucrative segment of the auto maintenance industry became businesses specializing in fast, low-cost oil changes.

Oil change specialists catered to customers who no longer had the time, a place, or the inclination to perform relatively simple automobile maintenance jobs for themselves. Car owners began keeping their cars longer and became more concerned with preventive maintenance, which included regular oil changes. Quick oil change shops also came to benefit from concern for the environment and legislation regulating the disposal or recycling of used oil. In the early 1990s, there were an estimated 6,000 oil changing service shops nationwide, accounting for about one-third of the $8 billion oil change industry. Most new-car dealers and some gas stations also offered oil changes and continued, collectively, to account for the majority of the U.S. retail oil change business.

Most quick oil change shops offered a standard set of services that, in addition to changing the motor oil, included checking other automotive fluids, such as the brake, transmission, power-steering, and windshield washer fluids, and topping them off if necessary. They also inspected the air filter and air pressure in the tires. Some quick oil change shops even washed the windows and vacuumed the car's interior.

In the early 1990s, many oil changing shops had begun offering tune-ups and other automotive services in an effort to expand their customer base. Likewise, small businesses that began as specialists in brakes or tune-ups were inclined to provide oil changing services. Though oil changes done by car dealers were usually part of warranty-maintenance or purchase-incentive programs—some offering free oil changes for the life of the car—car dealers also were beginning to match quick oil change shops in price, speed, and attention to customer service.

One of the latest trends in the quick oil change industry of the early 1990s was mobile service that catered to cus-tomers who found it inconvenient to drive to a shop and wait 10 to 15 minutes. Such businesses outfitted a van with all the necessary equipment and serviced cars at customers' homes or offices. Mobile oil changing services generally charged prices competitive with other oil change businesses; their labor cost per oil change was higher, but mobile businesses usually had much lower start-up costs and little overhead, so they needed fewer customers to be profitable.

Although many opportunities still existed, the quick oil change business was considered a mature industry in many areas of the United States, especially the Northeast, in the 1990s, and it was dominated by big-name franchisors. Some of the best-known companies were offering new franchises only on a very selective basis. Entrepreneurs entering the quick oil change industry needed to be prepared for stiff competition and be determined to offer exceptional service to ensure customer loyalty and repeat business.

FINANCIAL ASPECTS

Depending on whether you buy or lease a facility, start-up costs for an oil changing service are likely to run from a minimum of $80,000 to as much as $300,000; the average start-up cost is about $100,000. A successful quick oil change shop averages $45,000 to $60,000 in profit before taxes, based on a volume of approximately 40 cars per day.

Land, construction, equipment, and even operating capital can be financed. Investing your own money in any enterprise avoids several complications. Using your own funds is the fastest and easiest way to raise capital while avoiding interest charges and retaining greater control of your business. But, there are also greater risks involved with investing your own money, and you may not have the financial resources. In that case, you need to consider other sources of financing.

The first thing you should do is seek out a financial advisor. Some banks and community colleges offer small business assistance programs. There are also associations of retired business executives who volunteer to assist start-up businesses. These people can help you seek financing and also help create a business plan that will satisfy potential lenders.

Banks, in particular, are notoriously conservative in

FRANCHISE OPPORTUNITIES

Jiffy Lube International, Inc.: 6000 Metro Dr., Baltimore, MD 21215; phone: (800) 327-9532. Founded, 1982; purchased by Pennzoil Co., 1989; more than 330 company-operated outlets and 700 franchises in 46 states; considered the industry leader. Franchisor requires 2-week training program and assists in preparing a business plan.

Quaker State Minit-Lube Inc.: 1385 W. 2200 South, Salt Lake City, UT 84119; phone: (801) 972-6667. More than 370 company-operated outlets and 50 franchises in 20 states.

Valvoline Instant Oil Change, Inc.: P.O. Box 14046, Lexington, KY 40512. Founded, 1866; began franchising, 1982; initial franchise fee: $25,000; more than 330 company operated outlets and 50 franchises. Franchisor provides all equipment and requires 5-week technical training course.

Other Franchisors: All Tune and Lube: 407 Headquarters Dr., Millersville, MD 21108; phone: (800) 333-9263. **Grease Monkey International, Inc.:** 216 16th St., Denver, CO 80202; phone: (303) 534-1660. **LubePro's International:** 1900 N. Roselle Road, Schaumburg, IL 60195; phone: (800) 654-LUBE. **Oil Can Henry's:** 12000 N.W. Front Ave., Portland, OR 97209; phone: (800) 765-6244. **Oil Express National, Inc.:** 15 Spinning Wheel Road, Hinsdale, IL 60521; phone: (708) 325-8666.

their lending practices and will ask to see a sound business plan. They will also perform a thorough background check and require collateral, though you may be able to get an unsecured loan if you have an excellent credit rating and are putting up at least part of the capital yourself. Finance companies often will accept greater risk and may extend a loan in cases where a bank will not; however, they also charge higher interest rates. Another potential source of capital is to sell equity in your business. An equity investment is not a loan, and therefore there are no legal obligations for you to repay the investment. Instead, investors own a percentage of the business and share in all losses and profits. Although selling equity may seem to be a good way to raise capital, you may also lose some control over your business. Always check with a lawyer before entering any legal arrangement.

The **Small Business Administration (SBA)** is another source of start-up capital. The SBA is an independent agency of the U.S. government that promotes small businesses through loans, counseling, and other information. As far as financing goes, though, you generally must exhaust all sources of private financing before you are eligible for an SBA loan. There are Small Business Administration offices in most major cities. Check the U.S. Government section of the telephone directory for locations and telephone numbers; you can also reach the SBA at **1-800-U ASK SBA.**

FRANCHISE OR INDEPENDENT?

One of the hardest decisions to make will be whether to purchase a franchise or remain independent. Franchisors usually offer the benefits of a recognized business name, training, attractive equipment-purchase packages, a proven market strategy, and advertising programs. They may also help you secure financing, either directly or indirectly. In some cases, just being accepted by a franchisor indicates a better chance of success since reputable franchisors will do a market analysis to ensure that an area meets their requirements, infomation that may help you get financing through other sources.

The downside to becoming a franchise operation is that you give up some control over how your business is run. Franchisors establish general practices that they expect their franchisees to follow, often including hours of operation, products you use and sell, and uniforms your employees wear. In addition, there is usually a hefty up-front franchise fee that may range from $10,000 to $25,000. You may also incur some continuing financial obligations since most franchisors require franchisees to pay a percentage of gross sales as a royalty and for advertising.

Before deciding whether to stay independent or purchase a franchise, you should check the competition. Independent oil change shops have a tough time in areas dominated by franchises because of name recognition and marketing and promotional support. The local Yellow Pages telephone directory is a quick way to assess the situation. Do most of the oil change shops listed for your area appear to be franchises? Newspaper ads will also give you a good idea of how competitive the industry is and whether it is dominated by nationally known franchisors. If the majority of the oil changing service businesses in your area are franchises, you may want to hook up with a franchisor who is not already represented in the area.

If you decide to go with a franchisor, you should be aware that costs and services vary widely. Some franchisors provide help in selecting a site, raising capital, negotiating a lease, purchasing equipment, and hiring employees. They may even offer training programs for you and your employees ranging from a few days to several weeks and provide on-site assistance for the first three to 12 months of operation. On the other hand, some franchisors will sell you a name and a service manual and you may never hear from them again.

LOCATION

Choosing a location will be the most critical decision you make in opening your oil change shop. A poor location is the chief cause of all retail business failures, and the right location can help you overcome many early mistakes and shortcomings common to start-up businesses. A business advisor can help you do a market study, but you can also quite easily do some preliminary work yourself.

First, make sure the community can support another

quick oil change business. You need to be able to attract customers without setting off a price war, since established businesses are more likely to survive price competition than a start-up business. Check out the competition. Do those businesses appear healthy? Some things to consider are whether there seems to be a steady flow of customers and whether the facilities are well maintained. Have other oil change businesses opened recently, and if so, do they appear to be attracting customers without having to undercut the prices of more established businesses? Does the competition also offer services such as brakes jobs and tune-ups? If so, this may be an indication that there was not enough business to survive as an establishment that only offers oil changing services.

Also, learn as much as possible about the community, including average family income, employment trends, percentage of home ownership, and other demographic information that may give a clue as to whether the community is suitable for a new service-oriented business. The local chamber of commerce will be able to answer many of your questions, but remember that one of the chamber's jobs is to "sell" the community and it may present an overly optimistic scenario. The library, the Bureau of the Census, and many small business assistance programs can also supply detailed information about the local economy and population.

After you determine whether the market can support another quick oil change business, plot the competition and

INDUSTRY STATISTICS

- *Average Number of Years in the Quick Lube Business:* 6.
- *Average Number of Bays in Quick Lube Facility:* 3.
- *Average Cost of Basic Lube, Oil Change, and Filter:* $23.
- *Average Number of Cars Serviced Per Day:* 43.
- *Average Number of Cars Necessary to Break Even:* 28.
- *Busiest Day of the Week:* Saturday.
- *Busiest Month of the Year:* July.
- *Percentage of Quick Oil Change Facilities Leased:* 45%.
- *Percentage of Quick Oil Change Facilities Owned:* 55%.
- *Percentage of Quick Oil Change Shops Grossing Less Than $200,000:* 15%.
- *Percentage of Quick Oil Change Shops Grossing $200,000-$400,000:* 46%.
- *Percentage of Quick Oil Change Shops Grossing $400,000-$600,000:* 26%.
- *Percentage of Quick Oil Change Shops Grossing More Than $600,000:* 13%.
- *Percentage of Quick Oil Change Shops Using Lifts:* 21%.
- *Percentage of Quick Oil Change Shops Using Pits:* 89%.
- *Percentage of Quick Oil Change Shops Accepting Oil for Recycling:* 65%.
- *Average Hourly Rate Paid Lube Technicians:* $5.85.
- *Average Hourly Rate Paid Managers:* $9.75.

(SOURCE: *NATIONAL OIL & LUBE NEWS* SIXTH ANNUAL FAST LUBE SURVEY, 1993.)

population density on a map. Oil change shops generally draw customers only from their immediate market areas. You will not want to be too close to an established competitor, but you will need to be as close as possible to your potential customers. Locating your business close to other automotive services, such as brake repair and tune-up shops, may be a plus, but first determine whether those businesses offer oil changes as a sideline.

Most consultants recommend that a quick oil change shop be located in a secondary business district with a traffic count of at least 25,000 vehicles per day. Traffic information should be available from your state or city department of transportation. It is also better to be near a corner rather than on a corner so access to your business will not be affected by traffic backed up at the intersection. While busy streets are generally better for business, traffic congestion, median strips, high speeds, and other conditions that make entering or leaving your businesses more difficult will definitely work against success. Make sure you monitor traffic patterns during your projected hours of operation.

Although you are offering an automotive service, be sure to look into the nature of the pedestrian traffic. What brings people to the area? Do they fit your customer profile? Having popular stores nearby will give your customers someplace to go while they wait for an oil change or may convince others to have an oil change since they are in the area anyway. You will have to pay more for a prime location, but it should be worth it in the long run.

Other factors to consider in deciding on a location include the history of a particular site. Why is the space available? Did the previous business fail, and if so, why? Talk to nearby business owners. Are they doing well? Why do they think their neighbor failed? It may have been bad management, or it may have been a lack customers for that particular type of business. Go back to the department of transportation one more time to see if there are any major road construction projects planned for the area. The last thing you need is to open your business one day and then find the street torn up for six months of repairs the next.

FACILITY

As the potential owner of a start-up business, you are more likely to lease a facility than purchase one outright, which could cost as much as $250,000 for the land and building. However, you should not automatically dismiss the idea of buying a site if you can arrange the financing. Buying could save you money and aggravation in the long run, especially if you later lose your lease after paying for improvements and building up your business.

If you decide to lease, be very careful. Some advisors recommend signing the shortest possible lease, so if your business fails you are not trapped into making monthly payments on a facility you are no longer using. Others recommend a longer lease with an option to renew as protection against rent increases or losing your lease altogether.

PRIMARY ASSOCIATIONS AND SELECTED TRADE PUBLICATIONS

Associations:

Convenience Automobile Services Institute:
P.O. Box 34595, Bethesda, MD 20827; phone: (301) 897-3191.

Automotive Oil Change Association: 12810 Hillcrest, Suite 213, Dallas, TX 75230; phone: (800) 331-0329.

Publications:

National Oil & Lube News: 2541 74th St., Lubbock, TX 79423-1499; phone: (806) 745-7573.

Though you will most likely start off with a standard lease, everything should be negotiable, including who is responsible for remodeling, signage, and liability. If the site is part of a business complex, be wary of clauses that may regulate such operating conditions as the hours your business is allowed to be open. You will have greater flexibility with freestanding buildings. The best advice: If there is something about the lease that makes you uncomfortable, look elsewhere. The first site you find may not be the best.

Whether you buy or lease a site, most advisers recommend finding an existing lube center. Because service pits are preferable to lifts, the cost of converting a garage or other establishment to a quick oil change facility can be more costly than starting from scratch. Positioning a car over a service pit is faster than raising a car on a lift and also allows one technician to work under car while another works on ground level.

Once you have a site, about 80 percent of the facility should be devoted to work space. You should also have at least two work bays so that a problem with one customer's car will not delay servicing your next customer. The rest of the space should be divided among a customer order and payment area, a small waiting room, and an office and storage space. Most of your supplies, including motor oils, lubricants, and filters, can be stored in the work space, but you will need additional space for toiletries, cleansers, and extra equipment.

Although an oil change should take no more than 10 to 15 minutes, make the waiting area as comfortable as possible. If the waiting room is unpleasant, even 15 minutes may seem like a long time, and your customers may become impatient and less likely to authorize additional services. Your clients will also remember how they were treated when it is time for another oil change. At a minimum, the waiting area should be carpeted and equipped with coffee and soft-drink machines, soft music, current magazines, and comfortable chairs. Be sure to keep the waiting area, as well as your work area, clean. Customers will feel more relaxed in a tidy

waiting area and more confident if the work area appears clean.

MARKETING STRATEGIES

Marketing for an oil changing service naturally revolves around three basic selling points: preventive maintenance, convenience, and low price. At various times you will probably advertise your business based on each of these main themes: regular oil changes can prevent future mechanical problems; an oil change takes only a few minutes, no appointment is necessary, and it's much easier than doing it yourself; and an oil change at your shop is less expensive than one obtained somewhere else.

Price competition, however, is probably your least important selling point. Most quick oil change shops offer similar services for about the same price. Stiff competition already keeps profit margins very low in the oil change business. A price war with nearby competitors is likely to hurt more than help. In addition, full-service automotive repair shops often advertise extremely low-cost oil changes as a loss leader to attract customers to their more profitable services. A shop specializing in oil changes cannot compete with these low prices. On the other hand, full-service automotive shops may not be able to compete with your promise of fast service.

ADVERTISING

The best way to develop an effective advertising program is to ask successful businesses what works for them. Your competitors in the oil change business may not be willing to share their secrets with you, but other business will. Ask shops in the same business district, especially other automotive services, about their advertising. Most quick oil change shops advertise heavily in local newspapers. However, direct mail coupons have proven to be most effective in bringing in new customers. According to the *National Oil & Lube News,* direct mail coupons are the most popular form of advertising among oil change businesses, accounting for approximately one-third of their total advertising budgets.

Remember to target your customers. For example, apartment residents often have less time and no place to do their own oil changes. Fliers distributed to nearby apartment complexes may be very rewarding. You might also ask apartment managers to distribute coupons to new residents. Keep in mind that businesses fail without promotion. Develop an advertising program and budget at least six months worth of advertising with your start-up costs.

MANAGEMENT ISSUES

The most critical management issue facing owners of oil changing businesses may be the question of liability. Several owners have been sued by customers when something goes wrong with their cars after having the oil changed or other automotive service performed at a quick oil change shop.

These customers have claimed that the work was improperly done by poorly trained technicians, and there have been documented cases of the wrong parts or fluids being used and causing serious engine damage. There are insurance companies that offer coverage against liability claims; your best protection, though, is a properly trained work crew. Since most oil change technicians are paid near minimum wage, it is essential that a shop owner hire a dependable manager to supervise operations.

Another issue is whether to augment your oil change business with other automotive services. On the surface, expansion may seem to make sense: you already have the facility and the customer base. According to the *National Oil & Lube News,* about 20 percent of quick oil change shops also offer tune-ups or brake service, and transmission service is one of the most profitable add-ons. The drawback of appending your services is that oil changes generally do not require a skilled technician, but tune-ups do. Quick oil change shops that offer mechanical services must hire qualified personnel or risk the possibility of a lawsuit if something goes wrong.

Oil changing service business owners also have to deal with the disposal of used oil. About one-third of quick oil change shops currently use a licensed recycler to dispose of used oil, while more than half ship it off to a landfill. A few use it for heating purposes. In the early 1990s, there was increasing pressure to dispose of the oil in environmentally safe ways. In many communities, recycling is now mandatory. There are also efforts at both the national and local levels to have used oil declared a hazardous waste, which could significantly increase the cost of doing business. Do-it-yourselfers also generate about 350 million gallons of used motor oil annually, about two-thirds of which—the equivalent of five oil tankers—is dumped in the trash or poured down storm drains. Many quick oil change shops have begun accepting used oil as a community service and to generate goodwill.

In the final analysis, operating an oil change shop can be a profitable business. In an industry that is very competitive, a successful business is dependent on volume, and volume depends on repeat customers. Most quick oil change shops offer similar services for about the same price and with the same time guarantee. The only way to truly differentiate your business and develop a loyal customer base is by offering better service than the competition.

SOURCES:

Henry, Ed, "Survivor's Guide to Quick Lubes," *Changing Times,* April 1989, p. 41.

Madden, Michael, editor, *Small Business Start-Up Index,* Gale, 1991.

Martin, Susan A., editor, *Worldwide Franchise Directory,* Gale, 1991.

Quick Oil Change/Lube Shop, EntrepreneurGroup Business Start-Up Guide, 1989.

"Sixth Annual Fast Lube Survey," *National Oil & Lube News,* August 1993.

Vamos, Mark N., "Presto! The Convenience Industry: Making Life a Little Simpler," *Business Week,* April 27, 1987, p. 86.

—*Dean Boyer*

Baby Supplies Store

One of the first fads to wane at the end of the booming 1980s was lavish spending on children's clothing and accessories—right? Wrong! New parents and grandparents in the 1990s want their babies to have the best. And why not? They are more able to afford it than any previous generation. From elegant cribs and ornate strollers to high-tech safety devices, babies are enjoying the good life like never before.

Despite a recession in the late 1980s and early 1990s, spending on baby merchandise in the United States continued to grow to over $3.2 billion by 1993. As sales of adult apparel contracted, many savvy entrepreneurs found a prosperous niche supplying the demands of new baby-boomer parents and their high-style toddlers. And the baby supplies industry was expected to continue growing steadily into the twenty-first century. Although department stores are scurrying to get in on the boom, opportunities abound for starters of specialty shops that can appeal to this upscale market.

COSTS AND PROFITS

The average baby store owner generates about $30,000 each year in pretax profits, and more successful shops typically pull down closer to $60,000. Established stores with a great location and product mix can bring annual profits of $100,000 or more.

Typical start-up costs for baby stores total about $100,000, but you will probably need to start with at least $85,000 for a shop that offers multiple product lines. You might be able to get by with a lower investment for a highly specialized shop.

Your biggest up-front expense will be inventory. For a typical 2,000-square-foot store, you can expect to spend between $50,000 and $70,000 on stock. Your investment in store improvements and equipment will range from $30,000 to $45,000. Monthly rent will run from $3,000 to $4,000, depending on your location, and monthly payroll expenses will likely top $1,500. Finally, advertising, supplies, utilities, and other miscellaneous costs should push your initial outlay into the $100,000 range.

A viable alternative to opening a completely new baby store is purchasing an existing retail business. This allows you to bypass some of the headaches of establishing and marketing a new enterprise. You might be able to rejuvenate a sagging children's store, for example, by converting it into a baby store. If you are thinking about buying an establishment, be sure to consider why the store is for sale; outside influences specific to the local market or site, such as new competition; the shop's financial and tax records for the past three years; the worth of existing equipment and inventory; and remodeling expenses. You should also spend a few days in the store to get a feel for its clientele.

Because of high start-up costs, opening a baby supplies shop clearly is not a spur-of-the-moment endeavor. To secure financing, you will need to develop a detailed business plan replete with market analyses and strategy, management and operations plans, and cash-flow projections. If you don't have significant retail experience, a bank may require a hefty personal investment in the venture along with collateral sufficient to ensure your ability to cover the loan. If you are buying an existing shop, the owner may help you finance the purchase in exchange for a portion of future profits.

The **Small Business Administration (SBA)** can provide valuable information about assembling a business plan, and may even be able to help you secure a government-backed loan. Call the SBA at **1-800-U ASK SBA,** or write to: **Small Business Directory, P.O. Box 1000, Ft. Worth, TX 76119.** Your local SBA office, which can be reached by consulting the "U.S. Government" section of the Yellow Pages, will also be able to help. Other sources of financing information include national and regional retail trade associations.

LOCATION

Whether you start a new baby supplies store or buy an existing business, you will want to keep in mind the importance of an excellent location—it can make or break your venture. Is the surrounding community large enough to support your store? How many babies live in the area, and how many new parents will be around in three to five years? Studies show, for example, that a population base of at least 23,500 is needed to support one baby store. Your state census bureau will have valuable data on the number of competing retailers in each area and the demographic make-up of local communities.

SUPPLIERS

Furniture:

Child Craft: P.O. Box 444, Salem, IN 47167; phone: (821) 883-3111.

Evenflo Juvenile Furniture Co.: 1801 Commerce Dr., Piqua, OH 45356; phone: (513) 773-3971.

Gerber Furniture Group, Inc.: 9600 Valley View Road, Macedonia, OH 44056-9989; phone: (216) 468-2000.

Accessories:

Graco Metal Products, Inc.: P.O. Box 200, Elverson, PA 19520; phone: (215) 286-0150.

Noell Joaana, Inc.: One Mason, Irvine, CA 92714; phone: (714) 770-6303.

Strolee of California: 19067 S. Reyes Ave., Rancho Dominguez, CA 90224; phone: (213) 639-9300.

Clothing:

Ocean Pacific Childrenswear, Inc.: 4600 E. 48th Ave., Denver, CO 80216; phone: (303) 388-9696.

Oshkosh B'Gosh, Inc.: P.O. Box 300, Oshkosh, WI 54901; phone: (414) 231-8800.

The William Carter Co., Inc.: 400 West Main St., Ephrata, PA 17522; phone: (717) 733-2261.

In addition to selecting a viable community for your store, you will want to analyze site-specific traffic and spending patterns. You need to make sure, of course, that parking and accessibility are geared toward parents with babies. You should also try to situate your store near complementary businesses, such as anchor department stores or women's clothing shops. Factors to consider about the space itself include the number of electrical outlets and lights; the quality of heating and cooling equipment; the size and type of signs allowed by local zoning ordinances; ease of merchandise delivery; and insurance rates. Your local chamber of commerce will have maps and data to help you select a site.

The four major types of store locations are malls, strip centers, downtown, and freestanding. About 40 percent of children's wear retail companies are based in strip centers, 25 percent are in downtown centers, and 20 percent are in malls. Because baby shops have been growing faster than other retail sectors, mall managers are increasingly courting baby shop owners with favorable lease arrangements. Although mall leases are often much more expensive than those at other locations, a mall can generate a huge amount of traffic and provide the most convenient shopping environment for parents with children in tow. A mall store may also reduce advertising expenses you would incur at a location with less foot traffic. Plus, a mall setting is more amenable to the sale of high-profit goods that buyers purchase on a whim.

LAYOUT AND SETUP

A typical baby store has about 1,500 to 5,000 square feet of floor space. Larger shops are often 10,000 square feet or more. Stores that offer multiple product lines typically devote about 40 percent of their space to furniture, 10 percent to clothing, 5 percent to toys, and 30 percent to accessories. The checkout counter, office, and storage space will consume the remaining 15 percent of the floor.

If you are opening a mall store you will probably have much less space to work with, perhaps less than 1,000 square feet. Because you will be relying more on impulse purchases and casual shoppers, clothing and toys will probably be your biggest sellers, followed by accessories and then furniture. Emphasize catalog sales of space-consuming items, and display smaller high-ticket goods. Allocate your floor space accordingly, and then adjust your layout after you get a feel for customer demand.

Goods that are considered "impulse" purchases, such as toys and clothes, should be placed nearest to the front of the store. Clothes should hang on round racks or sit folded on tables. Place miscellaneous accessories against the wall. Furniture should be in the back of the store, and the cash register should be near the center of the space, facing the entrance. By keeping displays neat and orderly, you can increase your inventory without creating a cluttered appearance.

Plan on spending at least $12 per square foot on equipment, furnishings, and store improvements to set up your shop. You can easily spend more than $50 per square foot, though, if you go first class. You may be able to get your landlord to cover some costs, such as lighting fixtures and wallpaper. Most importantly, don't skimp on lighting. A generous amount light will reflect a clean atmosphere—an important attribute for a baby store. The trend in the mid-1990s was away from the cute baby-blue and pink decor to more fashionable chrome and glass, but you should create your own unique, cost-effective setting.

Save money on fixtures by purchasing them at auctions and installing them yourself. To find the best deals on used equipment, look in the Yellow Pages under "Store Designers and Planners" or under "Store Fixtures." To reduce your up-front expenses, lease as much of your equipment as possible. You should be able to lease a $2,000 cash register, for example, for less than $100 per month. Don't forget to budget for price-tagging machines ($300 apiece), inside and outside security systems ($2,000 to $8,000), shopping bags, and other items.

INVENTORY

Your mix of products will largely determine your market niche. You need to decide early, based mostly on local competition and demographics, whether you will appeal to upscale or low-budget buyers. In any case, start with a small inventory and then concentrate on proven sellers. Most importantly, you should devise an advanced, computerized inventory control system with the help of your accountant. Your suppliers can help you create an inventory control program that can save you thousands of dollars each year. Don't forget, your inventory will be your largest expense by far and should receive a proportionate amount of your management time.

Furniture will account for more than 50 percent of your entire initial investment and will take up the most floor space. However, if you are located in a mall you will likely place an emphasis clothes and other impulse items. Regardless of your store size, you should supplement your furniture inventory with catalogs from which customers can place orders. Cribs will be major sellers; plan on having about 20 cribs in a 2,000-square-foot store. One store uses cribs as its mainstay product, and has over 50 on display at all times in its 5,000-square-foot facility. Allocate 20 percent of your floor space to cradles, toy chests, lamps, changing tables, and other items.

Car seats, strollers, high chairs, and other accessories will make up 30 percent of your inventory investment. Items that are collapsible, convertible, and can be taken on the road will sell best to increasingly mobile parents. Although some

posh, high-tech strollers and high chairs offer big profit margins, be sure to offer traditional devices as well. Specialty safety accessories, such as electronic remote room monitors, were increasing in popularity in the mid-1990s. Toys, which don't sell well in non-mall baby shops, should account for five percent or less of your inventory.

Soft goods and clothing should each represent ten percent of your inventory expenditures, unless you are in a mall. Examples of soft goods are dust ruffles, sheets, pillows, and comforters. Placing them on the cribs will save floor space and help the cribs sell better. Since clothes are hard to sell in a non-mall setting, where few buyers make a special trip to purchase them, stick to popular styles and well-known brands. In an upscale mall setting, however, look forward to selling designer baby outfits priced at more than $200.

You may be able to cut your inventory costs by joining a local or regional buying consortium made up of small retailers that buy baby products. By pooling buying power, such associations are able to negotiate better prices and credit terms. They can also help you stay on top of new products and sales trends and will provide tips on inventory management. California-based Baby News Stores is one such organization. Ask the owner of a baby supplies store outside of your immediate locale if such an association exists in your region.

An effective means of differentiating your store from the local competition is finding a few specialty suppliers, such as independent craftspeople. A few distinctive items, like handmade cribs and rattles, can boost your store's image and set it apart from the mainstream retail crowd. Visit craft shows to find unique stock items.

PRIMARY ASSOCIATIONS AND SELECTED TRADE PUBLICATIONS

Associations:

Infant and Juvenile Manufacturers Association: 100 E. 42nd St., New York, NY 10017; phone: (212) 867-5720.

Institute of Store Planners: 25 N. Broadway, Tarrytown, NY 10591; phone: (914) 332-1806.

National Retail Merchants Association: 100 W. 31st St., New York, NY 10001; phone: (212) 244-8780.

Publications:

Earnshaw's Infants, Girls and Boys Wear Review: Earnshaw Publications, Inc., 225 W. 34th St., Rm. 212, New York, NY 10122; phone: (212) 536-2742. Monthly newsletter.
Fairchild Fact File: Children's Market, Infants', Toddlers', Girls', and Boys'—Apparel, Juvenile Products, Toys/ Dolls: Fairchild Publications, Seven W. 34th St., New York, NY 10001; phone: (212) 630-3880.
The Infant/Toddler/Preschool Market: SVP, Inc., 625 Avenue of the Americas, New York, NY 10011; phone: (212) 645-4500. Market data book containing forecasts for furniture, clothing, toys, and accessories.
Visual Merchandising and Store Design: ST Publishing Co., 407 Gilbert Ave., Cincinnati, OH 45202; phone: (513) 421-2050.

STAFFING

Plan on working at least 50 or 60 hours each week until you have the shop running smoothly. In addition, for a store of 1,500 to 2,500 square feet, you will probably need to hire a full-time assistant manager and one or two part-time salespeople. Be careful to hire workers who are mature and have a positive, friendly demeanor.

Your assistant manager should be very detail oriented, and should have a set of skills that make up for some of your own shortcomings. Important experience you may want to look for include inventory management and purchasing. Expect to pay the assistant manager about $300 to $400 per week. Salespeople will earn around $5 per hour. If you eventually hire a full-time manager to take over many of your duties, plan on spending about $400 to $500 per week.

ADVERTISING

Expect to spend at least $2,000 to $3,000 to market your shop's grand opening, which will ideally occur a few weeks after you have opened your doors for business. This will give you a chance to iron out any wrinkles before heavy marketing begins.

During your first year or two you may have to continue

INDUSTRY STATISTICS

- *Typical Start-up Expenses:* $90,000 to $130,000, depending on store size and location.
- *Typical Net Profit Before Taxes:* $30,000 to $40,000.
- *Typical Ongoing Inventory Investment:* $50,000 to $80,000.
- *U.S. Baby Supplies Sales (For Children Under 24 Months):* $3.2 billion in 1992 (excluding toys and clothing), up from $700 million in 1979, and $1.67 billion in 1986. 1992 sales topped $20 billion when clothes and toys are included.
- *Industry Growth Rate:* 8% per year average in the early 1990s.
- *Number of U.S. Children Under Five Years of Age:* 19 million in 1993, up from 16 million in 1980.
- *Number of U.S. Births:* About 4.1 million in 1992, up from 3.5 million in 1979, but down from 4.2 million in 1990. The birth rate is expected to decline gradually through 2000.
- *Children's Supplies Store Locations:* (Outdoor strip malls) 40%; (downtown shopping centers) 25%; (indoor malls) 20%; (freestanding buildings) 15%.

spending more on advertising than you would like, perhaps about 10 percent of gross sales. In addition, your local baby store clientele will constantly change as new parents enter your potential market. To keep up with a changing market base, many baby shop owners find that they must continue spending heavily on advertising. Thus, even after you are established, expect to spend more on marketing than the retail industry standard of two to five percent of sales.

Before you spend any advertising money, though, you will want to draft a detailed marketing plan. Seek professional advice. Qualified free-lance advertising consultants often work for as little as $40 or $50 per hour. And after a consultant helps you set up a marketing plan and put together some sharp advertising materials—brochures, newspaper advertisements, press releases, catalogs—you can manage your marketing program yourself with occasional help from your consultant.

Because you are serving a niche market, you should avoid advertising through costly media, such as radio, big newspapers, and television. You will get the most for your advertising dollars from targeted media, such as direct mail and community newspapers. Don't forget to call the Yellow Pages, a dependable and relatively inexpensive advertising tool, early so that your listing will appear when you open your shop.

One baby shop owner saves money by marketing her store through doctor's offices and hospitals. She also sends catalogs to expectant mothers, who usually begin shopping long before the baby arrives. One of your most important and least expensive marketing tools will be word of mouth, so go the extra mile to please your customers. And don't neglect grandparents in your advertising strategy. They may become some of your best customers.

Another important marketing tool you will want to

consider is trade shows. Most retailers attend at least one trade show per year. Besides boosting sales and increasing your visibility in the community, trade shows are also a great place to take a look at the competition and find out what trends are affecting the baby industry. Several books can tell you how to make the most of a trade show. Be sure to reserve your space far in advance so that you can secure a strategic display space. Your local chamber of commerce can tell you about upcoming events.

LICENSES AND INSURANCE

Before you open your doors you will need to obtain tax permits from the state and city, which may require a deposit of a few hundred dollars. You will also need a local business license and permission to stock inventory on your premises. It's a good idea to apply for a federal tax identification number if you are unincorporated. The SBA offers a comprehensive checklist of regulatory requirements for new business owners.

To minimize your liability, you will want to consider incorporating your business when it starts bringing in more than $50,000 per year in sales—Again, talk to your accountant. You will need good business insurance, of course, and before you open your facility, make sure that it complies with strict new accessibility requirements as outlined in the federal Americans With Disabilities Act.

TRENDS

The "baby boomlet" began waning in the early and middle 1990s, as the number of annual births started declining for the first time in about 15 years. But don't worry. Consumer purchases of baby products will continue to climb throughout the decade, for several reasons that you should consider as you prepare to enter the industry. For example, many more of today's babies are firstborns who require much more furniture and accessories than their future siblings. The average couple spends $10,000 on its firstborn child during its first twelve months of life.

In addition, working mothers, who were increasing in number in the 1990s, are much more likely to purchase expensive items that will make their lives easier. The rising number of double-income families will also create a greater market for pricey luxury items, such as $400 strollers and $100 baby bomber jackets. Furthermore, the average age of new mothers will continue rising through the end of the decade, resulting in a greater demand for safer and more expensive items. Finally, the wealthiest generation of grandparents in history will bring even more dollars into baby stores.

So what are your chances of success in the baby supplies store business? Major department stores and discount centers have tried to get in on the growing business by creating special baby supplies departments. This means that you will have to differentiate your shop by offering something those stores lack, whether it's personalized service, hard-to-find items, an attractive atmosphere, or some other distinction. But the growing market exists. With careful planning, keen inventory management, clever marketing, and a love for babies, you can prosper in this unique and enjoyable business.

SOURCES:

"Baby Store," *Entrepreneur Magazine's 184 Businesses Anyone Can Start and Make a Lot of Money,* second edition, Bantam, 1990.

Biederman, Danny, "Can We Shop?," *Children's Business,* March 1992, p. 120.

Colman, Gregory J., "Meet Me at the Mall," *Children's Business,* August 1992, p. 33.

Dunwiddie, Paul, "Hoping to Nurture Sales, Fletcher's Changes Its Focus," *Eugene Register-Guard,* March 30, 1993.

"Entrepreneur's 7th Annual Survey of 177 New Franchises," *Entrepreneur,* April 1994, p. 111.

Miller, Cyndee, "Brands Are Extremely Important," *American Marketing Association Marketing News,* June 8, 1992, p. 1.

Power, Gavin, "Catering to Pint-Sized Fashion Plates: Under-14 Set Is Reshaping the $30-Billion Children's Apparel Industry," *San Francisco Chronicle,* December 13, 1993, p. B1.

Salfino, Catherine, "Downsizing for Growth; Licensed Team Apparel Companies Seek Big Score in Kids' Market, Children Clothing," *Daily News Record,* April 12, 1993, p. 13.

Sloan, Kathleen, "Rain or Shine Spring Has Spring, the Grass Has Riz Kids Don't Care What the Weather Is," *Toronto Star,* April 22, 1993, p. FA1.

—*Dave Mote*

Beeper/Pager Service

Whether Americans like it or not, modern technology is weaving its way into their daily lives at a rapid clip. High-technology products that were once solely purchased by the rich or powerful have become necessary accessories for a vast number of people. And so it goes with pagers. Initially, only medical doctors or executives of giant corporations used pagers, while the rest of society made do with answering machines or nothing at all, relegating themselves to patiently waiting for their messages to catch up with them. But all of this has changed since the telecommunications industry hit its stride in the 1980s. Pagers, or beepers, have become so pervasive in U.S. society that it is not uncommon to see children playing in a park with pagers clipped to their waists, ready to receive a message from mom or dad. Indeed, nearly everyone can find a reason to purchase or lease a pager. Some people have two pagers, one for business messages and another for personal essages, while others have no professional need for pagers and own one exclusively for personal use.

As the pager industry crossed the line from commercial to consumer sales in the late 1980s to include both as revenue-generating market segments, the profit potential for pager operators skyrocketed. Some operators boast of recording 35 to 40 percent of their total revenues as profit, a margin that highly successful corporations would envy. Starting a pager business does, however, require a hefty amount of cash up front and a considerable amount of work to get off the ground. But once these obstacles are hurdled, the rewards can be extremely enticing. All that is required is persistence and patience on your part, a little bit of luck, and careful planning; then your efforts will begin to pay off.

COSTS AND PROFITS

The cost of starting your pager business will largely depend on the size of the market you intend to serve. Establishing your business in a small market—those trading areas with a population below 1.5 million—will generally require a $200,000 investment. For large markets, such as major U.S. cities, or a pager business that serves several segments, start-up costs can exceed $1 million.

Not every pager operator can expect to post a 40 percent pre-tax margin; instead, the percentage is indicative of the potential in the industry. On average, pager businesses operating in small markets with roughly 200 subscribers post annual revenues of $50,000, while larger markets generate up to $5 million in revenue annually by serving around 20,000 subscribers. Depending on the size of your market, annual pretax profits typically range between $17,500 and $2 million. Usually, it takes anywhere from one and a half to three years to overcome your initial investment outlay.

FINANCING

Obtaining the money to begin your foray into the pager business can be overwhelming, especially considering the large amount you will need to get started. On the other hand, the burgeoning growth of the telecommunications industry as a whole and the optimism characterizing its future can work to your advantage. Banks earn their money by providing loans, so your chances of obtaining financing should be increased by the very nature of the business you intend to enter.

Of course there is more to convincing a bank to lend you money than simply presenting them with a great idea. Any relationship you have cultivated with a bank representative, either through previous business loans you have been granted or just through your personal banking activities, will improve your odds. Before you meet with a loan officer you should prepare an estimated business balance sheet listing all assets and liabilities, which should include the amount that must be invested to begin your business. Also, prepare a detailed projection of earnings and expenses for at least the first year of operation, as well as a monthly cash flow projection. List the collateral you intend to offer as security for the loan, with an estimate of the current market value for each item offered, and include the balance of any existing liens. In addition, you should prepare an updated personal financial statement.

An alternative to securing financing from a bank is to apply for a loan from the U.S. **Small Business Administration (SBA),** which can be contacted at **1-800-U ASK SBA.** This avenue can only be pursued after first attempting to get a loan from a bank or other lending institution, since federal law prohibits the SBA from granting loans to applicants before other means are sought. In order to receive a loan

PRIMARY ASSOCIATIONS AND SELECTED TRADE PUBLICATIONS

Associations:

Telocator, The Mobile Communications Industry Association: 2000 M St. NW, Ste. 230, Washington, DC, 20036; phone: (800) 922-7626. Membership includes companies and individuals who supply radio paging and mobile telephone communication services to the public, including independent radio common carriers, cellular telephone companies, and telephone companies. Telocator fosters the development of industry standards for wide-area paging and mobile telephone systems and offers industry-wide support and information.

Telecommunications Industry Association (TIA): 2001 Pennsylvania Ave. NW, Ste. 800, Washington, DC 20006-1813; phone: (202) 457-4912. Membership includes companies that manufacture products for or provide services to the telecommunications industry. TIA sponsors seminars and promotes the industry in general.

Publications by TIA:

Industry Pulse, published by Telecommunications Industry Association.

Publications by Telocator:

Mobile Communications Industry Guide.
Nationwide Service Directory.
Telocator: The Magazine for the Mobile Communications Industry.
Telocator Network of America Bulletin: News and Analysis for the Mobile Communications Industry.

from the SBA, a potential borrower must meet certain requirements, a majority of which pertain to the size of the business in terms of employees and revenue. These requirements should pose no problem to the aspiring pager operator. To determine if you are eligible, locate an SBA loan application at your local library, which also houses additional information produced by the SBA that you will find helpful.

GETTING STARTED

Establishing a pager business requires a considerable amount of groundwork before you become involved in other areas of organizing your business. In fact, you are not officially engaged in the pager business until you locate an available radio frequency, obtain approval from the Federal Communications Commission (FCC), and begin using your licensed frequency. This is a difficult process, and some of the work necessitates hiring specialized consultants, money that may be wasted if you are unable to successfully obtain a frequency and begin conducting business.

Pagers are activated by information received via a specific radio signal, one on which you must be licensed to transmit. There are, however, only a limited number of radio

frequencies; once all the frequencies are occupied, no more can be created. Consequently, the FCC administers the allocation of radio frequencies, creating frustration and dejection for some and exhilaration for others.

To gain the FCC's approval, you must first locate an untapped radio signal, a chore the FCC will not help you complete. Since this information is nearly impossible for someone without specialized experience to discover, you should count on hiring a consultant, or at the least expect to spend a fair amount of money. Specialized research firms will scour FCC records for you, or you can purchase, for roughly $2,500, computer software that charts the market, provided you pay the monthly update fee of approximately $125.

Once you have located an available signal, you must demonstrate to the FCC that transmission on your selected frequency will not infringe upon other reception in your area of service. You will need to conduct an engineering study called a "channel interference study" that will again require the talents of a professional, in this case an engineer. Approximate fees for this service range from $300 to $500. But before you can determine if your signal will interfere with others, you must acquire an antenna. Typically, the cheapest way to do this is to lease space on an existing antenna tower, such as one used by a local radio station.

The next step is to file an application with the FCC, which will necessitate hiring a law firm that specializes in telecommunications; be prepared to pay between $800 and $2,000. It might be wise to contact a law firm before conducting a frequency search or engineering study, since many firms provide both of these services.

Once your application is filed, it may take from three to six months before the FCC will give you approval. Your request for a signal will be made public and other interested parties will have 30 days to file a request for the identical frequency. During this waiting period, make as many preparations as possible—without spending too much money—for starting your business, because once the FCC gives you the nod, you have 12 months to begin transmission on your frequency or your license will be forfeited.

Including your tower, which you should continue to lease since the costs involved in building your own tower are prohibitive, you will need a paging terminal, at least one transmitter, and pagers. A paging terminal will cost anywhere from $80,000 to $130,000, while a single transmitter costs roughly $20,000. (You may need more than one transmitter if your service area is especially hilly.) Different types of pagers run from $100 to $350.

An alternative to dealing with the lengthy and costly FCC process is to purchase a network that is already in operation, although this, too, is expensive. Fully developed systems typically sell for between $900 to $1,200 per subscriber, which would mean a minimum of $180,000 for a small market. Purchasing an already existing network may be your only alternative, however, if you are unable to locate an available radio frequency.

LOCATION

General rules apply to all types of retailers when selecting a store location. It is important to ensure that the site is easily accessible by both pedestrian and automobile traffic, that it is situated within an area supported by suitable demographics, and that a need exists for the particular product that will be offered. Specifically, you should target your pager business for middle-class and upper-income areas. A site near a densely populated business area or in a mall would be optimum, since customers not necessarily intent on acquiring a pager may nevertheless be drawn to your store. Of course, prime locations demand the highest rent, so it may prove imprudent to initially sign a binding lease for a property you may not be able to afford. If you decide to opt for a more economical route, be sure to ascertain which types of people reside in the area surrounding your selected site.

In assessing the population of a particular area, consult census surveys at your local library. The information included within these publications often focuses on small, neighborhood areas, or precincts, and will give you an indication of whether the population has declined, risen, or stagnated over the previous five or ten years. Also, census studies will tell you the size of the various age groups, their approximate income, and the cultural makeup of your area.

SMALL BUSINESS RESOURCE GUIDE

The following are a number of publications produced by the U.S. Small Business Administration (SBA) that are written for the small business owner. Although the materials listed below do not focus on establishing or operating a pager business, they do contain pertinent and valuable information for anyone contemplating a small business venture. The letters and number(s) following the titles are SBA publication codes and should be included when ordering a particular title. To obtain one of these guides, include the title, publication code, the amount of money required, your return address, and make your check or money order payable to **U.S. Small Business Administration.** Mail your order to: **SBA Publications, P.O. Box 30, Denver, CO 80201-0030.**

ABC's of Borrowing (FM1); price: $1.00.
Budgeting in a Small Service Firm (FM8); price: $0.50.
Recordkeeping in a Small Business (FM10); price: $1.00.
Selecting the Legal Structure for Your Business (MP25); price: $0.50.
Business Plan for Small Service Firms (MP11); price: $0.50.
Checklist for Going into Business (MP12); price: $0.50.
Pricing Your Products and Services Profitably (FM13); price: $1.00.
Inventory Management (MP22); price: $0.50.
Marketing Checklist for Small Retailers (MT4); price: $1.00.
Advertising (MT11); price: $1.00.

Valuable information can also be found in the SBA's **Small Business Start-up Information Package**, which can be obtained at your local library or small business development center.

Equally as important are maps of major trading areas pertaining to your subject area, which will indicate the major businesses in operation and the spending habits of the consumers surrounding your site.

MARKETING

Some of your marketing work will already have been completed by reviewing census surveys to assist in your selection of a suitable location. Keeping that demographic information in mind, note whether a majority of the residents in your target area are single occupancy tenants or whether your market is generally comprised of families. Identifying these and other demographic characteristics will give you a rough idea of which types of customers will be frequenting your store and will suggest which types of pagers to stock.

There are four broad categories of pagers, separated by varying degrees of technological sophistication and price, all of which you should become familiar with in order to gear your merchandise toward your anticipated market. The cheapest variety are tone-only pagers; as their name suggests, they emit only a beep when the pager is activated by a caller. Retailing for roughly $100, tone-only pagers would be perfect pagers for children. Consider selling tone-only pagers if your market area includes a substantial number of families.

Numeric display pagers beep and provide the telephone number of the caller, making them a suitable, inexpensive model for younger customers, or for those who do not require the features included with more advanced models. Numeric display pagers retail for anywhere from $140 to $200.

Tone and voice pagers emit a beep to indicate a page then play a brief voice message from the caller, much like miniature answering machines. These pagers, typically retailing for over $200, would be ideal for business purposes, enabling your executive clientele to quickly identify and prioritize messages without having to call each number.

The most sophisticated models are alphanumeric pagers, which display telephone numbers and detailed written messages up to 4,000 characters. Retailing for up to $350, alphanumeric pagers will most likely be purchased by upper-income customers demanding state-of-the-art products.

STORE SIZE, LAYOUT, AND STAFFING

Since pagers are generally smaller than a deck of playing cards, you will not need a lot of retail space to display your inventory. A minimum of 800 square feet should suffice, but if your finances enable you to lease a larger space, you may find that widening your options to include retail space from 800 to 1,200 square feet will give you a greater selection of sites from which to choose. Beyond budgeting concerns, the size of your transmission service area will largely decide the optimum size of your store. Small markets that serve 200

COMPUTERIZED DATABASES

Advanced Wireless Communication: Capital Publications Inc., P.O. Box 1455, Alexandria, VA 2213-2055; phone: (703) 739-6400; online: Newsnet, Inc.

Cellular Sales & Marketing: Creative Communications, Inc., P.O. Box 1519-GRI, Herndon, VA 22070; phone: (703) 787-4647; online: Newsnet, Inc.

FCC Week: Capitol Publications, Inc., P.O. Box 1455, Alexandria, VA 22313-2055; online: Newsnet, Inc.

Public Land Mobile Service Data Base: Comp Comm, Inc., Station House, 4th Fl., 900 Haddon Ave., Collingswood, NJ 08108-2167; online: Producer.

subscribers will obviously require less retail space than large markets serving 20,000 subscribers.

Put your marketing research to work in designing displays for your pagers. It might prove worthwhile to divide your floor space into sections according to different types of pagers and the different types of people that are likely to use a particular pager. Except for your office and storage area, a cashier counter, and several desks and chairs for customers to review and sign lease agreements (definitely an option you should provide to your customers), the remainder of the store should be devoted to product display and customer circulation. As a general guideline, 60 percent of your total square footage should be reserved for retail space, 20 percent for office and storage space, and 20 percent for cashier counter space.

You will need from one to 15 salespeople to assist you in your pager business, depending on the size of your business and projected volume of sales. If you find that you are initially unable to pay salespeople a salary, you can pay them on commission, or a base-wage plus commission.

MANAGEMENT ISSUES

Pagers are both sold and leased, but you will probably lease more units than you will sell. As a rough estimate, a pager is leased for between $13 and $30 a month, depending on the type of pager and the size of the area in which the pager can be activated. If a customer purchases a pager, then charge $8 to $15 a month for service. You can ascertain a more accurate figure by simply calling an existing pager business operating in a similar market, ask what they charge their customers, then structure your prices accordingly.

Since leasing a pager remains such a popular option for customers, you will need to provide repair and maintenance service. Until your pager business begins to generate handsome profits, you will probably be unable to afford hiring your own pager technician to perform such tasks, so it might be wise to purchase warranty coverage from the manufacturers of the pagers. Five-year warranties generally cost an additional $30 per pager. Keep in mind that part of your inventory will always be unavailable for customer use since your stock will rotate to and from the repair shop. Consequently, you should purchase more pagers than the number of subscribers you have enlisted, or plan to enlist. An approximate ratio to follow is 1,500 pagers for every 1,000 subscribers.

ADVERTISING

You should expect to spend from two to five percent of your gross annual sales on advertising and at least 10 percent during your first year of operation. If your budget allows, place advertisements in every available form of print media, including flyers, brochures, telephone Yellow Pages, newspapers, and magazines. Use a simple and direct style, imparting succinct information regarding the cost and various uses of pagers. As with a majority of products that at one time were exclusive, high-priced items, many people have no idea how much pagers cost and falsely presume they are too expensive.

FRANCHISES

As of the early 1990s, franchise opportunities did not exist in the pager industry, other than the option of purchasing an existing operation. What this means for the aspiring entrepreneur is less competition, so do not let the absence of franchises dissuade you from establishing your business. Your hard work and diligence will make you one of the select pager operators within your region.

COMPUTER REQUIREMENTS

Other than a standard computer, which you will find indispensable for managing daily operations, you will also need a paging computer to transmit signals to subscriber's pagers. For advice on purchasing and installing this sophisticated hardware and software, you should consult a qualified telecommunications/computer specialist.

According to informal industry studies, as the pager industry entered the 1990s, future growth was expected to increase by 25 to 35 percent annually until the year 2000. You can claim a share of this projected jackpot if you successfully enter the market by gaining the FCC's approval and by keeping apprised of the rapidly changing technology utilized in the industry once you are established. Pagers perform a variety of tasks, including providing stock quotes and news updates, that are becoming more in demand in the modern world. Your ability to match new technology with new customers will, to a large extent, determine the future prosperity of your pager business.

SOURCES:

Husain, Imran, ''Pagers,'' *Entrepreneur,* April 1992, pp. 87-89.
Kahn, Sharon, *101 Best Businesses to Start,* first edition, Doubleday, 1988.
Manusco, Joseph R., *Manusco's Small Business Resource Guide,* Prentice Hall, 1988.

Matulis, Scott, ''Paging All Profits,'' *Entrepreneur,* July 1988, pp. 152-58.

Schwartz, Carol A., editor, *Small Business Sourcebook,* fifth edition, volume 1, Gale, 1992.

Woy, Patricia A., *Small Businesses That Grow and Grow and Grow,* second edition, Betterway, 1989.

—*Jeffrey L. Covell*

Car Wash

In the early 1990s, there were more than 139 million privately owned passenger cars collecting dirt and grime along more than seven million miles of highway in the United States. With such a surfeit of clean-up work, the professional car wash industry shined as a $2.8 billion business, parceled out to more than 22,000 automated and self-service car washes across the country. Even so, *Entrepreneur* magazine estimated that roughly one-third of the nation's car owners have never used automatic or self-service car washes. Clearly, resourceful entrepreneurs were in a position to clean up on a promising deal.

Competition in the car wash industry has grown in tandem with demand. By the late 1980s, it was common for large gasoline companies to add free car wash facilities to their service stations in order to spur gasoline sales. Many car washes offered complex package deals or launched sideline businesses such as gift and snack shops, convenience stores, lube services, and gasoline sales. In addition, car wash businesses capitalized on studies demonstrating benefits beyond convenience and speed: most car washes—especially soft-rag and "less touch" services—were proven gentler than traditional home washing on car finishes and tended to use far less water and fewer toxic chemicals than most home jobs. With these advantages, the car wash business saw an average growth rate of ten percent starting in the mid-1980s, according to International Carwash Association/National Carwash Council (ICA/NCC) statistics.

The late 1980s, plagued by poor weather and a recession, brought a slump in car wash activity. By 1992, however, *Professional Carwashing & Detailing* identified favorable signs for renewed growth. While the greatest profits derived from larger, full-service operations, great potential remained in smaller, well-managed operations requiring far less capital.

COSTS AND PROFITS

The minimum start-up investment for a car wash business runs in the neighborhood of $120,000, with the average start-up investment falling at around $250,000 and an average net profit of $80,000 before taxes. In general, car wash operators shoot for profits of 23 to 29 percent of gross revenue. Many car washes can handle more than 20,000 cars per month, netting $250,000 to $300,000 a year before taxes. Compared with other small businesses, return on investment for a car wash operation is quite high.

Average costs and profits for the industry vary considerably depending on the type and size of car wash operation established. There are basically four types of car wash, three of which—full-service, exterior-only, and exterior rollover washes—are automatic. Self-service washes, the fourth type, are predominantly manual, though many are now including semiautomatic systems.

The simplest and least capital-intensive car wash design is self-service. Such a system is essentially made up of a coin-operated wash with covered bays, a central drain, and a wand attached to a flexible hose, which allows the customer to spray high-pressure water on the car and remove dirt. In addition to the basic soap and rinse cycles, more sophisticated self-service systems may offer presoaking, tire and engine cleaning, high-pressure soap spray, and wax features. A small, fully equipped, four-bay operation could be set up for approximately $140,000, with a financing down payment of roughly one-third up front. While self-serve car washes experienced a boom in the early 1980s, the market began a period of relative stagnation in the latter part of that decade. In response, many self-serve owners displayed optimism for the future by adding automatic bays. Other self-service washes offer convenience store facilities or basic tune-up and oil-change bays.

Unlike self-service washes, "exterior roll-over" systems delegate cleaning responsibility to automatic machinery. The customer remains in the stationary car while equipment—consisting of brushes made of plastic or cloth, high-pressure water nozzles only, or a hybrid system combining the two—passes over and around the vehicle to clean it. The benefits of such a system are low capital investment, low maintenance costs, and minimum labor. For those reasons, many oil companies have adopted it as the perfect solution to the "free wash" incentive with a minimum gasoline purchase. The chief drawback of the exterior roll-over carwash is the relatively poor quality of its wash.

In an exterior-only car wash, also known as a "drive through," the car is mechanically pushed or pulled through car wash equipment, which is located in a tunnel. As fully automatic machines, exterior-only car washes represent a

FRANCHISE OPPORTUNITIES

Detail Plus Car Appearance Systems: P.O. Box 14276, Portland, OR 97214; phone: (800) 284-0123; fax: (503) 231-7512. Founded, 1981; began franchising, 1983. 100 outlets located across U.S.; average cost: $30,500 for lower cost units and between $42,500 and $69,500 for moderate to higher cost units; offers complete car wash, detail, and appearance services; franchisor provides training program.

Express Wash: 908 Niagara Falls Blvd., N. Tonawanda, NY 14120-2060; phone: (800) 268-6792; fax (416)466-8293. Founded, 1986; began franchising, 1987. 300 outlets located throughout U.S., Mexico, and the Virgin Islands; offers mobile car washing and detailing services; units equipped with water tanks and other necessary items; after initial franchise fee of $1,695, franchisor provides comprehensive operations and business manual and financing assistance.

Mermaid Car Wash: 526 Grand Canyon Dr., Madison, WI 53719; phone: (608) 833-9274. Founded, 1983; began franchising, 1986. 3 outlets at a cost between $1,735,000 and $1,845,000; franchises full-service, soft cloth wash with beach theme/decor. In addition to $50,000 initial franchise fee, 1- to 3-week training period is required by franchisor (90 days training recommended); contracts for 20-year terms with 2% sales royalty; franchisor provides assistance with site selection, consulting services, construction inspection, etc.

Other Franchisors: Spot-Not Car Washes: 2011 W. 4th St., Joplin, MO 64801-3297; phone: (417) 781-2140. **Apollo Car-Truck Wash:** 3329 W. 5th St., Tulsa, OK 74127; phone: (918) 582-0025. **Classic Car Wash:** 871 E. Hamilton Ave., Ste. C, Campbell, CA 95008, phone: (408) 371-2414; fax: (408) 371-4337. **CleanCo, Inc.:** 2211 W. County Rd., C2, Roseville, MN 55113, phone: (612) 784-2293.

substantial investment in complex equipment, space to house that equipment, and land on which the operation can effectively run. An average building of 2,000 square feet, for example, would cost approximately $300,000 for the building and equipment alone. Heavy equipment expenses pay off in the form of two substantial benefits: exterior-only washes require only one or two workers, cutting down on labor costs, and they necessitate little, if any, handwork from those few employees. Everything from washing to drying is performed by machines.

Labor costs become a much more significant factor in the last, and most complex, system: the full-service car wash. As with exterior-only, the full-service wash depends on expensive, automatic machinery. Unlike exterior-only, however, full-service normally offers complete cleaning of the interior and often hand washing and drying of the exterior. In addition, full-service operations provide comprehensive cleaning packages that include various combinations of such services as sealer wax, polish wax, undercarriage wash, rust inhibitor, interior protectant, fragrance, whitewall cleaning, wheel treatment, floor mat cleaning, and more.

Though a full-service car wash is, by far, the most expensive operation to start up and run, it potentially generates the greatest profit. A full-service operation will require at least $100,000 to $300,000 down, with loans filling in the remaining $400,000 to perhaps more than $1 million. Labor can account for over 40 percent of total costs, according to Hanna Auto Wash, a major franchisor. Yet a larger labor force can translate into more efficient service and, ultimately, greater profits. Some car washes handle between 120 and 210 cars per hour, with an average profit of $1 per car.

FINANCING

As in any small business venture, one of the most bewildering yet essential steps is raising enough capital to start and sustain operations. Equipped with a sound business plan and a good measure of tenacity, you will find numerous financial sources, each with advantages and disadvantages that should be weighed against your particular circumstances—how much capital you have in personal reserves, how much interest you are willing to pay for given periods of time, what portion of your business (equity capital) you might be willing to offer to private investors in exchange for their financial backing, and so on. Usually, a combination of several financial sources is the preferred solution to funding.

As in all small business ventures, an advisable place to begin inquiry is the U.S. **Small Business Administration (SBA),** which provides invaluable information on diverse aspects of small business practice as well as small business loans. The SBA can be reached by calling **1-800-U ASK SBA** or by writing: **Small Business Directory, P.O. Box 1000, Ft. Worth, TX 76119.** Local SBA offices are also listed in the ''U.S. Government'' section of your telephone directory.

If you are not granted an SBA loan, there are more than enough other sources. Borrowing from banks is perhaps the most obvious solution, though banking institutions tend toward the conservative side of the financing spectrum. Personal or commercial loans can be backed with various forms of collateral, including your savings account, life insurance policy, real estate, inventory, equipment, or accounts receivable.

Finance companies offer another option. They are generally less conservative than banks but charge higher interest. A further means of raising start-up capital is equity financing, which entails dividing your business ownership among investors who contribute capital but do not necessarily participate in business operations.

Finally, obtaining capital through venture capitalists represents another option, though perhaps not the most advisable one for budding car wash operations. Venture capitalists typically expect a very large share of equity—between 20 and 70 percent—and a return of at least five to ten times their investment in three to five years. In addition, most venture capitalists are hesitant to consider investing in companies that will not be worth at least $30 to $50 million in five to seven years. Nevertheless, some venture firms do invest in smaller companies with exceptional growth prospects. For more information on venture capital companies, you may want to contact: **The National Association of Small Business Investment Companies (NAS-BIC), 1156 15th St., N.W., #1101, Washington, DC 20005; phone: (202) 833-8230.**

Some of the simplest and most obvious sources of funding are often overlooked. Though generally characterized by high interest rates, credit cards are a quick way to get cash with no paperwork. Another useful tip is to immediately establish good relations and credibility with suppliers for your new car wash. Any deferment of payment on merchandise will give you that much more money to work with during the crucial setup period.

Whether establishing credit with suppliers, applying for bank loans, seeking investors for equity financing, or trying just about any other means of raising capital, you will need an informed and presentable business plan. It should effectively explain your needs, what you intend to do with the requested money, and how that money will facilitate the development of your car wash. One of the better sources for more information is Entrepreneur Group's detailed guide to preparing a business plan, *Report No. X3402: How to Develop a Successful Business Plan,* which can be obtained by contacting **Entrepreneur, 2392 Morse Avenue, Irvine, CA 92714; phone: (714) 261-2325; fax: (714) 755-4211.**

LOCATION

Location is a high priority for success in the car wash business. Even the most advanced facility will fail miserably if it is situated in the wrong place. Before choosing an exact site location, it is wise to consider various general features marking prospective communities for the business: population; patterns in climate; economic profile, including information such as rates of employment and average family income; and demographics. Where a self-service wash may prosper, a state-of-the-art full-service facility may go broke. It is wise to check census data, business statistics, local bulletins, and trade associations, as well as to utilize other sources—including observing and talking to people—to determine whether the type of service you want to provide will fit in to a particular community.

Though every site possesses hidden wonders and problems that are largely up to chance, certain standard factors should always be carefully considered. Accessibility to potential customers is perhaps the most important. If drivers have to perform fancy maneuvers in order to clean their cars, they are more likely to drive to a less challenging facility. Corner lots are often desirable, as they offer access from two adjacent streets. Avoid any obstacles that may obstruct traffic, such as unbroken median dividers, no-turn signs, and intersections with traffic lights. Other factors to be considered in determining the suitability of a site are parking facilities, visibility, and proximity to other businesses that my either draw or repel customers. To help assess the value of a given site, you may want to enlist the services of industry specialists. Hanna Car Wash Systems, for example, conducts computerized site analyses that help determine business volume at a given location.

SETUP

Setting up an actual car wash facility on a chosen site requires expertise that most first-time operators lack. You will have to make key decisions: Should you buy or lease the property? Should you start construction from scratch or renovate an existing structure such as a gas station or existing car wash?

Generally, it is advisable to buy the land. In urban areas, however, that may not be possible. Furthermore, buying real estate may sap limited resources needed for actual operations. Leasing property is a viable option, but it should be done carefully; try to negotiate flexible conditions such as short-term leases that are renewable and leases that

---

INDUSTRY STATISTICS

Self-Service Car Washes:

- *Average Prices:* $2.99 for basic wash; $3.74 for wash and wax; $4.34 for Deluxe/Multiple Cycle Wash.
- *Average Total Annual Operating Costs:* $34,640.
- *Wash Volume Average (# of cars per location):* 13,300 in 1991; 13,800 in 1992.
- *Monthly Gross Per Bay:* $973.
- *Profile of Typical Self-Serve Car Wash Operator:* In business 10.1 years, owns 2.2 locations and 10.3 coin-op wand bays.

(SOURCE: 1993 SELF-SERVE STATISTICAL SURVEY, *PROFESSIONAL CARWASHING & DETAILING*)

Automatic Car Washes:

- *Average Prices:* (1993) $7.39 for full-service wash; $4.67 for exterior-only; $12.52 for top-selling combination package.
- *Average Total Annual Operating costs:* $350,000.
- *Wash Volume Average:* 63,900 for full-service; 46,300 for exterior-only.
- *Average Gross Revenue Per Car (excluding side-line business):* $8.61.
- *Profile of Typical Automatic Car Wash Operator:* In business 11.3 years; owns 1.8 exterior tunnels.

(SOURCE: 1993 AUTOMATIC SURVEY, *PROFESSIONAL CARWASHING & DETAILING*)

Other:

- 12% of carwash operators claim that auto detailing is their primary business (source: 1993 Detailing Survey, *Professional Carwashing & Detailing*).
- The average self-service or automatic car wash uses about 30 gallons of water per car; home washing uses an average of 150 gallons (source: *Business Wire,* April 15, 1991).

KEY PRODUCTS AND PROCESSES

- **Full-Serve Carwash:** A deluxe exterior wash in which the car is bathed with gentle cleaners and then dried. Service generally includes vacuuming of the floors, seats, and ashtrays; cleaning inside windows; wiping down the dashboard, console, steering column, instrument panel, and door jambs.
- **Exterior Car Wash:** Only the car's exterior is cleaned and dried.
- **Wheel Treatment:** Special products/cleaners are applied to wheel rim surfaces in order to impart a new look and help remove brake dust and prevent tarnishing and corrosion.
- **Foam Polish and Sealant:** A two-step, foam cleaning and polymer-based treatment that cleans and conditions in the first step and polishes in the second.
- **Poly Sealant:** A surface treatment that promotes beading action on the car's surface, adding protection against salt, sun, acid rain and other pollutants.
- **Clear Coat:** A foamy, surface treatment to enhance factory-applied clear coat and polyurethane paints on newer cars.
- **Underwash and Undersealant:** A two-step undercarriage treatment, including high-volume water spray followed by rust inhibitor applied to the underside of the car.
- **Vinyl, Rubber, or Leather Protection:** Any of several products applied to those areas of the car to restore lustre and durability.

contain provisions for subletting. Should your business fail, you do not want to be left with an expensive and useless lot.

You should look carefully at the pros and cons of starting from scratch versus working with an existing structure or business. Existing or abandoned gas stations are often convenient to refurbish since electrical, plumbing and other amenities are often already in place. Consider, however, that the renovation and rearranging of existing structures can often prove more expensive—and much more frustrating—than starting from scratch. Assuming control of an existing car wash also warrants careful planning and investigation. You should, among other things, determine why the facility is for sale; take a close and scrupulous look at financial records, using alternate methods—like records of water usage—to confirm figures for business volume; and weigh the costs and advantages of renovation against expected profits.

Among the numerous complexities of setting up shop, integrating a computer system into car wash businesses has become not only common, but extremely efficient. Integrated computer and software systems can tie together every facet of the operation, from monitoring and controlling automated machinery and merchandise to printing matching receipts. Valuable data—such as the exact time a car was washed, what extras were purchased, and the labor costs per car—can be collected and used to gain a competitive edge.

STAFFING

In most non-self-serve car washes, labor takes up the biggest chunk of operating costs, comprising up to 40 percent in some full-service washes. Even at less labor-intensive exterior-only businesses, over a third of costs may go to payroll. In addition to the substantial cost of labor, the industry places increasing emphasis on quality and friendliness of service. It is, therefore, crucial that you choose employees selectively in order to get the most out of your business.

Sources to use for recruiting or advertising for applicants include service stations, other car washes, public employment services and agencies, colleges, and civic groups. Referrals from your long-term employees are also valuable. Look for key traits that correspond with the nature of the job: car wash tunnel operators should enjoy working outdoors and using their hands, while cashiers should convey a sense of good cheer, sociability, and organizational skills. It is advisable to initiate an in-house training program followed by a 30-day probation period—time during which you and the employee confirm that the job fits the person.

It also pays to know the legal rights and expectations of your employees, as well as federal and state labor laws that affect you as an employer. The Fair Labor Standards Act requires minimum hourly wages as well as compensation of time and a half after 40 hours of work per week. The U.S. Department of Labor's Occupational Safety and Health Administration (OSHA) publishes a handbook designed to help small businesses manage their work site safety and health protection. Last updated in 1993, the booklet (OSHA 2209; order number 029-016-001-441) is available for $4 by writing **Superintendent of Documents, Government Printing Office, P.O. Box 371954, Pittsburgh, PA 15250-7954,** or by phoning **(202) 783-3238.**

MARKETING

With increasing competition in the car wash business, sound marketing practices are an essential tool for success. Before deciding on specific marketing strategies, it is wise to conduct thorough market research. For primary information, you can hire a marketing firm or personally organize campaigns through direct mail, telemarketing, personal interviews, and other avenues. Secondary data—information that is already compiled—is available from numerous sources, including census tracts, maps, media sources, yellow pages in the phone book, and community organizations.

Perhaps the most important marketing consideration in the car wash business is an emphasis on quality service. Discounted books of car wash tickets and incentives such as "Buy five car washes and get one free" are useful strategies to promote value. You should also consider maximizing business hours; many working customers prefer after-work hours or weekends to wash their cars. Most car washes are open at least 6 days each week from as early as 6 a.m. to 9 p.m., with more and more—especially self-service facilities—moving into 24-hour operation.

New technology also serves as a powerful marketing tool. New equipment—such as "soft-rag" and "less-touch" systems—is easier to operate and safer for cars.

Fewer customers will claim that the wash caused damage to their cars. In addition, economic hard times and rising car prices have prompted consumers to hold on to their vehicles longer (by 1989, the average automobile in the United States was 7.6 years old) and maintain them more carefully. Consequently, greater emphasis is placed on such extra services as engine cleaning, rustproofing, pinstriping, touch-up painting, window tinting, and cellular phone installation. Responding to this market, many car washes offer detailing services, or even full detailing shops, along with the standard wash.

Another fruitful marketing strategy is the development of a sideline business to supplement car washing. Such businesses include: gas pumps; on-site boutiques selling car-care products, auto accessories, and candy; video games and vending machines; and convenience stores (C-Stores).

ADVERTISING

Advertising in the car wash business typically draws two to three percent of gross revenue, compared to ten percent for most retail businesses. The smaller scale should not necessarily mean smaller effort; getting the most out of advertising spending can greatly increase business.

Whether you create them yourself or use an agency, ads should be clear and informative and should circulate in carefully chosen media. Plan a preopening campaign and grand opening blitz using direct mail, newspaper advertising, flyers, and a grand-opening party to attract as much attention as possible. Obviously, the initial ad budget will be substantially higher during this period. Once business is up and running, experiment with different media: newspapers; bus benches; Yellow Pages; direct mail; and specialty advertising on pencils, coffee mugs, shopping bags, key chains, and other items.

Careful research and planning can maximize ad spending. Before buying space in a publication, for example, check figures on its circulation and readership profile. One useful source for information on consumer and trade publications is **Standard Rate and Date Service (SRDS), 3004 Glenview Rd., Wilmette, IL 60091; phone: (312) 256-6067.** For direct marketing campaigns, you should shop around for affordable and effective mailing lists. While brokers are listed in the Yellow Pages under ''Advertising—Direct Mail,'' it is sometimes possible to trade lists for favors with other established businesses in your area.

LICENSES AND INSURANCE

As part of the planning process and prior to making too great a commitment with regard to funding and site construction, it is wise to check license and permit requirements for your area. In addition to a local business permit and sales tax permits, you should look into: zoning ordinances, fire-department permits, air and water pollution control permits, and even regulations controlling the design of your car wash sign. To save on water costs, many car wash operators dig wells of their own. If you plan to do the same, check for possible restrictions with the local business administration. Finally, standard business insurance is a necessity that should be factored into the working budget.

A 1990 survey by the International Carwash Association indicated that 95 percent of the people interviewed derived a psychological high from driving a clean car, while those who drove dirty cars tended to feel more depressed. That should be inspiration for even the car wash entrepreneur whose primary goal is not to make humanity happier. With careful planning and a focus on providing excellent customer service, a small business person can count on operating a car wash for a highly stable and potentially lucrative livelihood.

PRIMARY ASSOCIATIONS AND SELECTED TRADE PUBLICATIONS

Associations:

Car Wash Owners and Suppliers Association (COSA): P.O. Box 4067, Racine, WI 53404; phone: (414) 639-4393. Founded to foster a better public image and improve the operation of the car wash industry.

International Carwash Association (ICA): 1 Imperial Pl., 1 E. 22nd St., Ste. 400, Lombard, IL 60148-4915; phone: (708) 495-0100; fax: (708) 495-0144. Promotes the car wash industry and provides services to its member body of car wash owners, operators, managers, manufacturers, distributors and suppliers.

Publications:

American Clean Car Magazine: 500 North Dearborn St., Chicago, IL 60610; phone: (312) 337-7700; fax: (312) 337-8654.
American Car Wash Review: 13222-B Admiral Ave., Marina Del Ray, CA 90292; phone: (310) 397-4217; fax: (310) 827-2784.
Auto Laundry News: 370 Lexington Ave., New York, NY 10017; phone: (212) 532-9290; fax: (212) 779-8345.
ICA Letter: International Carwash Association, 1 Imperial Pl., 1 E. 22nd St., Ste. 400, Lombard, IL 60148-4915; phone: (708) 495-0100; fax: (708) 495-0144.
Professional Carwashing & Detailing Magazine: 13 Century Hill Drive, Latham, NY 12110; phone: (518) 783-1281; fax: (518) 783-1385.

SOURCES:

1991 Carwash Investors and Buyers Handbook, Professional Carwashing and Detailing Magazine, 1991.
''Automatic Carwash Survey,'' *Professional Carwashing & Detailing,* 1993.
Bochan, John J., ''Carwash Business: Not Just a Clean Sweep,'' *Business First-Louisville,* August 20, 1990, p. 25.
Car Wash, Business Start-Up Guide #1076, EntrepreneurGroup, 1989.
''Detailing Survey,'' *Professional Carwashing & Detailing,* September 1993.

Gould, J. Sutherland, *Starting From Scratch: 50 Profitable Business Opportunities,* John Wiley & Sons, 1987.

''In Search of Help,'' *American Clean Car,* June 1992, p. 40.

Madden, Michael, editor, *Small Business Start-Up Index,* issue 1, Gale, 1991.

Martin, Susan Boyles, editor, *Worldwide Franchise Directory,* Gale, 1991.

Schwartz, Carol A., editor, *Small Business Sourcebook,* fifth edition, volume 1, Gale, 1992.

''Self-Serve Statistical Survey,'' *Professional Carwashing & Detailing,* 1993.

Smedley, Peggy, ''How the Car Wash Industry Is Modernizing for the '90s,'' *National Petroleum News,* January 1990, p. 36.

—KERSTAN COHEN

Carpet Cleaning Service

A carpet cleaning service is one of the easiest and least expensive businesses to start. Along with a low initial investment, there is strong demand, low overhead, and almost immediate cash flow. The ease of starting a carpet cleaning business, however, renders the industry a highly competitive one.

FINANCING AND PROFIT POTENTIAL

It is possible to start a carpet cleaning business with nothing more than a rented carpet cleaning machine and a few customer referrals. More than one entrepreneur has lined up customers for one weekend and headed to the nearest equipment rental store on Saturday morning. In fact, such a simple approach might be the best way for people not sure about carpet cleaning to find out if the business is for them. The investment is minimal and carries no long-term obligations.

A few weekends spent cleaning carpets should be enough for the potential entrepreneur to get a flavor of the business, including the labor involved as well as the challenges of marketing and dealing with customers. The part-time carpet cleaner who is serious about business should invest in a work uniform, business cards, and temporary signs that can be attached to the sides of a car, truck, or van.

When the time comes to purchase equipment, most start-up businesses buy portable carpet cleaning systems that may cost from $2,000 for a new dry-foam or rotary-shampoo machine to $5,000 for a top-of-the-line, portable wet-extraction system. Do not overlook the market for used equipment. Some people who start carpet cleaning businesses later decide the work is not for them or they may move up to more sophisticated truck-mounted systems. As a result, it may be wise to purchase good used equipment, which is often available from individuals or local equipment dealers.

The most expensive carpet cleaning system is one mounted in a trailer or the back of a van. These systems may run from $10,000 to $40,000, plus the cost of the vehicle. In addition to looking more complex or professional, the biggest advantage to truck-mounted carpet cleaning systems is speed. They also include hot-water heaters that may help in cleaning; many people, though, believe that a portable carpet cleaning system, which is considerably less expensive, is just as effective in the hands of a trained technician.

In addition to a carpet cleaning system and a vehicle, the only other basic materials for start-up are various chemicals and cleaning solutions. These will vary depending on the carpet-cleaning system and represent a very small percent of the total investment.

Most small carpet cleaning businesses are run out of the owner's home. A business with one carpet cleaning system and crew—the owner and maybe one other person—should be able to gross between $40,000 and $60,000 a year.

EQUIPMENT

There are five basic methods of on-site carpet cleaning. The most popular among professionals, wet-extraction is a system in which hot water is injected deep into the carpet. The carpet is then immediately vacuumed, lifting both the water and the dirt loosened by the detergents. Wet-extraction is generally considered the most effective method of cleaning.

Another common cleaning process is known as dry foam. The dry-foam carpet cleaning system works much like wet-extraction with a moist foam cleaner that is brushed into the carpet and then vacuumed. Dry-foam systems are popular because the carpet dries much more quickly, and there is less risk of bleeding, fading, or other damage to the fabric. Dry-foam also costs less than wet-extraction.

The other three methods of carpet cleaning are rotary shampoo machines, probably most familiar to do-it-yourselfers who rent equipment, and dry-powder and bonnet systems, which use dry chemical absorbents to loosen dirt that can then be vacuumed. Chem-Dry, the largest franchiser of carpet cleaning businesses, uses chemical absorbents and carbonated water.

Because each carpet cleaning method has its particular advantages, some companies own more than one system and employ the one best suited for a specific job. For example, a company that normally uses a wet-extraction process may use dry powder if there is a risk of shrinkage or water damage to a particular carpet.

SKILLS AND TRAINING

Almost anyone can operate a carpet cleaning system, but there is more to cleaning carpets than running a machine. Professional carpet cleaners must be familiar with various

FRANCHISE OPPORTUNITIES

Chem-Dry Carpet Cleaning: 1530 N. 1000 W., Logan, UT 84321; phone: (801) 755-0099. Founded, 1977; promotes carbonated, low-moisture cleaning; Chem-Dry Charlie trademark; boasts more than 3,500 franchises in 22 countries; rated among top 10 franchisers by *Entrepreneur,* 1988-90. $15,000 franchise fee, plus monthly royalty; fee includes equipment, training program, business cards, uniforms, newsletter, and national advertising support.

The Von Schrader Company: 1600 Junction Avenue, Racine, WI 53403; phone: (414) 634-1956, or (800) 626-6916. Founded, 1935; manufactures dry-foam carpet cleaning equipment and sells complete business start-up packages beginning at $2,595.

Other Franchisors: COIT Drapery and Carpet Cleaners: 897 Hinckley Road, Burlingame, CA 94010; phone: (415) 342-6023. **Duraclean International, Inc.:** 2151 Waukegan Road, Deerfield, IL 60015; phone: (708) 945-2000, or (800) 251-7070. **Laser Chem Carpet & Upholstery Cleaning:** 126 Indian Avenue, Lawrence, KS 66046; phone: (913) 749-0936, or (800) 272-2741. **Rainbow International Carpet Dyeing and Cleaning Company:** P.O. Box 3146, Waco, TX 76707; phone: (817) 756-2122. **Rug Doctor Pro:** P.O. Box 7750, Fresno, CA 93747; phone: (209) 291-5511, or (800) 678-7844. **Stanley Steemer Carpet Cleaner:** 5500 Stanley Steemer Parkway, Dublin, OH 43017; phone: (614) 764-2007, or (800) 848-7496. **Town & Country Extraction Carpet Care:** 2580 San Ramon Valley Boulevard, Suite B208, San Ramon, CA 94583; phone: (415) 867-3850.

kinds of carpet fibers and their characteristics. They must also be knowledgeable about carpet installation, various kinds of dirt, and the chemicals used to eliminate stains. There is nothing worse for business than damaging a customer's carpet because the wrong chemicals or method of cleaning was used. Poor workmanship by incompetent or fly-by-night businesses have in the past given the carpet cleaning industry a bad name.

William R. Griffin, president of Cleaning Consultants Services in Seattle, Washington, stresses in *How to Start and Operate a Successful Service Business* that a carpet cleaner needs to know when to walk away from a job. Some customers have impossibly high expectations. Rather than mislead or disappoint the customer, Griffin believes the professional should explain that the carpet—or a particular stain—cannot be cleaned. If there is any possibility that the customer still expects a miracle, the carpet cleaning professional should decline the job.

Many companies, including carpet and carpet cleaning equipment manufacturers, franchisors, and industry consultants, offer training for professional carpet cleaners. Cleaning industry associations also sponsor training programs; contact the **Institute of Inspection, Cleaning and Restoration Certification (IICRC)** in Vancouver, Washington, at

(206) 693-5675. The IICRC is the largest certification agency in the cleaning industry. Griffin, who presents seminars on carpet cleaning, recommends pursuing a training program provided by an organization that is not in the business of selling equipment or franchises.

ADVERTISING AND MARKETING

A significant portion of your business plan should be devoted to how you will find customers. In the *Carpet Cleaners Guide to Sales and Profit,* Roy Moore and F. T. Smith state plainly: "One should be soliciting for work all the time." Many carpet cleaning companies report that the majority of their business comes through referrals from other customers. Referrals are the least costly and most effective form of marketing. But landing those initial customers can require considerable effort.

As a newcomer to the carpet cleaning industry, you should begin by soliciting friends and relatives, letting them know that you are in business. One approach is to offer to clean a friend's carpet for free in return for other referrals and recommendations. This will allow you to try out new equipment and quickly generate a list of prospective customers. Later, this approach can also be extended to regular customers; for example, you may offer a free cleaning for every five referrals that turn into paying jobs. Social or professional associations are also fertile ground for personal contacts that can generate business.

Some carpet cleaning companies rely heavily on cold calls, either canvassing a neighborhood or using a cross-reference directory to call homeowners in a particular area. Cold-call sales, however, are very difficult and can be tricky since many people resent the interruption. One method that appears to work without generating ill will is to talk the neighbors of a customer after a job is completed and offer them a "special deal."

Most carpet cleaning companies also make frequent use of fliers, door-hangers, and direct mail advertising, all of which have the advantage of being able to target selected neighborhoods. The most productive fliers offer a special price or discount on carpet cleaning done before an expiration date. Special offers can be especially effective shortly before such holidays as Thanksgiving and Christmas, when people do a lot of entertaining in their homes. Fliers and door-hangers, which can be distributed easily by youth groups, are probably the least expensive form of advertising, but direct mail can also be very affordable if it is tightly focused. One or two jobs resulting from direct mail advertising will usually cover the cost. One particularly popular form of advertising involves adding a coupon for your carpet cleaning service to an envelope filled with coupons for other businesses. Sharing the cost of postage with eight to ten other companies makes direct mail very inexpensive.

Many large carpet cleaning companies and franchisors advertise regularly in major metropolitan newspapers, a marketing method that poses two problems. First, the cost of a display ad may be prohibitive, especially for a single-unit business. Second, a broad circulation newspaper may generate leads so far away that a small company would lose money getting to the customer. Travel time is unproductive, so advertising in a neighborhood or community newspaper usually makes more sense, especially for a start-up business. Church bulletins and other community newsletters should not be overlooked. Another point to remember is that women make most of the carpet cleaning decisions, so advertising needs to be geared to their concerns.

Large companies have had success with advertising on television, but again, the cost is almost always prohibitive for a start-up business unless you can arrange a trade-off to clean the television station's carpeting. For start-up businesses on a shoestring budget, trade-offs may also be useful in arranging for business cards, stationary, signs, and other equipment. Almost every business has a carpet somewhere that needs cleaning!

Television also poses the same difficulty in targeting customers as broad circulation newspapers. Television advertising rates are based on total audience, but you will need to divide the price of a commercial by the number of viewers in the immediate market area to gain a true perspective of the cost. In addition, carpet cleaning companies are split about the usefulness of advertising in the Yellow Pages. In metropolitan areas with a large amount of carpet cleaning busi-

nesses, it is easy for an ad to get lost in the crowd unless the company's name begins with an ''A.'' In smaller communities, though, where there may be only one or two carpet cleaning businesses, Yellow Pages advertising can be very effective.

One form of marketing that is often overlooked by start-up businesses is signage on company vehicles. Neighbors who see a carpet cleaning truck or van in a driveway will often ask the crew for an estimate on cleaning their own carpets. A clear business identification reinforces a company's professional image, which is also a good reason for cleaning crews to wear uniforms. Uniforms and a professional appearance can help dispel any doubts that a customer may have about letting a stranger inside the house. Incidentally, signs do not have to be painted on a car or truck. Sign companies can make inexpensive magnetic signs that cling to the side of a vehicle, giving it a very professional appearance. The signs can be removed easily, which may come in handy if the company vehicle is also the family car. Magnetic signs are convenient for start-up businesses that plan to purchase a truck or van but do not want to make the investment right away.

Marketing for your carpet cleaning service should also include an effective follow-up program. Customers should always be asked whether they were satisfied with the work, and you should make improvements based on their responses. You should stay in touch with past customers, sending them reminders about the last time their carpets were cleaned or offering special deals for repeat business. Almost all start-up carpet cleaning companies concentrate on residential customers; however, there are also opportunities for small businesses in the commercial market. Cleaning vacant apartments, rental units, or offices for a management company can be especially profitable.

ADD-ON SERVICES

It is not uncommon for a carpet cleaning business to expand into related services such as on-site drapery and upholstery cleaning. Special equipment designed to clean draperies or upholstery is available for about the same cost as carpet cleaning systems. Some franchisors have begun adding ceiling and wall cleaning to their list of services. A particularly profitable market related to cleaning is restoring carpets damaged by water or fire for insurance companies.

RISK MANAGEMENT

As a smart business owner, you should carry liability insurance that will protect your business from having to pay damages arising from on-the-job injuries. Liability insurance should also cover accidental damage to a customer's premises. However, typical liability insurance will not cover damage to a customer's carpet caused by poor workmanship or the improper application of chemicals. It is possible to buy insurance to cover such destruction, and some franchisors offer insurance. In addition, if you belong to various

---

INDUSTRY STATISTICS

- *Percentage of Customers Who Choose a Carpet Cleaning Company Based on a Referral:* 48%
- *Number One Reason Customers Change Carpet Cleaning Companies:* "Never contacted by company again" (68%).
- *Percentage of Customers Who Change Carpet Cleaning Companies Because of Price:* 9%.
- *Percentage of Customers Who Change Carpet Cleaning Companies Because of Poor Work:* 14%.

(SOURCE: *CARPET CLEANERS GUIDE TO INCREASE SALES AND PROFIT*)

- *Percentage of Franchise Businesses Still in Operation 10 Years After Start-up:* 90%.
- *Percentage of Independent Businesses Still in Operation 10 Years After Start-up:* 18%.

(SOURCE: *U.S. DEPARTMENT OF COMMERCE*)

- *Size of the Residential Carpet Cleaning Market:* 8.5 million homes per year.
- *Percentage of Customers With Incomes Over $50,000 Hiring Professional Carpet Cleaners:* 68%.
- *Percentage of Customers Who Expect to Pay More Than $30 Per Room for Professional Carpet Cleaning:* 27%.
- *Percentage of Customers Who Expect to Pay Less Than $30 Per Room for Professional Carpet Cleaning:* 30%.
- *Percentage of Customers Who Picked Their First Carpet Cleaning Company by Word-of-Mouth Referral:* 46%.
- *Percentage of Customers Who Picked Their First Carpet Cleaning Company From a Yellow Pages Ad:* 16%.

(SOURCE: 1989 *J.D. CULLY SURVEY*)

PRIMARY ASSOCIATIONS AND SELECTED TRADE PUBLICATIONS

Associations:

Association of Specialists in Cleaning and Restoration (ASCR): 10830 Annapolis Junction Road, Suite 312, Annapolis Junction, MD 20701; phone: (800) ASCR-012.

International Institute of Inspection, Cleaning and Restoration Certification (IICRC): 2715 E. Mill Plain Boulevard, Vancouver, WA 98661; phone: (206) 693-5675.

International Society of Cleaning Technicians (ISCT): 3028 Poplar Road, Sharpsburg, GA 30277; phone: (404) 304-9941.

Publications:

Cleaning and Restoration: Association of Cleaning and Restoration, 10830 Annapolis Junction Road, Suite 312, Annapolis Junction, MD 20701; phone: (800) ASCR-012.
Cleaning Business: Cleaning Consultants Services, Inc., 1512 Western Avenue, Seattle, WA 98111; phone: (206) 682-9748, or (800) 622-4221.
Cleanfax Magazine: Cleanfax Publishing, 1566 W. First Avenue, Columbus, OH 43212; phone: (614) 486-5334.
Cleaning Management: National Trade Publications, 13 Century Hill Drive, Latham, NY 12110; phone: (518) 783-1281.

carpet cleaning associations, you may be able to obtain advice on dealing with particular problems that may develop, such as yellowing of a carpet after cleaning. Even though they may occasionally be forced to replace a client's carpet, few carpet cleaning businesses carry damage insurance because of the relatively high cost. Most take the position that the best protection against damage claims lies with skilled workers who are well versed in their trade.

Most states do not require a special license to operate a carpet cleaning business. That could change in the future because of mounting environmental concerns about the chemicals used in making and cleaning carpets and the health hazards posed by indoor air. Although it is purely voluntary, you can seek accreditation from the IICRC or some other industry organization. Carpet cleaning services that are certified often include that fact in their advertising, which may provide some additional credibility with customers.

STAFFING

One issue you may face almost immediately is the question of staffing. Although many carpet cleaning businesses consist of a single owner-operator or a husband and wife team, you may find it necessary to hire someone to help with either scheduling or cleaning.

In general, people do not like leaving messages on a telephone answering machine, so it is important that a business number be answered by a person whenever possible. This is especially true for a business like carpet cleaning. When people call a carpet cleaner it is usually because they need the work done soon. If there is no answer or they reach a recording, the most common response is to call someone else. Some carpet cleaning businesses hire an answering service that takes calls when nobody else is available. However, hiring someone who is trained to answer questions, give a preliminary estimate, and schedule the work may be much more effective in the long run for your growing business.

Even if you plan to do most of the work yourself, you should give serious thought to hiring someone to help with the actual cleaning. Cleaning a carpet is demanding physical labor, especially if there is a lot of furniture that needs to be moved. Hiring an assistant can greatly increase the lone worker's efficiency, and the additional jobs that can be done in the same amount of time usually more than cover the assistant's salary. You may also find it enjoyable to have a co-worker. Griffin recommends paying a knowledgeable helper between $7 and $10 an hour along with a commission on new referrals.

PRICING

To make a profit, the average residential carpet cleaning job should bring in between 20¢ and 30¢ per square foot. Ideally, of course, every job would be priced separately based on an inspection of the work to be done, since heavily soiled or stained carpets take more effort to clean. If it is not feasible to send someone to every customer's house for an estimate, you can offer a flat per-room rate based on average room sizes. You should have in your ads clearly outlined provisions for combined living spaces, rooms over a maximum size, or other special circumstances. In some cases, especially large jobs or carpets that are badly stained, it may be worthwhile to send someone to do an estimate.

Checking other carpet cleaning service ads will give you a good indication of what the going rate for carpet cleaning is in a particular area. Some carpet cleaning companies, though, advertise extremely low prices then add on extra charges for vacuuming, pre-treatment, spot removal, or stain-resistance protection. Such deceptive pricing tactics have been partly responsible for giving the carpet cleaning industry a bad name. Keep in mind that repeat business is the result of quality work and fair pricing.

FRANCHISE OPPORTUNITIES

There are a number of companies that offer carpet cleaning franchises. These franchisors usually provide equipment, training, a supply of cleaning materials, business cards, advertising materials, and telephone support. Each franchisor promotes a brand name and a particular method of cleaning, and fees range from about $5,000 to $15,000, plus monthly royalties. The same type of equipment and training is usually available from other sources at a lower cost and without ongoing royalties, so purchasing a franchise to start a carpet cleaning service may not be necessary. However, you may want to consider that, according to the U.S. Department of Commerce, five times more franchises are in business ten years after being started than independent businesses.

One important piece of information to know is whether a company has other franchises in the same general market area. If it does and if the other franchises have been providing quality service, then the goodwill associated with the franchise name will be a valuable asset. Consumers will have come to know and trust the franchisor. But if the other franchises have developed reputations for shoddy service, then the franchise name could be a detriment for a new business. Your business may also be hindered if your equipment or carpet cleaning process bears a brand name with a poor reputation.

In the final analysis, carpet cleaning may be an ideal business. It requires very little investment to start, it can be run out of the home, and it generates a positive cash flow almost immediately. It can be operated as a single-person business on a part-time or full-time basis, or, in the hands of an ambitious entrepreneur, can expand into a multi-unit operation with a number of add-on services. But a carpet cleaning service also requires hard work, both the physical labor of cleaning carpets and the effort necessary to market a service business. The best advice is to begin small, concentrate on cleaning carpets, and develop loyal, satisfied customers who will recommend you to their friends and neighbors.

SOURCES:

Bates, Owen, *How to Start Your Own Carpet Cleaning Business,* E. A. Morgan Publishing Co., 1986.

Griffin, William R., *How to Start and Operate a Successful Service Business,* Cleaning Consultant Services, Inc.

Moore, Roy, and F. T. Smith, *Carpet Cleaners' Guide to Increased Sales & Profit,* Cleaning Consultant Services, Inc., 1989.

—*Dean Boyer*

Check Cashing Service

If you have ever driven by a check cashing store and wondered how a business that cashes presumably bad checks can manage to survive, or why someone with a legitimate check would sacrifice a large percentage of its value just for immediacy's sake, consider that roughly one out of every five Americans does not have a bank account and that an overwhelming majority of the checks these 50 million people cash are in fact honorable. The common misconception regarding check cashing establishments in the 1990s is that they operate by charging exorbitant fees to shady individuals hoping to pass bad checks. This reputation was earned by early proprietors in the business who charged customers anywhere from 20 to 25 percent of a check's value, dealt almost exclusively with welfare recipients, illegal aliens, and transients, and were located only in the poorest urban settings.

The check cashing industry, however, has come a long way from its roots in the 1930s. Beginning as natural offshoots of liquor stores and supermarkets that served as "community banks," check cashing stores have evolved into respectable, burgeoning enterprises attracting a wide assortment of clients and charging service fees low enough to compete with banks yet sufficient enough to generate a sizeable profit.

Surprisingly, the financial risk involved in operating a cash checking business is not as high as many people would assume. Check cashing operators typically lose less than one percent of their total collected fees as a result of returned checks, and the losses incurred by honoring checks that pose a higher risk, such as personal checks, are usually offset by charging higher service fees. Since check cashing establishments are in no way associated with banks, their operation is not subject to federal regulation, allowing the aspiring entrepreneur to structure service fees to suit a prospective market and achieve maximum profit potential.

Growth in the check cashing industry was sparked by early 1980s deregulation of financial services, which immediately encouraged banks to charge higher service fees to their customers for basic banking services. Banks earn a majority of their money by providing loans, not by operating checking accounts, so the needs of customers who require only basic banking services are often overlooked, and those same neglected customers are asked to pay increasingly high service charges for minimal amount of service.

Another inconvenience suffered by bank customers is the seven- to ten-day hold that is often applied to certain types of checks. Many people do not want to wait for their money or simply cannot afford this delay. By focusing your efforts on providing quick, friendly service to customers who only want to cash checks and by adjusting your service fees to make your check cashing store a viable alternative to traditional banks, the possibility exists to woo customers away from banks and into your business.

COSTS AND PROFITS

First, the good news: Profits in the check cashing business can be very appealing. If your business does exceptionally well, your annual net profit before taxes could reach as high as $112,000. A less optimistic yearly expectation is a pretax net of $78,000. Some of the more successful stores rack up an average of $200,000 in gross annual sales, cashing 100 checks a day. For your first year of operation, the profit potential is somewhat lower and will most likely not exceed $40,000.

As a low-end figure, around $67,000 is needed to set up a cash checking store, but the average start-up investment generally climbs up to $80,000 and often exceeds $100,000. The amount you project for your initial investment will depend on what kind of deal you can get on materials, the size and location of your store, and how much you decide to invest in security measures.

FINANCING

Undoubtedly, the most daunting aspect of calculating investment costs is determining how to obtain the money in the first place, a task made more difficult by the nature of the check cashing business itself. Although check cashing proprietors have enjoyed considerable success in shedding the image of the industry as a collection of unsavory and unscrupulous cash merchants, banks generally look askance at the check cashing business and still regard it as an illegitimate stepchild of the banking industry. Consequently, you could experience more than a modicum of difficulty in obtaining a loan to start your check cashing business. That is not to say,

FRANCHISE OPPORTUNITIES

The following are several of the better-known check cashing franchisors. The royalty figure indicates the percentage of monthly gross sales the franchisee is obligated to pay. Advertising royalty represents the franchisee's contribution toward local and national advertising expenses incurred by the franchisor.

Cash Plus Inc.: 4020 Chicago Ave., Riverside, CA 92507. Initial franchise fee, $14,500; start-up costs, $30,000-$45,000; royalty, 6%; no advertising royalty; no financing provided.

Check-X-Change: 111 S.W. Columbia, #1080, Portland, OR 97201. Initial franchise fee, $6,500, $15,700, or $19,700; start-up costs, $33,000-$104,000; varying royalty; no advertising royalty; no financing provided.

Check Express U.S.A. Inc.: 5201 W. Kennedy, #750, Tampa, FL 33607. Initial franchise fee, $24,500; start-up costs, $103,000; royalty, 5%; advertising royalty, 3%; no financing provided.

United Check Cashing: 325 Chestnut St., #1005, Philadelphia, PA 19106. Initial franchise fee, $17,500; start-up costs, $50,000-$71,000; royalty, 0.3%; no advertising royalty; financing provided.

Check-Mart: 1055 Aurarian Pkwy., Ste. 100, Denver, CO 80204. Initial franchise fee, $25,000; start-up costs, $45,000; royalty, 5%; no advertising royalty; financing provided.

Nix Check Cashing: 17019 Kingsview Ave., Carson, CA 90746. Initial franchise fee, $25,000; start-up costs, $94,400; royalty, 6%; advertising royalty, 2.5%; no financing provided.

however, that banks should not be approached for financing. Keep in mind that lending money is how banks make money, so every effort should be expended toward persuading a bank to back you in your business venture. Any relationship you have developed with your banker, either through another business in which you are involved or just from your personal banking activities, will of course improve your chances.

Another avenue to pursue, not just for financing but for other matters related to establishing and operating a small business, is the U.S. **Small Business Administration (SBA),** which provides financing in certain circumstances and publishes a wealth of materials that address a broad range of topics, from preparing your small business taxes to calculating your yearly budget. In order to be eligible for an SBA loan, you must first attempt to obtain financing from a bank or other lending institution. Most of the SBA's pamphlets can be found in your local library, or you can call **1-800-U ASK SBA.** The SBA is a resource that should not be ignored.

Obtaining a check cashing franchise is an additional

alternative to approaching a bank for financing. Many, but not all, check cashing franchisors offer franchisees financing as well as a full spectrum of services for the potential check cashing operator. It is important to remember, however, that franchisors—some more than others—limit the control you have over the operation of your establishment, so you should thoroughly investigate what the franchisor expects of you and what you can expect of the franchisor before entering into an agreement.

CHOOSING YOUR COMMUNITY

The first step in selecting a site for your check cashing store is to identify a suitable community for your business. The area in which your store is located will be as important to your business' success as the particular site you choose within that area. In general, there are two types of communities in which check cashing stores can operate profitably: low-income and middle-class.

While it may seem strange to consider opening a new business in a vicinity you have identified as economically depressed, bear in mind that many banks have closed branch offices in these areas, limiting the number of places residents within the community can cash their checks and thereby creating a need for the services you propose to offer. The right middle-class or suburban community is also an area in which a check cashing store can operate successfully, provided the design and specific location of your establishment will encourage residents to frequent your business and you have properly identified a need for more convenient check cashing services.

To begin investigating a community, whether you opt for a lower-income or middle-class neighborhood or a mixture of both, conduct your own market survey of your chosen area. Much of this work can be accomplished by visiting your local library and chambers of commerce or business development centers, while additional information can be gleaned from canvassing other proprietors within the community. Business development associations and chambers of commerce will have maps of major trading areas that will show you the core businesses operating in your selected community and will indicate the spending habits of your target population.

At the library, take a look at census studies of your area. Often, statistical information is broken down into smaller, neighborhood areas, or precincts. Note whether the population within your vicinity has declined or expanded in the previous five or ten years, or if it has remained steady. As a rule, areas that have demonstrated a declining or static population base are not the best locales for opening a new business. Census studies will also give you an idea of the demographics of the area, providing you with an insight into the types of people that reside in the community, including the size of various age groups and the cultural make-up of the area.

SITE SELECTION

Once you have thoroughly researched a community and determined that its economic and population base will support the services you intend to offer, the next step is to locate a particular site for your store. Success for a check cashing store is predicated on achieving a high sales volume, so the accessibility of your establishment to both road and foot traffic is of paramount importance. A corner spot abutting a major thoroughfare would be the ideal location for your store, but of course prime locations demand high rent, a factor that must be considered during all phases of site selection.

Typically, rental fees for the shady side of the street are higher than the sunny side of the street, since retail studies have shown that businesses on the shady side fare better than those that must use awnings to block the sun. But of more importance to your check cashing establishment is which side of the street you are located on relative to traffic flow. A check cashing site that is located in proximity to a street that carries commuters to and from a major employment area—either downtown or near the area's major employer—will tend to receive more business if the location is on the same side of the street that commuters use to go home. Potential customers that need to cash a check are less likely to stop on their way to work, when time is particularly precious, than on their way home.

Also, imagine trying to reach your proposed location from various directions surrounding your site and different lanes of the main road that a majority of your customers will use. At first glance, what may look like a perfect location—a corner spot with high traffic density—may become a nightmare for customers trying to navigate toward your store. Note whether left turns are permitted from the other side of the street. If they are, will the driver be able to easily turn into your parking lot, or will a series of turns be necessary? Remember that the primary selling points of the services you will offer are speed and convenience; if customers cannot easily enter your premises, then business will suffer. Clearly, when attempting to combine high traffic density with accessibility, sacrifices must be made; the two qualities rarely mix harmoniously and you need to remain aware of problems that may occur.

Another crucial factor to consider before you become too involved with researching the viability of a location is whether you will legally be able to conduct business at your particular spot. Zoning codes and other restrictive ordinances often differ within three or four blocks; what may be approved on one block may be banned on the next. Consequently, if your selected area is populated by a broad range of businesses, that does not necessarily mean your particular site is zoned for check cashing stores. Be sure to check all restrictions that may apply to your site.

STORE SIZE

Check cashing establishments generally contain between 800 and 1,200 square feet of floor space, with yearly rental fees running anywhere from $6 to $36 per square foot. Store space in a mall will most likely be the most expensive per square foot, but the size of the space will be smaller—usually under 1,000 square feet. Determining how much floor space you will need depends largely on the amount you can afford based on your projected annual sales volume. Generally, high-volume businesses pay between two and four percent of their net sales for rental expenses, but this percentage can vary from as low as one percent to as high as ten percent. Calculating your budget for monthly rental expenses should be based on a careful market survey that will suggest your anticipated net sales.

STORE LAYOUT

When designing your store try to devote roughly 75 to 80 percent of the floor space for a customer service area. The emphasis should be on providing a large enough spot to easily accommodate your customers, even during peak periods of business. Several writing desks and a trash container should be placed away from the cashier windows and in such a way as to induce waiting customers to form lines naturally. In addition to the writing desks, several comfortable but inexpensive chairs should be available for friends or family members waiting for your customers. Other than these bare essentials, the customer service area should remain as uncluttered as possible to help quicken service.

SMALL BUSINESS RESOURCE GUIDE

The following are a number of publications produced by the U.S. Small Business Administration (SBA). Although the materials listed below do not focus on check cashing stores, they do contain pertinent and valuable information for anyone contemplating a small business venture. The letters and number(s) following the titles are SBA publication codes. To obtain one of these guides, include the title, publication code, the amount of money required, your return address, and make your check or money order payable to **U.S. Small Business Administration.** Mail your order to: **SBA Publications, P.O. Box 30, Denver, CO, 80201-0030.**

ABC's of Borrowing (FM1); price: $1.00.
Budgeting in a Small Service Firm (FM8); price: $0.50.
Recordkeeping in a Small Business (FM10); price: $1.00.
Selecting the Legal Structure for Your Business (MP25); price: $0.50.
Business Plan for Small Service Firms (MP11); price: $0.50.
Checklist for Going Into Business (MP12); price: $0.50.
Evaluating Franchise Opportunities (MP26); price: $0.50.
Small Business Risk Management Guide (MP28); price: $1.00.
Curtailing Crime—Inside and Out (CP2); price: $1.00.
Advertising (MT11); price: $1.00.

Valuable information can also be found in the SBA's **Small Business Start-up Information Package**, a copy of which can be obtained at your local library or a small business development center.

TRADE PUBLICATIONS, ASSOCIATIONS, AND MANUALS

Publications:

Checklist: A quarterly trade publication that, in addition to detailing the check cashing industry, guides you to appropriate state trade associations. Subscription price is $25 per year; for more information, call (212) 267-7712.

Associations:

NaCCA: The National Check Cashers Association provides members with a newsletter, access to representation in Washington, DC, and the opportunity to attend a national convention. For more information, call (201) 777-9870 or write to: NaCCA, 1 Mack Centre Dr., Mack Centre II, Paramus, NJ 07652. NaCCA does not offer start-up services to entrepreneurs.

Manuals:

Check Cashing and Fraud Prevention Guide: Produced by the Bank Administration Institute. Price is $15.00; for more information, call (800) 323-8552.

The check cashing windows should occupy approximately 50 percent of your total customer service area. Before tearing down an existing wall or building a partition to form your check cashing area, talk to a security consultant concerning the design of the teller counter. Most likely, the lower half of the counter, the "kick area," will have to be reinforced with steel. The counter itself should be from nine to twelve feet long with at least three feet of space provided for each teller. The cashier windows should be acrylic or bullet-proof glass. Bullet-proof glass is less expensive than acrylic but more costly to install, while both offer roughly the same amount of protection. One attractive feature of bullet-proof glass is that unsightly scratches can be removed, whereas nicks and scrapes on acrylic are permanent, an important consideration for maintaining the image of your store.

The remaining space behind the teller counter will be reserved for your office, a safe, a storage area, and a bathroom. In addition, you may want to set aside some space for your employees to sit while they are on break or engaged in some activity away from the counter.

MARKETING

Identifying exactly who your customers are is the most important aspect of your marketing strategy for operating a check cashing store. Generally speaking, there are four broad categories of customers that use check cashing services, all of whom may frequent your store. You may just cater to one particular group, depending on the composition of your target market. Many proprietors of check cashing establishments note that young, male, blue collar workers compose their largest market segment. Typically, these workers move frequently, especially those in the construc-

tion industry, and often forego opening a checking account at a traditional bank. Other blue collar workers, such as automotive mechanics or those involved in service-related fields, tend to purchase with cash instead of credit and depend on check cashing services to convert their paychecks to cash quickly. These customers, as well as nearly every type of customer you will serve, will be attracted to a place that is open late and provides speedy service.

Welfare recipients also gravitate toward check cashing stores to cash their government checks. Living from paycheck to paycheck with no savings, many need their checks cashed immediately. Your proximity to a low-income neighborhood as well as your courteous service could translate into a large and consistent customer base.

Although unpredictable, another large segment of people that may bring business your way are tourists. While it is risky to forecast a significant portion of your revenue coming from the tourist market, during peak travel periods tourists will fall back on check cashing stores either because they have exhausted their traveller's checks or simply because, in unfamiliar surroundings, they cannot find their particular bank. Again, your location is of singular importance; a store near major tourist attractions will obviously bring in more tourists.

If your store is situated near a university, students can provide a boost to your sales volume. Although many may have checking accounts, your proximity and accessibility could be the answer to their immediate need for money.

Virtually every successful check cashing operation offers additional services, such as money order processing, Western Union wiring service, photo identification, and postal services. Additional services usually are not profitable, but check cashing proprietors offer them as a very successful marketing device. Such extras often attract people who would not otherwise consider entering a check cashing store. Also, a full-range of services enables particular types of customers, such as nomadic construction workers, to take care of several chores in one stop.

To accommodate your customers, you should be open for business between 9 a.m. and 9 p.m., or from 8 a.m. to 8 p.m. If you must shorten your business hours, open later in the day. Once the banks close in the early evening, many people will have nowhere else to cash their checks. In addition, you should plan on staying open during weekends, especially Sunday.

SERVICE FEES

Collecting service fees is your method of generating income. Since you alone determine the percentage you charge per check, there are no strict rules governing your fee structure. Obviously, however, there is a limit to how much of their check customers will be willing to cede and a limit to how little you can charge and still earn a profit. Percentages vary according to the risk inherent in different types of checks. Typically, payroll checks written by local, reputable companies and government checks, such as welfare, social security, unemployment, and disability payments, present the least amount of risk and are charged from one to two percent of their value. Payroll checks from smaller, lesser-known companies are generally charged from three to four percent. The riskiest types of checks are personal, or two-party, checks, which some proprietors refuse to cash. Those that do cash personal checks charge as much as ten percent.

ADVERTISING

The effectiveness of your advertising will to a large extent determine the success of your business once you have selected and established a location. Perhaps your most important advertising tool will be the sign above your store. Pick a simple, easy-to-read sign that succinctly describes the services you are offering. All other forms of advertising, including newspaper, Yellow Pages, radio, signs on busses or bus benches, fliers, and direct-mailing, should adopt the same formula of making your message clear and concise.

In budgeting the amount of money you will spend on advertising, expect to spend from two to five percent of your gross annual sales. During your first year of operation, you should plan on spending at least ten percent of your projected gross sales. When you have calculated what this monthly figure should be, double it and spend that amount on your grand opening, which should take place several weeks after you open.

SECURITY

Protecting your establishment from theft will be your highest priority once you become involved in running a check cashing store, and it should be considered during all stages of organizing, establishing, and operating your business. The possibility of theft should, to varying degrees, influence your hiring of personnel, the selection of materials used to construct and fortify your store, and the type of equipment you purchase. No expense should be spared in purchasing a quality safe and a sturdy steel door. There are a multitude of security systems available, ranging from simple alarms to closed-circuit television systems and infrared alarms. A simple way to discover all the options available is to consult the Yellow Pages and explain your situation to a qualified security equipment salesperson. Another source of reliable information is an insurance agent, preferably one specializing in business insurance.

PERSONNEL

Since much of your success will depend on providing quick, accurate, and friendly service, considerable attention should be given to hiring employees who demonstrate such capabilities. They will serve as the linchpins of your operation and should be commensurately compensated. A check cashing store is not a good place to breed frustrated employees. Be sure to thoroughly screen prospective employees and search them out by placing an ad in newspapers or by using an employment agency, rather than by merely placing a "Help Wanted" sign in your window.

FRANCHISES

There are a number of successful franchisors of check cashing stores that are actively seeking franchisees. Obtaining a franchise may be your solution to the myriad obstacles that a new business owner must hurdle. Franchise agreements can include a broad range of services the franchisor will provide to the franchisee, including the hiring and training of personnel, financing assistance, budgeting and tax preparation, and advertising. In addition, by going the franchise route, you will benefit from either the regional or national name recognition the franchisor has established, which is part of the reason you must pay a percentage of your earnings to the franchisor. Whether you opt for a franchise plan or choose to go it alone, you should not neglect to investigate the franchise option. Often, just by talking with a franchise representative you can gain valuable insight into the operation of a check cashing establishment.

FUTURE PROSPECTS

As the success of cash checking stores increased, their popularity attracted the attention of the federal government toward the end of the 1980s, when the industry began displaying a need for some form of federal regulation. Federal intervention would likely signal the end of the proprietor's freedom to determine service charges and would establish a limit as to how much stores could charge per check value. If in the future, however, federal regulation is promulgated, the profitability of operating a check cashing service would most likely not change drastically. In fact, federal regulation could lend some legitimacy to the industry, which in turn could expand the sales volumes of check cashing stores nationwide.

SOURCES:

"188 New Franchises," *Entrepreneur,* April 1993, p. 124.

"Annual Franchise 500," *Entrepreneur,* January 1993, p. 214.

"Business Opportunity 500," *Entrepreneur,* July 1992, p. 214.

"Check-Cashing Service," *Entrepreneur Magazine's 184 Businesses Anyone Can Start and Make a Lot of Money,* second edition, Bantam, 1990.

Kotite, Erika, "A Run From the Banks," *Entrepreneur,* November 1987, pp. 53-58.

Lesonsky, Rieva, editor, *Check Cashing Service,* Entrepreneur Group, Inc., 1988.

Manusco, Joseph R., *Manusco's Small Business Resource Guide,* Prentice Hall, 1988.

Martin, Susan Boyles, editor, *Worldwide Franchise Directory,* Gale, 1991.

Schwartz, Carol A., editor, *Small Business Sourcebook,* fifth edition, volume 1, Gale, 1992.

Stodder, Gayle Sato, "Check-Cashing Services," *Entrepreneur,* July 1993, pp. 216-19.

—*JEFFREY L. COVELL*

Children's Day Care Center

Parents in the United States spend more than $10 billion annually on child care services. The average family may spend up to 20 percent of its income on child care. Organizations like the Child Care Action Campaign (CCAC) and the National Association for the Education of Young Children (NAEYC) have made it their business to educate the public about the importance of children's day care in the late twentieth century. As more and more women stay in the work force after having children, the child care industry has blossomed. Enterprising workers who want to start their own business can capitalize on the need for child care by opening a wide range of children's day care facilities. Options include family day care, which operates in the entrepreneur's own home for a few children, or a child care center for as many as 200 children.

Child care workers are among the worst-paid employees in the United States, but the industry is labor-intensive. In addition, high overhead costs keep profit margins down for owners of children's day care facilities. But the owners and operators of children's day care centers are providing something the public needs, and by the mid-1990s demand for day care still outpaced supply by a fairly wide margin. Downturns in the economy can effect day care centers, because parents who lose their jobs are more likely to pull their children out of the center.

It takes a special combination of talents for the owner and operator of a child care center to be successful. As important as good business and management skills are to the operation of the center, it is just as important to be dedicated to children. The most successful child care centers are those in which the owners convey their enjoyment with and concern for children to their staff, to the children, and to the parents. Word travels quickly in a community where the children thrive in a child care center, and that translates into a healthy business.

While day care centers are popular forums for child care, there are many other types of child care programs that can be opened and operated as businesses. Starting your own child care center is more expensive and labor-intensive than operating a family day care home. Some of day care options are: 1) In-home care, where nannies or caregivers live in the child's home. Salary usually includes room and board and is covered by minimum wage laws. Franchises in this field include A Choice Nanny and Any Situation. 2) Shared care, which is similar to in-home care but the nanny splits her time between two families. Sometimes the caregiver lives in one home but cares for children in two different homes. 3) Family day care, a situation in which usually a mother or grandmother cares for a few children, including her own, in her own home. Some of these people become licensed family child care providers with a specific number of slots available in her home, depending on its size and availability of play materials and play space. 4) Group homes, where a caregiver cares for a few children in her home and has other staff members to assist her. 5) Children's day care centers, in which the number of caregivers depends on number of children. Children are divided into groups for infants, toddlers, and preschoolers. Some of these centers also accommodate before- and after-school children.

FINANCIAL ASPECTS

If you opt against in-home child care opportunities, certain financial aspects must be considered before opening a child care center. There are two main types of child care centers. One is a for-profit child care center, which derives its income from fees charged to parents for bringing their children to the center. Some corporations support these child care centers by reserving and underwriting spaces for children of their employees. Another type of facility, not-for-profit child care centers, are tax exempt and may use government funds for day-to-day operations. These funds are available to enable children from low-income families to attend these centers.

Start-up costs include buying or leasing space, renovating the space, insurance, and such major equipment purchases as toys, furniture, and basic supplies, as well as initial marketing and advertising. Before starting up this type of business, you should investigate carefully the options of buying versus leasing and consider not only the community you will be serving, but the specific needs of the parents and children in that particular community.

The operating budget will depend largely on the kind and size of space you use. A full building with room to accommodate 100 to 200 children of varying ages will require much more staff and supplies, as well as more money for upkeep. The operating budget includes rent or

PRIMARY ASSOCIATIONS AND ORGANIZATIONS

American Child Care Services (ACCS): 532 Settlers Landing Rd., P.O. Box 548, Hampton, VA 23669; phone: (804) 722-4495.

Child Care Action Campaign (CCAC): 330 Seventh Ave., 17th Floor, New York, NY 10001; phone: (212) 239-0138.

Child Care Employee Project (CCEP): 6536 Telegraph Ave., Suite 201A, Oakland, CA 94609; phone: (510) 653-9889.

Families and Work Institute (FWI): 330 Seventh Ave., 14th Floor, New York, NY 10001; phone: (212) 465-2044.

National Association for the Education of Young Children (NAEYC): 1834 Connecticut Ave., NW, Washington, DC 20009; phone: (800) 424-2460, or (202) 232-8777.

National Association for Family Day Care (NAFDC): 725 15th St., NW, Suite 505, Washington, DC 20005; phone: (800) 359-3817, or (202) 347-3356.

Southern Association for Children Under Six (SACUS): Box 5403, Brady Station, Little Rock, AR 72215; phone: (501) 663-0353.

mortgage payments, utilities, telephone, staff salaries and benefits, insurance, food, equipment and supplies both for various ages of children and for office staff, and advertising.

Before drawing up your financial plans, it is helpful to consult the **Small Business Administration (SBA).** They can be reached at **1-800-U ASK SBA,** and most likely there will be a branch office located near you. The Service Corps of Retired Executives (SCORE), is also a good source of information. If you have any contacts in the industry, try to look at the budgets of other child care centers. If you plan to buy a franchise, the financial plans usually have already been drawn up, and much of the trial and error of budgetary development has been completed. You may still want to contact local business sources to adjust the franchise's plans according to the special needs and requirements of your own community.

Approach banks and other lenders once you have a general plan in mind. Be prepared to discuss the demographics of your area, mention prospective locations that you are considering, and show a sound budget. Sometimes, a local small business investment firm can provide start-up help.

LOCATION

Before choosing a location for your child care center, the owner must spend considerable time and effort in researching the need for care in the community. By contacting local social service agencies, churches, synagogues, PTAs, and businesses, you should get a sense of the numbers of working parents with young children who need child care. Find out if other child care centers are full and if they have waiting lists. When choosing a location, make sure to investigate outdoor space as well as indoor. Outside play should be in a safe area away from heavy traffic, while the location should also be convenient enough for parents to drop their children off without having to go far out of their way. Drop off procedures usually necessitate special traffic arrangements. Keep in mind that a site with an area in which cars are able to turn around might be very convenient for your child care center, as might a building with its own parking.

The owners of some child care centers advise against leasing space. They warn that buying a building or part of a building is the only way to safeguard your business from the whims of a landlord. Some centers do well in leased space, as long as the terms of the lease are favorable and flexible.

Some communities have very specific zoning ordinances that affect child care centers. Make sure you will be within the bounds of such ordinances and building and fire codes when you contemplate renting or buying a facility. If you are renting space for your child care center, check with local or state zoning and licensing offices about building-code requirements. Some landlords will make necessary modifications to accommodate you. If you are buying or building the center, you should work with architects and contractors who are familiar with child care facilities.

If the need is strong enough in your community, the possibility for donated space is worth investigating. Some low-income housing projects as well as some churches and synagogues prefer to open child care centers in their own buildings, but they do not wish to operate the programs.

MARKETING AND ADVERTISING

As with any new business, one of the keys to success is getting the word of your new venture out. Try to plan your opening in such a way that parents have already chosen your facility for their children before the official opening. Some facilities open at the beginning of the school year, so that the summer time, when older children are not in school, can be used to introduce yourself to the community. Aim your marketing efforts at specific communities. If you want to encourage children to attend who are in school during the day, contact the school officials, and try to arrange transportation to and from your facility for before and after school. Talk to the local PTA and introduce yourself to the teachers. Children enjoy continuity and can benefit from projects that complement the work they are doing at school.

Before opening, place notices on bulletin boards at local groceries and shops, churches, and synagogues. Use the local newspapers as much as possible. Try to get feature stories in the newspapers that working parents and other professionals read. Some children's day care centers have a specialized niche. Wee Care, in Birmingham, Alabama, for example, has a strong multicultural component, bringing African American art, music, and history into its program.

Consider marketing your facility to the local business community. Corporations are increasingly recognizing the need for child care among their employees. Consider opening a center at a workplace, or one conveniently located for several businesses. Even major companies that do not have on-site child care or resource and referral services often allow parents to put aside up to $5,000 per year tax free as payment for child care. These are known as dependent-care assistance plans, or DCAPs. If you know that local businesses offer these plans, contact them and discuss your children's day care center. Some companies reserve a certain number of slots for the children of their employees. Make sure to register with your local resource and referral agencies. **The National Association of Child Care Resource and Referral Agencies** can be reached at **(507) 287-2020.**

Another marketing priority is to price your services well. Make a scale that has prices that will stick, and compare your prices to what other local centers are charging. Most children's day care centers offer discounts for siblings enrolled simultaneously. You may, for example, consider

FRANCHISE OPPORTUNITIES

Goddard Early Learning Center: 381 Brooks Rd., King of Prussia, PA 19406; phone: (800) 289-2209, or (215) 265-5015. Founded, 1986; began franchising, 1988. Franchise fee, $25,000. Two-week mandatory training; sales royalty is 8% of gross sales, payable monthly.

Li'l Guys 'n' Gals Daycare International, Inc.: 10850 North 90th St., Scottsdale, AZ 85260; phone: (800) 634-4840, or (602) 451-0930. Founded, 1987; began franchising, 1990. Franchise fee, $40,000. Three separate day care programs for infants, toddlers, and preschoolers; week-long training session in Scottsdale; sales royalty is 6% of gross sales, payable monthly.

Primrose Schools Educational Child Care: 5131 Roswell Rd., NE, Marietta, GA 30062; phone: (800) 745-0728, or (404) 998-8329. Founded, 1982; began franchising, 1988. Franchise fee, $48,500. Educational child care for infants through kindergarten; offers training as well as lesson plans.

Tutor Time: 4517 NW 31st Ave., Fort Lauderdale, FL 33309; phone: (800) 275-1235, or (305) 730-0332. Founded, 1980; began franchising, 1989. Franchise fee: $25,000. Fast-growing franchise with comprehensive training and patented curriculum; sales royalty is five percent of gross sales.

Other Franchisors: Lollipop Lane, Inc.: 11811 North Tatum Blvd., Suite 3031, Phoenix, AZ 85028; phone: (602) 953-6682. **Prodigy Child Development Centers, Inc.:** 8601 Dunwoody Place, No. 714, Atlanta, GA 30350; phone: (404) 993-7211.

charging half-price for the second twin, or allowing two of three triplets to come for reduced fees. Make sure your hours are convenient for parents, but enforce the on-time pickup. Some children's day care centers charge a fee for every 15-minute increment that the parent is late.

In advertising, you must decide where to promote yourself as well as how to promote yourself. Your audience of working parents can often be best reached through newspapers and business magazines, as well as through parenting publications. Emphasize the cleanliness, safety, and highly qualified staff, and aim for small class sizes and a socially and academically nurturing environment.

STAFF TRAINING

Finding, hiring, training, and keeping an entire staff is more difficult for child care centers than for many other businesses, not least because child care workers are among the lowest ten percent of wage earners in the United States. In one respect, this is a plus for the owner of a child care center who does not have to pay top dollar for qualified workers. The flip side is that many workers get fed up with the work quickly. The turnover rate for child care workers is more than 40 percent each year. That means that the time and money invested in training them must be spent anew each year. Two thirds of all child care workers have been on the job for less than three years.

Decide how many child care workers you will need. Each state has licensing requirements that dictate the ratio of staff to children. Look for experience in child care, patience, energy, and creativity, and make sure to keep references. Also, consider whether all of your staff people need to work full-time. While the children enjoy the continuity of the same faces every day, some talented workers may only be available part time. Create a salary scale with room for growth and benefits if possible. Keeping an active roster of possible substitute workers is essential. Many child care centers have two shifts of workers to cover the 11 to 12 hour day. Try to hold staff meetings often enough that staff members feel a connection to each other, and so that they may air any grievances. Scheduling staff breaks during the long day caring for the children is also important.

In most day care centers, teachers or caregivers work in pairs. That way, if one teacher needs to change a diaper or mediate an argument between two toddlers, the rest of the children are not left to their own devices. Pairing caregivers who work well together is key, and allowing the caregivers to have input into the decision is helpful.

Local community colleges often have educational programs for child care workers. These can be sources of potential workers or students looking for unpaid internships. You may also find nanny-training classes offered in some vocational schools, where graduates can be hired as caregivers. Retired teachers or other educational specialists may be available to teach or to lead specialized activities such as

INDUSTRY STATISTICS

• Child care is a $48 billion industry (source: Tutor Time).
• More than 50% of working mothers are unable to find satisfactory child care (source: *CCAC Information Guide 3*; *USA Today*, June 1991).
• Approximately 57% of women with children under 6 years old were employed outside their homes in the 1990s (source: *USA Today*, June 1991).
• By the year 2000, 4 out of 5 infants and school children will have working mothers (source: *USA Today*, June 1991).
• Single parents head more than 25% of families in the United States (source: *CCAC Information Guide 3*).
• By 1990, 51% of mothers were working or looking for work before their babies' first birthday, up 60% from 1980 (source: *CCAC Information Guide 3*).
• More than 25% of working parents with young children use day care facilities (source: *Newsweek*, June 1992).
• A typical day care worker in the United States makes $5.35 per hour (source: *Newsweek*, June 1992).
• More than 40% of day care workers leave their jobs in under a year (source: *CCAC Information Guide 27*).
• Average families spend approximately 20% of their income on child care (source: *CCAC Information Guide 27*; *Good Housekeeping*, November 1992).
• Preschool child care costs an average of $300 to $500 per month per child (source: *Good Housekeeping*, November 1992).
• 13% of major companies provide on-site child care (source: *Good Housekeeping*, November 1992).
• 55% of major companies provide resource and referral services to help employees find day care options (source: *Good Housekeeping*, November 1992).
• There are no national standards for day care in the United States (source: *Newsweek*, June 1992).

music, art, drama, or languages. Refer to these experts in your marketing and advertising.

Some child care centers offer training in child development to their more valuable staff members. Child care workers are well placed to identify children with possible language or hearing problems. They also should receive training on identification of possible abuse victims.

RISK MANAGEMENT

In the field of children's day care, the entrepreneur must be thinking about safety issues at all times. Safety affects your choice of location, insurance coverage, and even schedule planning. Liability insurance and accident coverage are necessities. When obtaining insurance, make sure your general liability coverage includes bodily injury, property damage, medical costs, and legal defense in case of a lawsuit. A good security system is a must not only to protect your investment, but also to make parents feel safer about leaving their child. One franchise, Tutor Time, has identification cards and coded entries for parents to enter the facility and security cameras monitoring classrooms.

If you plan to take children off the premises for field trips or other outings, consider a comprehensive general liability package that covers accidents off-site as well as at the center. Family day care policies cost approximately $400 for comprehensive liability policies that include bodily injury, property damage, and incidental malpractice liability, as well as coverage while the children are on their way to and from the center.

Some states have instituted special plans to make insurance available to child care providers. States that have Joint Underwriting Authorities, or JUAs, make it a requirement for companies selling liability insurance to insure a share of applicants for child care liability insurance. Other states have Market Assistance Plans, or MAPs, in which insurance companies voluntarily participate in increasing availability of this liability insurance. Professional liability insurance is offered to groups such as the NAEYC and the National Association for Family Day Care (NAFDC).

Contact your state and local licensing office for information about local licensing requirements. In some states children's day care centers as well as family day care homes are licensed by the state. Staff screening is also essential, especially given the abusive situations that have been uncovered in child care centers. Train your staff in accident prevention, first aid, and CPR, and practice regular fire drills. Encourage parental visits, and review your safety and health procedures often.

LEGAL AND TAX ISSUES

Be prepared to protect yourself against potential legal action. It would be wise to meet with an attorney to discuss what waivers and forms should be required for parents before you can accept their children. One of these should be a medical treatment form, and another must have telephone numbers for each child's parents, physician, and emergency representative.

For family day care operators who work out of their homes, substantial deductions are allowed on income taxes. Contact your tax professional before you open so that you know what records to keep and how to maximize your savings. Limitations to these deductions concern the portion of your home that is "routinely used and available for use throughout the day," according to the tax code.

FRANCHISES

One of the benefits of entering the child care field by buying a franchise is that the franchisor has already had experience in the field. They often make other franchisees available to new operators, so that helpful hints can be suggested and mistakes can be avoided. Some of the franchises in the industry are Goddard Early Learning Centers in Pennsylvania, which began franchising in 1988 and had five outlets in the early 1990s; Li'l Guys 'n' Gals Daycare in Scottsdale, Arizona; Lollipop Lane in Phoenix, Arizona; Primrose Schools Educational Child Care in Georgia, which had 15 outlets in the early 1990s that specialized in educational child care with curricula for infants through kindergarten; and Tutor Time, based in Fort Lauderdale, Florida, which had learning centers for math and sciences as well as a miniature village and outdoor playgrounds.

Start-up costs for franchises involve more than the franchise fee. Franchisees must have capital to invest in furniture, equipment, and playground and kitchen equipment, among other expenses. Support is provided in various forms by the franchisor. Some franchisors help in site selection, lesson plans, staff training, and administrative details of registration and billing. Start-up costs depend on the franchise as well as on the size of the center. Some franchisors also provide on-site day care for businesses.

HELPFUL EQUIPMENT

Computer programs are available to keep track of registration, medical information, and other needs of the children's day care center. Some also can help owners order supplies, toys, or food, on a regular basis. Some of the franchisors will take care of these necessities, freeing the franchisee to focus on advertising and taking care of the children. For family day care centers, computer software is not always necessary, but it can make management easier. A database program and a word processor may be sufficient to make a difference.

Children's day care facilities need child-sized furniture and cots or beds, unless children bring their own mats for naps. Other necessary equipment includes shelves, teacher desks and chairs, play equipment for gross motor and small motor development, arts and crafts equipment, and possible musical equipment like record or tape players. Some children's day care centers have materials and equipment donated. Many others shop for some of these items at warehouses or other local sources of lightly used toys and equipment.

Like starting and operating any small business, managing a day care center has its risks. While the start-up costs, equipment needed, and possible liabilities may be daunting, given the increasing demand for quality day care in the mid-1990s, operating a child care center can be a rewarding experience.

SOURCES:

Ames, Katrine, ''Who's Minding Our Children?,'' *Newsweek,* June 8, 1992, p. 51.

Child Care Liability Insurance, Child Care Action Campaign, New York, 1990.

Facts about the Child Care Crisis, Child Care Action Campaign, New York, 1990.

Freeman, Michael, ''Hard Times Hit Day Care Providers,'' *San Francisco Business Times,* February 15, 1991, p. 1.

Harris, Richard W., ''Deductions for Use of Residence by Day Care Providers,'' *The National Public Accountant,* October 1992, p. 24.

How to Start a Child Care Center, Child Care Action Campaign, New York, 1990.

Jackson, Harold, ''Wee Care Academy,'' *Black Enterprise,* November 1993, pp. 78-87.

''KinderCare Workers Lose Jobs after Walkout,'' *Wall Street Journal,* January 5, 1994, p. B1.

Lurie, Theodora, ''Improving the Quantity and Quality of Child Care,'' *USA Today,* July 1991, pp. 68-71.

Madden, Michael, editor, *Small Business Start-Up Index,* Gale Research, Inc., 1991, pp. 32-33.

Martin, Susan Boyles, editor, *Worldwide Franchise Directory,* Gale Research, Inc., 1991, pp. 135-37.

McDonald, Jack, ''Day Care Fights Ills,'' *Health,* June 1991, p. 24.

Mitchell, Anne, and Diane Gage, ''Day Care in the '90s,'' *Good Housekeeping,* September 1992, p. 174.

''Rising-Star Franchises,'' *Working Woman,* November 1993, p. 103.

Schwartz, Carol A., editor, *Small Business Sourcebook,* sixth edition, volume 1, Gale Research, Inc., 1993, pp. 320-32.

Weissbourd, Bernice, ''A Day-Care Checklist,'' *Parents,* January 1993, p. 106.

Woy, Patricia A., ''Little Investment Becomes Big Business,'' *Small Businesses that Grow and Grow and Grow,* 2nd edition, Betterway Publications, 1989, pp. 19-24.

—*FRANCINE SHONFELD SHERMAN*

Clothing Consignment Shop

Contrary to popular belief, almost all consignment shops cater to the bargain hunter rather than to the low income person. Consignment shops therefore are not synonymous with thrift shops. A crucial difference between consignment shops and thrift shops is that consignors who contribute merchandise expect to be paid, and merchandise must be in very good or excellent condition. The unspoken rule of all consignment shops is: "second hand is not second best."

The clothing consignment business of the early 1990s was one of the fastest-growing small businesses nationwide largely because it is recession-proof, requires little or no experience to start, and has modest initial costs. Moreover, it is a business that lends itself to specialization; if there are too many general clothing consignment stores in your area, you may feature a particular kind of clothing, such as wedding gowns, athletic apparel, country/western clothing, evening apparel, maternity wear, or children's clothing. Unlike other retail clothing business owners, the clothing consignment shop operator also has the personal satisfaction of providing what amounts to a community service. You will essentially be recycling used clothing for those who are either environmentally conscious, just starting off in a job, or out for a good bargain.

COSTS AND PROFITS

All that is required of the prospective clothing consignment shop owner is a storefront—which is usually leased—a sign, and fixtures that can be begged, borrowed, or purchased at liquidation sales or at flea markets. You can negotiate with local printers or use your own computer to produce appropriate clothing tags. You will also need the right licenses, liability insurance, and money to pay a lawyer to examine your consignor contract and any other legal documents. While some consignment store owners have started their business with only a few hundred dollars, it is more realistic to estimate the minimum start-up cost at just under $10,000. If you want to add to that a cash reserve to tide you over the first six months and for emergencies, then the start-up cost will of course be higher. On the bright side, though, all of your inventory will be practically free, and you can

expect to eventually earn annual net profits of around $25,000 at the low end and perhaps up to $100,000.

FINANCING

If you cannot rely on a savings account or relatives for a loan, and if, considering the usurious interest rate, $10,000 seems like too high a sum to borrow on your credit card, then you should turn to the U.S. **Small Business Administration (SBA)** for lending advice. As a first step it is wise to avoid visiting or calling your local bank to secure financing. Instead, call your local chamber of commerce for the phone number of the local Small Business Administration office or call **1-800-U ASK SBA.** When calling the SBA, you are usually put on hold or will have a long message menu to choose from. Be patient and persistent; the SBA is there to help you, and a counselor will sit down with you and offer free advice on how to secure a loan and answer any other business questions you may have. The SBA also lends money and might prove to be a better choice than a commercial bank.

In addition, your local librarian is used to business queries and can quickly point you in the direction of the heap of books in every library dealing with small business loans and operations. Your SBA counselor will also be glad to recommend relevant books.

Taking the initial steps of contacting the SBA and obtaining information from the library should be taken since the task of applying for a loan can be a daunting one. Your consignment store as yet has no history. You must be able to prove convincingly—with the help of a sound business plan—that there is a market and future for your business. Therefore your own research and good, practical advice are crucial.

LOCATION

By the time you have your start-up costs covered, you probably have earmarked the likely location of your new store. There are a number of factors that come into play when selecting a successful store site, but undoubtedly the most important is proximity to good parking as well as to foot traffic. It is less important to worry about similar competitors in the area impeding your business. In fact, the

START-UP GUIDE AND SOFTWARE

Start-up Guide:

Consigned Clothing Business Guide, EntrepreneurGroup, Inc., 2392 Morse Ave., P.O. Box 19787, Irvine, CA 92713-9787; phone: (800) 421-2300.

Software:

Software constantly changes, and new packages appear frequently. The following are a list of some of the most popular brands. Prices cited are discount retail and approximate.

Peachtree Complete Accounting for DOS (also available for Windows): $189. A few main features are inventory for the small business, order entry, and accounts receivable/payable.
Peachtree Basic Accounting (DOS or Windows): $85. A simplified version of the above; provides online help; does not do inventory.
CA-BPI Accounting II for DOS (also Windows version): $164. Main features are payroll in addition to inventory, and accounts receivable/payable.
Quick Books & Quick Pay for DOS with Payroll: $109. Speeds up bill paying and invoicing.
One-Write Plus Accounting (DOS): $89. Features check writing, billing, inventory, and accounts receivable/payable.
FormTool 3.0 version: $50. This handy software creates every imaginable form on your PC, including price tags.
TurboTAX (DOS and Windows): $39. Claims to be the number one selling tax software; offers complete tax preparation.

presence of a number of consignment shops in the same vicinity often attract more customers—the kind who find it convenient to go from store to store in their hunt for the best bargains. Too much competition, on the other hand, might be an indication to specialize in a particular line of clothing that sets you apart from the herd.

Ideally, your location will be one where you can attract a mix of customers and a list of reliable consignors. There is a risk if your store is situated in an area primarily composed of students, who invariably go home for the summer and holidays; low income residents, who might flock to your store but might be unable to provide you with quality used merchandise; or an upper-income population, who might not value the bargain of secondhand clothing.

STORE LAYOUT AND SETUP

You have selected your store location in an area with good parking facilities and proximity to other stores and where pedestrians often pass by. Before opening day you have advertised and found out how easy it is to attract consignors to your store, so that you now have a basic inventory that will have to be sorted according to size and arranged on racks. A few factors that will in part determine the kind of store you select are whether or not you will have room for expansion (Is there a back room that could be used or an

upper or lower floor that could be opened up or leased in that eventuality?), and whether or not you will be able to have an eye-catching storefront.

Think twice before settling on a store that lacks a prominent storefront, which can be powerful advertising for your business. Make sure your sign is as appealing and inviting as possible. Select a name that is appropriate for the neighborhood where you are located and put your most attractive clothing in the display window. Make room for plants and dried flower arrangements and play soft background music; in short, appearance and mood should be part of your sales strategy.

Every clothing consignment store will need plenty of racks, some shelves or a corner set up with hooks, and possibly straw baskets in which you display such highly desired accessories as leather bags, belts, and scarves. If you can possibly afford it, have a display case for jewelry—if you decide to sell this—and your most expensive-looking handbags. Your cash register and receptacle for clothing tags, which identify the consignor by number, should be located where you will have the best eye contact with all of your customers and that will enable you to monitor all of your merchandise. Make sure that customers, including those pushing baby strollers, will have no difficulty maneuvering among your racks. It is also necessary to have a space set aside to try on clothing. For privacy in the dressing room, it is best to use a heavy curtain or drape that does not reach the floor, a deterrent against shoplifting. Finally, having plenty of mirrors in your store is not only a service to your customers but also a discouragement to the dishonest.

In setting up and arranging clothing on your racks, the crucial point to bear in mind is correct clothing size. You may notice some day that the premium brand silk blouse or wool skirt is not selling, perhaps because you carelessly placed it on the ''size ten'' rack instead of the ''size fourteen.'' Examine each item of clothing before laying it out on a rack—two skirts labeled size ten by the manufacturer may in fact be of dissimilar size when you look at them. If the space is available, some clothing consignment owners also provide chairs for customers, a table or two, and have a few toys on hand for restless children.

EMPLOYEE ISSUES

If your business is your first-ever consignment shop, it is usually not advisable to hire an employee. Even at minimum wage and part-time, the cost of hiring can put a serious dent in your profit margin. You also have to face a new set of problems—both legal and technical—when you hire someone. A wiser investment to make is appropriate software for your computer, which will facilitate such mundane but major matters as bookkeeping and keeping track of consignors and inventory, tasks that used to take up hours of an owner's time in the days before microcomputers.

If your business goal does include eventually becoming an absentee owner, then a part-time employee hired after your first year in business will be the ideal beginning. Once you have made up your mind to hire, you will have to be prepared to compose a job description and for the myriad forms you will need to fill out: tax, worker's compensation, social security, and wage forms.

INVENTORY AND CONSIGNOR MATTERS

By opening day, you will need to have acquired a basic inventory that fills up your racks and, if you have one, your display case. Where do you begin to obtain your merchandise? How do you price and tag it? After opening day, when do you accept merchandise—during regular store hours or by appointment? What about merchandise that has not been sold?

Before you open your shop, you will have advertised and invited consignors to deposit clothing. While you wait for them to come to you with clothing for sale, you can purchase good quality clothing from flea markets, discount stores, and garage sales. You can also ask friends for their good used clothing to add to your basic "start-up" inventory.

You are the boss and can set your own standards for quality. Some consignment store owners will accept only designer clothing in flawless condition. If your store is lo-

cated in an area where you think this is feasible, then you might highlight your high-quality inventory by means of your shop name—for example, "Next-to-New Chic Boutique"—and by printing up a sign that catches the consignor's eye and is either posted on the door or by the cash register. Whatever you decide, you must be firm about accepting clothing that is free of stains, rents, missing buttons, and damaged zippers. Your clothing, which must be cleaned and pressed, should reflect the season; summertime customers will not be flocking to your wool coat rack. Lastly, customers always look for clothing that is in style.

Most clothing consignment shops cater to women; men tend to wear out their clothes and are unlikely to be good, reliable consignors. Children's clothing should reflect the same standards as that of adult female clothing and should be in good condition and attractive looking.

After you have determined, in a friendly manner, what clothing to accept, you will give the consignor a number and a contract to sign. The agreement should indicate that when clothing is unsold after a specified period of time—the average rack life for a consignment garment is 60 days—either the customer can take back the merchandise or you will donate it to a charity. Because you will not want to be distracted during store hours with consignors bringing in clothing, accept garments by appointment only and discourage consignors from calling you during business hours about the status of their merchandise. Mail checks to consignors rather than having them come to the shop and pick them up.

With regard to pricing, a consignment garment usually sells for one-third the original retail price. You can often tell at a glance approximately how much a skirt or child's outfit cost originally. As the owner and operator of your own business, it is essential to visit discount and retail clothing stores in your area to keep up with what is in demand as well as with prices.

Once you have determined the price with your consignor (and most consignors are blissfully ignorant about your business and tend to accept your price), the usual method in all consignment shops is to split the purchase price of the garment after it is sold. Some owners take 60 percent but rarely more than that. It is also common practice to charge the consignor several dollars a year to register in an effort to recoup the cost of sorting and tagging garments.

There are computer software products that will generate tags, which ideally will identify the garment by the consignor's number, a description of the item, size, and price. Some store owners like to have different colored tags to reflect whether a garment has just been received or has been on the rack for a month. Clothing left on the rack for a month or more will probably have to be marked down; this is a matter you should discuss with your individual consignor.

Tags should be readily visible and firmly attached to discourage tag switching or loss. You should also have an easy method of removing the tag and depositing it in a box with a slot or in some other receptacle where there is

---

PRIMARY ASSOCIATIONS AND SELECTED TRADE PUBLICATIONS

Associations:

National Association of Resale and Thrift Shops (NART): 157 Halstead Street, Chicago Heights, IL 60411; phone: (708) 755-4561.

National Retail Federation (NRF): 100 W. 31st Street, New York, NY 10001; phone: (212) 244-8780.

Women's Apparel Chains Associations (WACA): 601 W. 25th St., 12th floor, New York, NY 10001; phone: (212) 675-6800.

Publications:

RTW Review: Danielle Consultants, P.O. Box 27688, Milwaukee, WI 53227-0688; phone: (414) 425-5503.
Sportswear International: VSI Publishing Corp., 438 W. 37th St., 4th floor, New York, NY 10018; phone: (212) 563-3470.
Stores: National Retail Merchants Association (NRMA), 100 W. 31st St., New York, NY 10001; phone: (212) 244-8780.
Women's Apparel—Retail Directory; Sportswear Retailers Directory; Clothing Retail Directory; Children's Clothing—Retail Directory: American Business Directories, Inc., American Business Information, Inc., 5711 S. 86th Circle, Omaha, NE 68127; phone: (402) 593-4600.
Directory of Women's and Children's Wear Specialty Stores: Chain Store Guide Information Services, 3922 Coconut Palm Drive, Tampa, FL 33619; phone: (813) 664-6700.

absolutely no danger of losing the tag, which records crucial information about your profit.

MARKETING AND ADVERTISING

Word of mouth and your own eye-catching storefront should generate customers, but it is good practice to tack your business card or a poster on public bulletin boards in supermarkets, churches, local libraries, and community centers. A weekly advertisement in your local newspaper, at least until your business is established, is also an effective method of garnering clients.

Your marketing strategy should be all-encompassing, however, and include more than a weekly ad in the local newspaper. There are many promotional opportunities that you can seize hold of. For instance, you have the opportunity to talk to your customers and to get to know them. Such small gestures as providing a toy or two to a fidgety child while his parent takes the time to browse in your shop; offering afternoon tea on a regular basis; keeping a log book of customer requests and calling them when the desired item is in your shop; and making your shop a cozy, inviting place to browse cost little, but definitely give your store the personal touches that virtually all retail clothing stores lack.

Finally, marketing can be fun: you can organize a fashion show, which can be especially enjoyable if you are the owner of a maternity or children's clothing consignment store. Also, if you do sell children's clothing, you could advertise a storybook hour or organize a birthday club.

TECHNICALITIES AND LEGALITIES

Before you even open your clothing consignment shop, you will want to review your store lease with a lawyer. Most landlords do have insurance to cover possible damage in common areas, but it probably will be necessary for you to take out your own liability insurance policy in case of theft or fire. You will also need county, state, and business licenses and tax permits. It is easy to find out exactly what you will need by calling your local chamber of commerce, which can direct you to the right office in your county and state. Business licenses may take time to obtain; in some states, the wait for the proper business license can take weeks.

By the time you are ready to accept your first consignment of clothing, you will need to have a contract drawn up for consignors to sign. Along with all of your other legal documents, this contract should be reviewed by a lawyer. It should specify the terms by which you accept the consignor's property, namely, how much of the purchase price of the garment he or she will receive, how long you will keep the garment if unsold, and a disclaimer of responsibility in case the garment is stolen or damaged. Your contract should also clarify what will happen to his or her garments if

unsold—most consignors will not bother picking up items that have been in your shop for two months. Before you open your business, it is a good idea to draw up a list of charities that might be interested in your unsold clothing. Remember, your clothes are all in good condition, so most charities running thrift shops of their own will not object to your consignments.

Finally, you should be willing to accept credit card payment from your customers. Therefore, calling area banks to get quotes on the fees charged for merchant accounts is a good idea.

COMPUTER SYSTEM AND PROGRAMS

If neither you nor anyone you know can design a software program to meet your bookkeeping needs, then you can turn to packaged commercial software for your IBM or Macintosh computer. There are many bookkeeping software packages available for under $200, as well as software that prints forms, labels, and tags, and software that does your check writing and compiles mailing lists. A simple phone call to your local software store and a description of your business needs will result in the right package for you.

In short, a consignment store can work well for you. Increasingly, recycling is becoming a way of life that will not wane in good economic times. With imaginative marketing and the right market niche—either general clothing, children's, maternity, wedding, or evening wear—your business can be a success.

SOURCES:

Budgar, Lawrence G., "Consignment Shop Businesses Thrive in Era of Thrift," *Wall Street Journal,* June 5, 1992, pp. B2(W), B2(E).

"Consignment Resale Clothing Store," *Entrepreneur Magazine's 168 More Businesses Anyone Can Start and Make a Lot of Money,* 2nd edition, Bantam, 1991.

Freese, Marjorie, and Sylvia Duncan, *How to Start a Consignment Shop & Make It Go,* Sylvan Books, 1984.

Gubernick, Lisa, "Secondhand Chic (TVI's Resale Stores)," *Forbes,* April 26, 1993, p.172.

Holmes, Kate, *Too Good to Be Threw, The Complete Operations Manual for Consignment Shops,* Chatham Communicators, 1988.

Kurland, Sheryl, "Market Niche for the '90s: High-End Consignment," *Baltimore Business Journal,* February 19, 1993, p. 61.

Menkes, Suzy, "Everything Old Is New (and Fashionable) Again; Thrift Shop Chic," *New York Times,* March 22, 1993, p. B3.

Stonesifer, Jene, "Setting up Shop, At Least Temporarily," *Washington Post,* July 6, 1992, p. WB8.

Woy, Patricia A., *Small Businesses That Grow and Grow and Grow,* Betterway Publications, 1989.

—*Sina Dubovoj*

Coffee Shop

With the surge in popularity of espresso, cappuccino, lattes, and gourmet coffee blends with exotic names, coffee has become big business. The United States is the world's largest consumer of coffee—each day, Americans down more than 400 million cups of java, according to the National Coffee Association.

Certainly, Americans have enjoyed coffee for decades, but since the early 1990s gourmet coffee has been the fastest-growing sector of the industry. Since 1990, gourmet coffee sales have risen from 10 percent to 13.2 percent of total coffee sales. In response to this rising demand for gourmet coffee, as well as the appliances needed to make espresso, cappuccino, and other coffee drinks, coffee cafes and gourmet coffee stores (often one and the same) have been opening in trendy shopping areas, college towns, and malls across the country. Entrepreneurs who open modern-day coffeehouses can expect to brew considerable profits selling coffee by the cup and by the pound—along with the machines that will let customers make their favorite coffee drinks at home.

Depending on the region of the country, competition can be stiff or almost nonexistent. On the East and West coasts, for example, coffee bars and shops abound—in some places, there might be three or four in a two-block area. In other parts of the country there may be only one coffee shop in an entire metropolitan area.

COSTS AND PROFITABILITY

A thriving coffee shop, on average, makes about $500,000 in gross sales annually. To achieve this amount, the entrepreneur should expect to invest about $250,000. Total initial investment and start-up costs can be higher depending on location, inventory size and type, number of employees, and insurance costs.

Franchising, which ensures a ready supply of new capital, represents the best prospect for a coffee shop's future growth. National coffee stores like Starbucks and Gloria Jean's Coffee Bean offer franchise opportunities. Both chains are expanding rapidly throughout the country and are enjoying high revenues. Most gourmet coffee franchisors require prospective franchisees to have $200,000 of equity in the form of savings, insurance, outside investment, or venture capital.

For the solo operator, the style of store you decide to create will determine your start-up costs. A gourmet coffee business can take the form of a traditional coffeehouse with tables and chairs; a cafe with a small kitchen where sandwiches and salads are prepared; or a coffee and tea store which mainly sells whole bean or ground coffee, packaged teas, and accessories, with perhaps a coffee bar where customers can buy a cup to go.

Most contemporary coffee shops are a hybrid of these three broad categories. In one visit, patrons can sit at a table or stand at a bar while drinking espresso and enjoying a light snack (anything from biscotti to a cup of soup), purchase a tea kettle, coffee mug, or espresso machine, and then buy a pound of whole beans to take home.

Whatever the setup, the start-up costs and overhead for a coffee shop are relatively low compared to other retail food businesses, such as full restaurants or bars. Coffee shops are traditionally small and cozy—thus, you can create an intimate atmosphere and keep costs down. "There's a high profit margin in coffee in general," David Levin, president of the Coffee Development Group in Washington, D.C., noted in an interview with *Entrepreneur.* "But with those specialty coffees, such as cappuccino, iced coffees and flavored coffees, people can really make some good money."

How much money is "good money?" you ask. The Coffee Mill in Oakland, California, reported sales of 8,000 cups per month at between 70 cents and $2.25 per serving in 1990. Arabica in Shaker Heights, a Cleveland, Ohio, suburb, grossed $800,000 in 1989, when the gourmet coffee boom was just beginning. And with the popularity of gourmet brews and blends increasing steadily during the early 1990s, the coffee business seems to be gathering strength. The primary liability for coffee shop operators are the standard accounts payable to suppliers and loans relating to starting and funding the business.

FINANCING

With their high profit margins and low overhead costs, coffee shops are viewed as a viable business venture by

**PRIMARY ASSOCIATIONS AND
SELECT TRADE PUBLICATIONS**

Associations:

National Coffee Association of U.S.A.: 120 Wall St., New York, NY 10005; phone: (212) 344-5596.

National Coffee Service Association: 111 E. Wacker Dr., Chicago, IL 60601.

Specialty Coffee Association: 1 World Trade Center, Ste. 800, Long Beach, CA 90831; phone: (310) 983-8090.

Tea Association of the U.S.A.: 230 Park Ave., New York, NY 10017.

Publications:

All About Coffee: William H. Ukers, Gale Research Inc., 835 Penobscot Bldg., Detroit, MI 48226.
Coffee Intelligence and *Coffee Annual:* George Gordon Patton & Co., 182 Front St., New York, NY 10038.
Coffee Technology: Michael Svetz, Avi Publishing Co., 250 Post Rd. E, P.O. Box 831, Westport, CT 10016.
John Conti Gourmet Guide: 4023 Bardstown Rd., Louisville, KY, 40318.
Tea & Coffee Trade Journal: P.O. Box 71, Whitestone, NY 11357.
World Coffee and Tea Magazine: McKeand Publicatons Inc., 636 First Ave., West Haven, CT 06516.

many financial institutions. Thanks to the robust health of the coffee industry and Americans' apparently unquenchable thirst for good coffee, opening a coffee shop is not a high-risk venture. The key to making it a success is twofold: first, find the necessary financing, and second, secure a prime location for the business.

Before arranging for loans and other financing, you should first conduct a market survey to determine a realistic sales forecast for the business. Lending institutions will want to see evidence of a plan firmly grounded in actual circumstances and market conditions. Demographics are a key component in a good market survey. The information you're after includes the population density and purchasing power, ethnic background and eating habits, median income and spending characteristics of people in your target location. You'll also want to determine the trade area and the present sales volume for coffee, tea, and other items you plan to sell. A vital next step is to estimate what proportion of this total sales volume you can expect to capture—particularly if there are other coffee shops similar to yours in the area.

Sources for the above information include the city and county governments, your local chamber of commerce and trade development commissions, and the U.S. Census Bureau. For information about similar businesses in the area, consult Dun & Bradstreet and check the local Yellow Pages.

In addition to approaching banks or other lenders for financing, you should investigate the Guaranty Loan Program of the **Small Business Administration (SBA).** The SBA is also an invaluable source of counsel and inexpensive publications about setting up and running a small business. The "U.S. Government" section of the phone book will have a listing for the SBA office in your area, or you can call **1-800-U ASK SBA.**

LOCATION

Ample financial backing and the quality of the coffee you serve won't amount to a hill of beans if you choose the wrong location for your business. One entrepreneur who's operated a coffee shop/dessert cafe in San Francisco for more than a dozen years noted that "location is everything, then design, and only third, the coffee."

You should probably target an area with plenty of upscale foot traffic. You may want to scout out a strip shopping center or a large mall. Look for "affinity" businesses—such as art galleries, gift shops, and high-end clothing boutiques—that attract your type of clientele. Once you've narrowed your search to a few areas, spend a few days watching the kind of people who patronize the stores surrounding these locations. A coffee shop generally attracts people between 25 and 45 with middle- to upper-incomes. About three-quarters of coffee shop customers are women, and people who earn more than $50,000 are high above the national average in their purchase of gourmet coffee.

Take a good, hard look at the competition. It's possible for two or three coffee shops or cafes to share a few city blocks if each one appeals to a particular segment of the population. For example, one might be a traditional coffeehouse that attracts the local college crowd by offering poetry readings and cozy tables conducive to studying. In contrast, the other two cafes might have limited seating and draw primarily morning commuters or the lunch-to-go crowd.

Since high profits in this business depend on heavy pedestrian traffic, be sure to locate your store in an area that's highly accessible. If your store is a free-standing building on a downtown commercial block, your sign should be visible from two directions. A large display window, through which pedestrians can see customers sampling coffee and customers can watch the passersby, serves as a powerful magnet. The aroma of brewing coffee should waft out the door to entice people who just happen to be walking past. For most coffee shops, Saturdays are busiest, followed by Fridays and Thursdays. December is the busiest month of the year.

In evaluating a location, keep in mind that a high volume of pedestrian traffic or a particularly chic shopping center can mean higher rent. Make sure that the rent is not beyond your capacity to pay, based on your projected sales volume. And investigate additional fees. For example, retailers in a shopping center or mall generally pay flat rents, percentages, a share of the total property tax, and "add-ons" that cover advertising, promotion, and maintenance.

DESIGN AND SETUP

The layout of your coffee shop has a very direct impact on your profit potential. Some cafes have the reputation of being hang-outs where customers linger for hours over books or newspapers and spend only a few dollars. If high volume and brisk table turnover is your goal, however, you can limit lingering by design. A stand-up bar or tiny tables with seating for only a few customers at a time sends an unmistakable message.

A distinctive ambiance can be created by color, lighting, accessory displays, and even equipment itself. Gleaming coffee urns, a chrome and brass Italian espresso maker, and glass-fronted wooden bins full of coffee beans create a different mood than bright lights, colorful walls, and marble-topped tables.

A word of caution about wood: although it creates a homey, warm atmosphere, porous wood is the worst material for storing coffee beans. It absorbs coffee oils, which then become rancid and can ruin the taste of new beans put in the bin. Make sure, if you buy wooden bins, that they are either nonporous wood or lined with nonporous, removable plastic that you can replace regularly. An alternative is nonporous bins made of acrylic, plastic or glass.

In creating your store's layout, keep in mind that the average coffee shop is 500 to 1,000 square feet and combines take-out and retail sales. Most sell coffee by the cup, light food items, whole-bean coffee by the half-pound or pound, a modest assortment of packaged teas, and accessories such as coffee grinders, automatic coffee makers, mugs, kettles, etc. Store layout will be determined by the scope of your menu and even your location—according to an article in *Restaurant Business,* downtown coffee shops mainly sell coffee by the cup, while mall shops sell more whole bean coffee and accessories.

Regardless of the size and variety of your menu, keep in mind that the bulk of your sales will come strictly from coffee. Starbucks, a popular Seattle-based chain and one of the leading gourmet coffee retailers in the early 1990s, noted in *Restaurant Business* that coffee was its top-selling product. In fact, in 1993, pastries represented just 11 percent of total sales for the chain.

Basic equipment needed to operate a coffee shop includes commercial coffee mills and scales; an espresso/cappuccino machine; display bins, jars, and cases; thermos carafes, mugs, and glasses; and scoops and bags for whole-bean or ground coffee purchases. Depending on the amount and kind of accessories you plan to sell, you may also need shelves, racks, display cases, and display tables. If you're planning to serve food, add silverware, dishware, and cooking utensils to your list.

In terms of inventory, *Entrepreneur* magazine recommends starting out with 400 to 700 pounds of coffee. Try to offer a wide variety of coffees from many different countries. Your supplier can tell you which types are best-sellers. Coffee loses its flavor and becomes stale quickly, so try not to overorder. According to the Coffee Development Group, a generally successful product mix is 40 percent flavored, 25 percent selects and blends, 18 percent decaffeinated, and 17 percent dark roast.

A reasonable goal is to sell 500 to 700 pounds of coffee per week. The most popular gourmet blends include French Roast, Italian Roast, Colombian Supremo, Mocha-Java Blend, Costa Rican, Vienna Roast, and Mexican. Remember to offer at least three varieties of decaffeinated coffee, and don't forget to concoct a special house blend. Don't be afraid to experiment in developing your house blend—it can help you create a unique identity for your store and become as distinctive as a signature.

STAFFING AND TRAINING

Most coffee shop owners start with a small staff of one or two employees. If you're serving a variety of food that has to be prepared or cooked in advance, consider hiring a manager with specialty food service experience. A good rule of thumb is to start with one full-time employee and two part-timers until you gain a good sense of the sales volume and traffic flow your store will generate.

You and your staff should learn as much as possible about coffee and tea. Everyone working in your store should be able to speak confidently about the aroma, body, and strength of each type of bean. Your supplier is a good source of background information about coffee—everything from where and how it's grown to the best ways to brew it. Encourage your employees to sample a variety of coffees so that they can make recommendations to your customers.

GOURMET COFFEE AND TEA SUPPLIERS

Becharas Bros. Coffee Co.: 14501 Hamilton Ave., Highland Park, MI 48203.

Coffee & Tea Ltd.: 1481 Third St., San Francisco, CA 94107.

Dallis Bros. Inc.: 100-30 Atlantic Ave., Ozone Park, NY 11416.

International Coffee Service: 680 Fargo, Elk Grove Village, IL 60007.

John Conti Gourmet Coffee: 4023 Bardstown Rd., Louisville, KY 40218.

Rose's Coffee Co.: 922 S. Boyle Ave., St. Louis, MO 63110.

Simpson & Vail Inc.: 53 Park Place, New York, NY 10017.

COFFEE AND TEA ACCESSORIES AND EQUIPMENT SUPPLIERS

Accessories:

AMA di G. Ardesi & C.: 3 Via Pavoni, 1-20159 Milan, Italy.

Filtrator Coffee Apparatus Co.: 31 Styertowne Rd., Clifton, NJ 07012.

The Gourmet Center: 1200 Dallas Trade Mart, Dallas, TX 75207.

Homewares of California: 1920 Freemont Ave., Signal Hill, CA 90804.

Melitta Co.: 1401 Berlin Rd., Cherry Hill, NJ, 08034.

Equipment:

Consolidated Paper Supply Co.: 2427 E. 14th St., Los Angeles, CA 90021.

Tempo Plastic Co. Inc.: 25 E. Providence Ave., P.O. Box 626, Burbank, CA 91503.

Toledo Scale: P.O. Drawer 1705, Columbus, OH 43216.

Some coffee shop owners hold tasting seminars for employees to acquaint them with the characteristics of different blends and brews.

MARKETING AND ADVERTISING

A grand opening is an ideal way to introduce your new business to the public. You may want to offer a free pastry with every purchase of a cup of coffee, or a free cup with the purchase of a pound of beans. Set up a coffee-tasting bar where customers can sample small cups of different beans and blends.

On a daily basis, the aroma of fresh coffee will be your most powerful marketing tool. The lush scent will draw in a steady stream of passersby who, in most cases, are already sold on your product. A staff well versed in coffee lore can further boost sales by introducing customers to new flavors and blends. To expand your customer base, set up a mailing list, sell gift certificates and hold coffee-tasting seminars. Take advantage of coffee's perishable nature and feature flavors of the day, week or month. Sell custom-made gift baskets and encourage customers to give coffee accessories as presents for weddings, birthdays, and holidays.

Because coffee is best when it's fresh, advise customers who purchase coffee for home consumption to buy only as much as they'll drink in a week. This is an excellent way to build a regular clientele, and it ensures that your customers will enjoy the most flavorful brew. Make educat-ing your customers' palates part of your marketing strategy. Their word-of-mouth recommendations are your best—and most inexpensive—form of advertising.

LICENSES AND INSURANCE

To open a coffee shop or cafe, you'll have to obtain a business license from the city or county where your shop will be located. Check to be sure that zoning ordinances permit your proposed use and allow for expansion. You'll also need a health-department permit, since you'll be selling food. The health department will probably want to inspect your store before selling you a permit, and may also require that your employees have certification.

Some jurisdictions require fire-department permits if flammable materials will be used in your place of business. Other locales have restrictive ordinances regarding size and design of signs, so you may need a special sign permit. You may also need state and federal licenses—check with your state government and the Federal Trade Commission (FTC) regarding these. You should also purchase standard business insurance. Investigate liability coverage as well; most food retailers buy this insurance to protect themselves in case of food poisoning or the presence of foreign materials in some imported goods.

According to a report on specialty coffeehouses by James Walton, gourmet coffee shops must comply with the federal Occupation Safety and Health Act (OSHA), the American Disabilities Act and the Immigration Reform and Control Act of 1986. More information about compliance can be obtained from the individual government offices, which should be listed in the phone directory under "U.S. Government."

With coffee sales climbing steadily, the prospects for launching a successful gourmet coffee business are good. Be aware, however, that a healthy bottom line ultimately depends on the world market. Coffee is a commodity, and fluctuations in the price of raw beans eventually trickle down to the gourmet coffee purveyor. But by blending together a prime location, an attractive, inviting decor, a variety of good coffees, strategic and creative marketing efforts, and an intelligent, coffee-literate staff, the aspiring entrepreneur can expect to make a comfortable living with his or her own coffee shop business.

SOURCES:

Coffee and Tea Store, American Entrepreneurs Association (AEA), AEA Business Manual No. X1202, 1988.

Durocher, Joseph, "Brewing Up Profits," *Restaurant Business,* February 10, 1992, pp. 158-160.

"How to Make Money on Coffee Breaks," *Entrepreneur,* March 1981, pp. 7-33.

Huffman, Frances, "Grounds for Success," *Entrepreneur,* September 1990, pp. 78-84.

Romano, Michael, "Coffee With a Kick: Gourmet Coffee Bars Are New Breakfast Niche," *Restaurant Business,* July 1, 1993, p. 142.

Scarpa, James, ''Gourmet Coffee Is Piping Hot,'' *Restaurant Business,* February 10, 1992, p. 24.

Walton, James, Michele Joseph, and Marc Rossen, ''Specialty Coffee House/Cafes in Northeast Ohio,'' *Basic Business and Industry Profile,* Cleveland State University, December 1992.

—*Marinell James*

Collection Service

A collection service, or agency, is a relatively easy business to start, but the industry is highly competitive and owning a successful business will require considerable skill and determination. The American Collectors Association suggests that anyone considering starting a collection agency be willing to work long hours and have the operating capital and the patience for the business to build slowly. The association also remarks that no amount of preparation or studying can replace the direct experience of collecting accounts. The good news, however, is that as long as there are creditors, there will be a need for collection agencies. And creditors are often willing to give new agencies a chance to prove their worth.

FINANCIAL ASPECTS

Start-up costs for a collection agency are typically very low. At the high end are collection agencies that lease enough office space for two or three collectors and spend $6,000 to $10,000 for furniture and basic office equipment. With rent, advertising, insurance, legal advice, and the first month's salaries, start-up costs could run as much as $30,000. At the low end are individuals who set up offices at home and work by themselves. Their start-up costs may run from a few hundred dollars, depending on what equipment they already own, to as much as $6,000 if they buy furniture and a personal computer.

A collection agency's earnings depend on how successful the sales manager is in attracting clients and how effective the collectors are in recovering unpaid debts. As a guideline, the American Collectors Association notes that a collection agency needs to generate $25,000 per month in new business for each employee in order to be profitable. Agencies generally charge clients between 30 percent and 50 percent of the money they collect, with pretax net earnings of 25 percent to 35 percent. In other words, gross revenues would range from $30,000 to $50,000 for every $100,000 an agency collects, with pretax net profit between $8,750 and $12,250.

Because start-up costs are relatively low, financing should not be a problem for a collection agency. New owners should first consider personal resources, the easiest and fastest source of financing. If outside financing is necessary, new owners should remember that banks are very conservative in their lending practices and require a solid business plan. Banks also usually require a thorough background check and collateral, although a person with an excellent credit rating may be able to arrange an unsecured loan. Finance companies often will accept greater risk and may extend a loan when a bank will not; however, they also charge higher interest rates. One source of financing that is often overlooked are personal credit cards. Although interest rates are much higher than a bank loan, start-up costs can be charged and paid off as soon as the collection agency begins to generate a positive cash flow.

The **Small Business Administration (SBA)** is another source of start-up capital. The SBA is an independent agency of the U.S. government that promotes small businesses through loans, counseling, and other information. The SBA is particularly sensitive to women and minority ownership. You must first exhaust all sources of private financing before you are eligible for an SBA loan. There are Small Business Administration offices in most major cities. Check the ''U.S. Government'' section of the telephone directory for locations and telephone numbers. You can also reach the SBA at **1-800-U ASK SBA.**

LOCATION

There are two aspects to selecting a location for a collection agency: choosing a community in which to operate and deciding on an office location within the community. Both are important, but choosing the right community may be the more critical. Although some collection agencies may do well in small communities, larger communities (some consultants recommend a population of at least 300,000) with healthy economic growth offer greater opportunities for success. The more economic activity in a community, the more bad debts are likely to be turned over to collection agencies. This is especially true for retail economic activity, since most collection agencies deal in consumer debt. The American Collectors Association suggests there should be at least 500 firms granting credit for each collection agency in a given area.

Office location may be important if you intend to concentrate on a particular market segment. A collection agency

INDUSTRY STATISTICS

• *Number of Collection Agencies in the U.S.:* 6,000.
• *Amount of Unpaid Debts Placed with Collection Agencies (1992):* $75 billion.
• *Average Rate of Collection for Unpaid Debts (1992):* 18.5%.
• *Bad Checks Written in the U.S. (1992):* 533 million, totaling $16 billion.

(SOURCE: AMERICAN COLLECTORS ASSOCIATION *COST OF OPERATIONS SURVEY*, 1993.)

• *Number of Credit Cards in the U.S.:* 950 million (source: Associated Credit Bureau, Inc.).

that works primarily with hospitals or other health-care providers, for example, may find it beneficial to be situated near a hospital or in a medical office complex. An agency that works primarily with banks or other financial institutions would be located suitably in a city's financial district. An office with a prestigious address may also carry some weight with potential clients. Most start-up agencies, however, are not able to specialize, and since clients seldom visit the agency and most collections are handled by telephone or mail, decisions regarding office location can be based on cost and convenience. Many one-person collection agencies operate successfully from the owner's home.

A collection agency does not require an elaborate office. Each collector should have a desk, telephone, and access to basic office equipment. Remember that you will generate a significant amount records, so you will also need to have plenty of storage area. The American Collectors Association recommends 75 to 100 square feet of office space, including filing space, for each employee. The sales manager will also need a desk, and may need an office—or access to a conference room—for meeting clients. Start-up businesses should also plan ahead and consider the possibility of future expansion.

As a prospective business owner, you should check with an attorney, who can decipher the fine print, before signing any lease. Collection agency offices have simple requirements, so there should be plenty of sites available. Most building owners will start off with a standard lease, but everything should be negotiable, including who is responsible for any improvements and repairs. As a lessee, you should also be wary of common costs and restrictions that could affect operations.

MARKETING STRATEGIES

Marketing a collection service is a matter of convincing a business with overdue accounts that turning them over to professional collectors is more efficient and profitable in the long run. Most marketing will be done through face-to-face presentations by you or a sales manager. Effective marketing techniques include a description of your collection methods, affiliations with other agencies, and your past success

rate. In addition, a dignified, professional-sounding name can help position a collection agency with its clients.

Many businesses are reluctant to assign overdue accounts to collection agencies, believing that in-house departments can collect the debts. By the time they turn to outside agencies, the debts are so old that collecting is nearly impossible. Potential clients are also cautious about questionable collection agency methods, since they can reflect badly on clients' businesses. The American Collectors Association emphasizes that listening to a potential client to learn his or her specific needs is critical to success. If you decide to align yourself with a particular industry, such as health care, financial services, utilities, or retail credit, you can develop an expertise and knowledge about the industry that may influence a client's decision.

ADVERTISING

Collection agencies generate much of their business by contacting potential clients and scheduling sales presentations. Other leads will come from recommendations provided by satisfied clients. Advertising can also generate interest, especially from smaller businesses that may not be contacted directly by the agency's sales staff. Most collection services advertise in the Yellow Pages and in trade publications. You should join your local chamber of commerce and other business and civic organizations and advertise in their publications. Although few clients will hire a collection agency on the basis of an ad, they will call to get more information. Direct mail can be especially effective in reaching specific industries. You may, for example, purchase a mailing list of all the health care providers or construction companies in a community and send them information about your services.

PRICING

In general, collection agencies are paid only when they are successful collecting money owed to their clients. However, some agencies may charge a minimum fee for taking on a new client or charge a flat fee for small accounts whether they collect or not. Agencies usually charge between 30 and 50 percent of the amount recovered, depending on how long overdue the account was when it was turned over to the agency. The longer an account has been outstanding, the harder it is to collect; studies show that 95 percent of accounts more than 90 days past due will not be paid by the debtor voluntarily. You may want to vary your fees based on the nature of the account. Retail accounts are often harder to collect than overdue hospital bills—at least for private hospitals—and command a higher commission.

Although most collection agencies have standard fees, in practice fees are often negotiated with individual clients, which means that sales managers must be able to estimate the chances of collecting on various accounts and the cost involved to ensure that the agency makes an adequate profit. There may be times when you accept a lower fee in order to get business from a client on a trial basis. Some collection agencies even go so far as to offer a ''no collection/no charge'' guarantee.

PERSONNEL

A collection agency has three basic job functions: collections, marketing and sales, and support. Although it is possible for one person to handle all three areas for a small collection agency, most start-up businesses will need to hire at least one person for additional help. Before taking on any employees, you should create a detailed job description outlining specific duties and necessary skills.

Collectors spend most of their time on the telephone either tracking down or talking with creditors whose accounts have been turned over to the collection agency. They are often paid an hourly wage plus, as an incentive, a percentage of the agency's commission on the money they collect. Most collectors can handle between 100 and 200 active accounts and should generate four to five times their base salaries in agency commissions.

A myth, according to the American Collectors Association, is that collectors need to be tough and intimidating. The most effective collectors are individuals who understand how to motivate people and can work with them to get the accounts paid. Desirable qualities include a quick mind, tact, and perseverance.

Sales personnel are responsible for generating new business by calling on potential clients and convincing them to turn their unpaid bills over to the collection agency. In many cases, salespeople also negotiate the agency's commission based on the nature of the accounts and the potential for future business. The salesperson may be the first and only person from the collection agency that a client ever deals with directly. In many agencies, sales personnel are paid strictly on a commission basis, receiving 15 to 20 percent of the new business they bring in.

Support staff handle much of a collection agency's clerical work, including bookkeeping, entering accounts into the computer system, and sending out collection letters. The more computerized an office is, the more such tasks as printing collection letters will be done automatically or by collectors themselves in the course of their regular work.

LAWS AND REGULATIONS

Collection agencies are highly regulated businesses. Most states require them to be licensed, while many require both a special business license and a bond. A few states also stipulate that potential collection agency owners pass a qualifying test. The American Collectors Association requires its members to be bonded and administers a professional certification program. You should contact the state regulatory agency or the American Collectors Association to determine specific requirements.

Collection agencies also must adhere to the federal Fair Debt Collection Practices Act, which places strict limits on how far a collection agency may go to collect on a past due account. In general, collection agencies are not allowed to threaten, harass, or lie to debtors to get them to pay. Collectors also must keep their efforts confidential. For example, you may ask former neighbors if they know where a debtor lives or works, but you are not allowed to mention the debt. It also is illegal for the outside of an envelope to indicate that the correspondence concerns an unpaid bill. You should become familiar with the Fair Debt Collection Practices Act, a copy of which may be obtained from most state regulatory agencies or by writing the American Collectors Association.

In some states, collection agencies are required to maintain two separate bank accounts, one as a regular business account and the second as a trust account. Money collected from a debtor is held in the trust account until a check is written for the client's share of the proceeds. The rest can then be transferred to the business account. Some clients ask that the full amount collected be forwarded to them, and they then remit the commission to the agency.

SPECIAL EQUIPMENT

Computers are essential to the efficient operation of a collection service, for both record-keeping and turning out form letters that are sent to creditors. An integrated database and word-processing software program can track all aspects of an account from the time it is turned over to the collection agency until it is closed. The right computer program can store and retrieve information on creditors, schedule calls, automatically print collection letters, and create financial reports for clients and the agency.

A consultant can recommend the most effective computer set-up for a specific collection agency, but in general, you should have a workstation for each employee that allows retrieval and input of information about active accounts. The cost of computers and computer programs can vary widely, but each workstation will probably cost between $700 and $2,000. Software developed specifically for collection agencies may cost between $2,500 and $3,500. You will also need a good quality printer and modem for

---

PRIMARY ASSOCIATIONS AND SELECTED TRADE PUBLICATIONS

Associations:

American Collectors Association and American Commercial Collectors Association: 4040 W. 70th St., Minneapolis, MN 55435; phone: (612) 926-6547.

Publications by American Collectors Association:

Collector.
Cred-Alert.
Currents.
Public Affairs Review.

FRANCHISE OPPORTUNITIES

American Lenders Service Co.: 312 E. 2nd St., Odessa, TX 79761; phone: (915) 332-0361.

Parson-Bishop Services, Inc.: 7870 Camargo Road, Cincinnati, OH 45243; phone: (513) 561-5560, or (800) 543-0468.

sending and receiving information by telephone. In addition, you may want to become a member of a credit reporting service and communicate with them electronically.

Finally, many people believe that hard economic times, which affected much of the United States in the early 1990s, meant a favorable business climate for collection services. And while it was true that more accounts were being turned over to collection agencies, it was becoming harder to collect from people who may have lost their jobs. Many collection agencies reported working much harder for far less reward. For the entrepreneur who was willing to learn the business, however, there was still plenty of opportunity

in an industry that would be around as long as there was credit.

SOURCES:

10 Myths of Debt Collection, American Collectors Association, Inc.

Andriatch, Bruce, "It's All in the Way You Ask; Collection Agencies Say a Calm and Professional Approach Is the Best Game Plan," *Business First of Buffalo,* February 10, 1992, p. 15.

Collection Agency, American Entrepreneurs Association, 1987.

Collection Fact Sheet, American Collectors Association, Inc., autumn 1993.

Selecting a Professional Collection Service, American Collectors Association, Inc.

Starting and Managing a Collection Service, American Collectors Association, Inc.

Thomason, Paul, "Walking the Line, Over the Edge," *Collector,* October 1993, p. 41.

"When to Use a Collection Agency and How to Find the Right One," *Profit-Building Strategies,* September 1987, p. 13.

Woy, Patricia, *Small Businesses That Grow and Grow and Grow,* Betterway Publications, 1989.

—DEAN BOYER

Compact Disc Store

Compact discs (CDs) revolutionized the recording industry in the early 1990s. After less than a decade on the market, compact discs surpassed records as the most popular form of recorded music. Every segment of the music-listening population—from teenagers to baby boomers—preferred the high-technology discs over records because of superior music quality and the fact that CDs were more durable, compact, and scratch-resistant. The market expanded as customers not only purchased new CD releases but also replaced old albums and cassettes with CDs.

As a retailer specializing in compact discs you have an advantage over a larger all-purpose record store because you can offer customers a greater variety of CDs in a smaller and more comfortable environment. A CD store is also easier to manage since you only keep inventory of one music format. If you plan your business carefully and creatively, you can carve yourself a lucrative niche in the CD industry.

START-UP COSTS AND PROFIT POTENTIAL

The minimum start-up investment for a CD store is about $50,000. Average costs, however, run closer to $75,000, with inventory making up the bulk of that figure. On average, compact disc retailers net $60,000 before taxes and may earn as much as $100,000. Some savvy CD entrepreneurs have earned millions of dollars by expanding into franchising businesses.

If you need financing, you might get a personal loan from a bank—provided your credit is strong enough. Choose a bank that offers all of the services you will need, including one that handles major credit cards. Before visiting your bank lender, prepare a detailed business plan describing your business, goals, and ability to attain those goals. In your financial statement, include several years of profit and loss estimates so that your lender knows that you are prepared to absorb losses. You might want to hire an accountant or a business consultant to help you with the statement; though it may cost several hundred dollars, it is worth the expense to have a professional, accurate, and complete statement.

Other sources of financial assistance include small business investment companies or other private investment firms. The U.S. **Small Business Administration (SBA)** may be able to offer you a loan or guarantee a loan, although the SBA generally helps firms after they have exhausted all other means of financial support. The SBA can be reached by calling **1-800-U ASK SBA** or by writing **Small Business Directory, P.O. Box 1000, Ft. Worth, TX 76119.** Local SBA offices are also listed in the "U.S. Government" section of your telephone directory.

LOCATION

The location of your store is of strategic importance. It is best to situate your store in or near an urban area with a population of more than 100,000. Conduct research on prospective neighborhoods to ensure that your offerings will attract residents or business people. Next, choose a site that is highly visible and accessible. A corner location at a busy intersection is ideal; if you provide parking facilities, however, make sure that accessing the lot is not difficult. Choose a cite near other small businesses and capitalize on the shopping traffic. Keep similar store hours as the neighboring shops and salons and accommodate tourists or evening shoppers. If you are seeking an after-work crowd, try to find a location on the side of the street which is used most by these pedestrians or motorists.

The size of your store should be from 1,000 to 2,000 square feet—although with creative design and storage plans, you could do well with as little as 500 square feet. A space in a high-volume shopping mall may be suitable for you. However, not all mall sites are visible, and malls generally charge higher rents for less space. In addition, in a new mall you may have to invest several thousand dollars for construction. In a shopping center you will need to do little advertising of your own, but you will probably have to pay small monthly fees for communal advertising and for the mall merchants association. Regardless of where you choose to locate, make sure the space has adequate facilities for your needs. Find out about licenses, permits, and zoning restrictions for your building and locality. Before signing your lease, you should be clear about all of your financial responsibilities.

PRIMARY ASSOCIATIONS AND SELECTED TRADE PUBLICATIONS

Primary Associations:

Recording Industry Association of America: 1020 19th St. NW, Washington, DC 20036; phone: (202) 775-0101.

National Association of Recording Merchandisers: 11 Eaves Drive, Ste. 140, Marlton, NJ 08053; phone: (609) 596-2221.

National Association of Music Merchants, Inc. (NAMM): 35 East Wacker Dr., Chicago, IL 60601.

Electronic Industries Association: 2001 Pennsylvania Ave. NW, Washington, DC 20006; phone: (202) 457-4900.

Decorating Retailer: 1050 N. Lindberg Ave., St. Louis, MO 63132-2994; phone: (314) 991-3470.

National Retail Federation: 100 W. 31st St., New York, NY 10001; phone: (212) 631-7400.

Publications:

International CD Exchange: ICE, P.O. Box 3043, Santa Monica, CA 90403.
Billboard: Billboard Publications Inc., 1515 Broadway, New York, NY 10036; phone: (212) 764-7300.
Jazz Times: 8055 13th St., #301, Silver Spring, MD 20910; phone: (301) 588-4114.
Rolling Stone: 745 5th Ave., New York, NY 10151; phone: (212) 484-1616.

MARKET RESEARCH

One of your primary tasks will be learning about the population of your intended area of business, since it will determine the types of stock you carry. Talk to neighborhood residents to determine their tastes and preferences in music and try to pinpoint the shortcomings of local music stores. You can find adequate demographic information from secondary sources at local chambers of commerce and small business development centers. Find out the average age, social class, and ethnicity of the residents. Ideally the locality will have a stable or growing population, diverse industry, and a strong economic base. Talk to local radio station managers for further advice on selecting your inventory. Contact the advertising divisions of local papers and radio stations for information on the buying patterns of the community. Consult with suppliers and other CD store managers with whom you will not be in direct competition. Find out where your competition is located by scanning the local Yellow Pages and visiting those stores.

LAYOUT AND EQUIPMENT

Your store will be divided into two areas, with about three-quarters devoted to retail space and the rest reserved for an office/storage area. You should work to personalize your retail space—for instance, it could be rustic and simple or sleek and high-tech. It is important to create an intimate yet professional setting so that you can compete with larger music stores. Remember that you are trying to put your customers in a buying mood, so make your store as enticing as possible.

When you're ready to unload your inventory, set up racks along the walls and place a few in the center of the store. Make the aisles about four feet wide to enable customers to move comfortably through the store. Position racks featuring special selections, such as discounted items, at the ends of the aisles. Customized shelving can cost more than $1,000, but depending on the look you want for your store, you may want to try making the racks yourself (or ask friends or woodworking students to help). For used equipment, check local papers for office sales and close-outs.

Once your shelving is in place, separate your CDs by category and then arrange them alphabetically. Include signs distinguishing the various sections so that customers may more easily locate titles. It is a good idea to install pegboards above the selections and mark the newest and most popular releases. You can also store discs above or below the display racks. Your most expensive items, however, should be locked in glass displays. Add variety to the layout by setting up special displays, such as used CDs casually arranged on a table. If your budget allows, it would be wise to set up listening booths with headphones.

Items with the most turnover should be placed at the front of the store, the location with the highest sales potential. Watch the way traffic flows through your store and arrange items accordingly. Some studies indicate that customers with particular purchases in mind move clockwise through the store to avoid other shoppers, while the browsers tend to saunter counterclockwise. The best-sellers should be placed at the left, allowing regular visitors to find their goods quickly and efficiently. Arrange a variety of other popular titles to the right for browsers. Remember that sales potential is lowest at the rear of your store, so keep the harder sells there.

Choose a store name that is unique, easy to remember, and clearly indicates that you are in the retail CD business. Post a creative, eye-catching sign outside—keep in mind that CDs are an impulse market and many passersby are potential customers. The exterior is one of the most important areas of the store. Be creative with your window displays to draw people inside. For decorating ideas, consult with your distributors; they may be able to provide you with free posters and other promotional aids. To draw attention to a particular title and to make up for the small size of CDs, display several copies of a title together. Set up some posters in the window as well as inside your store. You might also consider hiring an art student to redesign the windows periodically—either seasonally, during the Grammy Awards, or when a popular band is in town.

It is best to set up the checkout counter near the exit along a wall so it is not in the way of browsing customers. Position CD-related products, such as racks, portable cases, and cleaning kits, near the checkout. Set up a rack of music-related periodicals below or near the checkout, and leave counter space for promotional items, like key chains and pens, bearing your store logo. You should get an electronic cash register and develop a workable inventory tracking system. Initially you can lease a register for about $150 per month. Later you might want to invest in a computerized system that allows you to perform a number of functions automatically at the register.

Another important investment is a high quality stereo system, complete with CD player, an amplifier, good speakers, and perhaps an equalizer. Other equipment needs will include a typewriter, several multiple-line telephones, an answering machine, and tagging guns. In your office/storage space, you should also have a few chairs, a desk, cabinets, and a safe. Prepare professional business cards, letterhead stationery, and brochures. In all, your total equipment and miscellaneous supply costs, excluding inventory, will run about $20,000 or far less if you purchase used materials.

ADVERTISING

As with any business, promotion is crucial for success, particularly in the first year of operation. As a CD retailer, you should conduct preliminary market research and look for the most cost-effective advertising methods. It is important to keep your ads simple, clear, and informative. Be consistent with your message and run ads regularly, so that your message sticks with customers. You should strive to create visually appealing advertisements that stand apart from their surroundings. If your ads contain a significant

FRANCHISE OPPORTUNITIES

Sound Future Compact Disc Centers: Sound Future, Inc., 4411 Lemmon Ave., #101, Dallas, TX 75006-2162; phone: (214) 620-9969. Contact Walter Hawley, vice-president. Founded 1986; franchising since 1989; three company-owned units; two franchised units; features broad selection, knowledgeable employees, listening rooms. Start-up cost $19,500 to $475,000. No financing.

Compact Disc Warehouse, Inc.: 15601 Producer Lane, Bldg. A, Huntington Beach, CA 92649; phone: (714) 892-5433. Contact William E. Cline, general manager. Founded 1986; two franchises in California; maximum 2,000 square feet; features CDs, video discs, and related accessories. Provided by franchiser: one to two weeks of training at company headquarters and on-site; ongoing management assistance; advertising assistance as needed; inventory control help. Franchise fee $10,000; minimum start-up cost $140,000.

amount of small print, make sure you leave white space around your name, logo, and message.

To locate appropriate publications for your advertising, check reference materials such as the Standard Rate and Data Service (SRDS), which lists information—including data on subscribers—for various publications. You can also request media kits from the advertising representative of the publications that appeal to you. To test the success of your ads, advertise only one product per source and then compare the response rates.

There are additional ways to promote your store besides paid advertising. After your store has been open for about a month, orchestrate a grand opening that is a media event. If you let your suppliers know about the grand opening, they may offer promotional products free of charge. Distribute fliers inviting people to come for free food and drinks and hold a raffle. You could also hand out discount coupons redeemable on grand opening day or offer free pens with your company logo and name.

Send a press release and photo to your local newspaper describing your business credentials, the unique features of your store, and the store's value to the community. Keep the article interesting and informative to capture the attention of potential customers, and be sure to emphasize why your selection and service are better than that of your competition. It can also be beneficial to make yourself known and respected in the community by contributing to local charities and participating in local events.

Your goal in advertising is to try to develop a strong base of customers who will frequently visit your store. If you can provide superior service and selection, word of mouth should help boost your sales and allow you to reduce your reliance on paid advertising. For this reason, it is advisable to invest a significant amount of effort and capital—about ten percent of sales—on advertising for your grand opening. After your first year of operation, you should generally allocate a few percentage points of sales toward your advertising budget.

Some effective media sources include local papers, the Yellow Pages, radio, cable television, and direct mail. You might also want to prepare brochures and leave them at the check-out counter and send them to select customers. Handbills are a cheap and useful method of advertising, particularly for special occasions; you can prepare several thousand fliers for less than $100. You can utilize direct mail by getting lists of names from agencies (located in the Yellow Pages under ''Advertising—Direct Mail'') for about $40 per thousand names, although usually a minimum of 5,000 names is required. You might also consider offering quantity discounts for your customers to encourage larger purchases. If you offer special-order services for customers, this might help win their loyalty. Another promotional tack is to sell or give away T-shirts or shopping bags with your business logo on them.

INDUSTRY STATISTICS

- *Retail Sales of Recorded Music in U.S.* (1991): $7.8 billion (source: RIAA Consumer Profile).
- *Retail Sales of Recorded Music in the U.S., Japan, and Europe: 1988*—CDs: $5.9 billion, analog cassettes: $6.5 billion; vinyl LPs: $2.5 billion; *1991*—CDs: $13.3 billion; analog cassettes: $5.8 billion; vinyl LPs: $905 million (source: Electronic Business, from BIS Strategic Decisions).
- *Fourth Quarter Sales by Music Formats* (1993): average 62% of sales from compact discs, 12.2% higher than 1992; cassettes accounted for 30% (source: Macey Lipman Marketing, from *Billboard*).
- *Retailers Using Interactive Customer-Assistance Devices* (1994): 43%, offering such devices as listening posts (source: *Billboard*).
- *Types of Music Purchased Based on Dollar Volume* (1992): rock: 33%; urban contemporary: 17%; country: 17%; pop: 11%; classical: 4%; jazz: 4%; gospel: 3.5% (source: RIAA study).
- *Sales and Shares of Recorded Music by Format* (1991): cassettes: 360.1 million units, 45.3% share; CDs: 333.3 million units, 41.9% share; vinyl singles: 22 million units, 2.8% share (source: *Wall Street Journal,* from International Federation of the Phonographic Industry).
- *U.S. Sales of CD Players:* 1992: $1.9 billion; 1993: $2.2 billion, 10.5% of $21 billion electronics entertainment market (source: *Market Share Reporter,* from BIS Strategic Decisions).
- *U.S. Sales of Cassette Decks:* 1992: cassette decks: $850 million; 1993: $832 million, 4% share (source: *Market Share Reporter,* from BIS Strategic Decisions).

INVENTORY AND PRICING

A reasonable investment for initial inventory is $40,000 to $50,000, which will include multiple copies of two or three thousand titles. Since this is your greatest investment, be very discriminating in your selection. Concentrate on offering a wide selection of music categories that are proven sellers. The most popular categories of music are rock and pop; they account for about 60 percent of music sales. Rather than trying to compete with the larger stores, stock a good selection from the Top 40 releases for the teenage market. Rock appeals primarily to the 10 to 25-year-old middle-class market, while pop generally has its audience with slightly older students and professionals. Urban contemporary is quite popular with a variety of teens and young adults. Although country music is most popular in the South, it has gained popularity throughout the United States. Older customers often favor classical music or jazz and will probably want to replace their old records with higher-quality CDs. It is best to start out with small amounts from each category and expand in response to your customer demand. Make it clear to your customers that you can special order certain items.

It is important to manage your inventory carefully since it will determine sales. Remember that you pay overhead costs for unsold stock. If your inventory is turning over too slowly, you should select more popular releases. If your inventory is turning over too quickly, order larger volumes at a time. Check with an accountant for advice on your inventory control system. (You can purchase or lease a cash register which can keep track of inventory using specially coded labels on the CDs.)

To locate suppliers, scan trade journals, buyers' directories, and trade associations. You could save money buying your products directly through manufacturers, although it may be difficult to find a contact and you may have to purchase large quantities. Most likely you will purchase from distributors who buy from a variety of manufacturers. They generally offer a large selection of CDs and require small minimum quantities. Once you have developed a good relationship with your suppliers, you can negotiate for smaller orders when necessary. To encourage prompt deliveries, you should set a cut-off date after which you will not accept goods.

Try to get credit from the suppliers to defer payments for one to three months, but do not be discouraged if you initially have problems getting credit. You will probably have to pay by cash on delivery (COD) for a few months before you are extended credit. If you are prompt with payments, you should not have trouble developing a strong credit line. If possible, take advantage of discounts for early payments. Consider your supplier's freight costs when ordering; as this can amount to ten percent of the cost of the goods, you might be better off making less frequent, but larger, orders. Keep in mind that during the Christmas season you will have to double or triple your stock.

Price your goods according to wholesale costs, operating costs, freight expenses, and your profit. Wholesale costs generally run about 70 percent of the list price. If you purchase from distributors, your wholesale costs will range between $6 to $18 per CD and average about $10 to $12. Find the best prices and look for discounts on large orders. Compare your prices with other stores and try to be competitive. Also take into account that you may have to absorb some fluctuating costs, like insurance rates. To determine your net profits before taxes, estimate monthly sales per square foot and subtract fixed and variable costs.

RISK MANAGEMENT

Insurance is available for almost any risk. Figure out what types of insurance are required by law in your area and if there are others you feel are necessary. You must comply with safety standards according to the Occupational Safety and Health Act (OSHA) of 1970. For instance, emergency exits should be clearly marked and a fire extinguisher should be easily accessible. You will need to install a burglar alarm—an expense ranging from $500 to $2,000. For higher crime areas you may need a closed-circuit television which can cost several thousand dollars. You should be aware that thievery occurs frequently with the employees of a business; discourage it by offering your staff discounts on store items.

Post your policies on returns and used CDs on a sign

near the register. For defective products offer store credit or refunds—you will get credit from the manufacturer and keep your customers happy. Keep abreast of trends in recording technology and offer new items as soon as is feasible.

STAFFING

Your first staffing concern is deciding if you will manage your store. If you decide to hire a manager, look for such qualities as knowledge of the music industry, experience in buying and managing inventory, and courtesy with customers. Advertise for positions with placement agencies and with local and college newspapers. You should offer managers a competitive salary and five to ten percent of sales to encourage productivity. Your profit, of course, will be greater if you act as manager and hire an assistant manager. Initially, a two-person staff should suffice, but depending on sales volume you may need to hire part-time, weekend workers. Eventually you may need more full-time workers.

To encourage applications, pay above minimum wage and make sure you reward excellent work with bonuses or promotions. Provide free T-shirts with the store name and logo as a uniform for your workers. To reduce employee turnover, create a comfortable environment in which to work. Be courteous to your staff and set a good example of the way to treat customers. Encourage your staff to offer suggestions on improving your service and music selection.

Keep in mind that your staff will cost you about 15 to 30 percent more than their salaries, depending on the extent of benefits you provide and the amounts of required employment taxes. Determine the regulations concerning your employees and keep accurate and complete records of all aspects of your business for several years according to the statute of limitations. You may want to hire a part-time bookkeeper to do the payroll and expenses.

LEGAL ISSUES

Determine which legal form you would like for your business. For instance, you could be a sole proprietor, in which case your personal credit is merged with your business. However, if your business fails, you risk losing your personal property. Another option is a partnership, whereby each party is equally responsible for one another's financial activities. A limited partnership might be safer, since each partner is only liable for their share of the business. It would probably be best to form a corporation, so that your business functions separately from your personal finances. The process of incorporation is not very difficult, and you can avoid expensive lawyers fees by filling out the forms yourself. Reduce double taxation by giving yourself a large enough salary to eliminate business profits. Finally, you will probably need to acquire a sellers or tax permit from your State Sales Tax Commission, which will allow you to delay tax payments until after you sell your goods.

SOURCES:

Christman, Ed, "Cracking the Record Club Connection to Used CDs," *Billboard,* May 29, 1993, p. 66.

Compact Disc-Only Store, Entrepreneur Inc., American Entrepreneurs Association, 1987.

Schwartz, Carol A., editor, *Small Business Sourcebook: The Entrepreneur's Resource,* sixth edition, volume 1, Gale, 1993.

—*Audra Avizienis*

Computer Consulting Service

Are you a person who is not easily frustrated by a computer? Do you like to customize a new software package after it has been installed? Do you always find yourself coming to the rescue of friends and associates who can't seem to get their computers to work just right? Would you like to be your own boss?

If you have an aptitude for troubleshooting and solving problems with computers, you could be in business as an independent computer consultant providing high-tech solutions for businesses and individuals. Even though it seems like computers have invaded every aspect of life in the United States, there are still many people who are daunted by their desktop machines. For some people, just getting their computers to run after turning them on is a challenge. In addition, the computer industry is changing rapidly, and many people are unable to keep abreast of its many innovations. More computer consultants are needed to help guide the nation into the twenty-first century, when an "information superhighway" is expected to link every person in the world electronically.

Businesses choose to work with computer consultants because such experts can save them time and money by solving problems and providing information. Independent computer consultants are especially attractive because they are not selling a particular computer software package or hardware brand, nor are they normally on retainer for another business.

As an independent consultant, you can choose to offer your services on a temporary basis. In the economic climate of the early 1990s, the need for temporary workers was not likely to dissipate soon. According to Alan Radding in *Computerworld* magazine, corporate restructuring was likely to create more of a demand for consultants. But Radding warned that "the road to success as an independent consultant is strewn with pitfalls." Before going out on your own, determine whether you can handle not having a steady income.

Exact figures that describe the success rate for computer consultants are unavailable. However, the Independent Computer Consultants Association (ICCA) reported a 25 percent turnover rate in its membership due to people leaving the computer consulting business. Often, a beginning computer consultant succeeds in snagging a first assignment, but once it's completed, there is no hope of continuing business with a particular client. Radding quoted Gene Sutton, president of the Greater Boston Chapter of the ICCA, as saying, "As few as 25 percent of new consultants make it past start-up and sustain an ongoing operation." Success in computer consulting takes time, the ICCA explains. Some consultants even rely on brokers to link them to assignments as a way of maintaining cash flow.

FINANCIAL ASPECTS

Part-time or full-time computer consulting, like other consulting businesses, is very lucrative in the long run. You can work alone or in partnership in an office or out of your own home, although you will probably spend most of your time at your client's site. Consultants can earn about $42,000 before taxes and are able to start with an investment as low as $9,000. Depending on what a particular market will yield, consultants charge as much as $250 to $500 or more per day for their services. Their fees range from $10 an hour for data processing to $200 or more per hour for high-tech troubleshooting.

Your start up costs—which will average about $18,000—will be spent on computer equipment, telecommunications (possibly a car phone, beeper, voice mail, your own toll-free number, computer bulletin board, fax machine, and copier), office space, marketing and advertising, trade publications, insurance, and broker's fees. A larger capital investment will be needed if you elect to work off-site—that is, you accept jobs that are performed at your work site and not the client's. Off-site contractors, according to John Zarrella in *High-Tech Consulting,* earn more for their services than on-site consultants. If you use a broker, consider that their fees range from 10 to 30 percent. Section 1706 of the federal income tax code also limits the extent to which independent contractors can rely on brokered assignments.

PROFIT POTENTIAL

Though some consultants earn as much as $70,000 or more before taxes, the average income before taxes is around $42,000. According to some sources, a typical consultant bills an average of 14 days a month, bringing in anywhere from $600 to $900 a day. One successful computer consult-

PRIMARY ASSOCIATIONS AND SELECTED TRADE PUBLICATIONS

Associations:

Independent Computer Consultants Association: 933 Gardenview Office Parkway, St. Louis, MO 63141; phone: (314) 997-4633; fax: (314) 567-5133; CompuServe ID#: 70007, 1407.

Association of Electronic Cottagers: P.O. Box 1738, Davis, CA 95617.

Association of Managers and Consultants: 3950 N. Lakeshore Dr., Chicago, IL 60611; phone: (312) 525-7312.

Data Processing Management Association: 505 Busse Highway, Park Ridge, IL 60068; phone: (708) 825-8124.

Institute of Management Consultants: 19 W. 44th St., Suite 810-811; Consultants National Resources Center, 5000 Kaetzel Road, Gapland, MD 21736.

Publications:

Consultants News: James Kennedy, Templeton Road, Fitzwilliam, NH 03447.
PCWeek: One Park Avenue, New York, NY 10016.
PC Magazine: P.O. Box 54093, Boulder, CO 80322.
Home Office Computing: Scholastic Inc., 730 Broadway, New York, NY 10003; phone: (800) 288-7812.

ing group, Micro-Trek of New York City, supervises more than 40 employees and was grossing more than $3 million in the early 1990s. Micro-Trek began when its two partners plunked down $9,000 and developed their business to include computer programming, networking, accounting, financial systems, and computer consulting.

LIABILITIES

Sustaining cash flow, performing work without a contract, and improper billing can be major liabilities to becoming a computer consultant. Also, expect to put in long hours as an independent consultant. That means working on weekends or being on call for emergencies and traveling to your work sites. Remember, you have no paid vacation or sick leave, so you will need to work within the time frame you have negotiated. Much of your time outside of the actual consulting will be spent handling your own marketing, advertising, and budgeting.

It may be hard to estimate how much a job will cost until it is completed. You may want to charge for a preliminary consultation and then provide a written estimate for the entire project. You may also need to establish a pricing structure that encompasses whether you design software or whether you reconfigure hardware and networks then train people to use the entire computer package. Don't forget to price "rush" projects, as this type of assignment can generate more income. Other higher paying consulting jobs include saving failed projects within the an allotted frame.

According to Zarrella, consulting projects can be broken down based on the difficulty and risk involved. Risk and rewards are directly proportional; the higher the risk, the greater the reward. Whatever you do, use a standard contract that outlines your responsibilities from start to finish.

LOCATION

How do you determine how much office space you'll need? One formula suggests that 100 to 300 square feet are needed for a one-person business. But if you need room for additional staff, multiple computer systems, photocopiers, fax machines, an answering machine, telecommunications, tape back-up equipment, and storage for computer books, software, and materials, expect to double or triple the square footage. You may need to rent office space, but this can be expensive. Investigate your community's small business initiatives or "incubators" that enable you to share office space and equipment with other small businesses.

Working at home was becoming an increasingly popular alternative in the 1990s, but some find it hard to avoid distractions at home. Inventive home offices can be carved out of attics, closets, and bedrooms. *Home Office Computing* magazine profiles successful home businesses using computer technology and can provide you with ideas.

MARKETING STRATEGIES

Always determine who your target markets will be before you launch your computer consulting business. The first step is to develop an overall business plan that defines your markets. You need to decide if you will be serving individuals or businesses; if you wish to take on long-term or short-term assignments; if you will serve mainframe or personal computer users; and if you want to work within the private or public sector. People seek computer consultants with plenty of experience. Customers will check your references to determine your skills in certain areas.

Defining your market is crucial at the initial stages of setting up your computer consulting service. Paul H. Saluk, for example, was a professor of immunology and infectious diseases at Hahnemann Medical Center and Hospital in Philadelphia and at New York University Medical School. He and a partner decided to go into business for themselves in 1983 at the dawning of the information age. They formed MCS Systems, a computer consulting service that provides automated management systems for business. Specifically, Saluk's service focuses on UNIX-based multi-user, multitasking computer systems, and a programming language the partners developed to customize software packages much quicker than with COBOL or BASIC. By 1987 the company was predicting $2 million in revenues. Saluk noted the benefits of specializing: ''The main reason behind our success is not biting off more than we can chew,'' he told the

South Florida Business Journal. ''We want to be in control.''

Another entrepreneur, Joyce Creiger, became a high-tech art consultant after discovering an electronic method for organizing art slides. She initially used a computer consultant to store slides on computer videodiscs but then developed a system that allowed art brokers and others to view art on videodiscs from host locations across the country. Each disk stores approximately 110,000 color images. Anyone using the Omnivex system can search the catalog for a specific color, genre, artist, or type of work. In seconds the computer provides a summary of artwork fitting the description, and users can call up the images or scroll them at their leisure.

Creiger told *Working Woman* magazine that she had learned from several previous art company ventures what not to do in business. By the time she formed her Omnivex company, she had done extensive research. She worked with a lawyer to develop her business plan and hired a stock broker. By the late 1980s art galleries were advertising their slides on her Omnivex system. Creiger used an interest in art, her business skills, and computer technology to provide a unique service. Future ventures call for expanding her system's applications, perhaps to antiques.

The need for computer consultants to provide innovative solutions is endless. Advertising agencies, for instance, seek ways to make technology pay off for them and need consultants to create tailor-made media buying programs. But perhaps the hottest market in the 1990s—when more businesses were shifting their operations out of the office to individual employee homes—was the emergence of the telecommuter. Since managers and employees are often not computer experts, merely establishing a modem link from an employee's home to the company's mainframe can be quite frustrating. Businesses may need troubleshooters who can guide them in making such electronic connections.

While you hone your business acumen and target your skills to the right markets, investigate other methods of becoming a presence in your community such as joining your local chamber of commerce. In *Small Businesses That Grow and Grow and Grow,* Patricia A. Woy cited one

computer consultant who went one step further and designed software to help his chamber of commerce organize its membership files. Woy also recommends that computer consultants consider working with their city government for a minimal fee as a way of networking.

Monitor activity in the computer market by keeping up-to-date with such trade publications as *PC Week, PC Magazine,* and *Computerworld* as well as those specific to your computer specialty. In addition, three associations can benefit budding consultants by providing valuable information: Independent Computer Consultants Association, Association of Electronic Cottagers, and Data Processing Management Association.

Whatever market you choose to target, strive to make a good impression on everyone you meet and be prepared to offer a business card and brochure listing when you are accessible. A hot line or answering service is an effective method of putting you in touch with clients in trouble, keeping you in demand and in business.

ADVERTISING

By far the biggest expense you will face as a consultant will be advertising and promotion. Design your advertising strategy according to your client base; that is, the fewer clients, the more money you'll spend on advertising and vice versa. In addition to eye-catching business cards, allow your ad budget to include such media as the Yellow Pages, trade journals, and possibly even brochures and other sales promotional materials.

Referrals by either word of mouth or via recommendations from computer brokers or computer consulting organizations will be a key part of your business. Your advertising budget should include ads in trade journals and other publications. Depending on your target market, you may want to leave your business cards in areas frequented by people who may need your services.

One effective means of advertising is direct mail, a technique to use after you have targeted your markets. Send a cover letter, along with a business card and brochure, to selected prospects. Develop your mailing list from trade magazines or your local chamber of commerce. In *High-Tech Consulting,* Zarrella advises never ''under any circumstances'' send your letter to the personnel department of a company. Always call and ask for the name of the engineering manager, head of information services, or other higher level positions so that you can be sure you are contacting the people who need your services.

Press releases, another effectual advertising strategy, are an economical way of getting your name in the newspapers and mentioned in magazines and will cost you as much as a postage stamp. Your press release should be limited to one page if possible and should state who you are, what services you provide, and a phone number. Target as many newspapers, magazines, and journals in your market area as you can. As an expert in your field, you can also offer to

CERTIFICATION PROGRAMS FOR COMPUTER CONSULTANTS

Examinations are available for certification in the following areas:

• Certified Computer Programmer
• Certified Data Processor
• Certified Systems Professional
• Associate Computer Professional

For more information, contact the Institute for Certification of Computer Professionals, 2200 E. Devon Ave., Suite 268, Des Plaines, IL 60018-4503; phone: (708) 299-4227; fax (708) 299-4280; CompuServe ID#: 74040, 3722.

TIPS ON PRESENTING YOURSELF AS A QUALIFIED COMPUTER CONSULTANT

- Don't attempt to snow your potential clients with technical jargon.
- Listen to your clients' needs and objectives before offering solutions.
- Have solid and trustworthy references.
- Mention vendor relationships up front; you may have access to technical support needed to complete projects.
- Be objective in your recommendations for clients.
- Have a backup person who can complete your work if something happens to you and inform your client of your intended backup person up front.
- Provide regular status reports on your work to ensure credibility.
- Be ready to explain your fees and how you have determined them.
- Inform your clients of your professional affiliations.
- Specify early on how long a project will take and your cost estimate.
- Notify your client of possible delays.

(SOURCE: *INDEPENDENT COMPUTER CONSULTANT*'S "10 TIPS FOR HIRING A COMPUTER CONSULTANT," MAY 12, 1993.)

write a column in a local newspaper. Readers will know you are a consultant, and they will perceive that you are knowledgeable about your subject area.

LICENSES AND LEGALITIES

As an independent contractor in your community, you may need a business license to operate out of your home or rented work space. Investigate what licenses you will need to work in your town and state. You may also want to seek legal advice to help you establish your small business; an attorney can guide you in formulating work contracts with customers that outline your consulting responsibilities. Contracts are legal documents and should specify what and when you intend to deliver, when you will be paid, what will happen if you are not paid, and the amount of time it will take to complete a project.

INSURANCE

Your computer consulting business represents a significant investment. To protect it from failure, you will need insurance to offset losses in case of accidents involving your staff in the work space or destruction to your equipment and inventory. Keep in mind that you will be paying for your own health, life, and auto insurance. Consider plans that cover you in case a disaster interrupts your business; business interruption insurance will cover you against income lost during this time. Zarrella recommends that you purchase product and professional liability coverage as you may be responsible for injuries to customers resulting from use of your products or services. For example, if you design accounting software that incorrectly tracks expenses, you may actually be sued for damages.

You are not in the clear, however, just because you are making money on a regular basis and are adequately insured. To get the most out of your small business, consider investing your earnings to cover anticipated shortfalls and capital expenditures. Check with your bank to determine savings vehicles that can maximize your earnings so that you will stay in business.

LEGISLATION

In the early 1990s self-employed workers were increasingly coming under scrutiny by the Internal Revenue Service (IRS), which was attempting to reduce abuses to the tax system. According to the ICCA, "the IRS says that 3.4 million Americans working as independent contractors should be reclassified as employees," resulting in more than $500 million in penalties and back taxes. The IRS uses specific criteria to define employees and independent contractors based on the nature of the working relationship, services provided, and who controls the work. See an income tax accountant or consultant to determine if your computer consulting business will be penalized by existing federal and state taxing laws.

COMPUTER SYSTEM AND PROGRAMS

The type of computer and software you choose will depend on your clients' needs. You should at least be familiar with their equipment and software. The essentials for any computer consultant are at least two functioning personal computers with adequate memory and hard drives; laser-quality printers; tape back-up and storage—which should be located away from your office for security reasons—modems, including fax/modems; graphics; color monitors; and a back up supply of peripherals. Software programs run the gamut: an overall telecommunications package, word processing, spreadsheet, and possibly multimedia programs help make an independent business person's office complete.

All in all, in the electronically sophisticated modern world, an aspiring computer consultant has the opportunity for a lucrative career. With the appropriate mix of expertise and specific software and programs, an effective marketing strategy, and the means of obtaining financing, you can start and maintain a profitable service.

SOURCES:

Churbuck, David, "Consultant in a Bind," *Forbes,* November 13, 1989, p. 285.

"Choosing a Computer Consultant: Look for Custom Services," *Business Journal of New Jersey Annual,* 1990, p. 38.

Davidson, Gary, "Upgrading the Accounting System," *Small Business Reports,* January 1989, p. 70.

Entrepreneur Magazine's 168 More Businesses Anyone Can Start and Make a Lot of Money, second edition, Bantam, 1991, p. 143.

Harvey, Suzette L., "Transition Comes Easily for Computer Consultant," *South Florida Business Journal,* May 11, 1987.

''How to Choose a Computer Consultant,'' *Black Enterprise,* June 1988, p. 288.

Kirkpatrick, David, ''Why Not Farm out Your Computing?'' *Fortune,* September 23, 1991, p. 103.

Mortz, John R., *Make Money Moonlighting—The 4 Best Ways to Earn Money with Your Computer and the 4 Traps to Avoid,* American Institute of Computer Technology, 1989.

Oshins, Alice H., ''A Brand-New Way to Organize Fine Art,'' *Working Woman,* May 1987, p. 66.

''Proving Ground for Entrepreneurs,'' *In Business,* March/April 1990, p. 32.

''Putting Computers Together Again,'' *The Economist,* August 25, 1990, p. 55.

Radding, Alan, ''Consultants Walk a Rough Road,'' *Computer World,* January 23, 1989.

Simon, Alan R., *How to Be a Successful Computer Consultant,* McGraw-Hill, 1990.

Skigen, LoriBeth, ''Cashing in Their Chips,'' *Advertising Age,* February 25, 1991, p. 28.

U.S. Industrial Outlook 1992, U.S. Department of Commerce, 1992.

Woy, Patricia A., *Small Businesses That Grow and Grow and Grow,* Betterway Publications, 1989.

Wuest, Stephen G., ''Add a Computer Consultant Without Increasing Your Staff—the VAR,'' *Management Consulting Services,* autumn 1989, p. 37.

Zarrella, John, *High-Tech Consulting,* Microcomputer Applications, 1983.

—*Evelyn S. Dorman*

Dance School

Aerobics, jogging, and walking are all great forms of exercise. Isn't there a more rewarding path to fitness, though—one that also enhances your social life and teaches you some practical skills? Dancing is the perfect answer and may provide a great opportunity for you to capitalize on the American exercise boom.

Although the total number of people signing up for dance school classes declined in the late 1980s and early 1990s, several niche markets offered solid profit potential in the mid-1990s. More young people were becoming interested in ballroom dancing, for example, and some studios were finding a demand for country dance instruction. So if you love to dance and have a knack for sales, opening a dance studio could be your ticket to a fulfilling entrepreneurial career.

PROFITS AND COSTS

A typical dance school with an established core of clients will produce about $35,000 in profits annually. Larger schools can bring in $70,000 or more. With a savvy marketing campaign and low overhead, it is possible to generate a profit in your first year, but it may take two or three years to establish a fruitful customer base.

You will need at least $10,000 to cover your start-up costs and operating expenses for one year. One dance studio owner believes that "to do it right" you should plan to spend between $50,000 and $80,000. Keep in mind, though, your costs and profits will vary tremendously based on your location and type of school.

To open and operate a standard-sized, fully-equipped studio, plan on spending about $20,000 up front and approximately $3,500 per month on overhead. The up-front costs would cover the security deposit on your rental space; your first month's rent of $1,500; a $2000 sign; $1,500 worth of furniture; a computer and office supplies; about $5,000 for advertising expenses; and other miscellaneous costs. It also includes $8,000 for mirrors, railing, music, and other studio items.

The beauty of starting a dance school is that you can begin on a relatively small budget. All you really need is a large floor space, a simple sound system, and some office supplies. As your clientele grows, you can either move to a new space or gradually add the traditional accoutrements, including mirrors and wooden floors. One successful school started with only $3,000 and was able to operate entirely from cash-flow.

An attractive alternative to opening a dance studio is to offer dance classes at such satellite locations as community centers, YMCAs, health clubs, and corporate centers. This strategy reduces your start-up costs, allows more flexibility than a rental commitment, and broadens your potential customer base to surrounding communities. It also offers profit possibilities roughly equivalent to operating a studio.

FINANCING

Many banks will be reluctant to fund the start-up of a fully-equipped dance studio unless the proprietor has extensive experience operating similar facilities. If you don't have a lot of relevant experience in the industry, you will probably be required to put up enough collateral to cover the loan if the school fails. Getting a loan for a more spartan studio may not be an alternative because most banks find it unprofitable to make loans of less than $50,000 to new customers due to paperwork required by the government.

The **Small Business Administration (SBA)** may be able to help you secure a small loan if you have a good business plan and you do your homework. They will even help you with the business plan if necessary. Call the SBA at **1-800-U ASK SBA,** or write to: **Small Business Directory, P.O. Box 1000, Ft. Worth, TX 76119.** Another option is to find a partner that can help fund your venture—about six percent of all U.S. dance studio owners choose this route.

One way to help finance your studio once it is up-and-running is to rent your space to other business owners. Martial arts or aerobics instructors, for example, might prefer to rent your floor space for a few hours each week to teach classes rather than operating their own facility. You can charge them a set rental fee, though a common arrangement is to contract for a percentage of their gross income.

LOCATION

When selecting a community for your dance studio, a safe rule-of-thumb to follow is to consider one percent of the local population as your potential market. Of course this

PRIMARY ASSOCIATIONS AND SELECTED TRADE PUBLICATIONS

Associations:

American Dance Guild: 31 W. 21st St., 3rd Floor, New York, NY 10010-6807; phone: (212) 627-3790.

Dance Educators of America: 85 Rockway Ave., Rockville Centre, NY 11570; phone: (516) 536-6502.

International Tap Association: 3220 Connecticut Ave. NW, 112 Washington, DC 20008; phone: (202) 363-3960.

National Association of Schools of Dance: 11250 Roger Bacon Dr., Ste. 21, Reston, VA 22090; phone: (703) 437-0700.

National Dance Association: 1900 Association Dr., Reston, VA 22091; phone: (703) 476-3400.

Professional Dance Teachers Association: P.O. Box 91, Waldwick, NJ 07463; phone: (201) 769-2069.

United States Ballroom Branch of the Imperial Society of Teachers of Dancing: 68 Centennial R., Warminster, PA 18974; phone: (201) 491-9696.

United States National Institute of Dance: 38 S. Arlington Ave., P.O. Box 245, East Orange, NJ 08019; phone: (201) 673-9225.

Publications:

American Dance: American Dance Guild, 31 W. 21st St., 3rd Floor, New York, NY 10010-6807; phone: (212) 627-3790.
Dance Magazine: 33 W. 60th St., New York, NY 10023-6487; phone: (212) 245-9050.
Dance Teachers Now: SMW Communications Inc., 3020 Beacon Blvd., West Sacramento, CA 95691-3436.
Journal of Physical Education, Recreation and Dance: National Dance Association, 1900 Association Dr., Reston, VA 22091; phone: (703) 476-3400.
Spotlight on Dance: National Dance Association.

percentage would be split with your competitors, including aerobics and fitness centers. In general, an area with 25,000 people can support one studio. Areas with growing populations of upper- and middle-income professionals will offer the best opportunities. Contact your chamber of commerce for demographic information, and ask your local librarian for the Standard Metropolitan Statistical Area (SMSA) data for your region.

The location of a dance studio is less important than the quality of instruction and the size of the dance floor. Many students will opt for a distant studio with a good dance program rather than sacrifice quality for convenience. Although you will want to choose a location that is visible and accessible, you can save money by avoiding prime real estate that is better suited for high-traffic retail establish-

ments. However, keep in mind that most of your clients are likely to be women and children, so don't choose to situate your studio near a bar or in a neighborhood with a rough reputation that will discourage newcomers.

If you decide to start a dance school that holds classes at satellite centers rather than a rented studio, look first for free space. Indeed, many community organizations, for example the Jaycees and Elks Club, will let you use their facility for free, or at least for a nominal charge. Your classes will make a lot of noise, so be sure that you are able to reserve a long-term, regular class time that will not conflict with other activities in the complex.

LAYOUT AND SETUP

You will need at least 500 square feet of space for every ten students that are in your studio at once, plus space for bathrooms and an office. In addition, most studios are arranged so that two or more classes can proceed simultaneously, so you should try to find a space that can be divided as your business grows. In order to get a better idea of the amount of space you will need, find out how many students are enrolled in the classes of your nearest established competitor. Expect to attract one-fifth to one-half as many students in the first year or two after opening.

The layout and furnishings of your school will depend largely on the type of dance classes that will be taught. You can get by with a linoleum floor—the best are hardwood—and bare walls for ballroom or swing dance instruction, but ballet classes will require such equipment as mirrors and barres. The ideal studio has a large, furnished entry space where customers can congregate and socialize before and after their lessons. The dance floor should be visible from this space so that potential customers can observe your classes. If you have room, include an elevated platform in the corner where an instructor can view the entire floor and the sound system can be stored and operated. Try to leave enough space for a food and punch table at the back of the floor so that you can host non-instructional dances. Ideally, the front of your studio will be plate glass so that activity will pique the interest of outsiders.

You may seek additional income by selling ballet dancewear, dance books, and other retail items. These goods should be displayed neatly in your entry room where students congregate. A typical inventory investment is about $1,000, but most suppliers can arrange for you to make a deposit of only 50 percent of the wholesale inventory value in return for a percentage of your sales.

STAFFING

Your staff will define your dance studio and can make or break your venture. They will constantly interact with your patrons, both physically and verbally. If they are not enthusiastic, polite, clean and neat, attractive, and competent, you will lose customers. Hire instructors you know and like, or go to local dance classes and scout for recruits. If you are unsure of your ability to find sharp instructors, don't start a dance school.

Expect to pay your instructors between $20 and $50 per hour based on experience, the type and quality of dance your studio offers, and your local cost of living. Assuming you have enough dance experience to teach classes, you will likely provide most or all of the instruction initially, and you'll also be keeping up with advertising, paperwork, and maintenance. Plan on putting in 14-hour days, five or six days each week until you begin generating enough income to hire a few instructors and, possibly, an assistant manager.

A sensible and common alternative to hiring instructors at an hourly rate is to rent your facility to independent teachers. One dance school owner, for example, charges her three instructors a $15 to $25 per hour "floor fee" to teach in her studio. She splits the profits with the teachers based on the number of students that show up for their classes. This type of arrangement provides a greater incentive for instructors to cultivate repeat business, and it reduces the owner's management and payroll responsibilities.

MANAGEMENT ISSUES

If you plan to offer children's classes, make sure that you and your staff are trained to work with young people and their parents. While most adult students attend your classes by choice, the same is not always true for children. In addition to kids who don't want to be there, you will often have to deal with sick or incorrigible children. From a liability standpoint, you will have to document and strictly follow disciplinary and safety procedures. Finally, many parents will be quick to blame you when their child is not performing up to their expectations, but don't fail to consider their viewpoint—keep looking for new ways to encourage your students.

When dealing with adults, remember that your world is

INDUSTRY STATISTICS

- *Number of U.S. Dance Studios and Schools (1990):* 3,648.
- *Total Industry Sales Revenue (1990):* $334 million.
- *Percentage of Studios That Are Sole Proprietorships:* 47.
- *Percentage of Studios That Are Incorporated:* 47.
- *Percentage of Studios That Are Partnerships:* 6.
- *Minimum Population Required to Support One School:* 10,000 to 25,000.
- *Typical Annual Profits of an Established School:* $25,000 to $40,000.
- *Average Number of Employees:* Five.
- *Average Annual Sales Revenue Per Establishment:* $95,479.
- *Average Annual Payroll Per Establishment:* $27,989.
- *Average Annual Payroll Per Employee:* $5,689.
- *Largest Dance School Franchise:* Arthur Murray Dance Studios, 1077 Ponce de Leon Blvd., Coral Gables, FL 33134; phone: (305) 445-9645; start-up costs range from $12,500 to $100,000; 224 outlets in 1987.

not theirs. To many of them, dancing is just a small part of their everyday life—a recreational and social activity that they enjoy. Keep your classes professional, yet light-hearted. The more serious students can take your advanced classes or pay for individual instruction.

ADVERTISING

Your most important advertising medium will be a word-of-mouth network. In fact, some dance studio owners curtail advertising in newspapers and direct mail after they get their operation off the ground, having found that investing in customer satisfaction is the most cost-effective way to bring in new business. The best way to get your network started before you open your doors is to teach dance classes in the community—at the YMCA, youth centers, and community colleges. Even if you already have a good personal reputation established, to attract clients to a new studio you will have to implement a carefully conceived advertising strategy. Your skills and dedication won't get you very far if people don't know that your studio exists and how it can benefit them.

Go to a free-lance advertising consultant—an experienced professional that knows the local market. Ask owners of businesses similar to yours for recommendations. You should be able to find good advice for about $50 or $60 per hour. A consultant can help you draft a marketing plan and put some sharp advertising materials together. After that, you can run the advertising campaign yourself with occasional outside advice.

Advertisements in local and metropolitan newspapers will not bring great returns for your ad dollars, but they are necessary to announce the opening of a new school. Metropolitan magazines are a better bet for advertising an established studio, particularly if you want to reach an older audience. If you want to target the under-30 crowd, stick with billboards, direct mail, and radio. Your best advertising dollars will be spent on a Yellow Pages ad—reserve your listing before your studio opens. Stay away from pens, calendars, and other gimmicks that look neat, but fail to bring in new clients.

MARKETING

The success of any dance school or studio depends largely on the owner's ability to bring prospective students into the school and convince them to pay for classes. Many studios charge customers on a per-month basis and require an additional enrollment fee of $20 to $40. The student typically agrees in a written contract to pay the studio $20 to $25 per month for three, six, or twelve months. In return, he or she may attend the equivalent of, perhaps, three one-hour sessions each week. The primary advantages of such a system are that it motivates students to stay involved and generates dependable cash-flow for the studio operator.

Some dance school owners believe that membership contracts often scare away potential customers. Instead, they

RECOMMENDED READING

- *College Blue Book: Occupational Education,* Macmillan Publishing Co., 866 3rd Ave., New York, NY; phone: (212) 481-2659. Biennial directory of educational programs that include all forms of dance.
- *Dance Injuries, Their Prevention and Care,* by Daniel D. Arnheim; Princeton Book Co., P.O. Box 57, Pennington, NJ 08534; phone: (800) 220-7149.
- *The Dance Studio: Business Managing for Aerobics, Dance, and Gymnastics Teachers,* by Marie Zima; Mc-Farland & Co., Inc., Hwy. 88 box 611, Jefferson, NC 28640; phone: (919) 246-4460.
- *Motivation in Education,* by Samuel Ball; Academic Press, 1250 6th Ave., San Diego, CA 92101; phone: (800) 321-5068.
- *National Guild of Community Schools of the Arts— Membership Directory,* 40 N. Van Brunt St., Rm. 32, P.O. Box 8018, Englewood, NJ 07631; phone: (201) 871-3337.
- *Opportunities in Fitness Careers,* by Jean Rosenbaum and Mary Miller; VGM Career Horizons, 4255 W. Touhy Ave., Lincolnwood, IL 60646-1975.
- *The Super Studio: The Guide to a Successful Dance Studio,* by Debbie Roberts; Evanston Publishing, 116 Hinman Ave., Evanston, IL 60202.

charge students for each individual lesson, or sell them a group of sessions at a discount. One studio owner charges $45 per lesson for individual instruction and a fraction of that amount depending on class size. Set your own prices based on rates charged by your competitors and the type of dance you offer.

Market position also plays an important role in attracting clientele. You will need to position your service so that it provides something of value that your competitors don't offer. One shrewd dance school owner targeted her studio at children and adolescents. She offered weekly half-hour classes in tap, jazz, clogging, and ballet for $20 per month. Before opening day she enrolled more than 100 students, and two years later she had 200 students and four instructors.

Regardless of your fee structure, you must maintain an ongoing marketing program to replace students that quit. Don't relax your marketing efforts during the winter months when attendance is high, only to be surprised by a drop-off in revenues when spring arrives. You can provide students with the incentive to return by offering new classes and such services as hiring specialty instructors to teach completely different dance forms. Country dance classes, for example, were becoming popular in the mid-1990s, as were classes that combined aerobics and dance. Offering children's classes is also a great way to increase business and keep your studio busy when many adults are at work.

Help your students set goals that give their dancing a higher purpose. Provide financial incentives—such as free classes or reduced fees—that push them to master new dances and achieve expertise. Offer discounts or cash awards to students that convince friends to enroll. Contests, parties, and socials that are open to the public will bring new clients through the door and make existing customers feel appreciated.

OTHER INCOME

You can boost your dance studio's income by integrating add-on profit centers. With a $2,000 investment in video equipment, for instance, you can begin charging students to tape and assess their dancing. This service is suited primarily to artistic dance studios where dancers are looking for an effective way to identify and correct flaws in their technique. But you can also advertise the service on a free-lance basis, for recitals and other performances not affiliated with your school. In addition, parents will be willing to pay $25 or more for a high-quality tape of their child performing a dance or routine.

Recitals for ballet and tap schools can be big money makers. Because they give your students a goal, recitals tend to make your customers attend classes more regularly. Recitals will also significantly boost your retail clothing sales. In addition, a well choreographed show provides an excellent advertising medium for your studio. Finally, many school owners are able to turn a tidy profit from ticket sales. As an illustration, if you have 100 students participating in a recital you can expect to sell 200 to 300 tickets just to your students' families and friends. At $10 per ticket, you should be able to clear $1,500 to $2000 after expenses. You can even put your students to work selling the tickets.

One of the best ways to expand your client base is to offer classes away from your facility, in surrounding communities that don't have access to dance classes. After you have established one class, start sending one of your instructors to teach that group while you start a class at a different satellite location. Over time, this strategy can add a major profit center to your business.

LICENSES AND INSURANCE

There are usually no specific state or county licenses or accreditations required of dance schools or instructors. Nevertheless, check the regulations in your area. Your local SBA office can give you a business start-up kit that tells you which government offices regulate dance studios in your state.

Most serious dance instructors and studio owners belong to at least one of several associations and are certified by one or more industry organizations. Dance Masters of America, for example, requires their members to take three years of classes from member schools and pass a stringent test. Likewise, Dance Educators of America and Professional Dance Teachers of America both test and certify instructors.

Insurance costs for a ballroom, ballet, or swing dance studio are similar to those of most businesses. However, you should check with your insurance agent if you plan to integrate gymnastics or fitness activities into your program. In addition to general liability insurance, you should get incidental professional insurance. This protects you against claims by any of your instructors for bodily injury that they suffer on the job.

Although the number of dance studios and students declined in the late 1980s and early 1990s, plenty of opportunity to prosper in the industry still exists. Your chances of success depend on your ability to find a vacant market niche and build a satisfied base of clients. You may never get wealthy, but if you truly love the art of dance and are good at working with people, owning and operating a dance studio can bring rich rewards.

SOURCES:

Gray, Michelle M., ''Mother Daughter Act: Two generations carry on tradition of dance,'' *Tribune Chronicle,* August 25, 1993, business section.

Madden, Michael, editor, *Small Business Start-Up Index,* issue 1, Gale, 1991.

Martin, Susan Boyles, editor, *Worldwide Franchise Directory,* Gale, 1991.

Miller, Mary, and Jean Rosenbaum, *Opportunities in Fitness Careers,* VGM Career Horizons, 1991.

Mullins, Robert, ''A New Twist on Old Dance Steps,'' *The Business Journal—Milwaukee,* October 16, 1993, section 1, p. 1.

Occupational Outlook Handbook, 1992-1993 Edition, U.S. Department of Labor, 1992.

Schwartz, Carol A., editor, *Small Business Sourcebook,* fifth edition, volume 1, Gale, 1992.

Walters, Rebecca, ''Elite Dance Plans to Stay One Step Ahead,'' *Business First Columbus,* January 24, 1994, section 1, p. 9.

Zima, Marie, *The Dance Studio: Business Managing for Aerobics, Dance, and Gymnastics Teachers,* McFarland & Company, Inc., 1987.

—*DAVE MOTE*

Dating Service

"SWM, 35, tall, blue eyes, dark hair, handsome, bright, financially secure, likes tennis, theater, fine dining, conversation. In search of SWF, 30-40, attractive, outgoing, sensitive, loving, family-oriented, for serious relationship. Photo appreciated." If you were hoping to meet that special person, would you respond to this ad? If so, then you might meet your match.

The number of single people in this country has been growing every year; in 1992, nearly 40 percent of the entire American population—72 million people—was unmarried. This piece of the demographic pie has given rise to a host of dating services, from video dating to newspaper ads to personalized voice mail. With a minimal investment, some creative marketing, and a genuine desire to help singles "meet their match," a significant amount of money can be made in providing a dating service.

COSTS AND FINANCING

The start-up investment for a dating service could be as low as $500 if you plan to work out of your home, while a modest office in a mid-sized city might require an average investment of $12,500. A high-end investment approximates $200,000 and covers costs of setting up a lavish office in a major metropolitan area. Annual revenues for dating services are between $50,000 and $500,000, with annual pretax profits between $40,000 and $200,000, and a dating service owner can expect to break even in six months to three years.

Before you arrange financing for your dating service, consult an accountant and map out a detailed list of projected expenditures and revenues for the first three years of the business. These figures will help you estimate how much you'll need to start your operation. Entrepreneurs who are successfully running a dating service can be invaluable sources of information on start-up costs and financing, so don't overlook meeting with them and discussing your plans.

If you decide to open a small dating service and run the operation from your home, you can probably rely on your own financial resources. However, if you're planning something more elaborate, it will require more capital. Because commercial banks usually don't lend large amounts of money to new businesses, your best bet is to apply for a personal loan based on your assets and business experience. Or you can apply to the **Small Business Administration (SBA),** a federal government agency, for a loan. Check the government listings in your local phone book to see if the SBA has a branch in your area, or call **1-800-U ASK SBA.** You may also want to visit the local chamber of commerce for information on small business loan programs in your community. Although franchising is not widespread in the dating service industry, there are a few franchisors that will provide information on how to best finance and market your services.

LOCATION

The most important consideration in choosing a location for your business is whether there are enough singles living in the area to provide the clientele for a dating service. Check with the Census Bureau to find out how many single people live in your area; other sources of demographic information include local and community newspapers, and the city or town library. Remember that charging $500, you would have to get 200 people to sign up in order to gross $100,000. This money has to cover all of your expenditures, including rent, stationary, advertising, equipment, and salaries. If you hope to make more money than that, you'll need a higher membership fee or more members. Be sure to check if there are other dating services in the area and determine whether or not there is enough business for more than one such service. If so, how can you offer something different?

In selecting an office site, consider how easy it is for customers to find your business and then park nearby. It is especially important to operate your business in a safe location, because a significant part of your clientele will include women who will be meeting with you during evening hours.

LAYOUT AND SETUP

When you open a dating service, what you're selling is a reputation for bringing people together and making the right "match." Although it doesn't happen very often, there have been cases of suspicious or unsavory characters taking advantage of the participants in a dating service. Extensive application forms, two or three pieces of identification, and a personal interview should allow you to weed out those indi-

FRANCHISE OPPORTUNITIES

Great Expectations Creative Management:
17207 Venture Blvd., Encino, CA 91316; phone: (818) 788-7878; fax: (310) 477-5566. The largest of the video dating services in America, with 43 locations throughout the United States, Great Expectations is known as the McDonald's of the industry; the franchise claims more than 135,000 members nationwide through its video dating and singles introduction services. Provided by the franchisor: an initial training program, a month long follow-up program at the franchisee's place of business, an operations manual, management advice, and marketing assistance.

Other Franchisors: The Network Club: 1815 Hawthorne Ave., Ste. 248, Redondo Beach, CA 90278; phone: (310) 793-3000. **Selectra-Date Corporation:** 2175 Lemoine Ave., Fort Lee, NJ 07024; phone: (201) 461-8400. **Together:** 171 Main St., Ste. B-103, Ashland, MA 01721; phone: 1-800-635-3836. **Together Dating Service:** 790 Farmington Ave., Bldg. 3B, Farmington, CT 06032; phone: (203) 677-2534.

viduals. A one-time registration fee, paid up front, should also help to discourage those not seriously interested in finding a mate. These measures will ensure the safety of your service and minimize the possibility for bad experiences.

The amount of your registration fee will also distinguish the type of clientele you serve. For instance, if your fee is between $500 and $2,000, you will attract fairly affluent customers and, in turn, these individuals will know that their prospective matches have the financial security to afford your services. Registration fees toward the lower end tend to attract artists, therapists, police officers, musicians, and teachers, whereas higher fees attract business executives, doctors, lawyers, and independent entrepreneurs.

Many video dating service owners believed that a prestigious location in a convenient part of town was crucial to their success. Some even spent more money decorating their office than they did for video equipment. Because many people are initially apprehensive, embarrassed, or nervous about walking into the office of a dating service, a warm and friendly atmosphere helps to relax them. If you're opening a video dating service, the equipment should not be arranged so that it intimidates or frightens the customer; all equipment should be unobtrusively placed so that the studio looks more like a den, allowing clients to feel comfortable enough to reveal their personality. You can also enhance the ambiance of your office with subtle yet effective touches. Some dating services serve wine or coffee and other refreshments, while other services play music or greet clients regularly on a first-name basis.

The more willing you are to cater to your customers, the more your business will grow by word of mouth. One video dating firm in New York City goes an extra step for its clients—if a new member is too busy to schedule a session to tape an interview at the dating service office, the company arranges to tape an interview at the client's office or residence. The better you get to know your customers, with all their likes and dislikes, the more easily you can steer them toward potential matches. For people who don't have a great deal of free time to view videotapes or meet with you regularly at your office, the more personal service you are willing to provide the more likely your clients will be to trust your matchmaking suggestions.

STAFFING

Dating services are often owned by one or two individuals who also perform all the tasks associated with operating the business, including answering the phone, interviewing, and arranging the matches. In fact, many dating services are started by lone entrepreneurs who already have full-time jobs; relying on an answering machine in their home or an office, they arrange matches during their spare time in the evening or on weekends. Video dating services, however, are an exception. Taping an interview with a customer involves a certain amount of technical expertise, so it is usually best to hire one or two experienced people in order to make sure the taping is professional.

MARKETING

There are numerous formats a dating service can take to attract a clientele. There are video dating services, computer dating services, personalized voice mail, singles newspapers, singles dinner clubs, ''just lunch'' singles services, and personal matchmakers. Of course, catering to singles isn't new—a 10-cent publication featuring pictures and descriptions of women available for marriage was printed in Nebraska in 1915. However, the format you choose and the singles market you expect to capture will determine the revenues and growth of your dating service.

Before you decide upon the type of dating service you want to open, it's advisable to do some demographic research. J. Walter Thompson, a New York City advertising agency, released a market research report in 1989 on the topic of ''singles lifestages.'' The company discovered that there are four groups of singles: the single who lives at home with parents at the average age of 22; the single who is just starting out his/her career at the average age of 26; the mature, well-established single at the age of 45; and the left-alone, or older single with an average age of 70. This kind of information, along with singles' eating habits, consumer trends, cultural interests, disposable income, and travel habits, will enable you to make smart decisions in delineating a market for a dating service in your area.

The most successful dating services find a niche—especially if the area in which they are located is saturated with such services—and then cater to that specific category of singles. Gentlepeople, a dating service in New York City, was founded because the owner thought there was a need for pairing successful, highly educated, and culturally oriented singles. More than 75 percent of Gentlepeople's customers have advanced degrees, including doctors, lawyers, architects, and academics, but the focal point of the service revolves around their attraction to the arts. Even starving artists are welcome to join because of their relation to the arts. Although there are no rigid acceptance criteria, Gentlepeople is highly selective and rejects nearly half of all the people who apply.

Plump Pals is another dating service that caters to a specific category of the singles market. The owner's daughter, who weighed 350 pounds and worked at a hotel in Atlantic City, mentioned to her mother that European men were very attracted to her and, unlike Americans, were not put off by her weight. Thinking about the difficulty a heavier woman has in meeting the right man, the mother opened a specialized service that turned into an overnight success. There are no restrictions on membership in Plump Pals; interestingly enough over 95 percent of the male clients are average-sized customers searching for a heavier mate.

Generating membership is essential from the beginning. One way to do this is to offer reduced membership fees when you first open; another way is to offer a short trial membership period at a reduced rate. One innovative entrepreneur generates new clients by asking for only half of the membership fee up front and the other half when the cus-tomer actually gets married. Since many people are suspicious about or reluctant to join a dating service, this marketing technique has helped the owner create a reputation for trustworthiness and, in turn, results in new members through word of mouth.

Other marketing techniques that help generate new membership include, for example, a guarantee of at least one date per month for one year; a guarantee of either six dates the first six months, or an extension of membership for another year; a guarantee of six dates over a one year period and invitations to all the parties or special events arranged by the dating service; a get acquainted wine and cheese party at your office or home; or an arrangement with a restaurant for a gourmet night where individuals change seats after every course. With creativity, intelligent marketing, and a sincere approach to matchmaking, you can generate more than enough customers to get your dating service up and running.

ADVERTISING

Keeping a steady flow of new customers will always be important for the continuity and growth of your service. Just as a retail clothing store keeps its bins and shelves stocked with new merchandise, you must also keep adding to a large pool of available singles. Therefore, you should plan to set aside a significant sum of money in your budget just for advertising. The more successful you are at arranging matches, the less some of your clients will require your services—they'll get married. So you must constantly be on the lookout for ways to spur new membership.

Start your advertising campaign in city newspapers, then focus on magazines that reach the category of the singles market you want to capture. If it's the culturally minded client that you're trying to attract, for instance, you can advertise in the playbill of the local symphony, opera, and theater companies. Gentlepeople advertises in such publications as the *New York Times* and *New York Magazine* as well as highly specialized publications, including the *United Nations* newsletter and *The Law Journal.* Don't overlook advertising in local church publications and small community or ethnic newspapers. Some larger metropolitan areas also offer cost-effective cable television and radio advertising.

The more creative and successful you are in attracting singles to your dating service, the more you'll get free publicity. Some dating services have become so famous they have been profiled on talk shows and TV newsmagazine programs. If you have contacts that can inform you when newspapers and magazines are planning to run articles on various aspects of the dating scene in your area, you can provide the reporter with information about your own business. Publicity like this adds anywhere from 10 to 20 new clients to your eligible singles list.

INDUSTRY STATISTICS

- *Single Adults Living in the United States in 1992:* Approximately 66 million (source: U.S. Census Bureau).
- *Combined Earned Income of Singles in 1989:* More than $614 billion (source: 1989 J. Walter Thompson Advertising Agency Marketing Report).
- *Median Age of First Marriage for Men in 1993:* 26.3 years, up from 23.2 in 1970 (source: *Chicago Magazine,* 1993).
- *Median Age of First Marriage for Women in 1993:* 24.1 years, up from 20.8 in 1970 (source: *Chicago Magazine,* 1993).
- *Households Headed by a Single Person in 1992:* One out of every two (source: U.S. Census Bureau).
- *Consumer Profile of Seniors that are Singles:* Senior singles are the most diet and health conscious of all singles age groups, they are the most frequent mail order customers, and a large portion of them own pets (source: 1989 J. Walter Thompson Advertising Agency Marketing Report).
- *Number of Single Adults in Chicago in 1993:* 61% (source: *Chicago Magazine,* 1993).
- *Number of Single Women Exceeding the Number of Single Men in Chicago in 1993:* Approximately 136,000 (source: *Chicago Magazine,* 1993).
- *Chances that a 40-Year-Old, College-Educated, Single Woman Will Get Married:* 2.6% (source: a highly controversial 1986 Harvard/Yale Study as reported by *Newsweek Magazine*; more recent studies estimate that women in the same group have about a 20% chance of marrying).

ACCOUNTING, LICENSES, AND INSURANCE

Before starting a dating service, you should contact, in addition to an accountant, a lawyer to help you in devising a comprehensive business plan. Together, these professionals can suggest the most efficient way for you to fulfill federal and state tax requirements and guide you through the bureaucratic labyrinth of filling out the documents to open a dating service. The county clerk will provide you with information about any licenses and permits that might be necessary. Whether you work alone or hire a staff, you'll also need to arrange property insurance, health insurance, and apply for a federal employer identification number. Ask your accountant to set up an accounting system that best suits your needs, and rely on him or her to advise you on ways to keep your taxes as low as possible.

Starting a dating service, whether a home-based, personalized matchmaking business or a large video introduction operation in a major metropolitan area, requires careful and thorough planning. Targeting a specific category of the singles market, creating an intelligent marketing technique, and developing a reputation as a trustworthy matchmaker will start you on the road to becoming a successful entrepreneur.

SOURCES:

Entrepreneur Magazine's 111 Businesses You Can Start For Under $10,000, Bantam Books, 1991.

Entrepreneur Magazine's 168 More Businesses Anyone Can Start and Make A Lot Of Money, Bantam Books, 1991.

Jannot, Mark, ''Love Brokers,'' *Chicago Magazine,* February 1993, pp. 60-67.

Kahn, Sharon, and the Philip Lief Group, *101 Best Businesses To Start,* Doubleday & Co., Inc., 1992.

Madden, Michael, editor, *Small Business Start-Up Index,* Issue 1, Gale Research, Inc., 1991.

McLaughlin, Kevin, ''A Singular Sensation,'' *Entrepreneur Magazine,* April 1990, pp. 105-108.

Schwartz, Carol A., editor, *Small Business Sourcebook,* Volume 1, Gale Research, Inc., 1992.

Stodder, Gayle Sato, ''Meet Market,'' *Entrepreneur Magazine,* March 1994, pp. 174-177.

Wagner, Stephen, *Mind Your Own Business: The Best Businesses You Can Start Today For Under $500,* Bob Adams, Inc., 1992.

Woy, Patricia A., *Small Businesses That Grow And Grow And Grow,* Betterway Publications, Inc., 1989.

—THOMAS DERDAK

Delicatessen/Sandwich Shop

On a typical day nearly half of all adult Americans are food-service patrons. And while fast-food franchises often cater to many of these customers, a sandwich made with crisp lettuce, ripe tomatoes, hand-sliced meats, and cheeses—all layered between freshly baked bread—can for many people top a burger on a bun. Sandwich shops and delicatessens offer the same convenience as fast-food restaurants, in most cases at only a slightly higher cost. And these shops and delis reap tasty profits, generally preparing a sandwich in just a few minutes for under a dollar and then selling it for about three times as much.

Traditionally delis have been a standing favorite among the college-age market. And, as aging, more health-conscious baby boomers changed their eating habits, the sandwich segment of the fast-food market enjoyed considerable growth during the late 1980s; meanwhile, hamburger-oriented restaurants began losing market share to sandwich shops and delis, prompting such fast-food leaders as McDonald's, Burger King, and Hardees to experiment with sub and deli sandwiches. Feeding the growth in delis and sandwich shops was the fact that customers could actually see their food being prepared, instead of being handed a bag full of paper-wrapped burgers and fries through a drive-through window. With a lot of hard work, entrepreneurs who properly market a well-placed sandwich shop or deli can find it to be a profitable and rewarding business.

COSTS AND PROFITS

Minimum start-up costs for a sandwich shop are about $40,000; costs for a deli, which generally offers a larger menu and stresses the display of food more, will likely be greater. The average start-up investment for a sandwich shop or deli runs in the neighborhood of $70,000. Some sandwich shops and delis report pretax profits of more than $60,000 (some report as much as $150,000), while the majority earn closer to $40,000 annually. The primary liabilities of a sandwich shop or deli owner include working capital loans and the standard accounts payable. In addition, many sandwich shop and deli owners don't own the building where they do business and are thereby responsible for monthly rent payments.

FINANCING

Proper financing is essential when preparing to start a sandwich shop or delicatessen, particularly if you want to set up shop in the heart of a high-rent business or shopping district. It is therefore advisable to consult with foodservice experts to determine how much money you'll need to get your business started. Investigate real estate and facility costs carefully, talk with other operators to get their input on needed equipment and inventory, and consider what financial resources and potential collateral you have at your disposal. Probably your best source of pre-financing information will come from state and regional restaurant associations and trade publications, which can help detail your needs and offer suggestions for locating a sympathetic lender.

The more you do in the way of arming yourself with facts and figures before approaching a bank, the better your odds are of coming away with financing for your new business. A banker will want to see calculations that justify your requested loan amount and outline when you will break even. These figures should include financial projections for at least three years, your anticipated income and expenses, and proposed repayment schedules. In addition, you will probably be asked to provide a market analysis and a marketing strategy (including a pricing structure) which shows you can capture a profitable share of customers.

Ultimately a number of variables—including business track record, personal assets, and credit history—will determine whether a bank will loan to a prospective sandwich shop owner. While in the process of courting lenders you would do well to contact the U.S. **Small Business Administration (SBA)** about loan eligibility requirements. In order to receive an SBA loan, you must have been unable to secure financing on reasonable terms elsewhere; nonetheless, the agency can still provide a wealth of information and serve as a potential lender of last resort. To receive SBA information and/or loan eligibility requirements, call **1-800-U ASK SBA,** or write: **Small Business Directory, P.O. Box 1000, Ft. Worth, TX 76119.**

FRANCHISE OPPORTUNITIES

Subway Sandwiches & Salads: 325 Bic Dr., Milford, CT, 06460; phone: (800) 888-4848.

Blimpie: 1775 The Exchange, Ste. 215, Atlanta, GA 30339; phone: (800) 447-6256.

Schlotzsky's: 200 W. 4th St., Austin, TX 78701; phone: (512) 480-9871.

Mr. Philly: Restaurant Developers Corp., 5755 Grainger Rd., 2nd Floor, Independence, OH 44131; phone: (216) 398-1101.

Little King: 11811 I St., Omaha, NE 68137; phone: (402) 330-5030.

Sub Station II: 425 N. Main St., P.O. Box Drawer 2260, Sumter, SC 29151; phone: (803) 773-4711.

Togo's Eatery: 900 E. Campbell Ave., Campbell, CA 95008; phone: (408) 377-1754.

Mr. Submarine: 720 Spadina Ave., Suite 300, Toronto, ON, Canada M5S 2T9; phone: (416) 962-6232.

Joyce's Submarine Sandwiches: 1527 Havana St., Aurora, CO 80010; phone: (303) 344-1674.

Tubby's Sub Shops: 34500 Doreka Dr., Fraser, MI 48026; phone: (800) 752-0644.

Baldinos Giant Jersey Subs: 760 Elaine St., Hinesville, GA 31313; phone: (912) 368-2822.

O! Deli: 2000 Wayne Ave., San Leandro, CA 94577; phone: (510) 351-0405.

LOCATION

Site location is probably the prime factor in determining whether a sandwich shop or deli will be profitable. Because delis and sandwich shops tend to draw the majority of their customer base from a three-mile radius around their location, the ideal location for a sandwich shop would be in a heavily-traversed urban or suburban business or shopping district.

To reduce the amount of site research you have to do, you can contact local chambers of commerce and economic development agencies to inquire about favorable commercial areas. Your chosen location should be visible from the street and offer enough parking to accommodate peak business hours (one parking spot for every three chairs in your facility is a good rule of thumb). You should also check vehicle and pedestrian traffic counts before selecting a site. Local traffic and highway departments can provide fairly accurate traffic count data, as well as information on proposed street modifications. The speed of traffic flow is also important; look for a location where speed limits run between 25 and 40 miles per hour, allowing for easy ingress

and egress (another important location consideration) to and from your sandwich shop.

Cost will be a bottom line factor. When starting out you should need no more than 700 square feet; and if you limit your space requirements and lease a facility, you should be able to minimize your start-up investment. When negotiating a lease, seek the shortest term possible, such as a one-year agreement with a five-year renewal option. Rental costs will be lower if you select a freestanding building rather than a mall or shopping center location; but shopping centers typically share (and thus lower for each individual business) utility and advertising expenses.

You should in most cases avoid setting up shop near a similar type of operation, unless your research suggests there's enough customers to go around. On the other hand, an area without sandwich shops might be a danger signal; some locations have a history of failure. Before finalizing your site location you might wish to hire a market research and analysis firm or a foodservice consultant. You can locate the names of research firms by looking in the Yellow Pages under "Market Research & Analysis." Trade publications and foodservice associations can provide you with information on foodservice consultants, who can perform market and feasibility studies (as well as provide help in such areas as menu development and facility design).

LAYOUT AND DESIGN

The exterior of your sandwich shop or deli can be a powerful marketing device, so your sign should be highly visible and your building's external appearances should be attractive—connoting a shop that is bright, clean, and charming. Your logo design is paramount because it will be used on all your signs and advertisements; you may want to consider hiring an artist or logo designer to help. Sandwich shops located in malls and shopping centers often strive for eye-grabbing displays that employ large photos of taste-tempting sandwiches. Freestanding buildings are a little more limited in this regard, leading some operations to place their sandwich preparation area near windows in order to whet the appetites of potential customers passing by.

To avoid the overly-familiar look of fast-food hamburger restaurants, you should strive for a unique and pleasant internal decor—one that exudes creativity and cleanliness. Hanging plants, paintings, photographs, and posters can provide an inexpensive yet appealing look. For floors use an attractive tile—perhaps with colors used in your logo—that can be easily cleaned. Enamel-based paints or washable wall coverings should be used for walls; both can be easily cleaned, and cleanliness above all else (aside from your sandwiches) will determine whether customers return a second time.

Your floorplan should be designed on the basis of whether you are starting a strictly takeout operation or a combination takeout/sitdown business. If your plan is to offer only takeout, allocate about 75 percent of your floor space for a production area, about 15 percent for customer service, and about 10 percent for storage needs. If you offer dine-in service as well, your production/storage area will be reduced to about one-third of your floor space, while half of your space should be dedicated to a dining area and the remaining space used for production purposes.

About five percent of your production area floor space should be allocated for receiving and storage needs—refrigerator, pantry, etc.—and thus be accessible to supply vehicles. In addition, about five percent of the floor space near the receiving area should be allocated for an employee lounge and restroom. Your production area should also be designed to allow for a small manager's office and trash storage.

The layout of your production/storage area will vary according to whether you plan to offer only takeout service or include sitdown dining. If your operation is strictly takeout, the food production area should be streamlined as much as possible to allow for a smooth flow of sandwich preparation activities and customers. The design for your food preparation area will vary, according to whether you plan a deli or sandwich shop. The difference between sandwich shops and delicatessens revolves around food selection and display. Delis generally offer a wider array of cheeses and often include a selection of fish in their menus, as well as a wide variety of salads. In addition, deli food is typically displayed in tiered, refrigerated glass-front cases, which sandwich shops need not invest in.

A deli's production and customer services areas should be separated by display cases; in a sandwich shop a service counter will divide the areas. Your food preparation areas will include a sandwich preparation area and a soft-drink system and coffee maker, placed at either the beginning or end of the service counter/display case. If operating a sitdown facility it might be wise to use paper plates and cups and plastic utensils; if you don't, your facility design will need to include a dishwashing area (preferably towards the rear of the kitchen in a corner).

Your customer service area should be big enough to accommodate waiting customers during peak business hours and will include a cashier's station at the end of the counter or glass case nearest the entrance. Dining areas for sandwich shops and delis vary greatly in size; for a moderately sized operation of 500 to 700 square feet, 6 to 12 tables with 12 to 24 chairs should be sufficient. If you provide trash cans in your dining area no waitresses will be required; your tables need only be monitored and wiped down as needed.

EQUIPMENT

A small sandwich shop's equipment needs are minimal, while a deli often needs larger sized units of production and storage equipment and larger quantities of customer service items. A deli will need at least two refrigerated glass display cases and possibly a dishwasher. Those items, along with a larger refrigerator/freezer necessitated by a larger menu, could easily make a delicatessen's equipment expenses $20,000 higher than those of a sandwich shop.

Both delis and sandwich shops should be equipped with food and beverage preparation items that include a slicer, mixer, portion scale, meat grinder, roll warmer, toaster, microwave, sandwich unit/board, coffee maker, beverage stand and dispenser, and ice machine. You'll also need a cash register, garbage disposal, refrigerator/freezer, and shelving units. Both delis and sandwich shops will need a limited amount of office equipment: a desk, chair, file cabinets, and a good typewriter (or a computer with printer).

Before buying new equipment, consider used items. The Sunday classified sections of most metropolitan newspapers offer a range of furniture and equipment, often at bargain prices. In addition, vendors of new equipment often have used items which have been traded in. Or, if you want to limit your initial capital outlay but still get new equipment, you might want to consider leasing, which carries the advantage of being able to make reasonable payments on the latest models. You can obtain information on equipment vendors by subscribing to trade publications or contacting foodservice associations and other sandwich shop operators. Or, look for ''Restaurant Equipment & Supplies'' in the business-to-business Yellow Pages.

PRIMARY ASSOCIATIONS AND SELECTED TRADE PUBLICATIONS

Associations:

National Restaurant Association (NRA): 1200 17th St. NW, Washington, DC 20036; phone: (800) 424-5156.

International Dairy-Deli-Bakery Association (IDDA): 313 Price Place, Suite 202, P.O. Box 5528, Madison, WI 53705-0528; phone: (608) 238-7908.

Publications:

Restaurants USA: National Restaurant Association (NRA), 1200 17th St., N.W., Washington, DC 20036; phone: (800) 424-5156.
Dairy-Deli Digest: International Dairy-Deli-Bakery Association (IDDA), 313 Price Place, Suite 202, P.O. Box 5528, Madison, WI 53705-0528; phone: (608) 238-7908.
Dairy-Deli Wrapup: IDDA, 313 Price Place, Suite 202, P.O. Box 5528, Madison, WI 53711; phone: (608) 238-7908.
Deli-Bake Advocate: Gro Com Group, 1002 S. Fort Harrison Ave., P.O. Box 10378, Clearwater, FL 33517-0378; phone: (813) 443-2723.
Deli News: 7441 Garden Grove Blvd., Ste. H, Garden Grove, CA 92641; phone: (714) 373-0343.
American Deli-Bakery News: Jenkins Communications, Inc., 150 Spear ST., San Francisco, CA 94105; phone: (415) 777-0604.

INDUSTRY STATISTICS

- *Number of Meals Consumed Away From Home by Typical Person (1991):* 3.8 per week, 198 per year (source: National Restaurant Association).
- *Amount of Restaurant Traffic for Off-premise Consumption (1992):* Nearly half (source: National Restaurant Association).
- *Percentage of All Food Eaten Away From Home (1990):* (Eating out) 46%; (eating at quick-service restaurants) 34% (source: U.S. Department of Agriculture Economic Research Services).
- *Amount of Increase in Sandwich Shop Sales Between 1988 and 1990:* 36% (source: U.S. Department of Commerce).
- *Average Per-Person Check Amount at Restaurants (1992):* $3.98 (source: National Restaurant Association).
- *Ratio of Retail Outlets That Are Eating or Drinking Establishments:* More than one in four (source: National Restaurant Association).
- *Estimated Number of Sandwich Shops that Open in One Year:* 5,000 (source: U.S. Department of Commerce).
- *Estimated Percentage of Total Restaurant Industry Sales Attributed to Sandwiches:* 4.3 (source: NPD Research).
- *Median Pretax Income for Restaurants as a Percentage of Total Sales (1992):* 3.1% of sales for full-menu tableservice restaurants; 6.0% of sales for limited-menu non-tableservice restaurants (source: National Restaurant Association).
- *Foodservice Industry's Food and Beverage Purchases (1994 Projection):* $102 billion (source: National Restaurant Association).

INVENTORY

The basic inventory required for a sandwich shop or deli includes a range of breads, meats, cheeses and produce items—all of which will need to be as fresh as possible to keep customers coming through the door. You'll also need a supply of beverages, as well as paper products and eating utensils. The freshest bread you can buy will more than likely be found locally; look for a well-respected baker who can supply you (at wholesale price) with a range of rolls and bread—such as white, wheat, rye and pita—on a daily basis. You will probably want to use at least the more-popular meats, including chicken, corned beef, pastrami, roast beef, salami, and turkey, as well as several types of cheeses, such as American, cheddar, Jack, and Swiss. The basic produce items you will need are lettuce and tomatoes; you might wish to add others, such as hot peppers and onions. If starting a delicatessen, you will probably offer a fairly complete line of salads (including cole slaw, cucumber, green, pasta, potato, and three-bean), have several types of fish (such as cod, herring, salmon, and sturgeon), and offer a greater choice of cheeses.

For beverages, some sandwich shops sell canned soda pop and pints of milk, while others utilize dispensers and include iced tea and various carbonated drinks. Nearly all serve coffee. Shop around before signing on with beverage dealers; some offer beverage dispensers at a reduced charge or free. You will likewise want to talk with several food suppliers before agreeing to become one of their customers. Seek suppliers who are known for quality and can deliver on a "just-in-time" basis, whereby you receive shipments just before you need them. Suppliers can be located in the Yellow Pages under "Grocers, Wholesale" and "Fruits and Vegetables, Wholesale."

STAFFING AND MANAGEMENT

Your staffing needs will depend in large part on your shop's hours and whether you serve as an owner/operator. Most sandwich shops and delis open by 11 a.m. and close anywhere between 7 p.m. to midnight, depending upon their location. Peak hours (which should be staffed accordingly) are generally 11 a.m. to 2 p.m., although this may differ if you're located in a business or shopping district with theaters and bars.

If you begin as an owner/manager you might be able to get by with only one other full-time employee, who would preferably have experience making sandwiches. If sandwich making is your forte—which is definitely to your advantage—a part-time staffer/assistant could be all that you require, depending upon business volume. If you plan to stay open 12 hours a day, you will probably need an assistant manager as well as one or two other part- or full-time employees.

Your manager will need to prepare your sandwich shop for opening. S/he may also be responsible for greeting customers and supervising production workers, as well as making sandwiches during busy periods and waiting on customers. During slow times the manager can deal with necessary bookkeeping and supply matters. The assistant manager will likely be in charge of making sandwiches, running the operation when the manager is not "on the front line," and routing and washing dirty dishes if non-disposable tableware is used.

When hiring for your sandwich shop or deli, look for experienced foodservice workers. Employees should be enthusiastic, neat in appearance, and have tidy work habits which will keep your operation spotless. In training employees, you should stress the need to keep portions consistent and avoid waste, otherwise your profits will be eaten or thrown away. You should probably provide your staff with some type of uniform—if only matching t-shirts with your logo—which can reinforce your operation's image.

In setting wage scales, remember that well-paid employees are more likely to be cheerful and productive workers. Pay for an experienced manager begins at about $18,000 while other full or part time workers can be paid as little as minimum wage. You might want to consider using a "plate incentive"—paying employees from one to three cents per meal or plate served—and a gross profits incentive (two to five percent) for your manager or assistant manager.

If starting a new business on your own seems too overwhelming, you can hire a food-service consultant to advise you on issues with which you're not familiar. Or, you might wish to consider one of the host of franchise opportunities in the sandwich shop and deli markets. A franchisor can provide you with a range of support services, although it will cost you a franchise fee and more than likely a slice of your shop's profits.

MARKETING

Given the popularity of sandwiches, your marketing should be limited only by local demographics; typically sandwich shops and delis draw customers from business, shopping, and residential areas within a 10 minute walk or 15 minute drive of your store. What you will be marketing is your image. Your competition, no matter where you're located, will probably include fast-food hamburger restaurants, ethnic restaurants, and other specialty restaurants; your marketing goal should therefore be to distinguish your sandwich shop or delicatessen from other restaurants. Your logo, signage, decor, quality of sandwiches, and service should all work towards building a unique image that will linger in customers' minds.

One of your principal marketing tools will be your menu, which should be planned and designed carefully. Offer as many sandwich combinations as possible and don't just list items on a menu; give your sandwiches unforgettable and appetizing names and then describe them honestly and attractively, emphasizing ingredients and freshness. Be creative; even if your menu is only a sheet of paper, utilize graphics and color to blend with your overall image.

In pricing your sandwiches and other products, you should consider labor and supply costs as well as competition. Some sandwich shops and delis figure the cost of producing a sandwich and triple that figure to determine menu prices. Others use a more complex set of figures; if you need assistance in this area, a food-service consultant should be able to help determine an attractive yet profitable pricing structure.

ADVERTISING

Advertising for a sandwich shop or deli should be geared towards the surrounding neighborhood. If your store is located in a business district, you might want to send letters to new firms, offering to treat their staff to a meal; if you serve a lot of factory workers, your advertisements should emphasize fast service and convenience; and, if you are catering to a largely residential neighborhood, consider "family specials" or other promotions that will attract busy mothers, fathers, and children. Mostly, you should try to get inside the mind of your prospective clientele and try to deliver what they want.

Your menu can be an excellent form of advertising. One effective, low-cost means of advertising is to distribute menu flyers to surrounding residential neighborhoods and business and shopping districts. This can be done door-to-door by you, your staff, or a distribution service. If your budget allows, you can mail flyers to every address in your area; you might wish to include coupons for a discounted or free meal.

Other forms of advertising used by sandwich shops and delicatessens include the Yellow Pages and local newspapers and radio stations, but be careful that you're not wasting money by extending advertising outside of your local area. Probably your best form of advertising will be word of mouth by those who have eaten at your establishment, so service and quality are paramount. Remember customers' favorite sandwiches, talk with regulars, and get your patrons feedback on your operation. Remember, advertising can help get customers into your store the first time—but only a positive experience can get them to keep coming back.

LICENSES AND INSURANCE

In order to open a sandwich shop or deli you will need to obtain a local business license and the state and/or city sales tax permits required by law; to determine the specific licenses you will need, check with your city or county clerk. You'll also need to purchase a county health department permit required for all businesses that purvey and distribute food. If you're planning to serve beer and wine, you'll need to apply for the proper license through your local municipality or county—and remember, licenses to sell alcohol can be very expensive.

In order to protect your new business, business insurance is a must. Ask other operators for suggestions on insurance companies, or look in the Yellow Pages for an insurance company that writes business policies. Another needed form of protection is a security system. Silent alarms and/or on-site alarms are good deterrents to robbery and burglary and come in a variety of models. Industry trade publications and other operators are good sources of information on vendors of security systems, or you can look in the Yellow Pages under "Security Control Equipment and Systems."

In the final analysis, many restaurants do fail in their first year, but they need not. With the proper feasibility study and market research almost anyone can open and effectively run a sandwich shop or delicatessen. And a well-managed and promoted sandwich shop should be able to take a sizable bite out of the local hamburger-oriented restaurants' market share, break even in about six months to one year, and then maintain a healthy profitability for as long as it continues to satisfy its core clientele.

SOURCES:

Break-Even Analysis as a Profit-Planning Tool, Sunbelt
    Foodservice, September 1989.
Hill, G. Carlton Jr., "Getting the Loan You Deserve,"
    Restaurants USA, January 1992, pp. 15-16; "Putting
    Together the Pieces of a Business Plan," *Restaurants USA,*
    May 1992, pp. 31-34.
Horowitz, David, and Dana Shilling, "Restaurants," *The
    Business of Business: How 100 Businesses Really Work,*
    Harper & Row, 1989, pp. 121-124.

Kahn, Sharon, and the Philip Lief Group, *101 Best Businesses to Start,* revised edition, Doubleday, 1992, pp. 201-204.

Minno, Maurice P., ''How to Plug Into the Consultant Network,'' *Restaurants USA,* November 1985, pp. 25-26; ''Planning a New Restaurant Team,'' *Restaurants USA,* June/July 1985, pp. 24-26.

Moomaw, Paul, ''Building an Image with Advertising,'' *Restaurants USA,* August 1990, pp. 14-16.

Raphel, Murray, ''How to Find, Capture and Keep Customers,'' *Direct Marketing,* April 1993, pp. 26-27.

Regan, Claire, ''Menu Merchandising,'' *Restaurants USA,* October 1986, pp. 30-32.

Sandwich Shop/Deli, Business Start-Up Guide, EntrepreneurGroup, 1988.

Schwartz, Carol A., editor, *Small Business Sourcebook,* sixth edition, volume 1, Gale, pp. 546-552.

Tarras, John, ''Location, Location, Location,'' *Restaurant Hospitality,* September 1991, p. 84.

Weiss, Steve, ''The Comeback of the New York Deli,'' *Restaurants & Institutions,* November, 25, 1992, p. 74.

—ROGER W. ROULAND

Desktop Publishing Service

Computers have revolutionized the way people communicate, introducing media and methods that never before existed. Desktop publishing (DTP) is one high-tech service that can be performed by anyone with a computer and a flair for design. A desktop publisher can make a decent income publishing newsletters, magazines, newspapers, brochures, pamphlets, and even books. DTP is the fastest growing of all home-based computer businesses, and sales of DTP equipment have exceeded $6 billion.

Desktop publishing centralizes all aspects of the development, design, and production of printed material. Combining word processing, graphics, page layout, design, and typeset-quality printing, DTP also eliminates the large team of people previously needed to create and produce publications.

COSTS AND PROFITS

Desktop publishing is one of the easiest businesses for the lone entrepreneur to launch. There are three essential components to a DTP system: a computer and laser printer (hardware) and software. These basic and indispensable items can cost a total of $5,000 to $13,000. To pare down the cost of your basic DTP system, consider buying some used equipment and shop around for discount prices on software.

Start-up costs can vary considerably depending on the type of computer you choose, where you buy it, the kind of software you purchase and the other office machines you decide to include in your initial investment (Will you buy a copier, for example, or take advantage of the quick-copy shop down the street?). But the primary factor affecting the price of a DTP system is rapidly changing technology. An advancement this year can make last year's computer almost obsolete.

To determine which computer to buy, talk to other people in the business. There are those who swear by their IBM computers or PC-compatibles and others who won't work on anything but a Macintosh (Mac) computer. Visit several computer stores and give the equipment a "test drive." In the past, PCs and Macs were mutually exclusive systems, but recent technological advances have minimized the differences between the two. It is now possible for Macs to "read" material created with a PC's MS-DOS operating system.

Whether you eventually settle on an IBM or a Mac, get the most powerful computer you can afford. Look for a computer with more than 16 mhz and sufficient memory to run any software. In addition a hard disk with at least 100 megabytes will enable you to store all of your software on it and still have space to spare. A large-screen video display terminal (VDT), or monitor, will make page layouts easier. Prices vary widely, but in general, a monochrome or gray-scale monitor is cheaper than a color VDT.

For desktop publishers, a laser printer is a must. You'll be producing text as well as graphics, and clients will expect clear, crisp copy. Look for a high-resolution printer with 1.5 to 2 megabytes of memory, so that it can print out complicated graphics without faltering.

A complete DTP system calls for three types of software programs—word processing, graphics, and page layout. There are many varieties of each type; your best bet is to experiment in order to find the packages that are easiest for you to use. Popular programs include WordPerfect, Microsoft Word, Aldus PageMaker, Ventura Publisher, and Adobe Illustrator. And don't forget to invest in a good business software package, such as Lotus 1-2-3, for bookkeeping, billing, databases, and spreadsheets.

To fully outfit your DTP office, you'll need a fax machine or a computer with a built-in fax/modem and standard office furniture and supplies. Some desktop publishers buy scanners, which enable them to manipulate images and drop low-resolution versions of graphics into a page layout to check positioning. As technology progresses, scanners are fast becoming essential tools. A color scanner can run between $2,000 and $3,000; a gray-scale version can be had for $1,000 to $2,000.

Total start-up costs, then, can run between $15,000 and $20,000. The profit potential of desktop publishing can vary as widely as the cost of getting started. The authors of *Desktop Publishing Success* estimate that in order to cover expenses and make a net profit of $25,000, you'll need a pretax income of $50,000. This assumes a billing rate of $50 per hour for 1,000 billable hours a year.

The main pitfall to avoid in setting up your DTP business is charging clients too little. Keep in mind that

PRIMARY ASSOCIATIONS AND SELECTED TRADE PUBLICATIONS

Associations:

Association of Desktop Publishers: P.O. Box 881667, San Diego, CA 92168-1667; phone: (619) 279-2116.

Boston Computer Society: 1 Center Plaza, Boston, MA 02108; phone: (617) 367-8080.

Graphic Artists Guild: 11 West 20th St., New York, NY 10011; phone: (212) 463-7759.

International Association of Business Communicators: 1 Hallidie Plaza, Suite 600, San Francisco, CA 94102; phone: (415) 433-3400.

National Association of Desktop Publishers (NADTP): 462 Old Boston Rd., Boston, MA 01983; phone: (800) 874-4113.

Publications:

Desktop Publishing Success: Business One Irwin, 1991.
Desktop Publisher's Guide to Products & Services: Fox Pond Communications, 1990.
How to Start and Operate a Home-based Word Processing or Desktop Publishing Business: Bob Adams Inc., 1990.
National Association of Desktop Publishers Journal: NADTP, 462 Old Boston Rd., Boston, MA 01983; phone: (800) 874-4113.
Desktop Publisher: P.O. Box 3200, Maple Glen, PA 19002.
Publish!: PCW Communications, 501 Second St., San Francisco, CA 94107.

when you're starting out, you'll spend many hours mastering your software packages—time you will not be able to bill to a client. To improve the profit picture, many DTPer's charge more than $50 per hour or offer their services as consultants or marketers. Talk to other DTPer's to find out the range of hourly rates your market will support and consult sources such as *Desktop Publishing Success* for suggested rates for common projects.

To help with budgeting and cost projections, work up a realistic business plan, which will also be useful if you need to seek outside financing. Local chapters of the **Small Business Administration (SBA)** offer a free *Small Business Start-Up Information Package* and publish a number of other informative booklets at low cost. Small business owners can obtain funds through the SBA's microloan or guaranty loan programs. Check the "U.S. Government" section of your phone directory for the listing of your local SBA office or call **1-800-U ASK SBA.**

LOCATION

Unlike many other businesses, such as restaurants or retail stores, a desktop publishing office does not have to be located on a bustling main street in order to succeed. Desktop publishing naturally lends itself to a home-based setting. There are numerous pros to working at home, including a short "commute," exceptionally low overhead costs, greater control of the work environment, and considerable flexibility.

In setting up your DTP home-office, make sure there is sufficient space for equipment. Arrange your office ergonomically for maximum comfort and efficiency. Consider ordering a second phone line for your business number and perhaps a third for the fax machine. A further benefit of working out of the home is that living space used exclusively as an office is a deductible expense on your income taxes; check with your accountant for guidelines.

MARKETING YOUR DTP BUSINESS

To find clients and generate income, you'll need to develop a marketing strategy that encompasses informal and formal promotion, some advertising, referrals, networking, and cold calling. Use your computer to create work samples, such as brochures and flyers, to mail as a package to prospective clients. Befriend writers, photographers, printers, and creative directors at public relations firms and advertising agencies. Referrals can be the source of a substantial chunk of your business.

Before you can begin marketing your DTP business in earnest, however, you must determine the types of services you will offer. A DTP business can involve a wide variety of projects, including newsletters, brochures, manuals, business cards, annual reports, magazines, and resumes. Obviously, be careful not to spread yourself too thin.

You can increase your profitability as a desktop publisher if you find a specialty niche. Possibilities to explore include: slidemaking with presentation graphics software, business forms, a personalizing service, and the relatively new specialty of desktop mapmaking. Other alternatives emerge as quickly as technology makes them possible. You may want to investigate multimedia, image processing, and database typesetting, which enables DTPers to produce directories of all kinds.

If venturing into the uncharted waters of multimedia or image processing are not appealing options, you could opt for more conventional DTP staples, such as newsletters. Publishing an newsletter can be a profitable undertaking if you do your "homework," which includes researching your topic, studying the competition, and targeting your audience. When carefully conceived and well planned, newsletters are the most profitable undertaking for a DTPer.

A good rule of thumb is to publish what you know. You can turn your knowledge of a particular hobby into a how-to, consumer-oriented newsletter. You could also concentrate on organizational issues and propose an employee newsletter to one of your corporate clients. If you're savvy about stocks, bonds, and mutual funds, consider creating a newsletter for business or financial audiences. The key is to identify a marketable subject. Spend some time reading papers and magazines and watching TV to get a feel for trends and hot topics. Pay attention to the issues people are talking about. For a newsletter to be successful, it must offer specific information not available from other sources. The advantage of DTP is that you can pick up on and react to emerging trends faster than traditional publishers.

After you have decided on a subject for your newsletter, your next step is to develop a subscriber base. You can purchase mailing lists from publications or organizations that appeal to your target audience, then develop a direct mail package to entice subscribers.

In general, direct mail is an effective way to publicize your business. Advertising is expensive and usually beyond the budget of a start-up DTP business. Use your new computer system to produce slick, attractive direct mailers, flyers, and brochures that you can distribute to a select audience.

Perhaps starting a newsletter from scratch sounds a little too risky to attempt at first. Another option for the fledgling DTPer is to offer skills on a free-lance basis to business clients. By taking this route, you will be able to charge by the hour or by the project to do a variety of jobs, ranging from product brochures to training manuals. As your business grows, maintain a database of all past, current, and prospective customers and use desktop-published direct mailings to remind them that you exist or to let them know about new services you offer.

STAFFING

Most desktop publishing businesses begin as solo operations. Even when the volume of work increases, many DTPers prefer to subcontract work out rather than hire an employee. In all likelihood, you will start out as a do-it-yourselfer and handle every aspect of the business, from writing and designing to billing and bookkeeping. If your business is successful, it will eventually grow beyond a level that you alone can handle. You can expand by hiring temporary help or hooking up with other independents and free-lancers to create a high-tech "virtual office" of designers, writers, and graphic artists linked by phones, faxes, modems, and electronic mail.

MANAGEMENT ISSUES

Desktop publishing is a highly creative venture, and it's also a business. If you spend all your time brainstorming new ideas and beautiful designs, you could be headed for trouble. You must take into account at every step the viability and profitability of your business, and make necessary adjustments to your business plan. To address the array of practical management issues that confront the small businessperson—contracts, invoices, insurance, taxation—consult lawyers, accountants, other DTPers, and entrepreneurs with small business start-up experience.

Laws regarding professional liabilities and taxes are different in each state, while laws concerning copyright and incorporation, for example, are more standard regardless of your business' location. Make sure you investigate all legal issues thoroughly. A variety of books, articles, and newsletters for DTPers address these matters in depth.

To make your life and the operation of your business easier, develop a simple bookkeeping system. Create listings for income, expenses, assets, liability, and net worth and make sure your records are always current. The few extra hours each week will be well worth it at tax time, which for a self-employed person is four times a year.

LICENSES AND INSURANCE

Like any other enterprise, you will need a license from the city in which you plan to operate your DTP business. If as a sole proprietor you decide to name your business, you may have to register the fictitious name with the city, county, or state. Procedures differ from state to state, and the fee to file a fictitious name notice runs from $10 to $100. To determine if you need to file a notice, check with the county clerk's office.

Once your DTP business is up and running, you will want to explore the issue of copyright. If you are producing an original newsletter, magazine, or newspaper, you should copyright the material contained therein by including a copyright notice in the publication. For regulations regarding direct mail promotion of your publications, consult the Federal Trade Commission (FTC).

As a desktop publisher operating computer equipment that is fragile and complex, you will need to insure your equipment. If operating out of your home, keep in mind that your homeowner's insurance will not completely cover your equipment. Consult with your insurance agent to set up a separate policy.

Computer systems inevitably crash, software goes on the fritz, files are somehow erased and every once in a while, the power goes out when you have an impending deadline.

DESKTOP PUBLISHING SUPPLIERS

Computer Brokerage Services: New York City; phone: (800) 735-7856 (mostly supplies for Macintosh computers).

Dell Computer Corporation: Phone: (800) 365-1460 (MS-DOS supplies).

Desktop Publishing Corner: Phone: (800) 937-2387 (hardware and software).

Midwest Publishing: Phone: (800) 621-1507 (tools for pasteup, laser paper).

National Computer Exchange: New York City; phone: (800) 359-2468 (publishes the *Computer Classified Blue Book* listing prices for PCs).

INDUSTRY STATISTICS

• *High Net Pretax Profit:* $157,000.
• *Average Net Pretax Profit:* $43,000.
• *Minimum Start-Up Investment:* $16,200.
• *Average Start-Up Investment:* $39,500.
• *Average Return on Investment:* 109%.
• *Stability:* Moderate.
• *Risk Factor:* Moderate.
• *Industry Growth Prospects:* Excellent.

(SOURCE: *25 HOT BUSINESSES FOR THE '90S,* ENTREPRENEUR GROUP, 1992.)

To make sure these problems are interruptions and not full-scale disasters, buy a service contract for your computer, back up your software, keep hard copies of all your documents, invest in a surge protector, and avoid hooking your system up to the same electrical lines that run refrigerators and air conditioners.

In summary, for an entrepreneur with sufficient determination, energy, and creative drive, desktop publishing can be a lucrative, rewarding business. To make it a viable long-term business, it's important that you keep up with technology. Stay abreast of new developments and carefully consider their impact on your DTP business. Be prepared to upgrade your equipment, expand your services, or find a new niche. With foresight and careful planning, your DTP business can thrive and grow.

SOURCES:

"Desktop Publishing for Small Publishers," *25 Hot Businesses for the Nineties,* EntrepreneurGroup, 1992.

Kramer, Felix, and Maggie Lovas, *Desktop Publishing Success: How to Start and Run a Desktop Publishing Business,* Business One Irwin, 1991.

Loftus, Michele, *How to Start and Operate a Home-Based Word Processing or Desktop Publishing Business,* Bob Adams, Inc., 1990.

Newsletter Publishing, American Entrepreneurs Association (AEA), 1990.

Pennybacker, James S., editor, *Desktop Publisher,* Fox Pond Communications, 1993.

Woy, Patricia A., "Computer Careers Capitalize on Skills," *Small Businesses That Grow and Grow and Grow,* Betterway Publications, 1989.

Williams, Thomas A., *How to Make $100,000 a Year in Desktop Publishing,* Betterway Publications, 1989.

Zogbi, Dennis M., "Desktop Publishing: Start Your Own Small Press," *Income Opportunities,* March 1992, pp. 54-55, 62, 64.

—*MARINELL JAMES*

Diaper Delivery Service

Diaper delivery services were very common during the 1950s but began to disappear after the introduction of disposable diapers in 1961. By the late 1980s disposable diapers accounted for nearly 85 percent of the market, and most parents who still insisted on cloth diapers did their own laundering. However, the trend began to reverse itself in the late 1980s, when environmentalists began warning about the impact of dumping approximately 17 billion disposable diapers every year in overcrowded landfills—about one ton of waste for every child under two years old. In 1993 cloth diapers accounted for about 30 percent of the market, and diaper delivery services served an estimated 750,000 customers.

FINANCIAL ASPECTS

Starting a diaper delivery service can be an expensive proposition, especially considering the large initial investment required for diapers and commercial laundry equipment. Many consultants consider the minimum start-up cost to be about $125,000, with the average cost hovering around $170,000. You may, though, find inventive ways to lower expenses. For example, Diaper Dan, a diaper delivery service that received national recognition from *Inc.* magazine in 1991, reduced start-up costs significantly by contracting with a commercial laundry instead of buying its own equipment. Diaper services generally needed at least 200 customers to break even, with gross profits of 60 to 70 percent of revenues for successful companies.

The first thing any aspiring entrepreneur should do is seek out a financial advisor. Some banks and community colleges offer small business assistance programs. There are also associations of retired business executives who volunteer to assist start-up businesses. These organizations can help you seek financing and also guide you in creating a business plan that will satisfy potential lenders.

In general, banks are very conservative in their lending practices and require a sound business plan, a thorough background check, and collateral. Someone with an excellent credit rating, however, may be able to get an unsecured loan. Finance companies will often accept greater risk and may extend a loan when a bank will not; they also charge higher interest rates.

Another potential source of capital is for the owner to sell equity in the business. In an equity investment, investors own a percentage of the business and share in all losses and profits. An equity investment is not a loan, and there are no legal obligations to repay the money. Although selling equity may seem to be a good way to raise capital, the business owner may also lose some control over the enterprise. Check with a lawyer before entering into any legal arrangement.

Suppliers may also be a source of financing for a diaper delivery service. For example, though an initial supply of diapers may cost several thousand dollars, the cost can be paid from revenues if the diaper company postpones payment for 90 days. Likewise, laundry equipment can be expensive, but manufacturers may be willing to negotiate a payment schedule, thus reducing start-up costs.

The **Small Business Administration (SBA)** is another source of capital. The SBA is an independent agency of the U.S. government that promotes small businesses through loans, counseling, and other information. The SBA is particularly sensitive to ownership by women and minorities. You must first exhaust all sources of private financing before you are eligible for an SBA loan. There are Small Business Administration offices in most major cities. Check the ''U.S. Government'' section of the telephone directory for locations and telephone numbers. You can also reach the SBA at **1-800-U ASK SBA.**

SPECIAL EQUIPMENT

The heavy-duty, commercial-grade washers and dryers used by diaper delivery services are much different than their domestic counterparts. Commercial washers, which maintain the pH levels necessary for proper cleaning, range in cost from $50,000 to $200,000. Commercial dryers start at $22,000. However, start-up businesses can usually find used equipment for considerably less money. Other basic equipment includes rolling carts for moving diapers between operations, tables for sorting and folding, and possibly a steam presser to iron diapers before folding. You will also need to own or lease one or more delivery vans, which should be clean, well-maintained, late-model vehicles with the company name, logo, and telephone number clearly

INDUSTRY STATISTICS

• *Number of Disposable Diapers Sold Annually:* 17 billion (source: *New York Times,* October 23, 1992).
• *Number of Diapers Used During Infancy:* 4,500 (source: *New York Times,* October 23, 1992).
• *Percent of Market Using Cloth Diapers:* 30% (source: National Association of Diaper Services [NADS], 1994).
• *Average Cost of a Disposable Diaper:* $.25 (source: *New York Times,* October 23, 1992).
• *Average Cost of Cloth Diapers Delivered:* $.17 (source: NADS, 1994).
• *Average Cost for One-Week Supply of Disposable Diapers:* $15 (source: *Whole Earth Review,* 1988).
• *Average Weekly Cost of Diaper Delivery Service:* $12 (Source: NADS, 1994).

marked on all sides to draw attention to the business and promote a proper image.

SUPPLIES

Diaper delivery services must maintain a large inventory of diapers and cleaning supplies, including detergent, bleach, fabric softener, and a chemical "sour" that lowers the pH after the diapers are washed. A baby will use between 80 and 90 diapers per week, so a delivery service should stock about 200 diapers per customer—half in use and half being cleaned and prepared for delivery. A delivery service with 200 customers would need about 40,000 diapers at a cost of $.07 to $.10 each ($2,800 to $4,000).

The average diaper will last 50 washings, so the inventory needs to be replaced about once a year. The cost of cleaning supplies may vary depending on volume, but you will need about one pound of detergent per month for every customer and about a third as much chlorine bleach. Most consultants recommend keeping at least a three-month supply on hand. You should also provide your customers with diaper pails and deodorizer.

MARKET

There are two primary markets for diaper delivery services: parents of children under two years old and institutions that care for young children, including day-care centers and hospitals. Parents most likely to use a diaper delivery service are in their mid-20s to late 40s and have annual incomes of $30,000 or more. Although environmental awareness plays a major role in whether parents decide to use cloth diapers, the convenience of delivery is also a factor, especially for working parents with a total income of $50,000 or more. In addition, parents strongly believe that freshly laundered cloth diapers are better for their children.

Though most diaper delivery services focus on the residential segment of the market, a few are successful in marketing to day-care centers and hospitals. Day-care centers are often reluctant to use cloth diapers because they require more effort than disposables. But some day-care centers

actually advertise the fact that they use cloth diapers, and many others are willing to use cloth diapers if requested by their clients.

Hospitals also use disposable diapers, especially since manufacturers often provide them with free disposables as a way to reach new parents. Parents who received a week's supply of brand-name disposable diapers when they took their newborn babies home were very likely to continue buying the same brand. In the late 1980s, though, some hospitals returned to using cloth diapers because of environmental concerns and because some infants were sensitive to the chemicals used to make disposable diapers more absorbent. As a diaper delivery service owner, you could conduct a good sales presentation to convince a hospital to use cloth diapers.

LOCATION

In selecting a site for a diaper delivery service, the two most important factors are cost and distance to primary market areas. Since customers rarely, if ever, visit a diaper delivery service, facilities can be located in relatively low-rent industrial areas. Keep in mind that the closer the laundry facilities are to the primary market area, the less expensive and more efficient delivery will be. You should consider locating in an industrial park on a side of town where you expect to draw most of your customers. If you expect to target more than one community, you should situate your laundry facilities as centrally as possible. Be sure the site is properly zoned and that the local health department and environmental protection agency will allow the operation of a commercial laundry.

FACILITY

A diaper delivery service will need at least 2,000 square feet of space in an area that is properly zoned for a commercial laundry. The facilities will need adequate water, sewer, and electrical service to handle the equipment as well as plenty of space for sorting, folding, and storing clean diapers. Your establishment should also have convenient access for delivery vans to drop off soiled diapers and pick up clean ones. Other necessities are rest rooms, a lunch room for employees, and an office area.

The laundry facility should be laid out in an efficient "assembly line" pattern so that soiled diapers are dropped off near the washers. From there, they go into the dryers and then on to sorting and folding tables. Lastly, diapers will be either stored or loaded into the van for delivery. Water, sewer, and electrical hookups can be expensive and difficult to move, so your layout should be designed around the washers and dryers.

Check with an attorney before signing any lease. Most building owners will start off with a standard lease, but everything should be negotiable, including who is responsible for improvements and liability. If the facility is part of an industrial park, you should be wary of common costs and restrictions that could affect operations. A diaper delivery service needs little more than plenty of space and proper water, sewer, and electrical hookups, so there should be plenty of facilities available.

PERSONNEL

A start-up diaper delivery service will need at least three employees—a driver and two people to handle washing and preparing the diapers—and will need to increase the number of employees as the business grows. Washing, drying, sorting, folding, and preparing diapers for delivery can be hard and often unpleasant work. Some consultants suggest paying production workers 50 percent more than minimum wage. You may also consider paying workers a bonus based on volume.

Special care should be given to hiring drivers, since they will represent the company in all face-to-face dealings with customers. In addition to having a good driving record, a driver must be personable and well groomed. The driver must also be able to answer questions about prices, services, and the benefits of cloth diapers. Most importantly, s/he must understand that customer service is the first priority.

You may want to train your driver to sell add-on products such as baby food, baby clothing, and toys. Daniel Gold, founder of Diaper Dan, told *Inc.,* ''I thought of . . . the old-time milkman who began to sell his customers butter and eggs. So I wanted my customers to develop a relationship with my drivers, to be on a first-name basis and more like friends.'' Gold also found that women tended to be mistrustful of delivery men, so he hired female drivers whenever possible.

As your diaper delivery service grows, you may want to hire a manager to schedule pickups and deliveries, supervise laundry operations, and purchase supplies. That will enable you to focus on marketing and other business functions. Other employees may include a bookkeeper, working part-time at first, and a secretary to answer phones.

PRIMARY ASSOCIATIONS AND SELECTED TRADE PUBLICATIONS

Associations:

National Association of Diaper Services (NADS): 2017 Walnut St., Philadelphia, PA 19103; phone: (800) 462-NADS.

Publications:

NADS Newsletter: National Association of Diaper Services, 2017 Walnut St., Philadelphia, PA 19103; phone: (800) 462-NADS.

PRICING AND BILLING

Most diaper delivery services pick up soiled diapers and deliver clean ones once a week, charging about $12.50 for 80 diapers. The price covers labor and materials, overhead, and a profit generally ranging between 30 and 50 percent of gross revenues. Start-up delivery services should compare prices with the competition, but it will not always be possible or desirable to offer the lowest price. Established delivery services may have a customer base that allows considerable savings in operating costs. Lower prices may also indicate poorer service or low-quality diapers. You should set prices based on what you need to be successful. If your prices are higher than the competition's, then you must compensate by promoting how your service is better.

Customers should generally be billed each week with delivery, although some services mail invoices on a weekly, bi-weekly, or monthly basis. Institutional customers, including day-care centers and hospitals, are almost always billed monthly.

ADVERTISING

For a diaper delivery service, advertising has two primary objectives: to create an awareness of a particular company and to overcome a reluctance to use cloth diapers. The primary reason that parents choose disposable diapers is convenience. In addition, many parents have no experience using cloth diapers, are afraid of sticking their babies with safety pins, and may not understand the benefits. They may also believe that diaper services are more expensive than using disposable diapers. Along with promoting recognition of your company name, the most effective advertising will also address parent concerns.

One way to entice parents to try cloth diapers is to offer a week of free service. The customer has nothing to lose, and your investment is minimal. However, a general advertising campaign offering free service may generate a response from people who are not likely to continue with your company, so you may want to focus your advertising on a particular target market. This can be done by purchasing mailing lists, which provide demographic information on potential customers. Some diaper services have been successful in getting hospital childbirth classes to distribute promotional material and even teach how to diaper a baby using cloth as well as disposable diapers.

Given the cost compared to the market for diaper delivery services, it probably does not make sense for you to advertise in the mass media—radio, television, and general circulation newspapers. One exception may be if there is a local cable television show specifically targeted at new parents. However, you should definitely advertise in parenting magazines and in your local Yellow Pages directory.

RISK MANAGEMENT

As a smart business owner, you should carry liability insurance that protects your service from damages arising from on-the-job injuries. Most states do not require a special license to operate a diaper delivery service, though you may need special permits in some areas because of the large amount of discharge into the sewer system.

OUTLOOK

Environmental concerns over disposable diapers began to lessen in the early 1990s, which slowed the growth of diaper delivery services. Although 22 states were considering putting a tax on or banning disposable diapers in 1989, no laws were passed. In 1992 the *New York Times* reported: "Exhausted by the failure to convince parents that the nation's landfills have turned into reeking mountains of disposable diapers, many of the most zealous environmentalists have simply stopped trying." Cotton diapers were nonetheless holding on to about 30 percent of the market. Although most diapers were being washed at home, diaper delivery service industry analysts believed there were still growth opportunities. The key factor was convincing parents that a diaper delivery service is both convenient and affordable.

SOURCES:

Diaper Delivery Service, Business Start-Up Guide, Entrepreneur Group, 1992.
Finegan, Jay, "Diaper Dan," *Inc.,* March 1991, p. 80.
Specter, Michael, "Among the Earth Baby Set, Disposable Diapers Are Back," *New York Times,* October 23, 1992, p. A1.

—*DEAN BOYER*

Drug and Alcohol Rehabilitation Service

In waging the "war on drugs," U.S. government policymakers focus their efforts on reducing the supply of drugs, while others fight the battle to reduce demand in cities and towns across the United States. Some professionals have seized the opportunity to make their living by helping drug users battle addiction. To start a business in this socially relevant field, a major financial commitment is not required; you will, however, need plenty of compassion, understanding, and resolve.

Studies reveal that of the 70 million Americans who use drugs, 6.5 million of them are in need of treatment. Fortunately, society has recognized the merits of substance abuse treatment. By the late 1980s more people were seeking treatment for substance abuse than ever before. Not only was there less of a stigma on addiction treatment, financial assistance from the federal government as well as employer-sponsored coverage provided resources drug abusers needed to seek help.

Drug and alcohol rehabilitation is an established industry that uses various treatment methods and patient settings, including detoxification, residential treatments, halfway houses, and outpatient services. Starting any type of residential rehab program involves building a major medical facility and maintaining a large professional staff, a setup that would be prohibitive for the prospective small business owner. Outpatient practices, on the other hand, can be operated from the home or an office building and can potentially be lucrative.

An outpatient program typically offers individual and/or group therapy and family counseling and is appropriate for anyone interested in starting a substance abuse counseling program. If you possess a master's or doctorate degree in human services or psychology, the credibility of your program will certainly increase. Advanced degrees are not required in the rehab business, but an understanding of addiction is critical. In fact, some of the most successful counselors are former addicts themselves.

COSTS AND PROFITS

Costs and earnings in the rehab business vary considerably. Some determinants of profitability are location, degree of expertise, and most importantly, your ability to fill appointment space. Typically, substance abuse counselors bill at a rate of $75 to $125 for a 50- to 60-minute session. To remain competitive, however, many counselors operate on a "sliding fee scale"; they charge according to the client's income and other indicators of his or her ability to pay for services. A sliding scale can reduce billing rates to the $5-$25 range.

Most patients pay for private substance abuse therapy through private and group insurance and employee assistance programs (EAPs). Other major providers are Medicaid/Medicare, Blue Cross/Blue Shield, and public funds such as disability benefits. Keep in mind that most insurance plans put a cap on the amount of treatment for which they will reimburse annually. Insurance companies, moreover, have screening processes that determine which counselors they will accept as treatment providers. Contact the individual companies for their eligibility requirements.

FINANCING

Drug and alcohol rehabilitation programs have low start-up costs. You will need office space with a waiting room, a file cabinet that locks, and a telephone and answering service to begin your practice. Nevertheless, you are likely to require some financing to begin operating. Owing to the time associated with processing insurance claims, there is a lag between delivery of service and payment. A working capital loan, therefore, will help tide you over until you begin to collect receivables.

In order to obtain financing from a bank, you should present the loan officer with a credible operating plan and prove that you have some relevant experience. Most banks prefer to lend to someone with state or national licensure/certification and/or an advanced degree. You can enhance your lending profile by establishing a relationship with a recognized hospital or residential treatment program that could provide supplementary care for your patients as well as referrals. Other factors a loan officer may consider include your credentials, professional experience, areas of expertise, fee structure, and accessibility.

Before approaching a loan officer, be sure to talk with friends in the counseling, banking, and management industries. If you need assistance putting together a businesses plan, or finding loan programs, the U.S. **Small Business**

PRIMARY ASSOCIATIONS AND SELECTED TRADE PUBLICATIONS

Associations:

Alcohol and Drug Problems Association of North America (ADPA): 444 N. Capitol St. NW, Ste. 706, Washington, DC 20001; phone: (202) 737-4340.

Institute for Integral Development (IID): P.O. Box 2172, Colorado Springs, CO 80901; phone: (719) 634-7943.

National Association of Alcoholism and Drug Abuse Counselors (NAADAC): 3717 Columbia Pke., Ste 300, Arlington, VA 22204; phone: (703) 920-0497.

National Organization of State Alcohol and Drug Abuse Directors: 444 North Capitol Street, NW Suite 520, Washington, DC 20001; phone: (202) 783-6868.

Publications:

The Counselor: National Association of Alcoholism and Drug Abuse Counselors, 3717 Columbia Pke., Suite 300, Arlington, VA 22204; phone: (800) 548-0497.

Addiction Program Management: Manisses Communication Group, Inc., Box 3357, Wayland Sq., Providence, RI 02906-0357; phone: (401) 831-6020.

Alcoholism and Drug Abuse Weekly: Manisses Communication Group, Inc., Box 3357, Wayland Sq., Providence, RI 02906-0357; phone: (401) 831-6020.

The Alcoholism Report: National Council on Alcoholism and Drug Dependence, 1511 K St. NW, Suite 938, Washington, DC 20005; phone: (202) 737-7342.

Administration (SBA) is an excellent resource. They can be reached at **1-800-U ASK SBA,** or write: **Small Business Directory, P.O. Box 1000, Fort Worth, TX 76119.** You may also want to check the ''U.S. Government'' section in your telephone directory for the SBA office nearest you.

LOCATION

When deciding on a location for your drug and alcohol rehabilitation service, price and convenience are important concerns. Unless you are an established therapist who enjoys a lucrative hospital affiliation, elaborate office space will be prohibitively expensive. You may want to work out of your home or share office space with another counselor in order to minimize expenses.

Although it may require some leg-work, establishing a home office is an excellent way to reduce operating costs. If you decide to work out of your home, you will need to obtain a variance or local permit. This process is normally administered by the local zoning board of appeals that handles requests for permission to operate from a private residence; determine the appropriate local authority and contact it directly. To obtain the maximum tax benefit, be sure to consult your tax advisor when establishing a home office;

the Internal Revenue Service (IRS) scrutinizes home office deductions. Also, in the interest of professional decorum, be sure to build an entrance to your office that is separate from the family entrance.

It would also be prudent to consider your patients' needs when choosing an office location. Often a drug or alcohol addict will have had his or her driver's license revoked or suspended. Thus, proximity to public or some other form of alternate transportation is imperative. On the other hand, if you plan on treating upper-middle-class suburban clients, an office that is situated off the beaten track might assuage patient concerns about confidentiality.

MARKETING

The drug and alcohol rehabilitation business is extremely competitive. Thousands of counselors, self-help groups, and public and private programs exist throughout the United States. A small start-up program, therefore, must distinguish itself in order to succeed in the industry.

Your individual selling and networking ability may be your best marketing tool. You will need referrals to develop a client base. When targeting potential referrals, be sure to focus on the sources of drug and alcohol treatment funds. The U.S. Veteran's Administration, for example, dispenses disability benefits that cover substance abuse rehabilitation. One excellent resource at the state level is the Regional Alcohol and Drug Awareness Resource Network Agency (RADAR), which is responsible for distributing alcohol and drug abuse prevention and education materials. RADAR was established by the U.S. Department of Health and Human Services Office of Substance Abuse Prevention. Every state has a RADAR office; you may want to check with your state's department of public health for the office nearest you.

Some of the most fruitful sources of alcohol and drug abuse referrals are the courts, insurance companies, and human resources departments of large companies. Your patient appointment schedule should allow you to set up meetings with individuals from these organizations during normal business hours. Every effort should be made to establish a formal link with a specific EAP and/or a specific employer. If your specialty is teenage substance abuse, the local high school guidance department and college health center are excellent sources of referrals.

In order to avail yourself of the many referrals available through the court system, you may want to offer a Driving Under the Influence (DUI) program. A major national effort to rid the roads of drunk drivers created high demand for DUI programs, which are typically offered by large public institutions. A local probation officer, though, may know of some opportunities for the small business owner in the DUI segment of rehabilitation.

In addition to networking, price and service are two variables that a drug and alcohol counselor can use to gain a competitive advantage. By carefully managing your expenses, you should be able to price your treatment below that of large programs. One marketing strategy for a start-up business is to initially offer very low prices in order to attract patients. In a business of referrals, the more people you can treat, the better.

Attentive and flexible service will also differentiate your program from the competition. By offering appointments before and after regular business hours and on weekends, you will accommodate working clients who probably have insurance to pay for your services. Also, 24-hour operation is critical in the business of addiction therapy.

Finally, plan on joining one or more of the professional associations in the rehab industry. Many organizations work closely with families, law enforcement, and health agencies. The publications offered by professional groups are an excellent source of information concerning trends in treatment, which agencies are providing funding, and other marketing leads.

ADVERTISING

Although much of your business will be generated through referrals, formal advertising is a strategic priority. At the least, you should plan to advertise in the Yellow Pages and

in your local newspaper. Your advertisements should list a telephone number that patients can call 24 hours a day. You may also want to cite the types of insurance programs you accept. A quick flip through your Yellow Pages under "Alcoholism" and "Drug Abuse Addiction Treatment and Rehabilitation" might give you some advertising ideas. Keep in mind that you need to promote your business in specific media that are appropriate for your area of emphasis. For example, if you want to counsel teenagers, advertise in magazines that are marketed to teenagers.

Finally, you may want to purchase a listing in a national treatment directory. For a fee these directories list thousands of counselors and treatment programs and often accept advertisements. Some possibilities include: *Drug, Alcohol, and Other Addictions: A Directory of Treatment Centers and Prevention Programs Nationwide,* Oryx Press, 4041 N. Central, No. 700, Phoenix, AZ 85012; phone: **(601) 265-2651**; and *National Directory of Facilities and Services for Lesbian and Gay Alcoholics,* National Association of Lesbian and Gay Alcoholism Professionals, 204 W. 20th St., New York, NY 10011; phone: **(212) 713-5074.** Ask your librarian about the many other directories in print.

STATE OFFICE FUNCTIONS

Office of the Governor:
• Responsible for the implementation of substance abuse legislation.
• Responsible for designating the State agency that applies for federal drug law enforcement, education, treatment, and prevention funds.

State Legislature:
• Establishes funding levels for statewide drug law enforcement, treatment and prevention.

State Drug Program Coordinator:
• Establishes a statewide drug abuse action plan and coordinates the activities of executive branch agencies.
• Assists in the establishment of substance abuse program priorities.

State Health Offices:

RADAR: Regional Alcohol and Drug Awareness Resource Network Agency:
• State office responsible for distributing alcohol and drug abuse prevention and education materials.
• Activities are coordinated by the National Clearinghouse for Alcohol and Drug Information.

State Education Office:

State Coordinator for Drug Free Schools:
• Establishes school-based drug and alcohol prevention/ education programs.
• Administers Federal Drug Free Schools and Communities funds.

(SOURCE: *NARCOTICS AND DRUG ABUSE: A-Z,* 1993.)

GOVERNMENT REGULATION

From a regulatory perspective, the primary consideration for drug and alcohol rehabilitation programs is confidentiality. Congress passed specific legislation pertaining to the rehab industry entitled "Confidentiality of Alcohol and Drug Abuse Patient Records: General Provisions," which are published in the *Federal Register.* You must obtain and become familiar with these regulations if you intend to provide substance abuse treatment. The laws contain five parts—Introductory Statements, General Provisions, General Confidentially Regulations, Disclosure with Patient Consent, Disclosure without Patient Consent, and Court Orders—address a variety of confidentiality issues, and supersede all state laws.

The Food and Drug Administration (FDA) also regulates narcotic treatment programs. The FDA is particularly active in monitoring the use of methadone—a drug used in patient detoxification and maintenance. Because many of your patients may be on methadone maintenance programs, particularly if they recently completed detoxification, you should become familiar with methadone regulations even if you will not be prescribing the medication.

In addition to federal regulations, most states have specific requirements with regard to substance abuse treatment programs. To begin your state-level investigation, call your state's Department of Public Health Bureau of Substance Abuse Services. The phone number is listed in the government section of your telephone directory.

LICENSING AND ACCREDITATION

In an effort to increase the stature of drug and alcohol treatment, many states have developed Counselor Certifica-

INDUSTRY STATISTICS

- *Direct Costs for Alcohol and Drug Abuse Treatment in the U.S.:* $16.9 billion (source: *Professional Psychology Research and Practice,* May 1993).
- *Average Cost of 30-Day Inpatient Alcoholism Rehabilitation Program:* $6,000-8,000 (1993).
- *Growth Rate for Alcohol and Drug Treatment Centers:* (1978-84) 78% (source: American Hospital Association).
- *Average Number of Visits to a Health Care Professional Preceding Substance Abuse Diagnosis:* 4 (source: Mental Health Epidemiological Catchment Area survey).
- *Increase in Codependency (Addiction to Two or More Substances) 1982-86:* 20% (source: *Professional Psychology Research and Practice,* May 1993).
- *Number of Americans Involved in Alcohol-Related Fatalities:* (1979-89) Over 100,000 (source: *Professional Psychology Research and Practice,* May 1993).
- *Lifetime Prevalence for Drug Use Among High School Seniors:* (alcohol) 90%; (tobacco) 67%; (marijuana) 40%; (stimulants) 18%; (cocaine) 8%; (hallucinogens) 8%; (heroin) 1.5% (source: National Survey of High School Seniors).
- *Percentage of AIDS Cases Attributed to IV Drug Use:* 25%.

tion Programs for providers of drug and alcohol treatment. The certification process varies from state to state but usually includes an examination that tests knowledge and skills in such areas as prevention and education, intervention and counseling, medical support, recovery, and family support.

Again, you should contact your state Department of Public Health Bureau of Substance Abuse Services for information on state specific certification processes. Another resource for information of this nature is the **National Association of Alcoholism and Drug Abuse Counselors (NAADAC): 3717 Columbia Pke., Ste. 300, Arlington, VA 22204;** phone: **(703) 920-4644.** Membership in NAADAC, which provides training and education to substance abuse counselors and promotes national accreditation standards, is a must for the aspiring drug and alcohol counselor.

When considering the costs and benefits of accreditation, keep in mind that many insurance programs require accreditation in order for a counselor to be eligible for referrals. In addition, public funds are usually available only to accredited programs. Since accreditation may also help you secure a loan from a bank, it is probably in your best interest to obtain all certification or licensure that is available to a person with your education level.

INSURANCE AND LIABILITY ISSUES

Like most health services industries, the substance abuse treatment profession is quite risky from a legal standpoint. You should definitely plan on purchasing malpractice insurance. It would be wise to consult with an attorney before you begin your practice to discuss specific areas of liability.

Your responsibilities will vary according to the types of patients you treat. Treating teenagers, for example, will involve different legal responsibilities than those for treating adults. It is your responsibility to stay abreast of legal issues that pertain to the business. The regulations will change frequently. Joining a professional organization should help you stay informed.

MANAGEMENT ISSUES

Working with drug and alcohol addiction can be a stressful and emotionally draining experience. You may often feel unsuccessful because of the traditionally high rate of recidivism. Many counselors in the business suffer from burnout. Hiring part-time interns is one management technique that could minimize burnout and save you money. Contact the career services center at a local college or university and set up an internship for a psychology or social work major. You can decide how much responsibility to give the intern based on his or her level of maturity and experience. Above all, be sure that the student is compassionate and caring.

In addition to burnout, you should consider the health risks to you and your employees that accompany working with drug and alcohol addicts. You should require that your employees be immunized for hepatitis and tuberculosis. If you work with intravenous (IV) drug users, be sure to educate your employees on the transmission of HIV, which can cause AIDS.

Fortunately, according to national studies, marijuana and cocaine use is declining among the age groups most at risk for substance abuse. Alcohol use remains quite prevalent, however, and the number of cocaine-related deaths is increasing. Much work remains in the war against addiction. As a prospective substance abuse counselor, you can expect to operate in a highly competitive field, put in long hours, and often see no tangible signs of success. In the long run, however, you may save many lives.

SOURCES:

Craig, Robert J., *Clinical Management of Substance Abuse Programs,* Charles C. Thomas, 1987; ''Contemporary Tends In Substance Abuse,'' *Professional Psychology Research and Practice,* May 1993.

Cottler, Linda B., ''Establishing a Substance Abuse Treatment Program,'' *Hospital and Health Services Administration,* summer 1992, pp. 237-245.

McClellan, A. Thomas, et al., ''Private Substance Abuse Treatments: Are Some Programs More Effective than Others?,'' *Journal of Substance Abuse Treatment,* Pergamon Press, May/June 1993.

Sixth, Carol, editor, *Narcotics and Drug Abuse: A-Z,* Croner Publications, 1993.

Schwartz, Carol A., editor, *Small Business Sourcebook,* sixth edition, volume 1, Gale, 1993.

The Treatment Directory: National Directory of Alcohol, Drug Abuse and Other Addictions Treatment Programs, The U.S. Journal of Drug and Alcohol Dependence, 1991.

—*Kristine Dailey*

Dry Cleaning Service

The question of what happens to your clothing after you deposit it on the dry cleaner's counter can be answered by any of the United States' nearly 50,000 dry cleaning establishments. Industry employees know that the garments are placed in large machines that operate much like washing machines using such chemicals as perchlorethylene and carbon tetrachloride rather than soap and water. Subsequent pressing is done with either large steam machines, used primarily for jackets and trousers, or industrial grade irons, used for more detailed work involving pleats and tucks. Dry cleaning has become an increasingly essential and lucrative service industry that saves consumers the time and effort involved in cleaning, pressing, and preserving their wardrobes. Since clothing manufacturers who use such popular fabrics as wool and silk often recommend the specialized cleaning process, dry cleaners are assured a relatively steady business, which is bolstered by a seasonal demand for professional care of leather and fur apparel.

Several variations on the dry cleaning theme are available to potential facility owners. You may opt to start a "drop shop" that takes in and returns cleaning performed by outside dry cleaning plants, or you may wish to establish a facility that features on-site cleaning operations. Options within these two primary types of establishments center on the volume and variety of cleaning you wish to provide. In addition to dry cleaning, on-site facilities may offer laundering services, used primarily for men's cotton dress shirts. Some provide more specialized cleaning services for draperies, leather garments, and wedding dresses, while others subcontract these services to better-equipped plants. Furthermore, some dry cleaners offer alterations and storage space for winter clothing, particularly coats.

The type of service you choose will depend on the amount of capital you have to invest; drop shops call for a relatively low initial investment but require the subcontracting of dry cleaning plants, while on-site facilities incur expenses for machinery and additional staff. Several opportunities in franchising also exist, including the most popular chain, One Hour Martinizing, whose on-site facilities are capable of one-hour service upon customer request. Franchise operations offer stiff competition to independent dry cleaners, who must vie for market share against nationally known chains.

COSTS AND PROFITS

The cost of starting up an independent, on-site dry cleaning service can range from around $75,000 for a small cleaning plant to approximately $150,000 for a larger facility featuring laundry services. The amount of monthly rent paid to lease an adequate facility, of course, depends on its size and location; in general, a facility with an area between 1,000 and 2,000 square feet is recommended. According to dry cleaner Dominick Luce, as cited in Joe Sutherland Gould's *Starting from Scratch: 50 Profitable Business Opportunities,* basic equipment can cost about $50,000 and consists of a cleaning machine and dryer—each holding around 45 pounds of clothing—as well as a spotting board, on which clothes with stains are treated with chemicals and steam. Luce estimates the average monthly cost of dry cleaning chemicals, which were delivered to his shop and pumped into the machine, at $500. Additional expenses are incurred for such supplies as hangers and plastic bags. When considering the purchase of an already established dry cleaning shop, plan to spend about one year's projected gross revenues.

A dry cleaning business usually takes from one to three years to break even. Average annual revenues ranged from $100,000 to $400,000 in the late 1980s, while the industry reported a total of nearly $4 billion in revenues. Annual pretax profits per store during this time averaged between $8,000 and $100,000.

FINANCING

As is the case with most small businesses, adequate financing for starting a dry cleaning business is imperative. Funding a foray into dry cleaning generally requires a loan from a local bank or the U.S. **Small Business Administration (SBA),** which can be reached by calling **1-800-U ASK SBA** or sending a request for information to **Small Business Directory, P.O. Box 1000, Fort Worth, Texas 76119.** In addition to needing information on your proposed business plan—which will outline your ideas for location, marketing strategy, and services offered—most banks require the prospective business owner to prove that he or she has capital equal to 30 percent of start-up costs. Some franchisors offer loans to those who qualify, or will act as guarantor of

PRIMARY ASSOCIATIONS AND SELECTED TRADE PUBLICATIONS

Associations:

International Drycleaners Congress (IDC): P.O. Box 1, Cupertino, CA 95015-3009; phone: (408) 252-1746.

International Fabricare Institute (IFI): 12251 Tech Rd., Silver Spring, MD 20904; phone: (301) 622-1900.

Neighborhood Cleaners Association: 116 E. 27th St., New York, NY 10016; phone: (212) 684-0945.

Publications:

American Drycleaner: American Trade Magazines, 500 N. Dearborn St., Chicago, IL 60610; phone: (312) 337-7700.

Drycleaners News: Zackin Publications, Inc., P.O. Box 2180, Waterbury, CT 06722-2180; phone: (203) 755-0158.

Fabricare News: International Fabricare Institute, 12251 Tech Rd., Silver Spring, MD 20904; phone: (301) 622-1900.

The National Clothesline: BPS Communications, 717 E. Chelten Ave., Philadelphia, PA 19144; phone: (215) 843-9795.

Textile Maintenance Reporter: The J.S. Henderson Corp., 1806 Treadwell St., Austin, TX 78704-2143; phone: (512) 442-8771.

Western Cleaner and Launderer: Wakefield Publishing Co., 100 N. Hill Ave., Pasadena, CA 91106-1939; phone: (818) 793-2911.

a bank loan, while others, including One Hour Martinizing, do not.

LOCATION

Dry cleaning establishments are commonly located in shopping centers or in urban areas within street blocks that have easy access to curbside or deck parking. Prime locations in suburban areas may be found near other service or retail stores, such as grocery and video stores, shoe repair shops, and banks, allowing customers to take care of several errands in one trip. In larger, urban areas, dry cleaning establishments are best situated within walking distance of apartment and office buildings, appealing to city residents and commuters who have a limited amount of time and require easy access.

LAYOUT AND SETUP

Operating a dry cleaning drop shop, from which garments are sent on to a cleaning plant, requires minimal equipment. Such stores commonly consist of a sales counter, motorized clothing racks, a cash register, and a few other necessary supplies such as laundry bags for separating clients' orders

and a filing system for arranging clothing on racks. In addition, one or more delivery vans should be maintained for transporting clothing to and from the dry cleaning plant.

Drop shops should present a friendly, pleasant, and, of course, neat appearance and enough seating for customers should lines develop during busy morning and afternoon hours. Price lists are often posted in dry cleaning establishments, and decor may incorporate posters that inform patrons of new developments in dry cleaning techniques or provide tips on how to treat different types of stains at home before bringing a garment in for cleaning.

The equipment needed for a dry cleaning drop shop is also integral to the on-site cleaning facility. The plant facility, however, requires additional space for cleaning and pressing machinery as well as for prepping areas in which buttons are refastened, sleeves are stuffed with tissue paper, and complete orders are bagged before being hung on motorized racks. *American Dry Cleaner* magazine, as quoted in Sharon Kahn's *101 Best Businesses to Start,* noted that plant facilities generally require store space of about 2,000 square feet. Nevertheless, successful establishments with smaller staffs and more limited services have operated in areas of less than 1,000 square feet. As an owner of an on-site cleaning facility, you may wish to consider installing air conditioning in your store or equipping it with a large fan, as the cleaning equipment generates an uncomfortable level of heat, particularly in summer months.

At both drop shops and on-site cleaning facilities, ample and convenient parking is essential. Most customers prefer a short, direct route from their car to the establishment in order to avoid the risk of dropping articles of clothing while walking to the store and to transport freshly cleaned clothes back to their cars quickly. To this end, one welcome store feature is the drive-through or curbside service provided by some dry cleaners, which allows customers to remain in their cars during drop-offs and pick-ups.

An alternative to the conventional dry cleaning establishment was introduced in 1987, when Paul McDonald founded Commuter Cleaners. McDonald's operation initially consisted of one truck equipped with laundry bags and a clothes rack, which he drove weekday mornings to a suburban New York train station, meeting commuters bound for Manhattan and offering them dry cleaning pick-up and delivery. Customers of McDonald's service deposited their dirty clothes in the bags he provided and then filled out an order form, keeping a copy of the form as a receipt. McDonald then brought the cleaned clothes to his customers at the train station as they awaited return trains during the late afternoon rush hour. Commuter Cleaners saved customers the time and effort involved in dropping off and picking up their dry cleaning during traditional store hours. The operation quickly expanded its line of trucks and added several new routes to suburban communities in New York and Connecticut; McDonald's projected sales for 1993 were $1 million.

An operation similar in scope to Commuter Cleaners is

Pressed 4 Time, a mobile dry cleaning operation that began franchising in 1989. This franchise also experienced rapid growth and planned to expand operations during the 1990s to Canada, Australia, and Great Britain.

STAFFING

The number of employees required by a dry cleaning establishment depends on the hours it remains open and the extent of the services provided. Drop shops typically retain a manager (often the founder), one full-time or several part-time counter clerks, and a driver. On-site cleaning facilities feature management, counter clerks, and professional cleaners and pressers. During the first few years of business, an on-site dry cleaning establishment can operate with as few as two employees, one to perform the cleaning and another to handle customers and perform miscellaneous duties. For this reason, dry cleaning is frequently begun as a family business, with spouses sharing responsibilities and perhaps receiving assistance from their children or other family members.

The new dry cleaner can expect to put in long hours during the first few years; 12-hour work days are not uncommon. The busy season for dry cleaning typically occurs from October through December, when customers require cleaning for their heavier clothing, including sweaters, suits, and winter coats. During this time, additional part-time staff may be required.

While expertise in the field can be gained only through experience, a basic knowledge of the process is relatively easy to acquire. Training courses are available from the

FRANCHISE OPPORTUNITIES

One Hour Martinizing Dry Cleaning: 2005 Ross Ave., Cincinnati, OH 45212-2009; phone: (513) 351-6211, or toll-free (800) 827-0345. One of the oldest and largest dry cleaning services in the world, One Hour Martinizing has achieved national recognition, offering customers one-hour service through on-site cleaning facilities. The company was founded in 1949 and has expanded to include a network of more than 850 outlets in 15 countries. Franchising opportunities are available through parent company Martin Franchises, Inc., which requires its franchisees to have a minimum net worth of $150,000. Approximately $65,000 of the franchisee's net worth must be in liquid assets.

Other Franchisors: A-1 Discount Cleaners: 4105 S. 84th St., Omaha, NE 68217. **Clean 'N' Press Franchise, Inc.:** 655 Montgomery, Ste. 1200, San Francisco, CA 94111. **Dry Cleaning World:** 1234 Brittain Rd., Akron, OH 44310. **Dryclean—U.S.A., Inc.:** 12515 N. Kendall Dr., Ste. 400, Miami, FL 33186. **Jim Dandy Discount Dry Cleaning Stores:** 15155 Stagg St., Van Nuys, CA 91405. **Pressed 4 Time:** 48 Mechanic St., Newton, MA 02164-1436. **Star Cleaners:** 2502 N. Rocky Point Dr., Ste. 655, Tampa, FL 33607.

International Fabricare Institute (IFI) in Silver Spring, Maryland, which offers intensive three-week courses in cleaning, spotting, finishing, management, plant maintenance, and other operations. The Neighborhood Cleaner's Association in New York City also offers similar training over a period of ten weeks. Many franchises have instituted their own training programs, stressing that no prior experience in the field is necessary.

Most dry cleaners become members of the IFI, which develops new cleaning processes through the various studies it conducts on textiles and chemicals. For a fee, the Institute also offers its members an analysis of a specific stain to determine its content and the best means of removing it. In this capacity, the IFI is sometimes called upon to determine the origins of a stain in case a dispute arises between the dry cleaner and the customer. According to David Horowitz and Dana Shilling in their 1985 book *The Business of Business: How 100 Businesses Really Work,* "about one-sixth of the problems [analyzed by the IFI] were blamed on dry cleaners, the rest on careless manufacturers or owners."

MARKETING

The market for dry cleaning services experiences mild fluctuations in response to general trends in the fashion industry. During the 1970s, or example, when the leisure suit, made of polyester or other "wash and wear" synthetic fabrics, gained popularity, the demand for dry cleaning declined. Fortunately for both the industry and consumers, this trend was brief.

In the 1980s fashion in the business world returned to more traditional fabrics. The emergence of the young urban professional, or yuppie, signaled renewed concern for a clean and neatly pressed conservative appearance in the workplace. Yuppies valued dry cleaning services for their ability to clean the requisite three-piece suit and for the time saved in having someone else attend to clothing maintenance. Also during the 1980s, dry cleaning benefited from the increasing number of women entering the professional work force. Books and articles advising women on how to "dress for success" promoted wool and linen business suits as well as silk blouses and ties as appropriate office wear, all of which require dry cleaning.

Despite the ever-changing fashion industry, dry cleaning has remained a stable and profitable industry. People simply have less time to clean and press their own clothes, and more fabrics are requiring the special care afforded by the dry cleaner. Commenting on the effects of the national economy on the dry cleaning industry, Ken Faig of the International Fabricare Institute, was quoted in *101 Best Businesses to Start* as stating, "No business is depression proof, but this comes close. . . . In bad times, people don't buy clothes and have to keep the old ones in good shape."

ADVERTISING

Advertising budgets in the dry cleaning industry are typically small, as many independent dry cleaners rely solely on careful work and satisfactory customer service to draw and maintain a clientele. Dry cleaners can gain a customers' trust by presenting them with impeccably cleaned and pressed clothing—avoiding the common problem of double creases in trouser legs, for example—as well as by exhibiting expertise in the area of stain removal. Customers appreciate learning more about the service and how they can help treat their clothing before bringing it in to the dry cleaner. Furthermore, an honest approach in advising a customer on whether or not a garment actually needs to be dry-cleaned can result in better business relations.

Special price rates and coupons have also proved effective in bringing in a clientele, representing a method favored by the United States' many franchise dry cleaners, particularly in areas with strong competition. For example, in addition to regular coupon mailings, One Hour Martinizing has offered special incentive plans in conjunction with other companies, such as Royal Caribbean cruise lines: Book a cruise and receive a certificate worth $50 in dry cleaning services. The Clean 'N' Press dry cleaning franchise of Phoenix, Arizona, was founded as a discount cleaners, offering prices more than 50 percent below the industry average. While such large-scale programs and offers tend to be the domain of the larger franchise companies, similar local programs can also prove profitable for the independent cleaner. Coupons featured in local newspapers or in direct mail coupon packages tend to draw a positive response.

DRY CLEANING AND THE ENVIRONMENT

In the late 1980s and early 1990s, increasing concern about the effects of dry cleaning on both human health and the environment resulted in government regulations on the industry. After extensive research, the Environmental Protection Agency (EPA) determined that one chemical commonly used by dry cleaners, perchloroethlene (perc), is a potentially hazardous substance. Protective measures to ensure the safety of employees and the communities surrounding dry cleaning plants were enacted as a part of the Clean Air Act.

Specifically, dry cleaners were required to equip their machines with refrigerated condensers to help curb the dangerous emissions generated from perc. The carbon vapor absorber, a mechanism previously used by some dry cleaners to help combat perc emissions, was deemed less efficient than the refrigerated condenser and was therefore considered unacceptable for new businesses starting up in 1993. However, a grandfather clause allowed dry cleaners already equipped with carbon vapor absorbers before that year to retain this method of control.

As a result of the new regulations, all dry cleaning establishments were required to file an Initial Notification form in 1993, informing the EPA of their current practices and equipment. Furthermore, the act stipulated that dry cleaners keep detailed records of repairs made to their machines, particularly those involving chemical leaks. Government inspections of dry cleaning facilities were also initiated during this time, and failure to comply with the act resulted in fines and potential legal action.

EPA regulations meant added expenses for the owner of a dry cleaning establishment. Accurate assessments of the costs involved in updating and maintaining equipment as well as in the additional recordkeeping were not yet available in the early 1990s. Some industry analysts suggested that prompt efforts to comply with the regulations might result in improved business, since customers and employees would be afforded a safer environment.

Despite these environmental concerns, analysts regard dry cleaning as a profitable industry in which opportunity is afforded even those with no prior experience. The service remains in great demand, and with some training, hard work, and a commitment to satisfying customers, dry cleaners have generally found that the experience proves rewarding.

SOURCES:

Encyclopedia of Associations, 25th edition, Gale, 1991.

Friedlander, Mark P., Jr., and Gene Gurney, *Handbook of Successful Franchising,* Liberty Hall Press, 1990.

Gould, Joe Sutherland, *Starting from Scratch: 50 Profitable Business Opportunities,* John Wiley & Sons, 1987.

Horowitz, David, and Dana Shilling, *The Business of Business: How 100 Businesses Really Work,* Harper & Row, 1989.

Ingram, Leah, "Wash 'N' Go," *Entrepreneur,* July 1993.

Jones, Constance, *The 220 Best Franchises to Buy,* Bantam, 1993.

Kahn, Sharon, *101 Best Businesses to Start,* Doubleday, 1988.

Schwartz, Carol A., editor, *Small Business Sourcebook,* sixth edition, volume 1, Gale, 1993.

—*TINA GRANT*

Environmental Store

Environmental stores first appeared in the early 1970s in Berkeley, California, and began proliferating throughout the United States some 20 years later. In the early 1990s America's environmental consciousness was sparked after several ecological disasters occurred—including a major oil spill off the coast of Alaska, increased concern over scientific evidence of a hole in the earth's protective ozone layer, and the massive oil well fires set in Kuwait by fleeing Iraqi troops after the 1991 Persian Gulf War. After the highly publicized twentieth anniversary of Earth Day in 1990, the number of "green" stores—selling everything from environmentally friendly detergents and cosmetics to t-shirts that support environmental consciousness—soared from a handful to more than 300 just four years later.

The burgeoning environmental industry, which averages a 25 percent growth rate annually, offers vast opportunities for the creative and savvy entrepreneur. Green specialty retailers, unlike conventional retailers, provide customers with expertise as well as convenience. Many analysts argue that environmental retailers will maintain this advantage even as mainstream stores increase their stocks of environmental products. To succeed, the ecological entrepreneur need only find the right niche in a market which offers tens of thousands of environmentally friendly products.

START-UP COSTS

Start-up costs will probably run between $20,000 and $100,000 depending on size and location, though franchises may cost more. You should draw up a detailed business plan, which includes your short- and long-term goals, your assets, and how you wish to allocate your resources. A well-planned strategy will help you make more accurate financing and marketing decisions and will also allow you to evaluate your progress in the future. In drafting an expense list for capital investment, include all office equipment, display fixtures, security systems, insurance, and salaries. For variable expenses include federal and state taxes, health care plans, customer service, and utilities. Consult with the **Small Business Administration (SBA)** for advice about starting your business and getting loan guarantees (call **1-800-U**

ASK SBA). Check with state and local environmental agencies on eligibility requirements for low interest loans and tax deductions.

If you wish to take out a loan but have not established an adequate credit rating you may do so by simply taking out a small loan and repaying it immediately. When you apply for a business loan, present your business plan to the lending officer in person. To improve your chances of getting a loan you should also provide your lender evidence of your experience, your reputation as a reliable business person, and your ability to fulfill obligations. Win the lender's confidence in you and your project.

Be creative with financing. One green retailer, for instance, collected enough investment capital by offering future customers $120 in store credit in exchange for each $100 investment. Only resort to "plastic," or credit-card financing if you are sure you can repay the amount within a short period. Also, do not invest in luxury setups until you have generated enough sales.

To determine inventory costs consult with local distributors about their prices. As a potential client they should be willing to help you. Some green retailers reduce their margins of profit to be more cost-competitive with conventional stores. However, this may not be necessary as demand for green products increases and costs decline.

LOCATION

Selecting a good site is crucial. A corner location, especially at a major intersection, is best for maximum visibility. You could also benefit from a site near a busy supermarket. Find a location with adequate parking either on-site or nearby. Research your prospective neighborhood to find out about the demographic makeup, the buying trends among consumers of various ages and incomes, and the potential for market growth. Keep in mind that some environmental goods are priced slightly higher than comparable goods and thus may appeal to middle- and higher-income groups. Good sources for demographic statistics are local chambers of commerce, the Small Business Administration, and the *Statistical Abstract of the United States,* which is published by the U.S. Census Bureau.

PRIMARY ASSOCIATIONS AND SELECTED TRADE PUBLICAITONS

Associations:

Association of Corporate Environmental Officers (CEO): P.O. Box 4117, Timonium, MD 21093; phone: (301) 561-9296, or (800) 876-6618; fax: (301) 561-9738.

Environmental Management Association: 255 Detroit St., Ste. 200, Denver, CO 80206; phone: (303) 320-7855; fax: (303) 393-0770.

National Association of Environmental Professionals: P.O. Box 15210, Alexandria, VA 22309-0210; phone: (703) 660-2364.

Organic Food Alliance (OFA): c/o James Holt, 2111 Wilson Blvd., Ste. 531, Arlington, VA 22201; phone: (703) 276-9498.

Organic Foods Production Association of North America (OFPNA): P.O. Box 1078, Greenfield, MA 01301; phone: (413) 774-7511; fax: (413) 774-6432.

Publications:

Directory of Environmentally Sound Products: Department of Purchasing and Supply, City Hall, 100 Queen St. W., 18th Fl., West Tower, Toronto, ON, Canada M5H 2N2; phone: (416) 392-7311, fax: (416) 392-0801.
Environment: 4000 Albemarle St. NW, Washington, DC 20016-1851; phone: (202) 362-6445.
Environmental Report: National Press Bldg., Washington, DC 20045; phone: (202) 393-0031, or (202) 393-1732.
Garbage: P.O. Box 56519, Boulder, CO 80322-6519; phone: (800) 274-9909.
The Green Consumer: Find/SVP, 625 Avenue of the Americas, New York, NY 10011; phone: (212) 645-4500, or (800) 346-3787; fax: (212) 645-7681.
In Business: The Magazine for Environmental Entrepreneuring: 419 State Avenue, Emmaus, PA 18049; phone: (215) 967-4135.

A good indicator of a neighborhood's environmental awareness is the number of active environmental groups in the vicinity. By all means consult with these organizations for information on the local residents. They will probably be willing to assist you and may provide you with invaluable information about starting your business.

Ideally you will find a location that puts enough distance between you and potential competitors. If not, you should carve out a unique niche for yourself and begin to think about how you can improve on the services your competition provides—or if you can supply something your competitors do not. Once you have chosen your location you might want to demonstrate your environmental commitment to customers by joining local environmental organizations and attending seminars and conferences in the area.

STORE LAYOUT AND SETUP

Unless you have sufficient business experience and investment capital you should start out with a small retail space of about 700 square feet. Of course, it's easier to operate profitably in a smaller area if you intend to sell small items like cosmetics. If you wish to offer a larger selection of household, business, and recreational goods you will probably need closer to 2,000 square feet.

Create a pleasant and distinctive atmosphere for your customers. The Greenpeace Environmental Store in Los Angeles, for example, looks like a rain forest. Present your products creatively, display rock and mineral collections, or play sounds-of-nature music tapes. Make your store a haven for a fun and sophisticated shopping experience. Set up displays attractively and efficiently using environmentally safe materials and fixtures like non-toxic linoleum floors, recycled metals for shelving, and energy-efficient bulbs. Avoid fluorescent lights, which tend to wash out colors.

Arrange product categories strategically using color schemes to distinguish between different sections. Place sales items and ''impulse'' goods, like preservative-free candy and nontoxic pens, near the front of the store by the cash registers. Staple items should be located towards the back of the store. Provide a restroom for customer convenience and for promoting environmental products like soaps, tissues, and air fresheners. Let your customers know that all aspects of your store are environmentally sound.

Do not neglect the exterior of your store—use it as advertising space to attract passersby. Think of a unique ecologically related store name and logo and post them clearly. Paint the door and the trim in a bright attractive color or design. Indicate that the paint is environmentally safe and that you stock it in your store or that it can be special ordered. Be creative with the window displays and change them seasonally and for holidays and special events, such as Earth Day and Arbor Day. Coordinate window colors with those in the back of your store where you stock staple items so that you attract customers towards that area. If you are not artistic, hire a local art student to help.

FINDING YOUR MARKET NICHE

While you are scouting around for a location you should also be thinking about which types of goods will be most marketable in the area. You may discover product ideas you had not thought of earlier. Consult with local wholesalers and distributors for advice about appropriate types and quantities of stock. Contact environmental trade associations; they might be able to direct you to local brokers or recycling companies that want to market new products. Visit environmental exhibitions such as Eco Expo, which showcases the largest selection of green products, ideas, and services in the country. Exhibitions may help you get product ideas as well as establish links with green manufacturers and distributors.

Carl Frankel, publisher of *Green MarketAlert,* believes that ''small suppliers are trying to carve out a niche with 'deep green' products developed especially for the green market, while mainstream suppliers are working on improved packaging or coming out with new lines." Having researched the market thoroughly, use your expertise to determine which product niche will work best for you.

Determine whether you will offer general-store type goods or will specialize in a particular segment. Practical household items, for instance, would include recycled paper products, concentrated detergents, energy-saving light bulbs, and rechargeable batteries. You could offer nontoxic gardening products or focus instead on pet care. Sales are booming in the health and beauty aids segment, which includes special baby care products, medications, and cruelty-free (not tested on animals) cosmetics. Natural foods are also a popular green market, with items like preservative-free cereals, chemical-free produce, and other organic groceries.

Another new and expanding field is eco-clothing, with sales of $20 million in 1992 and projected sales of more than $80 million within four years. This category includes environmentally friendly clothing, sheets, and towels made of organic cotton and other natural fibers and colored with natural dyes rather than chemicals or bleaches. Other retail options might include arts and crafts made by indigenous

peoples, jewelry made of recycled metal, or global textiles. An environmental store geared toward children might specialize as a science-oriented learning center, offering products like instructional books, discovery kits with telescopes and star charts, and computer software. Or it could be a game-oriented kids store featuring environmentally safe and nonviolent toys.

Durable environmental goods, such as energy-efficient appliances like toasters, refrigerators, air conditioners, and washing machines, are another viable option. Or you could become a retailer on the cutting edge of the green market and specialize in introducing new and unusual items like recycled carpeting. You may have ambitions to start your own private label, or a franchise. Check with environmental journals for more information on existing franchises. If you are really ambitious you could open your own environmental mall, like Fred Segal's in Santa Monica, with a variety of green retailers.

STAFF SELECTION

Seek out knowledgeable staff members who care about the environment but will not become too didactic or preachy with customers. Screen out applicants in your ads to save you time and trouble in your personal interviews with them. You should train your staff well, demonstrating how you expect them to treat customers.

Your attitude toward your staff is very important. Win their loyalty and enthusiasm about your store by giving them an adequate salary and offering occasional bonuses. Be as courteous and responsive to your staff as you expect them to be to your clients. Unless you plan to be at your store full time, consider training someone as manager. And be prepared for greater business activity during holiday seasons, particularly around December, by hiring some part-time staff members. Incidentally, environmental gift items priced under $25 are especially popular.

ENVIRONMENTAL AWARENESS

While an environmental store is first and foremost a business, most green retailers also get involved in conservation efforts, and educate their customers about the products they sell. Some shoppers need to be reassured about a product's environmental benefits because of false advertising by some mainstream brands. Test the products yourself. Read environmental publications and trade journals to keep informed about environmental trends and events, new products and technology, changes in environmental legislation, and who's who in the environmental world. Encourage your staff to stay informed as well.

Keep in mind that a number of green consumers are highly knowledgeable about the environment themselves— and you could also learn from them. Be responsive to their concerns and seek out their advice so you can improve your operations. Set up an information desk or bulletin board on environmental activities and allow groups to leave bro-

---

FRANCHISE OPPORTUNITIES

Ecology House: P.O. Box 40428, Portland, OR 97240; phone: (503) 223-1842; Founded, 1983; began franchising, 1987; one company-owned unit; five franchised units; located in or near major U.S. cities; features environmentally themed gifts, such as t-shirts, toys, jewelry, sculptures, books, and environmental products like water-saving devices, rechargeable batteries, and energy-saving light fixtures. Provided by franchiser: two weeks hands-on training at a franchise, operations manual, point-of-sale computer software. Franchising fee, $20,000; royalties, 5%; total investment, $123,000-$211,000. No direct financing.

The Body Shop: 45 Horsehill Road, Cedar Knolls, NJ 07927; phone: (201) 984-9200. Founded, 1988; began franchising, 1990; over 167 outlets worldwide; features environmentally friendly and cruelty-free skin- and hair-care products; Franchising fee, $40,000; no royalties first three years, 3% fourth year, 5% fifth and following years.

The Gifted Gift Co.: 161 W. 61st St., Ste. 5D, New York, NY 10023; phone: (212) 262-2557. Founded, 1990; features art products made from recycled materials and designed by artists; product line called O Zonics. Franchising fee, $20,000; royalties, 5%; total investment, about $10,000.

Naturesafe Store: 133 E. De la Guerra #423, Santa Barbara, CA 93101; phone: (805) 682-9455. Founded, 1990; two outlets; features environmentally safe and nature-oriented products. Franchising fee, $5,000-$15,000; royalties, 5%; total minimum investment, $65,000.

INDUSTRY STATISTICS

- *Environmental Store Industry Sales (1993):* $36 million (source: *New York Times,* June 14, 1993).
- *Projected Environmental Store Sales (1997):* $95 million (source: *New York Times,* June 14, 1993).
- *Green Consumer Products Market (1992):* $110 billion (source: *Advertising Age,* May 10, 1993).
- *Projected Sales of Green Consumer Products:* (1993) $121.5 billion; (1994) $127 billion; (1995) $137 billion; (1996) $143 billion; (1997) $154 billion (source: *Los Angeles Times,* April 22, 1993).
- *Sales of Green Household Products (1991):* $2.1 billion, 7.1% of $30 billion household products market (*Research Alert,* April 10, 1992).
- *Projected Annual Growth Rate of Green Household Products (1993)* 30% annually through 1990s (source: *Research Alert,* January 1, 1993).
- *Sales of "Deep Green" Health and Beauty Aids:* (1991) $1.7 billion; (1996 projection) $4.8 billion (source: *Research Alert*).
- *Global Market of Environmental Products, Services, and Technologies:* $500 billion annually by year 2000 (projection; source: *Business Wire,* October 13, 1993).
- *Consumer Concern About Cost:* given two equal products, 89 percent of respondents preferred the environment-friendly selection, but only 20 percent were willing to pay 10 to 15 percent extra (source: *WWD,* July 16, 1993).
- *Green Catalogue Market:* (1994) $48 million; (1997 projection) $115 million (source: *DM News,* February 7, 1994).
- *Gender Differences in Purchasing Environmentally Packaged Soft Drinks (1993):* 27% of women actively sought out environmentally packaged items compared to 16% of men (source: *Super Marketing,* June 4, 1993).

chures or petitions. If you have enough space you could also provide some chairs, a table, and some environmental literature for customers and people waiting for other shoppers. Eventually you may use the space for evening readings with guest speakers, or as a meeting place for activists.

MARKETING STRATEGIES

There are a number of ways to promote your store and your products without having to rely on paid advertising. Nearly everything you say and do as a retailer is a potential advertisement. Remind your customers of your commitment to the environment through self-promotion, publicity, and media events. Provide free brochures to customers on environmental facts and statistics. Stage a community event, perhaps in collaboration with a local environmental group, and get the press interested. Be sure you are promoting a substantive issue and not just creating hype to promote your business. You can also have special sales in which you donate a percentage of your proceeds to nonprofit organizations, as a number of green retailers frequently do.

Another way stir up interest in your store is to write articles for local papers about newsworthy events and ideas. Present some new or controversial information or write about an unusual and exciting product that you happen to sell. To capture the attention of the editor or reporter you send your press release to, make your press release lively, upbeat, and interesting. Address your letter to specific editors and reporters so it will not get lost in the mail room of the newspaper or magazine. When your article is published, frame it and put it on the wall in your store, or use it as a newsletter and provide free copies to customers.

Get people to talk about your store enthusiastically. Offer promotional giveaways, like reusable shopping bags, t-shirts, and hats with your store name and logo. If you can afford to, start up a mail-order catalog. Offer special services, like bridal registries; you can make larger orders more attractive by discounting prices based on volume. Finally, keep abreast of how and why your competition is or is not successful and learn from their experiences.

RISK MANAGEMENT

Be sure you have all the necessary licenses and insurance you need for your area. You should have an adequate security system; install a sprinkler system, a burglar alarm, and, if necessary, window grating. To prevent shoplifting, keep the racks low and arrange them so that staffers can see the aisles. Place convex wall mirrors in corners and keep small expensive items behind the cash counter or locked in display cases. Keep in mind that about 30 percent of small business losses are due to petty thefts committed by employees. You can help to avoid this by keeping a good rapport with your staff.

COMPUTER DATABASES

Environmental marketing information can be accessed through a number of on-line databases, such as *Business and the Environment,* which provides data on trends in the environmental industry. Other good databases are *Green Marketing Report, Outdoor Forum,* and *Natural Products ALERT. FidoNet* connects 10,000 bulletin board services on a variety of topics, from nature trips to hazardous waste

ENVIRONMENTAL ORGANIZATIONS

Environmental Defense Fund: 257 Park Ave. So., New York, NY 10010; phone: (212) 505-2100.

Environmental Protection Agency: 401 M St. SW, Washington, DC 20460; phone: (202) 382-2090.

Greenpeace USA: 1436 U St. NW, Washington, DC 20009; phone: (202) 462-1177, or (202) 462-8817.

National Wildlife Federation: 1400 16th St. NW, Washington, DC 20036; phone: (202) 797-6800.

National Resources Defense Council: 40 W. 20th St., New York, NY 10011; phone: (212) 727-4400.

National Recycling Coalition: 1101 30th St. NW, Suite 305, Washington, DC 20006; phone: (202) 625-6406.

management. For on-line conversations between individual environmentalists, check with San Francisco-based *WELL* (Whole Earth 'Lectronic Link). CD-ROM databases include the *Natural Resources Metabase* and *Enviro/Energyline Abstracts Plus,* featuring multidisciplinary global literature on the environment.

SOURCES:

Bennett, Steven J., *Ecopreneuring: The Complete Guide to Small Business Opportunities from the Environmental Revolution,* John Wiley & Sons, 1991.

Campbell, Tom, "Green Movement Blossoms Into a New Leaf for Retailers," *Business First-Buffalo,* May 6, 1991, sec. 1, p. 1.

Ebisch, Robert, "Retail Goes 'Green'," *Boulder County Business Report,* May 1992, sec. 1, p. 13.

EcoLinking: Everyone's Guide to Online Environmental Information, Peachpit Press.

Emerson, Jim, "Real Goods Begins Consolidation Of Earth Care Paper's Operations," *DM News,* February 7, 1994, p. 12.

Harrison, Barbara, "Business and the Environment: Fashions in Green—Eco-Clothing Is a Long-Term Trend, Not a Fad," *Financial Times,* June 9, 1993, p. 18.

MacEachern, Diane, "Tips for Planet Earth," *Washington Post,* February 18, 1993, p. T8.

Manning, Anita, "Eco-Stores Catch Customers' Fancy," *USA Today,* June 27, 1991.

Martin, Douglas, "Save a Planet, Make a Buck: The 'Green' Industry Ripens," *New York Times,* June 14, 1993.

Parrish, Michael, "'Green' Business Policies Pay Off; Earth Day," *Los Angeles Times,* April 22, 1993, Business sec., Part D, p. 1.

Wolcott, John, "Retailers Answer Nature's Call," *Puget Sound Business Journal,* sec., 1, p. 4, November 13, 1992.

—*AUDRA AVIZIENIS*

Executive Recruiting Service

How would you like to start a business that requires no product inventory and a low start-up investment—a business that in a few years could earn you status, prestige, and six-figure profits? An executive recruiting service, which acts as a broker between employer and potential employee, offers a potentially lucrative opportunity for the entrepreneur. But unlike an "employment service," an executive recruiting firm receives its fee (typically about one-third of the annual salary of the person to be hired) from the employer. This "people placing" type of business will not only make you feel good about providing benefits for both employers and employees, but also about the connections you make along the way and the profits you earn as a result.

The executive recruiting industry got its start around the time of World War II but did not begin booming until the 1970s and 1980s, when more and more corporations began recognizing the need for outside placement assistance that preserves confidentiality and helps fill management openings. With the growing significance of small businesses, which often lacked personnel expertise, and the move towards corporate downsizing, which meant more available executives and fewer human resource departments, there was an increasing potential for success in executive recruiting in the 1990s. As a result, the prospective executive recruiter possessing adequate financing, a flair for sales and marketing, and a talent for research and screening had an opportunity to make money matching managers with companies.

COSTS, PROFITS, AND FINANCING

Minimum start-up costs for an executive recruiting service run in the range of $16,000, while average costs are about $27,000. Though some executive recruiting services report pretax profits of more than $250,000, most earn closer to $80,000. Liabilities are limited, especially if you start from a home-based office and operate your service by yourself; this would make advertising your primary ongoing expense. In addition, because it will take time to build client and candidate contacts and then conduct subsequent searches, you will probably need approximately eight months operating capital to see you through until your first successful executive placement.

When considering financing, keep in mind that to get an executive recruiting service off the ground you will probably need more money for operating capital than start-up expenses. To determine specifically how much money you will need and how to go about getting it, you should discuss your project with any contacts you might have in the banking and commercial lending fields who would advise you free of charge. More than likely, your best sources of pre-financing information will be the professional associations and trade publications that serve executive recruiters.

When dealing with a commercial lender, your own professionalism can go a long way toward making a favorable impression. After all, "you" will be your business, and a bank executive may very likely view your conduct as representative of how you will go about landing clients. In addition, it will help if you have significant personal assets and a clean credit history, as well as previous business ownership or management experience. A bank officer will also be looking at other factors to determine if you could run a viable executive recruiting service and thus be a reliable borrower. S/he will be interested in details of your marketing strategy and your ability to successfully implement a business plan; in this area, sales experience or a background in human resources could help a great deal. You will also need to compose the record-keeping procedures you will use to track financial activity and your proposed timetable for repayment.

While in the process of determining your financial needs and exploring financing options, you should contact the U.S. **Small Business Administration (SBA)** about loan eligibility requirements. In order to receive an SBA loan, though, you must have been unable to secure financing on reasonable terms elsewhere. Still, the agency can provide a wealth of business information and also serve as a potential source of financing down the road. To request SBA information and/or inquire about loan eligibility requirements, call **1-800-U ASK SBA,** or write: **Small Business Directory, P.O. Box 1000, Ft. Worth, TX 76119.**

INDUSTRY STATISTICS

- *Percentage of Executive Searches by Candidate Compensation:* (More than $200,000) 22%; ($100,000-199,000) 49%; ($60,000-99,000) 20%; (under $60,000) 9%.
- *Percentage of Executive Searches by Function:* (President and chief executive officer) 26%; (marketing and sales) 18%; (finance and administration) 13%; (special services) 13%.
- *Percentage of Executive Searches by Region:* (International) 24%; (Northeast) 24%; (Midwest) 18%; (South) 11%; (West) 11%; (Southwest) 5%; (Canada) 5%.
- *Leading Industry Users of Executive Search Firms and Their Percentage of Total Searches:* (Banking and finance) 21%; (professional services) 8%; (consumer products) 7%; (electronics and aerospace) 7%; (hospitals and health care) 6%; (pharmaceuticals, chemicals, plastics and medicines) 6%.
- *Growth in Executive Search Activity:* (4th quarter of 1992 to 4th quarter of 1993) 13%.
- *Growth (Reduction) in Executive Search Activity by Region:* 4th quarter of 1992 to 4th quarter of 1993: (Northeast) 23%; (Midwest) 39%; (South) 34%; (international) 29%; (West) -9%.

(SOURCE: MEMBERSHIP SURVEY OF EXECUTIVE SEARCH ACTIVITIES OF THE FOURTH QUARTER, 1993, CONDUCTED BY ASSOCIATION OF EXECUTIVE SEARCH CONSULTANTS.)

LOCATION

Because most executive search activity occurs in metropolitan areas, the ideal location for an executive recruiting service office would be in a large city or growing suburb, in a building that will enhance your professional image. Because executive recruiters typically use their office to consult with company clients and interview potential management candidates (and because appearances are important in the industry), a site in a high-rise office building—where your neighbors might be law firms, accounting agencies, and other professional services—could actually improve your prestige and ability to secure contracted searches.

Regardless of whether you choose to start from an office or your home, you will definitely need to be close to both clients and candidates, although a search for executive talent may occasionally take you out of your region. The area you choose should have a population of at least 100,000 and an economic base that has a sizable and diverse work force capable of supporting top management talent and of offering competitive salaries. You should also keep in mind that when seeking a location, the smaller the area, the less viable your business will be in the face of existing competition.

OFFICE LAYOUT AND SETUP

While contact with potential clients is essential, many independent executive recruiters start their business from home, meeting with prospective clients and candidates over meals or in client offices and later moving into an office as profits warrant. In the beginning you should need no more than 600 square feet, and a home-office of that size—particularly one that has a separate outside entrance and is well furnished—should be sufficient to get started.

While the decor of your office should be tasteful and professional in appearance, your equipment and furnishing needs will be minimal. An attractive set of furniture, including desks, chairs, tables, filing cabinets, and book shelves, should be almost all you need. To give your office style, you might buy a variety of large plants, as well as a few prints for your walls, which should be painted in neutral colors. Your equipment needs will also include a phone system. If working out of your home, you can purchase a quality answering machine, or better yet, hire a service that will answer calls using your company's name.

The ideal office will include separate rooms for phone work (to contact clients and search candidates), research work (to locate sources of candidates, screen candidates, and check their backgrounds), and interviewing candidates. Each of these phases of executive search and recruitment requires access to client and candidate records, which could all be placed on a multi-user database in a computerized filing system and be accessible to your staff from any area of your office.

While a computer system is technically an optional start-up cost, it could provide numerous benefits. In addition to speeding typing and billing processes, a computer with the proper software can generate an up-to-date executive candidate list for specific industries, which could become a major marketing tool. When investing in software, make sure to purchase both spreadsheet and database-management programs.

Another recruiter resource that is standard if not essential is a comprehensive business library. If you are unable to afford buying one, your office should be located near a large public or university library that houses such business reference books as *Standard & Poor's* and *Dun & Bradstreet,* both of which are used to locate top-notch executive candidates.

Your only "inventory" needs will fall under the category of paper products. In addition to standard office supplies, you should invest in business cards, letterhead stationary, printed envelopes, and promotional brochures. When selecting paper goods and choosing typefaces, opt for neutral colors and standard type fonts. Shop around to get the best buy; you can contact appropriate local services and suppliers by looking in the Yellow Pages under "Office Supplies," "Printers," or "Graphic Designers."

STAFFING AND MANAGEMENT

The staff of an executive recruiting service will typically be engaged in three types of work activities: soliciting accounts, researching candidates, and recruiting candidates. Areas of responsibility are rarely mutually exclusive, and in the initial stages of your business, you should be able to handle all of them yourself, while perhaps utilizing answering and secretarial services.

As an account executive, you will need to build your business by selling your service to client companies, a process that will involve maintaining records on potential clients, making endless cold calls, tapping contacts you have through various civic, professional, and trade organizations, and following up on leads you receive about companies that could become clients. Once you have landed a commissioned search, you will need to conduct research to find out what candidates are available and then to verify those candidates' qualifications. You can farm out much of this phase of operations, although initially it would be wise to learn the ropes of research yourself. There are a number of newslet-

PRIMARY ASSOCIATIONS AND SELECTED PUBLICATIONS AND BUSINESS RESOURCES

Associations:

National Association of Executive Recruiters (NAER): 222 S. Westmonte Dr., Suite 101, Altamonte Springs, FL 32714; phone: (407) 774-7880. Membership includes executive recruitment and search specialist firms; NAER's mission is to promote and enhance the public image, awareness, and understanding of the executive search profession; publishes directory, quarterly report, brochures.

Association of Executive Search Consultants (AESC): 151 Railroad Avenue, Greenwich, CT 06830; phone: (203) 661-6606. Professional association representing over 110 search firms and 2,500 consultants; AESC's mission is to establish, maintain, and enforce professional standards in the executive search industry; activities include compiling statistics.

Publications and Business Resources:

Executive Recruiter News: Kennedy & Kennedy, Inc., Templeton Rd., Fitzwilliam, NH 03447; phone: (603) 585-2200. Monthly newsletter covering industry trends and developments.

Recruitment Today: 245 Fischer Ave., B-2, Costa Mesa, CA 92626; phone: (714) 751-1883. Bimonthly magazine covering all aspects of the recruitment process.

Employment Marketplace Resource Directory: Employment Marketplace, P.O. Box 31112, St. Louis, MO 63131; phone: (314) 569-3095. Directory of firms and organizations supplying information, products, or services to the personnel and employment industry.

Executive Search Research Directory: The Recruiting & Search Report, Box 9433, Panama City Beach, FL 32407; phone: (800) 634-4548. Annual with quarterly updates covering researchers or research firms specializing in candidate locating, screening, and development.

Recruiting Trends: Remy Publishing Co., 350 W. Hubbard St., Ste. 440, Chicago, IL 60610; phone: (312) 332-3571. Monthly covering trends and practices in recruiting for hard-to-fill technical positions.

ters that sell candidate lists, as well as various free-lance and independent research operations. Probably the best sources of information on newsletters and research firms are the industry's trade publications and professional associations.

After compiling a substantial working list of potential candidates for a position, you will begin recruiting. Generally candidates will be unaware that they are being considered for a position. You must call them at home or at work—employing diplomacy and tact—and assess whether or not their interests and abilities mesh with the position you are seeking to fill. Because you will be calling out of the blue, it is extremely important to be able to give the name of a referring person to the candidate you are calling. You will usually interview those considered to be the best candidates and then weigh their verified experience and background—as well their personalities—against the needs and chemistry of the company client. After compiling a short list of top-notch, pre-screened candidates, you will pass it on to the company client and then facilitate interviews, acting as a go-between when necessary during subsequent negotiations.

In terms of workload, one recruiter can typically handle about five searches at a time, although this will vary according to the nature of the searches being performed and the amount of additional duties of the recruiter. If you are the sole operator of your service, you might want to consider hiring a part-time secretary to screen calls, sort mail, and maintain client and candidate records. However, it could be more cost-effective initially to locate a good secretarial service that can handle your written communications, record-keeping, and billing work, and also turn out high-quality letters and proposals on short notice.

As your business grows and you can afford it, you may want to hire a part- or full-time ''junior executive'' or trainee to assist you in answering the phone, handling various research and clerical duties, and making initial contact with candidates. An assistant could free you up to concentrate on courting company clients, paring down candidate lists, and working directly with companies as they interview your ''short list'' choices and move towards hiring a candidate.

Just as you would benefit from a background in sales, marketing, and human resources, so too would anyone you hire to assist you. Additionally a recruiter should be out-going and detail-minded. Those who have worked in personnel departments or college placement offices would be ideal; as a matter of fact, when looking for a part-time assistant you may want to hire a graduate student majoring in business administration or marketing.

Wages for executive recruiters vary; some recruiters are paid only a commission for placements, while others are paid a salary (junior account executive salaries generally start between $20,000 and $30,000) plus bonuses (25 to 30 percent of the profits from a successful placement). Many recruiting service owners feel that paying a salary plus a commission will attract better employees and also ensure that a recruiting assistant won't rush through searches and

FRANCHISE OPPORTUNITIES

Bailey Employment System: 51 Shelton Rd., Monroe, CT 06468-2415; phone: (800) 627-2712.

Bryant Bureau: 12801 N. Central Expressway, Ste. 700, Dallas, TX 75243; phone: (214) 239-7575.

Fortune Personnel Consultants: 655 3rd Ave., Ste. 1805, New York, NY 10017; phone: (800) 221-4867.

Future Centres: The Old Mill, Northgrove Rd., Hawkhurst, Kent TN13 4AP, England; phone: 580 752619.

The Hayes Group: 3020 E. Camelback Rd., Ste. 367, Phoenix, AZ 85016; phone: (602) 956-9010.

HRI Services, Inc.: 150 Wood Rd., Ste. 303, Braintree, MA 02184; phone: (617) 848-9110.

Management Recruiters: 1127 Euclid Ave., Ste. 1400, Cleveland, OH 44115; phone: (800) 875-4000.

Marshall Group Personnel Franchise Corp.: P.O. Box A-1, Carmel, CA 93921; phone: (408) 625-5700.

MTS Inc.: Box 456, Harrogate, TN 37752-0456; phone: (612) 626-5806.

The Murphy Group: 1211 W. 22nd St., Ste. 200, Oak Brook, IL 60521; phone: (708) 571-1088.

Netrex International: Lincoln Centre, 5420 LBJ Freeway, LB 4, Dallas, TX 75240; phone: (214) 770-2525.

Positions, Inc.: Faneuil Hall, Boston, MA 02109; phone: (617) 367-9200.

Roth Young Personnel Service, Inc.: 535 5th Ave., Ste. 1100, New York, NY 10017; phone: (212) 557-8181.

Sanford Rose Associates International, Inc.: 265 S. Main St., Akron, OH 44308; phone: (800) 759-7673.

provide company clients with an "average" candidate in order to make a quick commission.

If you find that running an entire operation with little experience and minimal staff support seems too overwhelming, you might want to explore some of the various franchise and business opportunities offered by well-established firms. Franchisors can often offer large databases of clients and candidates as well as other support services in exchange for an up-front franchise fee and an ongoing cut of your executive placement profits.

MARKETING

You can assume that about half of your time running an executive recruiting firm will be spent marketing your ser-

vice and developing recruiting savvy, while the other half will be devoted to assigned searches. In the beginning, though, you will be without profit-making commissions and should employ an "I'm here when you need me" marketing strategy.

You should plan on taking at least a month or two to compile a list of potential client companies before you can begin to tap businesses for commissioned searches. In the meantime, you will need to take an active approach to networking, contacting former business associates and acquaintances for names of potential clients, searching newspapers and trade journals for management vacancies, locating county and state agencies where incorporation papers are filed (new companies can be good sources of business), contacting local media sales representatives for information on local companies, and scouring a myriad of other sources that might turn up a client.

Eventually the key to building up your business will be your contacts. Word of mouth is often paramount in securing clients and locating strong candidates. Thus, successful recruiters are often well-known personalities in their communities as well as "joiners" who belong to a range of civic and professional organizations. And while cold calls and direct mail have their place in a marketing strategy, you will need to get a foot in the office doors of the people who do the hiring.

When making initial contacts with companies, remember to dress appropriately; a business suit and tie is essential in conveying an image of professionalism. You will need to find out who has the power to authorize job searches at your target companies—the head of the company, a human resources department, or sometimes department heads—and speak to those people in person. Be willing to go out of your way to meet busy people. Some company heads will refuse talk to you during business hours but will be greatly impressed if you meet them at a commuter station or ask them to breakfast.

When you meet with potential clients you should not only sell them on your searching and recruiting abilities, but also attempt to distinguish yourself from competitors. You can do this by stressing such factors as your contacts, price, convenience, and the quality and speed of your placements. Additionally, you may specialize in one industry, establishing an area of expertise for your business, but possibly limiting your profit potential.

Besides your own sales ability, one of your key marketing tools will very likely be a promotional brochure that explains your services. Your brochure should convey the sense that yours is a serious and professional business that can deliver high-quality candidates in a timely manner (the average time for a search is three to four months). The text of the brochure should contain no more than a minute or two's worth of reading, and be printed in a standard type font of at least ten-point. An effective means to display your message is on lightly colored paper of roughly seven-and-a-quarter by eight-and-a-half inches, which with one fold will fit nicely into a number ten envelope and accompany any direct-mail letters.

Your first mailing should be limited to nearby areas in order to minimize advertising and follow-up expenses. Start with about 100 to 200 letters, allowing you an opportunity to quickly change your approach if the first batch of letters fails to produce results. Your direct mailings should include your brochure and a personalized cover letter addressed specifically to the highest-ranking official you can find in the company. You should send out letters at least four times a year and follow up each with a phone call in two to four weeks. According to industry insiders, every 100 letters should get you about ten appointments, which should in turn yield three potential opportunities for work. You should then be able to turn one of four proposals into a contracted search.

When pricing your services you should consider competition as well as profit margin. There are two principal types of business approaches in the industry: contingency services (paid for only if a candidate is found) and retainer services. For both types of services, the final fee represents a percentage (typically 10 to 33) of the first year salary of the person to be hired. If you work strictly on a contingency basis, be aware that while you may get more clients, you are not guaranteed a fee for your services. Additionally, some companies hire more than one contingency firm at a time.

A retainer firm usually bills clients on a monthly basis for expenses and professional services—which are calculated in the form of a daily billing rate—rendered during the course of a recruitment. Daily billing rates range from $300 to $1,000 a day, with the average rate around $500. When calculating your daily billing rate consider labor costs, overhead, and profit margin (usually 10 to 25 percent). Some services work on a flat fee basis, with or without expenses; if you do this you will need to estimate the hours a search will take and multiply that by your daily billing rate. Other firms charge only for hours worked, taking their daily billing rate and dividing it by eight.

Like other businesses, there are pitfalls to executive recruiting. One is seasonality; during the spring many companies do their own recruiting on college campuses. Another concern is the ethics involved in executive recruiting, sometimes referred to as "headhunting." Some candidates will be turned off by your unsolicited approach. You should also guard against raiding a company where you have placed a manager; an unwritten industry code of conduct suggests you should not seek candidates employed by a former client for at least two years after working for that company. There will also be times when a client does not like your choice of candidates, or an ideal candidate cannot be found. When this occurs, it is best to evaluate the situation on a case-by-case basis, reviewing the terms of your contract and weighing future business considerations.

ADVERTISING

When first starting out, advertising will probably be your biggest ongoing expense. In determining your advertising budget, you should allocate a figure equivalent to about ten percent of your projected gross sales. The focus of your advertising strategy should be to build a professional image and be listed in all the right places.

Aside from direct-mailed handbills and brochures, advertising mediums that tend to yield results include newspapers, newsletters, trade magazines, and the Yellow Pages. If taking out a listing in the Yellow Pages you may want to have your business' name appear under more than one heading. Potential Yellow Page categories include "Management Consultants," "Executive Search Consultants," "Personnel Consultants," and "Employment Agencies." In addition, you should have your service listed in at least some of the numerous directories, particularly *Directory of Executive Recruiters.* Trade publications and professional associations should be helpful in locating information on available directories.

In addition to promoting their business to potential client companies, some recruiting services actively advertise for candidates, either to build their candidate base or to locate candidates for a specified search. Such advertising can result in a slew of unneeded resumes from unqualified people. But even if you choose to avoid this type of advertising, keep in mind that you may find it necessary at times when seeking to place someone in a difficult-to-fill position. If forced to advertise when conducting a search, trade journals of the appropriate industry may be the best place to start.

LICENSES AND INSURANCE

While most states have stringent laws regulating employment agency activities, an executive recruiting business that receives only employer-paid fees is usually exempt from state licensing and not responsible for paying state sales taxes. Be advised, though, that some states will not allow you to meet clients or candidates in a home-based office. For information on regulations in your area, consult with an attorney or a regional professional association.

In order to open an executive recruiting service, you will need to obtain a local business license and perhaps other permits. Check with your city and county clerks or an attorney to determine specific requirements for your area. You will also want to purchase standard business insurance as well as a sound security system to protect your records and equipment.

In the final analysis a properly managed and marketed executive recruiting service with a good location should meet with success, provided its recruiters have the ability to understand the needs of companies and the concerns of prospective candidates. A well-run service should not only place top managers with appreciative companies, but given time, should also place some heady profits in the pockets of its owner.

SOURCES:

Adshead, John, "Headhunting Without Tears," *Personnel Management,* October 1990, pp. 56-57.

"Executive Headhunters: Don't Call Us, We'll Call You," *The Economist,* March 28, 1991, pp. 78-79.

Executive Recruiting, Business Start-Up Guide #1228, EntrepreneurGroup, 1988.

"Executive Recruiting Service," *Entrepreneur Magazine's 168 More Businesses Anyone Can Start and Make a Lot of Money,* second edition, Bantam, 1991, pp. 92-94.

Executive Search Activity Ends Year on High Note, Association of Executive Search Consultants, January 26, 1994.

Horowitz, David, and Dana Shilling, "Headhunters," *The Business of Business: How 100 Businesses Really Work,* Harper Collins, 1989, pp. 408-410.

Martin, Susan Boyles, editor, *Worldwide Franchise Directory,* Gale, 1991, pp. 198-207.

Matusky, Greg, "Back to Basics: Master the Fundamentals and Overcome Any Obstacle," *Success,* March 1992, pp. 51-54.

Pouliot, Janine S., "What a Difference an Hour Makes: Pay-as-You-Go Recruiting Firm Leads to Savings," *Management Accounting,* May 1991, pp. 34-35.

"Pros & Cons of Search-Listing Newsletters," *Executive Recruiter News,* January 1994, pp. 1-2.

Schwartz, Carol A., editor, *Small Business Sourcebook,* sixth edition, volume 1, Gale, 1993, pp. 661-664.

Visconti, Ron, *Effective Recruiting Strategies,* Crisp Publications, 1992.

Woy, Patricia A., "Executive Search Firm," *Small Businesses That Grow and Grow and Grow,* second edition, Betterway Publications, 1989, pp. 117-123.

—ROGER W. ROULAND

Facsimile Transmission Service

Why spend $9.95 or more to have a high-priority document delivered by the next day—not to mention package the document, apply postage, and bring the wrapped document to a collection box—when you could transmit it for receipt within a minute via a facsimile (fax) machine for less than half the price? More and more business people are asking themselves this question and opting for faxing. Sure, you have to find a public fax facility, but the ubiquity of these fax machines, which can be found in hotels, motels, airports, train stations, travel agencies, and public libraries, have made them the most efficient way to transmit documents in the 1990s.

Conceived and implemented in 1843 by Alexander Bain, a Scottish clock maker and inventor, facsimile transmission involves scanning the original copy and sending signals over telephone lines and microwave relay. Although the procedure was used in the 1880s and early 1900s, it did not really catch on until the 1930s, when newspaper and magazine reporters began transmitting photographs via radio waves. Eventually transmitted fiber-optically over telephone wires, a facsimile of a document could be scanned and sent from one location to another in a minute or less.

By 1990 at least 9,000 public fax stations were flourishing in the United States, and that number increased rapidly. Industry observers predicted that by 1995 the fax market would skyrocket to $780 million for the 20 million people in the United States working at home and that revenues would soar to $1.2 billion by the same year. Accompanying the popularity of public faxing, however, was an increase in competition among fax service owners. Nevertheless, with sufficient financing, prudent management, and astute, service-based marketing, an entrepreneur had a decent chance of making money in the facsimile transmission market.

COSTS AND PROFITS

Minimum start-up expenditures for a moderate-cost facsimile franchise hover between $3,500 and $4,000 for the initial franchise fee, $2,000 for the major equipment purchase, $100 for the opening inventory, and $250 for miscellaneous costs, for a total somewhere between $5,850 and $6,350. Facsimile machines used by ActionFax Public Facsimile Service franchises cost from $3,200 to $4,750; additional expenses incurred by the franchisee include purchasing the cover sheets, brochures, banners, fax paper, and the logo needed to operate an ActionFax outlet.

Facsimile machines can be leased from ActionFax to reduce start-up expenditures. For a fee, ActionFax makes available all machinery, supplies, and business forms necessary to operate a public facsimile station. You may be able to reduce expenditures for office supplies by purchasing them at a mass-volume office-supply store such as **Staples, 100 Pennsylvania Avenue, P. O. Box 9328, Framingham, MA 01701-9328; phone: (800) 333-3330,** which offers free next-day delivery on phone orders over $50, and **PaperDirect, 205 Chubb Avenue, Lyndhurst, NJ 07071; phone: (800) A-PAPERS.** ActionFax, which sets all rates charged by its franchisees, also maintains a toll-free technical support hotline for minor problems and offers a warranty-extension program covering facsimile machines used by franchisees. ActionFax receives a total of $.35 on each call made from an ActionFax outlet; in addition, the franchisee is responsible for paying all line charges incurred.

In general, fax service revenues, according to some industry analysts, would top $1.2 billion by 1995. The primary liabilities of a fax service owner include the standard accounts payable and working capital loans. Also, you will most likely not own the establishment in which the service is located—unless, of course, you operate from your own home—and so you will be responsible for monthly rent payments.

FINANCING

One of the most far-reaching mistakes new small business owners make is not securing sufficient financing. Before signing a franchise contract, consult with experts in order to determine how much capital you will need to launch your project. Ask anyone you may know in the commercial lending field for tips, especially since fax service franchisors frequently do not provide financing. Check your local business college for referrals to a student or instructor who could advise you free of charge.

Diplomatically approached, successful fax service owners will often provide financing and other information. Join your local chamber of commerce and make your ser-

FRANCHISE OPPORTUNITIES

Fax-9: 1609 West Murray Boulevard, Colorado Springs, CO 80916; phone: (719) 380-1133; fax: (719) 380-1143. Founded and began franchising in 1988; in 1991, Fax-9 had 167 sites in 42 states and Canada; growth expected throughout Africa, Asia, Europe, and Central and South America. Provided by franchisor: financing and elective training. Fax machines must be purchased by franchisee.

For a moderate-cost unit, the initial franchise fee begins at $3,500; major equipment purchases start at $2,000; operating inventory begins at $100. Adding miscellaneous costs, the average start-up fees average $5,850; possible bank financing begins at $4,000, with the cash required for financing averaging $1,850; franchising contract runs for 7 years, with a renewal option for an additional 7-year term; sales royalties are $40 per month; advertising includes description signage and direct mail; selling a franchise requires a $500 transfer payment from the franchisee.

Other Franchisors: ActionFax Public Facsimile Service: 4851 Keller Spring Rd., Ste. 211, Dallas, TX 75248; phone: (214) 661-2914, or (800) 365-2329; fax: (214) 661-1120. **Fax Mail:** c/o Hotelecopy, 17850 NE 5th Avenue, Miami, FL 33162; phone: (305) 651-5176, or (800) 329-6245; fax: (305) 651-7731. **HQ Business Center:** 120 Montgomery Street, Ste. 1040, San Francisco, CA 94104; phone: (415) 781-7811, or (800) 227-3004. **Personalized to Personable:** 7321 Victoria Park Avenue, Ste. 204, Markham, Ontario, Canada L3R 2Z8; phone: (416) 754-5355; fax: (416) 479-9593.

vices known to other business owners. For specialized pre-financing information, join a trade organization such as the American Facsimile Association (AFaxA) or the International Facsimile Association (IFAXA) and talk with your colleagues. A simple question such as "How's your bank treating you?" will probably elicit a number of stories that will give you an idea of how much money business owners are borrowing and at what rate.

Look for a bank that knows your industry and a banker who has done business with franchises like yours. Try to seek out a loan officer with 8 to 10 years of experience. Knowing ahead of time what your banker can do independently and what has to be routed "to committee" will aid you in formulating your strategy. If your banker doesn't have final authority, seek out his or her superior; remember, you're looking for an individual with some personal knowledge of you and your prospective franchise. Expect to meet with a lot of bankers—and to experience no small amount of rejection—before finding a banker with whom you can do business.

Prepare a five-year business plan, a personal financial history, marketing strategies, and sales projections based on future usage of your fax equipment. If necessary, hire a good accounting and legal team to ensure that your paperwork is perfect. When approaching a bank for a business loan, have ready cash-flow projections and financial statements, since

in 1994 banks were focusing heavily on cash-flow lending rather than on straight asset-based lending. However, you should expect to put up assets, including personal ones, as collateral.

The loan officer will be looking at other factors in determining your reliability as a borrower: a lucrative prospective location; plans to offer customers adequate—if not superior—service; a detailed marketing strategy that encompasses store fixtures, point-of-sale promotional materials, and promotional events; and a profitable pricing structure (at least a $2.00 per page transmission and reception charge). A lender will also ask about your management practices, qualifications for personnel—how knowledgeable you will expect your staff to be about faxing—proposed booth layout, and record-keeping procedures to track financial activity and report operating data.

Ultimately, an amalgamation of factors will determine whether a bank will lend to a prospective or fledgling fax service owner. You might also want to contact the U.S. **Small Business Administration (SBA)** to inquire about eligibility requirements for its loan program and to request other valuable information. The SBA can be reached at **1-800-U ASK SBA,** or you can write: **Small Business Directory, P. O. Box 1000, Fort Worth, TX 76119.** You might also want to check the "U.S. Government" section in your telephone directory for the SBA office nearest you.

LOCATION

Since stores offering only fax services rarely survive, most facsimile businesses are located within the confines of other establishments—print and copy shops, convenience stores, office supply shops, hotels, motels, airports, train stations, travel agencies, and even public libraries. Therefore, to gain the obvious advantage of a ready-made clientele, consider starting a facsimile service at someone else's business location. By complementing various retail and service operations, including banks, typesetters, post offices, drugstores, and courthouse coffee shops, a "nested" fax service, acting as a "drawing card," will synergistically add value to a preexisting business by improving foot traffic.

For the fax service, heavy foot traffic and street visibility are the two key ingredients for success; a sign or banner prominently displayed on the front facade of the building would also be helpful. If you own a home, think about setting up your business in one of the first-floor front rooms (preferably a sun parlor). Of course, first check with your town hall for zoning regulations. As with a storefront, an eye-catching sign or banner placed in a strategic exterior position on your home will accelerate your chances of attracting customers.

If you go the franchise route, give considerable thought to situating your facsimile service in a motel or hotel that caters to business people and frequently hosts business seminars and conventions. Hotels and motels will welcome you because your fax service will enhance the attractiveness of their establishments as conference centers. Business people almost always need to send high-priority documents at a moment's notice. A fax service can deliver a message to virtually any machine in the world. Fax vendors can seek out major agreements with hotel chains—Holiday Inn, Howard Johnson, Hyatt, Marriott, and Hilton, to name a few—to place fax machines in each hotel and to rent or lease the machines and add any fax charges to a business traveler's room bill.

In 1986 fax systems were too complicated to set up in a phone booth-type location, but by 1994 stand-alone facsimile services became quite commonplace. This resulted from the fact that fax machines included telephone credit card systems and display screens, similar to those of customer calling card telephone terminals already found in major airports and business travel locations. Also, technology prompted the development of machines that automatically accepted dollar bills before a transmission was made. Like telephone booths, modern fax service booths eventually came to require no attendant—only regular revenue collection, paper replenishment, and equipment maintenance. As the operator of a fax service, you would be, in effect, an ''absentee owner,'' and your profits would increase even

INDUSTRY STATISTICS

- *Growth of United States Fax Services (1992):* 30-50%, gradually declining to 15% per year.
- *United States Fax Service Penetration:* 1,000 walk-up fax service locations as of January 1988 and at least 2,000 such locations as of January 1989. By 1990, Tandy's 8,000 stores and a few other newcomers were predicted to have brought the total to over 10,000. Distribution was uneven, with a very high proportion in California and several regional services.
- *Location (1989):* Several states had most of their fax services in hotel chains, with Howard Johnson offering the most sites. Hotels had by far the most expensive fax services at $9 to $12 per page plus the cost of the call for sending and a similar amount for receiving.

(SOURCE: *FACSIMILE AND PC-BASED IMAGE TRANSMISSION MARKETS.*)

- *Usage Fees (1990):* (Transmission) 1-2 pages: $5.50; next 3-10 pages: $1.50 per page; each page over 10: $.50 per page. (Reception) 1-2 pages: $4.00 per page; 3-10 pages: $1.00 per page; each page over 10: $.50 per page.
- *Predictions:* More than 9,000 public fax stations by 1990; $780 million fax market by 1995 for the 20 million people in the United States working at home.
- *Average Price of a Fax Machine (1990):* With cables, under $500.
- *Average Price of a Cellular-Operated Fax Machine:* (With accessories) less than $1,000; data interface, approximately $250 (source: *Business Wire,* November 12, 1992).
- *Projected Revenues for the U.S. Fax Industry:* More than $1.2 billion by 1995 (source: *Marketing News,* October 28, 1991).

more if, as analysts predict, hotels and motels install fax machines in each room.

LAYOUT, SETUP, AND FEES

For a fax service, booth layout is especially important because one of the primary disadvantages of faxing is lack of confidentiality. Most public fax machines are placed in an area where other customers walking by can, at the very least, glance at a document. Therefore, try to position your fax machine(s) so that confidentiality is maintained. If a customer requires assistance, offer your help, but be careful to ensure that the client does not interpret your concern as intrusiveness. If a document is dropped off to be faxed later, preserve confidentiality by having folders readily available into which you can place incoming documents. If a document to be faxed is not placed in a folder, the customer may never know how many people besides the intended recipient will know the contents of that paper.

When an individual transmits a document to a fax service, the addressee will not know the document has been sent until (s)he is contacted by the service (unless the sender has previously notified the addressee by telephone). Depending upon how busy your service is, a delay may result between the arrival of the fax and the notification of the recipient. You might offer customers the option that you will call the addressee to let him or her know that a fax is on its way. You can then add the cost of the phone call to your client's bill.

If you choose to operate a self-service public fax booth such as that franchised by the ActionFax system, you will find that it is approximately thirty-and-a-half inches wide and nineteen inches deep, with a telephone handset, cover sheet bin, and a modified fax machine. Users fill in the cover sheet with the usual information plus a credit card number for billing purposes. The recipient can be identified by name and address, rather than by fax number, since ActionFax maintains a database of registered users. With ActionFax, documents are sent to regional computers, and the recipient is notified via telephone. Recipients without fax machines can go to the nearest ActionFax booth and call in; documents are then transmitted to that booth.

By all means, if you operate your fax service in person, keep your cash register out of view of the public so as not to invite theft. Decorate your space carefully, perhaps using paintings to enliven the walls. You could also pin up advertisements for businesses that complement yours. Visit other fax service outlets or dealerships to study how the owners have laid out their facilities.

Charges should be approximately $4.00 for the first page transmitted, $2.00 each for 2 to 10 pages, and $1.00 thereafter. For a recipient, fees should be $3.00 for the first page received, $1.00 each for 2 to 10 pages, and $.50 thereafter. One advantage of owning and operating a fax service lies in accounts receivable: You almost always will receive cash—thereby eliminating the mandatory clearance

PRIMARY ASSOCIATIONS AND SELECTED TRADE PUBLICATIONS

Associations:

American Facsimile Association (AFaxA): 1528 Walnut Street, Philadelphia, PA 19102; phone: (215) 875-0975; fax: (215) 875-0987.

Associated Mail and Parcel Centers (AMPC): 10701 Montgomery Boulevard NE, Suite C, Albuquerque, NM 87111; phone: (505) 294-6425; fax: (505) 271-2050.

International Facsimile Association (IFAXA): 4023 Lakeview Drive, Lake Havasu City, AZ 86403; phone: (602) 453-3850.

Publications by American Facsimile Association (AFaxA):

AFaxA Journal (quarterly).
Fax Focus: The Weekly Facsimile Newspaper.
FaxPro (periodic publication).

Publications by Associated Mail and Parcel Centers (AMPC):

AMPC Newsletter.

Publications by International Facsimile Association (IFAXA):

Facsimile—Facts and Figures (annual). *Fax News* (monthly).
Fax Number Directory (annual).
IFAXA Members Directory (annual).
P. C. Fax and Figures (annual).

time for checks—and you will not have to worry about past-due accounts and collection agencies, unless of course you permit high-volume customers to establish credit accounts.

STAFFING

Staffing for your fax service will depend upon your location and hours. If you are operating a self-service fax booth, you need not be present but you will obviously have to check on it, perhaps two or three times a week, to collect monies deposited, replenish supplies, and maintain hardware. If you own a customer-assisted service, you should train and employ at least one other person, so that (s)he can step in for you and act as manager if you are out of town or ill. This individual should have some experience in retail management and be highly organized and computer-literate, preferably with a communications and/or publishing background. Salary should be determined by industry standards; periodic merit raises, however, will enhance the motivation of an already-eager employee. If you find yourself inundated by customers, you may, instead of hiring workers, need to lease or buy more fax machines.

INDUSTRY INNOVATIONS

In the early 1990s increased competition saw the demise of the ''plain vanilla'' fax service. In order to succeed, you need to keep abreast of fast-breaking technological advances. Subscribe to one or more fax publications, such as the *AFaxA Journal, Fax Focus,* and *Fax News.*

Fax services progressed in 1993, when an alliance was formed between Ameritech's messaging services and Apple Computer's much-touted Newton devices, a project that established accelerated stay-in-touch capabilities between the two companies. People who used Ameritech's voice messaging or facsimile services would be able to receive notice that they had messages waiting. Messages could then be retrieved using Apple's personal digital assistant (PDA)—a small, intelligent computer-like device that permitted users to send and receive messages with the aid of a special pen.

In 1994 more advanced plain-paper machines were appearing on the market, and color faxes had already been introduced. Plain-paper laser faxes, which were quickly replacing thermal-paper faxes, were offering customers such features as automatic document feeders, paper cutters, and speed-dialing capabilities. Users would soon be able to take advantage of new complementary services, including Facs-Route, which offered users a 40 percent discount on long-distance faxes.

But perhaps the most widely used fax service offered in the early 1990s was the broadcast or mass fax, which allowed multiple terminal transmission of a single fax. Among those championing multiple facsimile transmission in 1993 were the audiotex and information service providers, long-distance telephone companies, regional Bell operating companies, and telemarketing firms.

To keep up with fax technology, you will, at the very minimum, have to be computer-literate. Additionally, you should know how to repair the machines, or else you will have to call in a repairperson, who will no doubt charge you a hefty fee. Keep abreast of business applications, corporate developments, and industry trends. Your diligence will be rewarded: As your revenues increase, you will be able to obtain bank loans to purchase innovative equipment, and your customers will seek you out as a knowledgeable source for fax technology.

ADVERTISING

Be prepared to spend nearly 70 percent of your initial investment on advertising during your first six months in business. First, try to obtain a catchy toll-free telephone number, such as 1-800-FAX-SHOP, 1-800-FAX-SERV, or 1-800-TO-FAXIT, to attract customers from all areas of the country. Then, utilize your local and regional newspapers and circulars, enhancing name recognition of your fax service with display ads in the business and classified sections. Contact a local ad mailer and arrange to place an ad to reach potential customers who otherwise would not be aware of your service. Create a fax service logo—or find a reasonably-priced free-lance designer to create one for you—and have it emblazoned on T-shirts that can be worn by you and your employees. You may also want to offer customers a free T-shirt for every 20 pages faxed.

Be certain to take advantage of every promotional opportunity and be flexible and expansive. Send press releases to local media announcing any special promotions you might conceive. For an opening-week promotion, hold a "Send a Fax Free" special. After you've established a clientele, offer customers one free fax for every five purchased. Develop relationships with local printers who lack fax services in their places of business; in turn, refer your fax customers to these printers. Design an advertising flier, have it printed by several different typographers, and then allow the printers to pass the fliers on to their customers. In addition, post fliers in office complexes, hotels, motels, airports, train stations, travel agencies, and supermarkets.

LICENSES AND INSURANCE

In order to open a facsimile transmission service as a business entity or within the confines of a preexisting business, you will need to obtain a local business license and the state and/or city sales tax permits required in your area. Check with your city or county clerks to determine the details for such permits. You will also want to purchase standard business insurance and invest in a sturdy security system to protect your inventory from theft.

PROSPECTS

Despite the "Paperless Revolution" of the late 1970s, hard copy still played a vital role in daily business communication in 1994. Indeed, a document transmitted at an opportune place and time could often make the difference between losing and closing a sale. In a minute or less—sometimes 15 seconds—modern fax machines could transmit document copies anywhere in the world. Along with speed came a multitude of applications: Practically any document, from a photograph to a purchase order, that could be reproduced on an office copier, could be whisked to any point on the globe at the press of a button.

As fax machines became the favored medium for transmitting time-critical documents, the prepared and pragmatic entrepreneur stood to benefit. With research, diligence, smart management, and astute advertising, almost any computer-literate individual could open a facsimile transmission service within the confines of a pre-existing business—whether as a primary source of income or on a moonlighting basis—and expect to realize substantial profits.

SOURCES:

Barty, Euan, "Hong Kong Innovates with Packet and Facsimile," *Telephony,* January 23, 1989, pp. 22-24.

Bhargava, Sunita Wadekar, "Extra! Extra! Hot off the Faxes! Facsimile Services Are Feeding Americans' Appetite for Quick News," *Business Week,* December 23, 1991, p. 84.

Coleman, Lynn G., "It's A 'Wild' Fax Future for Marketers," *Marketing News,* October 28, 1989, p. 5.

Entrepreneur Magazine's 168 More Businesses Anyone Can Start and Make A Lot of Money, second edition, Bantam, 1991.

Facsimile and PC-Based Image Transmission Markets, International Resource Development, Inc., 1989.

Facsimile Equipment and Services Market: New Applications Drive Growth in Niche Segments, Market Intelligence Research Co., 1991.

The Facsimile Equipment Market in the United States, Frost & Sullivan, 1982.

Facsimile Equipment Services, Market Intelligence Research Co., 1991.

Facsimile Markets, International Resource Development, Inc., 1985.

Gormley, Mal, "Faxing on the Fly," *Business & Commercial Aviation,* February 1992, p. 64.

Hewer, J. M., "What's New in Fax?," *CMA—The Business Management Accounting Magazine,* December 1989/ January 1990, p. 21.

Hobbs, Marvin, editor, *Servicing Facsimile Machines,* Prentice-Hall, 1992.

Jordahl, Gregory, *Plugging Into the Fax Track,* Association for Information and Image Management, 1990.

Koek, Karin, editor, *National Fax Directory,* Gale, 1992.

Kueny, Barbara, "Smaller Hotel, Motel Operators Hope Meeting Mania Means More Business," *The Business Journal-Milwaukee,* May 23, 1992, sec. 2, p. 6.

Liebowitz, J., and I. Singh, editors, *Fax/Net Electronic-Mail Source Directory,* Pergamon Press, 1987.

Madden, Michael, editor, *Small Business Start-Up Index,* issue 1, Gale, 1991.

Martin, Susan Boyles, editor, *Worldwide Franchise Directory,* first edition, Gale, 1991.

McComb, Gordon, *Troubleshooting and Repairing Fax Machines,* TAB Books, Inc., 1991.

Nielson, Kelly M., "Canada's Stentor Alliance Selects Tandem Telecom's INFO24-Fax Enhanced Fax," *Business Wire,* November 9, 1992.

North American Fax Directory, Dial-A-Fax Directories Corp., 1992.

Pirani, Judith A., Raymond L. Boggs, and Lewis I. Solomon, *The U.S. Facsimile Equipment Market II,* Venture Development Corporation, 1985.

Quinn, Gerald V., editor, *The Fax Handbook,* TAB Books, Inc., 1989.

Riggs, Carol R., "Still Using Fax the Old-Fashioned Way?" *D&B Reports,* May/June 1991, p. 30.

Samuel, James, "Traveling with a Laptop," *Sales & Marketing Management,* January 1991, pp. 64-66.

Schwartz, Carol A., editor, *Small Business Sourcebook,* sixth edition, volume 1, Gale, 1993.

Wolff, Carlo, "An Essential Amenity," *Lodging Hospitality (LHO),* February 1991, pp. 57-58.

Zimmerman, Michael R., "New Spin on Fax Routing Introduced," *PC Week,* June 24, 1991, p. 47.

—Virginia Barnstorff

Financial Brokerage Service

Banks, as well as savings and loans, are notoriously conservative when it comes to making loans to finance start-up costs for a small business or to finance the purchase of equipment. Therefore, people who are unable obtain a business loan from a bank often turn to a financial broker to seek out alternative sources of funding. An independent financial broker in such cases becomes the middleman or liaison between a lender (often a non-conventional private institution, such as a venture capital firm) and the person seeking a loan. As a full-time financial broker running your own business, you can perform a valuable public service, make a comfortable living, set your own hours, and do interesting, challenging work at a modest start-up cost.

There is no special education or training involved in becoming a broker, although a license is required in most states. The most important requirement is a thorough knowledge of financial markets. Some financial brokers acquire this through a previous job they held at a bank, or you can acquire it by carefully studying the financial market in your area. All financial brokers compile a list of core lending institutions that they rely on for loans or for referrals in case there is no good match between the borrower and the core list of lenders. Coming up with the right match between borrower and lender is a good part of every financial broker's job. Once that match is made, the financial broker puts together a loan package and follows the progress of the proposed loan. In case the lending institution rejects the loan request, the financial broker still collects a fee from the unlucky borrower. A professional financial broker with a good reputation never promises anything, and offers no guarantee of success.

FINANCIAL ASPECTS

Start-up costs for your financial brokerage business will depend on many variables: whether or not you have office equipment of your own, office furniture, and enough operating capital for a year. To start with, you will probably work from your own home. Your start-up costs will range from $9,000 to as high as $25,000. This will include equipment, furniture, insurance, advertising, and such miscellaneous costs as phone lines and office supplies. Once you have established yourself in business with a clientele of your own, you can expect to gross from $35,000 to $50,000 in your first year. Operating capital for the first year of your business can be kept at a minimum when operating from your home. All business related expenses, including a separate office in your house, can be itemized on your income tax return.

As an aspiring independent financial broker, you will be in a better position to obtain financing for your own business than most entrepreneurs. You may possibly run into difficulties similar to those that your future clients will be experiencing, however. By starting out with a home office, though, you'll have time to establish your business, complete all of your own market research, and obtain clients before you even make the move into an outside office. You can also keep costs down by using your own furniture or buying secondhand furniture and equipment; you may not want to purchase elaborate equipment until you're sure you have the clients to make such a heavy investment necessary.

Keeping careful track of outgoing expenses and incoming payments also can be a significant cost-cutter. The drudgery of record keeping has been greatly simplified by computer software. Check your local discount software store for software that will fit your specific needs. There will be at least a half-dozen software products to choose from that take care of accounts receivable and payable as well as payroll if you happen to hire someone. These can be had for under $200. In addition, there are excellent and inexpensive (under $100) software products that help you organize your budget and pay your bills and compute your income tax.

LOCATION AND LAYOUT

Once you have completed the most important part of your job, which is compiling a list of core lending institutions, and you have a marketing and advertising strategy in place, you will need to move into an office outside of the home. Location will be of great importance—a prestigious business area is best. Professionalism and influence are the impressions you want to convey to your present and future clients.

Carefully investigate the site of your future office by studying the recent history of the site—i.e., what kinds of businesses operated there, how often did the space "turn

TRADE SOURCES

Financial Broker (business start-up guide): Entrepreneur Group, Inc., 2392 Morse Ave., P.O. Box 19787, Irvine, CA 92713-9787

American Bank Directory: 6195 Crooked Circle, Norcross, GA 30095.

Directory of Corporate Affiliations (Who Owns Whom Redbook): National Register Publishing Co., 3004 Glen View Road, Wilmette, IL, 60091.

Directory, National Venture Capital Association: 1655 N. Fort Myer Drive, Arlington, VA 22209.

Dow Jones Investor's Handbook: 1818 Ridge Road, Homewood, IL.

EZ Telephone Directory of Brokers & Banks: 106 Seventh Street, Garden City, NY 11530.

Financial Executives Institute Member Directory: 10 Madison Ave., Morristown, NJ 01017.

For Financial Assistance:

The National Association of Small Business Investment Companies (NASBIC): 1199 N. Fairfax Street, Alexandria, VA 22314; phone: (703) 683-1601. The membership directory of this organization lists small business investment companies (which charge higher interest rates than most banks, but are willing to assume more risk) for each state. Directory also lists loan limits and is available for $10 by writing NASBIC, P.O. Box 2039, Merrifield, VA 22116.

over,'' etc.—as well as finding out whether the area is zoned for your type of business, information which you can obtain from your county government. Most financial brokers lease their first office. The best lease is one that enables you to sublet, in case your business does not perform in that location. Good parking and easy access from local highways and expressways are major criteria you should use in selecting a location for your business. Make it a point to drive around and assess the traffic conditions at different times of the day; determine how easy or difficult it might be for a future customer to park nearby. Give yourself several days to assess the future site of your office.

Another tempting option is just to buy out another financial broker's business completely, should one become available. This is not a bad idea as long as the person selling the business has not gone bankrupt. In that case, your own firm will project unfavorably, despite your best efforts to the contrary. Before buying out an establishment, be absolutely sure that bad business was not a factor in the sellout.

Once you have settled on an office site and signed the lease, you need to furnish your office in a style that suggests comfort and affluence, but not luxury—unless you can afford it. Secondhand office furniture and inexpensive wall decorations are fine. Your license, diplomas, and any other certificates of distinction that would suggest professionalism should be displayed on the wall of your office. Initially, you will probably work without the help of a receptionist. A screen or possibly an extra room should separate your office from such office equipment as photocopy and fax machines.

Good office furniture can be obtained secondhand or from furniture closeouts or chain office supply stores. Furnish your office with a large desk, comfortable chairs for your clients, two or three file cabinets, and miscellaneous items such as a small bookcase and shelves, magazine rack for professional literature in your field, computer stand, and office supplies. These supplies must include professional letterhead stationery, envelopes, and business cards. The cost of these items can be deducted from your income tax. To ensure that your business address remains stable, you should consider renting a post office box with a suite number from the post office or a private mail box operation.

MARKETING STRATEGY

While it is not necessary to have a special background in finance or business in order to become a financial broker, you should map out a careful marketing strategy before you even begin to advertise your services. The essential elements of this marketing strategy are developing a core list of lenders and thoroughly studying the community in which you expect to operate. Before you can begin to develop your marketing strategy, however, you must decide what kinds of brokering you will specialize in. There are financial brokers who specialize only in real estate loans, others in equipment loans—such as tractors, computer equipment, airplanes, etc.—and still others in personal loans, most of which are earmarked to start up a small business—the riskiest loans of all.

Before you hang up your shingle for business, you should have made a thorough study of the market in your business area. If you want to help prospective small business owners, you must find out whether new businesses are coming to or leaving your area. You might conclude that many retail stores have been opening in your area, and decide that this would be your best customer base. Once you have decided to specialize in loans to small retail businesses, you have a better idea of where to turn for financing for this specific kind of business. The same holds true if you happen to live in an area where agriculture is important to the economy. Farmers constantly need loans for equipment, and often get turned down by conventional loan sources. Specializing in farm equipment loans facilitates the next stage of your strategy—building up a list of lenders.

Once you have studied the economic factors in your area (your county government will furnish the statistics you want) and have decided on the viability of a certain community and specialty, you can begin to approach prospective lenders. To develop this base of lending institutions, on which you will rely constantly for future loans for your clients and for referrals to other loan sources, you need to have an exhaustive knowledge of all possible lending sources in your area. Not all banks refuse small loans: it is important to pay attention to advertising in local and professional newspapers and newsletters to determine just when a bank seeks loan customers and the kinds of loans a bank or other lending institution will make. The personal touch is also important. Until you get to the point where your clients start coming to you at your convenience, much of your time will be spent visiting prospective lending institutions and cultivating a business relationship with them. It is impossible to pursue your profession without such a list of contacts and core lending institutions. These contacts will also provide you with future business by word-of-mouth referrals.

ADVERTISING

Until you reach the stage where your business contacts and clients refer you to other prospective customers, you will need to advertise extensively and continuously. Again, your advertising plan should be well prepared even before you open for business. Direct mail can be effective if you target the right market. For instance, if you are specializing in start-up loans to finance retail businesses, you would send a brochure and cover letter to retail store owners announcing your business. The mark of the professional financial broker

---

PRIMARY ASSOCIATIONS AND SELECTED TRADE PUBLICATIONS

Associations:

National Venture Capital Association: 1655 Fort Myer Drive, Arlington, VA 22209.

Independent Bankers Association of America: 1168 S. Main St., Sauk Centre, MN 56378.

Publications:

American Banker: One State Plaza, New York, NY 10004.
Bank Administration: 60 Gould Center, Rolling Meadows, IL 60008.
Barron's—National Business & Financial Weekly: 22 Cortlandt St., New York, NY 10007.
Commerce Magazine: 200 N. LaSalle Avenue, Chicago, IL 60601.
Credit & Financial Management: 520 Park Ave., New York, NY 10018.
D & B Reports: 99 Church St., New York, NY 10007.
Financial Analysts Journal: 1633 Broadway, New York, NY 10019.
Inside R & D: 32 N. Bean, Englewood, NJ 07021.
Journal of Commerce: 110 Wall Street, New York, NY 10015.
National Real Estate Investor: 6255 Barfield Road, Atlanta, GA 30328.
Pensions & Investment Age: 740 N. Rush Street, Chicago, IL 60611.
Coopers & Lybrand Newsletter: 1251 Avenue of the Americas, New York, NY 10020.
Dow Theory Forecasts: 7412 Calumet Avenue, Hammond, IN 46324.
Dow Theory Letter: 1118 Silverado, La Jolla, CA 90238.

---

is avoiding exaggerated claims or guarantees you may not be able to keep.

Direct mail can be supplemented by advertising in the local papers in your business area as well as in trade journals and newsletters. For a list of such periodicals, your local library will provide you with a copy of the Standard Rate & Data Service, or SRDS, which lists even minor consumer and trade publications with their circulation numbers. Some prospective financial brokers turn to hiring a telemarketer, or they do the phoning themselves. This is no more effective than direct mail, however, and can cost you money in terms of time spent on the phone. More effective than cold calling is following up on your direct mail. Wait a week after you have mailed your brochure and cover letter, then call and inquire casually whether the prospective client has received your mailing. Distributing brochures in target areas is another effective strategy. Lastly, don't overlook the Yellow Pages, a source that many people turn to first.

EMPLOYEE MATTERS

If you have done your research thoroughly and have drawn up a core list of lenders, you might soon find yourself with a bustling business. And despite the fact that you can set your own hours and have your clients come to you, you may find that you're working long hours and need some help. If you are sufficiently well off, you can hire a full-time receptionist/office manager or a part-time marketing specialist whose sole job will be to keep abreast of financial markets and do the advertising.

For those financial brokers who wish to avoid the entanglements—financial and personal—of hiring someone, there are other alternatives. For clerical help, you can turn to a temporary employment agency that will provide you with the office support you need, without your having to encumber yourself with workman's compensation and employee benefits. You can also rely on consultants who, albeit for a high fee, will take care of your advertising or marketing efforts and free you from the burdens of extra taxes and forms, as well as the risk that the employee or partner you hire will be unsatisfactory.

CLIENT ISSUES

An established independent financial broker usually will have no lack of clients. The important task of the financial broker is matching the right lender with the right borrower. However, you must also match yourself with the right client. In most cases, you will use the same criteria that a bank does in selecting a client, except that a bank commonly rejects a loan because of a weak loan proposal. Re-doing and tightening that loan package will consume part of your day; presenting it to the right lending institution on your core list and following through on that package will consume another part of your time.

Because you will be working closely with your client, selecting one with whom you can work will be an important

SOFTWARE

The following is just a partial listing of some of the better software packages available. Prices cited are discount retail and approximate:

Peachtree Complete Accounting for DOS (also available for Windows), $189. A few main features are inventory for the small business, order entry, and accounts receivable/payable.

Peachtree Basic Accounting (DOS or Windows), $85. A simplified version of the above, provides online help; does not do inventory.

CA-BPI Accounting II for DOS (also Windows version), $164. Main features are payroll, inventory, and accounts receivable/payable.

Quick Books & Quick Pay for DOS with Payroll, $109. Speeds up bill paying and invoicing.

One-Write Plus Accounting (DOS), $89. Features check writing, billing, inventory, and accounts receivable/payable.

FormTool (3.0 version), $50. This handy software creates every imaginable business form on your PC, including price tags.

TurboTAX (DOS and Windows), $39. Claims to be the best-selling tax software; offers complete tax preparation.

consideration. Once selected, you must avoid making promises and guarantees. It is also unprofessional to cultivate a personal relationship with your client outside of your office. Promise to phone him or her at stated intervals or if anything significant develops.

Despite your best efforts, some of your loan packages will inevitably be rejected. You will be required to do a great deal of work before you ever pitch the loan proposal, so it is in your best interest to charge the client an upfront fee. What price to charge depends on the area in which you live and what your competitors charge—an easy matter to find out.

LICENSES AND INSURANCE

Depending on what specialty you choose, you may or may not need a license to practice. The Federal Trade Commission (FTC) does provide this information, as will your state

government. Requirements vary from state to state. Even if a license is not a requirement, it does lend your business greater credibility.

Be sure to obtain the proper insurance for your business, whether you operate out of your home or in an office. The best guide for finding the right insurer is the Yellow Pages. Under the insurance listing, pick out those companies that advertise their specialty in small business insurance.

Choosing to be a financial broker can be a worthwhile and lucrative career. You are serving a clientele which needs alternative sources of financing, and providing that financing can become a heady challenge. Boredom will never afflict you, and the job outlook for financial brokers is a good one.

SOURCES:

Fleming, James, ''A Win for Investors (Competition in the Discount-Broker Business),'' *Financial Times of Canada,* August 7, 1993, p. 4.

Graham, John R., ''Blind Spots That Can Destroy Your Sales Efforts,'' *National Underwriter Life & Health-Financial Services Edition,* November 29, 1993, p. 7.

McConnell, Dan D., ''Specialty Firms Making Their Mark in the Bank Brokerage Marketplace,'' *American Banker,* September 29, 1993, p. 16.

McDermott, Kevin, ''A Bridge to Rio (Geofinance, Broker of Export-Import Deals),'' *D&B Reports,* September/October 1993, p. 42.

Mulcahy, Colleen, ''Canadian Brokers Face New Competitors in Banks . . . Independent Brokers,'' *National Underwriter Property & Casualty-Risk & Benefits,* May 18, 1992, p. 41.

Nation, Nancy Isles, ''Broker & Matchmaker: Bruce Owen Mates Borrowers & Lenders,'' *Northern California Real Estate Journal,* no. 10, March 30-April 12, 1987.

''Regulators Lose Patience With Telephone Solicitors (Agents/ Brokers)'' *National Underwriter Life & Health-Financial Services Edition,* June 3, 1991, p. 31.

Rosen, Jan M., ''Software to Help Monitor Finances,'' *New York Times,* December 21, 1991, p. 18(N), 34(L).

Schwartz, Matthew P., ''Planners Are Seeking Better Info Management from B/Ds (Financial Planners, Broker-Dealers),'' *National Underwriter Life & Health-Financial Services Edition,* September 20, 1993, p. 7.

—Sina Dubovoj

Financial Planning Service

Want to save for retirement, put the kids through college without going bankrupt, or set aside a little something to celebrate that thirtieth wedding anniversary in Hawaii? To find answers to these questions, more and more people are turning to financial planners. Financial planners take a person's entire financial life into consideration, including goals and commitments, and then create a strategy that successfully gets them where and what they want. Rather than just providing advice on investments, a financial planner will help with everything from budgeting an income to setting up a retirement plan.

For many years financial planning services were devoted exclusively to helping the wealthy, but during the 1970s and 1980s the industry changed dramatically. One reason is that the financial world has become so complex that even middle income people need advice to sort their way through the maze of available mutual funds, retirement programs, insurance opportunities, and tax shelters. In addition, the downsizing of corporations and the slashing of benefit packages have frightened people into taking their personal finances more seriously than ever before. Since many of these people do not feel qualified or comfortable managing their own money, they're asking for professional help.

In the mid-1970s there were only a handful of financial planners; however, by the early 1990s there were over 250,000. This growth rate reflects the high earnings potential. Hourly fees range from $100 to $250, and commissions for selling investment products can be very lucrative. Excluding schooling expenses, start-up costs for a financial planning service are quiet low. With adequate education and a good understanding of a client's needs, there is a significant amount of money to be made in opening a financial planning service.

COSTS AND PROFITS

The minimal start-up cost for a financial planning service is approximately $12,000, an amount that may require finding a partner or working in an established office. High-end start-up costs hover around $60,000, and this includes setting up an office from scratch with lavish decor and furnishings. Ordinarily, annual revenues range from $30,000 to $3 million, while annual pretax profits range from $15,000 to $1.5 million. Break-even time for the new financial planner is between three and twelve months.

FINANCING

Starting a financial planning service is not like opening a hair salon or a muffler shop; the product you're selling is competent advice and reliable judgement. So financing your business might be more difficult than raising capital to open a retail store. The first thing to do is consult an accountant who will help you devise a business plan, in which you will detail all your projected costs and income for the first three years of your business. Talk to practicing financial planners and find out how much they spent starting their businesses. Once you have a comprehensive business plan, you're ready to approach both individual and institutional financiers for support.

Applying for a loan from a commercial bank is a lengthy process, but one which might be rewarding if you are prepared. Rely on your accountant and lawyer to help you with the application for a bank loan. Although most commercial banks don't provide loans to small start-up businesses, the fact that you're in a field with large income potential makes you less of a risk. Another way to finance your business is to look for individual entrepreneurs willing to underwrite your initial costs. These financiers are most often found by word of mouth, but financial planning associations are good places to make these contacts.

An alternative is to apply for a loan through one of the U.S. **Small Business Administration (SBA)** programs. Check your phone book for your local SBA office or call **1-800-U ASK SBA.** Another source of information on financing is *Entrepreneur,* a monthly magazine that periodically features articles on how to start a financial planning service.

LICENSING, EDUCATION, AND SPONSORSHIP

The financial planning industry is an unregulated one, so almost anyone can become a financial planner. Many entrepreneurs who go into the industry have at least a bachelor's degree in a field such as accounting, finance, business ad-

INDUSTRY STATISTICS

• *Growth of Financial Planning and Investment Advisory Firms from 1980 to 1992:* From 4,800 to 17,500.
• *Number of Financial Planners in 1993:* Approximately 250,000.
• *Number of Full-Time Inspectors Working at the Securities and Exchange Commission (SEC) in 1992:* 46.

(SOURCE: SECURITIES AND EXCHANGE COMMISSION, 1993.)

• *Rate at Which an Investment Firm Could Expect to See an SEC Inspector:* Once every 30 years.
• *Number of States Requiring Financial Planners to Pass Licensing Exams:* 38.
• *Number of Financial Planners Listed in the Santa Rosa, California, Yellow Pages:* 32.

(SOURCE: *MONEY MAGAZINE,* NOVEMBER 1992.)

• *Average Amount of Money Needed to Become a Financial Planner:* $2,000 (source: Denver's College of Financial Planning, 1993).

ministration, or economics, but this has not prevented individuals who are doctors, teachers, and psychologists from also entering the arena of financial planning.

In order to set up shop and provide services to your customers, however, you have to obtain two different licenses. The first is a Securities License, which gives you permission to sell financial products, including mutual funds, stocks, IRAs, and investments in real estate and commodities. To obtain this license, apply to the **Securities and Exchange Commission (SEC)** in Washington, D.C., which can be reached at **(202) 272-7450**; for a fee of $150 you will become a Registered Investment Advisor (RIA). The second license you'll have to apply for is an Insurance License. Secured through your state insurance commission, this license allows you to sell insurance-related investment products.

In order to get your licenses, you have to fulfill two conditions. First, you have to arrange for an established financial planning company to be your sponsor during the period you are preparing to take the examinations required for the licenses. Contact the financial planning group **Waddell & Reed, Inc.,** at **(913) 236-2000** for information. The second condition involves the money you'll have to spend preparing for the licensing exams; expect to pay approximately $1000 for the necessary training and study materials.

It is advisable to take an additional year or two of intensive study in order to earn the designation of Certified Financial Planner (CFP). This title will give you added credibility and probably result in higher fees and commissions. Issued by the **Institute of Certified Financial Planners (ICFP),** this private financial planners organization offers courses in the six areas you need to know in order to gain CFP certification: employee benefits, estate planning, insurance, investments, tax management, and retirement programs. Over 40 colleges and universities offer undergraduate courses that help prepare students for the CFP

examination. Call the ICFP at **(303) 751-7600** for information on the school nearest you.

Another organization that promotes professionalism within the field is the International Association for Financial Planning (IAFP); the IAFP sets standards for planners and has over 1,000 members nationwide who take a comprehensive examination. Call **(800) 553-5343** for more information. Both the IAFP and the ICFP conduct continuing education programs.

LAYOUT AND SETUP

In contrast to entrepreneurs who work out of their home or consultants who visit a customer's office, financial planners must have an office to invite a client in for a meeting. Professionalism—from the cut of your suit to the appearance of your office—is expected from a financial planner. Decorating your office, therefore, is an important consideration, and you need to find the right mix between comfort and formality. Remember, you want to exude an aura of trust and competence so that your clients will feel comfortable accepting your advice and passing on your name to others.

At the onset, you will have to hire secretarial help for the mounds of paperwork involved in financial planning. In addition, you might also want to hire a "paraplanner," a person who will assist you in researching and keeping up to date on the myriad investment opportunities you'll need to know in order to be a good financial planner. A paraplanner can be hired on a part-time or full-time basis, depending on your own knowledge of stocks, bonds, insurance, and real estate markets.

One of the most important purchases to make when setting up shop will be a high-quality computer and software packages that are specifically designed for the financial services industry. You should plan on acquiring accounting software, data software, and market tracking software, all of which are essential for keeping track of financial investments and customer accounts.

Although you will need to set aside a sizable portion of your start-up investment for marketing and advertising, you can cut your overhead costs substantially by sharing office space with other financial planners. Either through personal contacts or through one of the financial planning associations, you can meet people with similar goals and arrange to share rent, utilities, secretarial help, the cost of subscribing to financial publications (which are very expensive), and sometimes even research facilities. Like doctors or lawyers who are just starting their practice, you should consider sharing office space with other financial planners who can provide guidance for minimal cost.

MARKETING

During the 1980s, financial planners developed a bad reputation; incompetence, conflict of interest, and fraud were some of the terms heard frequently within the industry. The Securities and Exchange Commission estimated that, from 1990 to 1992, clients lost more than $600 million in dealings with financial planners. With investigative reports turning up scandal within the industry and regulatory agencies becoming more inclined to look into client complaints about individual planners, it is extremely important that you develop a reputation as a competent, reliable, and ethical advisor. A straightforward, honest approach toward your clients will keep your name above reproach and bring you even more customers.

Financial planners can help clients in three ways. First, you can advise customers on how to clarify their financial goals and commitments and begin a savings plan. Second, you can help design an appropriate investment portfolio by assessing clients' resources and attitude toward risk and then guiding them to reliable and safe financial products. Finally, you can bring order to the complex details of the financial realm, advising clients on pensions, wills, estate planning, insurance, and taxes. Normally, a planner will develop both short- and long-term financial strategies and then make periodic adjustments and provide written reports on clients' portfolios.

One of the best methods to attract clients and enhance your credibility is to offer an hour of free financial consulta-

tion. Ask prospective clients to bring in a list of financial goals, recent tax forms, balance sheets, and anything else that might be suitable. During the consultation, be up front about your training and experience, informing your prospective customer of fees, commissions, and the brokerage or insurance company with which you are affiliated. You can establish a good foundation for a working relationship if you provide your clients with disclosure forms, which can be obtained from financial planner associations. If a prospective customer asks for the names and numbers of previous customers, be prepared to provide them with that information.

As a financial planner, you can make money in one of three ways: either by charging a flat fee ranging from $300 for a simple financial plan to $30,000 for more complex plans that involve millions of dollars; by charging an hourly rate ranging from $50 to $200, depending upon the type of work involved; or by working on commissions, which are built into the price of the financial products you sell.

Due to that fact that there has been a good deal of publicity given to the harm planners can cause clients when they sell products on a commission basis only, one association for financial planners promotes a flat-fee pay scale as opposed to commissions. Contact the **National Association of Personal Financial Advisors (NAPFA)** at **(800) 366-2732** to find out more about this issue. Whichever method of payment you choose to impose, be sure to inform your clients before providing them with any of your services. Once again, a forthright approach to clients will inspire trust in you as a financial planner.

ADVERTISING

Name recognition should be the first priority of any financial planner; the more prospective clients hear or know about you the more likely it is they will seek you out. Approaching family and acquaintances is the usual first step in advertising your services, and these contacts should lead you to others. Referrals are also an inexpensive way of getting your name known; if you know bankers, lawyers, accountants, presidents of corporations, and other monied professionals, ask them for leads. Cold-calling is still another alternative, which can be used, for example, with lawyers and doctors, who because of their high incomes, are likely to be interested in financial planning services.

Newsletters are one of the best ways to advertise your financial planning service. You can either advertise in the newsletter of another planner, write a column on an aspect of financial planning with which you are particularly well acquainted, or start your own newsletter combining pertinent and useful up-to-date financial information and advice. You might also want to contact local newspapers, magazines, and other publications to find out if they need a financial correspondent. The free exposure that writing gives you could result in many new clients.

Another advertising technique you should not overlook

PRIMARY ASSOCIATIONS AND SELECTED TRADE PUBLICATIONS

Associations:

International Association for Financial Planning (IAFP): Two Concourse Parkway, Ste. 800, Atlanta, GA 30328; phone: (800) 553-5343.

International Board of Standards and Practices for Certified Financial Planners (IBSPCFP): 5445 DTC Parkway, Ste. P1, Englewood, CO 80111.

Institute of Certified Financial Planners (ICFP): 70600 East Eastman, Suite 301, Denver, CO 80231; phone: (303) 751-7600.

The National Association of Personal Financial Advisors (NAPFA): Buffalo Grove, IL; phone: (800) 366-2732.

Publications:

ABA Banking Journal: 345 Hudson Street, New York, NY 10014; phone: (212) 620-7200.
Barron's: 200 Liberty Street, New York, NY 10281; phone: (212) 808-7200.
Financial Planning: Two Concourse Parkway, Ste. 800, Atlanta, GA 30328; phone: (800) 553-5343.
Institutional Investor: 488 Madison Ave., New York, NY 10022; phone: (212) 303-3300.
Investor's Business Daily: 12655 Beatrice St., Los Angeles, CA 90066; phone: (310) 448-6000.

is direct mail. If you want to provide services to a specific group, such as the elderly or those in a certain income strata, direct mail can effectively target a segment of the population and bring in new clients.

ACCOUNTING AND INSURANCE

Consult with your lawyer and accountant for suggestions on how to best meet federal and state tax requirements and to help you with the avalanche of paperwork necessary to start a financial planning service. A trip to the county clerk's office will take care of any state license or city permit that you'll need. You should also arrange for your own health insurance and property insurance and apply for a federal employer identification number, especially if you intend to hire a staff.

Starting a financial planning service can be a challenging and rewarding career. If your financial acumen serves you well, if you get proper training, and if you develop a reputation for competent and ethical advise, then you stand to earn a substantial amount of money in the field.

SOURCES:

Dunkin, Amy, ''The Perils of Picking a Planner,'' *Business Week,* December 14, 1992, pp. 112-113.

Entrepreneur Magazine's 111 Businesses You Can Start for Under $10,000, Bantam Books, 1991.

Entrepreneur Magazine's 168 More Businesses Anyone Can Start and Make a Lot of Money, second edition, Bantam Books, 1991.

Kahn, Sharon, and the Philip Lief Group, *101 Best Businesses to Start,* Doubleday, 1992.

Madden, Michael, editor, *Small Business Start-Up Index,* issue 1, Gale, 1991.

O'Reilly, Brian, ''Picking the Right Financial Planner,'' *Fortune Magazine,* February 25, 1991, pp. 144-147.

Rich, Andrew M., and Jill Arowesty, *The Expert's Guide to Managing and Marketing a Successful Financial Planning Practice,* Prentice Hall, 1988.

Schwartz, Carol, A., editor, *Small Business Sourcebook,* fifth edition, volume 1, Gale, 1992.

Simon, Ruth, ''The Broken Promise of Financial Planning,'' *Money Magazine,* November 1992, pp. 133-149.

Woy, Patricia A., *Small Businesses That Grow and Grow and Grow,* second edition, Betterway Publications, 1989.

—THOMAS DERDAK

Flower Shop

A small flower shop in a strong market may bring in annual revenues of $150,000 to $200,000 and provide the owner with an income of $40,000 to $60,000. However, in addition to hard work and an understanding of business, operating a successful flower shop requires a knowledge of horticulture and a flair for flower arranging.

FINANCIAL ASPECTS

A flower shop will require a minimum of 800 to 1,000 square feet of space in a high-traffic commercial area, special refrigeration equipment, and considerable initial inventory, so start-up costs will run from a minimum of $25,000 to as high as $80,000. You also will need another $20,000 in operating capital.

There are several sources of start-up capital, but the first thing you should do is find a financial advisor who can help you understand your options. Some banks and community colleges offer small business assistance programs. There are also associations of retired business executives who volunteer to assist new businesses. In addition to helping you weigh your options, these people can guide you in creating a business plan that will satisfy potential lenders.

Though they are the most obvious sources of capital, banks are very conservative in their lending practices, especially for small, start-up businesses, and will require a sound business plan. Banks will also require a thorough background check and collateral. You may be able to obtain an unsecured loan if you have an excellent credit rating and are putting up at least part of the capital yourself. Finance companies will often accept greater risk and may extend a loan when a bank will not, but they also charge higher interest rates and are not very flexible if there are problems repaying the loan. Again, a good financial advisor can help you evaluate your options.

Another potential source of capital is to sell equity in your business. An equity investment is not a loan, and there are no legal obligations to repay the investment. Instead, investors own a percentage of the business and share in all losses and profits. Though selling equity may be a good way to raise capital, you may also lose some control over your business.

The **Small Business Administration (SBA)** is still another source of start-up capital. The SBA is an independent agency of the U.S. government that promotes small businesses through loans, counseling, and other information. The SBA is particularly sensitive to women and minority business owners. You must exhaust all sources of private financing before you are eligible for an SBA loan. There are Small Business Administration offices in most major cities. Check the "U.S. Government" section of the telephone directory for locations and telephone numbers. You can also reach the SBA at **1-800-U ASK SBA.**

Finally, if you have the resources, it may be best to invest your own money. Not only is that usually the fastest and easiest way to raise capital, it also avoids the interest charges that can mean the difference between a new business being profitable or losing money. Investing your own money also can help avoid later complications, especially since you retain greater control of the business.

LOCATION

Once you determine that a certain community is large enough to support another flower shop—a good rule of thumb is a minimum of 10,000 people for every full-service florist—the most crucial decision you make will be where to locate the business. Many of the people who shop for flowers are impulse buyers, so you will need to be situated in an area with plenty of pedestrian traffic, such as a shopping mall or a busy commercial district.

Many florists prefer a storefront in a crowded business district, especially a corner location that allows them to create window displays that are visible from several directions. These shops target white-collar workers, who make up a majority of the market, especially at noon or when they are on their way home from work and more likely to stop and browse. Leasing space in a commercial building also may be less expensive than similar space in a mall.

Malls, however, offer their own particular advantages. Flower shops in malls tend to attract an even higher percentage of impulse buyers, rather than people wanting fancy arrangements, so not as much space is needed. In addition, shops generally have open fronts, so store owners can create attractive displays that encourage browsing. Of course,

FRANCHISE OPPORTUNITIES

Buning the Florist: 3860 W. Commercial Boulevard, Ft. Lauderdale, FL 33309; phone: (305) 486-3000.

Conroy's, Inc.: 6621 Pacific Coast Highway, Ste. 280, Long Beach, CA 90803; phone: (310) 594-4484.

Flowerama of America, Inc.: 3165 W. Airline Highway, Waterloo, IA 50701; phone: (319) 291-6004, or (800) 728-6004.

O'Malley's Flowers: 15303 Ventura Boulevard, Ste. 700, Sherman Oaks, CA 91403; phone: (818) 784-1897.

Wesley Berry Flowers: 15305 Schoolcraft Road, Detroit, MI 48227; phone: (800) 356-5690.

malls also attract customers even on cold, blustery days when people are rushing past storefront businesses without stopping. Many florists with mall locations also have found it easy and useful to set up a flower cart outside the store to generate more impulse buying or to attract attention to the main store.

Whichever type of location you chose, make sure the site is highly visible and easily accessible, with plenty of parking for your customers. Also make sure that there are no other florists nearby. Although some types of enterprises such as appliance stores often do well in clusters and generate business for each other, this is not true for flower shops. A new flower shop is unlikely to attract customers away from an established florist that has provided good service over the years. Pick a location that will be more convenient for the customers you hope to attract.

Once you have a tentative location, be sure the space is adequate. You may need as little as 600 to 800 square feet in a shopping mall, or as much as 2,000 square feet for a full-service flower shop. In a mall, look for a site with the widest possible opening to the common area to attract customers; as a potential storefront owner, look for the most window space.

More than half the space of your shop should be devoted to sales or customer service, including plenty of well-lighted display space. Be sure there is enough room for customers to browse comfortably. All flower shops will also need room for refrigerated display cases, while larger shops will need a walk-in refrigerator. You also will set aside room for a work area near the rear of the store for receiving, arranging, and shipping flowers, and a small space for an office and storage.

Once you have narrowed down your choices for a location, carefully consider the lease arrangements. Leases can be very complex, especially in a mall where you may be expected to contribute to common expenses, so make sure you understand all the conditions. Most building owners will ask you to sign a standard lease, but you should consider everything to be negotiable, including who is responsible for site improvements.

When it comes to the length of the lease, try to strike a balance between flexibility and security. You will not want to be locked into a long-term contract in case the location turns out to be a bad choice, but neither will you want to risk losing your lease at a good location and having to start over somewhere else. Your best option is probably a one-year lease with an option to renew for a longer period. Finally, if there is anything about the lease that makes you uncomfortable, consider looking elsewhere. The first site you find may not be the best. In general, you should not pay more than 10 to 12 percent of expected gross revenues.

MARKETING

Effective marketing is critical if you are to attract shoppers who can then be turned into loyal customers. In general, marketing consists of five major activities: market research, product development, distribution, pricing, and promotion.

Market research means learning as much as possible about your potential customers, especially when and where they buy flowers and what you can offer that other stores do not. There are many companies that do market research, but you can do a significant amount yourself simply by visiting other flower shops and talking to their customers.

Once you know more about your potential customers, you can begin product development. This includes determining the type of inventory you will need. Will your flower shop cater to people interested in formal arrangements or more simple cut flowers and green plants? When your flower shop is up and running, continue to talk with your customers—and with the people who browse but don't buy—to find out what they would like to see added to your product selection, especially any related products or services that would increase flower sales. For example, many flower shops offer a selection of small gift items; others even provide wedding planning services that range from helping select the flowers to planning the entire service.

Distribution encompasses when and where customers may purchase flowers and how they are delivered. Your hours of operation, how you handle telephone orders, whether you accept credit cards or checks, how long it takes to fill a request, and any special services, such as packaging and delivery, are all elements of distribution. Each can be tailored to attract a different segment of the market. A flower shop located near a popular restaurant or night spot, for instance, may stay open later than a shop in an office building that is deserted by 6 p.m.

Pricing, of course, can be another effective marketing tool, and special pricing may generate new business, especially during holidays. Barring weddings, though, the people who purchase flowers generally are not comparison shoppers. Undercutting the competition may be an attractive strategy, but new business owners need to remember that prices must cover not only the cost of inventory and overhead, but also yield a profit.

Finally, you must consider promotion, which encompasses all the ways you make your business known to your prospective customers. Promotion issues include the name of the business, signage, window and store displays, advertising, and programs such as speaking to garden clubs, writing columns for a local newspaper, and teaching flower arranging. As with other marketing activities, promotion can be tailored to attract different segments of the market. For example, the name you choose for your business can indicate the geographic area you serve, a strategy that may attract customers who prefer a local business, or it can give a clue as to whether you offer items in addition to flowers, which may attract customers searching for a gift. Whatever name you choose, be sure it clearly tells customers the type of business you intend to be.

Window displays should also be designed to attract specific customers. For example, a flower shop in a busy business district that hopes to invite impulse buyers may not want to fill display windows with wedding arrangements. But a florist in a suburban shopping center where customers are more likely to browse may choose to have more elaborate displays, especially if the flower shop is near a bakery or wedding boutique that also would attract potential customers. Of course, displays usually revolve around current holidays, especially Thanksgiving, Christmas, Valentine's Day, and Easter.

When, where, and how you advertise also will depend on the market segment you are targeting. A small shop in a mall that depends almost exclusively on impulse buyers may decide to advertise only in the mall itself. Most flower shops advertise in the Yellow Pages directory, but a flower shop that offers formal arrangements may want a second Yellow Pages listing in the wedding services section. The same shop will find it useful to advertise in magazines targeted at future brides, while a shop that specializes in live plants should perhaps advertise in publications for gardeners.

You will probably want to advertise holiday specials in the local newspapers, but again, this depends on your particular goals. If you take out ads in newspapers, be sure your advertising dollars are being spent effectively. A neighborhood flower shop may benefit from a small ad in the daily newspaper, but it may garner much more business from a

PRIMARY ASSOCIATIONS AND SELECTED TRADE PUBLICATIONS

Associations:

Society of American Florists: 1601 Duke St., Alexandria, VA 22314; phone: (703) 836-8700.

Florist's Transworld Delivery Association (FTD): 29200 Northwestern Highway, Southfield, MI 48037; phone: (313) 355-9300.

American Floral Services, Inc.: P.O. Box 12309, Oklahoma City, OK 73157; phone: (407) 947-3373.

Teleflora, Inc.: 12233 W. Olympic Boulevard, Los Angeles, CA 90064; phone: (213) 826-5253.

800 Flowers: 1600 Stewart Ave., Westbury, NY 11590; phone: (516) 237-6000.

Publications:

SAF: Business News for the Floral Industry: 1601 Duke St., Alexandria, VA 22314; phone: (703) 836-8700.
Florist's Review Magazine: 310 S. Michigan Ave., Chicago, IL 60604; phone: (312) 782-5505; or 3641 SW Plass Ave., Topeka, KS 66611; phone: (913) 266-0888.
Florist: 29200 Northwestern Highway, Southfield, MI 48037; phone: (313) 355-9300.
Flowers &: 12233 W. Olympic Boulevard, Los Angeles, CA 90064; phone: (213) 826-5253.

larger ad in a local weekly. One way to judge effectiveness is to promote a special in both newspapers and then ask your customers where they saw your ad. Flyers and direct mail advertising can also be very cost effective for flower shops.

INVENTORY

One of the most critical elements of running a flower shop will be learning to manage inventory. On one hand, a large and varied inventory will create a favorable impression on your customers and ensure that you can satisfy their needs. But cut flowers, which should account for about two-thirds of your inventory, are perishable. Customers will certainly not buy wilted flowers, and any waste will cut into your profits.

Most florists purchase flowers from wholesalers on Mondays, Wednesdays, and Fridays, which ensures fresh flowers for the weekend. Ordering often guarantees a steady supply of flowers without overstocking and allows florists to increase their regular orders for weddings, funerals, and holidays. Florists generally purchase about $5,000 worth of inventory for every $50,000 in retail sales.

Eventually, you should be able to estimate the flowers you need very accurately based on past sales experience. In the beginning, it is better to buy too much stock than too little. A flower shop that is understocked will disappoint prospective customers and prompt them to go elsewhere. Be

INDUSTRY STATISTICS

Number of Retail Flower Shops in the U.S.: 30,000 (source: Society of American Florists).
Annual U.S. Flower Sales: $10 billion (source: Perishables Research Organization).
Annual U.S. Retail Sales for Flower Shops: $4.3 billion (source: Society of American Florists).
Percent of Flower Shop Sales Through Franchise Outlets: (Estimate for the year 2000) 50% (source: U.S. Department of Commerce, Bureau of Industrial Economics).

sure to remove display flowers whenever they begin to droop. Wilted display flowers will create a bad impression and cause customers to go elsewhere. Florists often donate wilted or overstocked flowers to nonprofit organizations, making sure they get a signed receipt for tax purposes.

FLOWERS BY WIRE

Most flower shops belong to marketing organizations that also act as clearinghouses for orders placed with a florist in one city and filled by a florist in another. The largest of these is Florists' Transworld Delivery Association (FTD), which boasts more than 20,000 members worldwide. Another major organization is Teleflora, Inc. Depending primarily on the telephone for transmitting information, they have recently begun establishing computer networks. The flower shop that takes the order generally receives a 10 to 20 percent commission. Members complete a monthly report on orders taken and filled. The clearinghouse then submits a bill or sends payment to each member based on monthly activity. As much as 15 percent of your business may come from orders placed with florists in other cities.

Flower shops are only accepted into such organizations as FTD if they meet strict membership requirements that generally encompass personnel, signage, hours of operation, delivery facilities, and shop conditions, including lighting, displays, inventory, and supplies. They also offer marketing programs and provide training in marketing, flower designing, and flower shop management.

Finally, it is important to keep in mind that though hundreds of flower shops open every year, many of them fail. The Society of American Florists cautions that it may take up to five years for a new shop to become profitable. But for many shop owners who truly enjoy flowers and the pleasure they can bring customers, there is no better business to be in.

SOURCES:

Flower Shop, Business Start-Up Guide, EntrepreneurGroup, 1987.
''Thoughts on Flower Shop Management and Setting up a Retail Florist,'' *Sunlighting Florida Florists,* October 1990, p. 2.

—*Dean Boyer*

Food Delivery Service

W hy waste time driving to that great little restaurant, looking for a parking space, and waiting for a table or a take-out order when you can stay home and have your favorite restaurant entree too? Increasingly, a number of Americans are choosing to have their meals come to them via a food delivery service. The concept is simple: the food delivery service establishes delivery contracts with local eating establishments, which discount their food to the service; the delivery service takes phoned-in orders for restaurants, picks up the ordered meals, and then delivers food at menu price plus a small delivery charge. The concept is not only uncomplicated, it's profitable. Yet many communities are still waiting for a service to hit their town.

The food delivery industry was launched in the early 1980s when observant entrepreneurs like Domino Pizza's Tom Monahan recognized that big money could be made delivering pizzas to people either too busy or simply uninclined to cook or go out. Other pizza franchises followed Domino's lead, wetting the public's appetite for edibles other than pizza to be brought to the door. Since the mid-1980s the number of food delivery services has grown from a handful of operations to an estimated 1,000 services by 1994. Why? Because food delivery services capitalize on a number of growing socioeconomic trends: a shift towards a more service-based economy, a rise in the number of dual income families, an increase in carry-out orders, and a growing tendency towards cocooning or staying home rather than going out on the town. These facts, coupled with the vast amount of still untapped food delivery service markets, led industry observers to anticipate that this business will continue delivering profits to service owners throughout the 1990s.

COSTS AND PROFITS

Minimum start-up costs for a food delivery service run in the neighborhood of $19,000, with average start-up costs falling in the $40,000 range. Some delivery services report annual pretax profits in excess of $375,000, while most make closer to $70,000. The principal liabilities for a food delivery service owner consist of accounts payable, utility bills, payroll for dispatchers and drivers, and working capital loans. These can all be substantially trimmed by starting small—basing operations in the owner's home, paying drivers strictly on a per-delivery commission basis, and having drivers use their own self-insured vehicles.

FINANCING

Proper financing is necessary to be successful in any business, even an industry enjoying prosperous growth. So the first task in financing your new food delivery service is to determine how much money you will need based on projected start-up expenses. Costs will include equipment and fixtures, office rental, licenses/tax deposits, initial advertising, utilities, professional services, payroll, your own salary, supplies, a quarterly insurance payment, and a sufficient amount of operating capital to help see you through until you break even.

Sources of financing include equity investors, banks, finance companies, and the **Small Business Administration (SBA).** Before courting banks you may want to draw upon your own acquaintances who might be willing to participate in an equity investment. The disadvantage of this type of financing is that you may have to forfeit a portion of the control as well as the profits of your new business. The principal advantage is that you are under no legal obligation to repay the invested money.

Along with estimated earnings, expenses, timetables, and schedules for loan repayment, banks will want to know about your proposed management structure and personnel needs. The size of your market, your strategy for reaching sales projections, and what you will face in terms of competition will also be a concern. Starting a service in an area without food delivery will be to your advantage when trying to secure a loan. Be aware that in addition to collateral, banks may also ask you to post a cash reserve equal to 20 percent of a loan. Finance companies will be willing to accept a greater risk than a bank and be less concerned about the strength of your existing credit, but they will also charge a higher interest rate. Finance companies will want to know about your past financial record, the potential for your new business to be profitable, and what collateral you can offer.

The Small Business Administration may also serve as a loan source, but in order for you to qualify for an SBA loan

FRANCHISE OPPORTUNITIES

Take-Out Taxi: 1175 Herndon Parkway, Suite 150, Herndon, VA 22070; phone: (703) 689-4800. Founded, 1987; began franchising in May 1991. 75-plus outlets in the U.S.; have certain areas well covered, targeting smaller geographical areas than most services; represent variety of restaurants, from fast food to upscale; handle both lunch and dinner orders. Provided by franchisor: Classroom training program, on-site opening assistance, computer hardware and software, support service, office and delivery equipment, and supplies. Franchise start-up costs vary; typical 1994 costs ranged between $71,000 and $91,000.

Since its 1987 founding, Takeout Taxi has evolved into the nation's leading multi-restaurant delivery service company. Between 1991 and 1993 Takeout Taxi's number of outlets grew from five to more than 60 as total sales rose from $1 million to $17 million. In 1993 Taylor Devine joined Takeout Taxi as company president after five years with Blockbuster Entertainment, during which time the video franchisor grew from 270 stores to more than 3,000. Devine has pledged to turn Takeout Taxi into the Blockbuster of the food delivery service industry.

Other Franchisors: Waiters on Wheels: 425 Divisadero St., Suite 304, San Francisco, CA 94117; phone: (415) 252-1470. **Carry Out Cab:** 1100 E. Hector St., Suite 389, Conshohocken, PA, 19428; phone: (215) 413-7241. **Delivery Xpress:** 3321 Greenfield, Dearborn, MI, 48120; phone: (313) 336-3463.

you must be starting an independently owned and operated business and be unable to secure financing on reasonable terms elsewhere. For more information about SBA guidelines call **1-800-U ASK SBA,** or write: **Small Business Directory, P.O. Box 1000, Ft. Worth, TX 76119.** For the local SBA office nearest you, check the ''U.S. Government'' section in your telephone directory.

LOCATION

The office of a food delivery business should be centrally located within the planned service area and have adequate parking for dispatchers and drivers. Because customers will have no reason to visit your office, you need not look for a highly visible location. For financial reasons, you may want to start your business from home. Regardless of whether you choose a home-based operation or not, before deciding upon an office location you should talk with your local zoning officer about restrictive zoning codes and ordinances that may prohibit certain business operations or limit parking.

An area comprised of both residential housing and other potential day-time sources of orders—for example, colleges, hotels, and corporate offices—could boost sales significantly. In the beginning you'll need at least 20,000 households and seven restaurant accounts to be a viable business. More established food delivery services generally operate in an area with a four-to-six-mile radius yielding

30,000 to 60,000 households and 20 restaurants. So meals may be delivered within 45 minutes of an order, many services limit their area to that which can be reached in 15 minutes. Plotting the restaurants with which you would like to contract and the housing and business districts you want to target is one effective way of determining an ideal location for your company. When mapping out your service area, don't forget to plan for growth.

EQUIPMENT AND SUPPLIES

Sources of supplies tailored to the food delivery industry are continually coming into availability. By subscribing to relevant trade publications, you can keep abreast of these developments. You'll find that the necessary tools for food delivery help you keep in touch with two groups: your customers and the restaurants. The key to operating an efficient service will be your ability to communicate quickly and clearly with both.

The least expensive, though least efficient, means of relaying orders to restaurants is via telephone, although this method can work for smaller operations. If you choose to use a phone, you will need a minimum of two customer lines to avoid tying up calls. You will also want a separate line, preferably running directly to the kitchen, for each restaurant with which you contract. For information about calling features that may speed your operations and new business phone package deals, contact your local telephone company's business sales representative.

Alternative ways of communicating orders can be just as useful. Facsimiles can provide an efficient means of sending orders while simultaneously generating a copy of each order for both you and the restaurants. If you choose to send orders by fax or modem the restaurants you are working with will need similar equipment. The most expensive communications setup utilizes a computer modem, allowing orders to be sent straight from your computer to a restaurant's computer and printer.

Even if you use a fax to transmit orders, a computer system can still make your business more efficient. Besides simplifying and speeding up your bookkeeping, billing, and filing processes, computers can be used to compile demographic information on your customers—where they live, their food and restaurant preferences, and the frequency with which they order. With such information you can generate targeted mailing lists. Similarly, computers can be used to design marketing and promotional materials, including menu guides, a marketing necessity that lists the restaurants and their menus for your customers. In addition, computer software map programs can be invaluable in showing dispatchers the fastest route for drivers.

The ideal computer setup is a multi-user system that would link all of your computer terminals to a central processing unit (CPU). Ask your local computer retailer for information about computer hardware systems. The best sources of material on software programs tailored to the food delivery industry are other delivery service owners, custom-designed software manufacturers, and trade journals, such as *Meal Delivery Digest.*

You also need to keep in close contact with your delivery personnel. Each driver should have a two-way radio—either hand-held or car-mounted; this will help you convey customer orders and other directions. Then for deliveries you can use your own personal vehicle, lease or purchase a vehicle, or have your drivers use their own cars, which is what most food delivery businesses do. Vehicles should display signs—a relatively inexpensive advertisement—with your company name. If drivers use their own vehicles you can buy magnetic door signs or rooftop signs from a local sign shop. Your company's name can be painted on vehicles you own, or featured on vinyl signs that can be permanently applied.

To transport meals you should purchase insulated hot food boxes or bags that lose only two to three degrees per hour. You will need three to five of these bags or boxes for each driver. Depending on the size, bags range in price from $25 to $35, while boxes sell for $100 to $200. You may also want to purchase some type of matching uniforms that drivers can either buy from you or checkout from your office each day. Services often use a wide variety of uniforms, ranging from tuxedos to polo shirts or windbreakers.

INDUSTRY STATISTICS

- *Growth in Off-Premise Dining:* (mid-1980s to 1993) 40% (source: National Restaurant Association).
- *Number of Food Delivery Services:* (1986) less than a dozen; (1993) 800; (1994 projection) 1,000 (source: *Meal Delivery Digest*).
- *Amount of Restaurant Traffic for Off-premise Consumption:* (1992) nearly half (source: National Restaurant Association).
- *Total Sales Growth of All Food Service Businesses:* (projection, 1991 to 1994) 3.7% (source: National Restaurant Association).
- *Sales Growth in the Food Delivery Service Industry:* 19% between 1988 and 1991, from $5.7 billion to $6.8 billion (source: Hale Group).
- *Adult Satisfaction With Service at Table Service Restaurants:* (1992) 69% (source: National Restaurant Association).
- *Number of Adults That Were Food-service Patrons on a Typical Day:* (1992) slightly less than half (source: National Restaurant Association).
- *Number of Restaurants an Average Food Delivery Service Works With:* 10 to 15 (source: *Meal Delivery Digest*).
- *Percentage of Food Dollar Spent on Restaurant Bills:* 43% (source: 1994 *Money* magazine).
- *Leading Types of Food in the Take-out Market:* Pizza, 36%; sandwiches and hamburgers, 27%; chicken, 11%; Asian, 4%; retail host, 3%; all other, 19% (source: National Restaurant Association).
- *Sales Growth for Take-out Pizza:* (1982-87) more than 50 percent (source: National Restaurant Association).

OFFICE SETUP

Some food delivery services start from a home-based office in order to reduce initial costs. A spare room can easily be converted to an office if you have a business phone line installed, but keep in mind that the room must be used solely as an office in order to fully capitalize on business tax breaks. If you start your service from home, you should rent a post office box and enlist an insurance agent to find out if your present home insurance will protect you against business-related liabilities.

A service using six drivers and three dispatchers per shift can be accommodated by 800 square feet, while few operations will require more than 1,500 square feet. Ideally a food delivery operation should have enough room to set up desks for your dispatchers and provide you with a separate office. You should have a desk and a telephone for each dispatcher, and if you computerize right away, each dispatcher's desk should have a computer terminal and keyboard. Additionally you may want to include a room with chairs and tables for drivers not in the midst of a delivery.

STAFFING

A food delivery service area with 30,000 to 60,000 households can be covered effectively with four to six drivers and one to three dispatchers per shift. If you want to capitalize on business clients, you will want to be open from roughly 10 a.m. to 11 p.m. and may need more full-time staff than if you maintained shorter hours. Some services choose to start with only late afternoon and evening hours, while others run split shifts and don't offer services during mid-afternoon hours.

When hiring staff, consider what duties your workers will be performing. Dispatchers will be responsible for answering phones, taking orders, transmitting orders to restaurants, and dispatching drivers via two-way radio. Dispatchers should be paid an hourly wage that will attract potential employees with good communications and office skills; many services pay between $7 and $8. Drivers will be responsible for picking up and delivering food, so you should look for applicants with both a good driving record and a knowledge of the area to be served. Most food delivery services hire drivers who will use their own cars and act as independent contractors. Drivers are generally paid on a commission basis, which in most services means the driver earns the delivery charge (usually $3 to $5, though some services charge as much as $7 to $9), plus tips.

If you plan to be open 10 to 14 hours a day, you will probably need an assistant manager to cover for you when you can't be in the office. An assistant manger should be well versed in all phases of your service and should, therefore, be paid at least a few dollars an hour more than dispatchers. Aside from the wages you offer, any benefit program you put together will help you hire and retain qualified workers.

PRIMARY ASSOCIATIONS AND SELECTED TRADE PUBLICATIONS

Associations:

Food Marketing Institute: 1750 K St., N.W., Washington, DC, 20006; phone: (202) 452-8444.

National Restaurant Association (NRA): 1200 17th St., N.W., Washington, DC, 20036-3097; phone: (202) 331-5900.

Publications:

Meal Delivery Digest: Meal Delivery Ltd., 24275 La Hermosa Ave., Laguna Niguel, CA 92677; phone: (714) 495-4345. Meal Delivery Ltd. is a consulting firm owned and operated by *Digest* publisher Peter Hetherington. Aside from the quarterly publication, the firm also markets Hetherington's "Meal Delivery Manual"—offering an overview of the food delivery industry and a guide to marketing, operations, equipment, and supplies—and a "Presentation Folder," to help new services sign restaurants.
Restaurant Business, 633 Third Avenue, New York, NY 10017; phone: (212) 986-4800.
Restaurants & Institutions, 1350 E. Toughy Ave., P.O. Box 5080, Des Plaines, IL 60017-5080; phone: (708) 635-8800.
Restaurants USA, 1200 17th St., N.W., Washington, DC 20036; phone: (202) 331-5900.

MANAGEMENT ISSUES

Initially much of your time as a manager will be spent securing service contracts with restaurants and working with their managers. You should seek a diverse mix of restaurants with which to work. Keep in mind that it is not necessarily higher-priced restaurants nor high-income customers that generate the greatest profits. The prime restaurants to work with are those with a medium-priced menu that are known to serve quality food.

Be prepared to convince restaurants of the financial advantages your service can offer by creating a promotional package outlining the benefits of participating in food delivery. You should mention added exposure via your menu guide, new customers, and increased sales during days with inclement weather. Your promotional materials should also describe the logistics of your service and offer preliminary restaurant sales estimates. Let the eateries know how much you expect for a discount—traditionally 25 to 30 percent—and the delivery fee you will charge, but be willing to negotiate discount percentages. Sometimes a well-known restaurant will enhance your service's image or generate so much in sales that a smaller cut for you will still pay dividends.

In pricing your services you may want to establish a per-order minimum of $10 and, in order to encourage larger orders, you can offer free delivery for orders over a certain dollar amount. You may also want to explore other delivery opportunities. Some services have had success delivering products such as videos and flowers. If you want to deliver movies you should solicit video dealers and ask them to set aside a few copies of ten or 12 popular titles for your business. If you do choose to deliver videos you will probably want to establish a higher delivery charge for strictly movie orders—such as $5 to $7—and a lesser fee, such as $1, for each additional title or for a movie to be delivered with a meal. Securing a contract to deliver flowers, particularly from a florist that does not offer delivery services, should be relatively easy. Again you will want to establish higher delivery rates to address flower orders without meals.

Aside from the standard tax-related paperwork employers need to file, if you do hire drivers as independent contractors you will generally be required to file an annual information return (IRS Form 1099) for these workers. Legally a driver cannot be considered an independent contractor if s/he works for only one service without offering services elsewhere. If a driver is hired as an employee and earns more than $20 a month from tips, this income must be reported monthly using Form 4070. You must then withhold social security and income due on this amount of tips from the employee's wages, but you are only required to match the Social Security tax deducted from wages, not from tips. A driver working as a contractor must pay her/his own Social Security. For more information on tax matters, contact your local Internal Revenue Service office. Check your phone directory for the IRS location nearest you.

If you are overwhelmed by the thought of starting a business on your own, you may want to explore franchise opportunities. Franchises can offer business expertise, market advice, and a proven way of operating. The most established one, Take Out Taxi, can provide franchisees with computer software custom-designed for the food delivery industry. The disadvantages to franchises include fees and the slice of profits franchisors take.

MARKETING

Initially many food delivery business owners find they have to market a service unknown to the public. Consequently, it is imperative that you do your homework, surveying potential customers to find out what types of people would use delivery services and what foods they would like to see delivered. This data could be gathered via direct mail surveys, telemarketing, or personal interviews, all which could also help generate start-up mailing lists. Once your business is established, you can use the demographic information you have gathered through orders.

During the day many food delivery operations find success serving corporate clients; this is especially true in large cities. Hotels—particularly those too small to offer room service—also represent a market segment waiting to be draw upon. In the suburbs lunch orders will be limited while a majority of dinners ordered will be for dual-income families wanting meals from moderately priced restaurants.

Theoretically anyone with a small amount of disposable income can be attracted by food delivery service, and some services find that much of their business comes from moderate and low income apartment dwellers.

Promotions can help any food delivery service attract and retain customers. Some services send out postcards to first-time customers the day after they've ordered, offering the next order free. Other services attract customers through delivery discounts featured in coupon mailers. The key to promotions involves punching the right buttons to attract and retain customers; so the more you know about your customer base the better.

ADVERTISING

Advertising for a food delivery service is a two-fold task. You must first make potential customers aware of what a food delivery service is and how one operates and then make people want to use your service. A well-promoted grand opening—utilizing free publicity from local media, especially if your service is the first in your area—is crucial to getting the word out. Mailing handbills is also a fairly inexpensive means of debuting your service and later reminding customers of the service you offer. You may want to enhance your opening by giving away promotional items like pens, visors, calendars, or t-shirts with your company name. They too can serve as an ongoing source of advertising.

The best form of advertising for a food delivery service is a menu guide, and the best though most expensive means of distributing a guide is through direct mail. One way to offset the cost of printing menus, at approximately 10 cents per copy, is to require restaurants you work with to pay a fee for being listed. If this doesn't go over well, you can sell advertising space on your menus to other businesses. Menus may be bulk mailed, but this method is much slower than direct mail and perceived as less personal. Many services hand distribute their menus to the doorsteps of potential customers. You can also have restaurants you work with hand out your menu guides to their customers and ask hotels to leave guides in their rooms.

On top of menu costs, food delivery operations generally allocate about one percent of their projected gross sales for advertising. You may find that local newspapers and radio stations serve you well because they speak to your entire delivery area. An ad in the Yellow Pages can also represent a good annual investment once your service is known.

LICENSES AND INSURANCE

In order to start a food delivery service you will need to obtain a local business license and the city and/or state sales tax permits required in your area. Check with your city and county clerks for specifics. In some cases you may be required to obtain a county health department permit, although such permits should not be required if your drivers do not open food packages or handle food in any way. On top of standard business insurance, you may want to purchase a non-ownership automobile liability insurance policy that would compensate for any inadequacies of your drivers' liability policies.

In the final analysis almost anyone—armed with the proper research and a willingness to put in some long hours during the business start-up period—can effectively operate a food delivery service. By the third or fourth month a well-run service should break even, although there are sound business reasons for putting the first year's profits back into the operation. But once firmly established with a customer base and key communications equipment, a food delivery service can open the door to significant profits.

SOURCES:

Alderman, Lesley, "Eating on the Run: Fast Food Will Go Gourmet as Home Delivery Services Cater to All Tastes," *Money,* Forecast 1994 Issue.

Butcher, Lola, "Ahhh . . . a Loaf of Bread, a Jug of Root Beer—Call Takeout Taxi," *Kansas City Business Journal,* December 11, 1992, p. 1.

Casper, Carol, "Food-To-Go: Heady Growth Has Tapered off to Steady Increases," *Restaurant Business,* November 1, 1991.

Food Delivery Service: Entrepreneur Business Guide No. 1348, Entrepreneur Group, 1990.

"Food Delivery Service: Waiters on Wheels," *25 Hot Businesses for the Nineties,* Entrepreneur Group, 1992.

Hetherington, Peter B., "Delivery Services: Growth and History," *Meal Delivery Digest,* Spring 1993, p. 1.

Hetherington, Peter B., "Making PR Work: Publicity & Press Releases," *Meal Delivery Digest,* Spring 1993, p. 1.

Huffman, Frances, "Hot Opportunity: Delivering Profits," *Business Start-Ups,* November 1993, pp. 64-69.

Hughes, Paul, "Top 10 Businesses for 1994," *Business Start-Ups,* January 1994, p. 41.

Lee, Consella A., "Sustenance, Profits Found in Food-Delivery Business," *The Baltimore Sun,* December 9, 1993.

"Lunch Delivery," *Entrepreneur Magazine's 168 More Businesses Anyone Can Start and Make a Lot of Money,* second edition, Bantam, 1991, p. 15-16.

Madden, Michael, editor, *Small Business Start-Up Index,* Issue 3, Gale, 1991.

"New on the Menu: Takeout-Delivery Firms Dish out Marketing Services as Well," *The Wall Street Journal,* September 16, 1993, p. 1.

Ryan, Nancy Ross, "Food to Go Is on a Roll," *Restaurants & Institutions,* March 6, 1991.

Wernle, Bradford, "Can Concept Stand and Deliver: Franchisor Seeks to Bring Restaurants to Your Door," *Crain's Detroit Business,* July 12, 1993, p. 9.

—ROGER W. ROULAND

Golf Shop

olf has become the fastest-growing sport in the United States, surpassing tennis in popularity. In the 1990s, the number of golfers has grown by four percent annually, while the number of people taking up tennis has increased by two percent. Golf has exploded in popularity perhaps because it is a sport that can be played "from cradle to grave." Golf is the favored sport of senior citizens, a growing segment of the U.S. population, and is increasingly being played by women—who comprise the fastest-growing segment of the golfing public.

With the golf industry as a whole worth more than $20 billion, there are many business opportunities for the entrepreneur. Golf equipment and apparel command a $2 billion market, making golf shops a potentially profitable enterprise that can become recession proof. Golf shops are either pro shops owned by a country club, private, independent shops, or franchises.

COSTS AND PROFITS

Golf pro shops owned by country clubs are probably the least expensive golf shop operation, since the club owns the store and is in charge of payroll. The operator of the golf pro shop is the owner of the merchandise sold in the shop; the owner's only capital expenditure is for inventory. Because many vendors are willing to extend credit for merchandise, start-up costs for the pro shop owner are minimal, ranging from $3,000 to $10,000.

The privately owned, independent golf shop, selling mainly clothing and equipment, is a far more expensive and risky operation to own than a pro shop, due to stiff competition from discount franchises and the absence of club members, who are the main customer base for the golf pro shop. However, this might well be the most satisfying business for the golf lover turned entrepreneur who enjoys being his or her own boss and does not want to pay a franchise fee.

Start-up costs, of course, vary widely for the independent golf shop owner: at the minimum, one can expect to pay for a store lease, a burglar alarm system, cash registers, a computer system, and inventory—all of which can add up to anywhere from $75,000 to $200,000. What also must be taken into account is the near certainty of the shop's operat-

ing in the red for at least two years. Realistically, then, start-up costs will push well beyond the $75,000 range.

Initial costs for starting a discount golf shop franchise will run approximately $175,000, which includes the franchise fee, inventory, and store, making this alternative the most popular for golf shop entrepreneurs. Newly established golf shop franchises also tend to operate in the red the first year or two, necessitating a substantial reserve capital. Profitability can run as high as $100,000 a year before taxes, depending on many factors in the highly fragmented golf industry.

FINANCING

As a first step in securing financing, you should consider approaching your local **Small Business Administration (SBA)** for advice, rather than your local bank. Call your chamber of commerce for the phone number of the nearest SBA office or phone **1-800-U ASK SBA.** Be aware that the SBA is usually very busy. You may be put on hold or be routed through an automatic operator. Be patient and persistent—the SBA is there to help you, and a counselor will sit down with you and advise you for free on how to secure a loan, and answer any other business questions you may have. Your counselor will guide you through the steps of drawing up an effective business plan. The SBA also lends money, but only if you have exhausted all other financing options.

Another resource is your local librarian, who is accustomed to business queries and can quickly point you in the direction of scores of books in every library dealing with small business loans and operations. Your SBA counselor also will be glad to recommend relevant books.

The reason for taking these preliminary steps is that the task of applying for a loan can be a daunting one. Your business as yet has no history. You must prove convincingly that there is a market and future for it, which requires research, planning, and expert advice.

Once you have drawn up a detailed business plan, you're ready to present it to a bank for a loan. There are several types of bank loans with varying interest rates. If you're willing to pay a lot of interest, you may want to turn immediately to any number of finance companies that spe-

REFERENCES AND TRADE PUBLICATIONS

References:

Golf Equipment & Supplies—Retail Directory: American Business Directories, Inc., 5711 S. 86th Circle, Omaha, NE 68127; phone: (402) 593-4600.

Golf Tips: Werner and Werner Corp., 16000 Ventura Blvd., Suite 201, Encino, CA 91436; phone: (310) 820-1500.

Sporting Goods Retailers Directory: American Business Directories, Inc.; 5711 S. 86th Circle; Omaha, NE 68127; phone: (402) 593-4600.

Sports Market Place: Sportsguide, Inc., P.O. Box 1417, Princeton, NJ 08540; phone: (609) 921-8599.

Publications:

Golf Shop Operations: Golf Digest/Tennis, Inc., P.O. Box 0395, Trumbull, CT 06611-0395; phone: (203) 373-7231.

Golf Industry: Sterling Southeast, Inc., 1450 NE 123rd St., North Miami, FL 33161-6051; phone: (305) 893-8771.

Golf Market Today: National Golf Foundation (NGF), 1150 S. U.S. Highway 1, Jupiter, FL 33477; phone: (407) 744-6006.

Sporting Goods Business: Gralia Publications, 1515 Broadway, New York, NY 10036; phone: (212) 869-1300.

Sports Trend: Shore Communications, Inc.; 180 Allen Rd., NE, Bldg. N., Ste. 300, Atlanta, GA 30328; phone: (404) 252-8831.

cialize in lending to businesses and tend to take on greater risks than a bank.

Golf pro shop owners who are fortunate enough to operate a shop owned by a country club have the least amount of start up capital to worry about, and need not consider reserve capital. In this case, if you cannot rely on your savings or a loan from friends or relatives, then the quickest and easiest means of obtaining funds is your credit card, provided you can pay off the loan in six months. Virtually all banks offer short term loans for such cases, but they can entail a great deal of red tape you might wish to avoid.

LOCATION AND MANAGEMENT

For the independently owned or franchised golf shop, it is not enough to locate your store on or near a high traffic area. You should be accessible to foot traffic as well, and to public transportation. Ideally, you should be situated close to a public golf course and, if possible, in or near an affluent neighborhood. If that is not feasible, being situated in a shopping mall or near one can be a plus, although this can mean high rent expenses.

For a $2,000 fee, Integrity Golf in Edmond, Oklahoma will do a detailed survey of potential locations for your business, or will examine the location you have selected and help you with gauging your market and assessing your competition.

A country club golf pro shop will take its clientele from the club membership. In most clubs, members must go to the pro shop to make reservations and pay greens fees. Set up your counter in the rear of the store so that customers and members must pass by your merchandise each time they play golf. What the golf pro shop may lack in variety of merchandise or personal services is made up for in clothing and other merchandise that bears the particular country club's logo. Club members will naturally be interested in these personalized items, and, because they are usually affluent, they may be willing to pay higher prices for the latest fashions and merchandise.

Independently owned and franchised shops have the advantage of offering a great variety of merchandise. Franchise shops can attract customers with low prices, while the private, independently owned golf shop can offer special services that franchises and pro shops may lack, such as custom made golf clubs, golf equipment repair, and rentals. Any golf shop should have enough room for customers to take their clubs for a ''test drive''—which means you'll need high ceilings. Many successful shops have sophisticated setups, including computers and video screens, that allow for customers to hit balls into a net, analyze their swing, and even play simulated rounds of golf on famous courses. You can also devote land around the shop for use as a driving range for hitting practice balls. Ideally, your shop will be large, with room for expansion in the future.

MARKETING AND ADVERTISING

Marketing and advertising in a country club pro shop depends mostly on the good word of your customers. You should stress the latest fashion merchandise, especially clothing, and create an interesting, evolving floor display that will continue to intrigue customers who may be in your shop several times a week.

Advertising and marketing are much more involved for franchised and private golf shops. If you can afford the expense, have a firm like Integrity Golf do a marketing strategy plan for you. If your pockets are not quite deep enough for that, you can start marketing before you even open your shop. Decide what your shop can offer that will make it stand out and differ from those of your competitors. You'll need to purchase business stationery and business cards. It also helps to get your shop's name established in the trade and the community; you can send ads to all the local newspapers, involve your store in sponsoring local events or perhaps a Little League team or softball team, and advertise in trade magazines. If you provide good service and attempt to make your store stand out, you've won half the battle. The golf community is close-knit, and word of mouth can make your store a success.

STAFFING AND EMPLOYEE TRAINING

It is extremely difficult to run a golf shop alone. Having a partner is nice because you can share expenses as well as the work. Failing that, an employee can be a great asset, but is also an expense. Hiring an employee entails a whole new set of problems and requirements. Once you have made up your mind to hire, you will have to bear in mind the need for a proper job description, and the multitude of forms that you will have to fill out: tax forms, workman's compensation forms, social security and wage forms. You can pay as low as minimum wage—but you will probably get what you pay for in terms of job performance. Competitive wages are always the best rule of thumb to follow when hiring.

Unlike most retail stores, a golf shop will attract potential employees who are knowledgeable about the game and the equipment. A certain amount of expertise is, of course, indispensable for your employees, so you should include this criterion in the job description. Not all new employees will have experience in retail sales or computers, however, and this kind of training will be up to you. All employees must be willing to keep abreast of their sport and the golf shop business, so you may wish to make watching televised golf and reading the latest magazines a part of their responsibilities.

LICENSES AND INSURANCE

You will need a number of licenses to open your business; check with your state, county, and local governments about licensing and zoning requirements. You can also find out what business permits and licenses you need by calling your chamber of commerce or a librarian. Virtually every county

HELPFUL COMPUTER SOFTWARE

Golf Shop Software:

Proshop Retail: Handicomp, Inc., P.O. Box 87, 60 Baldwin St., Jenison, MI 49428-0087; phone: (800) 833-0033, or (616) 457-9581. This firm, in business for more than 25 years, sells a wide range of computer systems for the golf shop, running from approximately $1650 for the complete pro shop management system to $250 for wordprocessing software geared to the needs of the golf shop.

Software for the Retail Store:

Peachtree Complete Accounting for DOS (also available for Windows), $189. A few main features are inventory for the small business, order entry, accounts receivable/payable.
CA-BPI Accounting II for DOS (also Windows version), $164. Main features are payroll in addition to inventory, accounts receivable/payable.
Quick Books & Quick Pay for DOS with Payroll, $109. Speeds up bill paying and invoicing.
One-Write Plus Accounting (DOS), $89. Features check writing, billing, inventory, accounts receivable/payable.
TurboTAX (DOS and Windows), $39. Claims to be the number one selling tax software; offers complete tax preparation.

Note: Prices cited are retail and approximate.

FOR FURTHER ASSISTANCE

Financing:

The National Association of Small Business Investment Companies (NASBIC): 1199 N. Fairfax Street, Alexandria, VA 22314; (703) 683-1601. The membership directory of this organization lists, in each state, small business investment companies (which charge higher interest rates than most banks, but are willing to assume more risk). Directory also lists loan limits. This is available for $10 at NASBIC, P.O. Box 2039, Merrifield, VA 22116.

Associations:

National Golf Foundation (NGF): 1150 S. US Highway 1, Jupiter, FL 33477; phone: (407) 744-6006.

National Sporting Goods Association (NSGA): Lake Center Plaza Building, 1699 Wall Street, Mount Prospect, IL 60056-5780; phone: (708) 439-4000.

Professional Golf Club Repairmen's Association (PGCRA): 2053 Harvard Ave., Dunedin, FL 34698; phone: (813) 733-4348.

Franchisors:

Golf USA: 1801 S. Broadway, Edmond, OK 73013; phone: (405) 341-0009.

Nevada Bob's Pro Shops: 3333 E. Flamingo Rd., Las Vegas, NV 89121; phone: (702) 451-3333.

Pro Golf Discount: 31884 Northwestern Highway, Farmington Hills, MI 48018; phone: (313) 737-0553.

publishes an annual small business guide that lists relevant information and phone numbers. Do not expect to obtain the required permits and licenses instantly—you may have to wait several weeks. Check the Yellow Pages for insurance companies, and be prepared to ask a lot of questions. You want to find an insurer that specializes in helping small businesses.

COMPUTER SYSTEMS AND PROGRAMS

Unless you're a computer programming wizard and can design a software program to help you run your business, you'll be wise to invest in a packaged commercial program that can do your bookkeeping, track inventory, and much more. There are many bookkeeping software packages available for under $200, as well as software that prints forms, labels, and tags, and still others that do your checkwriting and mailing list(s). Call a good local software store and describe your business plan thoroughly; a knowledgeable vendor should be able to find a software that meets your needs. If you have a little more to invest, you can look into any number of computer systems and software designed specifically for golf shop operations. Proshop Retail, a company that offers a range of such products, will install a system for approximately $2,000.

Your golf shop can be tailored in any way you wish—provided you've found a solid, loyal customer base. But running a golf shop is not just about enjoying golf. Retail businesses require long hours and often years of patience before they can become profitable. Fortunately, golf is enjoying a booming popularity in the United States and more businesses will need to come forward to meet the demand.

SOURCES:

Durgin, Hillary, ''Golf Is Suburbs' New Way to Generate More Green,'' *Crain's Chicago Business,* June 28, 1993, p. 4.

Fiedelholtz, Sara, ''The Retail Trail; Pro Shop Merchandisers Count Department Store Training,'' *Women's Wear Daily,* September 15, 1993, p. G14.

Lippincott, Liz, ''Going Shopping (Women's Golf Clothing),'' *WWD,* September 15, 1993, p. G1.

Lloyd, Brenda, ''Golf Biz Proving Weatherproof in Southeast (Men's Clothing),'' *Daily News Record,* August 30, 1993, p. 46.

Nelson, Janet, ''Getting Into Golf (Salesmen),'' *Sales and Marketing Management,* July 1990, pp. 70-72.

Smith, Ron, ''Golf Industry Provides Lease-Sale Firm Option,'' *Implement & Tractor,* August/September 1993, p. 2.

Stogel, Chuck, ''It All Adds Up (Advertising in the Right Places at the Right Times Can Pay Off for Club Pros),'' *Golf Pro,* August 1993, pp. 58-60.

''Tee-Off Time (Acquisitions and Consolidation in the Golf-Course Industry),'' *Forbes,* November 8, 1993, p. 14.

''Tee Time,'' *Entrepreneur,* August 1989, pp. 50-57

Willwerth, James, ''Driving Reign (Golf Clubs),'' *Time,* September 6, 1993, p.50.

—*Sina Dubovoj*

Hair Salon

Just about everyone needs a haircut, even in hard economic times. Indeed, most consumers are willing to spend less or even forego other items rather than cut back on services such as haircuts. Traditionally considered one of the few genuine recession-proof businesses, hair salons are snipping, shampooing, wrapping, waxing, and massaging their customers more than ever before.

The hair salon business expanded rapidly during the 1980s, with sales growing at an annual rate of 15 to 20 percent near the end of the decade. In the 1990s, annual sales growth declined, but the beauty industry was working hard to persuade middle-class people that salon services are necessities rather than frivolous luxuries for the rich. The industry's marketing success was dramatic. No longer considered self-indulgent excesses, but healthy pursuits, the wide array of specialties at a full-service salon include aroma therapeutic massages, manicures, eyebrow arching, seaweed wraps, permanent waves, and coloring. If a person is not inclined to go to a full-service salon, there are numerous franchises that offer simply low-cost haircuts.

COSTS AND PROFITS

Start-up costs for a hair salon run from $2,500, to furnish a room at home with used equipment, up to $175,000 for a large, full-service salon. Average start-up costs are around $20,000. Depending on the amount invested and/or borrowed to start a salon, it generally takes two months to four years to reach the break-even point. Annual sales range from $20,000 to $300,000, while yearly pretax profits fall between $15,000 and $75,000, with an additional $2,000 to $10,000 in tips. Liabilities may include franchise fees, working capital loans or monthly rental payments, the purchase of equipment, and the normal accounts payable.

FINANCING

During the late 1980s and early 1990s, hair salons developed along two paths: full-service salons that offer manicures, eyebrow arching, skin care, massages, and the normal cuts and perms; and franchises that provide inexpensive haircuts with no-frills services and deal in high volumes. Before starting a salon, you should have a good idea of which path you wish to follow in order to encourage growth—either selling a full range of beauty and hair services to a small clientele, or bringing in numerous customers for affordable haircuts. The direction you take will determine your costs for advertising, your pricing, and your equipment purchases.

Once you've decided on the kind of salon you want to open, the next step is to figure out the amount of money needed to open a shop. Hairdresser, cosmetology, barber, and beautician associations and trade publications are invaluable sources for pre-financing and start-up cost information. You also might go straight to a beauty salon owner and inquire about how to best finance your own business within the beauty industry.

Financing a full-service salon involves very significant initial costs, and it is rare that a commercial bank will lend that amount of money to a brand new operation. As an alternative, you can arrange for a personal loan based on personal assets and previous business experience, or approach the U.S. **Small Business Administration (SBA)** and apply for a loan through one of its lending programs. The SBA can be reached by phoning **1-800-U ASK SBA.** If you decide to open a no-frills, high volume, cut and perm beauty shop, your best option—and one that is becoming more and more popular throughout the United States—is franchising. Becoming a franchisee minimizes the risk of starting your own beauty shop, since the parent company usually guides you every step along the way. Many franchisors offer financing and sometimes help to arrange a commercial loan against the purchase of a franchise store.

LOCATION

One of the most important decisions you will make in opening a hair salon is determining a location. Unless you intend to work out of your home, you will first need to find a site for your shop, and that means arranging to build, buy, rent, or renovate the premises. When selecting a location, be sure to evaluate the neighborhood and whether it has high traffic volume and good customer accessibility; you might even be able to negotiate a lower rent, for example, in a neighborhood where retail shops and storekeepers encourage new businesses to help build customer traffic. If you intend to open a full-service beauty salon and attract a wealthier

FRANCHISE OPPORTUNITIES

Supercuts: Northgate Drive, San Rafael, CA 94903; phone: (415) 472-1177, or (800) 999-2887. Founded, 1975; more than 550 outlets throughout the United States; franchises haircutting salons designed to provide affordable hair cuts, styling, and shampooing for women, men, and children. Provided by the franchisor: financing, training programs on topics such as record keeping, employee relations, and customer service; additional assistance in market research, public relations, site selection and construction, staff training and ongoing recertification. Fees range from approximately $90,000 to $200,000. It is recommended that the franchisee have a net worth of not less than $150,000. Franchisor does not require previous hair-care industry experience.

Other Franchisors: Accent Hair Salons: 211 S. Main St., Ste. 1130, Dayton, OH 45402; phone: (513) 461-0394. **City Looks:** 300 Industrial Blvd. NE, Minneapolis, MN 55413; phone: (612) 331-8500. **Cost Cutters:** 300 Industrial Blvd. NE, Minneapolis, MN 55413; phone: (612) 331-8500. **Custom Cuts:** 13846 Manchester, St. Louis, MO 63011; phone: (314) 391-1717. **Family Haircut Store:** 398 Hebron Ave., Glastonbury, CT 06033; phone: (203) 659-1430. **Fantastic Sam's:** 3180 Old Getwell Rd., P.O. Box 18845, Memphis, TN 38181; phone: (901) 363-8624. **Great Clips, Inc.:** 3601 Minnesota Dr., Ste. 475, Minneapolis, MN 55435, phone: (612) 893-9088. **Great Expectations Precision Haircutters:** 125 Service Rd., Jericho, NY 11753; phone: (516) 334-8400. **Femmina Beauty Salons, Inc.:** 3301 Hempstead Tpke., Levittown, NY 11756; phone: (516) 735-2828.

clientele, it would be advisable to lease premium space in order to create an upscale image.

SALON LAYOUT AND SETUP

Some beauty salon owners swear that the way a shop looks is a critical factor in its success. One entrepreneur who chose the full-service approach purchased a former residential site and renovated the entire house. She gutted it, stripped the floors, ripped out the attic, and created a cathedral ceiling with skylights. She also landscaped the area outside the house with apple and pine trees. For a total amount of $100,000, the woman gambled that the unique ambiance of her shop would give the impression to potential customers that she provided more than just cuts and perms. She succeeded; her first year gross was more than $150,000.

Not everyone, however, has the capital to invest in elaborate visual effects in order to decorate a store. Whether or not you decide to make that kind of investment, every store needs basic equipment for at least two to six hair stations. These stations are the focus of hair salons, and the surrounding layout can be extremely influential in marketing your services.

When the customer enters the store, there should be a waiting area with comfortable chairs and a coffee table to display the latest copies of trade publications and movie and fashion magazines. Many people get ideas for new hair styles from these sources. A checkout counter that can double as a display case for hair care items is also a good marketing tool. Remember to contact your local equipment dealers and used furniture suppliers to reduce the cost of outfitting your shop.

You should decorate your shop sparsely but elegantly. Tile or wood floors provide for easy and quick cleaning, and adequate lighting can give a bright and airy feeling to even the smallest shop. Using small spotlights and track lighting may be very helpful in creating the particular kind of ambiance you want. There should be enough mirrors so that both the hairstylist (or the beautician) and the customer have unobstructed views to see the work as it is done; at the same time, mirrors make any room look larger. The trick to decorating your shop is to design an attractive and inviting atmosphere so that customers will feel comfortable enough to return.

STAFFING

Your own training will be your initial expense, even before you set up your business. If you decide to cut hair yourself, rather than just manage a hair salon, you'll need to get a national license. You can get your license by going to school part time or in about six months if you choose full-time study. There are many schools throughout the United States and tuition varies somewhat according to location. Most beginning beauticians work at an existing shop in order to develop their skills and learn the trade, so that they know what to do when they open their own boutique.

Long operating hours are standard for most beauty shops, so you must arrange for adequate staffing. Hiring or training someone to manage the shop when you are away will help the business run smoothly. Ideally, this individual should have experience in beauty salon management, exhibit good organizational skills, have some knowledge of hair care products, and also a good enough memory to greet regular customers by their first name. In order to keep initial costs low, this person can also double as a cashier and/or receptionist. As your business grows, however, the manager should deal with more important matters such as scheduling, bookkeeping, inventory, and marketing.

Two of the most important considerations when hiring someone to work in your salon is how long an individual has been in the profession and previous places of employment. Experienced beauticians will bring the clientele they have built over time to your shop; the salon where they have worked will determine the kind of clientele they bring. Although you should always give a recent graduate the opportunity to develop his or her skills, it would be wise to hire a few people that will bring an already-established clientele with them. It is important to remember that customers who receive a good cut or perm from a beautician are inclined to follow that person no matter where they work. In short, the importance of cultivating good employees should not be underestimated; an experienced, congenial, and accessible staff will attract a loyal customer following.

Once you've covered overhead expenses, you need to consider how much to pay your staff. A manager's salary should be determined largely by industry standards, with periodic merit raises. Many salons pay a commission to other employees and arrange a 50-50 split of the price for each haircut, manicure, perm, or makeup job. Some beauty shops pay minimum wage and expect employees to make up for low salaries in tips. Often, however, salon owners who arrange to pay their staff more than minimum wage get a return on investment through employees who are happier and therefore less likely to move to another shop and take their clientele with them. One of the challenges store owners confront is holding on to staff in an industry where the turnover is very high.

ADVERTISING AND MARKETING

Plan to advertise not only in the Yellow Pages and local newspapers, but also in weekly community and church publications, and by distributing flyers announcing special promotions. Your most potent and effective marketing tool, however, will be your services and staff.

In deciding on the layout for your store, make every service that you provide in your boutique visible. A customer who is having her hair cut might see another customer who's getting a facial and realize how much she would like to have the same treatment. Services are contagious, and the more visible they are, the more likely people will purchase them. Ask employees to suggest manicures or other services while they're cutting or coloring a customer's hair; longtime clients have a tendency to accept the recommendations of their beauticians.

It is also important to display carefully selected products such as shampoo, conditioner, and makeup around the

PRIMARY ASSOCIATIONS AND SELECTED TRADE PUBLICATIONS

Associations:

Association of Cosmetologists and Hairdressers (ACH): 1811 Monroe, Dearborn, MI 48124; phone: (313) 563-0360.

Hair International: 1318 Starbrook Dr., Charlotte, NC 28210; phone: (704) 552-6233.

Intercoiffure America (IA): 540 Robert E. Lee, New Orleans, LA 70124; phone: (504) 282-4907.

National Beauty Culturists' League (NBCL): 25 Logan Circle, N.W., Washington, DC 20005; phone: (202) 332-2695.

National Cosmetology Association (NCA): 3510 Olive St., St. Louis, MO 63103; phone: (314) 534-7980.

Publications:

Modern Salon Magazine: 400 Knightbridge Pkwy., Lincolnshire, IL 60069; phone: (708) 634-2600.

hair stations and checkout counter. These items occupy very little space and yet can generate significant retail sales. Elegant brand-name items appeal to clients who want to look stylish and who will therefore pay a bit more for recommended products. This marketing technique can also serve as a motivational tool if you give your employees a certain percentage of the retail price as a commission for suggesting the better quality products you display.

Developing a loyal and ever-increasing clientele should be the main goal of your marketing strategy. Good techniques such as package treatments, for example, in which a customer is offered a facial, manicure, perm, and body massage for $150 and is told that the same services would cost $250 when sold separately, will encourage return business. Gift certificates and discounts during slow hours will also increase the amount of customer traffic through your door.

The best and most effective way to market your services will be through satisfied customers. It should be a normal procedure for your staff to give their business cards to customers, and to ask if clients would like to schedule regular appointments. Promotions such as a free perm or manicure for every customer who brings in three friends are also good sales techniques. You want your clientele to recommend your salon to their family, friends, and acquaintances, so be attentive to their concerns, and tell your staff to take time to teach customers how to use hair care and skin care techniques at home. Customers are walking advertisements; the better they look, the more likely their friends and acquaintances will ask for the name of their beauty salon.

INDUSTRY STATISTICS

- *Average Beauty Salon Revenues (1992):* 31% from haircuts; 17% from perms; 30% from hair coloring; the remainder from nail care, skin care, and retail sales (source: Business Information Services).
- *Average Amount of Study Time Needed for Beauty Salon Training and a National License (1993):* 1,500 hours (source: *Salon Magazine*).
- *Total Revenues for National Beauty Salon Industry (1992):* $35 billion (source: *Crain's Chicago Business*).
- *Total Revenues for Beauty Salon Nail Care Business (1992):* $3.4 billion (source: *Crain's Chicago Business*).
- *Total Revenues for Beauty Salon Skin Care Business (1992):* $1.4 billion (source: *Crain's Chicago Business*).
- *Percent of Salon Customers Who Are Men (1992):* 25% (source: *Crain's Chicago Business*).
- *Women-Owned We Care Hair Franchises (1992):* 8 out of a total 68 (source: *Beauty and Health Magazine*).

ACCOUNTING, LICENSES, AND INSURANCE

A beauty salon can be established in a number of different ways, so the best course of action is to hire a good accountant and lawyer to help you come up with a business plan. The accountant will advise you on the best way to meet your federal and state tax requirements, and an experienced lawyer will guide you through the maze of filing the necessary documents to open your shop. You'll need to contact your county clerk in order to get a local business license and sales tax permits. Property insurance, employee health insurance, workers' compensation, and a federal employer identification number are also needed. Rely on the professionals to help you devise an accounting system that suits the size of your salon, and to advise you on how to keep your taxes low.

Whether you decide to open a full-service salon or a high-volume haircutting business, and whether it's small or large, part of a franchise, or an independent store, you need to plan carefully. Competition in the hair salon industry is growing at a fast pace, but so are the opportunities. If you exhibit intelligent management and creative marketing and satisfy your customers, you'll be poised for success.

SOURCES:

"Equal Opportunity," *Beauty and Health Magazine,* July/August 1992.

Gearhart, Susan Wood, *Opportunities in Beauty Culture Careers,* Career Horizons, 1989.

Gould, Joe Sutherland, *Starting From Scratch: 50 Profitable Business Opportunities,* John Wiley & Sons, 1987.

Kahn, Sharon, and The Philip Lief Group, *101 Best Businesses to Start,* Doubleday, 1992.

Madden, Michael, editor, *Small Business Start Up Index,* issue 1, Gale, 1991.

Martin, Susan Boyles, editor, *Worldwide Franchise Directory,* Gale, 1991.

Perri, Colleen, *Entrepreneurial Women,* Possibilities Publishing, 1987.

Siegel, Eric, *The Arthur Young Business Plan Guide,* John Wiley & Sons, 1987.

—THOMAS DERDAK

Health Food Store

According to an early 1990s survey, 90 percent of grocery shoppers are interested in healthy food, that is, food that is free of or low in pesticides, chemical preservatives, cholesterol, and refined sugar. While more and more supermarkets stock their shelves with such items as wheat germ, vitamins, and preservative-free bread and breakfast cereals, almost all fruits, vegetables, meats and poultry, eggs, and household cleaning products are tainted with preservatives, hormones, or toxic chemicals harmful to the environment. Only health food stores have the variety and range of "natural" foods, vitamins, and environmentally friendly products that even the largest supermarkets lack. The market for health food products has grown 8 percent annually since 1986. Hence, despite the existence of approximately 10,000 health food stores throughout the United States, the health food business is still a potentially lucrative one.

COSTS AND PROFITS

Start-up costs for a health food store can vary drastically depending on whether you purchase your store or lease it and whether you are going in with a partner or going it alone with one or two employees. Buying a franchise is the exception rather than the rule, but a typical health food store franchise will require at least $50,000. While it is possible to set up a health food for only $15,000, successfully starting a store on a shoestring is rare. Typically, you can expect your start-up costs to be in the range of $50,000, depending on your location. A health food store in Indiana, for instance, is cheaper to start than one in Washington, D.C., or New York City.

As a prospective health food store owner, your most viable option is to lease a store and pay a deposit. In addition, you will need to pay for your store layout, which at minimum, will consist of a cash register or two, grocery store shelves and bins, and a computer. In addition, in the first few years of your business, you should plan on spending time and money traveling to trade conventions and networking. Your greatest expense, though, will be inventory. Costs can be contained by buying organic produce locally and by carefully researching which vendors you use; for instance, you may want to avoid vendors who insist that you purchase a specified amount of merchandise. Another way to defray costs is to sub-lease part of your store.

At the low end of the scale, the yearly average net profit for a health food store will be in the $25,000 range before taxes. A typical high-end profit before taxes is $80,000.

FINANCING

Most aspiring small store owners are not wealthy enough to finance their ventures out of their savings. Hence, you will most likely need to borrow money, and as an aspiring health food store owner, your loan will need to cover working capital, inventory, equipment, and in many cases, a lease or mortgage. The task of applying for a loan can be daunting. Before you contact a local bank, you should consult the U.S. **Small Business Administration (SBA)** by calling **1-800-U ASK SBA.** Almost always when calling the SBA, you are put on hold or will have to choose from a long message menu. Be patient and persistent; the SBA is there to help you, and a counselor will sit down with you and advise you for free on how to secure a loan and answer any other business questions you may have, including how to draw up an effective business plan. Incidentally, the SBA also lends money, but only if a commercial bank has turned you down.

Since your health food store as yet has no history, you must convince potential lenders that there is a market and future for it. Composing a solid business plan requires research and expert advice. Your local librarian, who is accustomed to business queries, can quickly point you in the direction of the heap of books in every library dealing with small business loans and operations. Your SBA counselor will also be glad to recommend relevant books.

Once you have completed a detailed business plan, you will present it to a bank for a loan. There are several types of bank loans with varying interest rates. If you are willing to pay a lot of interest, you can turn to any number of finance companies that specialize in lending to small businesses and that, more often that banks, tend to take on riskier ventures.

LOCATION AND STORE LAYOUT

In the booming health food business, location is crucial to success. If you can afford to set up your business in a middle-class neighborhood or where educational levels are

PRIMARY ASSOCIATIONS AND SELECTED TRADE PUBLICATIONS

Associations:

National Nutritional Foods Association (NNFA): 125 E. Baker Ave., Ste. 230, Costa Mesa, CA 92626; phone: (714) 966-NNFA.

African-American Natural Foods Association (AANFA): 7058 S. Clyde Ave., Chicago, IL 60649; phone: (312) 363-3939.

Natural Food Associates (NFA): P.O. Box 210, Atlanta, TX 75551; phone: (800) 594-2136.

Publications:

Health Food Stores Directory: American Business Directories, Inc., 5711 S. 86th Circle, Omaha, NE 68127; phone: (402) 593-4600.

Organic Food Mail Order Suppliers: Americans for Safe Food (ASF), Center for Science in the Public Interest (CSPI), 1875 Connecticut Ave. NW, Ste. 300, Washington, DC 20009-5728; phone: (202) 332-9110.

Health and Natural Foods Market: Find/SVP, 625 Avenue of the Americas, New York, NY 10011; phone: (212) 645-4500, or (800) 346-3787.

Health and Natural Foods: Business Trends Analysts, Inc., Industry Studies, 2171 Jericho Turnpike, Ste. 200, Commack, NY; phone: (516) 462-5454.

Vitamins, Minerals and Supplements: Find/SVP, 625 Avenue of the Americas, New York, NY 10011; phone: (212) 645-4500, or (800) 346-3787

Health Foods Business: Howmark Publishing Corp., Elizabeth, NJ 07208; phone: (908) 353-7373.

Health Foods Retailing: 6255 Barfield Rd., Atlanta, GA 30328; phone: (404) 256-9800.

Natural Foods Merchandiser: New Hope Communications, Boulder, CO; phone: (303) 939-8440.

high, as in a college town, this is the ideal location. The vast majority of health food customers earn middle-class incomes (or, as in a college town, have middle class aspirations) and are college educated.

It will be difficult to find an area that does not already have a health food store or even superstore. If another establishment exists, be sure to offer certain products that your competition lacks and implement promotional strategies that will draw in customers. Do the other health food stores rent out bicycles? Do they have tables and chairs and sell sandwiches and smoothies? Do they offer free samples?

It is not enough to locate your store in or near a high traffic area. Your store should also be accessible to foot traffic and public transportation. Ideally, there should be other types of businesses in the area that draw customers.

Store layout in a health food store varies widely from shop to shop. Despite the recent advent of the natural food superstore, health food stores for the most part are generally cramped places, a fact that does not seem to deter customers as it would perhaps if the store sold clothing, appliances, or furniture. Health food stores are unique in that they almost always incorporate a certain philosophy that stresses wholesome living, environmental consciousness, and in most cases, an escape from the hurried, impersonal pace of modern life.

Your store should be a reflection of your ideals and personality: some health food store owners play soft music, or decorate their stores with plants and antique objects or with attractive posters. Somewhere in your store you should have a nook with books and magazines that educate the customer about healthful living and the environment and encourage them to stay and browse. A bulletin board in your store may attract customers who come not only to put up announcements but also stick around to have a look. Your store should at all times be very clean, even if small and cramped, and should always be very well stocked. In short, you should strive to make your store as inviting as possible.

MARKETING AND ADVERTISING

Your marketing strategy should be all-encompassing. Unlike most retail stores, you can offer personal service and a marketing strategy that reflects who you are and what you stand for. Your values should be evident in the layout of your store, and in the interest you show in your customer's needs. There are many stories about health food store owners who earn the gratitude and loyalty of a customer for taking time out to order a particular product s/he needs, or ensuring that a particular item is always in stock. Health food stores have become synonymous with personal service and a personal, friendly approach. Thus, unlike most retail stores, they often feature tables and chairs, a juice bar, and a nook for reading. In addition, they may offer services that other stores lack.

It should be part of your marketing strategy to keep up with what other health food stores are doing and with the trends of the industry. Being a member of a trade association and keeping up with health food newsletters and magazines ought to be of particular importance in your sales strategy, especially in the initial years of your business.

Once you have decided what you can offer your customers by way of personal service and special products, you will need to advertise heavily, especially in the beginning. While one can read about successful owners who never advertise but rely solely on word of mouth, these are exceptions. Unless you have a good reason to think you can thrive with only the business obtained from the recommendations of already-established customers, you should advertise.

Public radio stations will acknowledge your store on the air in return for a contribution. If you cannot afford to advertise on commercial radio, then you should prepare flyers describing your store and leave them in public places such as churches, community centers, and senior citizen centers, where you may announce senior citizen discounts. Area restaurants should also know of your existence.

Other methods of making your business known should

not be overlooked. If you can possibly afford it, a mass mailing of your flyers would be effective. Weekly advertising in your local newspapers for the first six months of your business is a must. Organize promotional events, offering free samples or conducting an in-store demonstration of a product, and sponsor community activities. Pay attention to even the smallest means of advertising; make sure, for example, that each customer gets your business card by placing it in the grocery bag. Though the greatest assets to your business will be the quality of your service and word of mouth, you will be helped along with effective advertising and marketing.

STAFFING AND EMPLOYEE TRAINING

It is almost impossible to open a health food store and expect to work solo in the project. Having a partner, of course, is the ideal start-up solution, since you can share the expenses as well as work. If you are unable to secure a partner, an employee can be a great asset as well as expense. As is the case with many prospective health food store owners, you may be entering a business of which you know little, or you may lack experience in a retail business. An employee who has had that experience can be a real help. If you are familiar with the health food business and do have experience in retail, then you have the expertise to train an employee.

Training an employee to work in a health food store is not very different from training any retail store employee,

START-UP GUIDE AND RELEVANT SOFTWARE

Start-up Guide:

Health-Food/Vitamin Store, EntrepreneurGroup, Irvine, CA, 1992 (updated annually). Very detailed guide on how to start your own business from scratch.

Software:

The following is a list of some of the most popular brands of software for small business owners; prices are approximate.

Peachtree Complete Accounting for DOS (also available for Windows), $189. A few main features are inventory for the small business, order entry, and accounts receivable/payable.

Peachtree Basic Accounting (DOS or Windows), $85. A simplified version of the above; provides on-line help; does not do inventory.

CA-BPI Accounting II for DOS (also Windows version), $164. Main features are payroll, inventory, and accounts receivable/payable.

Quick Books & Quick Pay for DOS with Payroll, $109. Speeds up bill paying and invoicing.

One-Write Plus Accounting (DOS), $89. Features check writing, billing, inventory, accounts receivable/payable.

FormTool, 3.0 version, $50. This handy software creates every imaginable form on your PC, including price tags.

TurboTAX (DOS and Windows), $39. Claims to be the best-selling tax software; offers complete tax preparation.

except that the health food store employee must be knowledgeable about nutrition. S/he must be willing to read up on nutrition and vitamins. If you cannot afford to send your employee to a nutrition seminar or two, then provide a bibliography of the most important health books and make it a point to discuss the readings together. In addition, many local libraries offer films and videos on various aspects of nutrition. Since customers will constantly be coming in and asking for advice, you need to display knowledge about products, vitamins, and therapies.

Hiring an employee does entail a whole new set of problems and requirements. Once you have made up your mind to hire, you will have to bear in mind the need for a proper job description and to fill out a multitude of forms, including tax forms, workman's compensation, social security, and wage forms. You can pay as low as minimum wage, but in that case you will have few job takers. Competitive wages are always the best rule of thumb to follow when hiring.

MANAGEMENT ISSUES

It is possible to keep down costs by becoming knowledgeable about local produce and possibly contracting with local farmers for their fresh produce, eggs, and milk, if you choose to sell these items. It is usually not difficult to find organic farmers and hen breeders in your area. For a new product, you should buy in small amounts at first. However, some suppliers insist that you buy a certain amount from them, or they will not sell to you at all. That is when it pays to make careful preparations before you open your store. Some prospective health food store proprietors have studied suppliers for a year before contracting with them; good vendors can be one of your greatest assets. Delivering goods to your store also can cost a fair amount. This might be reduced if you negotiate with different delivery services or, if feasible, buy your own truck.

Besides reducing your costs and researching your suppliers, a matter that is unique to health food store owners is food spoilage. While people want preservative-free food, it is easy to forget that such food spoils soon. You and your employee(s) must be vigilant about food spoilage and ordering the appropriate amounts of certain products. Unlike unsold vitamins, food cannot be returned.

PRICING

Pricing is subject to demand and supply, and it is wise to keep up with prices in other food stores—health food stores as well as supermarkets. Conducting a sale on slow moving items is one way to solve a inventory problems and draw customers into your store. The bottom line in pricing, however, should not be whether or not your prices are comparable to other stores, but whether your operating costs will be covered. A price that is higher than your competitor may be offset by offering a customer a special service, such as credit or delivery. Lastly, there are state and federal laws that apply

FRANCHISE OPPORTUNITIES

General Nutrition Centers (GNC): 921 Penn Ave., Pittsburgh, PA 15222; phone: (412) 288-4600, or (800) 766-7099.

Great Earth, International: Phoenix Labs, 175 Lauman Lane, Hickville, NY 11801; phone: (800) 527-7965. A vitamin store.

Smoothie King: 725 Mississippi Ave., Ste. 7, Metairie, LA 70003; phone: (504) 467-4006. Sells nutritional drinks.

to retail sales, and you should find out if any of these apply to you.

LICENSES

You will also need numerous licenses from your state, county, and city. Double check the zoning laws in the neighborhood of your store. It is easy to find out what business permits and licenses you will need either by calling your chamber of commerce, which will provide you the right phone numbers, or asking your local librarian. Virtually every county publishes an annual small business guide that lists relevant information and phone numbers. Do not expect to obtain the required permits and licenses immediately; the wait can sometimes stretch for weeks.

COMPUTER SYSTEM AND PROGRAMS

If you are unable to design a software program to meet your bookkeeping needs, then you can turn to packaged commercial software for your IBM or Macintosh computer. There are many bookkeeping software packages available for un-

der $200, as well as software that prints forms, labels, and tags, writes checks, and compiles mailing lists. A simple phone call to your local software store and a description of your business needs will result in the right kind of software for you.

Not every health food store succeeds, and a number eventually close their doors for good. The market trend, however, is clearly in favor of healthy food, food free of chemical contaminants, and clean water. With the right products, location, and sales strategy, you can succeed as a health food store owner.

SOURCES:

Gould, Joe S., "Natural Food Store," *Starting From Scratch, Fifty Profitable Business Opportunities,* John Wiley & Sons, 1987.

Gutfeld, Rose, "FDA Again Planning Move to Restrict Nutritional Health Claims," *Wall Street Journal,* June 2, 1993, pp. B9(W), B8(E).

Lani, Luciano, "*Money*'s 1993 Store of the Year," *Money,* December 1992, pp. 104-113.

Litwack, David, "In This Health Food Store, Food Service Is a Natural Attraction," *Supermarket Business,* May 1993, pp. 79-82.

McMath, Robert, "New Products: Prognosis for the Natural Foods Business," *Brandweek,* October 5, 1992, p. 24.

Miller, Cyndee, "Health Food Sheds 'Hippie' Image: Mainstream Consumers Targeted," *Marketing News,* September 14, 1992, p. 2.

"A New Generation of Health Food Stores," *Chain Store Age,* April 1993, pp. 28-29.

Richman, Alan, "Spilling Over With Success (Mrs. Gooch's Opens Third Store, Seeks Broader Market)," *Health Foods Business,* October 1981, pp. 59-68.

Strischek, Dev, "Lending to Health Food Stores," *Journal of Commercial Bank Lending,* June 1987, pp. 11-22.

—*Sina Dubovoj*

Hearing Aid Testing and Fitting Service

If you asked a roomful of people to name ten or so small business opportunities that immediately jumped to mind, it is unlikely any in your audience would mention opening a hearing aid testing and fitting service. And that may be precisely why such an endeavor merits serious consideration. For years, hearing aid wearers suffered the embarrassment of wearing large, bulky hearing aid devices that pointed them out in a crowd. Consequently, many people with diminished hearing chose to forego the socially painful experience of wearing a hearing aid, while hearing aid retailers, in turn, stood behind their glass counters waiting for a slow trickle of customers to come through their doors. Rapid technological advancements, however, have reduced the size of hearing aids to the size of a penny and improved the sound quality to such an extent that the prospect of wearing a hearing aid in the 1990s no longer invokes the apprehensions it once did. Hearing aids now can be matched to the wearer's skin tone, or can be inserted inside the wearer's ear canal, out of sight, and can be programmed to adjust to different listening environments, enabling the user to hear the chirps of a bird in a forest then hear a speaker's voice over the cacophony of rush-hour traffic.

These ameliorations in design and quality have invigorated the hearing aid industry, increased the size of its market, and, most important to anyone considering testing and fitting hearing aids as a small business, created an opportunity to capitalize on a large portion of the hearing aid market that has been left untapped. According to government studies, there were 18 million Americans in 1993 who required some sort of hearing aid device, but were reluctant to try one. With this large reservoir of potential customers, your hearing aid testing and fitting business could realize enviable growth; all that remains is for you to convince a portion of these 18 million people that hearing aids are not what they used to be, and your profits will climb.

Of course, the chance to earn a sizeable profit is not the only reason to open a hearing aid testing and fitting business. By helping your customers to hear more clearly, you will be restoring one of life's most precious gifts, making the emotional rewards at least equal to the financial rewards. Indeed, the individual contemplating the establishment of a hearing aid business must care about his or her customers and the nature of the services provided to successfully operate. As proof of the lucrative possibilities within the industry, many disreputable hearing aid dealers emerged during the 1980s hoping to quickly cash in on the growing demand for hearing aids. This development led to pleas for stricter federal regulation of the industry in the early 1990s that augured an increase in the number of licenses required to operate a hearing aid business. Aside from the additional bureaucratic paperwork created, this closer examination of the industry is a welcomed change for business owners who truly care about providing quality service and merchandise. The image of the industry, tarnished somewhat by dishonest operators, will undoubtedly improve as a result of federal regulation, and the honorable hearing aid businesses will prosper further. If your desire to assist your future customers in recovering their hearing is strong enough to warrant your entrance into this exciting and rapidly changing field, then sales will inevitably follow. Every satisfied customer leaving your store will mean one more person in the world can hear sounds he or she previously could not, and, at the same time, will mean more money in your cash register.

COSTS AND PROFITS

Once you have decided to commit time and effort toward opening a hearing aid testing and fitting service, the next step is to consider the costs involved in establishing such a business. As a general guide, you should expect to invest upwards of $55,000 to begin operations, but this figure will vary according to the size and location of your store and other variables. When calculating your start-up costs, certain basic expenditures should be included, such as major equipment purchases, rent (plus deposit), site improvement, initial inventory, grand opening advertising, and, of course, the miscellaneous costs that can add up quickly. For equipment, your minimum cost should hover around $5,000, an amount that also should be set aside to defray miscellaneous expenses. You will not require much stocked merchandise in order to operate, since the manufacturers of hearing aids will be fabricating the devices according to specifications provided by you, the hearing aid tester and fitter. Consequently, you should be able to begin business with roughly $600 worth of products. An equal amount of money should be

PRIMARY ASSOCIATIONS AND SELECTED TRADE PUBLICATIONS

Associations:

Academy of Dispensing Audiologists (ADA):
3008 Millwood Ave., Columbia, SC 29205; phone: (803) 252-5646.

Hearing Industries Association (HIA): 1255 23rd St. NW, Ste. 850, Washington, DC 20037; phone: (202) 833-1411.

National Hearing Aid Society: 20361 Middlebelt Rd., Livonia, MI 48152; phone: (800) 521-5247.

Publications:

Audecibel: National Hearing Aid Society, 20361 Middlebelt Rd., Livonia, MI 48152; phone: (800) 521-5247. Published quarterly.

Between Friends: Beltone Electronics Corp., 4201 West Victoria, Chicago, IL 60646; phone: (312) 583-3600. Published bimonthly.

Hearing Journal: Laux Co., 63 Great Rd., Maynard, MA 01754-2025; phone: (508) 897-5552. Published monthly.

invested toward the acquisition of signage announcing the services you provide.

The profit potential in operating a hearing aid testing and fitting service can be very enticing, but your expectations should be modest at first; any new business needs to be in existence for a certain length of time before its full revenue generating abilities can be realized. As a benchmark figure, however, successful operators in the industry record gross annual sales of over $500,000 and report pretax net profits ranging from 20 to 25 percent, encouraging results considering the relatively low start-up investment required.

FINANCING

Obtaining the money to open a small business can be a formidable challenge, but only if you allow it to be. Banks earn their money by providing loans, so if your credit history is respectable and you present an organized, detailed business plan that demonstrates the financial viability of your venture, there is no reason for financing to be an insurmountable obstacle blocking your business aspirations. Before you meet with a loan officer, you should prepare an estimated business balance sheet listing all assets and liabilities, which should include the amount that must be invested to begin your business. Also, prepare a detailed projection of earnings and expenses for at least the first year of operation, as well as a monthly cash flow projection. List the collateral you intend to offer as security for the loan, with an estimate of the current market value for each item offered, and include the balance of any existing liens. For assistance in developing a business plan, the easiest and most inexpensive approach is to visit your local library, which will contain a wealth of information concerning the creation of a thorough business plan.

An alternative to securing your financing from a bank is to apply for a loan from the U.S. **Small Business Administration (SBA).** This source must be approached after first attempting to get a loan from a bank or other lending institution since federal law prohibits the SBA from granting loans to applicants before other means are sought. There are various requirements applicants must meet in order to receive a loan from the SBA, a majority of which pertain to the size of the business in terms of employees and revenues. These requirements should pose no problem to the aspiring hearing aid testing and fitting operator. To determine if you are eligible, locate a SBA loan application at your local library, which will also possess many of the pamphlets published by the SBA that address a broad range of topics, ranging from preparing your small business taxes to calculating your yearly budget. To contact the SBA directly call: **1-800-U ASK SBA.**

Another option is to consider obtaining a hearing aid testing and fitting franchise from one of the several franchisers involved in the industry. Although not all of the franchisers offer financing to their franchisees, many provide assistance in obtaining financing.

LOCATION

For any small business operator, the location of his or her store is of paramount importance and often determines, to a large extent, the success or failure of the business. Consequently, you should devote considerable attention to the selection of a suitable site. There are general rules to observe in selecting a site for a business, one of which is to insure that your proposed site is reasonably accessible to both pedestrian and automobile traffic. Also, a site near or abutting a major thoroughfare will lend your business greater visibility and bring in more customers.

Beyond these basic considerations, there are conditions peculiar to the proper placement of a hearing aid testing and fitting establishment that should govern your selection. Since some of your customers, presumably, will be coming to your store directly from their doctor's office, you should try to find a location near a cluster of hospitals, or medical clinics. Additionally, studies have shown that people generally begin to suffer from diminished hearing past the age of 40, so the demographics of the area surrounding your proposed location should include a considerable percentage of people over 40. To determine the population characteristics of your area, you should, once again, head to your local library and peruse U.S. Census Bureau studies. This is a resource you should also consult to conduct a market survey and to gain information that will assist you in your attempt to secure financing. Census studies will indicate the representation of various age groups in your area, their approximate income, and a bevy of other statistics that will help you form an idea of what your new neighborhood is like. Equally as important are maps of major trading areas pertaining to your subject area, which will indicate the major businesses in operation and the spending habits of the consumers surrounding your site.

Since health insurance plans usually do not cover the cost of purchasing a hearing aid, you should avoid locating your business in an economically depressed area; you can obtain this information from census studies, or, perhaps, by simply driving around your target neighborhood. Also, evaluate the accessibility of your site by public transportation. You will be catering to an older clientele, many of whom rely on buses or subways to get around, so your proximity to major public transportation routes could mean more business.

The square footage of your hearing aid testing and fitting establishment will be largely determined by the amount you will be able to allocate toward lease payments and dictated by the number of customers you project will visit your store each day. As a low end figure, however, some operators in the industry successfully run their businesses with as little as 600 square feet of space. Stores of this size can efficiently accommodate 20 customers a day.

LICENSES AND CERTIFICATION

A survey conducted by the hearing aid industry found that 40 percent of the people who purchased hearing devices were less than completely satisfied with the experience. This negative reaction was largely due to the proliferation of disreputable hearing aid dispensers who neglected to provide proper and courteous service. The industry has also suffered from a rash of dishonest dispensers who, posing as audiologists or medical doctors, inaccurately diagnosed their client's hearing needs, or just sold them the most expensive model. Consequently, the U.S. Food and Drug Administration (FDA) has intensified its efforts toward regulating the hearing aid industry. For the aspiring hearing aid testing and fitting business, these developments underscore the importance of obtaining the proper licenses and meeting the various certification requirements.

Legally, hearing aid dispensers are not allowed to sell a hearing aid to someone who has not been examined by a

---

FRANCHISE OPPORTUNITIES

Ear Labs (formerly National Ear, Inc.): 18662 MacArthur Blvd., Ste. 103, Irvine, CA 92715; phone: (714) 752-0993. Initial franchise fee, $18,000.

Hearing Aids Today: 270 Cobb Pkwy. S, Ste. A7-B, Marietta, GA 30062; phone: (404) 427-7100. Initial franchise fee, $22,000.

Miracle-Ear: 600 South County Rd. 18, Minneapolis, MN 55426; phone: (612) 542-1118. Initial franchise fee, $15,000.

---

licensed physician within the previous six months, unless a waiver is signed by the customer. Moreover, hearing aid dispensers are legally obliged to inform their customers that it would be in their best interest to undergo a medical evaluation. As a hearing aid dispenser, you will need to become licensed to operate as such, unless you plan to operate your business in one of the few states that do not require hearing aid dispenser registration. To determine what the licensing requirements are for your area, contact the National Hearing Aid Society (NHAS) in Livonia, Michigan. The NHAS will refer you to your local representative who will, in turn, advise you of what particular conditions apply to your business. Also, you should contact the National Board for Certification of Hearing Instrument Sciences (BC-HIS) to inquire about obtaining proper certification.

MARKETING

Once you have examined census studies and have a clear idea of who your customers will be, your initial efforts will be directed at, of course, getting those people to come through your doors. One approach is to talk with ear specialists in your area about referring patients to them, which may eventually lead to the referral of patients in need of hearing aids directly to you. To locate these specialists, look in the telephone book Yellow Pages under the following headings: "otolaryngologists," "otologists," and "otorhinolaryngologists."

Providing your customers with proficient and polite service is the key to maintaining your customer base once it has been established. While this may seem an obvious statement, it is something you should always bear in mind and impart to your staff. This simple business axiom has been sorely abused in the hearing aid industry. Customers will generally have to make several visits to your store to complete the fitting process, and some may require more time than others. After a certain amount of visits you may not be generating any revenue from a particular customer, but it is in your best, long-term interest to extend every courtesy to a customer in this situation. Hearing aids normally only remain effective for three to five years, so a customer that requires a little extra time for one purchase will tend to return for another purchase if fully satisfied. It is also a good idea to offer a 30-day trial period with each sale. Before you become too involved in your marketing endeavors, contact the FDA and the NHAS to receive their respective guidelines concerning suitable promotional activities.

ADVERTISING

In composing your advertisements, stress the service-oriented attributes of your business. It might prove helpful to put yourself in the place of your potential customers while constructing your advertising themes. For many people suffering from hearing loss, the prospect of purchasing a hear-

SOURCES OF SUPPLY

The following is a list of both print and computer database sources that will assist you in locating reputable hearing aid manufacturers across the United States.

Print:

International Directory of Hearing Health Care Products: Advanstar Communications, 1 East 1st St., Duluth, MN 55802; phone: (218) 723-9200.

Hearing Health Industry World Directory: Laux Co., 63 Great Rd., Maynard, MA 01754-2025; phone: (508) 897-5552.

Databases:

Health Devices Sourcebook: ECRI, 5200 Butler, Plymouth Meeting, PA 19462; phone: (215) 825-6000. Online: DIALOG Information Services, Inc.

MDR On-line: Medical Device Register, Inc., 655 Washington Blvd., Stamford, CT 06901; phone: (203) 348-6319. Online: Producer.

Medical Device Database: Bradford Communications Corp., Toriano Bldg., 2nd Floor, Beltsville, MD 20705; phone: (301) 345-0100. Online: Producer.

ing aid is a painful thought, fraught with the realization that their hearing is not acute enough for normal activity anymore and that they must now wear a potentially embarrassing hearing device. Your objective is to convince these people that their fears are unwarranted. Use a clear, brief, and reassuring style that imparts the reliability of your services and the much improved quality of hearing aids in the 1990s.

Aside from placing an advertisement in the Yellow Pages, contact the manufacturing company that will be supplying you with hearing aids before you spend any money on advertising. Frequently, hearing aid manufacturers offer cooperative advertising programs that will reduce your advertising costs and assist you in deciding the amount and location of advertising space you will need to purchase.

FRANCHISES

There are a number of successful franchisers of hearing aid testing and fitting stores that are actively seeking franchisees. Obtaining a franchise may be your solution to the myriad of obstacles that a new business owner must hurdle. Franchise agreements can include a broad range of services the franchiser will provide to the franchisee, including the hiring and training of personnel, financing assistance, budgeting and tax preparation, and advertising. In addition, by going the franchise route you will benefit from either the regional or national name recognition the franchiser has established, part of the reason you must pay a percentage of your earnings to the franchiser. Miracle-Ear, for example, one of the more successful hearing aid franchising operations, was ranked as the ninth-largest brand spender on cable television in 1991, spending $5.5 million.

Even if you are leaning towards going it alone, the franchise option should be investigated nonetheless. Often, just by talking with a franchise representative, you can gain valuable insights into the operation of a hearing aid dispensing establishment.

FUTURE PROSPECTS

One the most difficult tasks a hearing aid testing and fitting business owner faced in the mid-1990s was keeping pace with the rapid technological advancements in the industry. In 1994 digitally programmed hearing aids able to adjust to disparate listening environments represented the vanguard of the industry technologically. The ability of a hearing aid dispenser to convey these ameliorations to potential customers and, thereby, grab the attention of the 18 million people in the United States who are reluctant to try hearing aids, yet need them, will, most likely, dictate the level of success that his or her business enjoys in the future. Indeed, the industry has come a long way since the days of clunky and ineffective hearing aids—all that remains is for the diligent entrepreneur to take advantage of these tremendous changes.

SOURCES:

Berger, Kenneth Walter, *The Hearing Aid: Its Operation and Development,* National Hearing Aid Society, 1974.

Doeheny, Kathleen, "When Selecting a Hearing Aid Get Facts—Don't Play It by Ear," *Los Angeles Times,* October 19, 1993, p. E3.

Geiger, Bob, "Miracle-Ear Spots Are Making Some Noise on Cable," *Advertising Age,* April 6, 1992, p. S4.

"A Hearing Aid that Boosts the Drum's Beat," *Business Week,* August 23, 1993, p. 70.

"How to Buy a Hearing Aid," *Consumer Reports,* November 1992, p. 716.

Kirsch, Bernard, "Breaking the Sound Barrier," *New York Times Magazine,* October 8, 1989, p. S6.

Martin, Susan Boyles, editor, *Worldwide Franchise Directory,* Gale Research, Inc., 1991.

"Programmable Aids Improve Hearing," *USA Today Magazine,* October 1993, p.12.

Schwartz, Carol A., editor, *Small Business Sourcebook,* sixth edition, volume 1, Gale Research, Inc., 1992.

Sprout, Alison L. "Disappearing Hearing Aid," *Fortune,* May 17, 1993, p. 89.

—*JEFFREY L. COVELL*

Herb Farm

It all started with that herb kit you got for Christmas. Soon, meals started tasting better—once you learned how to season food naturally with your homegrown harvest of spices. And if growing herbs worked so well for you at home, you wondered, could those cute little pots of sage, rosemary, and thyme lining your window sill blossom into a business?

The answer is yes. Herbs are not just for decoration anymore. The growing and marketing of herbs is a thriving worldwide industry. Demand for fresh herbs is so high that people venturing into the business, provided they have a carefully prepared business plan, stand a good chance of succeeding. More and more Americans are seeking natural foods and ways to flavor the food they cook without salt and preservatives. The dawning of the so-called New Age, which stresses a more natural, holistic approach to mental and physical health, has given more significance to using ancient herbal remedies to cure everything from the common cold to cancer to AIDS.

Natural or organic farming also continues to evolve as an industry aimed at consumers who seek alternatives to chemically fertilized food. Companies such as Herbal Life, Celestial Seasonings, Traditional Teas, and Spice Islands have already etched out a niche in the billion-dollar herb market. Then there's the ethnic cooking market. Fresh herbs are essential ingredients in Mexican, Creole, Cajun, and Asian food dishes. The increasing use of these products by restaurants has created a demand for fresh and dried herbs grown in the United States. And, in addition to their use in culinary purposes, herbs are appearing in make-up, landscaping, and everlasting floral arrangements.

So there's plenty of room for the beginning herb farmer, but like any new business, it will require a lot of love, much sweat, and no fear. It also is imperative that you develop some agricultural know-how. Growing herbs requires farming experience—everything from planting to harvesting to processing to distribution.

FINANCIAL ASPECTS

Herb farming can generate a second income or be a totally self-sufficient business. Herb farming businesses are generally operated on a retail or wholesale basis, but wholesale is the way to go if this is to be your only source of income. It's possible to start an herb farming business with as little as $3,740. Average start-up costs, however, range from $30,000 to $45,000. Herb farmers earn an average net profit before taxes of about $45,000 and can make as much as $140,000 before taxes. The sweet smell of herbal success means a 93 percent return on your investment. The primary liabilities to being an herb farmer will be your overall debt load.

The U.S. market for herbs is expanding and herb sales increase each year, reports *Entrepreneur* magazine. In fact, the magazine cites these United States Department of Agriculture statistics: sales for herbs increased by 50 to 100 percent from 1986 to 1990. The market for fresh herbs alone ranges from $100 million to $400 million, with close to half of the volume going through foodservice channels, reported Barney H. McClure in *Supermarket Business*. Boston, California, Chicago, Dallas, Houston, New England, New Orleans, and New York are the top markets for fresh herbs. However, the Southern portion of the United States shows the greatest growth, McClure states.

But before you get dirt under your fingernails, it's best to contemplate the risks. Herb farming is like any agricultural venture. If you think you'll be immune to the natural disasters plaguing other farmers, think again. Arm yourself with knowledge of pest control, organic farming, and soil preparation, preservation, and irrigation. In short: it's best to educate yourself *before* you start to farm.

For the beginner, starting a business can be the most rewarding and scary time of a person's life. You will have to make so many decisions that ultimately effect the outcome of your business that you'll wonder why you even thought you could do it in the first place. But you don't have to do it alone. There is help in the form of free advice provided by the Service Corps of Retired Executives (SCORE), the **Small Business Administration (SBA),** and your local division of the International Herb Growers & Marketers Association. The most significant costs to the beginning herb farmer will be labor and equipment, processing facilities, and distribution—depending on the type of herb farming business you undertake. For more information on the Small Business Administration, contact the agency at **1-800-U ASK SBA** or write: **Small Business Directory, P.O. Box 1000, Ft. Worth, TX 76119.** For information on the Interna-

PRIMARY ASSOCIATIONS AND SELECTED TRADE PUBLICATIONS

Associations:

American Botanical Council: P.O. Box 201660, Austin, TX 78720-1660; phone: (512) 331-8868; fax: (512) 331-1924.

American Herbal Products Association: P.O. Box 2410, Austin, TX 78768.

International Herb Growers & Marketers Association: 1202 Allanson Road, Mundelein, IL 60060; phone: (708) 949-HERB.

The Herb Research Foundation: 1007 Pearl St., Suite 200, Boulder, CO 80302; phone: (303) 449-2265; fax: (303) 443-0949.

Publications:

Botanical and Herb Reviews: P.O. Box 106, Eureka Springs, AR 72632; phone: (501) 253-7309.
Business of Herbs: RR2, Box 246, Shevlin, MN 56676-9535.
HerbGram: American Botanical Council, P.O. Box 201660, Austin, TX 78720-1660; phone: (512) 331-8868; fax: (512) 331-1924.
Herb Quarterly: Box 275, Newfane, VT 05345
IHGMA Newsletter: International Herb Growers & Marketers Association, 1202 Allanson Road, Mundelein, IL 60060: (708) 949-HERB.
Journal of Herbs, Spices, and Medicinal Plants: Haworth Press, 10 Alice St., Binghamton, NY 13904-1580.
Natural Foods Merchandiser: New Hope Publications, 1301 Spruce St., Boulder, CO 80302.
Taylor's Herb Gardens (seed catalog): 1535 Loan Oak Road, Vista, CA 92084.
The Herb Market Report: OAK, Inc., 525 S.E. H St., Grants Pass, OR 97526; phone: (503) 476-5588.
Miller, Richard Alan, The Potential of Herbs as a Cash Crop: OAK, Inc., 525 S.E. H St., Grants Pass, OR 97526; phone: (503) 476-5588.

tional Herb Growers & Marketers Association, write: **IHGMA, 1202 Allanson Road, Mundelein, Ill. 60060; (708) 949-4372.**

LOCATION

A kitchen window, greenhouse, or plot of land are good places to let your herb farm take root. You do not have to buy several acres of farm land to be successful. In fact, with a little imagination, you can transform any rooftop, vacant lot, backyard or even greenhouse space into an herb garden. Small gardens can reap big rewards. Herbs are like precious gems and often command a higher price than regular produce, especially if grown domestically. Even though most herbs can be grown and imported for less, homegrown herbs are considered to be superior, according to McClure in *Supermarket Business.* Fresh herbs grown on the farm can be worth as much as $3,000 per acre, he says.

Herbs can be cultivated and sold to local markets—i.e., restaurants, grocery stores, gourmet food stores, and farmer's markets. Herbal tea companies and natural food and health stores are always seeking fresh mint, chamomile, lemon grass, raspberry leaves, and rose hips for aromatic teas. Other fast selling items that can be marketed to these businesses as well as boutiques and bath stores are dried flowers, pot pourri, and dried plant arrangements that are sold for their natural beauty and fragrance.

But if you want to sell to restaurants, advises Stephanie Renaker-Jansen, owner of the Reminiscent Herb Farm Inc. near Cincinnati, Ohio, you'll need to grow your crops year-round. Renaker-Jansen's herb farm business consists of a 13,000-square-foot greenhouse and a 120-acre farm in Boone County. She told the *Cincinnati Business Courier* in 1988 that she sold between 300 to 400 varieties of herbs and 200 types of outdoor shrubs and trees. She also provided fresh cut herbs to Cincinnati and Northern Kentucky chefs who had previously relied on produce from California.

As you set out to plan your farm or garden, determine which herbs grow best in your region of the country, the length of the growing season, and the type of soil. Your nearest agricultural department, university extension, or herb grower's association will be able to provide this information.

MARKETING STRATEGIES

Do your homework first, before planting a seed in the ground, and figure out if there is a market for specific herbs in your community, state, or region. Herb farming is a long term, highly speculative venture, and it will pay to take your time researching it—perhaps a full year before you plant your first crop. Don't forget to add at least $500 to your budget for books, magazines, and seminars for research. The most popular and commonly grown herbs are basil, dill, mint, chives, bay leaves, oregano, rosemary, sage, tarragon, and thyme. But don't just plant the top selling herbs—think about filling a niche with your specialty herb product.

Part of your research will involve asking yourself some of the following questions: Do the health food stores in your area sell fresh herbs? Who are the gourmet cooks who need an abundant supply of spices? Could you be their supplier? Are there landscapers or greenhouses that could benefit from homegrown ornamental plants and herbs? What would it take to establish a booth at the farmer's market? Could you sell herbs out of your home year-round?

According to Steven Foster in *Botanical & Herb Reviews,* the botanical market, which represents wholesalers, brokers, and manufacturers of plant materials for health food markets, is probably the easiest one to break into for the start-up herb farmer. Herb sales represented about 17 percent of total retail sales or $653 million in 1991. Foster writes that more than ''600 botanical commodities are sold as bulk or finished goods in health and natural food markets in North America.'' The American Herbal Product Association is the best source for information on the types of herbs listed in this category.

Another question you'll need to answer is whether there are professionals in the natural healing community who need a constant supply of fresh herbs for medicinal purposes. There are several markets for medicinal herbs: overseas exports, pharmaceutical and health stores, and natural food bulk distributors, Foster says. He writes that the growing interest in traditional medicine will help increase opportunities for producers of medicinal plants.

Approximately 220 companies manufacture herbal medicine in the United States, according to Susan Mitchell in an article for *American Demographics.* Three percent of Americans use herbal medicine. Mitchell wrote that the herbal remedy market may be growing faster than conventional, over-the-counter medicines. Estimated growth for this industry ranges from 12 to 15 percent a year. But even though pharmaceutical drugs contain plant and herbal extracts, opportunities for supplying herbal raw materials to this market are extremely difficult for the start-up grower, who has not yet developed a long-standing relationship with a company.

Herb farmers aiming for the medicinal market may consider setting their sites on Europe or Asia. European standardized herb products, known as phytomedicines, represented a $2.2 billion market in 1990 and was projected to grow 10 percent annually. Germany represents 70 percent of this market and Foster predicts that the number of phytomedicine consumers could increase from 60 million to 330 million by the mid 1990s, opening up a market for American producers. Asian markets are also promising. The countries and cultures of the Far East have used and cultivated herbs since ancient times. Developing this market requires time, investment, and knowledge of doing business overseas, however; it may not be for the start-up grower, but should be considered once one gains more business experience.

A sign that the demand for fresh herbs is strong and getting stronger is their presence—only in the past decade—in American supermarkets. Up until this time, the bulk of all herbs and spices, more than 90 percent, were imported from overseas. American farmers had little experience growing herbs for the mass market. Herbs were traditionally grown on contract for McCormick-Schilling, Durkee, Spice Islands, and other dried herb packagers/growers. Specialty, fresh produce wholesalers then began supplying fine restaurants. The transition to retail sales came about through the distribution of fresh herbs through health food and gourmet food stores. Then supermarkets caught on. Today, fresh herbs are no longer sold primarily in supermarkets serving upscale suburban consumers. Fresh herbs are produced in every major metropolitan market area and sold in most supermarkets nationwide. Some of the larger growers and distributors are in the process of establishing national brands. The USDA's Market News Service now reports fresh herb price information in 17 markets in which their service is available.

Valuable resources for the beginning herb farmer are the *Herb Market Report,* published by OAK, Inc., and the *Herb Quarterly.* The *Herb Market Report* provides market analysis of new crops and tips on making your herb business more profitable. The *Herb Quarterly* contains information on all aspects of herb growing and marketing. To obtain seedlings wholesale, write for a catalog from Taylor's Herb Gardens, Inc. By reading these publications, you will begin to understand what will be required of you in the marketplace. Also, information on brokers, wholesalers, and manufacturers, as well as trends, legislation, and market reports will be readily available.

Once you've determined where your operation can best fit in the marketplace, your next task will be selecting a buyer to purchase your products and put you in business. According to Steven Foster in *Botanical & Herb Reviews,* herb farmers must demonstrate that they can produce herbs and deliver the product on time before sealing a deal with an herb broker or other end-user. Presenting yourself to a buyer requires that you have done your marketing homework. You must convey confidence in your product and convince the buyer that you are the best person to fulfill his or her needs. You will have to price your product according to the current market and time of year—and be sure to have samples of your product on hand for interested buyers.

If you have time, it might also help to gain some experience in growing, harvesting, and processing your crop before you enter the market. And diversify. Stephanie Renaker-Jansen, for instance, not only grows herbs for res-

SOME OF THE MOST POPULAR HERBS AND SPICES

- Allspice
- Anise Seed
- Basil
- Bay Leaf
- Caraway Seed
- Carob (Roast)
- Cayenne (Hot; powdered)
- Cilantro
- Cinnamon—stick and powder
- Curry
- Dill Weed
- Fennel Seed
- Garlic
- Ginger Root
- Mint
- Nutmeg
- Onion—chopped and powdered
- Oregano
- Paprika
- Pepper (black; whole and ground)
- Rosemary
- Sage
- Thyme
- Vanilla Bean

(SOURCES: *THE POTENTIAL OF HERBS AS A CASH CROP,* RICHARD ALAN MILLER, 1985, 1992; *RESTAURANT BUSINESS, SUPERMARKET BUSINESS.*)

taurants, but her business also provides landscaping and architectural design and installation services, and conducts mail-order services for customers world-wide.

ADVERTISING

Once you have proven that you can produce a crop of herbs for market, you'll need to think about advertising to keep business flowing. But beware: *You are prohibited by law from making health claims in your advertising.* There are ways you can publicize your product without spending a lot of money on a slick ad campaign. In fact, many herb farmers do a lot of direct marketing (selling directly to the public), as well as word of mouth advertising. Of course, you may have already accomplished some of this by networking with other herb growers, buyers, and suppliers at conferences, through trade association meetings, or by cold calling.

Making a name for yourself at a farmer's market, or a local grocery or health food store, also helps advertise your produce directly to consumers. Noted television gourmet host Graham Kerr suggests that herb businesses create "Supertags" to advertise the contents of their produce. For example, information on individual herb tags should include planting instructions, companion plants, culinary uses and recipes, medicinal uses, decorative potential, household uses, and preservation tips. Even using a table tent card saying "Fresh herbs courtesy of My Herb Farm" in a restaurant goes a long way to notifying your consumers that you provide quality, fresh produce. So does having a roadside stand at your farm or home (check your community's zoning laws for sign placement and advertising of small businesses). Letting consumers "pick their own herbs" directly from your herb farm is a great way of saving labor costs and advertising your business at the same time—and it ensures that your customers get the freshest possible product they'll find anywhere.

Then there's what is known as "free advertising," or public relations efforts that can help you make a name for yourself in your community. A press release to your local newspaper could spark enough interest in profiling your farm in the business or feature sections. Public speaking on herbs and their uses gets you out into the public. So does teaching a course on cooking with herbs or herb growing. Otherwise, you may want to consider placing advertisements in your local publications and trade magazines.

LICENSING AND LEGAL ISSUES

Again, it pays to check your community's zoning laws regarding either home-based or agricultural businesses before obtaining the necessary business licenses. Part of your investment should also be in securing proper legal counsel to advise you properly in launching your business. Also know whether your state legislates "organic farming." Organic farming does not involve using chemicals (in the form of pest control or fertilizers). Investigate whether you will need to obtain specific health certificates. Again, your local herb

growers association will be available to help you out with these details.

Probably one of the biggest issues facing the herb growing industry is the 1990 Nutrition Labeling and Education Act. This law directed the Food and Drug Administration (FDA) to create guidelines for health claims and labels on food, dietary supplements, and herbs. Initially, the industry favored the new law, but herb growers and marketers oppose the way the FDA is implementing what they see as a "drug-like standard" for allowing health claims for herb products.

In a trade newsletter, International Herb Growers & Marketers Association President Pat Reppert said "this means that if an herb is put on the market with an intended health benefit beyond flavoring, seasoning, or fragrance that it must go through the testing process that is used for new drugs, i.e., millions of dollars of controlled tests to insure safety." She questioned why herbs, which have been used for centuries without ill side effects, should be rigorously tested. The IHGMA—a 740-member organization—is urging its members to ask their legislators for co-sponsorship on two bills in the House and the Senate that will delay the implementation of the labeling act and current FDA interpretations.

SOURCES:

Buchanan, Rita, "An Herb Gardener Visits Chicago," *The Herb Companion,* April/May 1991, p. 86.

Entrepreneur Magazine's 168 More Businesses Anyone Can Start and Make a Lot of Money, second edition, Bantam, 1991.

Foster, Steven, "Medicinal Plant Production: Breaking into the Marketplace," *Botanical & Herb Review,* 1992.

Herb Farming: Cash for Your Crops, EntrepreneurGroup, 1992.

IHGMA Newsletter, International Herb Growers & Marketers Association, September 1993.

Maftei, Michaela, "Prospects in European Market for Culinary Herbs," *International Trade Forum,* January/March 1992, pp. 4-9.

Meares, Portia, "Herbs: The Nurturing Connection," *The Business of Herbs.*

Miller, Richard Alan, *The Potential of Herbs as a Cash Crop,* Ten Speed Press, 1992.

Mitchell, Susan, "Healing without Doctors," *American Demographics,* July 1993, p. 46.

RMA Annual Statement Studies 1992, Robert Morris Associates, 1992, p. 778.

Scarpa, James, "Herbs," *Restaurant Business,* July 20, 1992.

Scott, Alexander, "Herb Garden Business Brings Cash to Back Yard Gardeners," *Successful Opportunities,* March 1991, pp. 24-32.

Simmons, Amy, "Success More Than a Matter of Thyme for Herb Business," *Cincinnati Business Courier,* October 17-23, 1988, pp. 1, 29.

Schwartz, Carol A., editor, *Small Business Sourcebook,* 6th edition, Gale, 1993.

Woy, Patricia A., *Small Businesses That Grow and Grow and Grow,* Betterway Publications, 1989.

—EVELYN S. DORMAN

Home Health Care Service

Home health care encompasses two related but clearly defined businesses. Home health agencies provide at-home medical care under the supervision of a primary-care physician. According to the National Association for Home Care, there were about 6,500 certified home health agencies in the United States in 1993. Home care services, on the other hand, provide nonmedical, assisted-living services, particularly for the elderly or children with disabilities or long-term illnesses who are unable to care for themselves. There were about an equal number of home care services in 1993.

Both areas offer opportunities for people interested in the growing health care industry, but you should be aware that home health agencies are highly regulated businesses, with initial start-up and operating costs easily running as high as $300,000 or more. Thus, home health agencies are often operated by hospitals or large medical services corporations. Home care services are much easier and less costly to start. Home care services generally operate as referral services for independent care providers, which means they can be operated by a sole proprietor as a home-based business. Start-up costs are often less than $5,000. Since home care services do not provide medical care, they are less regulated at both the state and federal levels.

FINANCIAL ASPECTS

Starting a home care service involves developing a network of nonmedical care providers who work as independent contractors. Start-up costs are limited to establishing an office, which could be a room at home, telephone service, business license, insurance, and advertising and marketing costs. Start-up costs may range from a few hundred dollars to $5,000 or more, depending on the office, equipment, and initial advertising and marketing expenses.

Starting a home health agency is much more involved. Start-up costs will include leasing an office and hiring at least two registered nurses and a director (unless the owner has a medical background—see the personnel section for more information). Office expenses, equipment, licenses, insurance (including medical malpractice), advertising, and first month salaries will be at least $100,000. The agency will also need three months operating capital, which could boost start-up costs to $300,000 or more. Industry experts caution against a new home health agency becoming overextended by hiring more staff or purchasing more equipment than it initially needs. It is safer to start small and grow. Home health agencies generally earn a net profit of 36 percent to 48 percent of gross revenues, depending on the ratio of Medicare patients, private-insurance patients, and private-pay patients.

A home care service may not need outside financing, since start-up costs are relatively low. But home health agencies can be costly and probably will require outside financial support to get started. Banks are an obvious source of financing, but banks are notoriously very conservative in their lending practices and require a solid business plan. Generally, banks also require a thorough credit history and sufficient collateral, although a person with an excellent credit rating may be able to arrange an unsecured loan. Finance companies often will accept greater risk and may extend a loan when a bank will not; they also charge higher interest rates. Some banks and community colleges offer small business assistance programs. There are also associations of retired business executives who volunteer to assist start-up businesses. These people can help create a business plan that will satisfy potential lenders.

Another potential source of capital is for the owner to sell equity in the business. In an equity investment, investors own a percentage of the business and share in all losses and profits. An equity investment is not a loan and there are no legal obligations to repay the money. Although selling equity may seem to be a good way to raise capital, the business owner may also lose some control over the enterprise. One source of financing that is often overlooked, especially for smaller loans, are personal credit cards. Although credit card interest rates are much higher than a bank loan, start-up costs can be charged and paid off as soon as the business begins to generate a positive cash flow.

The **Small Business Administration (SBA)** is yet another source of start-up capital. The SBA is an independent agency of the U.S. government that promotes small businesses through loans, counseling, and other information. The SBA is particularly sensitive to women and minority ownership. However, you must exhaust all sources of private financing before you are eligible for an SBA loan.

FRANCHISE OPPORTUNITIES

Home Care Services:

Abbey Home Healthcare: 3560 Hyland Ave., Costa Mesa, CA; phone: (714) 957-2000.

Kimberly Quality Care, Inc.: 695 Atlantic Ave., Ste. 800, Boston, MA 02111; phone: (617) 951-2700.

Staff Builders, Inc.: 1981 Marcus Ave., Ste. C115, Lake Success, NY; phone: (800) 342-5782.

Home Health Agencies:

Firstat Nursing Services: 1645 Palm Beach Lakes Blvd., Ste. 450, West Palm Beach, FL 33401; phone: (800) 845-7828.

There are SBA offices in most major cities. Check the "U.S. Government" section of the telephone directory for locations and telephone numbers. You can also reach the SBA at **1-800-U ASK SBA.**

LOCATION

Every new enterprise should conduct a market study of the community to assess whether there is enough potential business to be profitable. This includes not only the population base, but also economic conditions and the amount of competition. This information should be developed as part of the initial business plan. Information is available from many sources, including local chambers of commerce, the U.S. Census Bureau, and state and federal health care organizations.

After determining that a community can support another home health agency or home care service, the start-up business should consider office locations. Since home care services conduct business primarily by telephone, the office can be as simple as a room at home. However, some referral sources (doctors, hospital outpatient planning coordinators, social workers, ministers, etc.) and clients may want to visit in person to discuss the service, so even home-based offices need to be professional in appearance.

As a home care service grows, it may become advantageous to lease an office with space for full-time or part-time personnel. A leased office may also create greater credibility with both clients and referrals sources, and depending on location, may generate new business. For example, home care services catering primarily to the elderly may want to locate near retirement communities or senior citizens centers. Firms that provide home care services for children may want to locate near schools, day-care centers, churches, community centers, parks or other places where they may be noticed by parents of younger children.

On the other hand, home health agencies need considerable office space from the start and location can be ex-

tremely important. A start-up home health agency will probably need a minimum of 2,000 square feet with plans to expand as the business grows. This would provide a reception area and office space for a sales manager and medical services director. Although the nursing staff will spend most of its time at client locations, the agency should provide workstations for nurses to use while in the office completing paperwork.

Home health agencies depend on referrals from doctors and hospital outpatient planners even more than home care services, so the office needs to present a highly professional appearance. And, because doctors and hospital outpatient planners may also want to discuss treatment programs with an agency's medical director in person, home health agencies should consider locating near hospitals or in established medical services complexes. The original business plan should include a map showing the location of hospitals, major medical services complexes, and other home health agencies.

MARKETING

For both home health agencies and home care providers, marketing is seldom directed to the person who ultimately receives the service; rather, marketing efforts should focus on referral sources. For home health agencies, much of their business will be patients covered by Medicare or private insurance who are referred by doctors, hospital outpatient coordinators, or insurance company case managers, and most of their marketing efforts will be directed toward these referral sources. However, there is a potential for private-pay clients that home health agencies should not ignore, although reaching this market may require an entirely different approach.

Physicians are the only people who can authorize at-home medical treatment that is covered by Medicare, and most doctors will be more interested in the services a home health agency provides than the cost. Consequently, marketing to physicians and hospital outpatient coordinators should stress nursing staff credentials, range of services, and commitment to quality health care. Insurance case managers will be more interested in cost. It is also important that health care agencies present themselves as knowledgeable about Medicare and private insurance.

In some instances, physicians may refer patients to home health agencies even though the services will not be covered by Medicare or private insurance. Home health agencies may need to market both service and price to these private-pay clients. In addition, some parents of children with disabilities or adults with elderly parents may prefer a home health agency to a home care service even when skilled nursing is not necessary. Even though these clients are likely to be affluent, they may still balance service against cost.

Although home care services are not covered by Medicare or most insurance plans, referrals may still come from doctors, hospitals, and insurance companies involved in creating a patient treatment plan. In addition, home care businesses are more likely than home health agencies to market their services directly to the public. Many home care clients will be parents of children with disabilities or adults whose elderly parents need help with everyday activities, including bathing, dressing, or eating. Whether a referral or the result of direct marketing, home care clients will be paying for the services themselves, and cost will be a major factor in the purchase decision.

ADVERTISING

In general, advertising will be far more beneficial to a home care service that markets to the public than a home health agency that relies primarily on physician referrals. Home health agencies market directly to referral sources through telephone calls and personal visits. However, health care agencies may find it useful to advertise in local publications read by medical professionals. Direct-mail advertising may also be useful, and home health agencies should mail information describing their services to physicians and hospital outpatient coordinators on a regular basis. Again, this material should focus on staff credentials, range of services provided, and the ease of doing business.

Home care services have far more opportunities for advertising. In general, home care services should consider any advertising that puts the company name and services in public view and is cost effective. This may include billboards, radio commercials, newspaper ads, or direct mail. More than one home care service discovered that advertising on public buses and bus benches can be effective. However, home care services should remember to target their advertising to the people who will pay for the services, not the people who will receive them. Advertising in a publication

for senior citizens may not be as effective as advertising in a publication that reaches adults who may have elderly parents in need of services. A simple measure of cost effectiveness is cost divided by the number of people in the target audience that hears or sees the message.

Both home health agencies and home care services should ask doctors offices, hospitals, public health and social service agencies, rehabilitation centers, senior citizen centers, churches, day-care centers—or any other business or institution that potential clients are likely to visit—to distribute brochures describing their services. Brochures do not need to be elaborate, but should emphasize the firm's commitment to providing reliable services at affordable prices. Health care agencies should have at least two brochures: one targeted to referral sources that includes information about ease of doing business, and one for potential private-pay clients that includes information about the relative cost of hospital-based care versus at-home care.

PERSONNEL

The business owner may often be the sole employee of a home care service. The owner develops a network of reputable home care providers (often referred to as home health aides or personal care aides) who act as independent contractors. The owner also markets the home care service to referral sources and potential clients. When potential clients contact the home care service and describe their needs, the owner calls the appropriate home care providers who are then responsible for working out the arrangements. The owner also follows up periodically to make sure clients are satisfied with their services. As a home care service grows, it may need to add clerical support. It may also decide to offer some limited home health services, and add the appropriate personnel. Many businesses that start out as home care services eventually become full-service home health agencies.

On the other hand, home health agencies require several employees with different skills. The first employee a home health agency needs is a director who has an extensive medical background and administrative experience. The director is responsible for scheduling, ensuring that the agency conforms to state and federal laws, and dealing with insurance companies, Medicare, and the Health Care Financing Administration. The director is also responsible for all the records that a home health agency is required to keep. Owners may serve as their own directors, especially in a start-up agency—and save $40,000 to $80,000 in salary costs. But owners without extensive experience in medical services should hire someone more qualified to handle this crucial position.

The medical services staff for a start-up home health agency generally consists of at least one registered nurse and a physical or occupational therapist. These people administer the treatment plan authorized by the primary-care physician who provided the referral. The agency may also hire

INDUSTRY STATISTICS

- *Number of Agencies Providing Home Care Services:* 13,951.
- *Number of Medicare-Certified Home Health Agencies:* 6,497.
- *Percentage of Home Care Services That Are For-Profit and Independently Owned:* 35%.
- *Percentage of Home Care Services That Are Hospital Based:* 30%.
- *Amount Spent on Home Care Services (1993):* $21.2 billion.
- *Home Care Services as Percentage of Total U.S. Health Care:* 3%.
- *Percentage of Home Care Services Covered by Medicare/Medicaid:* 62.5%.
- *Number of Individuals Requiring Home Care Services:* 11 million.

(SOURCES: NATIONAL ASSOCIATION FOR HOME CARE, 1993; ESTIMATES BASED ON 1987 NATIONAL MEDICAL EXPENDITURES SURVEY; AND OFFICE OF NATIONAL HEALTH STATISTICS.)

PRIMARY ASSOCIATIONS AND SELECTED TRADE PUBLICATIONS

Associations:

American Academy of Home Care Physicians: 4450 W. 77th St., Ste. 100, Edina, MN 55435; phone: (612) 835-1973.

American Federation of Home Health Agencies: 1320 Fenwick Lane, Ste. 100, Silver Spring, MD 20910; phone: (301) 588-1454.

Foundation for Hospice and Homecare: 519 C Street NE, Washington, DC 20002; phone: (202) 547-6586.

National Association for Home Care: 519 C Street NE, Stanton Park, Washington, DC 20002; phone: (202) 547-7424.

Publications:

Caregivers: 9300 Oak St. NE, St. Petersburg, FL 33702; phone: (201) 768-0201.
Caring: National Association for Home Care, 519 C Street NE, Stanton Park, Washington, DC 20002; phone: (202) 547-7424.
Home Health Agency Insider: American Federation of Home Health Agencies, 1320 Fenwick Lane, Suite 100, Silver Spring, MD 20910; phone: (301) 588-1454.
Home Health Line: P.O. Box 250, Port Republic, MD; phone: (410) 535-4103.
Home Healthcare Nurse: J.B. Lippincott Co., East Washington Square, Philadelphia, PA 19106; phone: (215) 238-4273.
Homecare Magazine: Miramar Publishing Co., 6133 Bristol Parkway, P.O. Box 4630, Culver City, CA 90231; phone: (213) 337-9717.
Journal of Home Health Practice: Aspen Publishers, Inc., P.O. Box 990, Frederick, MD 21701-9782; phone: (800) 638-8437.

one or more licensed practical nurses, therapy assistants, or home health aides (on staff, unlike home care services) to provide services that do not require the same level of training. Many agencies also employ social workers. According to the National Association for Home Care, registered nurses working for home health agencies earned between $28,000 and $38,000 in 1992; physical and occupational therapists, $31,000 to $45,000; licensed practical nurses, $20,000 to $26,000; social workers (with a masters degree), $27,000 to $35,000; and health care aides, $13,000 to $18,000.

Most health care agencies also have at least one person whose sole responsibility is to market the agency to the various referral sources. This may also be the owner in a start-up agency, but again it is extremely important that the sales representative have knowledge of the health-care industry. The sales representative will be the primary contact between the health-care agency and the referral sources and must develop professional business relationships that bring in new clients.

PRICING AND BILLING

Home care services generally charge clients from $7 to as much as $20 per day, depending on the type of care provided. This is a service referral fee, and not the cost of the care itself, which is billed by, and paid to, the home care provider. For example, a client may pay $10 per day to the home care service and $10 per hour for three hours of care, for a total of $40 per day. Some home care services also require a one-time or annual registration fee before making a referral.

Although care providers set their own rates, the home care service should periodically review what they are charging to be sure rates are reasonable. Most home care services bill their clients twice monthly. They also may negotiate a one-time fee for long-term care.

According to the National Association for Home Care, the average cost of a nursing visit in 1993 was $84. Nurses averaged five visits per day. However, the cost of medical treatment provided by skilled home health agency personnel was set by Medicare or established in advance by the insurance companies paying for the services. Medicare rates are fixed, but insurance payments may be negotiable. Home health agencies submit their rates to the insurance companies, which may accept them or make adjustments. Agencies also set their own rates for private-pay clients.

REGULATION

All health care agencies that receive reimbursement from Medicare must be certified by the **Health Care Financing Administration (HCFA),** an arm of the U.S. Department of Health and Human Services. HCFA rules and regulations for home health agencies are enforced by state health departments, which also may impose their own licensing requirements. Home health agencies are also subject to periodic, unannounced inspections.

HCFA regulations are extensive and change frequently, especially as more medical services previously available only in hospitals are provided by home health agencies. However, to be certified, home health agencies must provide two or more treatment services. Copies of the latest regulations are available by writing the HCFA at **6325 Security Building, Room 700, Baltimore, MD 21207-5161,** or from one of several regional offices. Anyone who is considering starting a home health agency must also contact the state health departments about local rules and regulations.

Home care services are not as regulated as home health agencies because they do not provide medical services. Home care services that operate only as referral agencies are even less regulated, since the care providers are independent contractors. However, home care services should contact their state health departments, not only to ensure that they meet all necessary requirements, but also to understand the requirements their independent contractors must meet.

INSURANCE

In addition to liability insurance and other common business coverage, a home health agency will need medical malpractice insurance. Home care services will not need malpractice insurance, since they do not provide medical treatment. However, they will need liability insurance and other basic coverage, including fire and theft. Owners who operate from a home office should check their homeowners policy to see what it covers. Most homeowners policies do not cover equipment used in a home-based business.

Home health agencies also should consider becoming bonded since employees will be working in clients' homes. A fidelity bond will protect the business against employee theft. Home care services may want to require their independent contractors to be bonded, which would add a degree of respectability to the business and possibly prevent legal action or bad publicity if someone whom the service referred is accused of stealing. (Bonding companies also require background checks on all employees, which can help prevent problems before they develop.) However, it is important to understand that a bond is not a form of insurance; it is a guarantee that the business can pay any claims against it. For a fee, a bonding company establishes a fund and immediately pays legitimate claims up to the limit of the bond. The business must repay the bond, usually within 90 days.

MEDICAL EQUIPMENT

Home health agencies furnish most medical and non-medical supplies used in providing their services. However, because of the initial cost, most start-up home health agencies do not provide durable health care equipment such as wheelchairs or intravenous infusion devices. Instead, clients are referred to medical equipment providers and make their own arrangements for delivery and billing. However, as agencies grow, many do begin providing durable equipment. Many others handle all the arrangements with medical equipment companies and bill their clients for the added service.

In 1993 the National Association for Home Care estimated that more than 6 million people in the United States received some form of home care for acute or terminal illnesses, long-term health conditions, or permanent disabilities. And indications were that the home health care industry would continue to grow in the years ahead as the U.S. population grew older and health care providers looked for ways to hold down rising costs.

However, the industry also was becoming more competitive. The number of Medicare-certified home health agencies doubled between 1967 and 1980, and doubled again between 1980 and 1985. In August 1993 there were 6,902 certified home health agencies. In addition, in the early 1980s, most certified home health agencies were operated by public health agencies. But in 1993, hospital-based agencies and for-profit agencies accounted for two-thirds of the industry.

As a result, starting a home health agency was more difficult and more risky in the mid-1990s than it was in the 1980s. However, for those agencies able to carve out a market niche, there was still plenty of opportunity. There was less risk, and perhaps even more opportunity, for home care services.

SOURCES:

Abramowitz, Michael, "Paying the Price for Home Care," *The Washington Post,* October 6, 1991, p. H1.

"A Business Even the Patients Like," *Forbes,* May 14, 1990, p. 104.

Home Health Agency, Business Start-Up Guide, Entrepreneur Group, 1992.

"Home Health Care Industry Sees Explosive Growth, As More and More, Recuperation Means Returning Home," *Denver Business Journal,* May 21, 1993, p. 4B.

"House Calls," *Entrepreneur,* August 1992, p. 99.

Stout, Hilary, "Godsend for Many, Home-Care Industry Also Has Potential for Fraud and Abuse," *Wall Street Journal,* p. B1.

—*DEAN BOYER*

Import/Export Service

As the world economy grows more and more interdependent, vast opportunities are opening up for import/export entrepreneurs. The tasks of an import/export agent include selecting and pricing marketable products, locating manufacturers and sales representatives, and drafting plans and contracts. The import/export industry is not nearly as daunting as it might seem. Anyone with a minimal amount of business experience can learn how to coordinate trades between buyers and sellers in different countries. To assist the potential import/export service owner, there are myriad informational networks worldwide, many of which are government-sponsored agencies designed to promote and facilitate international trade.

As an agent your risks are minimal; you do not have to purchase any goods until sales are made by trade merchants. The import/export business can be quite lucrative with an average return on initial investment at about 600 percent. You also have the advantage of being able to work from your home.

FINANCING

Start-up investment costs for an import/export service range from a minimum of $13,000 to an average of about $20,000. A higher capital investment would be required for individuals who wish to be merchants. The net profit potential before taxes may be greater than $200,000, although the average net profit is closer to $120,000.

Numerous sources are available to help finance your business. A bank may extend credit to you if you have sufficient capital in your account or if your company is financially stable. If you do not have an established credit rating, you can do so rather simply and inexpensively: take out a loan for several thousand dollars and pay it back immediately. You should also open an account at an international bank with a separate department for ''letters of credit'' (LCs), which are a common form of international payment.

When you apply for your business loan, meet with your lending officer in person. You must present a detailed and convincing business plan with clearly defined objectives, including the marketability of your products, your potential foreign partnerships, and your expertise. Consult with trade associations and professionals in the business for advice. The **Small Business Administration (SBA)** should be able to assist you in your start-up efforts and may guarantee loans for you. The SBA can also offer you free counseling with trade experts from the Service Corps of Retired Executives (SCORE) and Small Business Institutes (SBIs).

The SBA also publishes a number of useful materials, including the *Exporter's Guide to Federal Resources for Small Business.* Call **1-800-U ASK SBA** or write to **Small Business Directory, P.O. Box 1000, Ft. Worth, TX 76119.** The Eximbank in Washington, D.C., may also assist you with financing your business. Find out about relevant federal programs and activities by contacting the **Trade Information Center** at **1-800-USA TRADE.** Another helpful source is your district office of the U.S. Department of Commerce (USDOC) and your state export promotion or export finance office, which you can locate through the National Association of State Development Agencies.

LOCATION AND EQUIPMENT

You can easily start an import/export business from your home, although be prepared for an occasional visit from a client or credit reporter. You should inquire about local regulations regarding commercial use of space in a residential area, which may include restrictions on warehousing and the number of employees. You may also need separate insurance or a rider for your home equipment. Though a separate office may be necessary if you wish to accept credit card payments from U.S. clients, the nature of the business is such that you will not need a prime location.

Your initial investment will be little more than the cost of office equipment and supplies and perhaps rental space. Since you will conduct most of your communications electronically, you do not need fancy furniture or office equipment. Used equipment will help you keep costs down (check under ''Office Sales'' in your local papers). You will need a desk, a chair, some shelves, and filing cabinets. A copy machine is essential, since you will often need to make copies of documents. Another necessary item is a telex machine, which costs around $1,000, though you can start out with a rental for about $50 per month, or hire a telex service. An alternative to a telex is a computer modem and

PRIMARY ASSOCIATIONS

American Association of Exporters and Importers (AAEI): 11 West 42nd St., New York, NY 10036; phone: (212) 944-2230; fax: (212) 382-2606.

American League for Exporters and Security Assistance (ALESA): 122 C St. NW, Ste. 740, Washington, DC 20001; phone: (202) 783-0051; fax: (202) 737-4727.

International Traders Association: c/o The Mellinger Co., 6100 Varial Ave., Woodland Hills, CA 91367; phone: (818) 884-4400; fax: (818) 594-5804.

National Association of Export Companies (NEXCO): P.O. Box 1330, Murray Hill Sta., New York, NY 10156; phone: (212) 725-3312; fax: (212) 725-3311.

National Association of State Development Agencies: 444 North Capitol Street, Ste. 611, Washington, DC 20001; phone: (202) 624-5411.

National Customs Brokers and Forwarders Association of America: One World Trade Center, Ste. 1153, New York, NY 10048; phone: (212) 432-0050; fax: (212) 432-5709.

Small Business Administration (SBA): Office of Business Loans, 409 3rd St. SW, Washington, DC 20416; phone: (202) 205-6570, or (800) U-ASK-SBA.

Trade Information Center: 800-USA-TRADE.

telecommunications software. You should also have a typewriter, a fax machine, a separate telephone line, an answering machine, a calculator, a postage meter, and Rolodex files.

A cost-effective way of achieving a professional appearance is by investing a few hundred dollars in high quality stationery with a distinctive letterhead. Select a name that is original and easy to remember. You may want to register your company name as well. Be creative with your logo, avoiding clichéd trains, planes, and ships. Other important office supplies are forms. You can find standard documents for exports in stationery stores, but imports may require special forms that can be obtained from either the consulate in your client's country or from **UNZ and Company,** which can be reached at **1-800-631-3098.**

GETTING STARTED

You should decide whether you will work as an agent or merchant. An agent performs fewer tasks and takes fewer risks than a merchant. A merchant purchases goods outright and may have to warehouse them, but a merchant earns more than an agent relative to the quantity of goods traded. Unless you have the expertise, hundreds of thousands of dollars in investment capital, and can afford to take some risks, you should begin as an agent.

You also need to choose between importing and exporting to simplify your initial operations. Importing may be easier to the extent that you would be marketing and distributing products in a familiar country. A large part of import business is conducted by small-sized companies. However, there are more export services, and they are more diverse. The international market is about four times larger than the U.S. market and has a larger growth rate. Also, since 85 percent of U.S. exports come from only around 200 large corporations, there are plenty of opportunities for smaller-scale manufacturers to sell abroad. As an export agent you can offer these small firms your special skills. Once you are more established you may consider expanding into a full-service import/export management company.

SELECTING PRODUCTS

Your success as an import/export entrepreneur will depend largely on your ability to sell goods. Select products that interest you and that you have some business knowledge about, either in sales, marketing, or trade. It is important for your clients to know that you are capable of promoting their merchandise intelligently and effectively. For product ideas subscribe to trade publications, such as *Trade Channel, Gifts & Housewares Accessories, Asian Sources,* and *Made in Europe.* For novelty items and lower-priced goods check with the *International Intertrade Index.* Still another source for product possibilities is the *Exhibits Guide,* which lists trade exhibits.

Research the market demand for your products. If you choose to import, keep in mind that foreign specialty items carry a high status with many Americans. The SBA offers a number of inexpensive market research publications, such as *Researching Your Market* and *Export Indicators.* An excellent statistical reference book is the *UN Statistical Yearbook,* published by the United Nations, which provides data on products as well as on importing nations and may help you evaluate potential competition. Good sources for demographic data on foreign countries are *World Population, World Factbook,* and other publications that are available through the **U.S. Government Printing Office, (202) 783-3238.** You should also check with U.S. international aid organizations, which often seek export agents to service foreign countries with needed products.

LOCATING MANUFACTURERS

You can find listings of domestic firms in the *Thomas Register of American Manufacturers.* Exporters should register with the USDOC's *American International Traders Index,* a listing of more than 20,000 domestic manufacturers and the products they wish to export. *Kompass* is a good directory of foreign manufacturers, as is the *Latin/American Import Export Directory.* To locate addresses of foreign firms check with *Croner's Reference Book for World Traders.* The U.S. Foreign Commercial Service, a subdivision of the USDOC, may assist you by providing names of potential firms. Consider visiting your target countries, where you can consult their chambers of commerce, and the suppliers themselves. Foreign governments will usually be helpful in locating export firms for you. And of course you may advertise your company in trade journals.

GETTING SAMPLES

Once you have chosen potential suppliers, contact them, introduce your firm, and explain your intentions. If you are an exporter, try to meet with the manufacturers in person. If they are wary of foreign trade, assure them that you will buy their product at factory prices and will take care of all the necessary documentation. Request suppliers' catalogues and price lists and tell them you need to do some market research. If you are interested in their products, ask for a few samples. Requests for free samples may take some time, especially from foreign suppliers. To speed the process, you might simply send an international money order for the cost of the samples plus an approximate cost for insured air mail, though you are not guaranteed a shipment.

Once you have your samples, test the products with buyers and consumers. Find out about competitive firms and products, including market demand and conditions, cost, and any specifications you must follow. Check with secondary sources for information on demographic, economic, and trade statistics. Dun & Bradstreet's *Exporters Encyclopedia* provides information on trade restrictions, special licenses,

and other product specifications. Watch for changes in trade legislation—especially for textiles and clothing—which may restrict the quantities of goods allowed into the United States. For imports, check with U.S. Customs for restrictions, duties, and proper labeling. Do not be surprised if you have to make some product modifications, which should also be considered to reduce a product's price.

Your cost analysis should be based on transportation, insurance, commissions, and potential profit. The two most common methods of pricing your services are commission and retainer. For merchandise with definite market potential, choose the commission method (generally 10-20 percent). For goods requiring more marketing effort on your part, the retainer method—a guaranteed flat fee—might be safer. The retainer is based on labor, supplies, overhead, and profit. Also, find out what quantities your suppliers can provide, how soon they can fill your order, and how much they are willing to contribute to marketing and advertising expenses.

REPRESENTATIVES, DISTRIBUTORS, AND RETAILERS

Once you have researched your product and have a price quotation, you should print up a small catalogue and a price list. You will then have to find distributors or sales agents. Distributors purchase goods outright, whereas sales representatives usually work on commission, are contracted for a specific time period, and do not assume responsibility for the goods.

You may find foreign partners through the Bureau of International Commerce at the USDOC, which compiles a *Trade List* of foreign buyers, distributors, and agents for numerous products. The USDOC's International Trade Administration (ITA) provides an agent/distributor service at a cost of about $50 for three contacts per country. The ITA may also be able to furnish you with export mailing lists of manufacturers, retailers, and government agencies. The Foreign Commercial Service, a subdivision of ITA, provides professional assistance to domestic exporting companies. You should also consider getting your products or your catalogue into trade exhibits overseas. Check with the *Overseas Trade Promotion Calendar* and the USDOC's *Commercial News USA* service. If you are importing, go to the foreign countries of your choice and visit their chambers of commerce.

To select the best partners, evaluate their sales records, marketing strategies, facilities, types of products, extent of territory, and customer profile. Try to find someone who has experience marketing products like yours and give them information on and samples of your products. Present yourself and your firm favorably. Impress potential business partners with your enthusiasm about the products and knowledge of the markets. Solicit their advice and offer them a better deal or a better product than your competition. If you are exporting, remember to provide your overseas

INDUSTRY STATISTICS

• *Increase in U.S. Merchandise Exports and Imports (1993):* Exports: 3.7% increase to record $464.8 billion; imports: 9% increase to record $580.5 billion (source: *New York Times,* February 18, 1994).
• *U.S. Merchandise Trade Deficit Worldwide:* (1993) $115.8 billion deficit, 37% greater than 1992; (1994 projection) $135 billion; (1995 projection) $137 billion (source: *Los Angeles Times,* February 18, 1994).
• *U.S. Merchandise Trade Deficit (1993):* (With Japan) $59.3 billion, 23% increase from previous year; (with China) $22.8 billion (source: *Los Angeles Times,* February 18, 1994).
• *U.S. Merchandise Trade Surplus (1993):* (With Central and South America) $562 million; (with Mexico) $155.6 million (source: *Los Angeles Times,* February 18, 1994).
• *U.S. Trade Surplus with Western Europe:* (1992) $6.4 billion; (1993) $280 million (source: *Los Angeles Times,* February 18, 1994).
• *Exporter Markets (1992):* 50% of U.S. exporters sell to only one foreign market; fewer than 20% of exporters— less than 3% of U.S. firms—export to more than five markets (source: *A Basic Guide to Exporting,* USDOC, International Trade Administration).
• *U.S. Export Production (1992):* 85% of exports produced by approximately 250 large manufacturing companies (source: EntrepreneurGroup).
• *Growth in U.S. GNP Due to Exports (1990):* 84% of record $394 billion in exports (source: *A Basic Guide to Exporting*).

SELECTED TRADE PUBLICATIONS

Business America: The Magazine of International Trade: U.S. Government Printing Office, Washington, DC 20402; phone: (202) 783-3238; fax: (202) 512-2233.

Business International: Business International Corp., 215 Park Ave. South, New York, NY 10003; phone: (212) 460-0600.

Commerce Business Daily: U.S. Government Printing Office, Washington, DC 20402; phone: (202) 783-3238.

Gifts & Housewares Accessories: P.O. Box 34-23, Taipei, Taiwan, ROC.

International Financial Statistics: International Financial Statistics, Publication Services, Room C100, 700 19th St. NW, Washington, DC 20431; phone: (202) 623-7430.

International Intertrade Index: New Foreign Products-Marketing Techniques: John E. Felber, P.O. Box 636, Federal Sq., Newark, NJ 07101; phone: (201) 686-2382.

Ports of the World: CIGNA, P.O. Box 7728, Philadelphia, PA 19101.

Trade Channel: American Business Communications, Tarrytown, NY; phone: (914) 631-1802.

World Bank Atlas: World Bank Publications, 1818 H St. NW, Washington, DC 20433; phone: (202) 473-1154.

customers with warranties and proper servicing, as well as instructions in their native language.

To find domestic buyers check with the *Directory of U.S. Importers.* Pinpoint retailers who are interested in importing in the publication *Stores of the World* or in directories of department stores and specialty retailers. You might also consider advertising to target markets through specialty newspaper and journals. A mail order catalog of your own might be too costly since it is a competitive market. You might instead try to get included in an established catalog. Check with *Facts on File Directory of Mail Order Catalogs* for more information.

CREDIT INFORMATION ON SUPPLIERS AND CUSTOMERS

Once you are satisfied that your product is salable and you have formulated a marketing plan, you should make sure your trading partners are reliable. Check their credit history and references through your bank, asking for a quick response by telex. You may check domestic partners with credit reporting agencies for about $40 and foreign firms with bigger agencies like TRW or Dun & Bradstreet for about $120. The USDOC offers a service through the *World Trader Data Reports* for about $70, though the data is less up-to-date. Other options for checking firms in more developed countries are *The Exporter's Guide to Foreign Sources for Credit Information,* published by Trade Data Reports, or a particular country's chamber of commerce, which can be located in *Johnson's Worldwide Chamber of Commerce Directory.*

INTERNATIONAL PAYMENT SYSTEMS

Draw up a contract with the manufacturer about the details of the transaction, like shipping, handling, and insurance. Decide when the "title" transfer occurs, that is, determine who is responsible for the goods at each point of the trade.

There are several methods of payment for international transactions. Payment in advance could save time and hassles, but if you are the importer be sure the supplier is trustworthy. A frequently used method is the letter of credit (LC), which guarantees payment to the exporter and allows the importer to place desired shipping conditions into the document. The importer applies for an LC through an international bank, which requires the applicant to have a sufficient amount in an account or provide some asset as security. Payment risks to both parties may be minimized by using such documents as "sight drafts" or "time drafts," which are payable upon sight of the documents or after an agreed upon time. These drafts are arranged by the exporter through banks and are not guaranteed. Still another method of payment is the open account, requiring the importer to pay at some point after receiving the merchandise. Finally, there are consignment sales whereby the supplier retains title and receives a percentage of sales after they are made. Consignment is sometimes used for perishable goods that arrive damaged or for expensive industrial goods.

You may want to arrange a supply agreement with your partner if you feel you need to protect your long-term interests. For instance, you may have invested a great deal of time promoting a particular product and setting up the deal and you want to insure that in the future you are not bypassed by the supplier and purchaser.

You will probably not have to worry about trading in foreign currency. About 90 percent of international trade is transacted in U.S. dollars. If you are offered foreign currency you should probably only accept if the payment is timely. Consult with your international bank officer for advice on hedging, or avoiding, risks, which involves agreeing to buy your trading partner's currency at a fixed rate at a particular time. Keep in mind that if there is a time delay before you receive payment, you are essentially financing your trade partner, in which case you may be eligible for export credit or loans from the SBA or the Eximbank and receive cash in advance.

INTERNATIONAL SHIPPING AND INSURANCE

Familiarize yourself with basic shipping terminology. There are two sets of definitions, American Standard Foreign Trade Definitions and INCOTERMS (International Commercial Terms), but the latter is more common. You can get a listing in the *Guide to Incoterms,* which is available through the ICC Publishing Corporation in New York City. An excellent glossary of general import/export terminology is *A Basic Guide To Exporting,* published by the International Trade Administration of the USDOC.

Determine which means of transportation will be most cost effective—by land, sea, or air. Check the packing costs, shipping rates, insurance, duties, and tariffs. For products without predetermined rates, you can avoid paying the higher general cargo rate by asking to have a rate set for your products. Find out whether your trading partner's country requires an importing or exporting license and be sure that is taken care of before you complete your transactions. You will also need a "certificate of origin" from the exporting country's chamber of commerce if you want your product to be duty-free.

There are several choices for export packing, from "break bulk" boxes to larger, well-sealed "containerized" boxes. Consult a marine insurance company for advice and be sure the supplier provides adequate packing or else hire a service. Protect your goods against damage, moisture, and pilferage. *Ports of the World* is the source to check for packing specifications and symbols for special handling.

For moving shipments across international borders, you will need a freight forwarder and customs broker. A forwarder firm charges the exporter a fee of about $125 by sea and $50 by air for packing, documentation, and booking space on the transport vehicle. At the other end, the customs broker fills out entry forms and pays duties and bonds. The importer pays a fee of about $75, depending on how many agencies the product must clear.

Choose all-risk, warehouse-to-warehouse insurance per shipment from a good company. You may obtain it through the forwarder company. Make sure you work out an adequate transportation agreement with your trading partner.

MANAGEMENT

Start your business small with trial orders to minimize risk, and manage your income and expenses using a consistent method, either on a cash basis or an accrual method. If you hire extra staff members, make sure they are well informed about your products and markets.

If necessary, exporters should instruct their foreign agents about marketing and business management. Importers should follow through with the marketing of their products by checking the effectiveness of displays and promotion of the products and find out about consumer response. Develop good and lasting relationships with your representatives and partners.

Always try to learn as much as possible about business etiquette appropriate to your trading partner's culture. Familiarize yourself with customs regarding dress, greetings, gift-giving, and negotiating techniques. Be careful with gestures; in Bulgaria, for example, nodding your head means "no," whereas shaking your head means "yes."

INSURANCE AND TAXATION

Importers and exporters share in liability associated with harm caused by the traded merchandise. Avoid problems by acquiring adequate product liability insurance. Find out about any restrictive state or local regulations. If you resell your merchandise across state boundaries you should get a sales tax number from your state tax department.

You can deduct full travel expenses if a trip is no longer than a week or if you spend 75 percent of your time while there working; otherwise only a portion of the trip is deductible. Rent can also be partially written off depending on the amount of space you use for your business. But be careful: Rent deductions may increase your chances of being audited.

COMPUTERIZED SOURCES

Several on-line and CD-ROM databases are available to help you with your research. The *Economic Bulletin Board* (EBB) can help you with trade leads and provide statistical information from several government sources, including the Bureaus of the Census, Economical Analysis, and Labor Statistics, for a minimum annual fee of $35. For information call **(202) 482-1986.**

The *National Trade Data Bank* (NTDB) provides data on export promotion programs and international statistics gathered from over a dozen U.S. government agencies. The NTDB also contains the CIA *World Factbook* and the complete *Foreign Traders Index,* listing more than 50,000 names and addresses of foreign firms seeking imports. You can access census information on specific products or by country. The CD-ROM database is available in hundreds of federal depository libraries, and discs may be purchased for $35 each. Also available on CD-ROM are the *U.S. Exports of Merchandise* and *U.S. Imports of Merchandise,* which are compiled by the Census Bureau and are some of the most extensive data on specific products.

In summary, starting an import/export service can be a lucrative endeavor. Whether you decide to be a merchant or an agent, you need to do extensive research on international trade regulations and determine which products will sell well. With the right mix of trading savvy and marketable goods, you can count on a successful career in the import/export industry.

SOURCES:

A Basic Guide to Exporting, USDOC, International Trade Administration, 1992.

Cohen, William, *The Entrepreneur and Small Business Problemsolver: An Encyclopedic Reference and Guide,* John Wiley & Sons, Inc., 1990.

Import/Export Management Business, Business Start-Up Guide, EntrepreneurGroup, 1992.

Weiss, Kenneth D., *Building an Import/Export Business,* John Wiley & Sons, Inc., 1987.

Wells, L. Fargo, *Exporting: From Start to Finance,* second edition, Liberty Hall Press, 1991.

—*AUDRA AVIZIENIS*

Information Broker

Over the years there have been a few individuals who have been gathering data for profit. Searching for information was once a slow, laborious process, involving research in library card catalogues, heavy reliance on interlibrary loans, and considerable waiting. However, the advent of the microcomputer radically changed information retrieval by allowing the broker to work at home and quickly gather vast amounts of information, often with little need to visit the library. The opportunity to work at home, set your own hours, and be your own boss, all at a very low start-up cost, are very attractive aspects of becoming an information broker.

In addition, competition is minimal. Currently there are several thousand information retrieval businesses in North America, and more than three-quarters of them are one-person operations. Demand for information from the biggest users of the information broker's services—including the business, financial, medical, government, and private endowment sectors—has been escalating annually. Recessionary times in the early 1990s spurred the growth of this cottage industry—a computer and a telephone line are just about all that's necessary to make a living, often a highly successful living, in this burgeoning field.

FINANCING AND PROFITABILITY

Start-up costs for information brokers have been estimated at $3,000 to $9,000, although the higher number is most frequently cited. For those who don't have one, purchasing a computer with the requisite software, a printer, and a modem will be necessary. Additional equipment you should install includes a second telephone line, fax machine, and a photocopier. Also, plan to buy business cards and stationery, which will contribute to the professional image of your business.

Other unavoidable costs that must be considered are the fees charged by such commercial database services as DIALOG and CompuServe on which every information broker depends heavily. These services not only charge a monthly or annual fee, but also for online time and document delivery as well. Running up a $100 bill for one hour of online time with one of the major services is not uncommon. However, these costs can be recouped in the fee charged to the client.

Membership in one of the industry associations, for example the Association of Independent Information Professionals (AIIP), sometimes includes a discount rate for certain online services. According to Sue Rugge in *The Information Broker's Handbook,* you should also count on costs for subscribing to professional journals—unless you live near an excellent library—as well as travel to conferences, trade shows, and seminars in order to keep up with the changes in this evolving profession.

If you do not have the financial resources to cover your initial costs, you can apply for a loan at a local bank. Keep in mind, however, that a loan officer will carefully examine your previous credit history and will expect a detailed market plan in order to determine the profit potential of the business. Because the start-up costs for an information broker tend to be low, an alternative to securing a bank loan is to charge your equipment purchases with a credit card, despite the high interest rate. The ease of obtaining quick credit without hassles can at times offset the burden of high interest. Another reliable source of outside financing is the **Small Business Administration (1-800-U ASK SBA),** a federal agency with branch offices in many major cities. Check the government section of your local Yellow Pages to determine if there is an office in your area.

The growing number of people entering the information retrieval field is an indication of how lucrative the business can be. In fact, the most frequently cited average annual income, after two or three years of breaking even, is between $50,000 and $60,000. Average fees for research time charged by information brokers run from $40 to $75, which does not include applicable online database charges. Highly successful information brokers have learned how to keep costs to a minimum, while passing on the remainder to the customer.

OPERATIONS

Although there are no special licenses required of information brokers—check with the municipal offices in your city to acquire a regular business license—they must be aware of copyright laws that will likely affect them. Making sure to pay all applicable fees when copying and selling information that may be protected by a copyright is extremely important.

MAJOR ONLINE DATABASE SERVICES AND DIRECTORIES

Online Database Services:

BRS Information Technologies: 8000 Westpark Drive, McLean, VA 22102; phone: (703) 442-0900.

CompuServe: 5000 Arlington Centre Blvd., P.O. Box 20212, Columbus, OH 43260; phone: (800) 848-8199.

DIALOG Information Services, Inc.: 3460 Hillview Avenue, Palo Alto, CA 94304; phone: (800) 334-2564.

Dow/Jones News Retrieval Service: P.O. Box 300, Princeton, NJ 08543-0300; phone: (609) 520-4000.

NewsNet: 945 Haverford Road, Bryn Mawr, PA 19010; phone: (215) 527-8030.

ORBIT Search Service: 8000 Westpark Drive, McLean, VA 22102; phone: (703) 442-0900.

VU/TEXT Information Services, Inc.: 325 Chestnut Street, Suite 1300, Philadelphia, PA 19106; phone: (215) 574-4400.

Print Directories:

CD-ROM Databases: Worldwide Videotex; phone: (617) 449-1603.
DataBase Directory: Knowledge Industry Publications, Inc. (KIPI); phone: (914) 328-9157.
Directory of Online Databases (semi-annual): Gale Research, Inc.; phone: (800) 347-GALE. *Quick Check of Online Business Databases* (annual): Gale Research, Inc.; phone: (800) 347-GALE.

However, at times you might be able to avoid paying the fees directly by contracting with a document delivery service that incorporates such costs into their fees.

Making arrangements for receiving payment can be difficult, especially for new information brokers or those dealing with clients who are invariably in a hurry for certain data and don't want to be bothered with binding legal contracts. Problems may be avoided by asking customers to sign summary agreement letters before you take their business. Such a letter should outline the specific assignment and the amount and terms of payment (you may want to consult a lawyer for help in drawing up the document). Potential clients who refuse to sign the agreement letter should probably be turned away. You may want to dispense with the letter for repeat customers familiar with your business practices.

Information brokers can become important sources of support to one another. Rather than turn away a potential customer, brokers will often contract out the business that requires expertise they don't possess or for which they don't have time. The cost of the subcontracted work is then included in the fee quoted to the customer. The resulting profit margin may be small, but the client, who may become a repeat customer, is retained.

MARKETING AND ADVERTISING

Perhaps the most difficult aspect of the business is finding clients, a process that often necessitates 60-hour weeks in the first year. Therefore, devising a workable marketing strategy is essential. You must first decide whether or not you want to specialize in a specific type of information and target a particular niche market, for example the legal or medical professions. You will also need to determine the range of services you will offer. Information brokers can provide graphs, charts, analytical reports, and delivery of documents via the fax machine or just limit themselves strictly to a particular aspect of information retrieval.

Once you have defined the parameters of your business, a direct mail piece or brochure can be designed. Be sure to highlight your various services and emphasize the convenience you offer. The target market you've chosen will determine to whom the brochure should be sent. The local chamber of commerce can probably provide you with a list of those types of businesses in the area. You may want to consider putting an ad in the business sections of the newspapers delivered in your community. Networking among friends at online conferences and seminars is also a good strategy. In addition, don't neglect to place an ad in your local Yellow Pages.

PRIMARY ASSOCIATIONS AND SELECTED TRADE PUBLICATIONS

Associations:

Association of Independent Information Professionals (AIIP): P.O. Box 71053, Shorewood, WI 53211; phone: (713) 537-9051.

American Society for Information Science (ASIS): 8720 Georgia Ave., Suite 501, Silver Spring, MD 20910-3601; phone: (301) 495-0900.

Information Industry Association (IIA): 555 New Jersey Ave. NW, Suite 800, Washington, DC 20001; phone: (202) 639-8262.

Publications:

Information Sources: The Companies, Products, and People of the Information Industry (annual): Information Industry Association (see address above).
Information Times (bimonthly): Information Industry Association (see address above).
Information and Marketing Handbook: National Federation of Abstracting and Information Services (NFAIS), 1429 Walnut St., 13th fl., Philadelphia, PA 19102; phone: (215) 563-2406.
National Online Circuit Directory (annual): National Online Circuit (NOC), 90 E. Ridge, P.O. Box 368, Ridgefield, CT 06877; phone: (203) 798-5155.

As our society moves into the "Information Age," information brokers will be more and more in demand. In addition, there is excellent profit potential in this nascent industry. Armed with a computer, good research skills, and a clear idea of your target market, the information retrieval field is a natural entrepreneurial move for those who like the idea of working for themselves and setting their own hours.

SOURCES:

Basch, Reva, "Information Brokers as Consultants: Semantics and the Bottom Line," *Information Today,* January 1992, pp. 9-11.

Emshwiller, John R., "Firms Find Profits Searching Databases," *The Wall Street Journal,* January 25, 1993, p. B1

Greco, Susan, "The Scoop on 'Info Brokers,'" *Inc.,* December 1992, p. 27.

"Information Brokering," *Entrepreneur Magazine's 111 Businesses You Can Start for Under $10,000,* Bantam Books, 1991, pp. 181-184.

Leak, Andrea, "Information Brokering Creates High-Tech Cottage Industry," *Springfield Business Journal,* August 3, 1992, p. 1.

Locke, Tom, "Minutia Is Bread and Butter of Access Information," *The Denver Business Journal,* March 6, 1992, p. 1.

Madden, Michael, editor, *Small Business Start-Up Index,* issue 1, Detroit: Gale Research, 1991.

Marsh, D., "Information Broker: Mary Madden Knew Something About Computers. Burton Goldstein Knew Something About Lawyers' Need for Access to Courthouse Records. The Result is Information America," *Georgia Trend,* December 1992, p. 50.

Nowline, Sanford, "For a Fee, She'll Search for Almost Anything," *San Antonio Business Journal,* October 9, 1992, p. 1.

Romain, Garret, "The World On-Line," *Oregon Business,* February 1993, p. 84.

Rugge, Sue, *The Information Broker's Handbook,* Windcrest/McGraw-Hill, 1992.

Schwartz, Carol A., editor, *Small Business Sourcebook,* sixth edition, volume 1, Gale, 1993, pp. 940-952.

Shepardson, Monty, "In Search of Damn Near Anything: Findologist Eileen Lizer Unearths Oddball Facts and Unusual Things for Clients," *Los Angeles Business Journal,* April 1, 1991, p.1.

—*SINA DUBOVOJ*

Lawn Care Service

A lawn care service is one of the easiest and least expensive businesses to start. All it requires is a lawn mower, a pick-up truck, and some gardening tools. But don't be fooled. Successful lawn care businesses require long hours, hard work, and a dedication to service. As the business grows, it can require special training in horticulture and the application of lawn care chemicals. It can also require considerable managerial ability. According to Rod Bailey, owner of Evergreen Services Corporation in Bellevue, Washington, and former president of the Associated Landscape Contractors of America, the lack of a basic understanding of business principles is what hurts start-up lawn care services the most.

FINANCIAL ASPECTS

Starting a mow-and-rake lawn care service may not require any initial investment for the person who already owns a lawn mower, a rake, and a pick-up truck. However, the start-up business should add a blower, an edger, and a weed trimmer to its list of equipment as soon as possible. As the business grows, the equipment should be upgraded to include a commercial-grade reel-type lawn mower. A lawn care business cannot afford to have its equipment out of service, and a commercial-grade mower will be more reliable. A reel-type mower is also easier to keep sharpened and provides a cleaner cut, which is better for the lawn.

Starting from scratch, a mow-and-rake residential lawn care business will probably cost between $5,000 and $10,000, including a good used pick-up truck. A business that targets commercial clients may need to spend more on equipment right away. How much either business earns depends on many variables, including the length of the lawn care season and any additional services offered, such as fertilizing and aerating lawns and pruning trees. However, a typical mow-and-rake lawn care business with a three-person work crew should gross between $60,000 and $80,000 per year.

Basic equipment can be financed if necessary. However, investing your own money in any enterprise avoids complications, including interest charges. If you do need to arrange financing, your first move should be to consult a financial advisor. Some banks and community colleges offer small-business assistance programs. There are also associations of retired business executives who volunteer to assist start-up businesses. These people can help you seek financing and also help create a business plan that will satisfy potential lenders.

Banks are notoriously conservative in their lending practices and require a sound business plan. Banks will also require a thorough background check and collateral, although you may be able to get an unsecured loan if you have an excellent credit rating and are putting up at least part of the capital yourself. Finance companies often will accept greater risk and may extend a loan when a bank will not— but they also charge higher interest rates.

The **Small Business Administration (SBA)** is another source of start-up capital. The SBA is an independent agency of the U.S. government that promotes small businesses through loans, counseling, and other information. The SBA is particularly sensitive to women and minority ownership. However, generally a start-up business must exhaust all sources of private financing before it is eligible for an SBA loan. There are SBA offices in most major cities. Check the U.S. Government section of the telephone directory for locations and telephone numbers. You can also reach the SBA at **1-800-U ASK SBA.**

LOCATION

A small lawn care business can be operated out of your home. However, it is important to have a place to clean, maintain, and store your equipment. You may also need a safe place to store fertilizer and other lawn care chemicals. It is probably better to find a garage in a properly zoned business district that can also double as an office. Negotiate the shortest lease possible since a permanent business address will not be particularly important. This way, if your business outgrows the garage, or if the location proves unsatisfactory for some other reason, you will not be trapped in a long-term commitment. Be sure the garage has plenty of secure storage space, and consult with an attorney before signing any legal agreement.

FRANCHISE OPPORTUNITIES

Barefoot Grass Service: 1018 Proprietors Road, Worthington, OH 43085; phone: (614) 846-1800.

Emerald Green Lawn Care: 5300 Dupont Circle, Milford, OH 45150; phone: (513) 248-0981, or (800) 783-0981.

Lawn Doctor, Inc.: 142 Highway 34, Matawan, NJ 07747.

Liqui-Green Lawn Care Corp.: 9601 N. Allen Road, Peoria, IL 61615; phone: (309) 243-5211, or (800) 255-2255.

NutriLawn International: 2319 McGillivray, Winnipeg, MB, Canada R3Y-1G5; phone: (204) 895-4232, or (800) 663-4772.

ServiceMaster Lawn Care: 855 Ridge Lake Boulevard, Memphis, TN 38119; phone: (901) 684-7500.

Spring-Green Lawn Care Corp.: 11927 Spaulding School Dr., Plainfield, IL 60544; phone: (815) 436-8777, or (800) 435-4051.

Super Lawns, Inc.: P.O. Box 5677, Rockville, MD 20855; phone: (301) 948-8181, or (800) 44-LAWN1.

U.S. Lawns: 9880 Sidney Hayes Road, Orlando, FL 32824; phone: (407) 859-9735.

MARKETING STRATEGIES

In starting a lawn care business you should develop a marketing plan that states clearly the services you plan to offer, the geographical area you plan to serve, and who you see as your customers. Most start-up lawn care companies provide basic mowing and trimming services, although some may also seed and fertilize lawns, or offer landscaping services such as pruning trees and planting decorative shrubs and flowers. However, unless you have considerable experience or training in horticulture, it is probably best to begin with the basics. You should also limit the geographic area you plan to serve since you will not be able to allow for lengthy travel time in the prices you charge—which hurts your competitive edge.

Most start-up lawn care businesses concentrate on the residential market, although it may be possible to land contracts with small apartment or business complexes. However, businesses and apartment owners are very cost-conscious. If the start-up business is not careful, it could wind up losing money by bidding on commercial accounts. Large commercial customers generally deal with more established companies.

Likewise, on the surface, the best prospects in the residential market may appear to be upper-income neighborhoods. However, upper-income families are also more likely to be interested in landscaping services that the start-up business may not be in a position to offer. The best prospects for a start-up business may lie with middle-income neighborhoods, where the homeowners are interested primarily in a no-hassle, well-tended lawn. Neighborhoods with elderly residents are also fertile ground for small lawn care business. The local chamber of commerce should be able to provide neighborhood demographic information, including the percentage of home ownership and average annual income.

Once you have determined your market focus, you can begin thinking about how to contact your prospective customers. Rod Bailey, of Evergreen Services, emphasizes that marketing is a process that never stops. It includes how the crew looks and acts on the job, the condition of the equipment, and the quality of the work, as well as advertising. Most of your business will come from the recommendations of satisfied customers.

ADVERTISING

When most people think of advertising they think of newspaper ads or radio and television commercials, which may be very effective for liquid lawn care treatment companies that rely on a broad customer base. But, with the exception of classified ads in the newspaper, they are usually too expensive and not worthwhile for a mow-and-trim lawn care service. However, there are several very effective, low-cost ways to advertise.

The most effective advertising for a start-up lawn care business may be flyers that list the services the company offers along with a telephone number. Flyers can be distributed door-to-door or posted on bulletin boards in grocery stores and community buildings. Direct-mail advertising that can target neighborhoods may also be effective, especially if you focus on seasonal services such as seeding, aerating, and thatching. As the business grows, you may want to consider producing a color brochure that can be mailed to prospective customers. Depending on your expertise, one source of free advertising might be to write a lawn care column for a community newspaper. Most newspapers publish special lawn care advertising sections in the spring and again in the fall. You could also offer to talk to garden clubs or other groups about lawn care.

When thinking about ways to advertising your business, don't overlook your personal contacts. Let friends, neighbors, and family members know about your business. If they don't hire you, they may recommend you to someone who will. If you belong to a church or service organization, ask them to put a notice in the church bulletin or newsletter. Bailey also suggests canvassing a neighborhood, knocking on doors, handing out business cards, and talking about how professional lawn care can improve the homeowner's lawn. This can be especially effective if you are knowledgeable about horticulture and can discuss specific lawn care problems, such as weed and pest control. You should also have your company name and telephone number painted on the side of your pickup truck. If you use a family car, have a

PRIMARY ASSOCIATIONS AND SELECTED TRADE PUBLICATIONS

Associations:

Associated Landscape Contractors of America (ALCA): 12200 Sunrise Valley Drive, Suite 150, Reston, VA 22091; phone: (703) 620-6363.

Professional Lawn Care Association of America (PLCAA): 1000 Johnson Ferry Road NE, Suite C-135, Mariette, GA 30068; phone: (404) 977-5222, or (800) 458-3466.

Publications:

Lawn and Landscape Maintenance: GIE Publishing Co., 4012 Bridge Ave., Cleveland, OH 44113; phone: (216) 961-4130.
Lawn Care Industry: Advanstar Data, 7500 Old Oak Boulevard, Cleveland, OH 44130; phone: (216) 826-2839, or (800) 225-4569.
Pro Magazine: Johnson Hill Press, Inc., 1233 Janesville Ave., Fort Atkinson, WI 53538; phone: (414) 563-6388.

magnetic sign made that can be put on the door when you are making business calls.

Ultimately, the best advertising will be word of mouth, as satisfied customers begin to tell their friends and neighbors about your good service. You can help this process along by asking customers for their permission to use them as a reference. You should make a point of contacting their neighbors personally. Not only will you be able to use the customer's lawn as a selling tool, the more customers you get in the same neighborhood, the more efficient your business will become.

INDUSTRY STATISTICS

- *Size of U.S. Lawn Care Industry:* $2.4 billion.
- *Number of Lawn Care Companies in the U.S.:* 7,000.
- *Average Number of Years in Business:* 10.
- *Average Number of Employees:* 7.6.
- *Average Number of Employees Certified to Use Pesticides:* 2.4.
- *Average Labor Costs:* 33% of revenues.
- *Average Equipment Costs:* 12.5% of revenues.
- *Average Amount Spent on Marketing:* 4% of revenues.
- *Percent of Lawn Care Businesses Offering Chemical Application Services:* 35.6%.
- *Percent of Lawn Care Businesses Offering Mowing and Trimming Services:* 27%.
- *Percent of Lawn Care Industry Revenues from Residential Customers:* 71%.
- *Percent of Lawn Care Revenues from Commercial Customers:* 26.5%.

(SOURCE: PROFESSIONAL LAWN CARE ASSOCIATION SURVEY, 1993.)

PRICING AND HIRING

Pricing your services will be critical to your success. Most customers will prefer to pay an agreed-upon price quoted in advance. Therefore, you must be able to estimate accurately the time and expense involved in each job and base your quote on an appropriate hourly rate. The amount you charge will need to cover all of your expenses, including travel and depreciation, plus the wages of anyone working for you. To be profitable, a one-person lawn care business will need to charge between $20 and $30 an hour. Remember to include the time it took to land the job in your calculations. You should allow for some profit beyond your own salary that can be re-invested in the business.

A survey by the Professional Lawn Care Association showed that the average lawn care company spent about 78 percent of revenues to cover expenses, including about 33 percent for labor, 12 percent for equipment, 12 percent for fertilizer and pesticides, 9 percent for fuel, and 7 percent for insurance. About 4 percent went for advertising.

Because labor costs are your biggest expense, you'll want to be careful not to neglect this important area. You will probably be able to hire people to work in your lawn care business for little more than minimum wage. However, be sure to pay enough that you attract hard workers who do a good job and will not quit unexpectedly, leaving the job undone. Your customers are paying for good service, and like most service businesses your greatest success will come from repeat business. Rod Bailey warns, "Some people try to figure out how little they can do for what they charge. Successful businesses figure out how much they can do for what they charge."

FRANCHISE OPPORTUNITIES

Most lawn care franchises are involved in treating lawns with chemical fertilizers and weed killers, rather than providing traditional mowing or landscaping services. Franchise fees are often based on the size of the market, and may run from $5,000 to as much as $200,000. Franchisers generally provide training, advertising and promotional materials, and specific lawn-treatment programs. They may also lease equipment. The spring months are generally the busiest for the franchise owner.

In recent years, the application of fertilizers, weed-killers, and pesticides was the fastest-growing segment of the lawn care industry, and almost all franchises focused on this market. However, the application of lawn-care chemicals has become the most regulated segment of the industry. The Environmental Protection Agency and individual states are becoming even more strict regarding the application of long-lasting and liquid lawn care chemicals. In most states, persons who applied lawn care chemicals were required to obtain special licensing.

Because residential lawn care businesses are so easy to start, it is a very competitive field. This is especially true in a tight job market. Many people start part-time lawn care services to supplement their income or turn to full-time lawn care when they lose their jobs. These start-up businesses are often temporary until other employment is found. Since the business is only temporary, the owners often invest very little in training or equipment. ''The mower is in the shop'' is little comfort to a customer whose lawn looks ready for harvesting. Some lawn care businesses are even known to fold-up and leave work undone if other opportunities arise.

The reputation of the residential lawn care industry has also suffered from unscrupulous contractors who underbid other services and then do shoddy work before disappearing. These business are often referred to as ''mow, blow, and go'' in the industry. Any new contractor without a history of good service will have to dispel the poor image created by these fly-by-night operators. However, Bailey points out that

customers will be very loyal to businesses that provide reliable service. Bailey's advice for someone thinking about starting a lawn care service is, ''Be serious, be a business person, learn the trade, be good.''

SOURCES:

Price, Laurence W., *Starting and Operating a Landscape Maintenance Business,* Botany Books.

Additional information for this profile was obtained from a 1993 interview with Rod Bailey of Evergreen Services Corporation, Bellevue, Washington.

—*Dean Boyer*

Limousine Service

Imagine yourself in a private world surrounded by tinted glass on the sides, plush carpeting at your feet, and moon roof up above. Included in this scene are a wet bar, color television set, and sophisticated stereo system. You're rolling down the road in a stretch limousine that is taking you to the destination of your choice. A limousine can provide just this type of custom-designed private world for its passengers. Likewise, starting a limousine service can bring operators a wealth of advantages, including the potential to create a business part-time from home, expand as profits and time allow, and build a full-time career—all while mingling with interesting and influential people.

The limousine service industry has grown substantially since the late 1970s and really began to take off in the 1980s. Between 1982 and 1987, the number of limousines in the United States more than doubled, stretching to 40,000. Industry profits slumped with the economy during the late 1980s, but began taking a turn for the better in the early 1990s. And while the boom years have passed, those livery service operators who have placed themselves in a good market and learned to shift gears with passenger tastes and economic trends have found continued, tremendous profit potential in the limousine business.

COSTS AND PROFITS

You can start a limousine service on a shoestring—renting a limousine on an as-needed or monthly basis—and make annual part-time profits of a few thousand dollars. To open a full-time owner/operator business you will need at least $15,000 to $30,000 (depending on your choice of limousine and amenities), which would cover the down-payment for one new vehicle, insurance and license fees, and initial advertising. Those start-up necessities—along with regular maintenance and servicing of your limousine and any working capital loans—would also represent your primary liabilities. The average start-up investment for a limousine service hovers around $90,000, which generally covers a down payment on a fleet of two or three vehicles that can bring in pre-tax profits in the neighborhood of $60,000, and sometimes as much as $165,000.

FINANCING

Before looking for capital to start a limousine service, it is wise to determine how much money you will need. Costs of vehicles can vary dramatically, from under $20,000 for a used limousine to about $40,000 to $50,000 for the average stretch limousine with limited amenities. Sticker prices will depend in part on whether you are buying a "stretch limousine" (a vehicle that's been cut in half and extended 48 to 120 inches, and often includes entertainment amenities), a "formal limousine" (generally without entertainment amenities), a "sedan" (often called a "town car" and frequently used for corporate clients and airport runs), or a van or bus (which some fleets use to make shuttle trips between designated areas).

Before purchasing a limousine you should consider the typical "stretch," which customers might expect. The normal limousine of the 1990s is stretched 64 inches, while trends towards longer vehicles have pushed some "super stretches" out 85 to 120 inches. Typically stretch limousines have a bar, ice chest, television, rear facing seats, magazine rack, overhead controls for stereo and heating systems, indirect lighting, plush carpeting, and at least one (if not two) dividers between the driver's seat and passenger area. Of course all of this comes with a cost. When seeking information on what types of vehicles are available, where, and at what price, industry trade journals and limousine operators can be invaluable sources.

Banks will generally finance the purchase of a limousine if you can post 20 percent of the cost and you have a good credit rating. If you are financing an office as well as a fleet, banks will probably want to know about your previous business experience, personal assets, targeted market, and plans to meet your projected sales goals. Your financial needs will be much less if you run your service from home (which almost half of all limousine operators do). Another way to cut start-up costs is to buy a used limousine (customers can rarely tell the difference between new and used limousines if the latter has been well maintained). Buying a used limousine will allow you to gain business equity, improve your credit, and later trade up for a newer model as profits warrant. Used limousines can typically be found at car auctions and through advertisements in industry journals and metropolitan newspapers.

FRANCHISE OPPORTUNITIES

Air Brook Limousine: P.O. Box 123, Rochelle Park, NJ 07662; phone: (201) 368-3974. Founded 1961; began franchising 1976. Over 125 outlets; located primarily in New Jersey with plans for national expansion. Service utilizes sedans, vans, or buses; a centralized reservation center and dispatching department coordinates operations for specific areas consisting of several franchisee drivers; exclusive relationships with major airlines provide large base of corporate clients. Provided by franchisor: training program on company policy, map reading, and airports. Typical franchise is one person and one vehicle; a multiple franchise consists of several drivers working for one franchisee. Franchise fees start at $7,500; qualified applicants can borrow up to $5,000 from the company.

Leros Point to Point: 861 Franklin Ave., Thornwood, NY 10594; phone: 1-800 888-6332. Founded 1984; began franchising 1989. Primarily located in Northeastern United States; plans to establish over 200 franchises in North America, Europe, and Asia. Franchise options include establishment of new franchise outlet or the conversion of an existing limousine company. Provided by franchisor: training program, share/referral network, savings through collective purchases, expansion financing assistance. Franchise fees start at $20,000; also offers non-franchise management contracts that include computerization of business, financial management consultation, and sales and marketing assistance.

Many beginning operators lease or rent a limousine, particularly if they are planning to initially run a part-time or weekend operation. If you plan to start a full-time operation, the **Small Business Administration (SBA)** may serve as a source of start-up capital, but in order to qualify for a loan you must be starting an independently owned and operated business and be unable to secure financing on reasonable terms elsewhere. To inquire about eligibility requirements or request other valuable business information, call the SBA at **1-800-U ASK SBA,** or write **Small Business Directory, P.O. Box 1000, Ft. Worth, TX 76119.** Local SBA offices are also listed in the "U.S. Government" section of your telephone directory.

LOCATION

The ideal location for a limousine service would be in the wealthiest and most prestigious part of a metropolitan area, which could guarantee a maximum supply of passengers and an office address and phone number prefix that connotes high class. A service headquarters centrally located amid corporate offices, an airport or commuter rail terminal, convention centers, and major hotels/resort locations would guarantee opportunities to keep your fleet busy.

A smaller community can support a limousine service if the area offers an opportunity to book a sufficient mix of corporate clients, hotel/resort customers, special events (such as weddings), and entertainment excursions. A small

owner/operator service can start from a home-based headquarters (there is no need for customers to come to your office), although before doing so you should check with your local zoning officer about ordinances that may prohibit business operations or parking.

SUPPLIES AND SETUP

A minimum amount of supplies are needed to set up a limousine service headquarters. If you are working out of your home, you should have a business phone line installed and purchase a post office box, or hire a combination answering/mail box service. At the very least your headquarters will need standard business furniture, including a desk and file cabinets. A computer could help facilitate your filing and billing systems, while custom-designed limousine service software could help in mapping out routes and aiding in other industry specific tasks a computer could handle. The best source of information on appropriate hardware and software is other limousine operators and industry trade journals.

Besides a room for an office, you will need a place to service and park your fleet. If you don't have a garage and can't afford to rent one, you should at least invest in a canvas vehicle cover, locks for custom wheels, and a vehicle alarm system. An owner/operator should have an inventory of cleaning materials, auto maintenance items, auto detailing supplies, and passenger supplies. If you have at least two limousines, you will probably need to rent a garage, acquire a sturdy security system, and keep additional auto supplies on hand.

Limousine service clients expect a luxurious-looking, clean smelling, well-tuned vehicle, so your fleet will need to be kept in pristine condition both inside and out, as well as under the hood. Limousines should be wiped down every day, while waxing and detail work should be done every few weeks. Inside limousines fixtures need to be polished and carpets cleaned. Vehicles should also be aired out after each trip. In addition, a limousine's engine needs to be tuned regularly—almost as if it were an airplane engine. A small fleet owner/operator can learn to do these tasks, or, if you can afford it, you can contract with a local mechanic or auto service that can provide servicing, maintenance, and detailing work, as well as 24-hour road-side emergency service.

You will also need to purchase passenger supplies. In compiling these supplies, keep in mind that a limousine service caters to peoples' desire to be pampered. Consider anything a passenger might ask for or have forgotten, such as cigarette lighter, cork screw, glasses, napkins, drinks and mixers, tissues, toothbrush and toothpaste, nail clippers, hair brush, aspirin, etc. You will also need to purchase on-the-road supplies for vehicles, including compressed air and sealant to repair flat tires, safety flares and flashers, a fire extinguisher, spray detergent, cleaning towels, and carpet cleaner, as well as extra fan belts, vehicle lights, fuses, radiator coolant, and motor oil.

Your chauffeurs should be attired so as not to clash with their passengers, so you will need to purchase or rent a variety of uniforms. For business trips a chauffeur should wear a three-piece suit; for weddings and special occasions a tuxedo or a formal black suit is appropriate; and for casual clients a chauffeur should wear a blazer or sport coat. (Chauffeurs should always be equipped with two pairs of driving gloves and a good pair of sunglasses.) Female chauffeurs are generally expected to wear the same type of clothes as men, although a dark skirt is an acceptable alternative to pants. For a start-up on a limited budget you may want to require that chauffeurs buy their owns suits. Most of the uniforms you will need can be found at a tuxedo rental shop where you can inquire about rental and purchase options.

STAFFING

Adequate staffing for a limousine service will depend upon your fleet size and whether you begin a part-time or around-the-clock service. It is feasible to start with a staff that only includes you as an owner/operator, although ideally you would have at least one or two relief or on-call chauffeurs. With proper marketing a one-car fleet can be kept busy, in which case you may want to hire a full-time driver and a

INDUSTRY STATISTICS

- *Percentage of Limousine Service Operators That Work out of Their Home: 47%.*
- *Percentage of Limousine Operators Who Saw an Increase in Business (1991-92):* 67%, all operators; 57%, home-based operators; 76%, office-based operators.
- *Estimated Total Monthly Revenue:* $10,287, home-based operator; $64,645, office-based operator.
- *Size and Composition of Average Limousine Service Fleet:* 9.89 vehicles, including 4.25 limousines, 0.42 formals, 3.73 sedans, and 1.49 vans or buses.
- *Size and Composition of Average Home-Based Operator Fleet:* 3.82 vehicles, including 2.13 limousines, 0.25 formals, 1.113 sedans, and 0.31 vans or buses.
- *Average Hourly Service Rates:* $50, stretch limousines; $43, formal limousines; $37, sedans; $52, vans or buses.
- *Average Monthly Payments Per Vehicle:* home-based operators: $478 for limousine, $458 for sedan; office-based operators: $680 for limousine, $504 for sedan.
- *Average Fleet Age:* 30%, 0-2 years old; 50%, 2-5 years old; 30%, more than five years old.
- *Breakdown of Limousine Service Business by Types of Work:* 32%, corporate; 23%, weddings; 20%, night on the town; 9%, hotel/resort; 4%, funeral; 12%, other.
- *Average Limousine Service Trip:* 72.7 miles.
- *Average Number of Chauffeurs Used by Livery Services:* home-based operators, 1.1 full time and 3.3 part-time; office-based operators, 5.9 full time and 6.6 part-time.
- *Average Chauffeur Pay Rate:* $7.63, all services; $7.24, home-based operators; $7.94, office-based operators.
- *Average Chauffeur Tip:* 18%.

(SOURCE: 1993 SURVEY OF LIMOUSINE & CHAUFFEUR READERS)

secretary/receptionist so you can devote your time to securing new clients.

Smaller and home-based limousines services tend to hire drivers as independent contractors who are paid a per-job or per-hour commission, while larger services generally hire chauffeurs as employees who are paid an hourly wage of roughly $7 to $8 (with most of a driver's income generated by tips). Either way, most chauffeurs are generally paid only when working, and a large part of their earnings will come from tips. As independent contractors, drivers will be responsible for taking care of their own taxes and insurance, although you may have to file income informational returns with the Internal Revenue Service (IRS). Legally, a driver cannot be considered an independent contractor if s/he works for only one service without offering services elsewhere. If a driver is hired as an employee you will have to report tips earned and withhold social security and income due on tips from the employee's wages. But you are only required to match the Social Security tax deducted from wages, not from tips. For more information on tax matters, contact your local Internal Revenue Service office.

When hiring chauffeurs look for people with good driving records and a chauffeur's license. Because passengers expect quality service with their limousine, the drivers you hire should be patient, well-groomed, and have a knowledge of etiquette. Equally important, your chauffeurs should exude an air of self-confidence that puts passengers at ease. It is also a good idea to require that your chauffeurs know first aid. If your service is to do more than operate part-time you will probably want to hire a secretary/receptionist, who should be well-organized and have a good phone voice (which will be representing your service). You might want to explore the use of temporary agencies, which generally keep a list of both secretaries and chauffeurs. These agencies will cost you a few more dollars an hour in per-employee wages, but it will allow you to devote more time to marketing. And, you can also hire a well-received temporary worker away from an agency.

In setting wage scales, you should pay your employees at least the industry standard in order to keep morale high. Remember that aside from your marketing skills, the booking of clients hinges to a degree on your secretary's response when answering calls, while the potential for repeat and referral business depends in large part on the impression your driver conveys to passengers.

MARKETING

Depending upon your area and the services you offer, your business may be comprised almost entirely of corporate accounts, or be a mix of corporate accounts, airport runs, and special events (such as weddings, which make up nearly a quarter of all livery service business). When establishing your marketing strategy and passenger rates you should consider your competition and your area's population, as

PRIMARY ASSOCIATIONS AND SELECTED TRADE PUBLICATIONS

Associations:

National Limousine Association (NLA): 1300 L St., NW, Suite 1050, Washington, DC 20005; phone: 1-800 NLA-7007. Membership includes limousine service owners and operators as well as limousine manufacturers and suppliers to the industry. The NLA seeks to promote and advance industry professional and the common interest of its members, including the increased use of limousines in both business and public sectors. The NLA also monitors legislation, organizes lobbying efforts, and sponsors seminars on safety/regulatory issues and management techniques.

Publications:

Limousine & Chauffeur: Bobit Publishing Company, 2512 Artesia Blvd., Redondo Beach, CA 90278; phone: (310) 376-8788.
Limo Scene: National Limousine Association, 1300 L St., NW, Suite 1050, Washington, DC 20005; phone: (202) 682-1426.
The Limousine Journal: Virgo Publishing, Inc., P.O. Box 5400, Scottsdale, AZ 85261-5400; phone: (602) 483-0014.
National Limousine Exchange: Turnkey Publishing, 4807 Spicewood Springs Rd., Suite 3150, Austin, TX 78759; phone: (512) 345-5316.
NSLA Limo Line: Nassau Suffolk Limousine Association (NSLA), 44 Royal Ct., Rockville Centre, NY 11570; phone: (516) 763-NSLA.

well as your ability to deliver chosen services to the customer base you wish to target.

You can operate a limousine strictly on weekends, catering to proms, parties, weddings, and entertainment excursions and gross $2,000 to $4,000 a month. Some weekend services have had success carving out a niche market, specializing in such things as weddings and funerals, dinner and theater trips, sightseeing and shopping trips, and Bar Mitzvahs and other special events. Other creative operators have made money inventing markets by offering services such as romantic "luxury picnics," or trips home for new mothers who are picked up at a hospital with husband and a large stuffed animal in-tow.

To establish yourself full-time in the limousine business you will probably need to secure corporate accounts (which represent nearly a third of all livery service business). Executives use limousines as moving offices and often the size and makeup of your fleet can determine whether you will land corporate clients, who tend to request sedans and may insist upon new cars with special amenities. As a new owner/operator, ultimately you will risk losing business and referrals if you don't have a second (or third) vehicle and don't diversify your fleet.

Referrals represent a major source of a livery service's customers and some services offer customers referral discounts, whereby customers receive a discount on billing when the name of a potential customer they give you uses your service. You should also be aware that within the limousine industry referral networking is a two-way street among livery operations, and a considerable amount of referral business can come from other services. A number of livery operations do a good business by cashing in on clients that other services can't accommodate. If you're booked or a regular customer is going out of your service area, you can often collect a finder's fee from the service you refer the customer to, or just expect reciprocation down the road. You can also join a formal referral network by becoming a member of the National Limousine Association.

Many limousine services network with other types of businesses, finding that a limousine can be kept busy by providing hourly shuttle services to and from restaurants, beauty salons, and grocery stores. This type of service requires that you be "on call" and works well if trips are made from a well-defined area. Some services participate in "package deals" with restaurants and caterers, taking a piece of the profits on a combination limousine trip/dinner outing. Regardless of the type of services you are offering, it is a good idea to join your local chamber of commerce where you can make contacts with travel agents, chamber officials, and other business owners who could later refer a potential customer to your service.

Other contacts that can provide you with referral business include country clubs, hotels, motels, resorts, and casinos. Many livery services make special arrangements with these types of establishments and offer their customers guest rates. The only drawback to this arrangement is that participating establishments often get a 15 to 20 percent commission on business they book.

In pricing your services, you will need to charge at least twice the amount of each excursion in order to make a profit. The average hourly charge for limousine service is $50 (the charge is slightly more for vans and buses, slightly less for formals, and about $35 for sedans). Most services have a minimum charge equivalent to three hours and discount $5 to $10 an hour for waiting time (as opposed to driving time). You can also charge extra for special amenities requested by clients and services such as the use of a car phone, marking up the per-minute cost of phone service by as much as 25 percent.

When a customer calls to make a reservation you will need to fill out a trip sheet, which should include such vital information as date of order, customer's name, address, business and home phone number, type of limousine requested, pick-up time and location, number of passengers, projected driving and waiting time, drop-off location, and special amenities requested. When booking a trip you may want to mention that a 15 percent tip is expected. You should generally require a deposit to reserve your time, with any remaining balance due at the end of the trip. When establishing rates and payment requirements you will need to be somewhat flexible with corporate clients, who you will probably bill monthly.

ADVERTISING

The two best means of advertising a limousine service are referrals and the Yellow Pages. Provided you have done your market research, a Yellow Page ad should pay for itself by about the second month. You should stage an initial advertising campaign, with area newspapers and radio stations tending to produce the best results. And don't overlook the opportunity to get free publicity; many newspapers carry announcements and articles about new businesses.

It is wise to advertise based on your targeted market. If you're seeking corporate clients, direct mail and personal calls work well; if targeting a weekend market you should make contacts with wedding services and party caterers; and if you are marketing services to a suburban, professional crowd, advertisements on a popular, local radio station would be appropriate. More than likely you will need to be a jack-of-all-markets, at least initially, but it's still advisable to know your market and advertise accordingly.

LICENSES AND INSURANCE

In order to start a limousine service business you will need to obtain a local business license and the necessary city and state permits required in your area. Check with your city and county clerks to determine specifics. In addition, as an owner/operator you will need to take a state test to receive a chauffeur's license. You will also need license plates for your fleet, which are usually less expensive than plates for a personal car.

If your vehicles cross county lines or carry clients more than 100 miles from home, generally you will be required to purchase a state permit from a PUC (Public Service Commission, which in some states goes by a slightly different name); and, if your fleet crosses state lines, you will also need a one-time permit from the Interstate Commerce Commission. You can usually find the location of relevant agencies in your phone directory's "Government" section. Trade associations and local limousine service operators should be able to help see you through governmental red tape.

You will definitely want to purchase a comprehensive auto insurance policy, including a substantial amount of liability insurance (the per-vehicle industry average for an annual premium ranges between $2,000 and $3,000, while services generally carry between $900,000 and $1.3 million in liability coverage). Some states regulate coverage minimums for livery services; check with the your local secretary of state's office or an insurance agent well-versed in the transportation industry.

In the final analysis, the heydays of the livery industry are gone; but nonetheless with proper marketing, adequate financing, and the ability to offer a quality service, almost anyone can st̃ and operate a limousine service—be it part-time or full time. A well-run limousine service can break even within three months to a year, expand as the bottom line improves, and ultimately generate some luxurious profits.

SOURCES:

Cummings, Mike, "How to Start a Limousine Service," *Income Opportunities,* February 1990, p. 74.

Englander, Donna, "Operations Across the Country Report Business on the Upswing," *Limousine & Chauffeur,* May/June 1993, pp. 24-29.

Flint, Jerry, "Where Did All the Hot Tubs Go?," *Forbes,* October 21, 1991, pp. 328-330.

Horowitz, David, and Dana Shilling, "Limousine Services," *The Business of Business: How 100 Businesses Really Work,* HarperCollins, 1989, pp. 262-264.

How to Start and Operate Your Own Limousine Service, Income Opportunities Booklets, Davis Publications, 1990.

Kahn, Sharon, and The Phillip Lief Group, "Limousine Service," *101 Best Businesses to Start,* revised edition, Doubleday, 1992, pp. 492-496.

Kingsbury, Karen, "Start a Limousine Service, " *Income Opportunities,* February 1991, p. 74.

Limousine Service, National Business Library, 1991.

Madden, Michael, editor, *Small Business Start-Up Index,* issue 3, Gale, 1992.

Martin, Susan Boyles, editor, *Worldwide Franchise Directory,* Gale, 1991.

"Retro Limo," *Entrepreneur Magazine's 168 More Businesses Anyone Can Start and Make a Lot of Money,* second edition, the Editors of Entrepreneur, Bantam, 1991, p. 198.

Schwartz, Carol A., editor, *Small Business Sourcebook,* sixth edition, volume 1, Gale, 1993.

—*ROGER W. ROULAND*

Mail Order Business

Mail order is not a specific type of business but a certain way of doing business. Unlike retail selling, in which there is contact between a merchant and a purchaser, mail order is conducted at a distance. Orders are received through the mail, by telephone, and more recently, by fax transmission or via computer modem. Although some people claim mail order is an easy way to get rich, the assertion is not entirely accurate. Mail order is neither easy nor a magic formula to wealth. The business requires thoughtful planning and careful management. Nevertheless, if you are willing to invest the time and capital necessary to learn, practice, and persist, you can reap reasonable, even substantial, rewards.

COSTS AND PROFITS

Mail order is an attractive business to many new entrepreneurs because it can have a low cost of entry. Depending on your product and chosen distribution system, you can get started for as little as a few hundred dollars. With this type of investment you can purchase an advertisement, rent a post office box, and make arrangements for a manufacturer to "drop ship" a product for you. In drop shipping, you do not take possession of the merchandise. Instead it is shipped by the supplier on your behalf to your customers.

While establishing a mail order business in which you handle your own product or products and manage a mailing list with a computer requires a much larger investment, it does hold the potential for greater profit. The *Entrepreneur Business Group* estimated that you can expect to make a minimum start-up investment of about $13,000, with average costs approximating $22,500. Average net profits before taxes were estimated at $33,000, with high end profits in the range of $48,000.

The relatively low cost of start-up makes mail order an ideal choice for home based entrepreneurs. Before quitting a full-time job to devote yourself to your new business, some industry advisors even recommend starting at home on a part-time basis because it will enable you to learn and gain experience while you still have other income. A slow-growth strategy can help you avoid costly mistakes. Finding one successful product on which to focus initially is also suggested. Then, when you find a product that works, look for another product to sell to your current customers. Ideally, it should be one you can handle with existing warehouse space, one that uses the same shipping arrangements, and if possible, one that takes advantage of your off-peak market times. Once you have a successful second product, look for a third. Gradually you will develop a product line capable of filling a brochure.

Starting a new catalog from scratch is a risky and costly venture. One estimate in 1992 put the minimum amount required at $500,000. Add products to your line slowly and "grow" a catalog. Such a practice helps to minimize risk. In order to achieve a national presence, industry analysts suggested, it would cost $3 million and take three years.

FINANCING

For these reasons, financing a new mail order venture can be a challenging undertaking. Depending on your circumstances, you may qualify for governmental assistance programs. Check with the **Small Business Administration (SBA)** by calling **1-800-U ASK SBA** or writing: **Small Business Directory, P.O. Box 1000, Ft. Worth, TX 76119** to find out about eligibility. Local community business development projects may also have funds available for loans or grants.

Many new entrepreneurs find that the best source of funds is their own resources. If you do not have the capital you need, the next best source is friends and relatives. When you borrow from people you know, unless you want partners, make sure your agreements clearly specify that you are only borrowing money. If you want to form a partnership, be sure to consult an attorney.

You may be able to borrow money from a bank or credit union if you have personal funds or assets you can use as collateral. Without such collateral personal loans will be difficult to get unless you need only a small amount for a short time and your credit is very good. You may also be able to borrow money against the cash value of a life insurance policy.

Finance companies generally have more liberal lending policies than banks and credit unions but they typically charge higher interest. You may also be able to use your personal credit cards to get funds on a short term basis, but

PRODUCT IDEAS AND SOURCES

Ideas:

Information: Recipes, "how-to" booklets, home study courses, magazine or newsletter subscriptions, books, re-packaged copyright-exempt information available from the government, instructional audio or video cassettes.

Gift, Specialty, and Novelty Items: Toys, games, stuffed animals, tools, small appliances, kitchen aids, personalized products, collector items.

Health and Beauty Aids: Jewelry, sunglasses, diet aids, exercise devices, hair care articles, cosmetics.

Sources:

- Rejuvenate old favorites.
- Search expired patents.
- Ask manufacturers for molds of discontinued products.
- Attend inventor shows and trade shows.
- Read classified ads for going out of business sales.
- Visit manufacturer showrooms in gift buildings.
- Buy closeouts.
- Develop a new twist on a current product.
- Consult *Thomas' Register of Manufacturers.*
- Ask corporations about abandoned R&D projects.
- Consult directories of foreign manufacturers.

high interest rates can add extra expenses to your business. A limited amount of funds may be available from venture capital firms or small business investment corporations. These kinds of organizations, however, will want to control your business. To get in touch with them, look under the "Business Opportunities" section of the classified advertisements in the *Wall Street Journal* or other large, daily newspapers.

If cash flow is a problem, your suppliers may be willing to offer you credit. You can arrange for delayed payment, purchase items on consignment, or on a drop shipment basis. Drop shipping is an attractive alternative for some small mail order companies because it eliminates the need to tie up capital in maintaining an inventory. Despite its advantages, however, this practice leaves you with no control over merchandise availability and customer service. Many drop shipping arrangements also offer lower profit margins than more traditional distribution plans. The practice of drop shipping works best when you are just starting out, when you are testing a new product, or when you sell a wide variety of expensive merchandise.

LOCATION

The main objective when choosing a place for your mail order business is to find a location with the most space for the least amount of money. Because your customers will not be dealing with you in person, such amenities as convenient access or a plush decor would be expensive and unneces-

sary. In many communities you may be able to operate out of your home if you adhere to guidelines regarding inventory storage and package delivery. Your local zoning board can tell you what is permitted in your neighborhood.

If you start your business at home, you will need to decide whether to use your home address or a post office box. Although many mail order entrepreneurs grapple with perceived pros and cons of this question, some industry analysts report that your chances of success are unaffected by the choice. If you want a post office box and your local post office has a waiting list, check with independent companies that rent box space and offer other mailing and packaging services. Many of these organizations also provide access to photocopiers and fax machines.

SETUP

When setting up your office, pay close attention to the mailing area. The ability to efficiently process incoming and outgoing letters and packages will determine how smoothly your business functions. Your sorting requirements will vary depending on the volume of mail you anticipate and the class of mail you intend to use, so be sure to discuss your plans with your local postmaster. Buy a good postage scale and use it. According to a report published by *Small Business Opportunities,* accurate weighing of out-going letters and parcels can save you up to 20 percent in postage expense. One company offering a complete line of mail room equipment is **Pitney Bowes (800-243-7824).**

Another important piece of equipment is your telephone. Unless you plan to receive orders by phone or conduct telemarketing activities, a single line will probably meet your needs. If you'll be using a modem or plan to receive orders by fax, you may want a separate line dedicated solely to those functions. Contact your local telephone company to discuss your immediate needs as well as your long term plans. If you'll be taking orders over the phone, consider obtaining toll-free service. You can get an 800 number from the telephone company, or you can subscribe to an answering service and share a line with other companies. One way to determine whether or not you need toll-free service is to examine the practices of your closest competitors.

STAFFING AND TRAINING EMPLOYEES

As your venture grows, you will likely need assistance with day-to-day operations so that you can devote more of your time to managing the business. If you are working out of your home, your local zoning authorities may restrict the number of employees you can hire. Some jurisdictions prohibit you from having employees other than members of your immediate family in your home.

To help new employees learn the business, or to gain knowledge for yourself, you may want to take advantage of available classes or seminars. The **Direct Marketing Association, 11 W. 42nd Street, New York, NY 10036; phone:**

(212) 768-7277, sponsors seminars on various topics and conducts training programs for industry participants throughout the year. Business schools and community colleges in your area may also offer instruction.

MANAGEMENT ISSUES

One of the most important issues you will need to address is what type of product you will offer. "One-shot" products are those for which you solicit orders and either make or loose money based on the response to that one item. Some industry analysts point out that as many as 90 percent of one-shot items fail, but the few that are successful can generate large profits. Other mail order companies develop products and product lines intended to be sold on a repeat basis to the same customers. Although the initial cost of obtaining customers is higher, the potential for long term profitability is increased.

Once you have selected your product or product line, the next step is to decide what type of guarantee to offer. In general, the stronger the guarantee, the better the response you can expect. Some advertising media may even refuse to accept your ads if your policy is anything other than a money-back guarantee. Although you may experience problems with illegitimate complaints and returns, your overall profitability will improve if you offer a good guarantee.

The ability to accept credit cards can also boost your business. More than half of all orders taken by mail order, telemarketing, and catalog companies are charged to credit cards. Credit card acceptance, however, can be costly. If you do plan to take them, obtaining merchant status will be necessary. This is not an easy task—VISA and MasterCard issuers are often reluctant to grant merchant status to mail

order companies, especially new ones. Some advisors may suggest that you make arrangements with another merchant to process your credit card orders, but this practice, known as "factoring," is against the law in three states and prohibited by both VISA and MasterCard.

According to Larry Schwartz, president of the National Association of Credit Card Merchants, less than one percent of the banks in the United States accept new mail order companies. The association helps its members find banks willing to work with them. Annual membership is $349.95, and members receive a manual titled *The Complete Guide to Getting and Keeping your Visa/MasterCard Merchant Status.*

In addition, Schwartz also offers an alternative for those companies that want to accept telephone orders, but lack the ability to process credit card charges. The service, called Checks by Phone, permits charges to be made against bank accounts in this way: when a merchant receives a phone order, rather than asking for a credit card number, the customer is asked to read the printed numbers on the bottom of his or her check. The merchant contacts Checks by Phone, which provides verification and authorization through the use of proprietary software. Checks by Phone then sends a copyrighted check to the merchant by overnight delivery. The check will clear the customer's account in the usual manner, but with all the speed and convenience associated with a credit card transaction. Setting up an account with Checks by Phone costs $349.95 plus $7.50 to cover the cost of shipping and handling the necessary software package. In addition to setup costs, the service charges a per transaction fee that varies according to the amount of the transaction and the merchant's preferred level of security. To contact either **Checks by Phone** or the **National Association of Credit Card Merchants** call **(407) 737-7500.**

INDUSTRY STATISTICS

- More than 100 million American adults made a mail order purchase in 1992 (Source: *Direct Marketing Association, 1993 Annual Report*).
- In 1980 there were an estimated 1,200 catalogs circulating in the United States; in 1990 there were 12,000 (Source: *Direct Marketing,* July 1992).
- In 1992 direct marketing sales were increasing twice as fast as retail sales (Source: Bernard Klein, *Mail Order Business Directory*).
- The catalog industry generated more than $51.5 billion in sales in 1992; sales via television shopping exceeded $2 billion in 1992; all forms of direct marketing in the United States generated more than $350 billion in total sales in 1993 (Source: *Direct Marketing Association, 1993 Annual Report*).
- In 1992 the most popular price range for mail order items was between $8.00 and $25.00 (Source: Bernard Klein, *Mail Order Business Directory*).
- An estimated five to six million people were employed by the direct marketing industry in 1993, representing more than five percent of all the people employed in the United States (Source: *Direct Marketing Association, 1993 Annual Report*).

MARKETING

As you develop your marketing strategy, keep in mind the reasons people order merchandise by mail. Convenience, availability, and price are the three most frequently cited. Other important reasons include the enjoyment of receiving packages in the mail, privacy, security and parking concerns when shopping at stores, the availability of credit, and liberal return policies that enable customers to try products without risk.

Timing should also be an important consideration for your overall strategy. For consumer goods, most selling is done during the three months prior to Christmas. The second most intense selling season occurs during May and June, which encompasses Mother's Day, graduations, weddings, and Father's Day.

ADVERTISING

The mail order industry survives by advertising. The major forms include classified, display, direct mail, and broadcast. Classified ads are popular with new mail order companies

PRIMARY ASSOCIATIONS AND SELECTED TRADE PUBLICATIONS

Associations:

Direct Marketing Association (DMA): 11 W. 42nd Street, New York, NY 10036-8096; phone: (212) 768-7277; fax: (212) 768-4546.

National Association of Credit Card Merchants: 217 N. Seacrest Blvd, Box 400, Boynton Beach, FL 33425; phone: (407) 737-7500.

Publications:

Catalog Age: Cowles Business Media, 911 Hope Street, Six River Bend Center, Stamford, CT 06907; phone: (203) 358-9900.
DM News: Mill Hollow Corporation, 19 W. 21st Street, New York, NY 10010; phone: (212) 741-2095.
Direct Magazine: Cowles Business Media, Six River Bend Center, Stamford, CT 06907; phone: (203) 358-9900.
Direct Marketing Magazine: Hoke Communications, 224 Seventh Street, Garden City, NY 11530; phone: (516) 746-6700.
Target Marketing Magazine: North American Publishing Co., 401 North Broad Street, Philadelphia, PA 19108; phone: (215) 238-5300.

because they are inexpensive to produce and purchase. In addition, because of their low cost, classified ads generally return more profit per dollar spent than any other type. Industry advisors recommend using classified ads for items costing under $10.00 or for soliciting inquiries.

Although classified ads may generate a high percent of return on your advertising dollar, your potential volume will be limited because of their relatively small audience. To reach larger numbers of potential customers you may want to consider display ads. These are printed in publications on part of a page, a full page, or even multiple pages. In general, you can expect to pay more for advertising in a trade publication than in a consumer magazine, but it is typically easier to reach a more specific target market in a trade journal.

One of the most effective types of advertising is direct mail. Direct mail consists of print advertising material that is mailed directly to potential customers. This kind of advertising usually allows more flexibility in selecting your target audience, identifying a precise time of delivery, controlling the form of content, and judging the appropriate length of your message.

Preparing and mailing a direct mail package is often more costly than other forms of print advertising. The success of your efforts will hinge on the offer you make and the appropriateness of your mailing list. The best list to use is a list of your customers. This is followed by a list of people who made mail order purchases of similar kinds of products or services. Other types of lists that may prove helpful are those that include mail order buyers regardless of particular

purchases made and compiled lists of people with specified demographic characteristics.

In order to secure the necessary list for a direct mail campaign, you may want to contact a list broker who acts as a go-between for companies that want to rent or buy lists from one another. To find a list broker you can consult the *Direct Mail List Rates and Data Directory,* published by **Standard Rate and Data Service (SRDS).** If the directory is not available at your local library you may contact the publisher at **(708) 256-6067.** Another directory of list brokers is the **Direct Marketing Association's** *List, Production & Mailing Services Service Directory.* It is available from the **DMA Publications Department (404-664-7284)** and costs $40 for non-members and $30 for members.

Other types of advertising include radio and television ads, "take one" display coupons, "bounce-back ads" (those mailed inside packages of ordered merchandise), matchbook advertising, and such customized novelty articles as calendars, key rings, and pens. Matchbook advertising is best for items with mass appeal and for situations where slow returns will not be detrimental to your offer. Advertising on novelty items works best when there is some logical connection between the item you are advertising and the vehicle you are using.

You may find it necessary to experiment with the many forms of advertising in order to find the right combination to maximize your profits. To get the most out of your advertising dollar you will need to keep careful records. You should include an identifiable and distinct "key" in all your advertising. A key may consist of a unique suite or department number in an address, a serial number on a reply coupon, or any other device that will enable you to identify the source of each customer. When keys are consistently used and tracked, you will be able to analyze the effect of all your promotional efforts and determine which variations are best.

LICENSES, INSURANCE, AND REGULATORY ISSUES

Before you begin operating your mail order business, you will be required to register your company name with your local county clerk's office. Unless you plan to sell a restricted class of merchandise like pharmaceuticals, you may not need any other special licensing. To be sure, check with your local chamber of commerce, city hall, and county and state licensing boards to find out if your community has any particular requirements.

You will also want to check with an attorney about liability insurance. The type and amount of insurance recommended for your company will vary according to your product line or services. During start-up time you should get acquainted with an accountant who can help you set up a record keeping system and make sure your tax records are done correctly. You will also need to contact your state's sales tax bureau about collecting and remitting local sales or use taxes. If you will be purchasing goods for resale you will want to apply for a tax number that grants you an exemption from paying sales tax to your suppliers on such merchandise.

The practice of demanding that out-of-state mail order companies collect local sales or use taxes has been a source of conflict between industry participants and taxing authorities. A 1992 Supreme Court Decision (Quill Corporation v. North Dakota Department of Revenue) ruled that state governments could not require out-of-state mail order companies to collect and remit state use taxes on sales to customers within the state. The Court's decision, however, did not rule out the possibility of future congressional action to mandate tax collection responsibilities.

Bear in mind that various activities of the mail order industry fall under the regulatory control or supervision of such government agencies as the U.S. Office of Consumer Affairs, the Federal Trade Commission, the Food and Drug Administration, the National Association of Attorneys General, the U.S. Postal Inspection Service, the National Association of Consumer Agency Administrators, and the Council of Better Business Bureaus. The Federal Trade Commission, for example, enforces provisions of the ''30-Day Mail Order Rule.'' This rule provides specific instructions—which must be precisely followed—governing the timely shipment of products and the manner in which you may communicate shipping information to your customers.

COMPUTER SYSTEM AND PROGRAMS

A good computer system and software package can help you in three important areas of your business: management, communication, and production. Managing your database by maintaining your mailing list and keeping up-to-date information about your customers can help you improve your overall profits. The ability to communicate with your customers can be enhanced with word processing programs, mail merge functions, and even by providing ''on-line'' access. Desktop publishing software packages will allow you to put together professional looking direct mail pieces, lay out entire catalogs, and design display advertising. If you decide to purchase a computer, shop for the software first to make sure the system you buy will be able to do the jobs you want done.

The mail order business is a challenging and rewarding industry. With hard work and ingenuity, you can build a respectable business. And occasionally a business begun at a kitchen table does grow into a multi-million dollar enterprise.

SOURCES:

Bond, William J., *Home-Based Mail Order: A Successful Guide for Entrepreneurs,* TAB Books, 1990.

Cohen, William A., *Building a Mail Order Business: A Complete Manual for Success,* second edition, Wiley, 1985.

''The Challenges of '90's Cataloging,'' *Direct Marketing,* July 1992.

Ethical Business Practice, Direct Marketing Association, July 1993.

Direct Marketing Association 1993 Annual Report, Direct Marketing Association.

Hellerstein, Walter, ''Supreme Court Says No State Use Tax Imposed on Mail-Order Sellers . . . for Now,'' *The Journal of Taxation,* August 1992.

''How to Begin Selling by Mail,'' *Nation's Business,* April 1991.

Kelley, Arlean, ''Direct Mail Dollars,'' *Small Business Opportunities,* September 1993.

Klein, Bernard, *Mail Order Business Directory,* 16th edition, B. Klein Publications, 1992.

''Mail Order: The Appeal of Mail Order,'' *EntrepreneurGroup,* 1992.

Simon, Julian L., *How to Start and Operate a Mail Order Business,* fourth edition, McGraw-Hill, 1987.

''Success Is in the Bag,'' *Small Business Opportunities,* September 1993.

''The 10 Most Frequently Asked Direct Marketing Questions,'' Direct Marketing Association.

—*KAREN BELLENIR*

Medical Claims Processing Service

A medical claims processor is essentially a case-worker who expedites for a client—usually a patient or physician—the preparation of medical claim forms. With little more than a basic knowledge of medical insurance and billing, you can start a business as a medical claims processor for a very modest cost.

The medical claims processing industry has developed as a result of the increasing complexity and proliferation of health insurance claims and supplemental benefits, as well as the rising population of senior citizens on Medicare. The number of medical claims processors in the United States is small compared to the enormous number of claims filed. This scenario was unlikely to change much with the possible implementation of a national health insurance plan; private, supplemental health insurance policies would still be in demand, and the Medicare population would continue to grow.

COSTS AND PROFITS

As a newly minted medical claims processor, even with insurance and billing experience and some clients at hand, you will most likely want to keep your start-up costs low and begin your business at home. Initial costs can therefore amount to as little as what your office furniture and computer, as well as photocopy and fax machines, are worth. If you set aside one room in your house or apartment as an office, you can claim this on your income tax as a deduction. You can also claim office furniture, a computer and other office machines, and a separate business phone line.

Your start-up costs will depend on what necessities you lack. If you need to buy a computer with a hard disk drive, a modem, fax machine, photocopier, answering machine, desk and chair, and one or two filing cabinets, this could add up to $5,000 secondhand. If you purchase new merchandise, count on initial costs being closer to $10,000, which will include the purchase of basic tools of your trade—code books such as *Current Procedural Terminology* and the *International Classification of Diseases*—advertising, travel to medical and insurance conventions, and electronic billing services with a clearinghouse. Rarely figured into start-up costs is reserve capital, which is needed for expenses at least until your business picks up.

Some medical claims processors charge as little as $15 an hour for their services, others as high as $50. As an alternative to having an hourly rate, you may decide to charge a certain amount per insurance claim. Whatever method you choose, you have a chance at earning a living for yourself—$25,000 is the average profit before taxes—and you may eventually pull in $100,000 in profits before taxes.

FINANCING

If you cannot rely on your own savings or on relatives or friends for a loan, the quickest, easiest, and most overlooked alternative to acquiring initial capital is your credit card, provided you are sure you can pay your credit card debts within six months. If you take longer than that, the high interest payments make this alternative a self-defeating one.

You can turn to the **Small Business Administration** for financial advice, rather than a bank. Call your local chamber of commerce for the phone number of your local Small Business Administration office or phone **1-800-U ASK SBA.** When calling the SBA, you will often be put on hold or have a long message menu to choose from. Be patient and persistent; the SBA is there to help you, and a counselor will sit down with you and advise you for free on how to secure a loan, answer any other business questions you may have, and guide you through the steps of drawing up an effective business plan. Incidentally, the SBA also lends money, but only if a commercial bank has turned you down.

Take advantage of print and on-line sources on the financial aspects of small business start-up. Your local librarian, who is accustomed to business queries, can quickly point you in the direction of the heap of books in every library dealing with small business loans and operations. Your SBA counselor will also be glad to recommend relevant books.

Since your medical claims processing service as yet has no history, you must prove to potential lenders that there is a market and future for it. Once you have conducted the necessary research and called on experts for advice, you can draw up a detailed business plan and present it to a bank for a loan. There are several types of bank loans with varying

SOFTWARE

Peachtree Complete Accounting for DOS (also available for Windows), $189. A few main features are inventory for the small business, order entry, and accounts receivable/payable.

Peachtree Basic Accounting (DOS or Windows), $85. A simplified version of the above, provides on-line help; does not do inventory.

CA-BPI Accounting II for DOS (also Windows version), $164. Main features are payroll, inventory, and accounts receivable/payable.

Quick Books & Quick Pay for DOS with Payroll, $109. Speeds up bill paying and invoicing.

One-Write Plus Accounting (DOS), $89. Features check writing, billing, inventory, and accounts receivable/payable.

FormTool, 3.0 version, $50. This handy software creates every imaginable form on your PC, including price tags.

TurboTAX (DOS and Windows), $39. Claims to be the best-selling tax software; offers complete tax preparation.

Claims Assistance Software:

Ameri-Claim (electronic billing software), P.O. Box 755, Lee's Summit, MO 64063; phone: (816) 524-4044.

Applied Software Technology (electronic claim processing software), 591 W. Hamilton Ave., #201, Campbell, CA 95008; phone: (800) 627-6383.

Microsoft, One Microsoft Way, Redmond, Washington 98052-6399; (800) 227-4679; phone: (206) 882-8080.

Moore Business Products Division, 3901 Morse St., #100, Denton, TX 76205-4519; (800) 634-7341; phone: (817) 566-8646.

Quarterdeck Office Systems, 1901 Main St., Santa Monica, CA 90405; phone: (310) 329-9851.

interest rates. You can also consult any number of finance companies that specialize in lending to businesses and, though they charge a higher interest rate, tend to take on greater risks than a bank.

LOCATION AND OFFICE SETUP

Initially, you will probably want to keep costs as low as possible and start your medical claims processing service in your home. As long as your business is small, your space should be adequate, but as it expands, you may want to rent an office space, preferably near doctors' offices where parking is adequate.

Before you begin a home-based business, check your zoning laws to ensure compliance with them. Parking may or may not be a problem, depending on whether or not you decide to visit your clients in their homes. If you expect a client to come to you, then you must provide a reception area in your home that should be uncluttered and quiet. Any distracting noise such as a television or washing machine,

toys strewn about, or general messiness will merely detract from the professional appearance of your business, which you should be careful to cultivate.

As your business grows, you may seriously consider renting office space big enough to allow for a future employee. Doctors may eventually constitute part of your clientele. Patients who seek your help with billing will often be senior citizens who will find it convenient to seek your help if you're located close to their doctors' offices, which should have ample parking that includes parking for the handicapped.

EMPLOYEE HIRING AND TRAINING

Initially, and probably for the entire first year in business, you will work by yourself to keep down costs. When the time comes to hire an employee, you will be faced with a whole new set of problems and requirements. Once you have made up your mind to hire, bear in mind the need for a proper job description and the multitude of forms that you will have to fill out, including tax forms, workman's compensation, social security, and wage forms. You can pay as low as minimum wage, but in that case you will probably have few job takers. Competitive wages are always the best rule of thumb to follow when hiring.

At first, your employee will probably work part time and take care of filing and reception duties. It is advisable to hire someone who you think can be trained to take on more professional responsibilities, such as the initial client interview and record keeping. Your medical claims processing service will eventually grow to the point where you will need a full-time worker, which you should remember when writing your job description and selecting employees.

PAYMENT

If you process claims mainly for senior citizens on Medicare, then you will be dealing only with supplemental insurance policies. However, if physicians are part of your clientele, then Medicare claims will be a major part of your job. You will have to decide whether you want to be paid by the hour or by the claim. With electronic billing and fax machines drastically speeding up the billing process, you might consider the latter.

You will most likely bill your clients by mail. Sixty days is usually the limit in recovering full payment for your service; thereafter, you will have to investigate the reason for nonpayment. Many medical claims processors will establish retainer fees with clients, especially those who have long-term medical problems. In such a case, you would be paid a lump sum for your services over a particular period of time. You may decide to charge doctors transaction fees ranging from $1 to $5 per claim transaction.

There are literally hundreds of claim forms, many, if not most, of which you can obtain from your computer via a modem. Then there are your own records of sales and payments. Because of the complexity of your business and the possibility of making errors, it is strongly advisable to secure an accountant to go over your records and to turn to for advice.

COMPUTER MATTERS

In the computer age of the early 1990s, it was impossible to consider opening a medical claims business without a computer. Large and small insurance companies have switched to electronic billing as well as transmitting forms and documents by downloading them via a modem. Consequently, the billing process is simplified, errors are more readily detected, and payment is expedited.

As the operator and owner of your own medical claims service, not only are a computer, modem, and printer indispensable to your business, but also the requisite software. You will need software to process medical claims and software to keep track of your business, including payments, sales, possibly payroll, and other records, such as your own insurance payments. Lastly, for approximately $50, you can obtain excellent software to complete your taxes. Computer software has not only eliminated much of the drudgery of record keeping, but made it virtually error-free.

To determine what medical claims software is best for

PRIMARY ASSOCIATIONS AND SELECTED TRADE PUBLICATIONS

Associations:

National Association of Claims Assistance Professionals (NACAP): 4724 Florence Ave., Downers Grove, IL 60515; phone: (708) 963-3500. Founded, 1991; 850 members; publishes *Claims Advisor* newsletter and membership directory; operates bookstore. The NACAP is involved in educating the public about medical claims processing and helps members through referrals, meetings, and publications.

Health Insurance Association of America (HIAA): 1025 Connecticut Ave. NW, Ste. 1200, Washington, DC 20036; phone: (202) 233-7780. Primary trade association of health insurance companies in the U.S.; has a library of 4,000 books and provides an information service. HIAA is helpful for its publications and technical reports.

Publications by HIAA:

Digest of Health Insurance Laws and Regulations: 1984 to the present.
Course in Individual Health Insurance: Chicago, HIAA, 1983.
A Course in Group Life & Health Insurance: 3 volumes, Chicago, 1979-1984.
Medical Prevailing Healthcare Charges System: Semi-annual.
Surgical Prevailing Healthcare Charges System: Semi-annual.
Source Book of Health Insurance Data: Annual.

---

your business, consult with the **National Association of Claims Assistance Professionals,** by writing, **4724 Florence Ave., Downers Grove, IL 60515,** or phoning **(708) 963-3500.** To obtain software for your business management needs, go to your local discount software store and check out the business software section. There are numerous software packages geared toward small business operations, all of them under $200.

LICENSES AND INSURANCE

To start with, you will need to find out if your home is in an area zoned for business. You will also need numerous licenses from your state, county, and city. It is easy to find out what business permits and licenses you will need either by calling your chamber of commerce, which will steer you to the right phone numbers, or ask your librarian. Virtually every county publishes an annual small business guide that lists relevant information and phone numbers. Do not expect to obtain the required permits and licenses instantly; the wait can sometimes last for weeks.

To find the right insurance for your business, consult the Yellow Pages. Simply go to the insurance listing, and pick out those companies that handle business insurance.

MARKETING AND ADVERTISING

A careful marketing strategy is essential for your business. Word of mouth and personal contacts, such as doctors and personal friends, will produce most of your clients. Networking, therefore, is indispensable. Traveling to medical and insurance conventions that give you the opportunity to meet people should be an important part of your marketing strategy.

If senior citizens will be your most important clientele, you should make a point of going to as many senior citizen centers, apartment buildings, and nursing homes in your area to post a flyer explaining your services. Few people may have heard of your profession, and educating the public about it will be a major part of your marketing and advertising. It is best if you can arrange to speak as often as possible before senior citizen gatherings.

Make sure that you have an ample supply of business cards and carry them with you wherever you go. Advertise in your local paper on a regular basis. Finally, join the National Association of Claims Assistance Professionals; with fewer than 1,000 members, they often give referrals to members and inform them about advertising possibilities and the latest trends in the medical claims profession.

With only several thousand medical claims processing services in the United States and a market of well over 30 million senior citizens—and millions of other people carrying supplemental policies and with long-term illnesses or physical handicaps—the market is a huge one. The potential to establish a thriving business is excellent for the entrepreneur possessing good marketing, advertising, and managerial skills.

SOURCES:

Davis, James B., *CPT & HCPCS Coding Made Easy: A Comprehensive Guide to CPT and HCPCS Coding for Health Care Professionals,* PMIC, 1992.

Ferbas, Denise, "Stratus and Shared Financial Systems to Develop Medical Claims Software," *Business Wire,* February 25, 1992.

Fletcher, M., "Medical Claims Audits Cut Costs: Can Lead to Discovery of Overpayments, Improvements," *Business Insurance,* February 15, 1993, p. 18.

Jones, David C., "A Move to Cut Costs of Health Claims Processing," *National Underwriter Life & Health—Financial Services Edition,* August 17, 1992, p. 9.

Knaus, Gary, *Getting Paid for What You Do: Coding for Optimal Reimbursement,* McGraw-Hill, 1991.

"Learning to Live with Electronic Billing," *American Medical News,* August 23, 1993, p. 11.

Maher, Thomas M., "Claims Service Fills Terrific Consumer Need," *National Underwriter,* August 20, 1990, pp. 13 and 15.

Morris, Barbara A., "Fee Based Processing of Medical Claims—A Potential Growth Business for Agents," *Rough Notes,* May 1991, pp. 34-36.

Punch, Linda, "Credit Cards and the Health Care Crisis," *Credit Card Management,* July 1992, pp. 28-40.

Rode, Dan, "The Quest for Uniformity in Billing Goes On," *Financial Management,* June 1993, p. 24.

Scott, Miriam Basch, "EDI Reduces Administrative Costs," *Employee Benefit Plan Review,* March 1993, pp. 35-36.

Shear, Carolyn F., *The Health Insurance Claims Kit,* Chicago, 1992.

Thompson, Kevin D., "Hot Industries for Small Businesses," *Black Enterprise,* March 1993, pp. 61-68.

—SINA DUBOVOJ

Mobile Frozen Yogurt Business

Mobile frozen yogurt sellers have used so many different approaches to deliver such a wide assortment of frozen yogurt products to their customers that the industry is united by only two common elements: its mobility and its primary product. Frozen yogurt gained widespread popularity during the late 1980s and early 1990s as many Americans turned their attention to health and fitness. Frozen yogurt sales benefited from two coinciding circumstances: first, it was perceived as a healthy alternative to traditional ice cream; and second, new frozen yogurt formulations resulted in better tasting products.

Some industry watchers predicted that traditional storefront frozen yogurt sellers would see diminished profits due to increased competition during the early and mid 1990s. Mobile sellers, however, held an advantage because of their lower operating costs and their ability to cater to an ever-growing demand for convenience.

COSTS AND PROFITS

The costs of entering the mobile frozen yogurt industry can vary greatly depending on how you set up and operate your business. On the low end, if you deliver a pre-packaged, afternoon snack product to workers in a single, large office building you may need only a small initial investment. For $200 to $300 you can buy a simple food distribution cart and provide a tasty alternative to traditional break-time fare. If the building you would like to serve has freezer space available, perhaps to serve a cafeteria, you may be able to rent shelf space for storing your inventory. If freezer space is unavailable, you may be able to rent space in an off-prime location, such as a basement, and install your own freezer.

Because the costs of getting your business established with a food distribution cart are low, this option might seem attractive. Your profit potential with the cart, however, may be restricted. Since the cart does not provide refrigeration, you will be limited to serving only those customers you can reach within a tightly defined time parameter. You will also be restricted to serving the same people day after day. As a result, your sales may diminish depending on the season or after the novelty of your presence wears off. If you are looking for a part-time opportunity with a minimum cash investment, however, an office building delivery route may suit your needs.

Another alternative is to sell frozen yogurt products from a push cart or tricycle. These types of vehicles are available with freezer compartments and will provide you with the flexibility to take your products to more locations. One manufacturer, **Worksman Trading, 94-15 100th Street, Ozone Park, NY 11416; phone: 1-800-962-2453,** sells push carts and tricycles to frozen yogurt vendors who peddle their products on street corners or at stadiums, carnivals, amusement parks, county fairs, and hotels. Worksman Trading offers a nonmechanical push cart for $1,200 and a nonmechanical tricycle for $1,600. Nonmechanical units use dry ice to keep products cold. Mechanical push carts with overnight rechargeable batteries cost $2,400. (Because batteries are too heavy for easy tricycle operation, Worksman Trading offers only nonmechanical tricycles). Although nonmechanical push carts are cheaper initially, their cost of operation is higher because the dry ice must be replaced daily. If you decide to operate a nonmechanical unit, be sure to consider the cost of dry ice blocks when calculating your potential profit.

Although push carts and tricycles offer you greater mobility, they still carry limitations based on their size. You may decide an investment in a trailer or vending truck will pay off in increased opportunities. One supplier of standard and customized vehicles such as trailers, vans, and trucks is **All Star Cart Company, 1565 D 5th Industrial Court, Bay Shore, NY 11706; phone: 1-800-831-3166.** All Star Cart Company's prices vary according to the type of unit and the kind of setup you order. If you already own a van, the cost of making the interior suitable for selling frozen yogurt and soft drinks can range from $5,000 to $7,000 and up depending on the options you select. A self-contained trailer with mechanical refrigeration and a dipper well for hard pack frozen yogurt products can run from $8,000 to $9,000 depending on its specifications. One model, available for $10,000, includes an area for toppings. A larger 15- or 16-foot trailer including areas for soft drinks, coffee, and hot food can run as much as $18,000 or $19,000.

If you want to capture part of the lucrative soft serve market, your initial investment will be higher than if you offer only pre-packaged or hard pack products, but your

FRANCHISE OPPORTUNITIES

Many frozen yogurt franchisors offer licenses primarily to storefront operators. Some also are willing to accept mobile operators:

Bridgeman's Dip Shoppe: 6009 Wayzata Blvd., Suite 113, St. Louis Park, MN 55416; phone: (612) 593-1455. Offers franchises for both frozen yogurt and ice cream shops; provides mandatory training program.

Emack and Bolio's: P.O. Box 703, Brookline Village, MA 02147-0703; phone: (617) 739-7995. Mobile franchise opportunity for hard pack, dipped frozen yogurt dessert products; features no-fat product with 90 calories per scoop; provides mandatory training program.

Gelato Amare: 11504 Hyde Place, Raleigh, NC 27614; phone: (919) 847-4435; offers 45 frozen yogurt flavors; some available in fat-free, cholesterol-free, low calorie, and sugar-free varieties; provides two-week training program, planning assistance, equipment, inventory, advertising help, promotional materials, and on-going aid.

I Can't Believe It's Yogurt: P.O. Box 809112, Dallas, TX 75380-9112; phone: (214) 392-3012; toll-free: (800) 722-5848. Offers alternative distribution options including kiosks and carts to traditional franchise holders; provides training and ongoing assistance.

The Ice Cream Club: 278 Ocean Blvd., Manalapan, FL 33462; phone: (407) 731-3331. Offers ice cream, soft serve yogurt, and frozen diet desserts; provides owner/manager operations manual.

profit potential will also be greater. One manufacturer estimated that gross margins of 70 percent or more could be attained on soft serve products. In addition, soft serve yogurt typically carries a higher margin than soft serve ice cream.

If you decide to operate a mobile soft serve machine, look for one with a quick freeze time, a rapid recovery cycle, and a compact size. If you will be operating inside a building, make sure it features quiet operation. **Wilch Manufacturing, 1345 S.W. 42nd Street, Topeka, KS 66609; phone: (913) 267-2762,** provides a line of soft serve machines it claims are ideal for installation in vending trucks. A single flavor machine carries a list price of $4,700, and a dual flavor (twist) machine lists for $8,800. The company's distributors, however, make discounts available to qualified industry participants. Other soft serve machine manufacturers include **Taylor Company, 750 North Blackhawk Blvd., Rockton, IL 61072; phone: (815) 624-8333,** and **Stoelting, Inc., 502 Highway 57, Department M, Kiel, WI 53042; phone: 1-800-545-0203.**

Although equipment costs will be a substantial part of your start-up expenses, other items such as storage shelves, a refrigerator and freezer, office furniture and supplies, transportation, initial inventory, spoons, napkins, and cleaning supplies will also be necessary. In addition, you will need

funds to provide for advertising and necessary licenses and insurance. According to the Entrepreneur Group, you can expect minimum start-up costs of about $11,000. Average start-up costs, however, run about $32,000.

Profits from mobile yogurt sales vary according to the skills of the individual operator, location, and product popularity. Retail prices run eight to ten times the actual product cost, and the Entrepreneur Group projected an average return on investment of about 156 percent. Industry-wide average net profit before taxes was about $50,000, with high end net profit before taxes reaching $98,500.

Geography also can impact your potential for profits. Geographic regions subject to cold or inclement weather provide less opportunity than other areas, such as Florida and Southern California. A favorable climate, however, is not always the most profitable. According to one report, Southern California was the most competitive region in the country for mobile frozen yogurt dealers, and as a result depressed prices were keeping profits down.

FINANCING

If you decide to set up your business as a franchise, financing for part of your estimated start-up costs may be available from the franchisor. If you decide to become an independent dealer, you may find it necessary to secure your own financing. Banks and credit unions may be willing to lend money for major equipment when the equipment can be used as collateral. When approaching a financial institution, you should have a solid business plan already written. If possible, bring letters of agreement from managers and operators of businesses and other locations you plan to serve. By doing so, you will demonstrate that enough interest in your product exists to make your venture profitable.

Local community development authorities and the Small Business Administration are other potential sources of funding. If you qualify for minority status, special lending programs may be available from federal, state, and local government agencies. In addition, some programs have been set up to help economically disadvantaged entrepreneurs such as the chronically unemployed or former prison inmates. In 1992, for example, Kansas City's Community Development Corporation helped ten food vendors get businesses established under a program called Carts for Success.

SETUP AND LOCATION

When you establish your mobile frozen yogurt business, you will have to evaluate your needs for storage and office space. If you plan to operate your business from your home, check with local zoning authorities and health department officials to make sure regulations permit the usages you have in mind. You may find that although you can have your office in a spare bedroom, the health department may not let you keep your freezer in your garage.

Your storage needs will vary according to the types of products you sell and on how much inventory you plan to keep on hand. Soft serve mixes and toppings may require refrigeration, while hard pack or pre-packaged items require sub-zero storage. Freezer manufacturers can help you evaluate your storage requirements and select the best freezer to meet your needs. To find a freezer manufacturer, consult the *Thomas Register,* available at many public libraries.

In addition to establishing your office and storage areas, you will need to give careful consideration to your selling area. Because you are operating from a small, compact unit, you need to plan carefully and maximize the space available. If you plan to sell only prepackaged items, consider how they will stack inside your freezer compartment. If you plan to sell hand-dipped hard pack frozen yogurt, you will also need to carry cones, napkins, and other paraphernalia.

A major part of your space planning will revolve around the products you carry and your route or location. The Entrepreneur Group estimated that, in order to be successful, a mobile frozen yogurt truck required 12 to 20 stops at locations with 20 or more people. Office parks were suggested as a good location because many office workers sit at desks and were inclined to be sedentary. As a result they tended to be diet-conscious and appreciated frozen yogurt as a healthful snack alternative. Other potential stops included college campuses, factories, and recreational facilities.

PRODUCT SELECTION AND COMPETITION

Because of space limitations, the number of yogurt flavors or the variety of pre-packaged products you can offer will be limited. Your ability to match your selection with your customer's tastes will be one of the keys to determining your

success. The most popular flavors have traditionally been chocolate, vanilla, and twist (a combination of chocolate and vanilla). Other popular choices include fruit flavors and nut flavors. The availability of toppings can also help boost sales.

Your primary competition will come from other vendors vying for your customer's snack dollar. Ice cream vendors with no-fat products may try to capture some of the health-conscious market where yogurt has traditionally held an advantage. If you face this type of competition, you may want to offer a blend of specialized products such as those with reduced calories, no cholesterol, low fat, or no sugar.

ADDING EMPLOYEES

If you start your mobile frozen yogurt operation with a single route or cart, you may not require any additional employees. As you become established and add routes and locations, you will need people to man them. In addition, you may find you need to run extra vehicles or carts during peak seasons. You may also need temporary or part-time help to handle parties and other special gatherings, such as grand openings, where you are unable to be personally present.

Whether you hire high school or college students or look to temporary job agencies to find workers for you, be sure to check any potential worker's references thoroughly. Your employees should be dependable and courteous. If you will not be with them, they should be able to work independently. In addition, you need people who can be trusted with cash receipts.

Once you have hired new employees, you should invest some time in their training. Employees should be familiar with the nutritional content of the products you sell as well as with the safe operation of your equipment. In addition, your local health department may require the performance of specific procedures to ensure product safety.

MANAGEMENT ISSUES

When you decide to begin a mobile frozen yogurt company, one important issue you will face is whether to be a franchise or an independent operator. Franchisees sometimes face additional costs such as franchise fees and royalties, but in return they receive training, start-up assistance, help with advertising, and on-going counseling. Independent operators function on their own. One company able to help you evaluate your start-up needs is **World Franchise Consultants, 15919 West 10 Mile Road, Suite 201, Southfield, MI 48075; phone: 1-800-745-1415.** World Franchise Consultants can help you measure your potential market and put together a business plan. The company can also help you make decisions about how to design your cart, trailer, van, or truck.

If you affiliate with a franchise, you will probably purchase your equipment and supplies from the franchisor. If you operate as an independent, you will need to find

---

INDUSTRY STATISTICS

- Frozen yogurt establishments accounted for nearly one percent of all quick-service customer counts in the third quarter of 1993 (Source: NPD/CREST Household Report, National Restaurant Association).
- Sales of frozen yogurt totaled $2.4 billion in 1992 (Source: National Restaurant Association).
- Frozen yogurt sales represented the second-most promising food-related category after catering (Source: National Restaurant Association).
- Although the number of ice cream shops declined in 1989, the number of yogurt shops increased 33 percent; further growth is expected in the 1990s; the estimated 11,000 purveyors of frozen yogurt in 1990 was expected to climb to 14,352 by 1993 (Source: *Nation's Restaurant News,* June 11, 1990).
- Approximately 40 percent of Americans have not tried frozen yogurt (Source: *Nation's Restaurant News,* June 11, 1990).
- U.S. production of ice cream and frozen dessert products totaled 1.5 billion gallons in 1991. Of this total, frozen yogurt represented 75 million gallons (Source: *Restaurant Business,* May 1, 1993).

PRIMARY ASSOCIATION AND SELECTED TRADE PUBLICATIONS

Associations:

National Association of Ice Cream Vendors: 5600 Brookwood Terr., Nashville, TN 37205; phone: (615) 356-4240. Publishes monthly newsletter.

National Restaurant Association: 1200 17th Street NW, Washington, DC 20036; phone: (202) 331-5900. Represents members from all facets of the food service industry; publishes variety of materials and sponsors annual trade show.

International Ice Cream Association: 888 16th Street NW, Washington, DC 20006; phone: (202) 296-4250. Publishes manuals and training videotapes as well as periodic publications.

Publications:

Ice Cream Reporter: Find/SVP, 625 Avenue of the Americas, New York, NY 10011; phone: (212) 645-4500; toll-free: (800) 346-3787.
National Soft Serve and Fast Food Association Newsletter: National Soft Serve and Fast Food Association, c/o Chauncey Blubaugh, 7321 Anthony Hwy., Waynesboro, PA 17268-9736; toll-free phone: (800) 535-7748.
NICYRA Bulletin: National Ice Cream and Yogurt Retailers Association, 1429 King Avenue, Suite 210, Columbus, OH 43212; phone: (614) 486-1444.

suppliers and product distributors. One company offering frozen yogurt products and supplies to independent operators is **International Yogurt Company, 5858 N.E. 87th Avenue, Portland, OR 97220-1312; phone: (503) 256-3754; toll-free: 1-800-YO CREAM.** International Yogurt Company makes a full line of frozen yogurt products including single serve cups, hard pack flavors, and soft serve mixes. Many items are available in premium and no-fat varieties. The company also sells push carts, patio umbrellas, kiosks, and advertising materials such as banners, signs, menu boards, and promotional materials.

Another way to identify potential suppliers is to attend a major trade show. For example, every May the National Restaurant Association sponsors an event held in Chicago's McCormick Place. By attending the show, you can meet frozen yogurt vendors, distributors, equipment manufacturers, and other industry-related people. For more information contact the **National Restaurant Association**'s show office: **150 North Michigan, Suite 2000, Chicago, IL 60601; phone: (312) 853-2525.**

INDUSTRY TRENDS AND MARKETING

According to statistics compiled by the National Restaurant Association, orders for frozen yogurt increased 18 percent in 1989 and 33 percent in 1990. The boom proved short-lived, however. As frozen yogurt gained acceptance, it lost its status as a novelty and entered the American mainstream. Even McDonald's began offering a frozen yogurt dessert product. In addition, frozen yogurt sellers noted declines during the early 1990s. The sales slump was attributed to unfavorable weather patterns and a slow economy.

Some industry watchers expected sales to rebound as the overall national economy improved. The National Restaurant Association, for example, predicted a 5.6 percent increase in sales during 1993, making frozen yogurt the second-most promising food-related category after catering. Some analysts felt these conditions presented a favorable outlook for the mobile frozen yogurt industry.

To make optimal use of national trends, you will need a marketing strategy. Some industry analysts advised frozen yogurt dealers to develop marketing plans that focused on potential customers in the middle to upper-middle socioeconomic groups irrespective of age or sex. Other analysts offered more specific recommendations. The Entrepreneur Group suggested aiming at the 18- to 34-year-old category and noted that women were more likely customers than men. One major yogurt chain, I Can't Believe It's Yogurt, described a typical customer as a well-educated female, interested in indulgence but concerned about avoiding fat and calories.

ADVERTISING

To promote your products and differentiate yourself from your competition, you may want to offer promotional materials such as buttons, caps, and T-shirts featuring your name and slogan. If your customers are especially sensitive to health issues, you may find it helpful to produce a brochure explaining yogurt's benefits.

Frozen yogurt is often perceived as being low in both fat and calories, but this is not always true. Many yogurt products are available in low-fat and no-fat versions, but some have as much fat content as regular ice cream. The main difference between yogurt and ice cream is that yogurt contains live, active bacteria cultures that aid digestion. (Yogurt cultures are not killed by freezing.) If you choose to promote the health benefits of your products, make sure to disseminate accurate information. Frozen yogurt suppliers can provide you with detailed nutritional data about their products.

In many areas of the United States, the best season for selling will be during warm weather months. People tend to prefer other types of snack products during cold and inclement weather. To help bolster sales during the off-season, you can offer coupons, deliver novelty products with holiday themes, or supply specially packaged items at sports events. In addition, you may want to consider taking orders and delivering yogurt cakes and pies for office parties and other events.

LICENSES AND INSURANCE

The types of licenses and insurance you will require depend on how your operation is set up and the specific requirements in your jurisdiction. Some localities are more friendly than others to mobile operators. In some cities, vending trucks are no longer legal, while others welcome them. Push cart acceptance also varies from city to city. Your local authorities can also tell you what types of insurance you will be required to carry.

Because you are offering a product for consumption, your local health department may also enforce certain guidelines. For example, if you have a soft serve machine, local ordinances may mandate a specific cleaning schedule. Health codes may also specify how long your product can be held in a machine on a "stand-by" basis. In other places, the health department may periodically inspect your storage area or check the quality of your products.

YOUR OPPORTUNITY FOR SUCCESS

As an ever-growing number of people enter the frozen yogurt marketplace, competition will increase; as the market becomes saturated, pricing will become more competitive. These factors do not have to impact your business in a negative way. If you successfully identify your potential customers, establish a profitable route or pinpoint an excellent location, and market your product based on its convenience and health benefits, you can operate a prosperous mobile frozen yogurt business either as a part-time, seasonal endeavor or as a full-time venture.

SOURCES:

"Frozen Desserts," *Nation's Restaurant News,* June 11, 1990.
Gelato Amare, Raleigh, NC.
Gose, Joe, "The Chuck Wagon of the '90's—Treats on the Streets," *Kansas City Business Journal,* July 3, 1992.
"Indie Yogurt Shops Predicted to Melt Under Big Chain Competition," *Nation's Restaurant News,* June 11, 1990.
Kochak, Jacque, "Frozen Assets," *Restaurant Business,* October 10, 1991.
"Mobile Frozen Yogurt: Just Desserts," Entrepreneur Group, 1992.
Scarpa, James, "Soft Serve," *Restaurant Business,* May 1, 1993.
Schwartz, Carol A., editor, *Small Business Sourcebook,* sixth edition, Gale, 1993.
Tanyeri, Dana, "Frozen Dairy Treats Offer Luscious, Low-Labor Dessert Options," *Institutional Distribution,* January 1993.

—*Karen Bellenir*

No-Alcohol Nightclub

In addition to the more than 18 million recovering alcoholics in the United States, there are people who abstain from alcoholic beverages for other health reasons, because of religious beliefs or pregnancy, or out of a desire not to drive while intoxicated. As more facets of society become aware of the dangers of alcohol abuse, the nondrinker has become a target market. Designated-driver programs that offer special gifts or coupons to abstainers are gaining popularity at sports arenas and restaurants, and beverage companies are capitalizing on the growing market for nonalcoholic beer and wine. Furthermore, many nondrinkers still want to enjoy an evening out with friends, dancing and listening to music without feeling the temptation to drink. Thus, the notion of a no-alcohol nightclub is growing in popularity and is a potentially lucrative option for the aspiring entrepreneur.

COSTS AND PROFITS

A no-alcohol nightclub has equipment and staff requirements similar to those of other bars and nightclubs, with two major exceptions. First, you will not incur the costs of a liquor license or have to wait until a license is issued before you open for business. Second, you will not have the expense of keeping your club stocked with liquor. However, you will need to apply for a food service license and check the specific regulations for a restaurant-type business in your area.

Start-up estimates range from $50,000 for a bare bones operation to $500,000 for a large, sophisticated nightclub in a major metropolitan area. The average is closer to $100,000. Profits before taxes, depending on the size of the club, can range from $40,000 to $1 million. Because you can sell nonalcoholic cocktails for the same price as cocktails with liquor, the profit on drinks will be higher. Many patrons, though, will also order soft drinks and no-alcohol beer, which sell at cheaper prices. Consequently, it could take longer than a regular nightclub to turn a profit.

FINANCING

Be prepared to invest your own money in your new business. In the banking world, small businesses are viewed as risky, and financial institutions are leery of putting money into them. You should accumulate as much of your needed capital as possible from your own savings and from friends, relatives, and business partners. If you still find it necessary to apply for a loan, you should develop a detailed business plan. Include background information about yourself, a market analysis of the area around your proposed location, projections for income and expenses for the first several years, a list of other clubs in the area, a detailed marketing strategy, and a statement of your goals for the business venture. You should also prepare a personal financial statement, including your tax returns for the previous two years. The **Small Business Administration (SBA),** an agency of the federal government, is an excellent source of information on where and how to receive financing and can be contacted at **1-800-U ASK SBA.**

It is a good idea before starting any business to hire an accountant and an attorney. Be prepared to pay professionals who have experience in your type of business; their fees are well worth the advice and guidance that you will receive. You may also be able to use their business contacts to secure financial backing.

LOCATION

Two factors will figure prominently in your choice of location: access to potential customers and zoning regulations. You will want to situate your nightclub in an area with a high concentration of middle- to upper-class men and women between the ages of 20 and 40 years old. You will also want to be located near other businesses that cater to this demographic group, such as theaters, restaurants, and fitness facilities.

Because your club will serve only nonalcoholic drinks, you are likely to attract a teenage crowd. You will have to decide early in the planning stages whether or not this is a market that you want to pursue, since older patrons may not frequent a club with a younger clientele. A possible solution would be to offer special teen nights and tailor the entertainment accordingly.

Spend some time both during the day and at night gauging pedestrian and automobile traffic in the area of your desired location. You may even want to canvass some of the passersby as to whether or not they would frequent a no-

RECIPES AND SOURCES FOR NONALCOHOLIC DRINKS

Aztec Fire

2 scoops vanilla ice cream
1/2 pint cold coffee
1 pinch cocoa powder
Cinnamon
Blend first three ingredients. Serve in a tall glass. Sprinkle with cinnamon.

Steffi Graff Cocktail

1 1/3 oz. pear juice
1 1/3 oz. apricot juice
1 1/3 oz. kiwi fruit juice
1 1/3 oz. orange juice
1 kiwi fruit slice
1 small cocktail pear
1 slice orange
Stir juices together. Serve in a cocktail class with speared fruits.

Virgin Mary

6 oz. chilled tomato juice
Dash Tabasco
Dash Worcestershire sauce
Dash salt and pepper
1/2 oz. lemon juice
Pour tomato juice into chilled beer mug filled with ice cubes. Add remaining ingredients. Mix and serve with a chilled celery stalk.

(SOURCES: BLUTEAU, ANDRE, *100 COCKTAILS WITHOUT ALCOHOL,* PRODUCTIONS LUCODA INC., 1981; "NO-ALCOHOL BAR," *ENTREPRENEUR BUSINESS START-UP GUIDE,* ENTREPRENEURGROUP, 1988; SPATH, SIEGFRIED, *DRIVER FRIENDLY DRINKS.*)

alcohol nightclub. Check the Yellow Pages or contact the local chamber of commerce to find out what other businesses are in the area. Are there enough businesses to attract a lunchtime or after-work clientele? Be prepared to spend money for a prime location, especially if the neighborhood attracts considerable pedestrian traffic.

It is very important to research the history of your chosen location. An unsatisfactory location is one of the primary factors in the failure of food service and related businesses. If other clubs, bars, and restaurants have once existed on your chosen plot, try to find out why they closed; if location is mentioned more than once, it would be wise to consider another spot.

Zoning regulations will play a large part in the selection of your location. Laws governing noise and parking vary across the country, and you will have to verify the specific restrictions in your area. You should also check ordinances governing loading and unloading of merchandise, since your suppliers will need to make regular deliveries.

FACILITY

Look for a building that has previously been used for food and beverage service. The most ideal situation is to take over an existing bar along with its equipment. If the liquor inventory is included in the price, try to renegotiate the deal excluding the unneeded inventory. If this is not feasible, find a buyer for the liquor.

You can also renovate a small coffee shop or restaurant, in which case you should plan to pay between $15,000 to $40,000 to add the necessary bar equipment, fixtures, and furniture as well as pay for plumbing, electrical, and carpentry improvements. To accommodate a bar and tables with a combined seating of 100 people, a dance floor, and a stage, you will need a minimum of 2,000 square feet. The bar itself can be stationed against one wall or stand freely in the center of the room and should be attractive and inviting.

Most municipal health regulations require separate bathrooms for men and women if your seating exceeds 50 people. Keeping the bathrooms clean and properly stocked is essential. Your customers will use the bathrooms often and will rightfully expect them to be clean. Cleanliness is also important in the kitchen. If you plan to offer food other than what the bartender can serve—chips, pretzels, and microwaved items—you will need to check the local health regulations applying to kitchens before you open for business.

Your necessary storage and office area can be combined if space is tight. In the office, you should have a desk, typewriter, stationary and envelopes, recordkeeping books, business cards, employee time cards, and sales slips.

ATMOSPHERE

In decorating your nightclub, choose a theme and a particular style, keeping in mind the image you want your establishment to project. Ask yourself the following questions: What type of customers do you want to attract? What type of music and/or entertainment will you offer? Do you want your establishment to be a quiet, intimate place where people can enjoy nonalcoholic drinks, eat, and talk? Or do you want to be known as a dance club? All of these variables will help determine how you will decorate your nightclub.

Lighting is perhaps the key to creating a unique atmosphere for your nightclub; lights can provide intimacy as well as excitement. Lighting in the seating areas should be muted, while bright lights should be saved for the dance floor. In addition to lighting, there are any number of ways that you can decorate to achieve a particular effect. Use posters, candles, and memorabilia to add character to your nightclub.

The type of music and/or entertainment you choose will determine your need for a stage or bandstand. Although a stereo system and CDs or tapes are less expensive than live bands, you will not generate the same level of income that live entertainment attracts. If you plan to install a dance floor, get estimates from contractors, carpenters, and floor installers. Generally, you will pay between $500 and $1,000 for a 15' x 20' dance floor and a 6' x 10' x 2' bandstand, unless you are able to do the work yourself.

EQUIPMENT

Whenever possible, try to purchase used equipment and furniture. If you are moving into an existing bar or club, much of the necessary equipment and fixtures will be included. If they fit in with your decorating plans, you are in luck. Check trade publications and local newspapers for used equipment and furniture. It might also be fruitful to browse through flea markets in your area and attend auctions and foreclosure sales.

Budgeting for comfortable, sturdy chairs is essential, and you should plan to spend between $125 to $175 per chair. At the bar, you will need to provide approximately two feet of space per customer. At a standard 24-foot bar, this translates into 12 people, or 12 chairs. Tables should provide seating for groups of two and four.

The bar area will account for a large portion of your initial investment. If you will be building a new bar, determine the size and style you want before getting prices. Decide if you want the front covered with tile, leather, wood paneling, or carpeting, and choose a material—perhaps wood, Formica, or Corian—that you want to use to cover the top of the bar. The back of the bar is usually constructed of Formica with a mirrored upper wall. The lower half of the bar will house several refrigerated compartments. As a guide for determining how big your bar should be, a 2,000-square-foot club with a capacity of 100 customers usually needs a 24' x 30' bar.

In the work area directly behind the front of the bar, you will need a bin that will hold 450 to 600 pounds of ice and a beverage-dispensing system for mixers, soda, and water. Check health codes in your area for sink and dishwasher requirements. The most common setup employs three sinks: one filled with soapy water, one filled with clear water, and one filled with sanitized water.

Spend time selecting glassware, which will not only

add to your club's image, but will determine your drink sizes. To ascertain the number of glasses you will need, multiply your seating capacity by three and then factor in a 20 percent pilferage rate. For your grand opening, you should have a combination of highball glasses, Collins glasses, all-purpose wine glass, whiskey sour glasses, champagne flutes, beer mugs for soft drinks and nonalcoholic beer, mixing glasses, and coffee cups.

Outfitting the bar with bartending tools is not unlike setting up your home kitchen for the first time. A basic needs list includes serving trays, cutting boards, and two of each of the following items: long bar spoons, bottle openers, ice scoops, funnels, shot glasses, jiggers, plastic jars, blenders, shakers (tin and glass), paring knives, and glass cleaning brushes. You should also have bowls for sugar and salt.

You will need a cash register that has the ability to run tallies by type and size of drink, server name or number, and brand name. It is wise to invest in a model that also updates inventory. If you anticipate a high-volume business, you may want to explore the possibility of a computerized dispensing system that allows the bartender to pour seven premeasured liquids at one time and automatically deducts the amount from your inventory.

FOOD AND BEVERAGES

Food and beverage supplies constitute an ongoing expense. In the beginning, purchase a minimum amount of inventory until you can properly gauge your volume. Don't worry about running out; your suppliers will be able to deliver reinforcements very quickly. To offer the full array of nonalcoholic cocktails, you will need lemon juice mix, red maraschino cherries, coconut snow, cream, half and half, Tabasco sauce, grapefruit juice, tomato juice, orange juice, oranges, lemons, limes, celery sticks, grenadine, pineapple juice and slices, pepper, salt, kosher salt, sugar cubes, granulated sugar, cinnamon, nutmeg, and cloves.

For bar snacks, you can order the basics—potato chips, nuts, and pretzels—from wholesale bar suppliers. An initial order of $125 to $150 should be sufficient. For beverages, you will also need a variety of sodas and flavorings, such as cola, ginger ale, concentrated lemon-lime juice, club soda, and tonic water. If you purchase generic brands, the costs will be in the range of $15 to $30 per gallon. Alcoholic flavorings are available from flavoring and extract manufacturers. Suppliers will be able to help you determine your initial order, but as a general guide, plan to spend between $150 and $250 on flavorings and between $200 and $300 on mixers.

The popularity of coffee in recent years has spawned hundreds of varieties, and the Yellow Pages lists the names of coffee suppliers in your area. You will be able to choose from regular grind, decaffeinated, and flavored coffees. Some suppliers will require a minimum order of approximately 25 to 30 pounds per month. You can arrange to lease a coffeemaker from your supplier or purchase one for ap-

PRIMARY ASSOCIATIONS AND SELECTED TRADE PUBLICATIONS

Associations:

National Licensed Beverage Association: 4214 King Street, W., Alexandria, VA 22302-1507; phone: (703) 671-7575; fax: (703) 845-0310.

National Restaurant Association: 1200 17th Street, N.W., Washington, DC 20036-3097; phone: (202) 331-5900; fax: (202) 331-2429.

Publications:

The New Age Beverages Market: Find/SVP, 625 Avenue of the Americas, New York, NY 10011; phone: (800) 346-3787; fax: (212) 645-7681.
Leisure Beverage "Insider": Whitaker Newsletters, Inc., 313 South Avenue, Fanwood, NJ 07023-0192; phone: (908) 889-6336; fax: (908) 889-6339.

proximately $250. An espresso machine can also be leased or purchased for about $2000.

You will also need to design a food menu before you open. If your club will be a casual place, your menu might include such things as sandwiches, microwaved pizzas, popcorn, and nachos. Simple fare can be prepared by the bartender, or you can purchase pre-made sandwiches. If you want to offer freshly made sandwiches and grilled items, or if your customer volume is high, you will need to hire someone to make sandwiches and snacks. Even for the most basic food preparation, you will need to purchase a refrigerator, microwave, toaster, cutting board, and food storage containers.

A more sophisticated menu might include shrimp, oysters, caviar, and crab claws as well as a variety of fresh salads and pastas; such a selection will necessitate hiring an experienced chef. For a nominal fee, the **National Restaurant Association**'s (**NRA**) Department of Information Services sells a packet of start-up information that offers guidance in designing a menu. Contact NRA at **1-800-424-5156.**

In addition to food and beverages, you will need to keep in stock cocktail napkins, paper towels, sandwich tissues, disposable plastic place settings and plates, prewrapped straws, swizzle sticks, menus, and ashtrays. Your suppliers will probably request that you pay cash on delivery for the first few months. After they receive assurance that your business is successful, your suppliers will allow you to set up accounts with them.

SOUND SYSTEM

Plan to spend ten percent of your budget on a sound system that includes a CD player, amplifiers, and speakers. Check trade publications or the Yellow Pages for companies that sell and install sound systems. While you may be tempted to purchase a home stereo system because it is less expensive, a home system is not made to withstand the heavy use that your club will demand. Remember that you are using music to draw customers into your nightclub, and you must be willing to install professional sound equipment. A company that specializes in sound system installation will be able to dcsign thc sound system that is best suited for your club and your needs.

One of the questions a sound system company's representative will ask is what volume level you want in your club. Do you want to limit music to the background or do you want the music to be a prominent part of the atmosphere? Dance music will require an especially high volume level. Also consider installing a paging system that can be heard throughout your establishment. In addition, if you are also planning to offer live music, you will need a band mixing console, amplifiers, and speakers.

ENTERTAINMENT

If live entertainment is what you have in mind, you may want to start with just one or two nights per week of live music. You can save money by hiring bands directly to avoid the ten percent agent fee. Advertise in the local entertainment publications and visit other clubs, booking acts that you think will be in line with the image of your club. Some bars designate one night a week as audition night, which gives the club owners an evening of free music and the opportunity to judge the crowd's reaction.

Once you have hired a band, promote its appearance at your club by hanging posters in your club and placing advertisements in local entertainment publications. Bands often have loyal fans, and you will want to take advantage of this opportunity to bring new customers to your place of business.

In addition to providing musical entertainment, you may want to install several leased or purchased amusement devices, which include video games, pinball machines, jukeboxes, and cigarette machines. Leased equipment is usually installed for free with a negotiated percentage or commission on the take. You should try to secure for yourself 50 percent on video games and pinball machines and 10 to 20 percent on cigarette machines and jukeboxes.

EMPLOYEES

The most important investment you can make in your business is an experienced, personable bartender. Not only can a good bartender offer invaluable advice when you are still in the planning stages, he or she will often be the reason that customers continually return to your establishment. Check trade publications and your local Yellow Pages for employment agencies that specialize in bartenders and wait staff employees.

A no-alcohol bar can technically remain open 24 hours a day. However, you will probably want to make your hours consistent with other establishments, usually 11 a.m. to 2 a.m. In that case, you will need to hire three bartenders: one to work the day shift, one for the evening shift, and a relief bartender to sub for the other two on their days off. In addition to preparing and serving drinks, the bartenders should be responsible for keeping the bar stocked and clean during and after their shifts. Expect to pay the industry standard for your regular bartenders.

It will also be necessary to hire one or two people per shift, depending on your customer volume, to wait on tables. Wait staff, which will be paid minimum wage plus tips, should be friendly yet professional; no one wants to be served by someone who is surly or inexperienced. Provide your wait staff with uniforms that fit in with your theme. Many clubs have t-shirts designed for employees to wear and offer the shirts for sale to customers. Depending on your volume of business, the wait staff, in addition to serving drinks, can remove dirty glasses and dishes from the tables and wipe the tables clean. You may want to hire a server assistant to help maintain cleanliness in your club during busy times.

As is often the case in a restaurant-type businesses, you

may find that your wait staff has a tendency to quit on short notice. You will then have to be ready to pitch in. It is a good idea to train one of your best employees as an assistant manager. Be prepared to pay a manager the current industry rate or to offer other incentives such as profit sharing.

Although the bartenders in a nonalcoholic bar will not have to deal with intoxicated patrons, some customers may try to smuggle liquor into your club. Train your staff to handle such situations. It is also a good idea to become acquainted with your local police precinct in case you need to call for assistance.

OPERATIONS

Unless it is common in your area or if you are offering top-notch entertainment, a cover charge is not necessary. However, you may want to impose a monetary, or two-drink, minimum for patrons sitting at tables, especially on weekends.

Many of your patrons will want to pay their tab with a credit card. Depending on the credit card used, you will have to follow a particular procedure for processing receipts and getting paid. Some credit transactions, such as those charged to Visa and MasterCard, are managed by local banks. Find a bank in your area that handles both Visa and MasterCard. Other cards, such as American Express and Diners Club, are independently processed. You can look up the toll-free numbers for these companies in the Yellow Pages, where you will also find a listing of credit card machines suppliers.

ADVERTISING AND MARKETING

Although the corner bar might survive on simple word-of-mouth advertising and customers who happen to walk by and stop in, the unusual nature of a no-alcohol nightclub requires that you conduct some special promoting. Plan to spend approximately ten percent of your projected gross sales for the first year on grand opening promotion and advertising. Schedule your grand opening after you have been open for a few weeks so that you have time to work out major kinks in your operation. There are a number of promotional ideas that you can use to attract customers in the beginning, including discount coupons; premium items, such as tee-shirts and key chains; and door prizes. Also, offer free hors d'oeuvres so that customers can sample your menu.

You will want to advertise in local weekly publications that feature nightlife information. You should also arrange to have commercials aired on radio stations that play the type of music that your club features. Contact the **Standard Rate and Data Service,** by writing **3004 Glenview Road, Wilmette, IL 60091** or phoning **(708) 256-6067,** to obtain market information on publications and radio stations in your area. The advertising representatives for each publication and station will be happy to send you media kits that provide demographics on readership and listenership and reveal ad rates.

Since you are targeting a very specific audience, your promotional and advertising campaigns should emphasize the fact that your establishment is a no-alcohol nightclub. Contact local chapters of Alcoholics Anonymous (AA), offering your club as a meeting site or for holiday parties. In addition, your local AA chapter may publish a newsletter that features advertising. Churches and schools in your area might also be interested in renting your club for special events, which can be scheduled on the slower weeknights.

Use your imagination to create interest in your nightclub, promoting it, for example, as a place to watch the World Series or Super Bowl. Plan theme nights for holidays such as Halloween and Independence Day, or do something a little off-beat and schedule a beach party in January.

You will want to put considerable thought into the creation of a name and logo for your nightclub. Hire a graphics designer if your budget will allow the expense. If you need to keep your costs down, a student at a local art school might welcome the chance to create a design that will be prominently displayed in the neighborhood and might be willing to work less expensively.

INSURANCE AND SECURITY

You will need to purchase business insurance for your club in order to protect your investment from liability, theft, fire, and water damage. You should also install some type of burglar alarm system. While researching the operations of other nightclubs, find out what they are using to deter burglars. Check the Yellow Pages for area installers, who will be able to advise you on what is appropriate for your type of business.

Owning and operating a no-alcohol nightclub is a business venture with many facets to its operation and requires large doses of creative and physical energy. The keys to a successful club are creating the right atmosphere, providing good entertainment, and becoming well known through proper promotion.

SOURCES:

Halloran, James W., *The Right Fit: The Entrepreneur's Guide to Finding the Perfect Business,* Tab Books, 1989.

Kahn, Sharon, and The Philip Lief Group, *101 Best Businesses to Start,* Doubleday, 1988.

"No-Alcohol Bar," *Business Start-Up Guide,* Entrepreneur Group, 1988.

Scarpa, James, "Coping with Neo-Prohibition," *Restaurant Business,* July 1, 1990, p. 145; "Drafts, Carafes & Spirits," *Restaurant Business,* May 20, 1991, p. 201.

Schwartz, Carol A., *Small Business Sourcebook,* sixth edition, volume 1, Gale, 1993.

"Small Business Special Section," *Chicago Tribune,* October 27, 1993.

Walsh, Thomas, "Nightspots Get Mixed News from Amended Rules," *Back Stage,* February 16, 1990, p. 145.

—MARY MCNULTY

Nutritional Consulting Service

Remember the old saying, "An ounce of prevention is worth a pound of cure?" Because of renewed emphasis on prevention, nutritionists are finally being recognized by many health professionals as a necessary part of an individual's overall health-care team. So many illnesses are resultant of poor dietary lifestyles that, according to a 1992 *Consumer Reports* article, eating and drinking habits in the United States have been "implicated in six of the ten leading causes of death—heart disease, cancer, stroke, diabetes, atherosclerosis, and chronic liver disease and cirrhosis." Nutrition counselling, particularly with much of the public's attention focused on the U.S. health-care crisis, is certainly one step in the right direction.

As conventional wisdom advocates the value of good dietary habits, more and more people are entering nutritional occupations, and many experts already in the nutrition and diet planning fields are operating their own businesses. Dietary managers employed in hospitals and long-term care facilities are beginning to see the benefits of working as consultants to the dietary management teams in hospitals, correctional institutions, schools, and other food-service settings. Nutritional consultants and diet planners going into business for themselves have clients that may include individuals, corporations, media, hotels, restaurants, sports or health-care facilities, or food companies. Some set up shop in home offices, while others work from storefronts or use one of their clients as a home base.

Not surprisingly, salaries of diet specialists and other nutritionists, most notably those specializing in the needs of athletes, rose quickly in the 1990s. Educational requirements in the field have not been standardized across the United States, but an understanding of nutritional principles and academic work from accredited institutions will give a new business operator a head start. Capitalizing on trends, some dietitians planning to work in schools or hospitals have been taking extra courses to prepare themselves for more lucrative nutritional fields. As a result, the number of registered dieticians (RDs) doubled from the 1980s through the mid-1990s.

ADA-RECOGNIZED SPECIALIZATIONS

The most widely respected professional organization for this field is the American Dietetic Association (ADA), which sponsors a Dietary Practice Group (DPG) known as Consulting Nutritionists (CN). All of the members of CN are RDs. CN publishes a product catalog and a quarterly newsletter among other products designed to help its members achieve financial and professional success in the field. Also helpful, the ADA publishes several books for those nutritional consultants considering starting a private practice. These include *Reimbursement and Insurance Coverage for Nutrition Services, The Competitive Advantage,* and *Becoming an Entrepreneur in Your Own Setting.*

The ADA lists six categories of dietitians. Business dietitians, who work for food manufacturers and other nutrition-related companies, may develop new products or be in public relations, sales, or marketing. Clinical dietitians work in hospitals, long-term-care facilities, and outpatient settings, with a team that includes doctors and nurses. Community dietitians work for businesses, government health programs, day-care centers, or health clubs, developing food plans for low-income families. Consultant dietitians in business by themselves may work on a contract basis with food companies, clinics, health clubs, or long-term-care facilities. Some also write on nutrition, or speak at professional workshops. Education and research dietitians have advanced degrees and perform research on nutrition. Management dietitians work in food services for hospitals, schools, or restaurants, planning healthy menus and supervising personnel.

FINANCIAL ASPECTS

People who want to open a nutritional consulting or diet planning company must consider certain business basics. Financing must be carefully conceived, with much thought given to fees, marketing, and advertising. A good first stop for anyone considering entering the field is the **Small Business Administration (SBA).** Before approaching bankers or other lenders for financing information, SBA officers can provide information on government loan programs, as well as other sources of financing. They are accessible at **1-800-U ASK SBA.** Affiliated with the SBA is The Service Corps of

PRIMARY NUTRITIONAL ASSOCIATIONS AND ORGANIZATIONS

American Association of Nutritional Consultants (AANC): 1641 E. Sunset Road, B117, Las Vegas, NV 89119; phone: (702) 361-1132.

American Dietetic Association (ADA): 216 West Jackson Blvd., Suite 800, Chicago, IL 60606-6995; phone: (312) 899-0040, or (800) 621-6469. The ADA has many Dietetic Practice Groups (DPGs), including **Consulting Nutritionists** and **Consultant Dietitians in Health Care Facilities.**

Dietary Managers Association (DMA): One Pierce Place, Suite 1220W, Itasca, IL 60143; phone: (708) 775-9200.

Natural Food Associates (NFA): P.O. Box 210, Atlanta, TX 75551; phone: (800) 594-2136.

Nutrition Education Association (NEA): P.O. Box 20301, 3647 Glen Haven, Houston, TX 77225; phone: (713) 665-2946.

Nutrition for Optimal Health Association (NOHA): P.O. Box 380, Winnetka, IL 60093; phone: (708) 786-5326.

Nutrition Institute of America (NIA): 200 W. 86th St. Suite 17A, New York, NY 10024; phone: (212) 799-2234.

Retired Executives (SCORE). Its members provide a wealth of information free to interested consumers across the United States. They have been providing this counseling for more than 40 years. Besides counseling on financial aspects, SCORE members can discuss other business areas such as marketing, management, and long-term planning.

The start-up costs for nutritional consultants and diet planners vary widely. Much depends on the kind of business you want to open. Many nutritional consultants work either out of their homes or in offices affiliated with hospitals or physicians that they worked with before starting their own business. Those who choose to begin their consulting careers working out of home offices usually have very little initial outlay of funds, since in most small enterprises, the single most expensive outlay is for working space.

For those nutritional consultants who plan to rent an office or storefront, it is helpful to take out working capital loans. The payments on these loans usually become one's primary liability. When you approach lenders for business loans, they will ask questions about the type of business you plan to have. Be prepared; you will need a prospective location, a business description, and a resume of your own experience in the field. If you have prospective clients, it is helpful to present a list of these as well.

LOCATION

Nutritional consultants have a wide range of choices in finding a place to work. If space is available at home, the consultant needs to consider the client base. Will clients be coming for consultations? If the consultant will be traveling to meet all of the clients, what is the commuting time to the hospitals, schools, or clients?

Essentially, the ideal location depends on who your clients will be. If an office is a better solution, some choose storefront offices with good visibility and easy access. Others choose mall locations or space in a building with other professionals. If you plan to work with large institutions, a downtown office space gives a professional look that appeals to those in hiring positions at hospitals or nursing homes. If, on the other hand, you plan to reach out to individuals, you may prefer suburban office space located near transportation, with adequate parking available. If your clients are corporate or media related, choose an area where they will find you easily.

Other office spaces to consider are in sports and recreation facilities, health clubs, or health-care facilities; sometimes hospitals have office buildings adjoining them. Some nutritional consultants share space with physicians or other professionals. Shared space offers two advantages: it is less expensive than renting alone, and the consultant may share office staff and supplies costs.

MARKETING

Your location may also help set you up with a network of referrals. In professional buildings and hospital annexes, many physicians establish relationships with dietitians and nutritionists, referring patients to them while the dietitians may send their clients to physicians to solve a medical problem. CN also offers state referral lists as means of obtaining clients.

Most who go into nutritional consulting have experience in the field. They have a sense of demographics of their area; many also come armed with a base of customer support from previous work. The most successful consultants reach out to a specific group. Corporate wellness programs, for instance, may be a target. Nutritional consultants working with corporations may present workshops for employees. Sometimes the workshops are part of a series of health-related speeches or sessions offered at the workplace. Market yourself by preparing a list of topics you could present to the group—about nutrition and health, about shopping for healthy foods while holding a full-time job, or other topics of interest to working people.

Restaurants are another potential source of clients. Many restaurant owners and chefs work with nutritionists to develop health-conscious menus. Consultants work with chefs to create healthy meals and may also work with waitstaff and hosts to help them assist customers who are interested in the nutritional component of their meals. An expert can help the restaurant keep menus attractive, while suggesting alternatives to removing all of a meal's fat, like decreasing portion sizes.

The interest of restaurant owners in the nutritional aspect of their business was demonstrated in the early 1990s. The trade magazine *Restaurant Hospitality* ran an article suggesting that hiring an RD as a food and nutrition expert to modify menus is a financially sound investment. In an unrelated event, a two-day competition paired RDs of the ADA with chefs from the American Culinary Federation. Teams of RDs and chefs worked together to prepare nutritious and good-tasting and appealing foods. Such teamwork is helping both the restaurants and the dietitians in their businesses.

Sports facilities may also be a marketing target. Many have nutritional experts either on site or on call. Customers who use the sports facilities should be informed of the availability of a nutritionist. Good marketing tools are articles in the fitness center's newsletter, posters in exercise rooms and locker rooms, and word-of-mouth recommendations from personal trainers, aerobics instructors, and other staff members facility.

Most large newspapers have periodic health or nutrition sections; television programs and radio shows use experts as consultants too. Nutritional consultants who wish to place themselves as media spokespersons must develop

SELECTED HELPFUL PUBLICATIONS

Trade Magazines:

American Journal of Clinical Nutrition: phone: (301) 528-4000. Monthly medical and nutrition journal.
Eating Well: phone: (802) 425-3961. Bimonthly food and health magazine.
Journal of Nutrition: phone: (301) 530-7050. Monthly journal of nutrition research in U.S. and abroad.
Nutrition: phone: (818) 845-3748. Bimonthly medical journal of applied and basic nutrition.

Directories and Other Publications:

Allied Health Education Directory: phone: (800) 621-8335, or (312) 464-5000. Published annually by American Medical Association (AMA), covering 2,800 health career educational programs.
The Consultant Dietitian: Developing Marketable Skills in Health Care: phone: (800) 342-9678. Business guide published by Food Products Press of Haworth Press, Inc.
Directory of Dietetic Programs: phone: (312) 899-0040. Published annually by American Dietetic Association (ADA), covering about 600 approved or accredited dietetic education programs.
1993 Product Catalog of Consulting Nutritionists: phone: (206) 956-1367. Affiliated with ADA, contains listings of books, teaching aids, videotapes, slide programs, computer programs, and marketing tools for consulting nutritionists.
Opportunities in Nutrition Careers: phone: (800) 323-4900, or (708) 679-5500. Published by VGM Career Books, career opportunities with educational requirements and qualifications needed, includes list of graduate programs and internships in nutrition.

marketing plans that are based on thorough research of local media. If you choose to market yourself to one of these institutional groups, you may also find yourself getting inquiries for private counseling from individuals who use the institutions as well. Your marketing plan should focus on your own area of expertise as well as on the needs of your potential clients.

The competition some nutritional consultants face comes from large weight-loss and diet clinics. While these businesses—many of which are franchises—spend lots of money on marketing and advertising, they usually offer far less specific nutritional benefit than a trained RD can offer. While such franchises as Weight Watchers, Nutri/System, Diet Center Inc., Physicians Weight Loss Centers of America Inc., and other diet companies like Jenny Craig Inc. may aim at the same population, your marketing should emphasize nutritional expertise.

ADVERTISING

In starting your own business, the key to advertising is finding the method that places your name in the minds of potential clients. Become familiar with trade publications, such as the *American Journal of Clinical Nutrition, Eating Well,* and *Nutrition.* Some nutritional organizations also publish their own newsletters, and even if these publications do not accept advertising, you may consider writing informational articles for them. Nutrition for Optimal Health Association, Inc. (NOHA), for example, is a non-profit educational organization in the Chicago area that offers a series of audio and videocassettes for rental. You may want to consider speaking to them, or sampling materials from their educational library.

If you have experience in hospital or long-term-care facilities, physicians can be essential to your network of opening contacts. Hospitals have their own trade publications and newsletters. Similarly, dietary managers should make use of the Dietary Managers Association (DMA) and magazine. Be creative. Some nutritionists advertise in programs for local sporting events. Others, who are more comfortable speaking to groups about helping them plan balanced diets, offer free lectures or charge a minimal fee. The exposure can bring many new clients into your practice.

LICENSES AND INSURANCE

Registered dietitians, dietary managers, and nutritional consultants all have different educational backgrounds. The professional who wants to run his or her own business must be certain that clients understand who they are coming to for advice. For that reason, nutritional consultants and diet planners must obtain and maintain proper licenses. For example, registered dieticians are licensed by the American Dietetic Association (ADA), while dietary managers become certified (CDMs) by passing an exam that covers nutrition, sanitation, safety, personnel supervision, and other

SELECTED COMPUTERIZED SOURCES AND LIBRARIES

Computerized Sources:

Food/Analyst and **SANTE:** phone: (612) 931-9376, or (800) 397-9211. Databases with nutritional information for thousands of foods; corresponds with Department of Agriculture's food database; nutritional breakdowns for nutrients.

Health Index and **Health Periodicals Database:** phone: (415) 358-4643, or (800) 321-6388. Citations to consumer health literature from journals and newspapers.

Nutrient Data Bank Directory: phone: (314) 882-8693. Covers software packages for analysis of nutrient content.

Libraries and Other Sources:

Archer Daniels Midland Co. Library: phone: (217) 424-5397.

Pet Incorporated Corporate Information Center: phone: (314) 622-6134.

Planetree Health Resource Center: phone: (415) 923-3680.

Price-Pottenger Nutrition Foundation Library: phone: (619) 582-4168.

Ross Laboratories Library: phone: (614) 624-3503.

Tufts University Health Sciences Library: phone: (617) 956-7481.

United Dairy Industry Association Information Services Department: phone: (708) 696-1860.

U.S. Department of Agriculture National Agricultural Library Food and Nutrition Information Center: phone: (301) 344-3719.

areas. For certification and licensing requirements, contact the ADA or DMA.

Likewise, make sure to be in accordance with city, county, or state regulations. A law regulating the educational and experience standards of dietitians and nutritionists in the state of New York went into effect in 1993. Insurance requirements for small business owners in this field also vary. When operating out of a storefront or office, it is essential to have proper business license and permits. The process can take anywhere from a few days to a few months. Contact local city or county clerks about processes for obtaining these licenses.

Nutritional consultants who rent or purchase office space should have adequate disaster insurance. Consider general liability insurance and be certain your policy covers the loss or destruction of such property as patient records,

office furniture, and supplies. Those who work out of home offices are usually covered under home-owner or rental insurance. The membership department of the ADA has information on professional liability insurance for nutritional consultants and other dietetic professionals in business for themselves.

MANAGEMENT

Many nutritional consultants work alone after opening their business. For some of them, managing the administrative aspects of their business becomes a burden. If business is good, hiring an administrative assistant is often helpful. Students studying to become dietitians might be interested in working part-time while they complete their training.

Pricing your services is an important management task. Some of your clients may need only one consultation, while other projects may require weekly visits for a few-month period. Other clients will hire you on a retainer basis. A diet planner working with athletes who are training for a specific event or season can perhaps create a plan and implement it in only a few sessions. Depending on the situation, some nutritional consultants bill for their services by the hour, while others negotiate project fees.

Before opening your business, it is important to investigate which of your services for individual patients or corporations are covered by local HMOs and other insurance policies. Health insurance policies were beginning to cover nutrition counseling in the 1990s. Blue Cross and Blue Shield of Western New York, Inc., for instance, was not covering nutrition services in the mid-1990s. Generally, hospital patients receive nutritional consultation as an included cost in the room rate. Medicaid pays for some nutritional consultation in outpatient clinics. Other outpatients pay up front for nutritional consulting and then negotiate reimbursements from their insurers.

Some nutritional consultants have branched out to include food preparation as an option in their program. For a pricing structure, compare the fees of local professionals such as social workers or tutors. Create a brochure that details all of the options for different types of clients. You may consider creating one brochure for hospitals and long-term-care facilities and another for individuals interested in nutrition.

LEGAL OR TAX ISSUES

Nutritional consultants must keep excellent documentation of consultations with clients. Those who work in hospitals have different responsibilities and different procedures than those who primarily work for restaurants or as media critics. In a long-term care setting, for instance, dietary changes prescribed by an RD usually need to be approved by other members of the patient's health-care team, including physicians and nurses.

As small business owners, keeping abreast of taxation policies is very important. Again, SCORE may be a helpful source in understanding self-employment tax, withholding, and other tax questions. CN provides a mentoring system for nutritionists starting private practices, and the mentors are available to help new nutritionists learn the ropes.

COMPUTER ISSUES

For most nutritional consultants a computer is probably essential. Certainly, correspondence and appointments should be kept in computerized format. Also, the nutritional analysis software programs available have become central to the work the nutritionist performs. Databases make accessible nutritional information on thousands of natural and prepared foods. Nutritional assessment software enables a nutritional consultant to determine an adequate program for a client.

Armed with all the available resources, nutritional consulting can be a very lucrative business venture as well as one that truly benefits society at large. The variety of options are virtually endless. And even more encouraging, licensed nutritionists—expecting to be part of the nation's corrective solution—are looking ahead in hopes that the health-care reform package being planned in the 1990s might introduce reimbursements for their services.

SOURCES:

Burros, Marian, "Eating Well," *New York Times*, October 6, 1993, p. C4.

Franczyk, AnneMarie, "Nutritionists, Dieticians Now Need to be Certified," *Business First of Buffalo*, May 17, 1993, p. 6.

Hadfield, Linda C., "A Job With Good Taste," *Current Health*, April 1992, p. 16.

Hawley, Melinda, "Consulting Can Give New Direction to Your Career," *Dietary Manager*, May 1993, p. 8.

Hayes, Jack, "Chefs, Dietitians, Wed Techniques in Contest," *Nation's Restaurant News*, August 10, 1992, p. 7.

Madden, Michael, editor, *Small Business Start-Up Index*, Gale, 1991, p. 51.

Maki, Kathleen E., editor, *Small Business Sourcebook*, seventh edition, volume 1, Gale, 1994, pp. 1313-1327.

Martin, Susan Boyles, editor, *Worldwide Franchise Directory*, Gale, 1991, p. 531.

Mendelson, Anne, "Nutribabble," *The Nation*, June 17, 1991, p. 825.

O'Neil, Molly, "Grocery Wars: Good for You vs. Indulge," *Supermarket Business Magazine*, May 1992, p. 87.

Schroeder, Michael, "The Diet Business Is Getting a Lot Skinnier," *Business Week*, June 24, 1991, p. 132.

Schwartz, Carol A., editor, *Small Business Sourcebook*, sixth edition, volume 1, Gale, 1993, pp. 1226-1242.

Tougas, Jane Grant, "How a Dietitian Can Help Your Menu," *Restaurant Hospitality*, March 1992, p. 58.

Weber, Joseph, "The Diet Business Takes It on the Chins," *Business Week*, April 16, 1990, p. 86.

Webster, Bryce, "Fatten Your Wallet: 4 Weight-Loss Programs," *Income Opportunities*, May 1991, p. 53.

—*Francine Shonfeld Sherman*

Packing/Shipping and Mail Service

How many times have you searched for the appropriate box to wrap a present in, searched again for a carton to put the box in, sealed it, and then stood in line at the post office to send it on its way? Probably more times than you care to think about. And did you notice, the last time that you moved, that grocery stores don't seem to keep large boxes around anymore? Many people encounter the same obstacles daily and the packing/shipping and mail services industry is cashing in. With close to three billion packages shipped each year by the United Parcel Service and another 600 million sent via fourth class mail, you can tap into this market by opening an efficient shop that simplifies and satisfies a variety of customers' packing needs.

START-UP COSTS AND PROFIT POTENTIAL

Depending on the scope of the business, start-up costs can range from $20,000 to $72,000. The Associated Mail and Parcel Centers (AMPC), a trade association for the industry, reports that it is very risky to start such a business on less than $50,000. Much will depend on your rent and equipment costs. To keeps costs at a bare minimum, consider starting your business at a kiosk in a shopping mall and purchasing used cash registers and scales. While some stores report net profits of $100,000 before taxes, the average is closer to $55,000. *Entrepreneur* magazine rates the packaging and shipping business high in stability with low to average risk. Rent tends to be the greatest liability in a packaging and shipping business. Store owners pay about $14 to $20 per square foot of store space.

Before you apply for financial assistance, you will need to develop a business plan to determine how much financing you will require. In this business plan, you should include background information on yourself, a market analysis of the area in which you plan to start your business, projections for income and expenses for the first several years (estimate monthly figures for the first year and then annual figures for the next two years), a list of the similar businesses in your area that would constitute your competition, a detailed marketing plan, and a statement of what you think you can accomplish. The lender will also want to see your personal financial statement and your personal tax returns for the past two years.

Because start-up businesses typically face the most difficulties in qualifying for financing, you may find it necessary to raise most of the money on your own or to seek outside investors before approaching a lending institution. The **Small Business Administration (SBA),** a federal agency, is another good resource for information on where and how to receive financing. SBA can be contacted at **1-800-U ASK SBA.**

DETERMINING THE SCOPE OF YOUR BUSINESS

The central function of your packaging and mailing business is fairly straightforward: customers bring items to be wrapped, packaged, and shipped in boxes that you supply and then pay you to act as a middleman with the larger shippers. Most businesses of this kind also offer other services to increase their profits. The most common is mailbox rental, particularly in areas where the waiting list for post office boxes is long and the market for them exceeds the supply. People who work at home and want a professional-sounding business address, students, and people who travel frequently are among those who are in need of mailboxes. Mailbox rental is a relatively easy process. Customers pay a monthly fee to use your address, with their mailbox number listed as a suite or box number. When the mail is delivered to your store from the post office each day, you sort it into the proper mail slots. Customers then use their mailbox keys to retrieve mail at their convenience. You can also offer package receipt and mail holding services.

Office services such as photocopying, fax transmittal, and telephone answering are also commonly offered by the pack and mail store, as is the retail sale of packing and office supplies, key-making, check cashing, funds transfer, and lamination of cards and documents. You will need to determine the scope of your business before you get started. Do you want to limit your services to packing and shipping? Do you want to offer mailbox rental? Will you offer package pick-up service? By developing a business plan, you will be able to calculate what supplies and equipment you need. Remember that banks will require this information when you apply for a loan.

PRIMARY ASSOCIATIONS AND SELECTED TRADE PUBLICATIONS

Associations:

Associated Mail and Parcel Centers (AMPC):
10701 Montgomery Boulevard, N.E., Ste. C, Albuquerque, NM 87111; phone: (505) 294-6425; fax: (505) 271-2050.

Association of Alternate Postal Systems (AAPS): P.O. Box 324, Millburn, NJ 07041; phone: (201) 376-4996.

Coalition of Non-Postal Media (CNPM): 1013 E. Highway 95, Cambridge, MA 55008; phone: (612) 689-4505.

Publications:

AMPC News and Ideas; Basics of Bulk Mailing; Promoting Your Mail/Parcel Business; Post Office Basics: Associated Mail and Parcel Centers, 10701 Montgomery Boulevard, N.E., Suite C, Albuquerque, NM 87111; phone: (505) 294-6425; fax: (505) 271-2050.
Association of Alternate Postal Systems—Membership Directory: AAPS, P.O. Box 324, Millburn, NJ 07041; phone: (201) 376-4996.

CHOOSING THE RIGHT LOCATION

Choosing the right location is extremely important in the packaging and shipping business. In addition to the amount of visibility your business receives, location will determine rental costs, customer base, and the kinds of services you will offer. You should research your location thoroughly. First and foremost, a package and mailing service should be located far enough away from the nearest United Parcel Service office that the service charge you levy outweighs the gas and time required to drive to UPS.

It is a good idea to gauge the traffic patterns, both foot and automobile, around your potential location. Do this over several days at various times of day. Is the location easily accessible? Is the parking adequate? Customers with packages to ship will not want to walk long distances. Research the history of the location. You will want to know if several businesses have failed at this location. If this is the case, try to find out why.

Pack and mail businesses depend on two types of customers. The first is the residential customer who needs to have items packaged and shipped. The highest volume of this business will naturally occur during the December holiday season. To attract ample residential customers, it is best to be located in a middle- to upper-income neighborhood. Customers with disposable incomes are more apt to purchase gifts and ship them.

The other major users of pack and mail businesses are small business owners who need the convenience of an office and shipping service nearby, but who cannot afford space or equipment in their own stores to handle such things

as fax transmittals, photocopying, and mailboxes. To determine the number of small businesses located in your area, contact the local chamber of commerce, financial institutions and/or newspapers. Look for those types of businesses that are not likely to have shipping departments of their own, such as art galleries, printers, bakeries, advertising agencies, public relations firms, and small manufacturers. The chamber of commerce, local banks and newspapers can also provide information on population trends and buying power. Check the local post office to determine if your area has a market for more mailboxes. The U.S. Bureau of the Census now includes packaging and shipping stores as a separate category on its forms and, as the industry grows, more information will be available on customer bases and locations.

While mall locations provide the most visibility, especially for residential customers, rental rates are very high. Instead, consider a strip shopping center nearby that will benefit from mall traffic. You can also take advantage of the fact that customers are shopping for gifts at the mall and might want to have the gifts wrapped and shipped right away.

In addition to finding the right location with sufficient parking space, you need to find the right type of building. Is the building zoned for your type of business and can you count on fire department approval? Is heat and air-conditioning provided? Will you need to install carpeting? What type and size of sign does the landlord allow? Does the roof leak? What is the cost of burglary insurance at that location? Does the back of the store have a shipping door that is large enough to accommodate the package carrier's truck loading bed? Asking these kinds of very detailed questions before you rent space can help you avoid potential disasters and financial problems that might ruin your business in the future.

SETTING UP SHOP

You will need a minimum of 1,200 to 1,500 square feet divided into three basic areas: a customer lobby and packing room that are separated by a counter, an office, and storage space in the back. Install mailboxes in the customer lobby area and use the walls to display the boxes and wrapping paper that you offer. Mailboxes are available in two styles: lock and key or combination. The lock and key mailbox is cheaper, but you will face the nuisance of lost keys and changing locks for each new customer. If you are planning to install a key machine, this may offset the cost of replacing keys and you will be able to make the new keys yourself. Regardless of which style you choose, you will need to give each mailbox customer a non-copyable key to the front door so that they can retrieve their mail after store hours. To protect your inventory and property, install a retractable metal guard from the floor to the ceiling behind the counter that can be lowered each evening before you leave.

Install a cash register and weight scales on or behind

the counter. A telephone, shipping forms, pens, and pricing information should be within easy reach. In the packing room, which should be visible from the customer area, you will need a worktable and the necessary tools and materials for packing a variety of items. These tools and materials should include 8 to 12 different sizes of cartons, a full selection of gift boxes, plain newsprint and styrofoam peanuts for packing, tissue, shredded newsprint, transparent tape, box-sealing tape, and tape dispensers. Some pack and mail shop owners also invest in a foam-producing machine. During the holiday season, plan to order 30 to 40 percent more inventory than usual and place that order three or four weeks before Thanksgiving.

In the office, you will need a desk, files and a file cabinet, a typewriter and/or computer, and a telephone. A computer is not absolutely necessary for a pack and mail business but it can streamline your operation. There are software programs on the market that are designed specifically for pack and mail businesses. They typically feature UPS and postal rates and delivery timetables, package tracking, weighing and pricing capabilities (you can actually wire your computer into a scale), and account management. You can find suppliers in your local Yellow Pages or contact AMPC. The latter also offers training and assistance in site

FRANCHISE OPPORTUNITIES

American Post 'N Parcel: 315 W. Pondera Street, Suite F, Lancaster, CA 93534-3681; phone: (800) 2-PARCEL; fax: (805) 945-5271.

Express Postal Centers: 2775 44th Street, S.W., Wyoming, MI 49509; phone: (616) 530-9605.

Mail Boxes Etc. U.S.A.: 6060 Cornerstone Court West, San Diego, CA 92121; phone: (800) 456-0414.

Pack 'N' Mail Mailing Center: 5701 Slide Road, Ste. C, Lubbock, TX 79414; phone: (800) 759-2424; fax: (806) 797-8142.

Packaging Plus Services Inc.: 20 S. Terminal Drive, Plainview, NY 11803; phone: (800) 922-PACK; fax: (513) 349-8036.

Packy the Shipper: 409 Main Street, Racine, WI 53403; phone: (414) 633-9540; fax: (414) 633-8567.

Pak Mail Centers of America: 3033 S. Parker Road, Suite 1200, Aurora, CO 80014; phone: (800) 833-2821; fax: (303) 755-9721.

Pony Mailbox and Business Center: 13110 N.W. 177th Place, Woodinville, WA 98072; phone: (206) 483-0360; fax: (206) 486-6495.

Postal, Business, & Communications Centers: c/o Coserco Corp., 2225 E. Flamingo Road, Bldg. 2, Suite 310, Las Vegas, NV 89119; phone: (800) 234-3377.

selection and store set-up. You can reach **Associated Mail and Parcel Centers** at **505-294-6425.**

MANAGING YOUR OPERATIONS

Before you start your new business, it is a good idea to familiarize yourself with basic business practices, such as billing, inventory control, determining pricing, etc. Local community colleges usually offer courses for beginning entrepreneurs.

Another important first step you will need to take is to contact the local United Parcel Service headquarters and ask for a customer supply kit. You will receive instructions on how to schedule your store as a regular UPS pick-up point, how to package correctly, a rate chart, tracking information, and samples of order forms and labels. Your store will be the UPS customer. As such, package tracking or other problems must be handled between you and the UPS. Your customers will not have any contact with the carrier. To become a pick-up center you will be required to sign a letter of agreement, which includes instructions on how to use the UPS name in your advertisements. While United Parcel Service is the most widely recognized package carrier, you can find others in the Yellow Pages.

Familiarize yourself with postal regulations by obtaining copies of the reference manuals for the industry. Three key publications are the *National Five-Digit Zip Code and Post Offices Directory* (**United States Postal Service, National Address Information Center; phone: (800) 233-0453**), the *Domestic Mail Manual* (**Superintendent of Documents, U.S. Government Printing Office; phone: (200) 783-3238**) and *Bullinger's Postal and Shippers Guide for United States and Canada* (**Bullinger's Guides, Inc.; phone: (201) 664-7691**). Study them at your local library before deciding which ones to purchase.

The average handling charge per package is $3; prices can vary, however, depending on whether your customer brings in a ready-to-ship package or you provide the packing materials and perform the labor. Mailbox rental charges range from $10 to $25 per month depending on the size of the box. If you also plan to sell shipping, wrapping, and office supplies, you will need to determine your mark-up percentage. This will be based on the profit margin you want to achieve and what is competitive in your area. Suppliers are a good source to check for the current market rate.

Gift-wrapping prices can range from $5 for a simple wrap with ribbon to as much as $100 for something very elaborate. If you plan to offer this service, it is very important to research the rates at the department stores in your area because competition with them will be fierce. Unless your rates are lower or your wrapping style is unique, it will be difficult to convince the public to travel to another location to have their gifts wrapped. Keep in mind that gift-wrapping is very time-consuming and requires special skills.

You will want to establish a method of invoicing for your business customers and a policy for late or non-pay-

MENU OF SERVICES OFFERED BY PACKING/SHIPPING AND MAIL SERVICE

- Packaging and shipping
- Mailbox rental
- Photocopying
- Fax transmittal
- Envelope stuffing and mail sorting
- Gift wrapping
- Key-making
- Western Union/fund transfers
- Retail sale of office, packaging, and mailing supplies
- Money orders
- Telephone answering service
- Word processing and electronic mail services
- Document laminating

ment. Ask your regular customers for a list of their bank references. You can also check your customers' business and payment records by contacting **Dun & Bradstreet Information Services** at **800-234-3867.** A recommended policy for dealing with non-payment of mailbox rental fees is to send a notice after two months of non-payment stating that the lock will be changed in 15 days if payment is not received. If you do not receive payment within the allotted time, change the lock and return the mail to the sender.

STAFFING YOUR STORE

Initially, the owner or owners of a pack and mail store constitute the staff. This means that you can put in up to 72 hours per week, depending on your store's hours of operation. You will want to be open on Saturdays and have slightly extended hours in the evening during the week in order to accommodate customers who work. These hours also allow you to compete with the post office. After store hours, you will need to update your record-keeping and check your inventory. In the morning, you will need to finish packing any items that were left from the day before. If you find that customers are standing in line frequently, you should consider hiring one or two part-time employees, especially during the busy holiday season. This is particularly important if you are promoting your store as an alternative to long lines at the post office.

Many small business owners are wary of hiring employees, fearing the extra work that hiring and training employees requires as well as the possibility of theft. However, management studies show that you will not advance to higher income and profit levels if you do not free yourself from some of the routine work of your business. If you plan properly, hiring employees can be a beneficial experience which can work to your advantage as the business grows. Have a written job description and a list of the qualifications before you advertise for the position. Although high school and college students might be willing to work for minimum wage, you should offer the industry standard. Once again,

small business courses offered at local colleges will include information on management and employee issues.

As your business expands, you can hire or train an existing employee to be an assistant manager. This allows you to take some much needed time off. An assistant manager should be paid the industry standard and you will have to provide some insurance benefits.

If your business is going to offer package pick-up service, you will need to hire a messenger. Make sure that this person has a current driver's license and a good driving record. Your messenger will need to know the route thoroughly and have a pleasant personality—just as if he or she was working at the counter in your shop.

ADVERTISING AND MARKETING

Advertising will constitute a large share of your initial budget. Plan to spend between $2,500 and $5,000 during your grand-opening period. You will need to flood the area with the announcement of your company name and the services it provides. Emphasize the efficiency and friendliness of your store's service. Have flyers distributed and place ads in the local newspapers and Yellow Pages. Look for other avenues such as putting your business' name on church bulletins or score sheets at local bowling alleys. If zoning regulations allow it, use balloons or other attention-getters to create an awareness of your store.

Obviously, you will want to step up your advertising during the traditional gift-giving periods. However, use your imagination to promote your package and mailing store during other times of the year. Advertize your store's services to students returning to colleges and universities in the fall and winter. Show how you can help customers with odd-sized or shaped items. Offer coupons for discounts or two-for-one deals on your products and services. Throughout the year, use your storefront creatively to promote your business. Make sure your windows are clean and display colorful, attractive signs.

Remember that repeat business is very important for a pack and mail store. Once your advertising has convinced someone to enter your store, make sure they receive the high quality of service and products that you have promised.

OBTAINING LICENSES AND INSURANCE

Before opening your pack and mail store, you will have to obtain a local business license and state and/or city sales tax permits. Visit or call the city or county clerk in your area to find out what is involved in obtaining these documents.

You will need to purchase insurance for your business. If you are leasing space in a shopping mall or strip center, some insurance may be provided by the lessor, but on the whole you should be prepared to provide adequate insurance against theft, vandalism, fire and water damage, and liability.

It is also a good idea to hire an attorney and an accountant who are knowledgeable about your type of business.

They will be able to provide a wealth of information that far outweighs the cost of their services.

EXPLORING FRANCHISE OPPORTUNITIES

A number of pack and mail franchises are available and you should explore these possibilities while you are developing your business plan. Franchise fees average $15,000 with some as high as $19,500. In return, you receive a fairly extensive training program, assistance in selecting a location and guidance in setting up your store. You also can take advantage of national advertising, group rates on equipment, and group discounts from the national package carriers. Some franchises offer financial assistance as well. You may be required to turn over a percentage of your profits (usually about 5 percent of your gross income), so it is important to be aware of what is required before you decide to purchase a franchise.

The market for packaging/shipping and mail service stores is growing. However, the number of franchisors and franchises is also increasing—and squeezing out the independent shop owners. If your choice is an independently owned business, you must research your location thoroughly, plan carefully and employ creative marketing techniques to compete with the large chains.

SOURCES:

Associated Mail and Parcel Centers Fact Sheet, 1993.

Bustiner, Irving, *The Small Business Handbook,* Simon & Shuster, 1989.

"First Class Biz," *Small Business Opportunities,* September 1993.

Gould, Joe Sutherland, "Mail Box Rental," *Starting from Scratch: 50 Profitable Business Opportunities,* John Wiley & Sons, 1987.

Martin, Susan Boyles, editor, *Worldwide Franchise Directory,* Gale, 1991

Packaging & Shipping Service, Business Start-Up Guide No. 1287, EntrepreneurGroup, 1991.

"Packaging and Shipping Store," *111 Businesses You Can Start for Under $10,000,* Bantam Books, 1991.

"Private Mailbox Service," *Entrepreneur Magazine's 168 More Businesses Anyone Can Start and Make a Lot of Money,* second edition, Bantam Books, 1991.

Schwartz, Carol A., editor, *Small Business Sourcebook,* sixth edition, Gale, 1993

Woy, Patricia A., "Packaging Service: Making Money as a Middleman," *Small Businesses That Grow and Grow and Grow,* Betterway Publications, 1989.

—MARY MCNULTY

Party Supply Store

According to the trade magazine *Party & Paper Retailer,* the party supply store is a specialty outlet that has seen tremendous growth in the 1980s and early 1990s. Despite the encroachment of warehouse stores and other off-price retailers who sell similar goods at discount prices, consumers are turning increasingly to the specialists. When people with busy lives want to entertain, they have far less time to plan and prepare their events, and the party supply store is often their first stop. There they can accomplish everything from selecting a color or theme to purchasing invitations, decorations, and paper goods. Though party planning was primarily the responsibility of women in the United States for many years, more men are participating in shopping for parties, and they often feel more comfortable in one-stop party supply stores than in other broad-based stores.

In the years following World War II, as Americans began to celebrate birthdays, graduations, and other occasions without the wartime sense of impropriety, many small party and paper-goods stores opened across the country. Most of these were "mom-and-pop" operations run out of small spaces. In the 1980s and 1990s, the party supply store was increasingly found in spaces ranging from 2,000 to 8,000 square feet.

Because of the demands of dual-career families and overburdened schedules, the convenience of the party supply store has become more appreciated. As a business, the party supply store is adaptable to the changing retail environment. Though technology may change, celebrations of such landmark events such as births, weddings, and graduations are a constant. People choose stylistically different ways to celebrate, but they will continue to plan parties. An increasing interest by consumers in the environment, for instance, has led many party supply store operators to carry more paper than plastic goods. The design possibilities on these paper products are endless, and have enabled stores to increase the color and diversity of their wares. Sales in the field have also grown, averaging above 15 percent annually in the early 1990s.

Aspiring entrepreneurs considering opening party supply stores must consider certain business basics before entering the field. Financing should be carefully planned, even if you plan to buy a franchise. Each store must be managed with thought given to staffing, pricing, marketing, and advertising. Most of all, as the operator of a party supply store, you must be enthusiastic and committed to helping people celebrate their special life events.

COSTS AND PROFITS

Probably the most significant initial investment for a party supply store is rent. You will most likely end up renting rather than owning your retail space. Many party supply store owners take out working capital loans, and the payments on these loans become their primary liability.

The initial investment for a party supply store ranges from $30,000 to $100,000 depending on the type of store, the location, and the square footage of the store. Many owners of party supply stores find that they recover their initial investments relatively rapidly. One of the benefits of operating a party supply store is that your inventory is not perishable and will not be harmed by extended time lapses between purchase and sale.

Before approaching bankers or other lenders for financing information, it is helpful to talk to the **Small Business Administration (SBA).** SBA officers can provide information on government loan programs, as well as other sources of financing, and can be reached by calling **1-800-U ASK SBA.** Another organization, the Service Corps of Retired Executives, or SCORE, is affiliated with the SBA. Its members provide a wealth of free information to interested consumers across the United States. SCORE has been providing counseling for more than 40 years on not only financial matters, but on such issues as store location, marketing, and management.

When you approach lenders for business loans, they will ask questions about the type of business you plan to own and operate. Be prepared to show them a detailed business plan in which you put forth a prospective location, pricing structure, management strategy, possible store layout, and staffing ideas.

It is often helpful to meet with store owners in your area. If there is a franchise you are considering, it is worthwhile to talk with other franchisees. Another consideration in planning a party supply store is the selection of suppliers. While a large warehouse store can fall back on other mer-

FRANCHISE OPPORTUNITIES

Party City: 1440 Route 46, Parsippany, NJ 07054; phone: (800) 883-2100, or (201) 335-8900. Founded, 1986; began franchising, 1989; franchise fee, $25,000; discount party supply superstores measuring 6,000-8,000 square feet; one week of training required.

Party Fair: Pond Road Center, Route 9, Freehold, NJ 07728; phone: (908) 780-1110. Founded, 1983; began franchising, 1987; franchise fee, $24,000; retail party supply store.

Party Land: 44 Second Street Pike, South Hampton, PA 18966; phone: (215) 364-9500. Founded, 1986; began franchising: 1988; franchise fee: $20,000; party supply stores measuring from 2,000-3,000 square feet; two weeks extensive training required prior to opening of unit.

Party World: 10701 Vanowen Street, North Hollywood, CA 91605; phone: (818) 762-7717. Founded, 1979; began franchising, 1987; franchise fee: $20,000; approximately 5,000-square-foot discounter of party supplies; three-week training period required.

Other Franchisors: Paper First/Papertown: 4420 Monroe Road, Charlotte, NC 28205; phone: (704) 342-5815. **Paper Outlet:** 445 Hanover Ave, Allentown, PA 18103; phone: (215) 797-1222. **Paper Warehouse:** 7634 Golden Triangle Drive, Eden Prairie, MN 55344; phone: (800) 229-1792, or (612) 829-5467.

chandise if a delivery fails to arrive on time, a small party goods retailer can suffer large losses in such a case. Suppliers should be investigated carefully by consulting with other party retailers and by asking pointed questions of the suppliers themselves about shipments, billing, and availability of popular merchandise.

LOCATION

Choosing a location for your store is one of the first issues—and arguably the most important issue—you should resolve in planning your party supply business. The volume of traffic is crucial to your business, as is the kind of consumer the area attracts. Pay attention to other key tenants, noting whether or not those stores attract the same consumers that would also shop at your establishment. Try to find a corner lot if possible or a location that is at least visible from the street.

You have many different options in terms of location. Some party supply store owners find that a strip mall is ideal, while others praise independent malls. Landlords may be willing to upgrade store spaces before you move in; others are quite flexible in lease negotiations.

It is possible that a franchisor will help you find a location for your stores. Some will participate in lease negotiations and check for important lease clauses, such as a kickout clause, which allows the franchisee to get out of a

lease contract with a specified amount of notice to the landlord. This is useful in the event that a large, key tenant in a mall or store center decides to leave, or if other conditions change unexpectedly.

STORE LAYOUT AND SETUP

The size of your store is also an important factor to consider. Some party supply stores are as small as 800 square feet, while others are superstores with thousands of square feet. Between these two extremes are sizes that may lend themselves to good profit margins in upscale locations.

In designing your store, keep in mind the clients you will serve. They approach your store when they are planning events. Your establishment should be brightly but tastefully decorated and should make customers feel comfortable, with such amenities as wide aisles and ease of checkout. Party supplies should be organized in a coherent fashion, so that customers can find items quickly. Matching paper goods, invitations, and novelties, for instance, should be kept near each other without the "interruption" of other items. Maintain a brightly lit and clean store and create displays for seasonal merchandise or specials.

Party & Paper Retailer often contains feature articles on store layout. One suggestion for store layout is a design that emphasizes seasonal events. Engaging displays close to the entrance, for example, may encourage a customer who was initially only planning a birthday party to also purchase prom or graduation decorations and materials.

MANAGEMENT, STAFFING, AND INVENTORY

In a party goods store, the staff must be very well trained, enthusiastic, and helpful. Hiring decisions are essential to the smooth operation of your store. Some stores hire part-time employees, while others prefer to keep fewer full-time employees, who often develop a closer relationship to the store and its customers. During the hiring and training processes, emphasis must be placed on customer relations. Make sure your staff greet customers and offer assistance. A good salesperson in a party supply store can easily turn a small sale into a much larger sale by suggesting related merchandise. Also, if there are few customers, workers should be comfortable checking inventory, keeping displays neat, and organizing promotional events.

Management of your staff is critical, and planning should include methods of firing as well as hiring. Most owners and managers of party supply stores spend quite a bit of time in the store. It is usually necessary, however, to hire another manager or assistant manager who can be there when you are not. Develop an outline of training and decide how soon you will have new employees working in the store. Use industry sources to determine payment structures for full- and part-time employees. Again, franchisors often assist franchisees with these decisions and many offer training assistance with on-site help, written materials, and videotapes.

Choosing which products to carry is an essential management decision for the party supply store owner. Many shops experiment with various product lines and stick with the ones that are profitable. Retailers may find it helpful to buy closeouts or rely on suppliers to recommend successful lines.

MARKETING

The entrepreneur interested in starting a party supply store would be wise to do some preliminary market research. A basic understanding of the demographics of an area will help you determine the kind of customer base you want to establish, as well as how to reach that potential clientele. Before choosing what products to sell, you must decide who is going to be shopping at your store. The location of the shop, window displays, and store design all contribute to attracting the right customers and to encouraging those customers to buy.

Some people entering the party supply market target a very narrow audience. Even a small target segment necessitates your store carrying a wide selection of items to be profitable. Working couples, for instance, prefer to spend extra money on paper goods rather than go to the fuss of using and washing dishes. Often, the materials they choose come with matching decorations, which helps them complete their party planning in one store. If your target consumer group does consist largely of two-career families,

research has shown that even matching party sets that are higher priced move well.

You may find it necessary to avoid competition with local drugstores, supermarkets, and discounters by focusing on personalized service. You need to determine what products and services potential customers are not getting at the bigger stores and make them available. Drugstores and supermarkets, for example, generally carry party supplies, but they do not stock a wide variety of patterns. Party supply stores can therefore focus on a significant selection of designs as well as on higher-end goods. If you have a prime location and efficient and knowledgeable salespeople, you are more likely to make a profit despite competition.

In entering the party retail field, some business owners choose to make available additional party-related services. Some offer personalized centerpiece creation, while others have on-staff party planners. Try developing a list of local entertainers for your customers and their parties. Musicians, puppeteers, and magicians will be eager to have your help in advertising, and your customers will appreciate the efforts you make to find them good entertainment.

ADVERTISING

During your first months in business, you might spend as much as two-thirds of your initial investment on advertising. In order to introduce yourself to the neighborhood, advertising investment is essential. Your outlay will be smaller later on, but advertising should remain an item in your spending budget.

In-store promotions can be effective advertising tools. Overstock items lend themselves to two-for-one sales, and merchandise that is out of season can be offered at great discounts. Creative promotions set your store apart and encourage customers to shop often. Certain in-store events may be covered by the local press, providing you with free advertising. For instance, a party supply store might have a party-planning session featuring centerpiece designers or speakers from talent or entertainment agencies.

Local schools, especially high schools and junior colleges, often offer low-cost advertising in their athletic or drama programs. Local newspapers are an invaluable source, as small retailers begin to get their name established among potential customers. It is effective for more-established party supply store owners to go to trade shows and read trade magazines to find out what items are selling and to get tips from colleagues in the industry on advertising techniques.

FINANCIAL INVESTMENT

The typical financial investment for a party supply store varies widely. Differences arise when considering such factors as whether or not the store is a franchise and the size of the space. Franchise fees, which may be between $10,000 and $25,000, are not included in the calculation below.

Estimated Expenses to Include in Computing Initial Financial Outlay:

Rental security deposit: $4,000-$8,000 plus one month's rent

Site improvement: $4,000-$12,000

Equipment: $1,500-$6,000

Opening inventory: $25,000-$62,000

Outside signs: $1,000-$4,000

Grand opening advertising: $1,000-$2,500

Miscellaneous costs: $1,000-$10,000

Total: $37,500-$104,500

LICENSES AND INSURANCE

Before opening a retail store, you must check your city and county regulations regarding business licenses and sales tax permits. Check with local city clerks about procedures for obtaining proper licenses, which can take anywhere from a few days to a few months. Be prepared to discuss a general

HELPFUL PUBLICATIONS

Party & Paper Retailer: 70 New Canaan Avenue, Norwalk, CT 06850; phone: (203) 845-8020; fax: (203) 845-8022. Published by Russell Ward; monthly magazine for retailers, wholesalers, and manufacturers of paper tableware, decorations, balloons, stationery, greeting cards, and other party-related supplies; maintains reprint offerings of articles available for $1.00 each; features trade fair information, retailing tips, supplier information, and industry updates; subscription rates: $33 for one year; $48 for two years; $64 for three years; $4 newsstand.

Party Goods/Gift Store Business Guide: Entrepreneur, Inc., 2392 Morse Avenue, Irvine, CA 92713-9438; phone: (800) 421-2300, or (800) 864-6868; fax: (714) 851-9088. Business start-up guide #1283; features step-by-step instructions for starting a party goods or gift store; includes information on profits and costs, market potential, financing, advertising and promotion, finding the right location, and attracting customers; price: $59.50 with a 30-day money-back guarantee.

Party Supplies Directory: American Business Directories, 5711 South 86th Circle, P.O. Box 27347, Omaha, NE 68127; phone: (402) 593-4600; fax: (402) 331-5481. Directory of party supply stores; contains 8,911 listings of companies, each with name, address, phone number, number of employees, and name of owner or manager; price: $395.

business plan with city or county executives, as some places require such information before granting licenses.

Insurance is also a necessity for retailers. Whether you lease or own your store, disaster insurance can prevent unplanned occurrences from destroying your business. In some areas, flood, fire, and general liability insurance are sold separately. Give all types of insurance careful thought and consider coverage of both the store and the merchandise. Most store owners invest in security systems, and some landlords provide them as a part of the lease.

FRANCHISES

There are several franchise opportunities for those interested in opening a party supply store. Some are exclusively party stores, such as Party Land and Party City. Others, like Paper Warehouse and Paper Outlet, are paper franchises that carry party supplies as well as other paper products. A franchisor may help you make decisions concerning location, setting up your store, and selecting, purchasing, and renting equipment. One important benefit of entering the field as a fran-

chisee is that the franchisor has done research in the field and therefore your store is less likely to fail.

COMPUTER ISSUES

Computerized point of sale, or POS, cash registers have become standard equipment for party supply stores. They are used not only for traditional checkout and payment but also for inventory status maintenance. These registers generally tie into data bases that track inventory and are beginning to use technology that enables orders to be placed with manufacturers when inventory reaches a designated level. Also, as in most retail stores, you will need to buy and use credit card machines.

You may also want to invest in a system that produces computerized greeting cards, which made their debut in the early 1990s. Some party retailers who originally did not stock greeting cards bowed to their customers' demand for them, and others were considering purchase of machines that enabled customers to personalize their own cards.

As the popularity of party supply stores increased in the early 1990s, the prospects for success for the potential business owner were favorable. With a focus on catering to the party planner's needs and an effective means of promoting your enterprise, you could turn a handsome profit.

SOURCES:

Bond, Robert E. and Jeffrey M., editors, *The Source Book of Franchise Opportunities,* Irwin, 1993, pp. 463-72.

Dixon, Ted, editor, *The 1993 Franchise Annual,* Info Press, 1993, pp. 136, 174.

Franchise Opportunities Handbook, United States Department of Commerce, 1991, pp. 260-61.

Liparulo, Robert, "United We Stand . . . Starting a Buyers Group," *Party & Paper Retailer,* November 1993, p. 40.

Madden, Michael, editor, *Small Business Start-Up Index,* Gale, 1991, p. 120.

Maki, Kathleen E., editor, *Small Business Sourcebook,* seventh edition, Gale, 1994, volume 1, pp. 838, 841, 1354-55.

Mariani, Joanne R., "Minding Your P's," *Party & Paper Retailer,* November 1993, p. 52.

Martin, Susan Boyles, editor, *Worldwide Franchise Directory,* Gale, 1991, pp. 500-501.

Michelle, Amber, "Let's Party Creates a Bash That's a Blast!," *Gifts and Decorative Accessories,* March 1992, p. 68.

Shaw, Jan, "Streamers Seeks Venture Financing of 100 New Stores," *San Francisco Business Times,* April 5, 1991.

Swanson, Kathy, "Teaming with Quality," *Special Events,* September 1990, pp. 22-25.

—*FRANCINE SHONFELD SHERMAN*

Personal Shopping Service

As we enter the twenty-first century, the once routine tasks of shopping for groceries, clothing, and gifts are quickly becoming nuisances in our fast-paced society. In the past 20 years, more and more women have entered the work force leaving them precious little time for such errands. A growing senior citizen class means that more people with decreasing mobility need help meeting the demands of daily living. The pressures on small businesses have also increased, and the owner, who once personally chose corporate holiday and retirement gifts, no longer has the time to shop. If you're interested in a small business that can be run from your own home on a part-time basis, starting a personal shopping service is an option you should consider if you truly enjoy such tasks. Shopping expertise cannot be emphasized enough—this business requires "power shopping."

Before you open for business, you'll need to decide what types of shopping services you want to offer. Do you want to focus on clothing and gift purchases? This kind of service requires a good working knowledge of stores and mail-order companies. You should also possess a sense of style, a fairly extensive knowledge of clothing design, and be able to judge the quality of workmanship. Would you prefer to concentrate on grocery shopping? A grocery shopper should be familiar with bulk-shopping programs and have some knowledge of nutrition and food preparation. Do you want to include running such errands as picking up the dry cleaning or mailing packages? Perhaps you want your business to offer a combination of services.

COSTS AND PROFITABILITY

Starting a personal shopping business requires a relatively low initial investment—sometimes less than $5,000—especially if you have room in your home for an office. For this reason, and the fact that inventory is almost completely unnecessary, personal shopping services have a low risk factor. On the other hand, you are not going to make a million dollars overnight. According to the American Entrepreneur Association (AEA), net profits before taxes for a personal shopping service range from $28,000 to $46,000. However, an ambitious person with the creativity to expand the business can conceivably turn a profit of $500,000.

Because three-quarters of your time will be spent traveling, a car or van in good working condition is essential. A vehicle with a high mileage rate per gallon and the capacity for frequent stops and starts is the most economical. If you decide to purchase a car or van specifically for use in your business, explore the possibility of leasing the vehicle. A down payment is not required when leasing, and you can deduct the lease payments from your income taxes. Purchasing a vehicle will constitute your major start-up expense and liability.

In addition to office furniture, you will need a telephone and an answering machine with a beeperless remote feature. The latter is essential because you'll be spending so much time away from your office and you won't want to miss any calls from customers. If you're working from your home, have a separate telephone line installed with a call-waiting option. More telephone lines can be added as your business grows.

Purchase a calculator with a tape and a cash lockbox with compartments for receipts, currency, checks, and charge slips. You might also want to consider purchasing a Polaroid camera. As you get to know your customers' needs and preferences, you will be on the lookout for clothing and gifts. You may find an item that you think would be appropriate, but want to check the customer's opinion before making the purchase. A photograph of the item in question will enhance a verbal description.

A computer is not absolutely necessary for a personal shopping service. If you already own a personal computer, you can certainly put it to good use for record-keeping purposes. However, it is possible to run your business simply with a typewriter and a good filing system.

CHOOSING A LOCATION

Because you will be spending more time shopping than meeting with customers, your business should be located near large retail areas, instead of closer to your clients. However, you will have to choose an area in which to market your personal shopping service. Towns of at least 100,000 residents or those with easy access to a large metropolitan area are the best locations for a personal shopping service.

POTENTIAL CLIENTS FOR A PERSONAL SHOPPING SERVICE

- *Executives*—Gifts, groceries, wardrobe consultation.
- *Senior citizens*—Groceries.
- *Corporations*—Gifts for clients and employees.
- *Brides*—Trousseau planning.
- *Vacationers*—Wardrobe planning and travel needs.
- *Recent college graduates*—Wardrobe planning.
- *Working mothers*—Back-to-school needs, groceries.

Professional, two-income families living in upper-middle-class urban areas or affluent suburbs will constitute your primary market. Not only do these families have the disposable income to pay for a shopping service, they often lack the time to shop for themselves. If grocery shopping will be part of your service, you should also look for communities with a high percentage of senior citizens.

The Census Bureau and the chambers of commerce in your area are good sources for demographic information. The advertising department of local newspapers will also have information on purchasing power in the communities they serve. You will want to check the citizens' degree of disposable income, whether the residences are rented or owned, the types of businesses in which the residents work, age groups, family status, and the types of leisure activities in which the residents are engaged. Look for an area with a high concentration of professionals who own their own homes and travel frequently.

FACILITY

Whether you are going to set up shop in your home or will be renting space elsewhere, you will need a 200- to 300-square-foot space that can be divided into two sections. The front section will serve as a reception area that should be large enough for you and your client to sit and review purchases. Two comfortable chairs and a table that can hold shopping catalogs and double as a wrapping service are ideal. For the most part, you will call on your customers rather than the reverse, but you should be prepared in the event a client decides to drop by to pick up purchases. The reception area should be neat and uncluttered—you want to project a professional and organized image that coincides with the service you are selling. If your work area is messy and disorganized, customers will wonder how you can possibly organize their shopping tasks.

In the space behind the reception area there should be enough room to install a desk, file cabinet, telephone, and typewriter or computer. A bookcase for catalogs and miscellaneous office supplies is also a good idea. If you are planning to work at home, have an electrician check your wiring to ensure that your circuits are not overloaded.

Delivery trucks will need to have easy access to your business without disturbing your neighbors; therefore, if you live in an apartment building, you should consider locating

your office away from home. In addition, if a lack of room in your house or a poor location force you to rent retail space, look for a ground floor spot in a unique place. A converted house or storefront in a strip shopping center with boutique-type businesses are good choices, but avoid shopping malls where rents are high.

PRICING

Personal shoppers bill for their services in several different ways. Some charge a flat hourly rate, which is the most profitable approach for shoppers who also provide wardrobe planning or shop for one customer at a time. If you plan to combine shopping trips, however, it will be very difficult to calculate the amount of time you spent on each customer. The most widely used method is to charge a price-based fee that is calculated as a percentage of the client's bill. For example, you could charge a minimum of $25 for any purchase up to that amount; 35 percent of the total for purchases between $25 and $50; 30 percent for purchases between $50 and $150; and so forth. Grocery shoppers typically charge less because they do not spend as much time researching the purchases. For purchases exceeding $500, you might consider asking the customer for 50 percent of the price beforehand. One drawback to this method is that your profit margin could suffer if a customer prefers discount-priced items. Personal shoppers with a large corporate client base may work on a retainer basis. Others, particularly those who also provide wardrobe consultation, receive a monthly budget from their customers so they can continuously update the clients' wardrobes.

Researching the prices charged by your competition before you determine your rate is advisable. In addition, you will need to calculate your overhead (rent, automobile expenses, utilities, insurance premiums) to determine what you need to make a profit. If you find that your prices are being undercut by a competitor, reconsider your overhead costs and decide whether you can cut costs. Be very careful about undercutting your services—you should treat your personal shopping service as a serious business, not a hobby. You may find that in some cases it is better to lose a few customers than to cut your prices, and consequently, your profits.

Charging a premium for last-minute shopping requests or those that require an inordinate amount of time is not unusual. On the other hand, you can offer discounts for long-term projects or such simple errands as picking up dry cleaning and mailing packages. Be wary of accepting too many simple tasks, however, unless you have decided to make them a regular part of your business because such errands will cut into your shopping time, but yield very little return.

OPERATIONS

Whenever you meet with clients or potential clients, be sure to dress in a professional manner. Your customers will view your image as representative of the services you provide and your ability to choose the appropriate merchandise. The first time that you meet with a customer, you will need to interview him or her extensively. Create a form on which you can record the client's name and contact information and a description of the merchandise to be purchased, making sure to note sizes and color preferences. If you are providing grocery shopping, record brand and portion preferences. You will want to know as much about your customer's shopping needs as possible. Make a file for each customer and add catalog items or sale information that might be of interest to him or her.

You will need to subscribe to a variety of home and fashion magazines and catalogs. Most mail-order companies share mailing lists so that once you order an item from one catalog, you can quite possibly become inundated with catalogs from other companies. Most major department stores also issue catalogs, and you should request that you be put on those mailing lists as well.

Conduct research on the various grocery store bulk-purchasing programs and warehouse clubs in your area. Some chains charge a membership fee, others do not. While it is true that your customers will request specific brand names on many items, you may be able to save money by purchasing such items as paper towels and toilet tissue in bulk.

Plan your shopping trips for weekday mornings because stores are less crowded at that time, and the merchandise tends to be freshly stocked. Make a list of the stores you want to visit and items you need to purchase. Go to the furthest store first, then make your way back to the office. Budget your time wisely by calling ahead to make sure the items you want are available. While you are out shopping, check in for messages several times a day using a telephone credit card to make calls from pay phones. Return calls promptly—this not only lets your customers know that you are working for them, but you might also be able to combine shopping trips.

Grocery items usually have to be delivered to the customer immediately. If you are grocery shopping for several customers at one time, place coolers in your car or van to keep perishable food fresh. Otherwise, schedule times to deliver the items or arrange for the customer to pick them up at your office. Corporate clients can be visited during the work day, but if many of your customers are working men and women, it may be necessary to spend your evenings making deliveries. However, unless you must take advantage of certain sales or need to travel a long distance for a certain item, you should be able to keep your weekends free. When you return to the office, label packages for customers, record the purchases, and calculate your billing. This time can also be used to wrap gifts. Don't forget to budget time for perusing catalogs, clipping items for customer files, and soliciting new business.

If a customer is unsatisfied with a purchase and asks you to return it, never argue. To do so would negate any of

the benefits of your service. If you find that you are spending more time than you planned exchanging or returning items, re-examine your interview process. Perhaps you're not getting enough information about what the customer wants. Try to establish a refund/return policy at the stores you frequent. Because you are a steady customer, it may be possible to even return final sale items. In any event, it is imperative that you always save the sales receipts.

Many customers will want to pay for their purchases and your services with a credit card. Contact your local bank for information on becoming a VISA or MasterCard dealer. If you want to accept Diners' Club or American Express as well, you will need to contact those companies directly.

Checking the credit history of corporate clients or individual customers who contract for large merchandise orders might be a good idea. You can do this by contacting **Dun & Bradstreet Information Services** at **1-800-234-3867.** You can also ask your high-volume customers for a list of bank references. In addition, develop a policy for dealing with non-payment of accounts. For example, set a limit on the number of past due reminders that you will send before making a telephone call to the customer. If the bill remains unpaid, contact your lawyer for the appropriate legal action.

MARKETING AND ADVERTISING

In order to build a core group of clients, a personal shopping business requires an aggressive marketing plan with a clear idea of the intended target market. Once that has been established, you can begin advertising by having fliers printed and sent via third class mail to the homes in your target area; placing fliers on the windshields of cars in the commuter train station; visiting the department and specialty stores with which you plan to do business and asking permission to leave your business cards on the checkout counter; and calling on the local chamber of commerce or other business groups—their members are usually busy professional people, just the potential clients you are looking for. Becoming an active member of the business community is a good idea because it will allow you to increase your visibility as well as meet potential clients. A grocery shopping service can be promoted by leaving fliers on the cars in grocery store parking lots. You will also want to send fliers to retirement homes. Your promotional material should accentuate the time-saving and personalized aspects of your service: emphasize your ability to find unusual and unique merchandise; enhance your grocery shopping service by offering nutritional menu ideas.

Of course, business will peak during the holiday shopping months from October to January. Use imaginative ideas to attract customers during this time, then contact them again during other frequent shopping periods. One personal shopper, who also works as a wardrobe consultant for professional women, invites her clients' husbands to a ''Men Only'' night before the holidays and shows them potential gift ideas that she has chosen according to their wives' preferences and needs. Because many men feel uncomfortable shopping—especially in women's departments—you could also offer your service for birthdays, anniversaries, and Mother's Day. In addition, target women executives who might be interested in having you shop for their children's back-to-school clothes. Promote your services to brides who need to put together a honeymoon wardrobe and new college graduates requiring advice on purchasing work clothes.

EMPLOYEES

Although the reputation of a personal shopping service rests on the talents of the owner, extra help may become necessary, particularly during the hectic holiday season. You can hire a college student with some retail experience to make telephone calls locating merchandise, place catalog orders, pick up and deliver packages, and handle returns and simple exchanges.

If you find that you need an assistant on a full-time basis, hire someone to run the office while you continue to shop and meet with customers. The next step is to train someone to be a personal shopper. Be sure to instill in your employee the same commitment to service that earned loyal customers for your business. Take your assistant to the stores you frequent and introduce them to the salespeople that usually wait on you. Teach them to recognize value and quality. Remember that your employees will represent your company and they should present the same professional, efficient image that you have established.

LICENSING AND INSURANCE

Before you start your personal shopping service, you will need to acquire a license to conduct business. Contact the municipal office in your area to find out what is required. You will also want to secure insurance to protect your business against liability, theft, water damage, and fire. In addition, hiring an accountant and an attorney is always a good idea when you decide to start your own business. The professional advice that they can provide is well worth the cost of their services.

A personal shopping service is an excellent middle-income business venture for someone who likes to work independently and enjoys the retail industry. The personal shopper should always be organized and strive to present a professional image. If he or she can accomplish that, their business will thrive.

SOURCES:

Hausman, Carl, *Moonlighting: 148 Great Ways to Make Money on the Side,* The Philip Lief Group and Avon Books, 1989.

Kahn, Sharon and The Philip Lief Group, *101 Best Businesses to Start,* Doubleday, 1988.

Personal Shopping Service, Business Start-up Guide, EntrepreneurGroup, 1988.

Schwartz, Carol A, "Personal Shopping Service," *Small Business Sourcebook,* sixth edition, volume 1, Gale, 1993

Woy, Patricia A., "Personal Shopper," *Small Businesses That Grow and Grow and Grow,* Betterway Publications, 1989.

—MARY MCNULTY

**Andrew Carnegie Library
Livingstone College
701 W. Monroe St.
Salisbury, NC. 28144**

Private Investigation Service

Private investigators (PIs) have existed in the United States since Allen Pinkerton established the first private investigation service in Chicago in 1850. Hollywood helped create the image of the trench coat garbed "gumshoe" scouring back alleys and seedy motels. And on television, PIs are glamorized, gun-toting individuals who live and work in a state of high tension and danger. In reality, barely ten percent of PIs carry guns, and those that do are generally involved in security or bodyguard work. With the advent of microcomputers, the private investigator is more likely than ever to be an office sleuth, sitting behind a computer or talking on the phone. While there are still PIs who engage in surveillance and go undercover for information, this is no longer the rule. If you are good at tracking down information on a computer and are willing to put in long hours every week, you can begin a private investigative business at a low or quite modest start-up cost. The work is always varied and can be lucrative. A private investigator must be skilled at information retrieval—the real specialty of this profession. To be a successful PI, it is helpful, but not necessary, to have a background in law or criminal justice.

TYPES OF INVESTIGATIVE WORK

Because investigative work is time consuming and complex, most private investigator specialize. Traditionally the main work of the PI was checking up on cheating spouses or lovers. In the mid-1990s, few U.S. private investigators concentrated on this type of work (although it remains the most popular specialty in Japan). Some of the most readily available lines of private investigative work are background screening of prospective corporate employees and bankruptcy investigations. It is estimated that nearly half of bankruptcy filings are fraudulent, and the majority of banks and other lending agencies do not have the time or staff to investigate them all. Private companies have a wide variety of uses for the private investigator, from pre-employment screening, to investigating on-the-job theft or computer fraud, or investigating some aspect of their international operations.

Private investigators may choose to focus on missing persons, including missing heirs, bail jumpers, and recalcitrant debtors. An estimated $25 billion of unclaimed property remains in limbo because of missing heirs. The investigator who successfully tracks down a blood relative of the deceased is entitled to 50 percent of the value of the newly claimed property. Locating a bail jumper—by computer search or by interviewing family members and acquaintances of the accused—often results in ten percent of the bail as payment. As bail can range into the hundreds of thousands of dollars, this area of investigation can prove lucrative. In many instances, the reward of finding a missing person transcends monetary payment, especially in locating a missing child. (Statistics indicate that over two million children are abducted annually—either by a kidnapper or divorced parent.)

Another lucrative avenue is specialization in insurance claims, workers compensation, and liability claims—10 to 15 percent of which are believed to be fraudulent. Such work often involves surveillance, especially photographing the alleged wrongdoer. In addition, doctors sometimes turn to PIs to investigate malpractice suits against them. Many attorneys lean on private investigators to conduct fact-finding searches on difficult cases or to track down a crucial witness. In some instances, PIs take the witness stand. Finally, the federal government occasionally hires free-lance investigators, or independent contractors, for specific assignments.

START-UP COST AND PROFIT POTENTIAL

Most prospective private investigators begin their businesses at home. The advantage to this route is the considerably lower overhead. In addition, unless you are absolutely sure about obtaining enough clients to justify office space, the pragmatic approach is to start your business at home. If you set aside one room in your house or apartment as an office, you can claim these expenses as deductions on your income tax.

Your initial start-up expense will be your office equipment. For instance, a complete office—including a computer and printer, a modem, fax machine, photocopier, business phone line and answering machine, desk and chair, and one or two filing cabinets—could require approximately $5,000. In addition, expenses could increase, depending on what line of investigative work you choose. If you investigate criminal cases, you may have to purchase sophisticated

START-UP GUIDES AND DATABASE SERVICES

Start-up Guides:

Investigator's Data Base and Records Research Training Manual: How to Investigate by Computer (1988): Thomas Publications, P.O. Box 33244, Austin, TX 78764; (512) 832-0355.

Private Investigator Business Guide: Entrepreneur, Inc., 2392 Morse Ave., P.O. Box 19787, Irvine, CA 92713-9787 (1992; updated annually). Exhaustive guide on how to start your own private investigating firm from scratch.

Private Investigation: Methods and Materials (1991): Charles C. Thomas, Publisher, 2600 S. 1st Street, Springfield, IL 62794-9265; (217) 789-8980.

Obtaining Your Private Investigator's License (1985): Paladin Press, P.O. Box 1307, Boulder, CO 80306; (303) 443-7250.

Database Services:

BRS Information Technologies: 8000 Westpark Drive, McLean, VA 22102; phone: (703) 442-0900.

CompuServe: 5000 Arlington Centre Blvd., P.O. Box 20212, Columbus, OH 43260; phone: (800) 848-8199.

DIALOG Information Services, Inc.: 3460 Hillview Avenue, Palo Alto, CA 94304; phone: (800) 334-2564.

Dow/Jones News Retrieval Service: P.O. Box 300, Princeton, NJ 08543-0300; phone: (609) 520-4000.

NewsNet: 945 Haverford Road, Bryn Mawr, PA 19010; phone: (215) 527-8030.

ORBIT Search Service: 8000 Westpark Drive, McLean, VA 22102; phone: (703) 442-0900.

VU/TEXT Information Services, Inc.: 325 Chestnut Street, Suite 1300, Philadelphia, PA 19106; phone: (215) 574-4400.

cameras, walkie-talkies, debuggers, and a cellular car phone, and possibly a camcorder, tape recorder, binoculars, and a gun. These items could tack on at least another $5,000 to your start-up costs.

You might also want to invest in computer software for record keeping. Check your local discount software store for software that will fit your specific needs. There are at least a half dozen software products, priced under $200, that take care of accounts receivable and payable, and payroll. There are also excellent and inexpensive (under $100) software products that help you organize your budget, pay your bills, and compute your income tax.

Regardless of the line of work you select, you must pay for advertising costs, insurance, and electronic data services (although the last cost can be recovered by adding it to your client's fee). Another important item—one rarely figured into start-up costs—is reserve capital to get you through until you have steady business. Consequently, your total start-up cost could range from $5,000 to $25,000, depending on your intended line of work and the amount of equipment you need.

Once you establish your business, you can charge fees from $35 to more than $85 per hour, depending on your experience, geographical location, and success rate. If you choose to work as a free-lance private investigator for the federal government, you can generally charge at the high end of the scale. All of your expenses, such as travel and other miscellaneous expenditures, are charged to your client. As a private investigator, your income before taxes can range from $70,000 to $120,000.

FINANCING

If you cannot rely on your own savings, or on relatives or friends for a loan, the quickest, easiest, and most overlooked alternative is a credit card. If you choose this route, make sure you can pay off your card within six months—otherwise the high interest payments make this alternative a self-defeating one.

If you are unable to finance your business yourself, an advisable place to begin is the U.S. **Small Business Administration (SBA),** which provides invaluable information on diverse aspects of small business practice. The SBA can be reached by calling **1-800-U ASK SBA** or by writing **Small Business Directory, P.O. Box 1000, Ft. Worth, TX 76119.** Local SBA offices are also listed in the ''U.S. Government'' section of your telephone directory. An SBA counselor will sit down with you and advise you for free on how to secure a loan and answer any other business questions you may have. The counselor will guide you through the steps of drawing up an effective business plan. Incidentally, the SBA also lends money, but only if a commercial bank has turned you down. Another resource is your local librarian, who is accustomed to business queries and can quickly point you in the direction of books pertaining to small business loans and operations.

The reason for taking these preliminary steps is that the task of applying for a bank loan can be daunting. Before visiting your bank lender, prepare a detailed business plan describing your business, goals, and ability to attain those goals. You might want to hire an accountant or a business consultant to help you with the statement; though it may cost several hundred dollars, it is worth the expense to have a professional, accurate, and complete statement.

If you are willing to pay additional interest, you can turn to a finance company that specializes in lending to businesses and tends to take on greater risks than a bank. For more information on such companies, contact: **The National Association of Small Business Investment Companies (NAS-BIC): 1199 N. Fairfax Street, Alexandria, VA 22314; phone: (703) 683-1601.**

MARKETING/ADVERTISING

Even if you possess stellar qualifications—for instance, a background in law enforcement—your private investigation business cannot succeed without a marketing strategy. Most private investigators are located in or near cities because of the proximity to potential clients such as lawyers, corporations, insurance companies, physicians, and psychiatrists. Before you open your business (unless you start off with a good roster of clients), you should be listed in the Yellow Pages. Call to verify the inclusion deadline. The name of your business should be professional but also reflect the kind of business you're doing. Yet, for most beginning PIs, a mere listing in the Yellow Pages is not sufficient. Besides advertising weekly in your local newspaper, you should mail

brochures to those in your target markets. You might also try sending in an announcement advertising your services to professional associations in your area.

Word of mouth, of course, will garner most of your business in the long run. Once you establish yourself, advertising will decrease in importance, since your business will largely be repeat referrals. Always be sure that you have plenty of business cards handy. Rather than turn down a particular assignment because it is not quite in your specialty, you might sub-contract it to a free-lance private investigator who can do the job as competently as you would. Part of your marketing strategy ought to be knowing not only your competition, but how your competition may serve your needs.

PRIMARY ASSOCIATIONS AND SELECTED TRADE PUBLICATIONS

Associations:

Council of International Investigators (CII): P.O. Box 266, Palmer, MA 01069; phone: (800) 852-5073, or (413) 283-7003.

International Bodyguard Association (IBA): 9842 Hibert St., Suite 161, San Diego, CA 92131; phone: (619) 674-4840.

International Foundation for Protection Officers (IFPO): Bellingham Business Park, 4200 Meridian, Suite 200, Bellingham, WA 98226; phone: (206) 733-1571.

International Security and Detective Alliance (ISDA): P.O. Box 6303, Corpus Christi, TX 78466-6303; phone: (512) 888-6164.

National Association of Investigative Specialists (NAIS): P.O. Box 33244, Austin, TX; phone: (512) 928-8190.

Publications:

Detective Agencies Directory: American Business Directories, Inc.; American Business Information, Inc.; 5711 S. 86th Circle, Omaha, NE 68127; (402) 593-4600.
CD-ROM Databases: Boston: Worldwide Videotex; phone: (617) 449-1603.
DataBase Directory: White Plains, NY: Knowledge Industry Publications, Inc. (KIPI); phone: (914) 328-9157.
Directory of Online Databases (semi-annual): Gale Research, Inc.; phone: (800) 347-GALE.
Investigators Directory: American Business Directories, Inc.; American Business Information, Inc.; 5711 S. 86th Circle, Omaha, NE 68127; (402) 593-4600.
The Legal Investigator: (National Association of Legal Investigators or NALI); quarterly.
Nine Lives Associates Network: (Nine Lives Associates or NLA); quarterly.
P.I.: (Robert MacKowiak, editor); quarterly magazine.
Protection Officer News: (International Foundation for Protection Officers or IFPO); quarterly.

LICENSES AND CONTRACTS

Only about half of the 50 U.S. states require private investigator licenses. If you happen to be a retired police officer or detective, operating without a license probably won't hurt your business. Investigators from all other backgrounds, however, would do best to obtain a license. Most attorneys will not hire an unlicensed PI, since evidence they gather may not be admissible in court. In addition, a license lends your business credibility. If you live in a state requiring licensing, you will also be subject to a training requirement—usually two to three years or the equivalent number of hours of investigative or criminal justice experience—before you can take the written licensing examination. This training requirement, however, is waived for retired police officers. Once granted, a license is not permanent and must be renewed periodically.

There are books available on obtaining a license that outline requirements and give tips on how to prepare for it. Check your local library or call or write a professional organizations for private investigators. The test is almost always long and rigorous, and the failure rate is high—around 50 percent. If you choose to work as an investigator for the federal government, you also will need to undergo a security clearance. A "top security" clearance requires many months to complete.

Contracts are always required between you and your clients. These are legally binding, and almost always contain a confidentiality clause that prevents you from publicizing your case. Most PI contracts request prepayment of up to half of their anticipated costs and a retainer fee. The client, in turn, may demand that you regularly inform him or her of your progress on the case. The contract must state that if no results are produced, the client is still obligated to pay the stated amount. Several books on private investigative work contain sample contracts that can give you an idea of the kind of contract required. You should also have a lawyer peruse all of your contracts and other documents.

EMPLOYEE HIRING AND OFFICE MATTERS

It is possible, and often desirable, to work at home, considering the long and often odd hours that you will put into your cases. Initially, and probably for the entire first year in business, you will work by yourself to keep down costs. Because of the great demand for private investigative work, you may eventually need help. Hiring an employee entails a whole new set of problems and requirements. Once you have made up your mind to hire, bear in mind the need for a proper job description and the multitude of forms that you will have to fill out: tax forms, workman's compensation, social security and wage forms.

Many private investigators are fortunate to start off their business with a partner, so that training is unnecessary. If you are the sole owner of your business, securing an untrained employee will be easier than finding a trained one. The difficulty will lie in finding the time to train this employee since you would eventually want him or her to be licensed. Unfortunately, there are no schools offering courses in investigation. Until you are very firmly established in your business, you might instead subcontract your work to a free-lance PI, at a markup to the customer, and resort to temporary employment agencies for your clerical needs.

If you intend to open an office rather than work from the home, it should be as simple and inexpensive as possible, since you will most often end up visiting your clients at their homes and offices. You should check with your county about the zoning laws of the neighborhood. Make sure your lawyer reviews the lease before you sign it, and find out what kind of insurance the owner of your building has, or lacks. That will help you in determining your own insurance needs.

ON-LINE DATABASES

It used to be that the PI, or "gumshoe," would spend hours or days seeking records and information on a case. Nowadays, this can be reduced to a matter of minutes, with the right on-line databases at your fingertips. With a modem attached to your computer, and with access to the major on-line commercial databases, thousands of public records and current names and addresses can be brought up immediately.

While searching records via computer can cost hundreds of dollars a month, this charge is always passed on to the client.

SOURCES:

Blackwell, Gene, *The Private Investigator,* Security World Publishing Co., 1979.

Crabtree, Penni, "Move Over, Sam and Sherlock: Detectives Are Turning High-Tech," *San Diego Business Journal,* October 12, 1992, p. 1.

Green, Marilyn, *Finder, The True Story of a Private Investigator,* Crown, 1988.

Hill, Robin Mackey, "Private Eyes Dig Up Dirt for Law Firms (Private Investigators)," *Alaska Business Monthly,* March 1993, p. 24.

Hutchinson, Ty, "Private Eyes Can Help Battle Fraud (Auto and Workers' Comp Claims)," *National Underwriter,* May 3, 1993, p. 9ff.

Kabay, Mitch, "It Pays to be Paranoid When You're Hiring," *Computing Canada,* April 26, 1993, p. 21.

MacHovec, Frank J., *Security Services, Security Science,* C.C. Thomas, 1992.

MacHovec, Frank J., *Private Investigation: Methods and Materials,* C.C. Thomas, 1991.

Make $100,000 a Year (and More) as a Private Investigator, 1994.

"Private Investigating," *Entrepreneur Magazine's 111 Businesses You Can Start for Under $10,000,* Bantam Books, 1991, pp. 237-239.

Noel, Lorna Johnson, "Entrepreneurs: Private Investigators Specialize in Paper Chase," *Miami Review,* May 3, 1993, p. 1.

Queenan, Joe, "Uncle Sam's Private Eye: Peter Peterson is Murder on S&L Scamsters," *Barron's,* March 15, 1993, p. 15ff.

Romine, Linda, "Master Sleuth: Missing Children Are His Quarry," *Memphis Business Journal,* October 14, 1991, p. 1.

Shellum, Bernie, and Barbara Demick, "Lowly Gumshoe's Legwork Uncovered BCCI Scandal Ahead of Feds," *Journal of Commerce and Commercial,* August 21, 1991, p. 14A.

Thomas, Ralph D., *How to Find Cases Anywhere: PIs Guide to Obtaining Cases, Obtaining Free Publicity and Marketing Investigative Services,* Thomas Publications, 1988.

Thomas, Ronald L., "How to Pick a Private Investigator," *Security Management,* June, 1991, pp. 64-67.

Woy, Patricia, "Private Investigator," *Small Businesses That Grow and Grow and Grow,* Betterway Publications, 1989.

—*Sina Dubovoj*

Recycling Consultant/Broker

As the saying goes: "One person's trash is another person's treasure." These words ring especially true in the late 20th century, and they hold the key to a burgeoning new industry filled with opportunities. Finding innovative ways to reduce and reuse waste in this throwaway society is big business. By going into business as a recycling consultant/broker, you might be able to find a profitable niche in helping businesses and governments grappling with a trash problem that is out of control.

We now refer to it as recycling, but the concept of reusing what we throw away has been around for centuries. The peddlers and junkmen of yore collected scrap, paper, wood, old books—practically anything—and sold it on the open market to be reused. In fact, paper in the form of textile fiber was recycled from as far back as the 17th century until the mid-19th century before wood pulp was used.

However, the 20th century gave birth to a consumer society hungry for material possessions. Cheap, mass-produced, disposable products and packaging items became ubiquitous in the late-20th century—until we started running out of places to throw away our junk. Overflowing landfills and pollution have prompted changes in the way we handle our garbage. It is estimated that by the year 2000, more than half the nation's landfills will reach capacity. Burying it will soon be out of the question. Incineration, which causes possibly even more harmful air pollution, is no longer tolerated by most communities; neither is flushing waste out to sea. Recycling is no longer regarded as a fad favored by hippies and "back-to-nature" advocates, but as one of the few viable and acceptable ways to reduce waste and conserve resources. In the 1990s, recycling is a $1 billion to $2 billion business that has created a variety of business opportunities.

But trash these days is much more complex than textile fiber paper scraps, precious metals, glass, and wood. Now there are plastics, toxic chemicals, motor oil, toner cartridges, tires, and machine parts to reuse. Recycling is becoming more complex and technical; the person who becomes a recycling consultant/broker will need to have the technological know-how to resolve the waste crisis for companies.

Recycling know-how is constantly evolving because it is based on market forces. Businesses often do not have the workforce to devote to developing a full-scale, viable recycling program. The entire process involves several steps: recyclable waste is collected, then separated and processed into a reusable form—that is, if it can be reused by consumers again. Otherwise, it stays trash, and that's the problem. There has to be a demand for recycled products or it won't be recycled. Thus, even waste that is designated for recycling often ends up in a landfill anyway, at a growing expense that is felt by every government, taxpayer, business, and consumer throughout society. According to Gustav Berle in *The Green Entrepreneur,* recycling is cheaper than throwing garbage away: "It costs $50 a ton to bury our garbage in a landfill, and as much as $75 a ton to incinerate it. Recycling's bill is $30 a ton."

Though many businesses perform both consultancy and brokerage functions, it is important to distinguish between the recycling consultant and the recycling broker. The recycling consultant is involved in helping clients dispose of their trash in an economical manner by finding people who will process it and, ultimately, *use* the recycled material. Part of the consultant's job is to educate consumers to repurchase recycled products. These entrepreneurs also make cash from trash by providing businesses with solutions to their waste disposal problems. Many of those currently in the field have some recycling background. As consultants, they must be objective in how they select appropriate recycling programs for their clients. It is their job to implement profitable in-house programs, negotiate payment for recyclable materials with local processors and recycling collection companies, and encourage others to purchase materials once they have been recycled. Recycling consultants are paid on an hourly or daily basis and do not receive commissions for selling recycling programs.

Recycling brokers, on the other hand, actually *purchase* waste products at one price and then sell them at a higher price to earn their profit. They need a larger cash investment when starting up because they deal in large quantities of waste. According to Gina M. Farrell in *Entrepreneur* magazine, profit margins for recycling brokers is "relatively low," ranging from five cents to 30 cents on the dollar. Rarely do they take a percentage of the deal, or "cut," for arranging deals between clients. Recycling brokers provide a valuable service because they have an active

INDUSTRY STATISTICS

- *Garbage Disposal Costs as Much as the Police:* The average U.S. city spends as much on its waste disposal as it does on its police department year to year (source: *Newsweek*).
- *Landfill Space Running Out:* More than half the nation's existing landfills are expected to reach capacity before the year 2000 (source: *25 Hot Businesses for the Nineties,* EntrepreneurGroup, 1992).
- *People Make Trash:* A company with 120 employees who generate only .5 pounds of waste paper per person each day will have generated nearly 500 pounds of waste in eight working days or a full ton of garbage in less than five weeks (source: *25 Hot Businesses for the Nineties,* EntrepreneurGroup, 1992).
- *Four Pounds Per Person Every Day:* Every American generates about 4 pounds of waste a day, according to the Environmental Protection Agency. Less than 15 percent of this amount is currently recycled (source: *Entrepreneur,* 1991).
- *Environment Top Concern Among Americans:* A 1990 Gallup poll indicated that Americans consider the environment the third most important noneconomic crisis facing the United States after drug abuse and poverty and homelessness (source: *Entrepreneur,* 1991).
- *Landfills Cost:* Opening up a new landfill takes an investment of $2 million to $4 million, or four times what it cost in 1980 (source: *The Green Entrepreneur,* 1991).

network of contacts in the industry and the finances to successfully market reusable materials. In a sense, they have taken the profession of the junkman/peddler to a more sophisticated level.

It is possible to aspire to combine both a recycling consultancy and a brokerage as long as each function is performed independently. Consultants help their clients get the most money for their waste and brokers make their money by actually buying that waste—then turning around and selling it. Some consultants do earn a percentage of the profits from selling recycled products if their specific program succeeds. However, you would not be in business very long if, as a consultant, you bought your client's garbage at one price, then donned your broker's hat and sold it at a higher price for profit.

FINANCIAL ASPECTS

As a recycling consultant, start-up costs can be kept to a minimum because you will not need to invest so heavily in office equipment and supplies. The average office will have a staff of two persons. However, brokers, as stated earlier, will need more of a cash investment since they are in the business of buying and selling waste materials at a slightly higher price. The minimum start-up investment for a recycling broker is about $46,000; the average is $80,000.

Your office inventory will consist of a good computer and printer, fax machine, phones, photocopier, answering machine, office furniture, letterhead, business cards, and sales promotional materials. According to *Entrepreneur*

magazine's *25 Hot Businesses for the Nineties,* some recycling consultant/brokers use audio-visual presentations or rent videos on the environment as part of their sales presentations.

Before mapping out your office, consider the costs. You may elect to establish your own home office, which will eliminate the need to rent office space. If you do, install separate phone lines for your business and fax machine. Also check with your community zoning laws regarding operating a business out of your home. The more income you want to generate, the more you will spend on start-up costs, which will include staff salaries.

In terms of an initial investment, generally consultants can start with as little as $8,000. The average start-up cost for consultants is about $18,000. If you need help securing a business loan, contact your banker or obtain free advice on loans and business plans provided by the Service Corps of Retired Executives (SCORE), or the **Small Business Administration (SBA).** The SBA has created the Pollution Control Loan Program, which provides financing for small businesses that plan, design, and install pollution-control facilities. For more information on the Small Business Administration, contact the agency at **1-800-U ASK SBA**; the SBA Pollution Control Loan Program at **(202) 205-6552;** or write: **Small Business Directory, P.O. Box 1000, Ft. Worth, TX 76119.**

PROFIT POTENTIAL

Consultants earn as much as $70,000 or more before taxes, but the average income before taxes is around $42,000. But with the valuable knowledge recycling consultant/brokers have, profit potential is much higher. Consultants can charge as much as $50 to $100 an hour for their services. A person entering this profession can earn an average of $110,200 before taxes, a 137 percent return on the typical initial investment. The highest net profit before taxes is around $550,000.

MARKETING STRATEGIES

Networking with scrap processors, manufacturers, brokers, mills, and other recyclers in the industry will be the best way to keep in touch with your markets and make a name for yourself and your business. In fact, much of your time will be spent establishing contacts with organizations that have been doing business for years. You'll also need to do your research to stay abreast of all the changes in the recycling field. Once you solidify these relationships, your business can get underway.

Recycling, when profitable, generates a steady cash flow. Consider John Fearncombe, president of his own company, Bottom Line Consulting Inc. of Lake Barrington, Illinois. His firm serves the plastics and recycling industries by helping them separate plastics for recycling. His company also provides market-based programs and seminars, environmentally friendly product/package designs, and environmental risk assessments for clients. Fearncombe initially left the corporate world to start consulting in plastics recycling because he saw an opportunity to use his background in chemical engineering and resins to resolve ways of recycling plastic.

"The biggest problem is identifying markets for plastic," Fearncombe says. "A lot of people ask me, why don't you go into paper recycling? Well, I don't have the experience in that. And I suggest that if you're going to consult on something, you better have experience because when you're meeting with a company president, he can pick you apart pretty quick."

Fearncombe's extensive education no doubt smoothed his transition to the recycling industry. He has a master's in business administration, degrees in chemical engineering, and work experience with companies that manufacture food containers. He credits his master's in business administration with teaching him about marketing. "As a consultant, you've got to look for a niche, otherwise you end up in a competitive bidding process," he says. "There's money to be made, but if you don't know what you're doing, you'll lose money. Make sure there's a market for what you're selling and develop your network of contacts from day one. This type of consulting job takes a lot of commitment. It's not a part-time job."

MAJOR RECYCLING MARKETS

By the early 1990s, practically every state and municipality was implementing laws governing waste disposal and recycling. Potential markets exist anywhere enough trash or surplus material is being produced. That means your target markets could be virtually any organization, provided it produces enough quality recyclable materials. How do you narrow your potential client list so that it is manageable and

PRIMARY ASSOCIATIONS

National Recycling Coalition: 1101 30th St. NW, Ste. 305, Washington, DC 20007; phone: (202) 625-6406; fax: (202) 625-6409.

Institute of Scrap Recycling Industries: 1627 K St., NW, Ste. 700, Washington, DC; phone: (202) 466-4050; fax: (202) 775-9109.

National Association of Chemical Recyclers: 1875 Connecticut Ave., NW, Ste. 1200, Washington, DC; phone: (202) 986-8150; fax: (202) 986-2021.

Recycling Legislation Action Coalition: c/o Richard D. Wimberly, 177 Winthrop Road, Apt. 1, Brookline, MA 02416; phone: (617) 232-9038.

Steel Can Recycling Institute: Foster Plaza X, 680 Anderson Dr., Pittsburgh, PA 15220; phone: (412) 922-2772, or (800) 876-7274; fax: (412) 922-3213.

profitable at the same time? According to *Entrepreneur* magazine's *25 Hot Businesses for the Nineties,* "recycling consultants are most useful and effective in implementing profitable programs for organizations with 250 or more people."

Entrepreneur also cites the following key target markets for recycling consultants: Fortune 500 companies; utilities; government offices; non-profit agencies; hospitals; hotels; retirement communities; universities; defense and aerospace plants; real estate developers; high-rise office buildings; theme parks; stadiums; convention centers; and manufacturing plants. For information on local recycling opportunities for entrepreneurs, the *Directory of Local Governments' Recycling Practices* can be obtained for $10 from **The Council of Governments, 777 N. Capitol St., Washington, D.C. 20002.**

The markets for recycling brokers include scrap processors, paper mills, and manufacturing plants. Brokers acting as go-betweens between buyers and sellers of waste and scrap will have to diligently watch supply and demand for certain products. Therefore, brokers should be knowledgeable about several different products and their prices on the market.

As noted previously, it is not only necessary that consultants and brokers can find and recycle waste products—there also must be a market for the recycled material that is the end product. The recycling of post-consumer plastic containers—from one-liter pop bottles to high density plastic milk jugs—is hot, thanks to the work of entrepreneurs who practically initiated recycling of these materials into useful products that had a market, such as lumber-type products, carpeting, piping, plastic grocery bags, and clothing. Polystyrene food packaging (egg cartons, plates, fast food packaging), are also gaining in recycling popularity. And entrepreneurs are finding a profitable market for mixed plastics, according to *In Business* magazine.

Other opportunities exist in the following materials (which is not an all-inclusive list), according to Gustav Berle in *The Green Entrepreneur:*

• **Glass**—New technology is making glass recycling more efficient. Berle states that in 1989, more than 5 billion glass bottles and containers were recycled into new ones.

• **Steel**—New techniques have enabled this metal to be recovered and recycled efficiently and cleanly.

• **Motor Oil**—Efforts are underway to step up recycling of this product, which, until recently, was often dumped into sewage systems where it pollutes underground water sources. Recycling old oil is likely to be profitable as oil prices escalate.

• **Chemical Products**—Automatic transmission fluid, batteries and battery acid, diesel and motor fuels, fuel, dry cleaning solvents, paints and solvents, kerosene, and gun cleaners.

SELECTED TRADE PUBLICATIONS

Fibre Market News: G.I.E. Publishing, 4012 Bridge Ave., Cleveland, OH 44113; phone: (216) 961-4130.

Flashpoint: National Association of Chemical Recyclers, 1875 Connecticut Ave. NW, Ste. 1200, Washington, DC 20009; phone: (202) 936-8150; fax: (202) 936-2021.

Gildea Review: Community Environmental Council, 930 Miramonte Dr., Santa Barbara, CA 93109; phone: (805) 963-0583; fax: (805) 962-9080.

The Plastic Bottle Reporter: Plastic Bottle Information Bureau, 1275 K St. NW, Ste. 400, Washington, DC 20005; phone: (202) 371-5244.

Plastic Waste Strategies: Washington Business Information, Inc., 1117 N. 19th St., Ste. 200, Arlington, VA 22209-1798; phone: (703) 247-3424; fax: (703) 247-3421.

Plastics Recycling Report: Plastics Recycling Institute, Rutgers University, P.O. Box 1179, Piscataway, NJ 08854; phone: (908) 932-1766.

Recycling Technology Reports: CAE Consultants, Inc., 41 Travers Ave., Yonkers, NY 10705; phone: (914) 963-3965.

Recycling Today: G.I.E. Publishing, 4012 Bridge Ave., Cleveland, OH 44113; phone: (216) 961-4130.

Recycling Update: Update Publicare Co., Prosperity & Profits Unlimited, P.O. Box 570213, Houston, TX 77257-0213; phone: (713) 867-3438.

Resource Recovery Report: Frank McManus, 513 38th St., NW, Washington, DC 20015; phone: (202) 362-3034; fax: (202) 362-6632.

Resource Reycling: Resource Reycling, Inc., P.O. Box 10540, Portland, OR 97210; phone: (503) 227-1319; fax: (503) 227-6135.

Reuse/Recycle: Technomic Publishing Co., Inc., 851 New Holland Ave., P.O. Box 3535, Lancaster, PA 17604-3535; phone: (717) 291-5609; fax: (717) 295-4538.

FRANCHISES

Meg Whittemore in *Nation's Business* describes franchising in the environmental protection industry as "one of the strongest-running currents of the 1990s." Recycling franchises are a part of this trend of new businesses that are "meeting consumers' changing preferences with innovative products and services."

Python Recycling of St. Cloud, Minnesota, for example, has operated five recycling franchises since 1989 that conduct collection and redemption of waste products throughout the state. Waste haulers deliver curbside collections to Python, or Python comes to the consumer in the form of accessible drop off sites, according to company president and owner Stuart Hamilton. These sites handle aluminum can, nonferrous metals, glass, plastic bottles and jugs, newspapers, cloth, and office paper collections for recycling. Franchisees are trained in marketing and accounting and sell collected materials through Python's network of buyers or others for a royalty fee of $2 per ton. The idea, Hamilton told *Nation's Business,* is to "make the franchise worth something and make it convenient."

Start-up costs for such an enterprise ranges from $12,000 to more than $50,000, depending on the size of the center. Plans were underway to establish Python franchises in other states. Hamilton told *Nation's Business* that his company was interested in working with entrepreneurs who had enough capital to start their own processing centers.

ADVERTISING

Once you target your markets, you can approach them either by direct mail or by cold calling. Cull business relationships through your local Chamber of Commerce and via networking. Most of your business will probably be generated by referrals and how well you sell yourself on your sales presentation. Always try to contact company presidents or building engineers in charge of waste disposal. Your sales promotional material should include your qualifications, your specific area of expertise (i.e., paper, plastics, etc. recycling), and solutions you've provided for current and past customers.

RISK MANAGEMENT

Other than a business license, recycling contractors and brokers will not need licenses to work in the recycling industry. Establishing a good reputation is important. You may want to investigate being certified or obtaining college degrees in chemical engineering, environmental science, or related academic subjects to demonstrate your credibility. As Farrell writes in *Entrepreneur:* "Anyone willing to visit recycling plants, study the markets, and keep up on environmental and recycling issues has a chance to make it."

SOURCES:

Berle, Gustav, *The Green Entrepreneur,* Liberty Hall Press, 1991.

Churbuck, David, "Consultant in a Bind," *Forbes,* November 13, 1989, p. 285.

Farrell, Gina M. "Spinning Garbage into Gold: Trashing In," *Entrepreneur,* February 1991, pp. 146-53.

Glenn, Jim, "Proving Ground for Entrepreneurs," *In Business,* March/April 1990, p. 32.

Glenn, Jim, "Plastics Recycling Moves Ahead," *In Business,* January/February 1991, p. 42.

"Recycling Consultant/Broker: Spinning Garbage into Gold," *25 Hot Businesses for the Nineties,* EntrepreneurGroup, 1992.

Rose, Ronit Addis, "EcoPreneurs: Turn Your Business into a Lean, Green, Profit Machine," *Success,* October 1990, p. 51.

Whittemore, Meg, "The Adaptable Enterprise," *Nation's Business,* November 1990, p. 47.

Williams, Susan, *Trash to Cash,* Investor Responsibility Research Center, 1991.

—EVELYN S. DORMAN

Security Systems Service

The Federal Bureau of Investigation (FBI) reported 13 million property crimes in 1991. One of every 20 homes was burglarized, with an average property loss of $1,281. Approximately three million burglaries—one every ten seconds—are committed each year. Given such figures, it is not surprising that more and more Americans are investing in security systems and that increasing numbers of entrepreneurs are riding the wave to make an honest dollar off crime.

The security systems industry covers a wide range of services beyond burglary and robbery control. Other services include entry monitoring, central switchboard monitoring services, medical and other alert services, energy use monitoring, and fire-related services, such as smoke detection, sprinkler, and extinguisher maintenance. While different companies may specialize in different combinations of these services, the principal focus is usually on theft protection. The small businessperson new to the industry will most likely start out installing electronic security alarm devices of one sort or another.

Focusing business on burglary and robbery control does not mean limiting business. Within the rapidly growing field of security systems, burglar alarm installation has become not only the fastest growing segment, but the most profitable as well. While the bulk of business for security devices falls in the commercial and industrial sectors, the largest rate of growth in that area shifted to home sales (individual consumers) starting in the 1980s. From the late 1980s to early 1990s, the number of U.S. homes with some form of electronic security system jumped by nearly 40 percent; by 1993 approximately one in six homes was protected electronically, according to Dolores Kong in the *Boston Globe*. Over that same period, the average price of a security system dropped by 30 percent, bringing costs within reach of middle-class Americans, according to statistics compiled by J.P. Freeman & Co., a Connecticut security industry research firm. Lower costs reflected tighter competition as well as new technology, which made security systems less obtrusive, easier to use, and less expensive. *Entrepreneur* estimated the yearly rate of growth for the alarm industry at roughly 15 percent, attributing a good portion to the residential market.

For the small businessperson interested in security systems service, the industry offers an upward growth curve and an exciting variety of services to accommodate a growing customer base. Moreover, this sales-and-service business requires minimal facility and personnel in the initial phase, relatively little start-up capital, and background skills that can be easily trained and/or acquired in the field. Partly because of these benefits, the industry does have its drawbacks: 30 to 40 percent of all alarm dealers fail each year. Yet, with careful planning and perseverance, an entrepreneur in security systems services can make crime pay.

COSTS AND PROFITS

One of the main advantages of the securities systems service business is that it is perfectly suited for the sole proprietor to start single-handedly. Profits can start rolling in immediately after the first sale. Minimum start-up costs run in the neighborhood of $5,000 with average costs hovering around the $30,000 mark. Some established direct sales organizations report yearly profits before taxes between $40,000 and $50,000. Organizations at the high end have reported net profits of $100,000. The primary liabilities of a security systems business include the standard accounts payable and working capital loans. Most operations install the alarms they sell and thereby absorb equipment costs into the income of retail sales (and installation fees). Additional installation work is generally done on a contract basis for alarm systems that the client may purchase from another source. Alarm system inventories generally vary between $2,500 and $20,000, depending on the size of the operation and the types of security systems to be serviced. In addition, retail walk-in trade is of little importance, making a home or existing business office perfectly suitable for start-up or even permanent operations. Thus, monthly office rental expenses—common to most other small businesses—can be deferred until (if ever) more space is required for sales staff, inventory, or permanent display space.

FINANCING

As in any small business venture, one of the most bewildering yet essential steps is raising start-up capital. Invaluable pre-financing information is available from the professional associations and trade publications catering to the security

PRIMARY ASSOCIATIONS AND SELECTED TRADE PUBLICATIONS

Associations:

American Society for Industrial Security: 1655 N. Fort Myers Dr., Ste. 1200, Arlington, VA 22209; phone: (703) 552-5800.

Committee of National Security Companies (CONSCO): 2714 Union Ave., Extended, Ste. 310, Memphis, TN 38112; phone: (901) 323-0173.

Locksmith Security Association: 200 S. Washington, Royal Oak, MI 48067; phone: (313) 589-0318.

International Association of Professional Security Consultants (IAPSC): 13819-G Walsingham Rd., Ste. 350, Largo, FL 34644; phone: (813) 596-6696.

International Security Management Association (ISMA): Deere & Co., John Deere Rd., Moline, IL 61265-8661; phone: (309) 765-4987; fax: (309) 765-5772.

Private Security Liaison Council: P.O. Box 2255, Jackson, MS 39205; phone: (601) 948-55424

Security Equipment Industries Association: 2800 28th St., Santa Monica, CA 90405; phone: (213) 450-4141

Publications:

Computer Security Alert: Computer Security Institute (CSI), 600 Harrison St., San Francisco, CA 94107; phone: (415) 905-2370; fax: (415) 905-2234.
Locksmith Ledger: 1800 Oakton St., Des Plaines, IL 60018; phone: (312) 298-6210.
SECURITY: Cahners Publishing Co., 1350 E. Touhy Ave., P.O. Box 5080, Des Plaines, IL 60018; phone: (708) 635-8800; fax: (708) 299-8622.
Security Distributing and Marketing: P.O. Box 5080, Des Plaines, IL 60018; phone: (312) 635-8800.

76119. Local SBA offices are also listed in the "U.S. Government" section of your telephone directory.

Many other sources of financing also exist. Borrowing from banks is perhaps the most obvious solution, though banking institutions tend toward the conservative side of the financing spectrum. Personal or commercial loans can be backed up by using various forms of collateral, including savings accounts, life insurance policies, real estate, inventory, equipment, or accounts receivable. Finance companies offer another option; they are generally less conservative than banks but charge higher interest. Another means of raising start-up capital might be taking the equity financing route: dividing your business ownership among investors who contribute capital but don't necessarily participate in business operations.

Some of the simplest and most obvious sources of funding are often overlooked. Though generally characterized by high interest rates, credit cards are a quick way to get cash with no paperwork. Another useful tip is to establish credit with equipment suppliers and merchandise wholesalers. Many suppliers may put you on a cash on delivery (COD) basis for several months before issuing a line of credit. Either way, any deferment of payment on merchandise will give you that much more money to work with during the crucial setup period.

Whether establishing credit with suppliers, applying for bank loans, seeking investors for equity financing, or trying just about any other means of raising capital, you will need a presentable business plan. It should effectively explain your needs, what you intend to do with the requested money, and how that money will facilitate the development of your security systems business. Entrepreneur Group's detailed guide to preparing a business plan, *Report No. X3402: How to Develop a Successful Business Plan,* is available by writing: **Entrepreneur, 2392 Morse Avenue, Irvine, CA 92714, phone: (714) 261-2325, fax: (714) 755-4211.**

LOCATION

Careful planning of the location for your security systems office can greatly enhance success. The first step is to decide what kind of clientele you plan to serve, and what types of products and services you want to offer. It is wise to check census data, business statistics, local bulletins, trade associations, and other sources to determine whether your planned security service will fit into a particular community. In evaluating the community, important considerations include the purchasing power of the average resident, the prevalent types of residences, types and places of work, means of transportation, family socioeconomic status, and leisure activities. Home security systems, for example, are in especially high demand where people tend to be worried about being home alone or where well-to-do residents own expensive artwork, jewelry, or other valuable property that insurance cannot replace. Once you have chosen the community

systems industry. Once you're equipped with a sound business plan and a good measure of tenacity, you will find numerous financial sources, each with advantages and disadvantages that should be weighed against your particular circumstances—how much capital you already have, how much interest you are willing to pay, what portion of your business (equity capital) you might be willing to offer to private investors in exchange for their financial backing, and so on. Usually, a combination of several financial sources is the best solution to funding.

An advisable place to begin inquiry is the **U.S. Small Business Administration (SBA),** which provides invaluable information on diverse aspects of small business practice as well as tips about small business loans. The SBA can be reached by calling **1-800-U ASK SBA** or by writing **Small Business Directory, P.O. Box 1000, Ft. Worth, TX** most appropriate for your line of security services, you must set up a site within that community.

Since the securities services rely little, if at all, on walk-in retail business, there is no need to invest precious start-up capital on office design and layout. Space in buildings off the beaten track, in industrial parks, or even in homes is often sufficient. Your choice of even the purely functional office space should nevertheless follow certain useful tips. Locating your office within 10 to 15 miles of your main customer base, for example, is a good way to reduce travel time and costs, especially in the consumer/residential market. It is also important to check up on local zoning codes to avoid a site that prohibits your particular line of business. (Consult the nearest small business association for more details on zoning ordinances.) Finally, it often pays to locate your business next to other businesses that also supply homes or offices with installation or improvement services and merchandise. If your security system service operates near lumber yards, plumbers, industrial supply outfits, or the like, you may draw and share a common body of customers.

LAYOUT AND SETUP

Though your office may not need polish and marketing appeal to draw retail trade, careful planning in other areas will maximize its functionality. The space should accommo-

date business records, inventory, work stations for telephone salespeople, and a workshop for testing, maintenance, and repair equipment. If used efficiently, an area of 200 square feet should be fully sufficient for all operations. As you will shuttle regularly between your office and clients, you will also want to maximize your vehicle's use as a mobile workshop/office. Some operations are completely built into vans. Rand and Marshall Mueller, founders of Code-Alarm Inc., a Michigan-based company, started operations in their home basement in 1979. By the early 1990s, the company was touted as one of the largest car security alarm companies in the nation, reaching sales of $50 million in 1990 and employing over 600 people in several states. Beginning in small quarters clearly does not mean staying in small quarters.

Resourcefulness can stretch limited resources a long way. Consider purchasing used equipment from businesses that are being liquidated or sold, or by checking big-circulation newspapers under "Classified" or "Business Opportunities" sections. If your start-up capital is very limited, you may also want to explore leasing equipment, which entails substantially less initial cash outlay, but usually ends up costing more than purchasing equipment outright or via an installment plan.

FRANCHISE OPPORTUNITIES

Alliance Security Systems: 6-140 McGovern Dr., Cambridge, Ontario, Canada N3H 4R7; phone: (519) 650-5353; fax: (519) 650-1704. Provides state-of-the art electronic protection to institutional, industrial, commercial, and residential customers.

Chambers Franchised Security Systems, Inc.: 1103 Fredericksburg Rd., San Antonio, TX 78201; phone: (512) 736-2075; fax: (512) 736-3461. Provides electronic security services.

Dictograph Security Systems: 40 9th St., New York, NY 10001; phone: (212) 760-0530. Franchisor assists dealers in sale, installation, maintenance, and monitoring of all security-related systems.

Dynamark Security Centers, Inc.: P.O. Box 2068, Hagerstown, MD 21783; phone: (301) 797-2124, or (800) 342-4243; fax: (301) 797-2189. Markets and installs residential and light commercial security and fire protection devices.

International Loss Prevention Systems Corp.: 1350 E. 4th Ave., Vancouver, British Columbia, Canada V5N 1J5; phone (604) 255-5000; fax: (604) 254-2575. Offers a complete line of shoplifting prevention products and systems to retail businesses.

Sonitrol Corp.: 424 N. Washington St., Alexandria, VA 22314; phone: (703) 549-3900; fax: (703) 549-2053. Specializes in audio intrusion alarm systems.

STAFFING

Starting up a security system business is primarily a one-person job, requiring active involvement and long hours, as well as diverse skills ranging from sales to installation. Once the business is up and running, however, getting other hands involved is an important step for growth. If your business is not large enough to justify hiring full-time installers and telephone salespeople, their valuable input can be arranged on a contract basis as needed.

Qualified installers are not difficult to find. Most craftspeople with experience as electricians, television repairmen, appliance technicians, locksmiths, and general handymen can quickly develop security system installation expertise.

Skilled salespeople, with skills in both telemarketing and direct sales techniques, are invaluable assets. These workers should be capable of arranging appointments and then following up with personal visits, demonstrations, and presentation of estimates. Some field experience and background training in security systems for sales staff helps instill customer confidence. It is also important to provide sales staff with attractive incentives, ranging from straight commission to bonuses, finders fees, and combinations of these incentives with salaries and fringe benefits (insurance, paid vacations, profit-sharing, pensions, etc.). Once the sale is made, you should focus on sustained service and maintenance to promote customer goodwill and increase the chance of referrals.

COMMON SECURITY SYSTEM DEVICES

Taping: A common method of perimeter protection by which doors and windows are outlined with a metallic tape of foil that conducts electricity. If the glass or door is broken, the circuit is broken and an alarm sounds.

Light Beams: Involves substituting a photoelectric cell for a pressure mechanism; this device serves much the same purpose as a mechanical switch with the added advantage of low visibility and convenient installation in hallways, stairwells, etc. When the beam is broken by an intruder, the switch is activated.

Infrared Light Beams: An invisible version of conventional light beam switches.

Sonar (Ultrasonic Movement Detectors): Transmission of high-frequency signals between a receiver and a reflector responds to changes in wave frequencies by triggering an alarm.

Sound Frequency Detection: Devices that are tuned to specific noises—like a dog's bark or human command—to trigger an alarm or monitoring system.

Glass-Breakage Detectors: Sensitive devices fastened to widows or glass doors and set to trigger alarm if glass is broken.

Pressure Mats: Flat switches—often placed under door mats—that are activated by pressure, as of a footstep.

Microwave Detectors (Radar): Governed by the same principle as ultrasonic devices, but cover a range up to 400 feet, thereby detecting motion or ambient disturbances over large spaces.

Passive Infrared Detectors (PIR): Devices that respond to body head, not motion.

Capacity (Proximity) Detectors: Establish a close electrical field around valuable objects, triggering an alarm when field is broken.

MARKETING

Your security systems service will have to continuously match the changing needs of customers to rapidly changing technology. These factors will vary according to your line of specialty and the community in which you operate. The most effective way to keep abreast of such changes is to conduct careful, ongoing market research. You can gather useful information through direct mail campaigns, telemarketing, and personal interviews, or by gathering secondary data from census tracts, maps, media sources, the Yellow Pages, community organizations, and so on. Tailor your merchandise and sales strategies to the trends you discover. Finding answers to specific questions will help your business fill the appropriate market niches and compete with the proliferation of other security system services.

Despite the endless variables affecting the market, one factor is common to all security system customers: they seek peace of mind. Crime experts are quick to point out that no security system is fail-safe; if a burglar is absolutely determined, little can be done to stop the crime. But for the home or business owner uneasy about rising crime rates or afraid to be alone on their own premises, a well-marketed security system *can* offer a sense of safety, if not perfect protection. In a high tension society, the luxury of such a feeling is increasingly valuable.

Various other marketing strategies may help highlight the convenient and affordable nature of your services. Many insurance companies offer discounts to homeowners with security systems, a benefit you should emphasize to prospective customers. One of your chief responsibilities is to stay in touch with the latest innovations in technology and system design and market them aggressively. Not only does high technology often lower the cost to you and your customer, but it helps reinforce the impression of efficacy in the system (even when a more conventional system might work just as well). Code Alarm Inc., for example, markets a high-end car alarm which is wired to a car's cellular phone and which tracks a stolen car to its location before killing the motor. Other innovations in the car alarm industry include automatic and remote door locks, remote trunk release, and remote panic features, enabling an owner to trip the alarm if accosted near the car. Residential and commercial security systems more frequently employ central monitoring services and high-tech detectors capable of differentiating between common disturbances and those most likely to reflect criminal activity (sensors, for example, that might ignore a moving dog but would sound at broken glass).

ADVERTISING

Expect to spend about ten percent of gross revenue on advertising costs when your business is established, but substantially more during the first few years and particularly during the start-up period. Experiment with different ad media, from newspapers to bus benches, the Yellow Pages, billboards, and specialty advertising on pencils, bags, telephone pads, and the like. Since much of your security systems business will be drummed up over the phone, direct-mail advertising is a particularly good medium. Brochures are also useful tools, as your sales staff and installers can use them to walk prospective customers through important features assisted with visuals. You will probably want to incorporate the more current FBI facts and figures on crime—periodically updated by the FBI Crime Statistics Division—into your main brochure.

Also take advantage of every promotional opportunity possible from premiums such as low-cost chain guards and home inventory lists for prospective clients to news releases and demonstrations at trade shows. A well-presented demonstration can go a long way toward selling systems that might otherwise fall by the wayside.

LICENSES AND INSURANCE

In order to open your security systems service you will need to obtain a local business license as well as the city and state tax permits required in your area. Check with city and county clerks for details. You'll also want to invest in standard business insurance and, for good measure, a solid security system of your own—both to try your wares and protect them in the process.

Licensing and training permits for the security systems business vary substantially according to your location. You may be required to pass a test or have a master electrician on staff before you can be licensed. Before you can buy or sell merchandise at wholesale prices, you will probably need a sales tax permit (or sellers permit), usually obtainable through the Equalization Board, the State Sales Tax Commission, or the Franchise Tax Board. Your locale may also require a contractor license (the state of California, for example, requires completion of an exam plus four years of field experience within the past ten years). One way to cope with such regulations is to hire a qualified person as a so-called ''silent partner'' until you have met the qualifications yourself. Other snares to beware of include false alarm fines for systems that repeatedly alert crime-control officials when nothing is wrong, and legal suits by disgruntled clients. It is advisable to investigate these areas before finding yourself ensnared in problems that could have been avoided.

COMPUTER SYSTEMS AND HIGH TECHNOLOGY

Security system services are increasingly tied in with computerized equipment and communications and extremely high-tech equipment that you will use daily. Digital communications, printed circuits, and microprocessors have not only increased the flexibility and sensitivity of sensors and communication devices, but have helped bring down costs. At the American Society for Industrial Security (ASIS) show in Washington, D.C., in August of 1993, for example, Sensormatic Electronics Corp. introduced its VRS 2000, a ''visual reality'' security system integrating access control, closed circuit television (CCTV), electronic asset protection, and alarm point monitoring on a computer-based graphical

work station. While that example is at the high end of the industry, even small operations can capitalize on similar technology. Trade publications and shows are goods ways to keep track of the ever-changing technological blitz; falling behind can mean losing valuable business and, ultimately, losing your competitive edge.

Computer technology has often given rise to a completely new—and very diverse—field of security services. The information protection business may be regarded as the information-age offspring of the conventional security services industry. As computers become increasingly prevalent, and as plans for informational superhighways evolve, the protection of electronic information, data, and communications will virtually explode in importance.

The securities systems service is a rapidly growing industry rife with entrepreneurial possibilities. With hard work, business savvy, a flair for fast-changing technology, a crack sales team, and competent back-end service staff, a small businessperson should see significant returns on his or her investments. With rising competition, the failure rate is high. Nonetheless, properly marketed and installed alarms are an unbeatable way to make crime pay, with interest.

SOURCES:

Brydolf, Libby, ''Sales of Vehicle Security Systems are Revving Up,'' *San Diego Business Journal,* October 4, 1993.

Burglar Alarm Sales and Installations, EntrepreneurGroup, 1988.

''Burglar Alarm Sales and Installations,'' *111 Businesses You Can Start for Under $10,000,* Bantam Books, 1991.

''Burglar Alarm Sales and Installations,'' *Entrepreneur Magazine's 168 More Businesses Anyone Can Start and Make a Lot of Money,* second edition, Bantam, 1991.

Fadel, Karen, ''Safety Pays,'' *New Business Opportunities,* June 1991, pp. 42-48.

Madden, Michael, editor, *Small Business Start-Up Index,* issue 1, Gale, 1991.

Manning, Ric, ''Safe at Home: Americans Spend $1 Billion on Security Systems,'' *Gannett News Service,* May 12, 1993.

Martin, Susan Boyles, editor, *Worldwide Franchise Directory,* Gale, 1991.

Schwartz, Carol A., editor, *Small Business Sourcebook,* sixth edition, volume 1, Gale, 1993.

Weinstein, Bob, ''Code Warrior; Security Alarm Maker Locks Up Success,'' *Entrepreneur,* May 1991, pp. 100-106.

—*Kerstan Cohen*

Self-Storage Service

Whether they are college students leaving campus for the summer, apartment dwellers between two leases, or business executives swamped with files rarely used, nearly everybody could use some extra storage space. For a modest fee, self-storage services can take these loads off of people; yet only about one in ten Americans even knows what a self-storage facility is, suggesting there is a vast, untapped market for businesses that rent space.

The self-storage, or mini-storage, industry was born in the mid-1960s in southwestern states where many houses lacked basements, and garages were not enclosed. The first facilities found immediate success, prompting the proliferation of self-storage centers throughout the United States. New facilities or remodeled warehouses eventually replaced many of the converted old sheds and garages used in early operations.

Accompanying the boom in self-storage center development during the 1980s was increased competition, leading to over-saturation in some areas and making market research a definite prerequisite to starting a storage operation. Nonetheless, the entrepreneur with the proper financing and the willingness to put necessary time into conceptualization, planning, and management of a self-storage service could still reap the industry's traditional rewards of a steady cash flow, high profit returns, and low maintenance requirements.

COSTS AND PROFITS

Minimum start-up costs for a self-storage service using a converted facility are about $70,000. The typical investment for a new facility runs in the $350,000 to $750,000 range, while real estate and construction costs for a state-of-the-art operation in an urban area can push costs above $2 million.

Some self-storage center owners earn annual pretax profits of $125,000 or more, while the majority earn in the $60,000 to $90,000 range. Aside from working capital loans, the principal liabilities of a self-storage operator are real estate taxes, utility bills, and management costs. These expenses can be reduced, though, by serving as an owner/operator and leasing rather than buying property.

FINANCING

The most attractive method of financing a self-storage operation will depend upon your personal resources as well as your plans for a facility, so by all means discuss your project with any contacts you might have in the finance, real estate, and construction fields. Perhaps the best source of prefinancing information, though, will be professional associations and trade publications.

The money you will need to start a self-storage operation will be largely contingent upon land costs and capital required to convert or construct a facility. You will need about two-and-a-half acres for an average one-story facility with about 40,000 square feet of rental space. The necessary flat land for a self-storage facility can be purchased for $20,000 to $40,000 an acre—and possibly leased for considerably less—although real estate in growth areas could run much more.

In addition to contractor's charges, conversion costs can be held to $25,000 to $50,000 if using nonunion labor, while costs for bare-bones construction designs in rental units with no heating, air conditioning, or carpet start at about $9 a square foot, including land preparation. Banks, however, may shy away from loans for low-cost facilities or demand faster repayment schedules and impose higher interest rates.

Before approaching a commercial lender for a loan to start a self-storage center you will need to do your homework. While the high profit potential of a storage operation is attractive, a bank may be concerned about the ''saturation factor,'' as well as rising land and construction costs. A bank officer will probably want to see a detailed market analysis, which should illustrate that there is a customer base for your services. You should also be prepared to discuss your prospective location, rental rates, anticipated profit margins, proposed management structure, and estimated repayment schedule.

In addition to banks, there are a number of insurance, finance, and mortgage companies specializing in financing self-storage operations. Your best sources of information on these firms are industry associations and trade publications. Many self-storage operations have also been financed through joint ventures, limited partnerships, and syndicates, often comprised of a mix of parties with a range of experi-

PRIMARY ASSOCIATIONS

Self Storage Association (SSA): 4147 Crossgate Dr., Cincinnati, OH 45236; phone: (513) 984-6468. Members are owners and operators of self-storage facilities. The purpose of SSA is to improve the public's awareness of the self-storage industry. The SSA conducts educational meetings on a variety of self-storage topics, lobbies for state legislation recognizing the self-storage industry as a separate business, compiles statistics, and publishes a variety of periodicals. The SSA has four regional offices:

Central Region, (314) 997-6603; Northeast Region, (410) 730-9500; Southeast Region, (601) 969-0132; Western Region, (310) 855-8393.

Other Associations:

International Storage and Transport Association: 11150 Main St., Ste. 402, Fairfax, VA 22030-5066; phone: (703) 934-9111.

Collier County Self-Storage Association: P.O. Box 8366, Naples, FL 33941; phone: (813) 394-5900.

Greater Arizona Mini-Storage Association: 2425 E. Camelback Rd., #550, Phoenix, AZ 85016; phone: (602) 381-8525.

Minnesota Self-Storage Association: P.O. Box 583223, Minneapolis, MN 55458-3223; phone: (612) 338-1009.

New Jersey Self-Storage Association: 250 Lackland Dr., #8, Middlesex, NJ 08846; phone: (908) 271-9415.

New York State Self-Storage Association: 85 Parkledge Drive, Amherst, NY 14226; phone: (716) 839-1099.

Texas Mini-Storage Association: 2350 Lakeside Blvd., Ste. 850, Richardson, TX 75082; phone: (214) 669-1068.

Washington Area Self-Storage Association: 10 Corporate Center #400, Columbia, MD 21044; phone: (410) 730-9500.

ence in real estate and construction. In general these types of partnerships tend to divide business ownership among investors contributing capital. While you may or may not have to give up a portion of management control, you will be obligated to split the profits with your investment partners.

A combination of factors will ultimately determine whether a lending institution will loan money to a prospective self-storage service owner. Because you will likely be financing the purchase of land and the construction of a facility, any experience you or your investors have in the real estate and land development field will be a distinct advantage when trying to secure financing. It will also help if you have significant personal assets and business manage-

ment experience. Unless you have a guaranteed source of financing, you may want to contact the U.S. **Small Business Administration** about a loan. To inquire about eligibility requirements or request other information, call the SBA at **1-800-U ASK SBA,** or write, **Small Business Directory, P.O. Box 1000, Ft. Worth, TX 76119.**

LOCATION

Because most self-storage center customers choose a facility within three to five miles of their home, location is key to operating a successful self-storage business. The ideal location for a self-storage facility would be in a highly visible, densely populated area with little opportunities in a five-mile radius for new competition. A site along a major traffic artery between where people work and live—preferably on the drive-home side—would also improve the exposure of your business.

Typically the best locations for self-storage facilities are in growth areas where at least 30 percent of residential dwellings are multifamily units or where a large percentage of homes lack basements or enclosed garages. The existence of military bases as well as nearby boating and recreational areas can also be a boon to business. Look for signs of saturation, which may include declining rental rates, high vacancy rates at nearby storage facilities, and frequent bonus promotions offering such things as one month's free rent.

While generalizations can be made about favorable sites, before deciding on a location you may want to hire a marketing research and analysis firm to do a thorough study of several potential locations. You should be able to find a listing of such firms in the Yellow Pages or Business to Business Yellow Pages under "Market Research and Analysis."

FACILITY DESIGN AND CONSTRUCTION

After determining a location for your self-storage operation, you will need to develop a facility design plan. Most storage facilities built in the 1990s have 32,500 to 45,000 square feet of rental space and include an office for rental transactions—usually 120 to 400 square feet—and often a resident manager's apartment—generally 900 to 1,100 square feet.

One of the principal considerations in designing a facility plan is the mix of your rental unit. The average combination of storage unit sizes is about 15 percent 5' x 5', 25 percent 5' x 10,' 20 percent 10' x 10' (the most popular unit in most markets), 15 percent 10' x 20', and the remainder a mix of larger units. An area with a large number of multifamily dwellings will probably require more smaller units since residents of these homes typically accumulate less possessions, while a service targeting business and professional customers would require more 10' x 10' and larger units.

To give you an edge on competition, you may want to consider installing climate control systems, which include heating, air conditioning, and ventilation systems, in some of your units. Most facilities that have such systems pass on the cost of climate control to their tenants, charging as much as 30 percent more for these amenities. Ultimately the final decision for a unit mix should be based on soundly researched conclusions about your area's needs.

If land can be purchased at a reasonable cost and weather is moderate, you may want to consider including outdoor storage space, typically constructed with a parking lot surface and secured by internal fencing. If land costs are high or you are building in an urban or downtown location, you should think about constructing a multistory facility in order to maximize your lot size. Another cost-saving measure is conversion; old multistory warehouses sometimes make good choices, but make sure that any building you are considering is made of brick or masonry and includes an open interior in good condition.

Before building a new facility you will need to select construction materials. For the assemblage of walls and piers there are three principle types of materials: concrete block, prefabricated material, and wood. Prefabricated metal and concrete block are the most popular materials, while only about ten percent of all facilities use wood walls. Tilt-up concrete construction—whereby cement is poured into cast-aluminum forms that are then lifted into place—was becoming increasingly popular in the early 1990s. Tilt-up concrete can be colored during the mixing process while

molds come in a variety of designs. Tilt-up is well insulated and, like prefabricated metal, is movable and can be disassembled, allowing you to change your unit mix to fit changing market patterns.

For unit partitions, most operators choose prefabricated material while wood is also occasionally used. The most popular choice of materials for unit doors is roll-up metal—which uses less interior space and is does not restrict passageway movement—as opposed to hinged metal or wood. Rooftops are generally constructed using a standing-seam metal, which works well with prefabricated metal buildings.

Your design plan should also include signage and fencing stipulations. Your company sign will ideally be large, include your phone number, and be placed in a location visible from access roads. Fencing can be both an aesthetic and security consideration. Many operations use steel chain-link fencing topped with barbed wire, while those wanting to avoid the "prison look" choose wrought iron and install burglar alarms on the doors of each rental unit. To cut costs you may also want to consider using the back wall of buildings to form part of your grounds' outer perimeter.

Other design plan considerations include roads and landscaping. To learn more about your construction options, it would be wise talk to a reputable contractor. You can obtain a list of potential contractors simply by looking under "Contractors" in the Yellow Pages. Information on companies selling construction materials can be ascertained by consulting with vendors listed in industry publications. The construction techniques you ultimately employ will depend in part on fire, building codes, and zoning regulations, so before finalizing a design plan you should also contact local agencies regarding regulatory specifics.

TRADE PUBLICATIONS AND BUSINESS RESOURCES

Publications:

Self-Storage Journal: Self Storage Association, 60 Revere Dr., Ste. 500, Northbrook, IL 60062; phone: (708) 480-9660.

The Mini Messenger and *Self Storage Now:* MiniCo, Inc., 2531 W. Dunlap Ave., Phoenix, AZ 85021; phone: (800) 528-1056. *Mini-Storage Messenger's* April issue offers the Self-Storage Buyer's Guide, including nationwide listings of self-storage industry vendors of products ranging from construction and management services, to security systems and computer software. *Self Storage Now* is a free publication.

Inside Self-Storage: 4141 N. Scottsdale Rd., Ste. 316, Scottsdale, AZ 85281; (602) 990-1101. Also publishes annual *Inside Self-Storage Fact Book* and *Inside Self Storage Data Services' Industry Trend Reports.*

Business Resources:

MiniCo, Inc.: 2531 West Dunlap Ave., Phoenix, AZ 85021; phone: (602) 870-1711. MiniCo sells a variety of products and services to self-storage operators, including insurance, security products, and a bookkeeping system. In addition to two self-storage industry magazines, the company publishes a catalog of self-storage industry products, and the annual *Self-Storage Almanac,* which includes comprehensive demographic information.

EQUIPMENT AND COMPUTER SYSTEMS

Aside from a few hand carts or trucks you may wish to purchase for your tenants' use, the equipment you will need to start a mini-storage business will largely revolve around your office needs. While most operators could make do with a typewriter and the use of manual labor, a computer can speed typing, billing, and filing tasks and also be integrated with security systems.

Before choosing a computer vendor, select a software supplier and ask for that supplier's input on appropriate hardware. Several software companies, which typically advertising in trade publications, have custom-designed programs for self-storage operators. When selecting a hardware vendor look for a dealer that offers on-line service.

SECURITY AND LEGAL MATTERS

Providing for the security for your storage facility can be an important factor in marketing your service as well as in protecting you against costly law suits. Security systems used by self-storage operators include various padlocks, gate

INDUSTRY STATISTICS

- *Occupancy Rates According to Region of the United States (1993 and projected 1994):* (Northeast) 81.8% and 88.1%; (Southeast) 88.4% and 92.7%; (North Central) 91.5% and 92.7%; (South Central) 89.1% and 91.7%; (West) 89.3% and 91.8%.
- *Occupancy Rates by Immediate Market Area (1993):* (Heavy industrial) 88%; (commercial/retail) 87.4%; (urban/downtown) 84.4%; (residential) 89.5%; (rural) 90.5%.
- *National Rental Rates of Units (1993):* (5' x 5') $25.25; (5' x 10') $35.57; (10' x 10') $54.28; (10' x 15') $71.60; (10' x 20') $83.27; (10' x 25') $101.01; (10' x 30') $112.59; (20' x 20') $158.65.
- *Percentage of Climate-Controlled Facilities by Region:* (Northeast) 8%; (Southeast) 27.9%; (North Central) 10.7%; (South Central) 8.1%; (West) 12.1%.
- *Average Square Footage of Facility Rental Space by Region:* (Northeast) 42,537 indoor, 6,950 outdoor; (Southeast) 39,902 indoor, 13,495 outdoor; (North Central) 33,021 indoor, 37,856 outdoor; (South Central) 38,529 indoor, 10,272 outdoor; (West) 46,193 indoor, 10,300 outdoor.
- *National Percentage of Facilities Using Various Security Features:* (Padlocks) 85.9%; (automated gate access) 47.7%; (24-hour access) 41.9%; (manual gate access) 32%; (camera/video surveillance) 21.5%; (microwave/infrared motion detectors) 15.7%; (individual door alarms) 9.6%; (canine security patrol) 8.8%.

(SOURCE: *SELF-STORAGE ALMANAC: 1993-1994.*)

- *Average Rental Rates for a 10' x 10' Unit:* (Constructed prior to 1980) $49; (opened between 1990 and 1992) $65 (source: 1992 MiniCo Self-Storage Survey).

access systems, surveillance cameras, motion detectors, and watch services, including security guards and dogs. Many services have numeric keypads to provide gate access for tenants, while surveillance systems are becoming increasingly popular. Before investing in a security system, it is wise to consult with a security/protection firm.

Self-storage operators are not the insurer of their tenants' belongings, but in order to avoid lawsuits or liabilities stemming from stolen or damaged goods you do need to provide reasonable care for the protection of customers' property. If you sell padlocks to customers, these locks should be of high quality. In addition, you need to make sure your rental contract with tenants—as well as your advertising—honestly reflects the type of security you offer. To minimize liabilities, some self-storage operators include a provision in rental contracts limiting the value of goods that can stored.

You also need to be aware that while most tenants make timely payments, occasionally you will be forced to take legal action to secure past-due rent from tenants or take possession of their property in lieu of payment. Generally operators use "overlocks," which cover a tenant's padlock, when customers fail to pay two consecutive bills. Most states have enacted legislation that prescribes means for dealing with the property of delinquent tenants and for

taking possession of their goods in the event of nonpayment. Laws also detail circumstances in which you can auction off a tenant's belongings. To learn more about the applicable legislation in your area, talk to other operators in your state or consult with an attorney well versed in the storage industry.

MANAGEMENT AND STAFFING

Your staffing needs will depend largely on your security needs and whether you choose to serve as a resident manager. A self-storage facility staff can be limited to an owner/operator, while a number of operations hire retired couples to serve as a management team. But innovations in self-storage security and increased competition in the industry have led some services to move away from the traditional retired resident manager and opt for someone with management and sales experience to help bring in new customers.

At a minimum your manager should be able to do bookkeeping, handle rental transactions, and do light maintenance and groundskeeping work. If your bookkeeping or security operations are computerized, your manager will need to know how to use a computer and the appropriate software. Because managers work in isolated environments, when hiring look for candidates who are self-motivated. Your manager will need time off, so you may want to hire an assistant manager to provide relief help as well as part-time staff to do heavy maintenance work. College graduates make fine assistant managers while high school graduates are good candidates for part-time help.

When offering room and board, self-storage operations generally pay resident managers in the range of $500 to $1,800 per month. If you don't have a resident manger you'll probably need to pay higher wages and hire night security guards. By offering your manager competitive wages and a small percentage of profits, you should be able to woo a well-qualified person and provide him or her with an incentive to keep occupancy rates high.

MARKETING

During the early days of the self-storage industry, entrepreneurs could open a facility and do little in the way of promoting their service and still be assured a steady cash flow. By the early 1990s, though, it was necessary to engage in a thorough feasibility study before deciding upon a location. The owner of a new self-storage service also needed to actively market the operation to a customer base.

Self-storage centers generally cater to people who own more than they know what to do with, people who are in the midst of a move, and people who have recently been through a traumatic experience such as a divorce or the death of a loved one. The largest markets for self-storage customers traditionally have been apartment and condominium dwellers, college students, military personnel, recreational vehicle owners, senior citizens, and businesses and professionals. As a self-storage operator, what you are selling—or renting—is convenience, privacy, and security.

When marketing your service, design your message according to your targeted customer base. It helps to personalize ads with such titles as ''RV Owners'' or ''Students'' and stress how you can serve those people in particular. Students will be more interested in convenience and low cost, senior citizens and businesses will likely be more concerned about security, and apartment dwellers will probably value the fact that you are within a close distance to their home. Marketing can also be enhanced by emphasizing what makes your mini-storage business stand out from the pack. Some operators offer 24-hour access, some offer pickup and delivery services, and some stress availability of climate-controlled units; if possible find a specialty and promote it.

When pricing your storage units, consider industry standards as well as local competition. Smaller units always have a higher per-foot price than larger units. For instance, the average monthly cost for a 5' x 5' unit is about $25, while a 10' x 10' unit runs about $55. These rates can vary dramatically from region to region, though, so it's best to check the competition's rates and factor in what services you are offering and what market segments you are targeting. Typically, operators who advertise tight-security, extended gate hours, and live-in management can charge more than a lower-quality operation and still maintain their share of the storage market.

In addition to the unit rental fee, some operators charge a one-time fee for setting up bookkeeping for each tenant and offer to disinfect and spray units for bugs for an additional fee. If you are providing such unit preparation services but not charging, you should let your customers know. After securing the first month's payment, you may choose to bill your customers monthly or only send out notices to delinquent tenants.

To enhance your operation's marketability, you may want to consider offering auxiliary services. Many operators sell padlocks that can be purchased in bulk and sold at a 50 to 60 percent markup. Other potential services include the sale of boxes, packing materials, and tarpaulins, and the rental of moving equipment. You may also want to install snack and soft drink vending machines, which many customers will appreciate after unloading their belongings into one of your units.

ADVERTISING

Aside from your facility's highly visible sign, the best form of advertising for a self-storage business is the Yellow Pages, because those who need storage space and don't know where to find it will probably go to the phone book first. One warning: avoid advertising under the category of ''Warehouses,'' which can potentially give you a higher degree of legal responsibility for your tenants' belongings.

Your advertising should work in tandem with your marketing strategy. If you're targeting students leaving for summer vacations, place an ad in a campus newspaper or drop flyers in dormitories announcing ''special summer rates.'' If you have a military base nearby, find out if there is a base newspaper in which you can advertise. If you offer outdoor storage lots, you can purchase mailing lists of boat and recreational vehicle owners and target this group through direct mail, marketing your service to wider area. Seniors living in nursing homes or condominiums can be targeted by direct mail or fliers distributed door-to-door or left at a manager's desk. If you're after a business or professional clientele, phone calls can be an inexpensive way to let these customers know about your services, while direct mail—which tends to be more costly—can serve the same purpose.

When targeting a broader audience you might want to join other businesses in a coupon mailer, or utilize billboards, which if properly placed can provide an excellent, albeit expensive, form of advertising. Other forms of advertising include newspapers and local penny papers. Facility banners may be used to announce your grand opening. And don't forget that referrals can sell your space. Contact moving companies, real estate brokers, truck rental firms, and landlords and let them know about your service.

You should also prepare a brochure or handbill containing information about your service—including unit sizes, rental rates, and special features of your operation—for customers who stop by. When a potential customer calls, keep in mind that you have about an 85 percent chance of closing a rental booking right then; so do what you can to turn phone inquiries into effective one-on-one sales pitches.

LICENSES AND INSURANCE

To open a self-storage center you will need to secure a local business license and the city and/or state tax permits required in your area. Check with your city or county clerk for specifics. You'll also want to purchase business insurance. Contact one of the several insurance companies, often found advertised in trade journals, that specialize in writing policies for storage operations.

Ultimately, increased competition and sophistication of facilities has meant the departure of risk-free, easy-profit self-storage entrepreneurship; ''mom and pop'' teams can no longer convert a garage and make a bundle renting space. Nonetheless, just about anyone who does the proper research can open and manage a self-storage operation. And a well-designed and properly marketed self-storage center in a good location can achieve the traditional prerequisite for profitability of 85 percent occupancy within a year, breaking even in the process, and then netting its owner sizable profits.

SOURCES:

An Introduction to Self Storage, Self Storage Association.

Donahue, Gerry, "Get Rich Quick?," *Builder,* February 1993, pp. 226-28.

Kahn, Sharon, and The Phillip Lief Group, "Self Storage Center," *101 Best Businesses to Start,* second edition, Doubleday, 1992, pp. 287-91.

Leder, Steven E., "Your Duty to Provide Security," *Mini-Storage Messenger,* December 1993, pp. 45-8.

Madden, Michael, editor, *Small Business Start-Up Index,* issue 2, Gale, 1991, pp. 129, 170.

Ruloff, Charlene, "What Makes a Good Manager," *Mini-Storage Messenger,* December 1993, pp. 43-4.

Schwartz, Carol A., editor, *Small Business Sourcebook,* volume 1, sixth edition, Gale, pp. 1396-1402.

"Self Storage," *Entrepreneur Magazine's 168 More Businesses Anyone Can Start and Make a Lot of Money,* second edition, Bantam, 1991, pp. 131-32.

Self-Storage Almanac: 1993-1994, MiniCo, Inc., 1993.

Self Storage, Business Start-up Guide, EntrepreneurGroup, 1993.

—ROGER W. ROULAND

Sign Shop

Gone are the days when a custom-made sign took weeks to prepare, for personal computers have completely revolutionized the sign industry. In the 1990s, all a business owner had to do was call *you,* the instant sign store proprietor, wait 24 hours, and pick up or have delivered a professionally made sign.

Because modern sign-making equipment is so easy to use, you don't even need sign-making experience—although a flair for the graphic arts certainly would help—or creative skills, since the client provides the finished artwork. What you will need is the right equipment and solid advice on marketing, location, hiring employees, and running a business. You can obtain the essentials for a sign-making business by becoming partners with a franchisor or becoming a part of a nationwide network, such as SignBiz! Inc. In addition to enjoying a healthy income, you'll be in the enviable position of selling to professionals—sophisticated business people who value excellence.

COSTS AND PROFITS

As an entrant in the instant sign business, you should expect minimum start-up costs—excluding working capital—to run in the neighborhood of $31,000, with average costs hovering around the $54,000 mark. If you decide to become a franchisee, you will incur franchise, advertising, and license fees and training and special membership benefits costs. In the case of joining a nonfranchise network, such as SignBiz! Inc., the nation's largest chain of this type, you will not incur a franchise fee, and can expect a long list of benefits, which include a protected territory, for the network's one-time membership fee.

Some instant sign stores report yearly net profits before taxes of over $289,000, while the majority of sign-making services earns closer to $92,000. Linda Levitan, owner of Sign-Age of Tampa Bay, Inc., a nonfranchised SignBiz! Inc., store in Clearwater, Florida, won a $30,000 Pepsi account and a $40,000 Coca-Cola account in just one month in 1992. Klaus Hindrich of Affordable Signs, another SignBiz! store, in Illinois, landed a $45,000 banner order for Chicago's O'Hare Hilton in 1993.

The primary liabilities of a sign store owner include the requisite accounts payable and working capital loans. Furthermore, most retail sign shop proprietors do not own the building in which their businesses are located and so are responsible for monthly rent payments.

FINANCING

One of the most far-reaching mistakes new small business owners make is not securing sufficient financing. Before signing a franchise contract, consult with experts in order to determine how much capital you will need to launch your project. Ask anyone you may know in the commercial lending field for tips, especially since sign business franchisors frequently do not provide financing. Check with your local business college for referral to a student or instructor who could advise you for free.

Diplomatically approached, successful sign business owners are a fountain of financing. Join your local chamber of commerce and make your services known to other business owners by attending trade shows. For specialized prefinancing information, join a trade organization such as the National Electric Sign Association (NESA) or World Sign Associates (WSA) and talk business with your colleagues. A simple question such as ''How's your bank treating you?'' will probably elicit a potpourri of stories that will give you an idea of how much money business owners are borrowing and at what rate.

Spend time preparing a five-year business plan, a personal financial history, your marketing strategies outlined in detail, and sales projections based on future sales of your signs. If necessary, hire a good accounting and legal team to ensure that your paperwork is perfect. When approaching a bank for a business loan, be prepared with cash-flow projections and financial statements, since in 1994 banks were focusing heavily on cash-flow lending, rather than on straight asset-based lending. However, you should expect to put up assets, including personal ones, as collateral.

Look for a bank that knows your industry and a banker who's done business with independently owned firms or franchises like yours. Try to seek out a loan officer with eight to ten years of experience. Knowing ahead of time what your banker can decide independently and what has to

FRANCHISE OPPORTUNITIES

American Fastsigns, Inc.: 4951 Airport Pkwy., Ste. 530, Dallas, TX 75248; phone: (214) 702-0171, or (800) 962-0267; fax: (214) 991-6058. Founded and began franchising, 1986; has over 89 outlets in 35 states; franchise fee, $20,000; other expenses include an additional $90,000 to $125,000, which includes $40,000 for equipment, training expenses (mandatory), leasehold improvements, rent and utility deposits, and mandatory signs and graphics. Contracts run for 20 years, with a renewal option of 10 years; sales royalty: 6% of the gross weekly sales, beginning 60 days after the opening of the franchise; advertising fees: $2,500 prior to opening and 2% of gross monthly sales upon the opening of the store.

Other Franchisors: All American Sign Shops: 5100 Poplar Ave., Ste. 2116, Memphis, TN 38137; phone: (901) 761-3084; fax: (901) 761-3087. **The Best Instant Sign Co.:** 6363 NW 6th Way, Fort Lauderdale, FL 33309; phone: (305) 938-8448. **Custom Signs Today:** 2398 Mount Vernon Rd., Dunwoody, GA 30338; phone: (800) 783-9206; fax: (404) 698-0607. **Design 'n' Sign:** 30569 Dequindre, Madison Heights, MI 48071; phone: (313) 583-2525; fax: (313) 585-7898. **Franz Sign Co., Inc.:** 8 Glover St., Portsmouth, OH 45662; phone: (614) 353-1470, or (800) 447-1470. **Next Day Signs:** 2234 S. Hamilton Rd., Columbus, OH 43232; phone: (614) 575-9696, or (800) 766-4665; fax: (614) 575-9699. **S&S Signs:** Hwy. 31-W., S., P.O. Box 55, Woodburn, KY 42170; phone: (502) 529-5892, or (800) 523-1958; fax: (502) 529-9504.

be routed "to committee" will aid you in formulating your strategy. If your banker doesn't have final authority, seek out his or her superior; remember, you're looking for an individual with some personal knowledge of you and your prospective business. Expect to meet with a lot of bankers—and to experience no small amount of rejection—before finding a banker with whom you can do business.

Loan officers will be looking at other factors in determining you reliability as a borrower: a lucrative prospective location; plans to offer customers an adequate—if not superior—product; a detailed marketing strategy that encompasses store fixtures, point-of-sale promotional materials and promotional events; and a profitable pricing structure. A loan officer will also ask about your management practices, qualifications for personnel—how knowledgeable will you expect your staff to be about sign making?—proposed store layout, and record-keeping procedures to track financial activity and to report operating data. Some industry consultants, such as SignBiz! Inc., provide not only business plans, but also store layouts, staffing data, and background statistics to new store owners, thereby easing the process of seeking a loan.

Ultimately, an amalgamation of factors will determine whether a bank will lend to a prospective or fledgling sign shop owner. You might also want to contact the U.S. **Small Business Administration (SBA)** to inquire about eligibility

requirements for its loan program and to request other valuable information. The SBA can be reached at **1-800-U ASK SBA,** by writing: **Small Business Directory, P. O. Box 1000, Fort Worth, TX 76119.** You might also want to check the "U.S. Government" section in your telephone directory for the SBA office nearest you.

LOCATION

Sign businesses are typically located in retail centers with high visibility and accessibility. The ideal location for a retail instant sign shop would be on a corner side street near the central business district of a town or city with a population of at least 50,000. On this corner side street you can prominently display the name of your store, as well as have plenty of room in the back of the facility to stock your inventory and to discard used supplies such as wood or signs that did not end up being used.

You may set up shop in as few as 1,400 to 1,600 square feet, but you would be wise to figure in advance how much space you may need as your business grows. In addition to your store showroom, you will need to incorporate an office area into your rental space. Outside of your store, consider patron parking and the ease of entering your lot from the main business district).

LAYOUT AND SETUP

Store layout is perhaps one of your most important marketing tools. By the very nature of your business, your store will be "cluttered." This clutter can serve you well if you let customers interpret it as an indication of prosperity. If the entire shop is filled with signs and a great many samples of company logos that patrons would be likely to recognize, then passersby—potential customers—will look in the windows, see you and your staff so busy, and think that you must be in great demand.

Since research pointed to the fact that 60 percent of decisions to purchase in a retail environment are made while the customer is shopping around, your showroom should be inviting and tastefully decorated; remember, your typical client will be a professional with an eye for art. Keep a photo album with pictures of signs that you have designed so that customers may get an idea of the kind of work you do. A coffee table with chairs would be ideal in this situation; you might also leave a few catalogs on the table. And do have a coffee urn and small cookies for the sake of hospitality—the aroma of freshly brewed coffee can act as a tremendous sales stimulant.

You will need a great deal of equipment: software and a computer system; phone and alarm systems; an electric sign; store graphics; a photocopier; a telephone answering machine; a file cabinet; a computerized engraver; a vinyl cutter; a quality color printer; signage materials and supplies; a 25-inch roll laminator; a cutting table; general office equipment;

business forms; and stationery. If you take the franchise route or join a large network with substantial buying power, most of those concerns will offer discounts on the needed computer equipment and materials, and most will provide a starter supply of letterhead, envelopes, statements, and price lists.

The SignBiz! network, which offers the opportunity to own independently an instant sign business, will furnish the new owner with major manufacturers' equipment and national service/warranties along with its comprehensive training program, consulting and marketing support, protected territory, regional workshops, and national conventions. SignBiz! Inc.'s equipment package includes a 486 PC system with a 245 MB hard drive, a Hewlett-Packard scanner and color printer, and a 48-inch vinyl cutter that cuts at 31 inches per second. SignBiz! also includes a year's membership in NESA (National Electric Sign Association) in its new store package, and, through this affiliation, fax equipment is available, as are many other business services and equipment, at greatly discounted rates.

However, for the remainder of your requisite business office supplies, you definitely will want to visit or call one of the numerous high-volume Staples office-supply stores, whose headquarters are located at **100 Pennsylvania Avenue, P.O. Box 9328, Framingham, MA 07101-9328; phone: (800) 333-3330.** A paper mill such as **PaperDirect,**

205 Chubb Avenue, Lyndhurst, NJ 07071; phone: 1-800-A-PAPERS, can be a wonderful source of office forms and stationery.

EQUIPMENT AND COMPUTER CONSIDERATIONS

Sign shops can be separated into 3 types: commercial, which specialize in screenprinting, neon electrical signage, architectural signage, and monument signs; traditional, producing hand-painted, wood-carved, and (possibly) vinyl signs; and instant, which offer vinyl, using the latest scanning technology and cutting services to provide quick turnaround service and are located in retail space very accessible to other businesses. In general, as a sign shop owner, you may be producing such high-tech items as banners, window lettering, vehicle graphics, point-of-sale signage, magnetic vehicle signs, neon signage, carved wooden signage, silk screening, printed and engraved name badges, self-adhesive vinyl lettering and logos cut by computer for vehicles and corporate sign programs, modular framing and mounting systems, graphs and charts, awnings, and corporate trophies and awards. In addition to laminating services, you should also consider offering popular eight-foot-tall vinyl greeting signs to announce births and anniversaries, to wish "Happy Birthday" and "Congratulations," or to convey "Get Well" or "Welcome Home" messages.

Your emphasis should be on producing quality signs quickly, usually within 24 hours. Instant sign stores produce computer-designed signs and banners in a manner that is similar to desktop publishing. The design is composed on a computer, transmitted through a plotter to a vinyl sheet, and then transferred to the sign or banner. The signs and letters are constructed of vinyl and will adhere to hard, nonporous surfaces such as wood, plastic, metal, acrylic, and glass. The cut letters can be used for vehicles, boats, and on windows. Vinyl banners can be produced in any width by any reasonably required length. Signs produced by most instant sign stores are covered by a five-year or longer guarantee against fading. Many times, your customer will bring you prepared artwork or artwork on disk. Use of design computers permits accurate reproduction of logos and recall for repeat customers.

Franchises exist that offer training programs and follow-up services, which cover computer operation, layout input and creation, and hands-on activities. Designed to teach the nonartistic individual the sign business, not just how to run a piece of equipment, a program such as this will acquaint you with the computer equipment you might be using, including hardware and software. You definitely will need an IBM-compatible personal computer and sign-making software, and in many cases the hardware and software may be either leased or purchased. Scanning equipment will help you to duplicate a customer's logo in seconds.

INDUSTRY STATISTICS

- *Annual Sales of Electric Signs Per Employee (1992):* $90,500.
- *Annual Sales of Electric Signs (1992):* $3.12 billion.
- *Material Expenditures by the Electric Sign Industry (1992):* $1 billion.
- *Material Costs of Electric Signs as a Percentage of Sales (1992):* 32.5%.
- *Electrical and Architectural Sign Shop Payroll Costs as a Percentage of Sales:* (1991) 34.8%; (1992) 38.9%.

(SOURCE: *SIGNS OF THE TIMES,* JULY 1993.)

- *Profit Potential:* (High net profit before taxes) $289,500; (average net profit before taxes) $92,000; (minimum start-up investment) $31,000; (average start-up investment) $54,000 (source: *Entrepreneur,* August 1989).
- *Profile of the Average Sign Shop Owner:* 35-55 years old, has left a long-term employment history with one company (often with an early retirement incentive or other benefits package), has come from upper management, may have an engineering background, and is looking for fulfillment in an endeavor of his or her own (source: SignBiz! Inc.'s 1993 research).
- *Consumer Purchase Decisions:* 60% of decisions to purchase in a retail environment are made while the customer is shopping—and looking (source: *Business Opportunities Journal,* January 1990).
- *Average Monthly Royalty Fee:* 6% of the monthly gross (source: International Franchise Association, 1993).
- *Projected Nationwide Growth of Instant Sign Stores in Retail Locations:* From approximately 750 in 1990 to 3,000 in 1996 to 5,000 in 2000 (source: SignBiz! Inc.'s 1993 research).

PRIMARY ASSOCIATIONS AND SELECTED TRADE PUBLICATIONS

Associations:

National Electric Sign Association (NESA): 801 N. Fairfax St., Ste. 205, Alexandria, VA 22314; phone: (703) 836-4012; fax: (703) 836-8353.

World Sign Associates (WSA): 8774 Yates Dr., Westminster, CO 80030; phone: (303) 427-7252; fax: (303) 427-7090.

Publications:

Perspectives: National Electric Sign Association (see address above).
Sign Business: National Business Media, Inc., P. O. Box 1416, Broomfield, CO 80038; phone: (303) 469-0424; fax: (303) 469-5730. Provides the most coverage in its content of the instant sign industry.
Sign Control News: Scenic America, 21 DuPont Cir. NW, Washington, DC 20036; phone: (202) 833-4300.
Signals: National Electric Sign Association (see address above).
SignCraft: SignCraft Publishing Co., Inc., P. O. Box 06031, Fort Myers, FL 33906; phone: (813) 939-4644; fax: (813) 939-0607.
Signs of the Times: ST Publications, Inc., 407 Gilbert Ave., Cincinnati, OH 45202-2285; phone: (513) 421-2050, or (800) 925-1110; fax: (513) 421-5144. Monthly trade journal of the electric sign industry since 1906; covers all aspects of sign making; subscription fee: $36.00 per year, includes 12 monthly issues, a free 13th issue, and the Buyer's Guide, which lists all the suppliers, manufacturers, and distributors of sign-making materials, as well as related schools, associations, and consultants and a list of industry trade names. *Signs of the Times* is the most comprehensive of all the sign industry periodicals.

STAFFING

Staffing for your sign shop will depend upon your location and hours of operation. Be prepared to put a lot of time into your business. As Jerry Duncan, proprietor of Quick-Signs, a SignBiz! store in Fresno, California, stated, "When you think you're done, there is always something to do. [But] I wanted the freedom, the ability to make an impact and the chance to be financially successful. There is a satisfaction that is unbelievable. . . . You get out of it what you put into it."

A sign shop is an ideal employment situation for a husband and wife; together, they can train their children in the business. David and Marilouise Fudge, proprietors of Sign Wiz, a SignBiz! store in Sunnyvale, California, trained their 14-year-old son Mike in sign making. In addition, the Fudges employ five full-time people and an occasional part-time and temporary staff.

Ideally, you should train someone to act as manager when you are unable to be in the store. This individual should have some experience in retail management and be highly organized and computer-literate, with a communications and/or publishing background. Salary should be determined by industry standards; periodic merit raises, however, will enhance the motivation of an already-eager employee.

MARKETING

Since more and more sign shops are offering 24-hour service, your business will have to prove its individuality by means of marketing to your target customers, which will include corporations, large and small businesses, and clubs and associations. If you decide to become a franchisee or a member of a network such as SignBiz! Inc., you will enjoy the guidance of your partner, who will provide local and regional advertising materials for publication and distribution (at your expense). Other marketing tools will include posters, direct mailings, brochures, newsletters, local and regional newspaper ads, Yellow Pages ads, television spots, telemarketing, and toll-free telephone numbers.

Besides selling signs and banners (a staple of the instant sign store industry), you will want to consider renting, maintaining, and repairing them, as well as providing letters and parts to sign owners. And of course you will want to store logos and designs on computer to facilitate return business.

There are many other ways to market your business. Dave Fudge, owner of Sign Wiz, for example, attends "networking" breakfasts, where Sunnyvale's small-business people meet, just to get acquainted. Over time, he gained much work through the people he met at these breakfasts. As another technique, when business was slow during the Persian Gulf War, all of Sign Wiz's employees made outside sales calls.

ADVERTISING

Be prepared to spend fully 66.7 percent of your first year's advertising budget in the first 4 to 6 months. Enhance the name recognition of your sign company with display ads in the business and classified sections of your local and regional newspapers. Your business' presence in the Yellow Pages is a must. To start out, a double-quarter- or triple-quarter-column-sized ad is recommended. You can increase your ad size as your business matures each year. Create a sign business logo—or find a reasonably priced free-lance designer to create one for you—and have it brandished on T-shirts. Wear the T-shirts while you work and ask your employees to wear them as well. Offer customers a free T-shirt with every three signs purchased.

Be certain to take advantage of every advertising opportunity. Of course, emblazon your sign shop's name and logo on all your delivery trucks. Be flexible and expansive. Send press releases to local media announcing any special promotions you might conceive. For an opening week promotion, offer a Buy A Sign, Get A Sign Free special or a 20 percent discount on first purchases. By joining your local chamber of commerce, you can cultivate relationships with area merchants who might someday avail themselves of your services; in turn, encourage your customers to patronize these same merchants by displaying their ads in your store. You will also want to have business cards printed. Besides distributing them to business associates, you might check out mass-volume office-supply stores such as Staples; most Staples branches display a vinyl-pocketed business-card bulletin board where any entrepreneur can post a deck of business cards for customers to take.

LICENSES AND INSURANCE

In order to open a sign shop, you will need to obtain a local business license and the state and/or city sales tax permits required in your area. Check with your city and county clerks to determine the details. You will also want to purchase standard business and motor vehicle liability insurance. Another good idea is to invest in a sturdy security system to protect your inventory from theft.

Increased competition in the sign business in 1994 saw the demise of the "plain vanilla" sign shop. In order to succeed, you will have to stay abreast of fast-breaking technological advances. To keep up with breakthroughs, subscribe to one or more sign shop publications, such as *Signs of the Times, Perspectives, Sign Business* (which devotes a large percentage of its format to the instant sign industry), *Signals,* and *SignCraft.*

As your revenues increase, you will be able to obtain

bank loans more easily to purchase innovative sign-making equipment. The dinosaur days of the old style sign shops, when sign makers plied their trade by applying paint, have made way for an era in which modern sign shop owners let technology look after production so they can concentrate on developing the business. With research, diligence, smart management, and astute advertising, almost any tenacious individual can open a sign shop and expect to realize sizable profits.

SOURCES:

"The 1992 State-of-the-Industry Report," *Signs of the Times,* July 1993, pp. 114-127.

Beamer, Suzy, editor, *National Electric Sign Association— Membership Directory,* National Electric Sign Association, 1992.

Bustner, Irving, *The Small Business Handbook,* revised edition, Simon & Schuster, 1989.

Collins, Bill, "On Time, On Budget," *Signs of the Times,* July 1993, pp. 112-113.

Facade and Sign Design, Books Nippan, 1990.

Fitsgerald, Bob, *Practical Sign Shop Operation,* seventh edition, Signs of the Times Publishing, 1992.

Gould, Joe Sutherland, *Starting From Scratch: 50 Profitable Business Opportunities,* John Wiley & Sons, 1987.

Gregory, Ralph, *Sign Painting Techniques,* Signs of the Times Publishing, 1993.

Horowitz, David, and Dana Shilling, *The Business of Business: How 100 Businesses Really Work,* Harper & Row, 1989.

Instant Sign Shop, Business Start-up Guide, EntrepreneurGroup, 1992.

Larsen, Sonja, *Signs That Sell: The Handbook of Successful Merchandise Signing,* Insignia Systems, Inc., 1991.

Madden, Michael, editor, *Small Business Start-Up Index,* issue 3, Gale, 1991.

Martin, Susan Boyles, editor, *Worldwide Franchise Directory,* first edition, Gale, 1991.

Mikoda, Naoki, *Store and Sign Design,* Rockport Publishers, 1988.

Nax, Sanford, "Signs of Success in the Instant Sign Business," *The Fresno Bee,* May 10, 1993.

New Sign Shop Electrician's Workbook, American Technical Publishers, Inc., 1990.

Nichols, Paula, "Start Your Own Sign-Painting Business," *Business Opportunities,* November 1990, p. 52.

Richards, Terri, "Sign 'Em Up," *Entrepreneur,* August 1989, pp. 113-120.

RMA Annual Statement Studies, Robert Morris Associates, 1992.

Schwartz, Carol A., editor, *Small Business Sourcebook,* sixth edition, volume 1, Gale, 1992.

Sign Companies Directory, American Business Directories, Inc., 1992.

Sign Maintenance and Repairing Directory, American Business Directories, Inc., 1992.

"SignBiz! Takes Inside Track with Technology As Partner," *Business Opportunities Journal,* January 1990.

"Signs of Success," *Income Opportunities,* March 1988, pp. 65-66, 88-94.

"Signs of the Times," *Entrepreneur,* January 1989, p. 121.

Sims, Mitzi, *Sign Design,* Van Nostrand Reinhold Co., Inc., 1991.

NONFRANCHISE OPPORTUNITY

SignBiz! Inc.: 10 Corporate Park. Ste. 130, Irvine, CA 92714; phone: (714) 263-0400, or (800) 633-5580; fax: (714) 263-1555; the largest chain of nonfranchised sign stores in America; founded in 1989 by Michael Farley, who developed the first instant sign network in the United States, totaling 300 instant sign centers nationwide. Offers full-service marketing and toll-free telephone technical support and consulting services to its network members, without the penalties of franchise fees and royalties. Provided by company: site selection and lease negotiation assistance; demographic analysis at no additional charge; extensive vendor list and vendor discount programs; all sign-making equipment and proprietary software programs; protected territories; comprehensive training program conducted by instructors in a fully equipped training facility in Orange County, California; quarterly visits and consultations by a seasoned industry consultant in the first year; store layout and design plans; first year's membership in NESA (National Electric Sign Association); regional workshops and national conventions each year; full-color promotional mailers available at less than $.025 each; seasonal newsletter for developing market awareness; and a marketing program built on market research study conducted by an outside agency.

Successful Sign Design, Retail Reporting Corp., 1989.

"A Survey About Franchised Signshops," *Signs of the Times,* June 1991, pp. 74-89.

"A Survey About Nonfranchised Vinyl Signshops," *Signs of the Times,* August 1991, pp. 80-84.

Webster, Bryce, "It's Plain to See: Custom-Made Signs Are Booming," *Income Opportunities,* November 1990, pp. 51-52.

—VIRGINIA BARNSTORFF

Sports Cards/Memorabilia Store

While player cards have long been collectors' items among young people in the United States, more and more adults have become collectors in recent years. This trend, along with increasing interest in fitness and collegiate sports, has made the business of sports cards and other memorabilia a multi-billion-dollar industry.

Although the growth of national sporting goods stores—with heavy advertising and "lowest price" guarantees—has stiffened the competition for independent shop owners, success is still possible for the entrepreneur who loves sports, possesses keen business sense, and fosters a genuine team spirit among customers and staff.

COSTS AND PROFITS

The minimum start-up investment required for a sports cards/memorabilia store is about $50,000, with an average reported to be $95,000. High net profit before taxes runs to $204,000, with an average of $133,000. Usually even first-year net profit before taxes exceeds $100,000. Liabilities include repayment of loans, accounts payable to manufacturers for stock items, monthly rental payments for store space, and payroll for staff members.

FINANCING

The first step in getting a new business started is to secure adequate financing. To determine how much capital will be necessary, it is wise to consult with other store owners in the area who can provide first-hand knowledge and helpful hints concerning start-up and maintenance. If this is not possible, there are many other sources of information, such as Robert Morris Associates, publishers of *Lending to Different Industries,* and the local Small Business Administration, which not only provides free counseling and educational training but also may act as guarantor for loans made by banks or private lenders. The chambers of commerce, libraries, and sporting goods manufacturers can also assist in answering questions about the industry. Robert Morris Associates (RMA) can be contacted at (814) 946-6687. The Small Business Administration has a toll-free number (1-800-368-5855) and can also be contacted through the local field office listed in the telephone directory.

Once a projected monetary need has been determined, the next step is to consider funding. The primary resource for new businesses is personal savings and private loans. However, in most cases short- or long-term loans are also necessary. Short-term loans are usually paid back within a year. Long-term loans can be used for start-up costs, equipment, and commercial mortgages, and are usually paid back within seven years. Loan terms depend upon the size of the loan and an educated estimate of how quickly the loan can be repaid. An important factor to consider is the length of the "break-even period"—the time it takes for a business to make enough money to cover start-up expenses—which generally averages nine months to three years in this industry.

LOCATION

Perhaps the single most important factor in establishing a sports cards and memorabilia store is location. Many customers will be shoppers who, upon seeing the store, suddenly consider sports memorabilia as a gift. Hence, visibility is key, especially if the store doesn't advertise frequently. A centralized position in or near a college town is ideal, but shopping or strip malls are also convenient and attract people of all ages. The size of the store largely depends upon rental fees; mall rent can be quite expensive, so a smaller store in a mall is more cost-effective. Stores outside of malls can afford to be larger, allowing room for growth. Included in measurement considerations should be a small office and rest room area and adequate parking facilities.

STORE LAYOUT AND SETUP

The general layout of the store will depend upon the types of items to be sold. If sports cards are to make up the largest percentage of sales, they need to be given a prominent place in the store. Many owners report a greater demand for baseball cards, something that should be kept in mind in determining inventory selection. Collectors' cards of highest value should be kept in a display case to prevent damage—even a slight bend in a corner of a card can drastically reduce market value. Cards of current players should be placed in racks for easy selection. Cards bought in bulk can be sorted and repackaged in quantities of 50 or 100 to give customers

SPORTS CARDS MANUFACTURERS AND SELECTED TRADE PUBLICATIONS

Manufacturers:

Hi-Pro Marketing, Inc. (Action Packed Cards): Northbrook, IL 60062.

Fleet Corporation (Fleet Ultra): Mt. Laurel, NJ 08054.

The Topps Company, Inc. (Topps Baseball, Series 1): Duryea, PA 18642.

Publications:

Confident Collector Baseball Guide: Avon Publishers, Hurst Corporation, 1350 Avenue of the Americas, New York, NY 10019; phone: (800) 238-0658.
Sports Collectors Digest: Krause Publications, Inc., 700 East State Street, Iola, WI 54990.
Sportstrend: 180 Allen Road, N.E., Suite 300 S., Atlanta, GA 30328; phone: (404) 252-8831.

what they're looking for—the coveted rookie and superstar cards—at a lower price.

Other items on hand might include caps, sportswear, pennants, sports trivia games, card price guides, sports books, and autographed items. The hottest sellers will be memorabilia of local sports teams and teams ranked number one in the current standings. Sports knowledge is a definite plus in being able to assess team and player statistics to decide what and how much to order for the next year. Surpluses are not necessarily a problem when a team is playing below expectations, because items can be shelved until the team is back on top. And no sports item is ever out of date!

Windows are an excellent means of exhibiting sportswear. This commodity attracts all types of customers, especially since fitness gear has become increasingly popular. An appealing window set-up can make any store its own advertisement; therefore, much care and attention should be focused on this area.

MANAGEMENT ISSUES

Although staff members should have a sports background or general knowledge of sports, administrative and interpersonal skills are much more important. Sports cards/memorabilia stores often have seasonal highs and lows; hence inventory control and strong management abilities will be key factors in the success of the business. During peaks, store hours should increase, especially on the weekends when more customers are in the mood for leisure shopping. Several part-time staff members should be available to help with customer purchases. A full-time staff member or two—acting as managers—should be responsible for inventory, scheduling, price changes, and customer complaints. All

personnel should be friendly, courteous, and professional, since customer service and satisfaction may provide the competitive edge against larger retail stores.

MARKETING

As has already been mentioned, the small sports cards/memorabilia store faces stiff competition from the national sporting goods chain stores in terms of pricing and selection. The advantage of independents is the ability to specialize and to be oriented toward customer service. If a small business focuses on a relatively few sports, it can offer a wider selection of unique, hard-to-find items in those areas and be able to present knowledgeable advice to customers. This will not only draw customers in, but will also bring them back for repeat business.

Another way to serve customers is to provide request forms for items they are looking for but cannot find in the store. This should only be done, however, if there is a serious commitment to finding the item requested or an acceptable substitute. These order forms can also be used to help select future inventory items, as they give a clear indication of customer needs.

Personal attention is always good policy, and the sales staff will be very effective if attempts are made to become acquainted with customers on an individual basis, acknowledging preferences and past purchases and even contacting a customer when an item that would be of interest is received by the store.

Utilizing the various sports' seasonal schedules and main events as a marketing tool can bring about the largest percentage of sales for the year. Christmas is always a good time to have the store well stocked and opened for longer business hours, but college bowls, the Superbowl, the Stanley Cup Finals, NCAA tournaments, NBA championships, and the World Series are all major selling opportunities if appropriate stock is on hand.

INDUSTRY STATISTICS AND PRIMARY ASSOCIATION

Statistics:
• Sporting goods represent almost $15 billion in sales per year.
• Sports memorabilia stores average annual gross sales of $300,000 to $400,000.
• Sports trading cards represented $4 billion in annual sales for 1992, with 60% of that being baseball cards.
• There are an estimated 5 to 6 million card collectors in the United States.
• Competitor Spectathlete breaks down sales percentages as follows: college merchandise, 25%; baseball, 20%; basketball, 15%; hockey, 10%.

Association:

National Sporting Goods Association: 1699 Wall St., Mount Prospect, IL 60056; phone: (708) 439-4000.

Demographics will also play a role in determining what to sell and when to sell it. Stores in college towns require trendy, inexpensive sportswear and regalia that cater to the local college teams, while collectors' items usually sell best in more affluent areas. The socio-economic makeup of an area cannot be underestimated.

ADVERTISING

Heavy advertising should begin immediately after start-up and continue for at least six months thereafter. If it is possible for a local player to make a personal appearance at the store, newspaper ads and fliers announcing autograph sessions will draw in sports fans, celebrity gazers, and maybe even a sports writer or two. Children and adults love to have sports cards, books, and other memorabilia signed by a favorite player.

Local sports publications or cable television productions may be a more expensive source of promotion but may attract the more serious-minded sports enthusiast, with resulting sales thereby offsetting the advertising costs. Printed and televised ads should be brief, to the point, and memorable. A key phrase or creative approach will often spark interest or curiosity. Any other special engagements, merchandise sales, or unique acquisitions should be advertised. As mentioned above, making the connection between the store and a sporting event such as an NCAA tournament game stimulates a desire to buy; hence ads should run predominantly when sports excitement is at its peak.

LICENSES AND INSURANCE

Opening a sports cards/memorabilia store requires a local business license, as well as state and/or city tax permits. Fire, theft, and property insurance is a must to insure valuable collectors' items. General liability insurance should also be purchased to cover slip-and-fall and other accident cases. Care should be taken to review the different types of insurance policies before making a commitment.

SOURCES:

Brecka, Jon, editor, *Baseball Cards—Questions and Answers,* Krause Publications, Inc., 1990.

Entrepreneur's Sports Memorabilia Business Guide, February 1992.

Kahn, Sharon, and the Philip Lief Group, *101 Best Businesses to Start,* revised, Doubleday, 1992.

Madden, Michael, editor, *Small Businesses Start-Up Index,* Gale, 1991 cumulation.

Perry, Robert, "High-Scoring Money-Maker: Sports Cards," *Income Opportunities,* Volume 26, May 1991.

"Sporting Goods Store," *Entrepreneur Magazine's 168 More Businesses Anyone Can Start and Make a Lot of Money,* second edition, Bantam, 1991.

Weinstein, Bob, "Good Sports," *Entrepreneur,* April 1993.

—*Edna M. Hedblad*

T-Shirt Shop

The retail T-shirt industry has been growing steadily for decades. T-shirts are the largest segment of casual wear and appeal to a broad market, from students and sports fans to tourists and businesses. T-shirts are a fun and simple way to display personalized messages and advertisements. A retail T-shirt business is easy to run and requires minimal investment, equipment, and space. It is also a relatively stable enterprise and has very good profit potential. The T-shirt business is also ideal for those seeking absentee ownership.

START-UP COSTS AND PROFIT POTENTIAL

Start-up costs for a retail T-shirt business can range from $6,000 to more than $10,000. You can expect more than 50 percent of your gross to be profit, but your total income depends on whether you concentrate on the personal purchase market or the corporate promotional market. A low-volume store that concentrates mainly on personal purchases can gross about $3,200 per month, while a store that develops a strong business promotional segment can gross $20,000 per month.

LOCATION

Location is essential to success, particularly if you rely on the personal purchase market. You should research your potential region thoroughly. Local chambers of commerce and small business development centers should have adequate information on the economic and demographic profiles of the population. You could also get advertising and sales information from various local media. Find out the average ages, incomes, and types of occupations of the community's residents. Their purchasing power should be stable or increasing. Diverse industry in the region will increase your chances of developing corporate promotional clientele.

Keep in mind that the T-shirt business is largely an impulse market. To generate high-volume sales, your location should be accessible to pedestrian traffic, clearly visible to passers-by, and near a similar cross-section of small businesses. High pedestrian areas, such as tourist attractions or college campuses, are ideal. Malls have the advantage of dense shopping traffic. However, not all mall cites are visible, and malls charge higher rents for less space. In addition, in a new mall you may have to invest several thousands of dollars for construction.

In terms of size, you will need as little as 300 square feet for retail and storage/office space. (If you intend to operate on a larger scale and keep greater amounts of stock, you may need as much as 1,000 square feet.) Make sure the space accommodates your needs; make sure the electrical lines are adequate and determine if you will need a separate insurance and security system. If you allow customers to use your rest room, you should have one for women and another for men. You might also consider installing a small dressing room. You can use the retail space for most of your storage needs and leave only a small room for office work. Rent varies greatly by region, but the average cost is $500 per month, and a mall space runs at least $1,000 per month. To minimize risks, negotiate for a one- or two-year lease. Your contract could include an option to renew annually for several years.

STORE LAYOUT AND EQUIPMENT

It is important to design your store in a creative but efficient way. To display your T-shirts, you will need one or more center islands—low enough for the salespeople to observe on everyone in the store. Set up display racks along the walls and shelves above or next to them for stacking T-shirts. If you have limited capital, you might try making the shelves yourself or ask some woodworking students or friends to help you with customized shelving. If you have enough room, set up a round display rack at the front of the store. Display the heat transfers on boards to make them visible to customers. You should also set up several full-length mirrors.

Probably the most important piece of equipment for a T-shirt shop is the "heat seal press" which you will use for pressing on decals and lettering. You can locate press manufacturers through the Screen Printing Association and trade journals. A new machine costs about $2,000, but for a few hundred dollars you can buy a used press or a new press intended for smaller volumes. You could also put a down payment on a machine or lease one for under $100 per

INDUSTRY STATISTICS

- *T-Shirt Market (1991):* estimated $1.68 billion market (source: Investext, from *Market Share Reporter*).
- *Screen Printing Sales in the U.S. (1993):* $20 billion industry (source: *Crain's Detroit Business*).
- *Growth of the Licensed Sports Apparel Market:* sales grew 65% from 1990 to $7.1 billion in 1992, one of the fastest-growing segments of men's apparel (source: *Chicago Tribune*).
- *T-Shirt Market:* dominated in the 1990s by Fruit of the Loom Inc. and Hanes (source: *New York Times*, from The Fashion Network Report).
- *Youth Segment of T-Shirt Sales (1993):* 34% of T-shirts sold for the 7 to 17-year-old market; average cost of $8.20 (source: *Youth Markets Alert*).
- *Non-Sports Apparel T-Shirt Market for Kids (1993):* 98%; only 2% for active sports (source: *Youth Markets Alert*).
- *Youth Segment of Printed T-Shirts (1993):* 57% units with message: 40% with non-sport message; 10% with major sports license emblem (source: *Youth Markets Alert*).

month. If leasing, try to get title of your product immediately so you can write it off as an investment. The press is easy to use and can be mastered quickly.

The high-tech alternative method of printing T-shirts is screen printing by computers. If you decide to take this route you will have to invest several thousand dollars on a machine. Being on the cutting edge of technology, however, may be a worth the investment. One company was enormously successful by setting up their store so customers could watch the process of designing patterns on a computer monitor. The advantages of screen printing include a greater variety of available designs, easier pattern layout, and on-site production rather than sending orders to manufacturers. You can also personalize individual patterns rather than order the dozen or more of each design as required by most manufacturers. The higher-quality screen printing process is also often favored by older clientele and businesses seeking a professional look.

Another piece of equipment to consider buying is a stereo so you can play music that will draw young customers. An inventory tracking cash register is also a good investment; you can buy one or rent one for several hundred dollars per month. You will also need a phone and answering machine as well as filing cabinets for storing decals. Keep a dictionary at hand so your salespeople and customers can check the spelling of their messages. Other office supplies you will need are pens and paper, business cards, letterhead stationery, and a record-keeping system.

MARKETING STRATEGIES

You should strive to create an interesting image for your store. One of your first tasks is thinking of a distinctive store name—which includes some variant of T-shirt—so people can quickly associate name with product. Design an eye-catching sign and place it clearly at your storefront. Be sure to take full advantage of your exterior display windows—they are an excellent source of advertising for your store.

About two-thirds of your business will probably be the personal market and one-third corporate promotional. If you develop a good balance of both markets, you could gross more than $250,000 annually. Try to get as much of the business market as possible since it usually commands larger quantities. Send out direct mail brochures to potential businesses and make it clear that your company can handle large-volume customized jobs creatively and efficiently. Display samples of previous orders from companies and sports teams on the walls to inspire purchases of T-shirts as promotional items. (If you are just starting out, design samples of customized promotional T-shirts.) Try to come up with innovative gimmicks; for instance, T-shirts for dogs have become a $500 million industry. Let customers know that you are willing to place special orders by mail and offer them mail order forms along with your brochure. Offer discounts for larger quantity orders.

ADVERTISING

Initial places to advertise include local and student newspapers, the Yellow Pages, and brochures. Radio can be quite inexpensive and effective as well. You could attract the college crowd by featuring students in your local ads or by offering competitions for the best T-shirt designs. Your first

PRIMARY ASSOCIATIONS AND SELECTED TRADE PUBLICATIONS

Associations:

T.S.H.I.R.T.S. (The Society Handling the Interchange of Remarkable T-Shirts): 2554 Lincoln Blvd., #400, Venice, CA 90291.

Screen Printing Association International: 10015 Main St., Fairfax, VA 22031; phone: (703) 385-1335.

National Decorating Products Association: 1050 N. Lindberg Ave., St. Louis, MO 63132-2994; phone: (314) 991-3470.

National Outerwear and Sportswear Association: 475 Park Ave. S., New York, NY 10016; phone: (212) 686-3440.

National Retail Federation: 100 W. 31st St., New York, NY 10001; phone: (212) 631-7400.

Publications:

Impressions: 10015 Main St., Fairfax, VA 22031; phone: (703) 385-1335.
Decorating Retailer: 1050 N. Lindberg Ave., St. Louis, MO 63132-2994; phone: (314) 991-3470.
Interiors: Billboard Publications Inc., Time Publishing Co., 407 Gilbert Ave., Cincinnati, OH 45202.
Sportstyle: Fairchild Publications, Inc., 7 E. 12th St., New York, NY 10003; phone: (212) 741-5971.

FRANCHISE OPPORTUNITIES

T-Shirts Plus: The Plus Companies, 4732 W. Waco Dr., Waco, TX 76710; phone: (817) 776-8872. Contact David Byrd, executive vice-president; founded 1972; franchising since 1973; 175 units; located in regional malls; features imprinted sportswear and customized active wear, on-site customized imprinting service, special orders for businesses, clubs, and sports teams. Provided by franchiser: two weeks training at company headquarters (must pay own travel and lodging), newsletter, seminars. Franchising fee $35,000; royalties 7% plus 2% for advertising; total investment: $83,000 to $111,000. Financing available.

Wild Tops: National Development Group Inc., P.O. Box 2601, Framingham, MA 01701-0407. Contact Richard Gold, president. Founded 1985; franchising since 1985; four company-owned units; 18 franchised units; located in 400-1000 square-foot retail site in a mall, strip center, or other suitable facility; features sportswear such as T-shirts, sweatshirts, and fashion tops imprinted with contemporary designs; customized service, using heat transfers, flock lettering, screen printing. Provided by franchiser: one-week training program at the headquarters and in-store training at an outlet. Franchising fee $18,000; royalties 6% gross sales; total investment $40,000 to $150,000. No financing.

Nationwide Screenprinting of Alabama: 820 Rockford, Birmingham, AL 35209. Contact Rebecca Yates, president. Founded 1984; franchising since 1984; over 1000 units; features silkscreen for T-shirts and other items. Provided by franchiser: complete silkscreen set-up, training, a "Tech Help" hotline number, buying sources for suppliers, and a one-year warranty on all equipment. Total investment $8,999. No financing.

big media campaign should be your grand opening. After your store has been in operation about a month, celebrate the event by offering free food and drinks, discount coupons, or a special contest drawing. Publicize your grand opening by sending a press release and photo to local papers. Conduct occasional publicity campaigns and involve yourself in the community so your clients become familiar with you and your business.

INVENTORY AND PRICING

Your suppliers should be able to help you decide on appropriate T-shirt styles and decals for your target market. Start out with about 15 dozen T-shirts of each size: small, medium, large, and extra-large. Stock 100 percent cotton shirts, blends, and perhaps some of the environmentally safe, organically grown cotton shirts, to see which do best with your market. Pure cotton holds decals better than 50/50 cotton blends, although blends have the advantage of being shrink resistant. Keep in mind that darker-colored shirts tend to discolor slightly during the heat transfer process but can be countered by using screen printing. Choose several couple

dozen decals to start and increase to as many as a hundred as you go along. Make sure you have several styles of lettering on hand. Also, stock up on popular pre-printed shirts depicting famous personalities, sports teams, and advertisements.

To price your goods, double the wholesale cost of the T-shirts and triple the cost of transfers. To determine your net profits before taxes, calculate average monthly sales per square foot and deduct costs. Try to be competitive with other T-shirt retailers but do not undersell your products. Justify higher costs than your competition by offering better quality, service, and selection. Always be accommodating with customers.

STAFFING

When placing ads for job applicants, be as specific as possible with requirements to save you time during interviews. Advertise in local papers, schools, and agencies. Because T-shirt customers tend to be under 35 years old, you may want to seek fairly young staff members. One salesperson can handle about 25 sales per day. If you make more than about 75 sales per day, you will need a third salesperson and another press. (Be prepared for higher-volume sales during holiday seasons by hiring part-time staff members.) Keep your staff loyal to you by treating them well and offering discounts, occasional bonuses, and raises based on merit. Group insurance will cost you under $100 per month per employee. Remember that you must pay social security and other taxes for your employees. If you plan to hire a manager, you should add an override of one to three percent of sales to increase their productivity. You or your manager should do the bookkeeping of payrolls and expenses each week, or you can hire someone to do it for you for about $15 per hour.

SOURCES:

Heerwagen, Peter, "Signet Screen Printing Expands Operations," *North Valley Business Journal,* November 1991, p. 10.
"Hot Products '89," *ADWEEK Eastern Edition,* October 16, 1989, p. 32.
Maurer, Michael, "Wash And—Where Is It? Not These Shirt Designs," *Crain's Detroit Business,* August 9, 1993, p. E-5.
"1993 Outstate Michigan Private 50: The Top Three," *Outstate Business,* April 1993, p. 9.
Ryan, Nancy, "Sports Firm 'a Good Fit' For Loom," *Chicago Tribune,* October 12, 1993.
Schmitt, Jane, "T-Shirt Painting: From Basement to New Building," *Business First-Buffalo,* September 30, 1991, p. 1.
"T-Shirt Manufacturers," *Market Share Reporter,* Gale Research, Inc., 1993.
T-Shirt Shop, Entrepreneur Inc., American Entrepreneur Association Manual, 1988.
"T-Shirts With a Message," *Youth Markets Alert,* October 1993.

—*AUDRA AVIZIENIS*

Temporary Employment Service

Listed in the early 1990s as the third-largest developing industry in the United States, temporary help services have grown into a $20 billion business. Nine out of ten companies hire temporary employees from such services, and an increasing number of people are opting to work on a temporary basis because of the flexibility and varied experiences available in this type of working arrangement. Temporary employees are used extensively in the clerical, computer consulting, technical, professional, and medical fields. Profits for a new temporary employment service accrue quickly after a two- to three-year start-up period, with revenue potential between $250,000 and $20 million, depending upon the size and type of temporary service. Competition in the industry has increased as franchises continue to develop, but the need for temporary staff continues to grow as the economic structure fluctuates; thus there is tremendous potential for success with a highly organized, well-marketed, detail-oriented business.

COSTS AND PROFITS

Minimum start-up costs for a temporary help service range from $15,000 to $50,000, depending on whether the business is clerical or professional in nature. Many temporary services report an average start-up cost of about $35,000. Annual net profits before taxes vary from $12,000 to $500,000, with an average of $45,000. Revenues can extend from $250,000 to $1 million and up. Liabilities include payroll, advertising, insurance coverage, and office rental space.

FINANCING

"Anybody can succeed with a temporary employment company if you have enough capital," says Philip D. Cox, president of StaffAmerica Management Group, Inc. Having enough capital means being able to pay temporary employees a weekly salary while waiting 30 to 60 days for payment to be received from corporate clients. Thus, the beginning entrepreneur must first establish a "slush fund" or line of credit to cover payroll expenses and carry the new business through the break-even period, a duration of usually six months to a year. Since approximately 35 percent of the initial investment should be liquid assets, most entrepreneurs use personal savings and other personal resources as principal capital, coupled with private sources such as small loans at little or no interest from friends and relatives.

Banks and credit unions offer short-term and long-term loans to business ventures that appear to have the potential for profit. To obtain a bank loan, borrowers must present a clear and concise loan request stating exactly how much money is needed, how it will be used, and how it will be repaid. A written proposal is considered the best means of applying for a loan. The U.S. Small Business Administration suggests including the following elements in the proposal: general information stating the name of the business, principals involved, and purpose and amount of the loan; a brief description of the nature and structure of the business; a management profile describing the background, experience, and education of each principal; market information outlining services provided, anticipated competition, and customers targeted; and financial information including a projected balance sheet and income statement, personal financial statements from each principal owner, and a delineation of all collateral used to secure the loan.

When reviewing requests, bank loan officers consider how much personal savings an entrepreneur plans to invest in the new business, which should equal at least 25 to 50 percent of the intended loan. For example, if the borrower requests a loan of $100,000, he or she should be prepared to invest at least $25,000 to $50,000 of personal equity. A sound credit record is also important; however, the most important factor in determining whether a loan request will be granted is a projected cash flow sufficient to make payments on the loan. Therefore, the borrower must assure lenders of an efficient, productive, and profitable establishment.

The **Small Business Administration (SBA)** can provide further financial assistance as a guarantor—guaranteeing a loan made by a bank or private institution for up to 90 percent of the loan balance. The Administration, through its Small Business Development Centers, also offers management and technical assistance to small businesses. Copies of the *Small Business Directory* or other resource information published by the SBA can be obtained by writing, **Small Business Directory, P.O. Box 15434, Fort Worth, Texas, 76119,** or calling **1-800-U ASK SBA. Rob-**

FRANCHISE OPPORTUNITIES

Dynamic Temporary Services/Norrell Services:
3535 Piedmont Rd., NE, Atlanta, GA 30305; phone: (404) 240-3000, or (800) 334-9694. Began franchising in 1966; over 250 outlets in the U.S. and Canada; provides skilled employees with specialization in clerical and secretarial services; expansion plans project continued development of outlets in the United States and abroad. Start-up costs: no franchise fee, equipment such as computers, telephone system, office furnishings, miscellaneous office supplies. Provided by franchisor: initial printed supplies, assistance in establishment including site selection, marketing, employee selection and training, processing of payroll and taxes, and ongoing training programs. Start-up investment: $50,000 to $90,000.

Todays Temporary: 18111 Preston Rd., Ste. 800, Dallas, TX 75252; phone: (214) 380-9380, or (800) 822-7868; provides personnel for short- and long-term office assignments; founded in 1982, began franchising in 1983; 39 outlets in 15 states, with plans for continued expansion throughout the United States. Start-up costs range from $60,000 to $100,000.

Other Franchisors: Career Blazers: 590 5th Ave., New York, NY 10036; phone: (800) 284-3232. **Five Star Temporaries:** 1415 Elbridge Payne, Ste. 255, Chesterfield, MO 63017; phone: (314) 532-2777.

ert Morris Associates also publishes a financial guide entitled *Lending to Different Industries* and can be contacted at **(814) 946-6687.**

LOCATION

Temporary help services can be based in the home, which affords the beginning entrepreneur the advantage of minimal overhead expenses. Billing and other accounting can be done on a personal computer, and prospective clients can be visited at their offices. However, a conference room or other office space is necessary for interviewing temporary employees. Rental fees for such space average about $80 per day; entrepreneurs should count on using office space several days a month for a dozen or so interviews each day.

The fastest-growing segment of the temporary help industry has been specialty services such as data-processing and accounting. Since training on various computer software packages is required in these specialized areas, renting an office in a business district—near companies targeted for business—is advisable. Office space should include a working area for employees of the temporary help service, a training and testing room for temporary employees, and a conference room for interviews and meetings with clients.

LAYOUT AND SETUP

A temporary employment agency should look professional without being extravagant. An open-office arrangement works best, with no partitions separating the general work area. The atmosphere should be cheerful and relaxing, to calm nervous potential employees who have come to be interviewed. If possible, an office with many windows should be chosen to help create a bright, energetic look. Decor and furnishings should be transitional or contemporary, with tasteful art work that complements the office space and appeals to all types of clients and personnel. Plants also provide an inviting atmosphere.

A large conference table with several chairs, three or four desks (depending upon the number of staff), file cabinets, and tables for computers are necessities. Most services have a reception area or lobby where clients and job applicants are greeted and directed to appropriate personnel.

STAFFING

Two to four staff members are needed for start-up operations. Success in this industry depends upon the ability to manage diverse details in a timely and organized fashion. Thus staff should possess skills in three distinct areas: personnel, sales, and administration. The management team must be able to sell the service to clients who may be skeptical of temporary staffing and then continue marketing efforts to increase volume. Staff should also be able to hire reliable, productive employees for the temporary positions that need to be filled and perform the many and varied administrative duties which include handling time cards, paychecks, tax and insurance deductions, bills to clients, reports to the government, and client and temporary employee files. Responsibilities can, of course, be compartmentalized. Many services hire expert salespeople, accountants, and managers for specific tasks.

MARKETING

Effective marketing strategy is vital to the success of the temporary employment agency. Once a business district has been selected as a marketing target according to demographic studies, sales representatives or managers with a business background should begin contacting heads of corporations to inform them about the service. Personal visits are the best method of contact, as they provide more time for discussion and usually result in greater commitment by the client. However, time, effort, and expense can be reduced through telemarketing. This involves a 30 to 60 second sales pitch in which objections are quickly overcome and advantages of employing temporary help are emphasized. Clients should be reminded that temporaries do not contribute to their overhead in terms of benefits that can amount to as much as 33 percent over wages. Thus the company actually saves on the hidden costs of full-time employees.

Agencies training employees for specific word processing systems, computer programs, or other specialties attract their own customer base as they are sought out by clients with particular needs. Simple company surveys can help determine training necessary in a very cost-effective manner. Another option is to buy existing lists of clients and personnel, thereby reducing start-up expenditures of time and money; however, this usually involves a significant amount of capital and can be a difficult procedure.

Once a customer base has been established, effort must be made to maintain it. Louise Bruechert, president of MarKit Marketing Packages in Atlanta, GA, terms this practice "relationship marketing." Emphasis is placed upon dialogue between agency and client, building upon "client budget percentages." Increasing overall market share is relatively less important and less profitable than receiving a larger percentage of each client's operating expenses—especially for a small agency. A newsletter can serve both communication and volume purposes, reaching key clients, occasional users, and even prospective customers. Quarterly newsletters are frequent enough, but the main objective is consistency. A publication schedule should be set and followed or the agency will appear to be undependable. Dialogue will exist if readers are given the opportunity to respond: contests, surveys, and soliciting input on industry issues help to engage the reader and also strengthen the relationship between client and agency.

MANAGEMENT ISSUES

Management and administrative duties present the biggest challenge to the entrepreneur starting a temporary employment agency. *Entrepreneur Magazine's 168 More Businesses Anyone Can Start and Make a Lot of Money* states: "A typical day might include interviewing applicants, testing candidates, pitching clients, solving problems, handling payroll, taking orders, and making assignments."

A newly established agency must have a labor force in place before clients are contacted, but recruiting should not begin too early or applicants may grow impatient waiting for work and look elsewhere. Interviews for temporary staff

INDUSTRY STATISTICS

- The growth rate in the temporary help services field is three times that of all other service industries combined.
- Nine out of ten U.S. companies utilize temporary employees.
- 37% of temporary employees are placed in medical, professional, or industrial positions.
- The U.S. government expects 1.25 million jobs per day requiring temporary employees by 1995.
- 80% of all temporary employees are female, with 29% being 25 to 34 years old and 9% over 55.
- There are more than 3500 national and independent temporary services operating in the United States
- Annual revenues for a single agency average between $250,000 and $1 million; pre-tax profits range from $12,000 to $500,000.
- The national temporary payroll exceeds $15 billion per year.
- The temporary help industry has a projected growth rate of 5 to 10% per year through the year 2000.

workers generally should run 30 to 45 minutes, assessing skills, education, and qualifications for the types of jobs to be filled. Applicants should provide their own resumes, if possible; this enables the temporary agency to send a copy to the client, and having resumes ready speeds the placement process. It is helpful to create interview and order forms for the agency's own use, as well as stationery, business cards, mailings, and brochures. Mailings to clients and temporary staff should look as professional as possible, with no expense spared in contracting with a printing company that will provide creative, unique, and attractive materials.

The procedure for testing applicants might include typing, filing, and proofreading assignments, all designed to match appropriate employees to the hiring company. Constant recruitment and training are needed as temporary workers set their own schedules of availability. Some agencies offer benefits, profit sharing, vacations, trips, and prizes to attract and keep workers on the payroll. Free computer training serves both the agency and temporary staffer, encouraging workers to make themselves more marketable. Many companies allow temporary staff to train themselves on various computer software packages at their own pace and level.

Once workers are in place, financial and administrative duties must be addressed. Profits are determined by the mark-up charged to a hiring company for services rendered. Generally, mark-up rates run between 50 and 80 percent of the hourly rate paid to the temporary worker, with an average of 65 percent. For example, if a temporary receptionist is paid $10 per hour, the hiring company would be charged $16.50 per hour, with the difference being the agency's gross profit. The rate of pay before mark-up is added will depend upon the job assignment, the skill required, and the going rate in the local labor market. At the end of the pay period, time cards must be verified, paychecks must be cut with taxes deducted, and clients must be billed. Temporary help services are recognized in each state as employers for tax purposes, obligating services to pay all employment taxes, including social security, federal, and state employment taxes. For more information concerning tax and legal issues, contact the local General Services Administration (GSA), Small Business Administration (SBA), and State Division of Taxation.

ADVERTISING AND RECRUITING

Temporary employment agencies have to advertise for clients as well as employees. Since specialty services are the most sought after, ads that focus on specific skills can be placed in different sections of the local newspaper or phone book to attract companies in need of assistance. Local business journals and professional publications are other print options. Personal visits with clients are advantageous as well, as they help to build relationships with hiring companies and enable the temporary service to better assess and meet the needs of the companies.

PRIMARY ASSOCIATIONS AND SELECTED TRADE PUBLICATIONS

Associations:

National Association of Temporary Services: 119 S. Saint Asaph St., Alexandria, VA 22314; phone: (703) 549-6287.

National Staff Leasing Association (NSLA): 1735 N. Lynn St., Ste. 950, Arlington, VA 22209-2022; phone: (703) 524-3636.

American Association of Temporary and Contract Employees: 1621 19th St., N.W., Washington, DC 20009.

Publications:

Contemporary Times: National Association of Temporary Services, Inc., 119 South Saint Asaph Street, Alexandria, VA 22314; phone: (703) 549-6287.
EMA Reporter: Employment Management Association, 4101 Lake Boone Tr., No. 201, Raleigh, NC 27607; phone: (919) 787-6010.
The Employee Leasing Advantage: Aegis Group, 155 W. Hospitality Ln., Ste. 215, San Bernadino, CA 92408; phone: (714) 381-4800.
Office Magazine: 1600 Summer St., Stamford, CT 06904; phone: (203) 327-9670.
Office Systems: 941 Danbury Rd., P.O. Box 150, Georgetown, CT 06829; phone: (203) 544-9526.

A common difficulty among temporary employment agencies is meeting the demand for workers. If free training on computers or other office equipment is available, this should be mentioned, as employees appreciate the experience and added marketability. As an additional recruiting tool, many services offer bonuses for employees who refer friends or relatives.

RISK MANAGEMENT AND INSURANCE

All employees in the United States are required to provide workers' compensation covering medical expenses and partial wages for job-related injury or illness. Although health insurance is not mandatory, many temporary employment agencies have health plans established, especially for those employees with long-term assignments. General liability coverage insures against negligence resulting in injury or property damage on the part of the insured or its employees. However, since these policies are most often limited to the premises of the insured, effort must be made to seek out an insurance policy that will extend to operations on the premises of the client. Property coverage should include fire, theft, and computer policies to protect both hardware and software. Since employee fraud has increased dramatically in the last decade or so, it is advisable to purchase some type of employee dishonesty coverage that will protect against falsified time cards, deceptive workers' compensation claims, and other fraudulent acts.

Starting an independent or franchised temporary agency is a challenge requiring personal investment, a great deal of start-up time and effort, and excellent management and administrative skills. Nevertheless, the temporary employment industry continues to grow dramatically, providing the potential for great success for the determined entrepreneur.

SOURCES:

Entrepreneur's Temporary Help Service Business Guide, February 1992.
''Franchise Finds,'' *Small Business Opportunities,* November 1993.
''How to Start and Operate a Temporary Help Service,'' E. A. Morgan Publishing Co., 1986.
Innerview, Todays Temporary, Volume 7, Issue 1, Winter 1994.
Kahn, Sharon, and the Philip Lief Group, *101 Best Businesses to Start,* Doubleday, 1992.
Lesberg, Eileen, ''Updating Your Insurance Portfolio,'' *Contemporary Times,* winter 1986.
Madden, Michael, editor, *Small Business Start-Up Index,* Gale, 1991.
Martin, Susan Boyles, editor, *Worldwide Franchise Directory,* Gale, 1991.
Schwartz, Carol A., editor, *Small Business Sourcebook,* Volume 1, Gale, 1993.
''Temporary Help Service,'' *Entrepreneur Magazine's 168 More Businesses Anyone Can Start and Make a Lot of Money,* Bantam, 1991.
''Temporary Services Thrive,'' *Entrepreneur,* July 1987.
Woy, Patricia A., ''Temporary Employment Agency,'' *Small Businesses That Grow and Grow and Grow,* Betterway Publications, 1989.

—EDNA M. HEDBLAD

Travel Agency

In the early 1990s travel agencies constituted an $86 billion industry. While there were a few large companies in the field—including the Carlson Travel Network and American Express with more than 400 and 700 outlets, respectively—of the 32,000 travel agency locations in the United States in 1991, more than 70 percent were independently owned firms occupying a single office.

In addition to general business savvy, managing a travel agency required specialized knowledge of the travel industry, and a great many agencies were started by former travel agents. Starting a travel agency was also a popular option for business executives who wanted to make a mid-life career change. Some people were attracted to the business primarily because of such industry perks as free or reduced travel costs. However, by 1993 airlines and other travel providers had begun cutting back on such discounts, and consultants cautioned against confusing a love of travel with the desire to run a travel agency. Travel agencies, in general, operated on very small margins and needed large volumes of business to be even moderately profitable.

FINANCIAL ASPECTS

Opening your own travel agency can be fairly inexpensive, with start-up costs ranging from $15,000 to $60,000. These costs will include leasing and furnishing an office, hiring a staff, and purchasing equipment. In terms of the latter, all that will be necessary initially are a telephone system and a computer.

Most of your start-up expense will be allocated for leasing an office and hiring a staff. Based on where you plan to locate your business, rent will range from moderate to high. An office in a suburban area of retail establishments will be less expensive than leasing an office in a downtown business district. Handling corporate accounts will hasten your need for access to an airline reservation system and ARC accreditation—meeting accreditation requirements may double your minimum start-up costs. Purchasing a franchise could add another $8,000 to $30,000.

You will also need working capital until you begin to generate a positive cash flow, which may take anywhere from six months to a couple of years. An important point to understand is that travel agencies make their money from commissions paid by travel suppliers—airlines, tour operators, hotels, tourist attractions, car rental agencies, etc.—on ticket sales and bookings. The average commission is about 10 percent. Therefore a travel agency generating $1 million in sales grosses about $100,000 from which expenses must be paid. While the average agency had sales of $2.7 million in 1991, 30 percent of all travel agencies had sales of less than $1 million.

Starting a travel agency may put you in a position to take advantage of a unique source of financing that may be unavailable to other small businesses. People who invest in travel agencies often expect little or no interest on their investment in exchange for travel-related perks or simply to be associated with the industry. Investors who also act as outside sales agents may be eligible for low-cost travel or other perks based on the amount of business they send your way. However, in addition to cutting back on discounts, travel providers were cracking down on people misrepresenting themselves as travel agents.

The **Small Business Administration (SBA)** is another possible source of start-up capital. The SBA is an independent agency of the U.S. government that promotes small businesses through loans, counseling, and other information. The SBA is particularly concerned with women and minority ownership. However, you must exhaust all sources of private financing before you are eligible for an SBA loan. There are Small Business Administration offices in most major cities. Check the U.S. Government section of the telephone directory for locations and telephone numbers. You can also reach the SBA at **1-800-U ASK SBA**.

Keep in mind that in order to issue airline tickets, a travel agency must be accredited by the Airlines Reporting Corporation (ARC). As of the early 1990s about 96 percent of all travel agencies were accredited. However, accreditation is an expense that start-up agencies with limited ticketing may be able to postpone. In such a situation, an accredited agency can usually be found to issue tickets in return for a share of the commission, but at some point accreditation probably will become necessary. In addition to the convenience of issuing your own tickets—and not sharing commissions—some reduced rates on airline tickets, car rentals, and hotel accommodations are available only to accredited agencies. ARC also is responsible for the settlement process

FRANCHISE OPPORTUNITIES

Carlson Travel Network: P.O. Box 59159, Minneapolis, MN 55459-8206; phone: (612) 449-8207. Carlson Travel is the largest and oldest travel network in the U.S., dating back to 1888 when Ward G. Foster founded Ask Mr. Foster Travel in St. Augustine, Florida. In 1979 Ask Mr. Foster was purchased by Carlson Companies, Inc., which changed its name to Carlson Travel Network in 1990. In 1993, in addition to 400 company-owned agencies, there were more than 1,100 Carlson Travel Network "associate" travel agencies in operation. A Carlson Travel Network franchise cost $3,750, plus a percentage of the agency's commissions. However, Carlson franchised only existing agencies and did not provide start-up support.

Other Franchisors: Cruise Holidays International (cruise travel only): 9665 Chesapeake Dr., Ste. 401, San Diego, CA 92123; phone: (800) 866-7245. **GalaxSea Cruises:** 1400 E. Oakland Park Blvd., Ste. 103, Fort Lauderdale, FL 33334; phone: (800) 821-1072. **International Tours:** 5810 E. Skelly Dr., Ste. 400, Tulsa, OK 74135; phone: (800) 777-9691. **Pal Travel International:** 5180 Park Ave., Ste. 310, Memphis, TN 38119; phone: (901) 761-3084. **Travel Agents International, Inc.:** Box 31005, St. Petersburg, FL 33731-8905; phone: (800) 234-8241. **Travel Network Ltd.:** 560 Sylvan Ave., Englewood Cliffs, NJ 07632; phone: (800) TRAV NET. **Travel and Cruise Professionals International:** 10172 Linn Station Rd., Ste. 360, Louisville, KY 40223; phone: (800) 626-2469. **Travel Pros:** 3030 N. Rocky Point, Ste. 100, Tampa, FL 33607; phone: (813) 281-5670. **Travel Travel International:** 8855 Villa La Jolla Dr., La Jolla, CA 92037; phone: (800) 800-2410. **Travelhost Agencies, Inc.:** 8080 N. Central Expressway, 14th Fl., Dallas, TX 75206; phone: (800) 537-2732. **TravelPlex International:** 655 Metro Place S., Dublin, OH 43017; phone: (614) 766-6315.

that distributes commissions. Accreditation requires travel agencies to meet minimum requirements for experienced personnel and financial liability. For more information, contact the **Airlines Reporting Corporation, P.O. Box 96194, Washington D.C. 20090-6194; phone: (703) 816-8085** or the **International Association of Travel Agents Network, 300 Garden City Plaza, Garden City, NY 11530; phone: (516) 747-4716.**

Some states have passed laws requiring travel agencies to meet minimum standards for experience and financial liability. These regulations often mirrored the requirements for ARC accreditation. Travel agencies in a number of states must also contribute to an assurance fund that protects customers if a firm defaults on its obligations. The majority of states require agencies to deposit their clients' money in a separate bank account until it is paid out to the travel providers.

Another expense to consider is subscription to one of several computerized airline reservation systems, which would provide access to a database containing current rates and booking information on more than 650 airlines, 2700 hotels and motels, and 50 car rental companies. Prices for the systems—the most popular was Sabre from American Airlines—vary widely, but in all cases the more you use the system, the less it costs. Book only a few flights, and the system could cost hundreds of dollars a month; book a lot of flights, and it might pay for itself. Of the agencies with less than $1 million in revenue, 89 percent had an airline reservation system.

SPECIALIZATION

In general, start-up travel agencies should focus on a market niche, because it takes more experience and resources to be a full-service agency. By focusing your efforts, you will be able to provide the type of service that generates repeat business and word-of-mouth advertising. As your business grows, you may expand into other areas to meet customer needs, but you should develop your specialty and your agency's reputation first. The exception is if you plan to locate in a small community that may not be served by other travel agencies. You will then want to offer a full range of services from the beginning. There are generally two types of travel agencies—those that focus on business travel and those that cater to vacationers.

The biggest advantage to handling corporate travel is that commissions generally are paid on full-price tickets because business travelers make their plans too late to take advantage of special rates. Often corporate clients also will ask travel agents to book an entire trip, including airline tickets, hotel reservations, and car rentals. There are drawbacks to handling corporate accounts, however. Most business travel is domestic, which generally pays lower commissions. In addition, businesses may want you to invoice them, causing a possible delay of up to three months before payment is received. This will cost you money in either lost interest or finances charges, depending on your cash flow. Corporate customers are also more likely to request additional services, including ticket delivery and special accounting, reducing your profit margin even further. Because travel plans often change, in many cases you may have to book a trip over again, but no matter how many times a client changes his or her mind, you receive only one commission.

Business travel also is the most competitive arena—nearly 90 percent of all travel agencies handle at least some corporate travel. Large corporate clients often expect rebates based on total sales, a practice that cuts into profits, and if the service is not up to expectations, clients will not hesitate to go elsewhere. Therefore, additional staff with a broader range of skills and experience will be necessary to service business accounts. Pursuing these clients is not usually recommended for a new agency.

The vacation market can be subdivided into a great many niches, each of which can be fertile ground for a start-up travel agency. Some agencies simply focus on particular destinations. An example is Down Under Connections, Inc.

in Marietta, Georgia, which started out by serving only clients traveling to New Zealand and Australia. Other agencies concentrate on serving such specific client groups as unmarried travelers or the elderly, while some firms offer particular kinds of travel, for example scuba diving vacations. In recent years several agencies have been established to serve the gay community.

Vacation travel agencies may cater to individual clients or specialize in group travel. The biggest attraction to working with groups is that a single sale can result in a very large commission. Concentrating on group travel may also work well for a start-up agency with a small staff, especially if your agency focuses on destinations with which you or your staff are personally familiar or works with travel providers that have a good professional reputation. Travel agencies should sell the destinations and tours that the staff knows well; having been there oneself is the best advertising available.

On the other hand, group sales can be very demanding. Groups are much more likely to shop around for the best price. Whatever price you quote will be compared closely with the competition, and a large price differential will often be the deciding factor, even if your agency has more experience and a long list of satisfied customers. You may spend many hours putting together a top-notch travel plan and meeting with the group to present your proposal, only to lose the sale to another agency. To be successful selling group travel, you must be extremely creative and able to negotiate the best possible deals for your customers with the travel providers; good contacts in the travel industry are essential.

INDUSTRY STATISTICS

- *Total U.S. Travel Agency Revenues: $85.9 billion.*
- *Number of Travel Agency Locations: 32,066.*
- *Number of Unaffiliated Single-Office Travel Agencies: 22,000.*
- *Average Revenue Per Travel Agency Location in 1991: $2.7 million.*
- *Percentage of Travel Agency Locations with Less Than $1 Million in Revenues: 30%.*
- *Percentage of Agency Revenues from Domestic Travel: 69%.*
- *Percentage of Agency Revenues from Business Travel: 52%.*
- *Percentage of Agency Revenues from Personal and Vacation Travel: 48%.*
- *Percentage of Travel Agencies with Computerized Reservation Systems: 96%.*
- *Most Common Computerized Reservation System: American Airlines—Sabre (35%).*
- *Percentage of Travel Agency Revenues Generated by Airline Ticket Sales: 56%.*

(SOURCE: 1991 *TRAVEL WEEKLY*/LOU HARRIS & ASSOCIATES POLL.)

LOCATION

Choosing a location for your travel agency will depend on the clientele you hope to attract. If you plan to concentrate on business travel, walk-in traffic will not be essential, though you will need to be fairly close to your clients for pickup or delivery of tickets. Therefore an upper floor in an office building may be an ideal location. Likewise, walk-in traffic will not be especially important should you decide to focus on group travel. For the most part, "selling" will involve giving presentations at the group's location. A simple office with a desk and a telephone would be adequate, but be sure there is a lobby directory or other signage that makes it easy for customers to find you if necessary. You will also need a storage area so the office can be kept neat and clean.

However, if you plan to be a broad-service vacation travel agency your office should be situated in such an area of high visibility as a shopping mall or a busy business district that attracts a good deal of foot-traffic. Be sure that surrounding businesses attract people with discretionary income who may be interested in vacation travel. Also remember that not all travel agencies will necessarily be your competitors, so there is no need to avoid a location simply because another agency is nearby. Agencies situated in the same general area may actually enhance each other's business, provided they specialize in different types of travel.

Whenever you are looking for an office, be sure to ask why a location is vacant. Was the location unsuitable for the previous business? Is it zoned properly for a travel agency? If you expect customers to come to you, be sure there is plenty of convenient parking. The office probably will not require major modifications, although a reception desk or counter will be necessary if considerable walk-in traffic is expected. An important issue to consider is security, especially if you will be issuing airline tickets because blank tickets are almost like cash. Some consultants recommend locating the agency near a bank so that supplies of blank tickets can be kept safe yet accessible. Be sure the bank has Saturday hours because that is likely to be a walk-in travel agency's busiest day.

There seems to be no formula for setting up a travel office. A good example, however, is provided by the winner of *Travel Weekly*'s 1993 award for Best Office Design (for small agencies), Adventure Travel & Cruise Center in Las Cruces, New Mexico. The magazine noted that the agents had oversized L-shaped desks with plenty of room for clients to spread out brochures. Low-rise dividers provided each agent with some privacy without the feeling of being confined in a cubicle. The agency also included a playroom that was originally designed for after-school use by the employees' children, but also became a great place for customers' children to spend time while their parents were conducting business. In addition, there was a combined lounge and consultation area for customers to watch travel tapes.

PRIMARY ASSOCIATIONS AND SELECTED TRADE PUBLICATIONS

Associations:

American Society of Travel Agents (ASTA): 1101 King St., Alexandria, VA 22314; phone: (703) 739-2782.

Association of Retail Travel Agents (ARTA): 1745 Jefferson Davis Highway, Suite 300, Arlington, VA 22202-3402; phone: (800) 969-6069.

Greater Independent Association of National Travel Services (GIANTS): 915 Broadway, New York, NY 10010; phone: (800) 442-6871.

Independent Travel Agencies of America Association (ITAA): 1945 E. Ridge Road, Rochester, NY 14622; phone: (716) 436-4700.

International Gay Travel Association (IGTA): P.O. Box 4974, Key West, FL; phone: (800) 448-8550.

National Association of Business Travel Agents (NABTA): 3255 Wilshire Boulevard, Los Angeles, CA 90010; phone: (213) 382-3335.

Publications:

Travel Agent Magazine: 801 2nd Ave., New York, NY, 10017; phone: (212) 370-5050.
Travel Weekly: 500 Plaza Dr., Secaucus, NJ 07096; phone: (201) 902-2000.

MARKETING STRATEGIES

One of the things you will need to consider when setting up your office is your marketing strategy. Marketing encompasses everything you do to convince people to purchase travel through your agency, beginning with the type of agency you open and extending to the atmosphere in the office. If you focus on corporate accounts, your office should appear business-like and efficient in order to give clients the immediate impression that you are hard at work meeting their needs. You should also develop a professional presentation outlining your services—with an emphasis on convenience and cost—and target smaller firms that may not have been approached by larger agencies. Find out who usually makes travel arrangements for a company and schedule an appointment. Also, do not forget your personal contacts— ask friends and business acquaintances for suggestions and introductions.

Should you plan to serve walk-in customers with vacation travel arrangements, then your window displays, office layout, and signage are among the most important parts of your marketing strategy. Airlines and tour operators are good sources for brochures, posters, and advertising displays. You will want to present a friendly, festive atmosphere that encourages customers to wander in. Do not,

however, sacrifice professionalism or you may find that your agency has plenty of customers, but little business.

Most travel agencies advertise in newspapers, although direct mail is usually more cost-effective because you are able to focus specifically on your target audience. Interest in a new travel agency may also be sparked by organizing seminars for community groups on travel to specific destinations. An Hibernian group might be interested in learning about travel opportunities to Ireland, while a local adventure club may want to explore wilderness tour options. Some agencies give very general presentations on organizing group trips and then offer to provide additional information about specific destinations at a later time. No matter how you choose to market your agency, however, the best advertising is word of mouth from satisfied customers.

PERSONNEL

Most travel agencies employ two kinds of sales agents— inside agents and outside agents. Inside agents are full- or part-time employees who handle day-to-day sales. They usually are paid a straight salary, although by the early 1990s more agencies had begun to offer a base salary plus commission. In 1991 a little more than 20 percent of all inside travel agents received a combined salary and commission, while about six percent received commissions only. Sales agents should generate between two and three times their salaries for an agency to be profitable. In addition to good sales experience, inside staff should be able to write airline tickets and use computer reservation systems. Some community colleges and technical schools offer courses for travel agents, but many airlines offer sales and ticketing courses that are less expensive. Training is also available through industry associations.

Outside agents generate their own leads and contacts, then make referrals to the agency for a share of the commission and travel perks. Such agents may prove invaluable because they can generate substantial revenue for the agency without adding overhead. However, using outside agents who refer a lot of "prospects" that do not result in sales wastes the time of the inside staff and is counter-productive.

In addition to sales agents, you also may want to employ an experienced office manager, unless you know the travel industry and plan to run the agency yourself. The person hired should be thoroughly familiar with the industry and knowledgeable about paperwork requirements. Because the ARC requires that an agency have at least two experienced employees for accreditation purposes, employing such a person will put you a step closer to that goal.

ADDITIONAL OPPORTUNITIES

If starting an independent travel agency seems too daunting, you may want to consider purchasing a franchise from an already established chain. In the early 1990s several companies were offering travel agency franchises. The industry's largest travel-agency network was the Carlson Travel Network, formerly Ask Mr. Fister, with nearly 1,000 franchise outlets. However, Carlson franchises were awarded only to existing travel agencies. Other companies offered both conversion and start-up franchises for fees ranging between $8,000 and $30,000.

Franchisors offered the benefits of training programs, national marketing campaigns, discounts on airline reservation computer equipment, and the possibility of better rates on cruises and other travel options. However, travel agencies seeking similar benefits without the cost of a franchise often joined an agency consortium. About 40 percent of all vacation travel agencies were members of a consortium, while only 20 percent of those agencies focusing on businesses travel were members. In addition to the training programs offered, industry associations also provided networking opportunities simply for the cost of membership.

Operating a small travel agency can be an exciting and relatively easy way to become an entrepreneur. However, stiff competition, low profit margins, and disappearing travel perks may make it less rewarding than other small business ventures. Also, the travel industry was expected to change radically in the coming years. In his 1993 keynote address, Travis Tanner, then president of the Carlson Travel Network, told the Travel Industry Association that the travel agent could become "tomorrow's milkman." According to Tanner, "Interactive television is made for travel shopping. The family can sit at home and preview a trip to Hawaii by punching a few buttons on their remote. . . . And here's the scary part for travel agencies: it'll let them punch a button or two and make the reservation." Therefore, in order to survive, travel agents will need to offer exceptional customer service. "The most important product we have to offer . . . is our professionalism," Tanner went on to say. "Our knowledge . . . and above all, our integrity—you can't get that from a TV screen."

SOURCES:

Cropp, Richard, and Barbara Braidwood, *Start and Run a Profitable Travel Agency,* Self-Counsel Press, 1993.

Madden, Michael, editor, *Small Business Start-Up Index,* Gale Research, Inc., 1993.

Martin, Susan A., editor, *Worldwide Franchise Directory,* Gale Research, Inc., 1991.

Tanner, Travis, Keynote Address, Travel Outlook Forum, Travel Industry Association, Washington, DC, October 20, 1993.

—*DEAN BOYER*

Videocassette Rental Store

Why spend up to $7.00 to see a movie in a commercial theater—not to mention stand in line for tickets and pricey snacks, contend with chattering moviegoers and crying babies, and brave bad weather and parking woes—when you can rent it for less than half that price? More and more Americans are asking themselves this question and opting for home viewing. Sure, you may have to wait a few months for a film's release on video, but the comfort you gain in watching it snuggled up on your couch with your own homemade popcorn—pausing and rewinding if you like—may be well worth the wait.

The retail video rental industry has exploded since its humble beginnings in the early 1980s. Three fourths of American households have videocassette recorders (VCRs) and that number is increasing rapidly; industry observers predict that VCRs will soon be as prevalent in American homes as television sets. Accompanying the popularity of home video, however, has been an increase in competition among video retailers. Nonetheless, with adequate financing, careful management, and creative, service-based marketing, there is money to be made in the video business.

COSTS AND PROFITS

Minimum start-up costs for a retail videocassette rental business run in the neighborhood of $75,000 with average costs hovering around the $125,000 mark. Some video store owners report yearly net profits before taxes of over $100,000, while the majority earn closer to $60,000. Monthly rental revenues can range from $5,000 to $20,000. The primary liabilities of a video retailer include the standard accounts payable and working capital loans. Furthermore, most video store owners do not own the building in which they are located and are thus responsible for monthly rent payments.

FINANCING

One of the biggest mistakes new small business owners make is in not obtaining adequate financing. It is wise to consult with experts in determining how much money you will need to get your project off the ground. By all means ask anyone you may know in the commercial lending field for tips. Check your local business college for referral to a student or instructor who could advise you free of charge. And if you approach them diplomatically, successful video store owners are certainly a font of financing—and other—information. Perhaps your most important sources of prefinancing information, however, will be the professional associations and trade publications that have sprung up around the industry.

Ownership of a previous business and/or significant personal assets, of course, encourage a lending officer to lend to you. But s/he will be looking for other factors in determining your reliability as a borrower: a promising prospective location; plans to offer customers adequate stock; a detailed marketing strategy that encompasses store fixtures, point-of-purchase promotional materials, and promotional events; and a profitable pricing structure (at least a $2.25 per night rental charge). A loan officer will also ask about your management practices, qualifications for staff—how knowledgeable will you require them to be about your products?—proposed store layout, and record-keeping procedures to track financial activity and report operating data.

Ultimately, a combination of factors will determine whether or not a bank will lend to a prospective or fledgling video store owner. As a matter of course, you should contact the U.S. **Small Business Administration (SBA)** to inquire about eligibility requirements for its loan program and to request other valuable information. The Small Business Administration can be reached at **1-800-U ASK SBA**, or write: **Small Business Directory, P.O. Box 1000, Ft. Worth, TX 76119.** You may also want to check the "U.S. Government" section in your telephone directory for the SBA office nearest you.

LOCATION

The ideal location for a retail videocassette rental business would be a corner space, which allows visibility from several directions, in a commercial area frequented by the type of customer you wish to attract. You may set up shop in as few as 600 square feet, but it would be wise to figure in advance what your space needs may be as your business grows. In addition to your store showroom, you will need to incorporate an office/storage area and bathroom into your rental space. Consider customer parking and the ease of

FRANCHISE OPPORTUNITIES

Blockbuster Video: 901 East Las Olas Blvd., Ft. Lauderdale, FL 33301; phone: (305) 524-8200. Founded 1985; over 2,000 outlets in the U.S. and abroad; located near high-traffic commuter routes; 8,000 titles per store; spacious, well-stocked superstores that cater to families, feature knowledgeable staff, fast check-out procedures, a drop-off area, and long, convenient hours. Provided by franchisor: Training program, store design, product selection, merchandising assistance, national print and broadcast ads, ongoing promotional programs; heavy emphasis is placed on local advertising leading up to grand opening. Franchise fees start at $300,000.

In 1987 H. Wayne Huizenga and two partners spent $19 million to buy 43 percent of Blockbuster Video stock. As chairman and president, Huizenga proceeded to buy out his competitors. By the end of 1989 Blockbuster had grown from 19 to 1,000 stores. By mid-1991 the chain boasted 1,800 outlets in 43 states, Canada, and England, making it by far the world's largest retail video chain. Huizenga's plan of turning Blockbuster into the McDonald's of video chains resulted in 1991 sales of more than $1.6 billion.

Other Franchisors: Palmer Video Stores, 1767 Morris Ave., Union, NJ 07083-3598; phone: (800) 288-3456. **Video Biz,** 2981 West SR 434, Ste. 100, Longwood, FL 32779; phone: (800) 572-8347. **Video Galaxy Franchise, Inc.,** 101 West Rd., Vernon, CT 06066; phone: (203) 653-2420. **Video Update,** 287 East 6th St., St. Paul, MN 55101; phone: (800) 433-1195; **West Coast Video,** 9990 Global Rd., Philadelphia, PA 19115; phone: (800) 433-5171.

entering your parking lot from the main thoroughfare. If you live in or near a college town, look for a location that is within walking distance of student and faculty housing.

LAYOUT AND SETUP

Store layout can be a powerful marketing tool. If possible, position store fixtures so that aisles lead toward your checkout counter. Your video monitor should also attract customers to the checkout counter, but should not be so close as to interfere with checkout procedures. A glass-topped check-out counter can also function as a display case. A bench or a few chairs near the counter for people waiting for their friends to make a selection is another good idea. (Add a coffee table to display copies of your catalog—a marketing must). Before outfitting your store, check the yellow pages for rental fixture suppliers and used equipment dealers to maximize cost savings.

You will need enough space behind your counter to house most of your tapes and to allow staff to do their job efficiently. Further space behind the counter should be allotted for record keeping and cash-exchange procedures. A good rule of thumb governing space decisions is to commit 60 percent of your store to display and customer circulation,

20 percent behind the counter, and another 20 percent to office/storage space. Again, see how successful video retailers have done it.

Decorate your store carefully. You want it to be a warm and inviting space where people feel comfortable enough to spend some time. Contact movie distributors and local theaters to obtain "one-sheets"—the movie posters that adorn theater lobbies. Imagination is key here. Some retailers have opted for miniature marquees, spotlights and track lighting, old film reels, glossy photographs of stars or movie stills, newspaper clippings, and other Hollywood memorabilia to spice up their decor.

Most stores open with at least 500 titles in stock. Videocassette tape prices range from an often negotiable $30.00 to $80.00. The average life of a tape is about 400 viewings. Titles are purchased from video distributors; an average store may work with as many as a dozen of these (check out the **"Video Store" Guide to Prerecorded Videocassette Distributors; phone: 1-800-854-3112**). As your inventory is your primary asset, you should keep the actual videocassette behind your sales counter; display the tape jackets for customer perusal. Some stores place magnetized labels on the shelf below the cassettes to indicate whether or not a movie is in-house or out on rental. Several magnets listing the same title represent multiple copies of a specific film. Customers take the magnets to the counter where they are exchanged for the actual title. If the customer does not see a magnet, the film is out on rental.

Rental prices and terms (how long you can keep a video) vary widely across the industry. $3.00 is fast becoming the standard rental rate. Although the larger chains will allow you to keep a movie as long as three days, most smaller stores have a version of the "back before 10:00 p.m. tomorrow" policy; if you start out with a fairly small stock, you can't really afford to let your videocassette leave the store for more than 36 or so hours. Most stores levy a strict penalty (usually the cost of the rental for each day the tape is out of the store beyond the limit indicated on the rental agreement) if tapes are not returned promptly. (Good customers, however, should be allowed a little leeway).

Some store owners have had good luck establishing a "video club" to which members must pay a membership fee and are thus entitled to special privileges. Others offer their "no membership fee" policy as a principal selling point. Either way, store owners are largely at the mercy of their customers to return tapes once they leave the store. In order to better their assurance that tapes will be returned, some ask for a deposit equal to the value of the tape (usually in the form of a check that is returned to the customer); others require a major credit card number, which they will charge if a tape is not returned. But a large number of video store owners simply enact a rental agreement for which they require payment up front and the customer's name, telephone numbers, address, and driver's-license or state identification card number in exchange for a rental. If you adopt this policy, it is wise to develop a good relationship with your local police precinct; though the instance is rare, most errant customers will return a videocassette once a warrant is issued for their arrest.

Make sure to review your daily rental agreements every evening. This will not only help you keep track of which tapes are out and expected back on any given day, but will also enable you to see which tapes are moving. This will help you determine where you need to stock multiple copies and where you should cut back (tapes that don't move can be traded in through a video broker.) For the most part, it is better to stock a few extra copies than to make customers wait for the most popular films. To keep your cash flow healthy, you should aim to rent roughly half your inventory at all times.

STAFFING

Adequate staffing for your videocassette rental store will depend on your hours. If you want to maximize sales by

INDUSTRY STATISTICS

- *U.S. VCR Penetration* (1991): 76.6%; approximately 71 million households (source: Arbitron).
- *Growth of U.S. Video Specialty Stores:* 1980: 2,500; 1991 (projection): 27,000 (source: Entertainment Business Research).
- *Average Daily Rental Rates:* New releases: $2.54; other titles: $1.98 (source: 1991 *Video Store Magazine* Retailer Survey).
- *Average Video Store Revenues* (1991): $192,685 (source: 1991 *Video Store Magazine* Retailer Survey).
- *Consumer Intent to Rent After Seeing the Movie Theatrically:* Females under 25: 60%; males under 25: 42%; females 25 and over: 40%; males 25 and over: 38% (source: CinemaSource "Intent to Rent" research).
- *Consumer Preference to Videos as Opposed to Theatre* (1991 national survey of 1,000 adults): 67% of those polled would prefer to watch a movie at home, compared to 22% who would prefer to go out (source: Electronic Industries Association).
- *Composition of an Average Video Store's Total Inventory by Genre:* New releases (title available less than 3 months): 34%; catalog: 40%; children: 9%; adult: 7%; classics: 4%; music and sports: 2% each; exercise and foreign: 1% each (source: 1991 *Video Store Magazine* Retailer Survey).
- *Rental Profile* (1990): Average % of VCR households renting per month: 70%; average # of tapes rented per month: 7.1; average household expenditures per month: $12.80; average rentals per trip to video store: 2.3; average revenue per trip: $5.96; average # rental trips per month: 3.10 (sources: Fairfield Research Inc.).
- *Consumer Spending on Buying & Renting Videocassettes:* 1987: $6.4 billion; 1991: $11.2 billion (source: Paul Kagan Associates).
- *Demographics of the Frequent Renter* (rents at least once a week or more): The largest percentage of frequent renters are 20 to 29 years old, have household incomes of $30,000 to $50,000, and are about equally divided between men and women (source: 1991 *Video Store Magazine* Consumer Survey).

staying open seven days a week, for 12 or 13 hours per day, you will need more staff than if you maintained shorter hours, especially on the weekends when business is heaviest. Ideally, you should train someone to act as manager when you are unable to be in the store. This person should have some experience in retail management, be highly organized, and have a broad knowledge of, and love for, movies. S/he should also display a creative approach to promotion and sales. Salary should be determined by industry standards; periodic merit raises, however, will further motivate an already motivated employee.

You will also need several part-time employees to prevent customers from having to stand in line. You or your store manager should select and train this support personnel carefully. Keep your trade and film-related mainstream periodicals in your store and require that your staff read these between customers; if you don't have what a customer is looking for, or it's out on rental, your employees should be able to recommend several other related titles. If you pay your staff more than the legal minimum wage, you will most likely see a return on your investment through happier, more productive salespeople. Again, industry standards should be your guide.

MARKETING

More and more video retailers are discovering that they must develop a special marketing niche to compete with the large video chains. Since they can't offer the depth and breadth of videos available at the national and regional franchises, these smart managers are offering what the chains can't deliver: a focus on personal service and a unique selection of titles.

Some say that service is a lost art in American retail operations; it is an art well worth cultivating. Talking to customers—remembering their names, preferences, and something about their lives—is your marketing secret weapon. Keep this in mind when hiring staff. A knowledgeable, pleasant, and accessible staff will go a long way toward attracting loyal, long-term customers from the ranks of those who are no longer satisfied (or never were) with the automated check-out routine at the local chain. Word-of-mouth promotion courtesy of these customers can be a boon to your business.

Even if you are committed to a service-oriented marketing approach, you may wish to consider offering another "alternative" to the large video retailers. In fact, "alternative" video stores—stocking anywhere from 800 to 5,000 titles—are beginning to pop up in urban areas and university towns throughout the country. These establishments stock their shelves heavily with foreign, documentary, cult, classic, adult, and independently made films. Alternative video stores also usually offer a more mainstream catalog that includes new releases, dramas, comedies, horror and science fiction offerings, and movies for children. But the real selling point of these businesses is their hard-to-find titles. If

Associations:

American Video Association (AVA): 2885 North Nevada St., #140, Chandler, AZ 85225; phone: (800) 421-2300.

Video Software Dealers Association (VSDA): 3 Eves Dr., Ste. 307, Marlton, NJ 08053; phone: (800) 257-5259.

VIDION/International Association of Video (IAV): 1440 N St. NW, Washington DC 20005; phone: (202) 332-7166.

Publications:

PRC News: Corbell Publishing Co., 12335 Santa Monica Blvd., Ste. 129, West Los Angeles, CA 90025; phone: (213) 641-9767.

Twice: Twice Publishing Corp., 902 Broadway, New York, NY 10010; phone: (212) 477-2200.

Video Business: Diversified Publishing Group, 825 7th Ave., New York, NY 10019; phone: (212) 887-8408.

Video Extra: Home Viewer Publications, Inc., 8380 Old York Rd., #404, Philadelphia, PA 19117-1543; phone: (215) 629-1588.

Video Investor: Paul Kagan Associates, Inc., 126 Clock Tower Pl., Carmel, CA 93923-8734; phone: (408) 624-1536.

Video Marketing Newsletter: Vidmar Communications, Inc., 1680 Vine St., Ste. 820, Hollywood, CA 90028; phone: (212) 462-6350.

Video Store: Edgell Communications, Inc., 1700 East Dyer Rd., Ste. 250, Santa Ana, CA 92705; phone: (714) 250-8060.

you do some research at the chains (in itself a must for any would-be video store entrepreneur), you will get a feel for what they do not stock.

Combining personal service and unique stock in the form of special ordering will also sell customers on your store; it may be worth your while to track down an obscure video—despite the expense this sometimes involves—if a good customer is sure to rent it and let his/her friends know you have it. Whether you maintain a special order policy or not, listen to your customers. Find out what they're watching, recommending, and would like to see in your store.

Some video store owners have begun offering customers free popcorn and coffee, a "sneak preview" on the store VCR (an important marketing device) of a film they might like to rent, and even drive-through service. Other videocassette retailers have been lucky with two-for-the-price-of-one specials, 99-cent deals on a changing group of selected genre-related titles, and a free rental after a specified number of paid rentals. All of these ideas will help generate excitement about your store and thus bring in more customers.

Computer software packages that offer information on movies available for home rental are becoming increasingly popular. One of these—*Videohound*—will search 20,000 titles by several criteria and give you a plot synopsis, date of release, cast, and indicate whether or not your store stocks it, among other pertinent facts. If you can afford a computer terminal and the software, this may be a good investment. Customers generally enjoy browsing through electronic files even if they don't have a specific movie in mind.

A final word on marketing: Think long and hard about the area in which you wish to locate. Talk to area merchants and their customers. Assess the type of customer you are likely to attract. If you are located near a residential area with young families, make sure you stock plenty of children's videos. If you are situated in an urban area or near a college or university, make sure you acquire the requisite cult and foreign films. In suburban or rural areas, you may wish to stick with a more generalized catalog, including instructional and sports-oriented tapes, among others. Wherever you are, study the socio-economic and cultural character of the area and stock accordingly.

ADVERTISING

You should plan to spend fully two-thirds of your initial investment on advertising during your first six months in business. Utilize your local newspaper. Display ads in the weekend entertainment section can be extremely effective in encouraging name recognition. Create a store logo (or find a reasonably-priced free-lance designer do it for you) and have it emblazoned on t-shirts. Wear the t-shirt while you work and ask your employees to do the same. Give them away to customers who rent a specified number of movies. If you have display room in your store window, install a television and VCR there (perhaps on a mobile cart) and continuously play your most popular videos.

As a rule, you should take advantage of every promotional opportunity. Be creative. Send press releases out to local media announcing any special promotions you dream up. One clever angle is to develop a relationship with a VCR repair/rental business or dealer in your area. If customers complain of a VCR in need of repair or cleaning—or worse, say they don't own one—refer them to this VCR repair/rental or sales business. Meanwhile, design an advertising flyer that the VCR repair business owner or dealer can routinely pass on to his clients.

LICENSES AND INSURANCE

In order to open a retail videocassette rental business you will need to obtain a local business license and the state or city sales tax permits required in your area. Check with your city and county clerks to determine the specifics on these. You'll also want to purchase standard business insurance. Another good idea is to invest in a sturdy security system to protect your inventory from theft.

In the final analysis, increased competition has seen the disappearance of the easy-money days of risk-free video entrepreneurship; ''mom'' and ''pop'' can no longer open their doors with a few videos on the shelf and expect to garner substantial profits. Nonetheless, with research, smart management, and inventive marketing, almost anyone can open a retail videocassette rental business—whether as a primary source of income or as a sideline—and expect to see significant returns on their investment.

SOURCES:

''1991 Video Industry Statistics,'' Video Software Dealers Association, 1991.

Bates, Owen, ''How To Set Up and Operate Your Own Videotape Rental Store,'' Premier, 1986.

Gould, Joe Sutherland, *Starting From Scratch: 50 Profitable Business Opportunities,* John Wiley & Sons, 1987.

Horowitz, David, and Dana Shilling, *The Business of Business: How 100 Businesses Really Work,* Harper & Row, 1989.

Landsburg, Harry F., ''Lending to Video Stores,'' *The Journal of Commercial Bank Lending,* August 1990.

Madden, Michael, editor, *Small Business Start-Up Index,* issue 1, Gale, 1991.

Martin, Susan Boyles, editor, *Worldwide Franchise Directory,* Gale 1991.

Schwartz, Carol A., editor, *Small Business Sourcebook,* fifth edition, volume 1, Gale, 1992.

''Videocassette Rental Store,'' *Entrepreneur Magazine's 168 More Businesses Anyone Can Start and Make a Lot of Money,* second edition, Bantam, 1991.

Wallach, Van, ''Three Men and Their Baby,'' *Video Store Magazine,* October 1990.

Woy, Patricia A., *Small Businesses That Grow and Grow and Grow,* second edition, Betterway, 1989.

—*JULIA RUBINER*

Wedding Planning Service

Historically, most weddings were planned by the bride and her mother or another close relative accorded special standing as bridal consultant. Likewise, there was almost always someone who had read Emily Post and served as social arbiter on matters of etiquette and "proper" weddings. Increasingly, however, especially with the resurgence of big weddings in the 1980s, brides have turned to professional wedding planners. These consultants are paid to worry about all of the details, including finding the perfect site to exchange vows, addressing the invitations, and helping the newlyweds head for their honeymoon in style. Many wedding planners are women who arranged their own nuptials, only to realize how much easier it would have been with professional help.

FINANCIAL ASPECTS

Starting a wedding planning service is not expensive. Because wedding planners are selling a service based on their personal expertise, there is little equipment to buy, with the exception of a typewriter, telephone, answering machine, and office furniture, which can often be leased or purchased used. You will also need business cards and stationery. By spending carefully, the wedding planner working from home should be able to get started for less than $1,000. A computer for word processing and keeping records would increase minimal start-up costs to about $3,000. Leasing an office could cost anywhere from $300 to $1,200 a month, depending on size and location, and the first month's rent and security deposit should be included when estimating start-up costs.

Wedding planners usually charge between $2,000 and $3,000 per event, plus expenses. According to *Entrepreneur,* the average wedding planning service nets $57,000 per year. However, many wedding planners enter the business on a part-time basis, so earnings could be substantially less than those of a full-time service.

LOCATION

The two best locations for a wedding planning business are affluent suburbs and urban areas with a high concentration of upscale condominiums or town houses. Neighborhoods with trendy restaurants and shops frequented by young, upper-income couples are also appropriate. Statistics show that the average couple hiring a wedding planner are in their mid-20s, with an income of about $50,000.

Many wedding planners operate from their own homes. This works well because planners generally go to their clients' homes for consultations and planning sessions. However, if you plan to work from home, setting up a modest office is a good idea in case a customer would prefer to meet there. The home office should be decorated tastefully as it will be a reflection of your personal style and may greatly influence the prospective customer's decision to hire your services. You may also want to set up a post office box rather than using a home address on business cards and brochures. A second telephone line exclusively for the wedding planning service also will help establish a professional image.

If you decide to lease an office, you might want to consider a location near other wedding-related businesses, perhaps in the same building as a bridal shop or wedding photographer. These allied operations may spur increased business for a wedding planner. However, any business owner setting up an outside office should consider carefully all aspects of the lease. Like the home office, a leased office should be decorated to reflect the wedding planner's flair. The office does not need to be large, but there should be a consultation area with comfortable furniture as well as a work area with a desk, telephone, and typewriter or computer. The telephone is the wedding planner's most important tool.

MARKETING

Most of your clients will be couples who plan to have a large wedding. Traditional weddings can be expensive and most of the first-time brides who turn to professional wedding planners come from upper-income families. Therefore, marketing efforts should target families with such demographic characteristics. Large weddings are not for first-time brides alone, however. People getting married for a second time may want a big celebration, and they often have successful, established careers that would leave them little time to plan a wedding, but would provide them with the resources to hire the services of a wedding planner. They will be grateful for

INDUSTRY STATISTICS

- *Average Cost of Getting Married:* $19,000 (source: *Forbes,* 1991).
- *Annual Amount Spent on Weddings:* $32 billion (source: *Forbes,* 1991).
- *Average Age of Newlyweds:* Men, 26.4; women, 24.5 (source: U.S. Department of Health & Human Services, 1987).
- *Number of Weddings Annually in the United States:* 2.3 million (source: ABC Dialogue, 1993).
- *Percentage of Wedding Costs Spent on Reception:* 28% (source: Association of Bridal Consultants, 1993).
- *Percentage of Wedding Costs Spent on Wedding Rings:* 11.5% (source: Association of Bridal Consultants, 1993).

the convenience you offer and are a viable market for the wedding planner to consider.

There are a number of ways for a wedding planner to identify prospective customers. Wedding-license applications are public record and usually available from the city or county clerk. Most newspapers still publish engagement announcements, department stores maintain bridal registries, and it may be possible to purchase mailing lists from magazines that target brides-to-be. Many wedding planners mail brochures describing their services to the names they cull from these sources. Others telephone prospective brides and offer to discuss their services at a convenient time. This offer may take the form of a no-cost consultation or an invitation to a wedding planning seminar. Some planners distribute free wedding checklists, bringing home the point that planning a wedding can be a complicated business.

A less direct, but sometimes equally effective way for wedding planners to contact prospective customers is to arrange for other bridal service businesses to recommend or distribute literature about your planning services. Wedding planners often contract with many other vendors, including bridal and tuxedo shops, caterers, florists, photographers, engravers, bakeries, limousine services, and musicians. These businesses, which can be found in the Yellow Pages, may be willing to promote a wedding planning service, especially when a friendly relationship could result in more business being sent their way. You could also ask department store bridal registries to distribute brochures or small promotional items, but keep in mind some bridal registries offer their own consultation services. Mothers often make many of the important planning decisions for first-time brides, so you should be sure to include them in your marketing efforts.

ADVERTISING

Advertising serves several purposes, including creating a need. Planners must convince potential clients that they need help arranging their weddings. Advertising must also convince potential clients to choose a particular wedding plan-

ner over competitors, usually by emphasizing service, experience, or other attributes that create a favorable image of the business. Most couples choose a wedding planner because they know someone who was happy with the service or because they liked a wedding they attended. That makes a successfully planned and orchestrated wedding the best possible advertising.

However, you have several other advertising options, including traditional media, brochures, and direct mail. Traditional media takes the form of newspaper and magazine ads as well as radio and television commercials. These media may be too expensive or too broad to be effective, but should be considered. This is especially true if there are local publications or cable TV shows that target young women. You may also want to advertise in the Sunday section of a newspaper that carries wedding announcements. Many newspapers devote special sections—usually in June—entirely to weddings, providing another good opportunity to advertise. Another way to publicize your business is to contact the newspaper's editors and offer to write articles for these inserts or act as a source of information on wedding trends.

Brochures may be more cost effective than traditional media depending on distribution channels. Wedding planners should attempt to negotiate arrangements to distribute pamphlets with other wedding-related businesses, including bakeries, florists, jewelry stores, caterers, bridal shops, and bridal registries. Such distribution may range from a display with brochures free for the taking to a more active arrangement by which brochures are given to people who express an interest in wedding-related products or services. Pamphlets should also be made available to churches, reception halls, newcomer organizations, and women's groups. Although brochures do not need to be expensive, they should be tasteful and clearly explain the benefits of a wedding planning service.

Brochures can also be used for direct mail. Many wedding planners purchase mailing lists from publications that target brides-to-be and send personalized letters and information about the service. Others create their own lists from engagement announcements in local newspapers. A tasteful announcement offering congratulations and a telephone number for information about planning weddings can also be effective. These may be actual invitations to wedding-planning seminars or bridal shows organized by the planner. A follow-up telephone call adds a personal touch and gives you another opportunity to sell the service.

Wedding planners should also contact ministers and priests who perform weddings. Many young couples expect their churches to help with the wedding arrangements, and clergymen and women are often willing to recommend a planning service. In addition, you should be sure to place an ad in the local Yellow Pages.

RISK MANAGEMENT

In general, wedding planning services do not need a special license or certification beyond a regular business license. However, if necessary, some planners also provide catering services, especially if the wedding is being planned on short notice or the scheduled caterer is unable to fulfill its obligations. If you plan to handle or offer food services, you'll need a food permit from the county health department.

The more involved a wedding planner becomes in the actual wedding the greater the possibility that a client will sue if something goes wrong. For example, if you arrange for food service and the caterer forgets the wedding, both the caterer and the wedding planner may find themselves the objects of a lawsuit. To avoid this, most wedding planners only make recommendations. The actual contractual arrangements are between the client and the service provider. If you intend to play a more active, general contractor role, however, look into acquiring insurance that would cover any liability.

MANAGEMENT ISSUES

Most wedding planning services are one- or two-person businesses that do not hire employees. The exception to this is when it becomes necessary to hire people to set up the reception area or perform other activities that require temporary help. Some planners also occasionally hire artists, calligraphers, or other skilled personnel for special projects. As your business grows, however, you might find you could use some help with marketing efforts or office management. Wedding planners may spend up to half their time in marketing and paperwork. In any case, planners who work alone should consider training someone on a part-time basis. This person is then able to fill in, if necessary, on those occasions when two weddings are scheduled for the same day or the work load suddenly doubles. You might also get sick or

decide to take a vacation and need someone who can make sure the planning gets done. In addition, there is a point beyond which your business will not grow unless you expand and take on employees.

Many wedding planners, perhaps most, charge a flat fee for their services, which usually include consultations with the client and planning and coordinating the event. Clients will often prefer this because they know precisely what the service will cost. Over time, planners often develop a knack for estimating the cost of a job, but charging a flat fee can be costly for the novice planner who underestimates the work and time involved.

Other wedding planners prefer to charge by the hour, usually setting a minimum fee, much like other consulting services. For example, a wedding planner who charges $50 an hour may bill a minimum of 10 hours. Established wedding planners will sometimes charge a percentage of the total cost of the wedding, usually between 10 percent and 15 percent. Wedding planners should determine the going rate for similar services in their market area and set their fees accordingly. Higher fees are reasonable if a client has unusual demands.

Billing also varies among wedding planners. Some planners handle all arrangements, including paying outside vendors, and submit a single bill to their clients. However, most wedding planners simply recommend vendors to their clients for such services as catering, flowers, and photography. Deciding which vendors to employ and making the financial arrangements is left up to the customers. You may then be able to collect a commission from those vendors hired by your clients. While most wedding planners expect to be paid at the end of the reception, if you're handling the financial arrangements with outside vendors you should require a deposit to lessen the risk of nonpayment.

Working as an assistant to a wedding planner is probably the best training for people who are considering starting their own businesses. However, there are formal training courses offered by professional associations. The **Association of Bridal Consultants (ABC)** offers a series of correspondence courses for wedding planners and issues a certificate upon completion. The courses cover etiquette; sales and marketing; the wedding reception; planning, counseling and consulting; and related services. For more information, contact the ABC at **200 Chestnutland Road, New Milford, CT 06776; phone: (203) 355-0464.** The **National Bridal Service, Inc.,** offers the Weddings Beautiful Program for people who want to be wedding consultants. Those who complete the course receive the registered title of Certified Wedding Specialist. Contact the National Bridal Service at **3122 W. Carey St., Richmond, VA 23221; phone: (804) 355-6945.** Such books as *The Bride's Book of Etiquette, Emily Post's Complete Guide to Wedding Etiquette,* and *Emily Post's Wedding Planner* are excellent reference sources for wedding planners. Training in psychology, interior decorating, and the theater, along with a basic understanding of business principles, can also prove to be helpful.

PRIMARY ASSOCIATIONS AND SELECTED PUBLICATIONS

Associations:

Association of Bridal Consultants: 200 Chestnutland Road, New Milford, CT 06776; phone: (203) 355-0464.

National Bridal Service, Inc.: 3122 W. Carey St., Richmond, VA 23221; phone: (804) 355-6945.

Publications:

Bride's: Conde Nast Publications, 140 E. 45th Street, New York, NY 10017; phone: (212) 880-8539.
ABC Dialogue: Association of Bridal Consultants, 200 Chestnutland Road, New Milford, CT 06776; phone: (203) 355-0464.
Modern Bride: Cahners Publishing, 475 Park Avenue, New York, NY 10016; phone: (212) 779-1999.

In 1991 a correspondent for *Forbes* reported that "if American consumers in the 1990s are rejecting the ostentatious consumption of the 1980s, you would never know it from the wedding business." According to the article, weddings constituted a $32 billion industry and "the nuptial business shows no sign of slowing down." Based on pages of advertising, *Bride's* was the nation's largest magazine, ahead of *Business Week* and *Forbes. Modern Bride* was number four. All this was good news for those people with the right combination of skills who hoped to become successful wedding planners.

SOURCES:

Schifrin, Matthew, "The Newlywed Game," *Forbes,* September 2, 1991, p. 85.
Wedding Consultants, Chronicle Guidance Publications, 1989.
Wedding Planning Service, EntrepreneurGroup.

—*Dean Boyer*

Women's Accessories Store

Standing before a dressing-table mirror, women throughout history have looked down at their rings, necklaces, bracelets, and earrings and wondered, "What'll I wear?" There's an art to matching accessories to ensembles, and the women's accessory business has applied commerce to that art by providing today's fashion-conscious consumer with a quick, easy, and often cost-efficient way to build just the right "look."

The term "accessory" applies not only to jewelry, but also to belts, bags, shoes, socks, scarves, hats, headbands, and other "secondary" wearables. The price range of these accessories, too, proves vast—from the valuable diamonds and gold of high-fashion jewelry to the funky fashions sold on streetcorners. The women's accessories that are the most popular, however, are the medium- to lower-priced off-the-rack jewelry and wearables of a kind usually seen in mall or plaza specialty stores and stands.

START-UP COSTS

According to *Entrepreneur* magazine, earrings are the most popular of fashion accessories; indeed, many accessory shops highlight racks of earrings for every occasion. Since earring-based shops can often occupy smaller spaces than other boutiques, start-up costs can be considerably lower than the retail norm—from a minimum of $17,000 to an average of $28,000. But along with lower start-up costs comes relatively lower net profits. As *Entrepreneur* detailed it, profits for an earring shop begin at a pretax average net of $39,000, and go as high as $57,000 or more. On the other hand, a low-overhead earring shop can be a profitable enterprise for the small-business entrepreneur who might use the profits of one shop to open another.

Buying into a franchise can offer the security of corporate support, at the extra expense of corporate policy. One nationwide chain, Faux Pas, Inc., which specializes in discount versions of high-fashion jewelry, listed start-up costs of $29,000 for a lower-cost unit, $48,750 for a moderate-cost unit, and $71,000 for a higher-cost unit. These costs included an initial franchise fee, rental security deposit, one month's rent, "site improvement," major equipment purchase, freight charges, outside signage, opening inventory (ranging from $12,500 to $30,000 depending on store size), miscellaneous costs, and Grand Opening advertising.

FINANCING

In an uncertain economy, obtaining financing for one's own shop can be a risky venture. First of all, competition is everywhere. Virtually every women's fashion retail outlet—from department store to specialty boutique—has at least one rack of jewelry. Banks and other lending institutions will likely want to make sure you have proper collateral, and will probably check into your credit record and experience in the field. You may have to provide a breakdown of competitive stores in your areas. But the accessories entrepreneur has an ally in the **Small Business Administration,** which provides several different services ranging from guaranteed loans to technical advice; their number is **1-800-U ASK SBA.** You can speak directly to an adviser, and may be encouraged to contact your state Small Business Administration office for more specific details on finance, insurance, and limitations regarding your business. The best advice, of course, comes from someone who's been through the experience. Querying accessory shop owners may be the most effective way to find out how to obtain financing.

In the case of two partners in Des Moines, Iowa, who worked on opening a wearable and home accessories shop, "the bank loan of $31,000, plus the partners' initial investment of $15,000, [wasn't] enough to start this business," according to Louise Washer in a *Working Woman* article. "The only way [they] could make ends meet [was] by getting at least 60 percent of their inventory for free." To that end, the partners asked artists to place their jewelry and crafts into the store on consignment.

LOCATION

Malls and plazas provide a prime location for the accessory entrepreneur. Look for a safe location with a good reputation. If you can obtain space in the "main drag" of a mall—as opposed to one of the less-visited side areas—you can look forward to more traffic.

A typical earring shop can be small but should include back rooms for office and storage. If your budget does not allow for a permanent mall residence, consider a kiosk or

FRANCHISE OPPORTUNITIES

Faux Pas, Inc: P.O. Box 51273, Jacksonville Beach, FL 32250; phone: (904) 390-4172. W. H. Bonneu, president; founded, 1975; began franchising, 1985. More than 70 retail outlets nationwide, generally located in malls or high-traffic shopping centers. Training provided by franchisor. Franchise fee: $5,000. Other expected costs: Rental security, one month's rent, site improvement, major equipment purchase, signage, inventory, Grand Opening advertising.

Faux Pas offers belts, bags, scarves, jewelry, and other accessories at discount prices.

cart. "You'll cut down on your inventory and lease costs, and still enjoy the benefits of mall traffic," as *Entrepreneur* pointed out. "Kiosks or carts also work well at tourist attractions or other heavily trafficked locations."

LAYOUT AND SETUP

Accessory shops beckon to the shopper by virtue of color, light, and space. Aisles should be wide enough to accommodate several shoppers at once, allowing "passing space" to get by browsers who linger at displays. Some earring-based shops find that having the checkout counter as an "island" in the middle of the store while lining the walls with stock is an effective attention-getter. Others are laid out so that shoppers can pass by every display before reaching the checkout. Mirrors, of course, must be plentiful, and mirrored walls would be ideal.

Make your shop layout easy to understand at a glance. If you concentrate on earrings, they should be grouped together, and perhaps subgrouped by make, style, or price. Keep the earring displays neat throughout the day; customers are wont to examine jewelry, then leave it laying on a shelf. (Keeping a staff member constantly on the move to replace stock is also a good way to deter shoplifters.) Any additional accessories you choose—belts, scarves, socks— also must have their own place. Allow for room to hang signs and other advertising material. Many accessory shops reserve a special place for sales and special end-of-season markdowns.

Your checkout counter can be a selling tool as well. A lock-equipped, glass-encased counter can store your more valuable stock, such as pure gold or silver items, wristwatches, or anything with precious stones. With such stock in an enclosed case, a staff member can personally retrieve these items to show customers—adding not only security, but a sense of "cachet."

You might like to add to your store the benefits of a sound system, which can be as simple as a radio/tape player with small speakers mounted at either end of the store. Depending on whom you are trying to attract, choose music that can blend into your atmosphere. Loud rock and roll or other raucous sounds should be avoided, as should the bland

and monotonous "elevator" music. Well-recognized popular and classic soft rock can help create an image for your place; do not underestimate music's ability to hold customers for just a few more minutes so they can "finish" a favorite song. Be aware, though, that your sound system may clash with the piped-in mall Muzak that characterizes many venues.

Once you have established your business environment, you may find that obtaining stock for your store can be challenging. Many retailers choose from a trusted group of suppliers, but suppliers can number in the hundreds. With a firm grasp of the kind of jewelry and accessories you want— upscale, downscale, unusual, or any combination—look into a trade journal like *Accessories* (a Business Journals, Inc., publication), 50 Day St., P.O. Box 5550, Norwalk, CT 06854; phone: (203) 853-6015. Closeouts from other manufacturers are a good way of obtaining low-cost stock; as *Entrepreneur* noted, your markup can be as high as 100 percent to ensure profit.

When working with suppliers, though, be aware that start-up businesses can be perceived as risky. That's what the Des Moines partners found when they tried to obtain vendor credit, as Washer related in the *Working Woman* profile: "Start-ups, they discover, have to pay up front or COD [Cash on Delivery] for goods they order—which puts them at a disadvantage, since their money is tied up for four to eight weeks during delivery and even longer when there are back orders."

STAFF

A good staff can add real value to your accessories store. If you are located in a mall or plaza, you will probably feel obliged to stay open seven days a week, so having adequate people to work day and evening shifts is a must. Generally speaking, choose the kind of staff that matches your desired clientele. If you want to attract young women, for instance, high school and college students can be your employee base (you may also want to hire a college marketing graduate full-time to act as manager when you are not there). If your styles include more upscale jewelry, a mature woman can present the proper image. In any case, your staff should be well groomed (preferably modeling some of the stock) and well oriented, eager to offer help and suggestions. Customer service has become a watchword for the 1990s: gone are the days when shoppers will tolerate employees who ignore them or conspicuously make personal small talk on company time.

Your customers generally will fall into two categories: those who are looking for a particular piece to complete an ensemble, and those who are "just looking." Whatever the customer, your staff should take time to greet her, ask if there is anything they can do to assist, point out any special promotions, and be ready to steer the customer to the kind of accessory she is looking for. Male customers often come in looking for gift ideas; a prepared "box set" of matching jewelry, scarves, and bag can prove attractive to this prospect, especially on Valentine's Day and during the holiday season.

Insight and tact are of the utmost importance in dealing with any customer. An unsure shopper may rely on the salesperson's judgement on how a particular accessory fits her style; under no circumstances should the staff be encouraged to "push" inappropriate stock just to make a sale. The reverse of this situation is the "customer is always right" concept that may have the customer insisting that an inappropriate piece is right for her. In that case, the staffer must rely on tact to persuade the shopper otherwise; showing alternative pieces can help the staffer's cause.

Your store should have a comprehensive, clearly stated return policy. Typically, all regularly priced stock should be cheerfully refunded within 30 days and with a receipt. If you opt to exclude "sale" items from that policy, make sure the customer is aware of a final sale before any money is exchanged. After 30 days, you might ask the customer to exchange the purchase or take a due bill. If the purchased product proves defective, the buyer should have the option of choosing refund or exchange. Holiday-based gift items should also have a liberal return policy. Whatever your policy, your goal is a satisfied customer: remember that haggling over a relatively small amount of money can cost you goodwill—and business—over the long run.

MARKETING AND PROMOTION

The accessories business is highly competitive, so you will want to make your store stand out. Presumably, you have already defined your market and price range. If your main competition is from department stores, you might counter by offering a wider selection. If higher-end jewelry shops compete for shoppers' attention, stress the affordability of your stock. You also have the option of offering pieces no one else has. Some possible alternatives are one-of-a-kinds from local artists, antique pieces, and do-it-yourself beading.

When your location is in a mall or plaza, getting attention during your store's opening should not pose too much difficulty. Signs displayed outside your venue, staffers passing out handbills, and public-address announcements can help get people in your door. Send a press release to your local newspaper's business section, and news of your opening might end up in print. Some kind of "Grand Opening" event also can mark your debut; think about a two-for-one promotion, or a one-cent sale (buy one item, get the second of equal or lower price at one cent).

Sales promotion can take many creative forms. One mall-based accessories store positioned a staffer just outside the door to hand out "today only" 25-percent-off handbills good for only two hours. The store gained long lines at the checkout, especially when the "five-minute warning" was called. Customers who wrote their names and addresses on the coupon were put into contention for a $10 gift certificate drawing. The addition of these "captured" names and addresses on the handbills meant a customer database that can be used later in mailings. Drawing up a preferred-customer list, in fact, can help alert your "regulars" of upcoming sales and promotions.

ADVERTISING

The amount of traditional media advertising you place depends on your budget. If you can afford nothing but signs, then make those signs as professional-looking as you can. Target any newspaper ads to your market: a placement in the local college paper is inexpensive yet attractive to young women—especially if a coupon is included.

You might be interested in broadcast advertising. This can be expensive, but the audience is often far wider. A radio ad announcing a special promotion can be targeted to your customers on their favorite stations. Cable television companies offer "inserts" into blocks of local ads that they run; because cable is less expensive to buy than broadcast television and capable of reaching a more select audience, this medium deserves the consideration of shop owners with a compatible advertising budget. Of course, before placing any advertising or running any promotion, check with a business attorney for special terms or restrictions.

SOURCES:

Bustner, Irving, *The Small Business Handbook,* revised edition, Simon & Schuster, 1989.

Entrepreneur Magazine's 168 More Business Anyone Can Start and Make a Lot of Money, the editors of *Entrepreneur,* second edition, Bantam, 1991.

Madden, Michael, editor, *Small Business Start-Up Index,* Gale Research, Inc., 1991.

Washer, Louise, "Opening Day: We're in Business," *Working Woman,* May 1990.

—SUSAN SALTER

INDUSTRY STATISTICS

• Average annual expenditure, per reported consumer, on women's accessories: $34.46. (Source: *Consumer Power: How Americans Spend Their Money,* by Margaret K. Ambry, New Strategist Publications, 1991.)
• Percent of accessories among total annual expenditure spent on apparel and apparel services, by total before-tax income: 0.13% (Source: *Consumer Power: How Americans Spend Their Money*)

Word Processing/Secretarial Service

Why start a word processing/secretarial service business? For one thing, the demand for such services has shown steady growth as increasing numbers of employers seek cost-effective alternatives to hiring full-time staff. For another, a word processing/secretarial service entails relatively low start-up costs and minimal space requirements. Moreover, this type of business lends itself well to being home-based—a distinct advantage for many would-be entrepreneurs. And still another plus is the profit potential, which can be considerable.

Although estimates vary as to the overall size of this industry, the competition is generally keenest in the more densely populated areas of the country and moderate to virtually nonexistent in outlying regions. Yet even when situated in a highly competitive locale, these businesses can, through strategic marketing and promotion of their services, gain the competitive edge. While industry experts reported no franchising opportunities in this field as of 1993, many operators of word processing/secretarial service businesses have realized growth to the point where they have opened one or even several branch offices to accommodate increasing demands in the marketplace.

PROFITS, COSTS, AND OTHER FINANCIAL ISSUES

In large measure, the profits and costs of these operations depend on their size, location, and scope of services. Gross annual earnings in this industry can range from $30,000 to $100,000; liabilities include the standard accounts payable, as well as any loans obtained for working capital. In 1993 the Entrepreneur Group's *Secretarial/Word Processing Service* business guide cited $57,000 as the average before-tax net profits of these operations. The same source also reported average start-up costs of $27,500, although other sources, especially those centering on home-based enterprises, quoted lower figures, closer to $10,000 and often less.

Figuring prominently in the size of your own start-up investment will be the kinds of services you decide to offer. An operation providing desktop publishing services, for example, will need to invest in more sophisticated equipment and peripherals than one whose primary output comprises term papers, résumés, and business correspondence. Part of your initial outlay will go to licensing and insuring your business. You'll also need to purchase basic equipment and supplies, as well as maintenance contracts for your equipment, and perhaps engage the services of an accountant or lawyer. Advertising costs, too, are likely to be more heavily concentrated during the start-up phase of your operation.

How should you finance these expenses? Among the methods used by people starting out in this field are their own resources, those of family and friends, and loans from various institutions, including banks and the U.S. Small Business Administration; often a combination of these methods represents the best approach. If you decide to apply to a lending institution to help launch your business, you'll need to develop a business plan, which is a formal document that outlines your goals, qualifications, intended markets, competition, and so forth, and provides assorted financial projections and forms, such as a profit and loss statement and a balance sheet. For help in developing a business plan, obtain a copy of the booklet *Business Plan for Small Service Firms,* published by the U.S. Small Business Administration, or visit your local library or bookstore to investigate the many publications devoted to this topic. In addition, you may well find that you can trim initial costs through tapping such resources as ''superstore'' and/or mail-order office supply outlets, computer hardware and software warehouses, used-furniture stores, wholesale paper suppliers, and equipment rental or leasing firms.

LOCATION AND SETUP

A word processing/secretarial service can be set up in a home, an executive suite, or an office building. As a rule, these businesses require little space; often they can be hooked up with another enterprise, such as a bookkeeping service, and in the process reduce their overhead and come into contact with prospective clients who might otherwise be unaware of them. Whatever location you choose, be sure to consider your clients' needs. Adequate seating, a work surface on which to spread out projects, rest room facilities, and perhaps a coffee or tea arrangement will ensure client comfort and convey an atmosphere of professionalism.

Regarding your own work space, you will need a desk or other workstation, file cabinets, one or more sturdy chairs,

TYPICAL AREAS OF DIVERSIFICATION OR SPECIALIZATION

- Résumés, cover letters; related consultation services
- Notary public services
- Proofreading; copyediting; writing ad/newsletter/brochure copy
- Translating
- Desktop publishing; calligraphy
- Statistical/financial/legal/medical typing
- Dictation and transcription
- Telephone answering; mail receiving and forwarding; shipping services
- Photocopying
- General correspondence; repetitive letters and mass mailings
- Theses and dissertations
- Manuscripts, filmscripts, playscripts
- Bookkeeping
- Meeting minutes
- Fax services

a telephone and answering machine (or answering service), a calculator, and storage shelving. You will almost certainly need a computer (plus a typewriter as backup), monitor (screen), and printer (laser printers are recommended), along with solid word processing software that has such features as spell checking, mail merge, and a thesaurus. Depending on what kinds of services you offer, you may also need a modem, fax machine, photocopier, postal meter, transcription equipment, additional computer software, and specialized reference books. And, of course, you'll need to acquire and make room for all the supplies these items involve—file folders, computer diskettes, typewriter ribbons and correction tape, mailing envelopes and labels, and, most important of all, paper, in various sizes, weights, and colors.

In designing your office layout, strive for an arrangement that puts frequently used items within easy reach. Also be sure your setup takes client confidentiality into account: your clients' names and projects should not be readily visible to other clients or prospects with whom you may be meeting.

Those setting up a home-based office have special issues to consider, such as keeping work and home matters separate, deciding whether or to what extent evening and weekend work will intrude on family or personal needs, and dealing with home-related callers and repairpeople during business hours. However, the countless individuals who have opted for a home-based business have shown remarkable ingenuity in working out these issues and designing attractive, professional work spaces that rival those of their executive-suite-based counterparts. If you choose the home-based option, open your mind to the creative possibilities: could a dining room or a spare bedroom be refashioned into an office? Might extra garage space or a sun deck be converted to an office? What about annexing a section of the basement or transforming a loft or attic into your work

space? As you contemplate your own housing situation, you may well find that possibilities abound.

Among the preliminary tasks you will need to attend to during the start-up period are deciding on a business name and determining your opening and closing hours. You will also want to design and have printed a good supply of business cards, letterhead, envelopes, and the like. Useful, too, is a basic brochure detailing your services, prices, policies, hours, qualifications, and so forth.

MARKETING CONSIDERATIONS

Industry experts agree that offering a range of services and developing a specialty niche are key to achieving success in this field. Hence, taking stock of your own skills and researching the market to determine what kinds of services to offer to which types of clients are critical. With this information, you can gear your advertising and promotional efforts appropriately and cost effectively.

Besides being able to type—accurately—at least 70 words per minute, you should possess solid office, grammar, spelling, proofreading, organizational, and communication skills. You should also be knowledgeable about marketing and management, as well as about the word processing equipment and programs you'll use to complete clients' work. Particularly useful is expertise in one or more specialty areas. Some entrepreneurs in this business have, for example, a background in medical or legal transcription, experience preparing filmscripts or financial reports, graphic design know-how, or foreign language proficiency. In assessing your capabilities, do not overlook any volunteer work you may have done, such as preparing a newsletter for your church or synagogue, helping a friend develop his or her résumé, or typing your spouse's master's thesis or doctoral dissertation. If you find yourself lacking some essential ingredient, look into course offerings at local adult education programs, workshops offered through the U.S. Small Business Administration, and similar opportunities for expanding your skill and knowledge base.

Researching the market involves investigating who in your community might use your services. According to Jan Norman, author of *It's Your Business,* "the potential client base [for secretarial services] is huge." Basically, the market for these services comprises three categories. First are small businesses. Often home-based, these operations may not have the need, resources, or facilities to employ a secretary full time, yet still have numerous projects needing clerical attention. Consultancies, law firms, and doctor's offices, as well as community organizations and neighborhood stores, fall into this category.

The second market for word processing/secretarial services comprises larger corporations, which, during times of staff vacations, work overload, or downsizing, often find it advantageous to farm out their projects to independent services. Hospitals, manufacturers, schools, municipal agencies, publishers, and a host of other organizations make up this segment of the market. The third market is made up of individuals—the general public—whose need for secretarial assistance takes myriad forms. Students, professors, retirees, professional writers, and job seekers all have needs that can be met by a word processing/secretarial service.

In researching the market for your services, you should tap as many sources as possible—among them the Yellow Pages, state and local government agencies, the library, the chamber of commerce, and local newspapers. As part of this effort, you'll also need to survey the competition, ascertaining who else is "out there" and how you might fit in. Consulting the Yellow Pages or industry-specific directories will help determine how many competitors are in your area, what services they offer, and where they are located.

Many owners of word processing/secretarial service

USEFUL RESOURCES

Trade Associations:

National Association of Secretarial Services:
3637 Fourth St. N., Suite 330, St. Petersburg, FL 33704; toll-free phone: (800) 237-1462. Publishes print materials and software regarding industry production standards (including bidding and pricing guidelines) as well as a monthly newsletter, industry-specific manuals, and a handbook for starting a secretarial service.

Professional Secretaries International: 10502 Northwest Ambassador Dr., P.O. Box 20404, Kansas City, MO 64195; phone: (816) 891-6600. Offers international, division, and chapter memberships and sponsors a Certified Professional Secretary (CPS) certification program.

Government Agencies:

U.S. Small Business Administration: 1441 L Street NW, Washington, DC 20416. Provides a wealth of information and services to entrepreneurs. For general information, call the SBA Answer Desk at (800) 827-5722; for a list of publications (for example, *Business Loans from the SBA*), write SBA Publications, P.O. Box 30, Denver, CO 80201-0030.

Internal Revenue Service: 111 Constitution Ave. NW, Washington, DC 20224. Publishes helpful guides pertaining to tax issues (for example, *Recordkeeping for a Small Business*); call toll-free (800) 829-3676 to request copies.

Other:

Keyboard Connection: News, Information, and Support for Secretarial and Office Support Service Business Owners, P.O. Box 338, Glen Carbon, IL 62034; phone: (618) 667-4666. Quarterly newsletter.
Word Processing Service and *Secretarial Services* annual directories. Published by American Business Information, Inc., 5711 South Eighty-Sixth Circle, P.O. Box 27347, Omaha, NE 68127; phone: (402) 593-4600.

businesses have formed professional associations or informal networks. These can be well worth joining, not only because of the opportunities they offer for exchanging information but also because they often result in collaborative, complementary arrangements whereby services refer business to one another when vacations, work overloads, or projects requiring special expertise arise. If such groups exist in your area, members might well be willing to talk with you about, for example, what equipment they use and what they charge for their services. One source to contact is the National Association of Secretarial Services (NASS), the industry's primary trade association, which has various chapters nationwide.

After conducting this basic research, you must then decide how will you price your services. In this industry as in others, pricing depends largely on setting—urban, suburban, or rural—and the going rate among competitors. While some operations charge by the line, by the page, or by the project (for instance, charging a flat fee for a single-page résumé), most use an hourly rate as the basis for structuring their prices. NASS, which publishes pricing guidelines and conducts surveys of its members' rates, reported average hourly rates in 1993 to be in the range of $18.00 to $24.00 for basic word processing of double-spaced copy. Word processing/secretarial service businesses usually charge extra for more complicated work—statistical typing, for instance—and for rush jobs, hard-to-decipher originals, weekend work, and the like. In pricing your services, you'll need to take into account not only the type of work performed but also your indirect costs: overhead expenses, such as the costs of supplies and utilities, and "unbillable hours," such as the time you spend marketing your business and attending to administrative tasks.

ADVERTISING AND PROMOTION

Plan at first to take an aggressive approach toward advertising and promoting your services. Although a wide array of advertising and promotional techniques are available for you to choose from, strive always to appeal to the needs of your target audience and to stress the benefits they stand to gain by using your services. Owners of word processing/secretarial service businesses frequently cite the Yellow Pages as their major source of new business. Accordingly, consider running display ads under several headings in the Yellow Pages. A well-designed ad that specifies your capabilities will go far in attracting the eye of prospective clients.

Other strategies you might use include placing ads in the classified section of local newspapers and in the house organs of trade associations or civic groups. To reach students, post flyers on campus bulletin boards; to reach writers, run an ad in the "We Type Manuscripts" section of *Writer's Digest* magazine and/or contact local writers' groups for permission to publicize your service at one of their gatherings. Direct mail, while lending itself to a variety of uses, is especially suitable as a vehicle for attracting area businesses both large and small. Include in such mailings your business card and a copy of your brochure; also consider enclosing a discount coupon or making some other type of special offer, perhaps free pickup and delivery for a business's initial use of your service.

Because repeat business and word-of-mouth referrals constitute another major source of revenue in this industry, pay particular attention to maintaining harmonious customer relations. Stay in touch with your customers by calling them regularly. You may also want to send them thank-you notes, business tips, announcements of new services, and other materials that will keep them aware of your enterprise. Several word processing/secretarial services have developed newsletters, typically produced quarterly, as a means of enhancing communication and fostering customer relations.

Be ever alert to opportunities for promoting and publicizing your operation. Some things to consider, for example, are addressing a group of health care workers about advances in medical recordkeeping; holding an open house for publishing-industry staff wherein you offer tips on using a particular software program; or designing a set of résumé guidelines to distribute to participants at a community-sponsored workshop for job seekers. Use your imagination and ingenuity, make it a point to keep abreast of community events, and never overlook special occasions like Secretary's Day or Be Kind to Editors Week as prime opportunities to promote your enterprise.

ADMINISTRATIVE CONCERNS

Administrative tasks often consume as much as 25 percent of the business owner's time in this industry. Yet investing time in ongoing marketing and maintaining accurate records can pay off in the long run by bringing in business and helping the entrepreneur focus energies on key profit centers within the operation. Several authorities in this field recommend tracking as much information as possible about the enterprise: certain statistics worth noting are which clients generate how much income, which categories of services account for what percentage of revenues, which forms of advertising bring in what proportion of clients, and how much business comes from new versus old clients. Such data will help you pinpoint where to spend your time and dollars. Equally important is keeping thorough records of all income and expenses; you will need these at tax time (for lenders and creditors) and as tools for planning and forecasting. You'll also need to develop a number of forms to use in the day-to-day running of your business—project estimates, work orders, invoices, and billing statements, for example.

While probably the majority of word processing/secretarial services are, at least during the first several years of business, one-person operations, you may decide to hire part- or full-time staff for various aspects of your operation. If so, you will need to consult with a professional—for example, an accountant, an attorney, or a representative from the U.S. Small Business Administration—about the

appropriate forms and financial responsibilities associated with being an employer. An alternative arrangement—one commonly used in this industry—is to subcontract with independent workers (who use their own equipment at their own facilities) or with other word processing/secretarial services during times of overload or for special tasks, such as bulk mailings. If you opt for such an arrangement, you'll need to develop work agreements and perhaps application forms, typing tests, and the like.

LICENSES, INSURANCE, AND RELATED MATTERS

At the outset, you'll need to decide on the form your business will take—sole proprietorship, partnership, or corporation. You will probably need to obtain a business license, as well as a sales tax/resale permit, and you may be required to register your business name with state or county offices. Information on these various requirements and regulations can be obtained from state and local government agencies.

Those interested in a home-based business face special issues and must check with state and local authorities to determine whether they meet requirements for operating a business from the home. Renters, in particular, must verify that their rental agreement allows for a home-based enterprise. And, of course, any prospective home-based entrepreneur should seek expert advice on the tax implications and requirements associated with self-employment from the home. You will find that insurance, too, needs early attention. Speak with your insurance agent about obtaining coverage for fire, theft, vandalism, liability, business interruption, and other pertinent areas. In the case of home-based enterprises, such coverage is often available through a special rider attached to the regular home owner's or tenant's policy.

Given the favorable ratio of profits to costs, coupled with positive projections for growth in this industry, a word processing/secretarial service business represents a good option for prospective entrepreneurs. With the right combination of technical skill and marketing savvy, an individual can achieve success in this field while at the same time enjoying the variety and challenge that come with expanding or tailoring one's services to meet needs not filled by competitors.

SOURCES:

Bustner, Irving, *The Small Business Handbook,* Simon & Schuster, 1989.

Edwards, Paul and Sarah, *Making Money with Your Computer at Home,* Tarcher, 1993.

Entrepreneur Magazine's 111 Businesses You Can Start for Under $10,000, Bantam, 1991.

Fox, Frank, *Starting a Successful Secretarial Service,* National Association of Secretarial Services, 1988.

Glenn, Peggy, *Word Processing Profits at Home,* revised edition, Aames-Allen, 1989.

Hodson, Marcia, *Word Processing Plus,* CountrySide, 1991.

Madden, Michael, editor, *Small Business Start-up Index,* 1991 cumulation, Gale Research, Inc., 1991.

Melnik, Jan, *How to Open and Operate a Home-Based Word Processing/Secretarial Services Business,* Globe Pequot, 1994.

Norman, Jan, *It's Your Business, Orange County Register,* 1993.

Schwartz, Carol A., editor, *Small Business Sourcebook,* sixth edition, volume 1, Gale Research, Inc., 1992.

Secretarial/Word Processing Service, business guide #1136, third edition, Entrepreneur Group, 1993.

Smith, Lynette M., *How to Start a Word Processing Business at Home,* Qualitype, 1992.

25 Hot Businesses for the Nineties, Entrepreneur Group, 1992.

Werner, Tom, ''Former 'G-man' Strives for Letter-Perfect Product,'' *Philadelphia Business Journal,* October 28, 1991, p. 12B.

Woy, Patricia A., *Small Businesses That Grow and Grow and Grow,* second edition, Betterway, 1989.

—*ROBERTA H. WINSTON*

Master Index

Franchise Index

80.28

127456